Microsoft® Windows® XP Plain & Simple, Second Edition

Jerry Joyce and Marianne Moon

PUBLISHED BY
Microsoft Press
A Division of Microsoft Corporation
One Microsoft Way
Redmond, Washington 98052-6399

Library of Congress Cataloging-in-Publication Data pending.

Printed and bound in the United States of America.

5 6 7 8 9 QWT 9 8 7 6 5 4

Distributed in Canada by H.B. Fenn and Company Ltd.

A CIP catalogue record for this book is available from the British Library.

Microsoft Press books are available through booksellers and distributors worldwide. For further information about international editions, contact your local Microsoft Corporation office or contact Microsoft Press International directly at fax (425) 936-7329. Visit our Web site at www.microsoft.com/learning/. Send comments to *mspinput@microsoft.com*.

Acquisitions Editor: Alex Blanton
Project Editor: Laura Sackerman
Manuscript Editor: Marianne Moon
Technical Editor: Jerry Joyce
Typographer: Kari Fera
Proofreader/Copy Editor: Alice Copp Smith
Indexer: Jan Wright (Wright Information Indexing Services)

Body Part No. X10-80207

Dedicated with love to the memory of dear Auntie Mimi, who will live in our hearts forever.

Contents

Acknowledgments

This book is the result of the combined efforts of a team of people whose work we trust and admire and whose friendship we value highly. Kari Fera, our talented typographer, did the work of two people and did it superbly. She not only refined and produced the interior graphics but also laid out the complex design, wrestling heroically with problems ranging from limited space to logical arrangement of numbered steps. She does beautiful work. Our dear friend Alice Copp Smith has helped us improve every book we've written. Alice does so much more than proofread and copyedit: Her gentle and witty chiding on countless yellow sticky notes makes us groan but always teaches us to write better. And we are fortunate indeed to be able to work with indexer extraordinaire Jan Wright, whose index reveals in microcosm the soul of the book. We thank this dedicated and hardworking trio for their exceptional work and their unwavering good humor. That such a small group of people, working from "virtual" offices, can consistently produce award-winning books is an example of the real meaning of the word "teamwork."

At Microsoft Press we thank Alex Blanton for asking us to write this book, and we thank Laura Sackerman for her valuable insight and helpful suggestions. Thanks also to Jim Kramer and Gregory Beckelhymer, who provided assistance along the way.

On the home front, as always, Roberta Moon-Krause, Rick Krause, and Zuzu Abeni Krause provided love, laughter, and inspiration. We also thank the Krause puppies, Baiser and Pierre, for being gracious enough to allow us to publish their private playlist and to chat with us over the Internet.

About This Book

In this section

If you want to get the most from your computer and your software with the least amount of time and effort—and who doesn't?—this book is for you. You'll find *Microsoft Windows XP Plain & Simple, Second Edition* to be a straightforward, easy-to-read reference tool. With the premise that your computer should work for you, not you for it, this book's purpose is to help you get your work done quickly and efficiently so that you can get away from the computer and live your life. Our book is based on the Home Edition of Microsoft Windows XP with Service Pack 2 installed, but if you don't have the latest service pack installed or don't know whether it's installed, don't worry—we'll help you figure it out. If you're running Windows XP Professional, you can still use the information you'll find here. Just be aware that our book doesn't deal with some of the Professional version's special features: joining a domain and working with offline network files, for example.

No Computerese!

Let's face it—when there's a task you don't know how to do but you need to get it done in a hurry, or when you're stuck in the middle of a task and can't figure out what to do next, there's nothing more frustrating than having to read page after page of technical background material. You want the information you need—nothing more, nothing less—and you want it now! *And* it should be easy to find and understand.

That's what this book is all about. It's written in plain English—no technical jargon and no computerese. No single task in the book takes more than two pages. Just look up the task in the index or the table of contents, turn to the page, and there's the information you need, laid out in an illustrated step-by-step format. You don't get bogged down by the whys and wherefores: Just follow the steps and get your work done with a minimum of hassle. Occasionally you might have to turn to another page if the procedure you're working on is accompanied by a *See Also*. That's because there's a lot of overlap among tasks, and we didn't want to keep repeating ourselves. We've scattered some useful *Tips* here and there, pointed out some features that are new in this version of Windows, and thrown in a *Try This* or a *Caution* once in a while. By and large, however, we've tried to remain true to the heart and soul of the book, which is that the information you need should be available to you at a glance.

Useful Tasks...

Whether you use Windows XP on one home computer, on several computers that are part of a home network, or in a home office or small-business environment, we've tried to pack this book with procedures for everything we could think of that you might want to do, from the simplest tasks to some of the more esoteric ones.

...And the Easiest Way to Do Them

Another thing we've tried to do in this book is find and document the easiest way to accomplish a task. Windows XP often provides a multitude of methods to achieve a single end result—which can be daunting or delightful, depending on the way you like to work. If you tend to stick with one favorite and familiar approach, we think the methods described in this book are the way to go. If you like trying out alternative techniques, go ahead! The intuitiveness of Windows XP invites exploration, and you're likely to discover ways of doing things that you think are easier or that you like better than ours. If you do, that's great! It's exactly what the developers of Windows XP had in mind when they provided so many alternatives.

A Quick Overview

Your computer probably came with Windows XP preinstalled, but if you do have to install it yourself, the Setup Wizard makes installation so simple that you won't need our help anyway. So, unlike many computer books, this one doesn't start with installation instructions and a list of system requirements.

Next, you don't have to read this book in any particular order. It's designed so that you can jump in, get the information you need, and then close the book and keep it near your computer. But that doesn't mean we scattered the information about with wild abandon. The tasks you want to accomplish are arranged in two levels. The overall type of task you're looking for is under a main section title such as "Exploring the Internet," "Managing Files and Folders," and so on. Then, in each of those sections, the smaller tasks within the main task are arranged in a loose progression from the simplest to the more complex.

Section 2 covers the basics: starting Windows XP and shutting it down, using the Fast User Switching feature to change users without having to log off, starting programs and working with program windows, using shortcut menus, taking a class at Mouse School, and getting help if you need it.

Section 3 focuses on running programs, including some of the programs that come with Windows XP. You'll find information here about everyday tasks: composing, editing, saving, opening, and closing documents; copying material between documents; using the Calculator; and what to do if your computer "freezes up." There's a short section here for all you MS-DOS fans. And if you like playing computer games, either by yourself or with other players over the Internet, you'll find the information you need here. You'll also find information about the programs and games that are part of the Microsoft Plus! For Windows XP packs.

Sections 4 and 5 are all about using Windows XP as your window on the world at large—exploring, communicating, and using some of the tools that let you work and play in cyberspace. We'll help you as you explore the Internet—searching for people and places, finding and revisiting Web sites, designating your home page, viewing Web pages off line, saving and copying material from Web sites, and so on. We'll talk about communicating with friends and coworkers via e-mail—composing, sending, receiving, and forwarding messages; subscribing to newsgroups; managing and adding to your Contacts list; sending instant messages; and even having online voice and video chats or meetings. We'll also discuss some of the major security measures you can use to protect your computer and your personal information from prying eyes. You'll learn how to block those annoying and occasionally dangerous pop-up windows whose bullying takeovers of your screen drive you crazy when you're using Internet Explorer. We'll show you how to keep your e-mail account information safe when you're using a public computer, and how to prevent the purveyors of spam from persuading you to download pictures and thus unwittingly provide information about yourself.

Sections 6 and 7 are all about having fun—working with different types of pictures, including drawings and photographs; scanning pictures; working with pictures from digital or analog cameras and VCRs; assembling slide shows; making great little movies with narration, soundtracks, and fade-in/fade-out transitions between clips; playing and recording CD music; creating and listening to your own music playlist; and trying out Narrator—a program that actually reads aloud to you. The possibilities are endless, and we know you'll be thrilled by the professional results you can achieve with the combination of your own imagination and the Windows XP tools—among them Media Player and Movie Maker—that let you give free rein to your creativity. You'll also see the additional tools you can use if you purchase the Microsoft Plus! For Windows XP Digital Media Edition pack.

Section 8 is the place to go if you have questions about printing your documents or problems setting up your printer. There's a nice feature in Windows XP that makes it a snap to print your photographs, and we'll also show you how to print readable Web pages. This section of the book also covers sending, receiving, and annotating faxes, as well as creating useful fax cover pages.

Section 9 covers managing and organizing your documents, files, and folders: moving or copying files, and creating a system of folders in which to keep them; sharing files with other users; creating quick access to files and folders; recovering deleted items; using compressed folders to minimize large files; storing files on CDs or other types of removable disks; arranging the items on your Desktop; and navigating with toolbars.

Section 10 is about networking—the different types of networks you might encounter, how to find what you need on your network, and how to use the power of a network to your best advantage. We'll show you, among other things, how to share files and folders, and how to connect to your network in several different ways.

Sections 11 and 12 will help you make Windows work the way you want: You'll be selecting your default Web browser, music player, e-mail program, and instant messaging program; adding or removing Windows XP components; installing programs; adding hardware; and setting up your printer and your network, dial-up Internet access, Outlook Express, and Fax Service. We'll talk about customizing Windows XP: reverting to the classic Windows look; reorganizing the Start menu; customizing your Desktop, folder windows, and toolbars, and even the way you enter information, so that everything looks and works exactly the way you want.

Section 13 deals with what's possibly the most important topic in the whole book: Security, with a capital "S"! In this section, we cover all the ways you can protect yourself and your computer from the activities of others, whether they have direct access to your computer or are lurking in some faraway place from which they attempt to prey on you over the Internet. We'll show you how to set up secure passwords to deny access to your computer when you're not around; set up your firewall to prevent intrusions from the Internet; protect your personal information on the Internet; and increase your protection against dangerous e-mail viruses.

Last but not least, section 14 concentrates on those troublesome activities that we all try to ignore but know we must get around to eventually—preferably sooner than later. So, just as you'll occasionally need to do some basic maintenance on your car or bicycle, you'll also need to tune up Windows once in a while. And if something does go wrong with your system, we'll help you diagnose the problem, get help, and get the system running correctly again.

What's New in Windows XP?

Throughout this book you'll see *New Feature* icons identifying features that weren't available when Windows XP was initially released. If you're familiar with the original version of Windows XP, however, you'll see that most of the new features are those that provide increased security. You'll also find updated versions of some programs that were released after the original version of Windows XP, and all the new and interesting features that come in the Microsoft Plus! For Windows XP packs. This section of the book, however, might be more aptly entitled "What's New for *You* in Windows XP?" That's because Windows XP has taken the best features from both Windows Me and Windows 2000, improved on them, and added new ones. So, if you've been using Windows Me, you'll find many powerful features that come from Windows 2000 in addition to the completely new features of Windows XP. If you've been using Windows 2000, you'll find that the features incorporated from Windows Me make computing more friendly and more fun. And if you've been using Windows 95 or Windows 98, you'll see all sorts of features that will be completely new to you.

If you've upgraded your operating system from a version prior to Windows XP, the first thing you'll notice is Windows XP's new interface. This dramatic change isn't merely cosmetic—there are substantial changes to the way Windows functions. For example, Windows detects the content of a folder and then displays the content in the most advantageous view, listing the tasks you can do that apply to that type of content. No more searching around for the right command or window—just click the task you want to accomplish. You'll find that you can customize many items: You can change the look back to that of Windows 2000 if you like, or just change parts of the interface—the Start menu, for example. You can change what the computer does when you insert a music CD or a program CD. You can change the way you log on.

So what's new for *you?* If you've been using the Windows 95/Windows 98/Windows Me family of operating systems, the robustness, security, privacy, and power of Windows XP are new for you. You can use the powerful and secure NTFS disk format to protect your files from prying eyes, even if those eyes belong to other people who use your computer. You'll also be able to use some of the powerful tools of Windows 2000, such as Fax Service to send and receive faxes, and the Computer Management Console to manage just about everything on your computer.

If you're coming from the Windows 2000 and Windows NT family, the friendliness, compatibility, and fun of Windows XP will be new for you. You'll be amazed that you can use so many different types of hardware and software. You can fix problems simply by restoring your computer to an earlier configuration, you can log on easily, and you can customize the system in so many ways. And *yippee*—you can make movies and play games!

You'll find the Windows XP logon very friendly, and you'll appreciate the Fast User Switching feature—no need to log off when someone else wants to use your computer. Just switch users, and then, when the computer is free, resume work with all your documents and settings intact. If you need to store some files on a CD or make your own music CD, just send the files to your CD recorder, and Windows XP does the rest. The new versions of Internet Explorer, Windows Media Player, and Windows Messenger turn the Internet into your personal service provider—a source of endless information, entertainment, and communication. If you get into trouble, you can ask a friend or colleague for help over the Internet and let him or her take control of your computer and diagnose and fix the problem. And you can avoid evildoers lurking in cyberspace by installing a firewall that protects your computer from intrusion.

If you're upgrading from the original version of Windows XP with the installation of Service Pack 2 or later, you're going to see a significant increase in security. Many of these powerful security features are buried so deeply inside the operating system that you're unlikely to even know they're there—except by the reduction in problems you'll encounter. Other features, such as the Windows Firewall, are more obvious. The Firewall is a rigorous sentry patrolling the doors to your computer, challenging anyone or anything that approaches from the outside, and stopping anything that tries to slither away from the inside carrying your secret information with it. You might get *really* tired of the frequency with which you'll encounter the Windows version of *"Halt, who goes there?"* However, if the challenge stops a virus or destructive worm from infiltrating your computer, or prevents a file from a spyware program on your computer from escaping with your password or credit card number, you'll know it was worth the effort.

The increased security also encourages you to use all the available methods to prevent trouble. The new Security Center monitors your security settings and warns you if you haven't installed the latest critical updates from Microsoft. It tells you if your anti-virus software needs updating or if the Windows Firewall isn't protecting you as well as it should. The Security Center doesn't just warn you about problems—it shows you how to apply the strongest, most effective settings and how to get the downloads you need. And the increased security isn't limited to the operating system. You'll find that Internet Explorer and Outlook Express also provide settings that increase security and help prevent problems.

But improved security is certainly not the only enhancement you'll find in your updated Windows XP. For example, if you'd prefer not to use the programs for Web browsing, e-mail, instant messaging, and playing music that come with Windows XP, you can easily designate other programs as your default programs.

Some of the programs that came with the original version of Windows XP have also been upgraded; you'll find that they work a bit differently and often contain new and useful features. Among them are new versions of Internet Explorer, Outlook Express, Windows Messenger, and Windows Movie Maker. And, as we point out throughout the book, you'll find that the Microsoft Plus! and the Microsoft Plus! Digital Media Edition packs that became available after the original release of Windows XP will really enhance your work and play in Windows XP.

What's new in Windows XP? Perhaps, finally, the feeling that *you* control the computer rather than the computer controlling you!

A Few Assumptions

We had to make a few educated guesses about you, our audience, when we started writing this book. Perhaps your computer is solely for personal use—e-mail, surfing the Internet, playing games, and so on. Perhaps your work allows you to telecommute. Or maybe you run a small home-based business. Taking all these possibilities into account, we assumed either that you'd be using a stand-alone home computer or that you'd have two or more computers connected so that you could share files, a printer, and so on. We also assumed that you had an Internet connection.

Another assumption we made is that—initially, anyway—you'd use Windows XP just as it came, meaning that your folder windows and the Control Panel would show common tasks, and that you'd use your little friend the mouse in the traditional way: that is, point and click to select an item, and then double-click to open it. If you prefer, you can easily set your folder windows not to list common tasks, and you can use the mouse as if you were working on a Web page—pointing to an item to select it and then opening it with a single click. However, because Windows XP's default setup makes accomplishing your work so easy—and because our philosophy is that work should be as stress-free and pleasant as possible—that's what we've used in the procedures and graphics throughout this book.

A Final Word (or Two)

We had three goals in writing this book:

- Whatever you want to do, we want the book to help you get it done.
- We want the book to help you discover how to do things you *didn't* know you wanted to do.
- And, finally, if we've achieved the first two goals, we'll be well on the way to the third, which is for our book to help you *enjoy* using Windows XP. We think that's the best gift we could give you to thank you for buying our book.

We hope you'll have as much fun using *Microsoft Windows XP Plain & Simple, Second Edition* as we've had writing it. The best way to learn is by *doing,* and that's how we hope you'll use this book.

2 Jump Right In

In this section

Microsoft Windows XP is designed to work for you, not you for it. Don't be afraid to jump right in and try out some features. You'll find that there are often several ways to accomplish one task. Why? Because people work differently. Because different tasks have different requirements. And because you want to find the way that works best for you, get your work done quickly with a minimum of hassle, and then get away from the computer and live your life!

You'll find that the procedures described in this book are simple and straightforward and that you can often use automated methods to get some of the more complex tasks done easily. This doesn't mean that you can't get stuck or get into trouble, but there are so many safeguards built into Windows XP and so many places where you can get help that you'll have to work pretty hard to get into any *real* trouble.

This section of the book covers the basics: starting Windows XP and shutting it down, starting programs, using Fast User Switching to switch users without having to shut down all your running programs, accessing your documents, arranging your open windows, using the mouse, getting online help, and so on. There's also a handy visual glossary on the following two pages that will help you become familiar with the various components of the Windows XP environment.

Don't change or delete anything just yet—you'll want to feel comfortable with the basics before you do any customizing. The best way to learn about running programs, managing windows, and getting help if you *do* get into trouble is to jump right in and try things out.

What's Where in Windows XP?

Microsoft Windows XP is your working headquarters—the *operating system* that lets you run different programs simultaneously and share information among programs if you need to. Most of the programs you'll use have common characteristics that were designed to work together in the Windows XP environment so that once you learn how to do something in one program, you know how to do it in other programs.

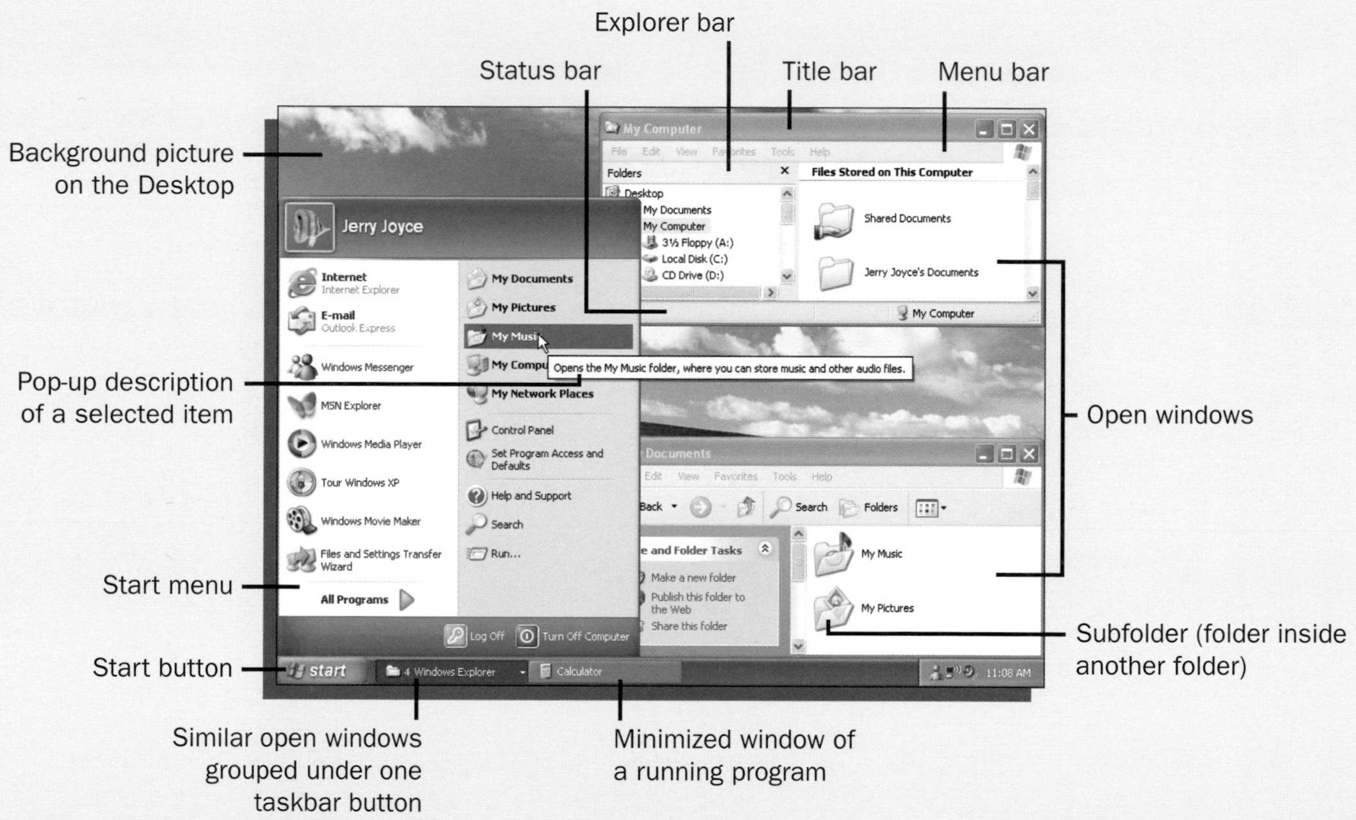

Take a look at the different parts of the Windows XP environment displayed on these two pages—what they do and what they're called—and you'll be on the road to complete mastery. The way Windows XP was set up on your computer, as well as the many ways in which you can customize Windows XP, can make drastic changes to the look of your Desktop, but the basic concepts are the same. And if you need to, you can always come back to this visual glossary for a quick refresher on Windows XP terminology.

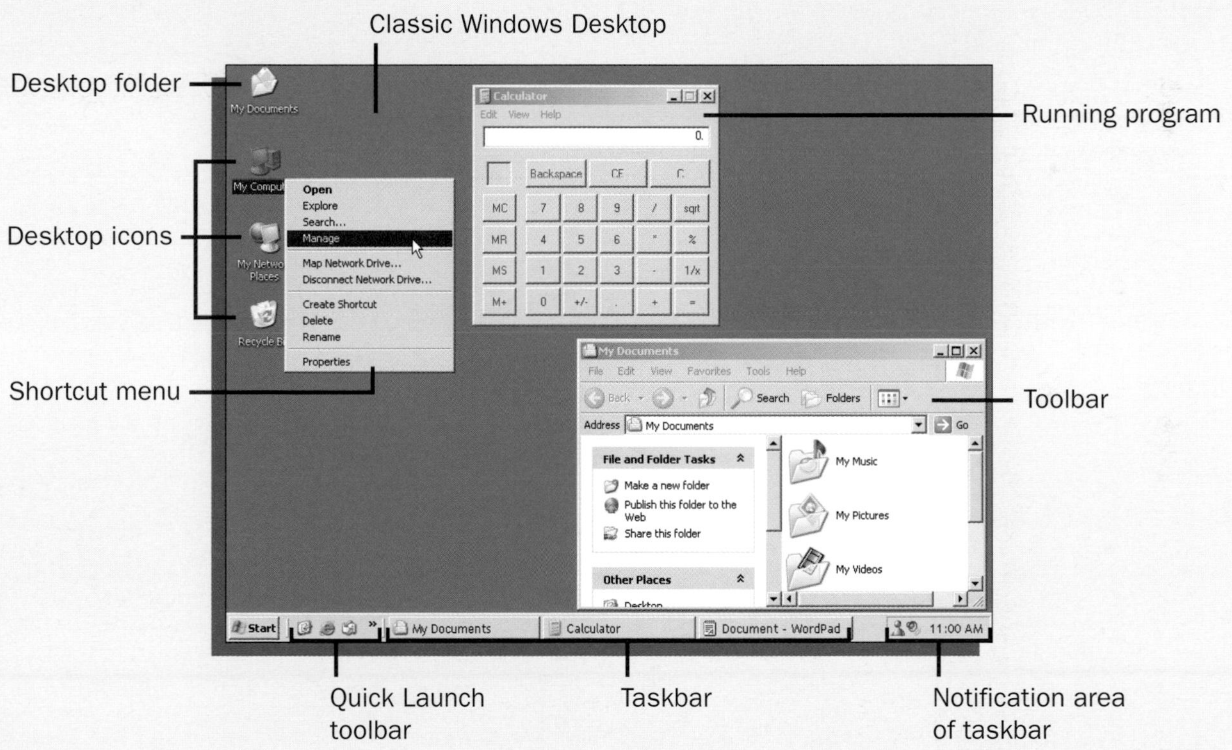

Starting Up and Shutting Down

When you turn on your computer, you're also starting Windows XP. Startup time depends on your computer's speed, configuration, and connections, and on the programs that are set up to start automatically. When you've finished your work, don't just turn off the computer! Windows XP needs a little time to close any open programs or connections and to save your current settings.

Start Windows XP

1. Turn on your computer, your monitor, and any peripheral devices—your printer, for example.
2. Wait for Windows XP to load.
3. Click your name.
4. If a box for a password appears, type your password.
5. Click here or press Enter to log on to Windows XP.

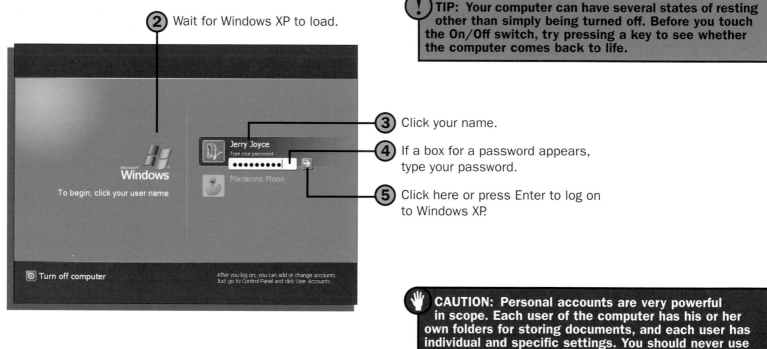

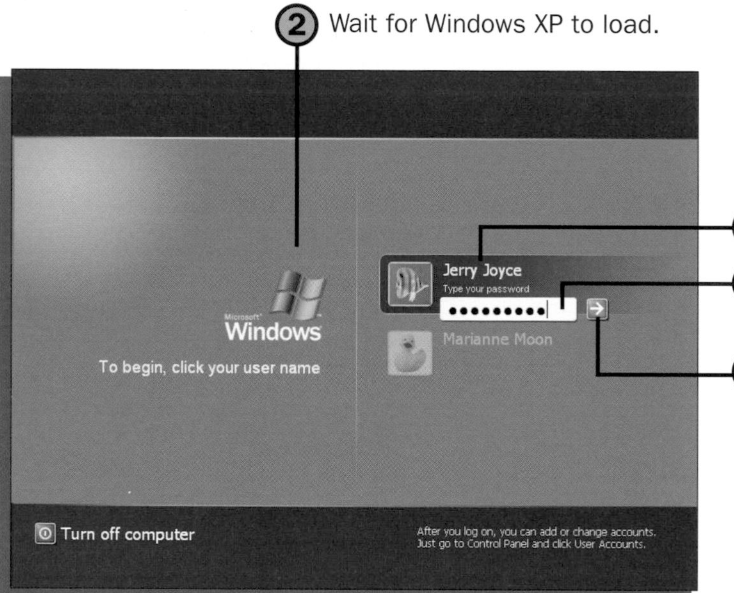

SEE ALSO: For information about logging off and about fast switching of users, see "Switching Users" on page 12.

For information about what to do if you're having problems when you try to quit Windows XP, see "Quitting When You're Stuck" on page 50.

For information about changing the way you log on, see "Changing the Logon" on page 235.

TIP: Your computer can have several states of resting other than simply being turned off. Before you touch the On/Off switch, try pressing a key to see whether the computer comes back to life.

CAUTION: Personal accounts are very powerful in scope. Each user of the computer has his or her own folders for storing documents, and each user has individual and specific settings. You should never use someone else's account! If you do, everything from files to e-mail messages could be misplaced or lost.

Shut Down Your Computer

1. Click the Start button, and then click Turn Off Computer.

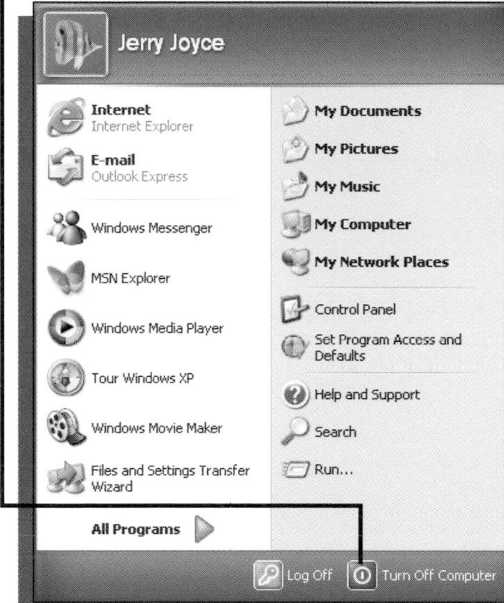

2. Click the appropriate option. The options available depend on the configuration of your computer.

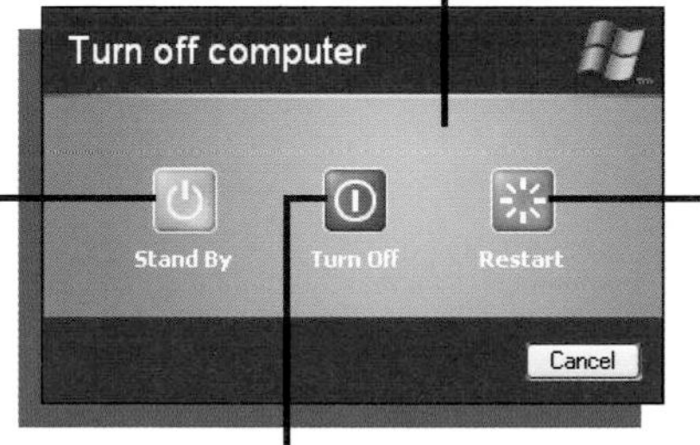

Switches the computer to low-power mode, but your programs are still open. Press any key or move the mouse to reactivate the computer. (On some portable computers, you might have to press the power button.)

Exits Windows XP and then restarts the computer.

Exits Windows XP and prepares the computer to be turned off.

3. To place the computer in Hibernate mode, hold down the Shift key, and click the Hibernate button when it appears.

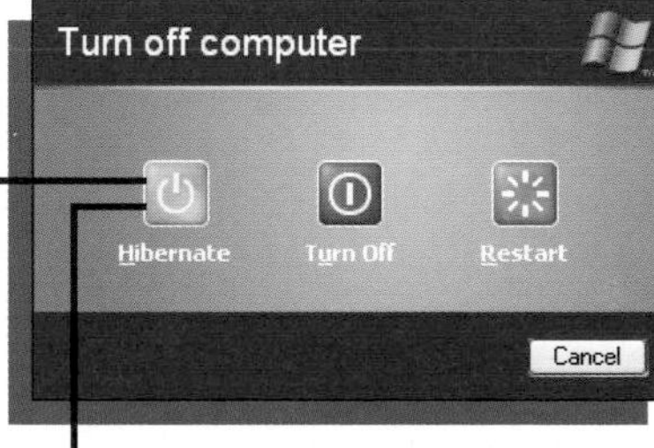

Records onto the hard disk all the items contained in the computer's memory, and then shuts down the computer. All the items are restored when you restart the computer.

TIP: You'll probably want to restart Windows XP after you've made changes to the computer's configuration or if you're having any software problems.

TIP: If the Stand By option isn't available on your computer, it's probably because one or more hardware components can't support Stand By mode. It's usually easier to forgo this feature than to try to figure out which components are preventing you from using Stand By mode.

Switching Users

If someone else wants to log on to your computer and use his or her own settings, you have two choices: You can log off and thereby close all the programs and network connections you were using, or you can simply switch users. Switching users is obviously a great idea! You can leave all your programs running, and as soon as the other person has finished with the computer, you can get back to work and find everything just as it was before you switched users.

CAUTION: Leaving your programs running uses some of the computer's resources, so the other person who's using the computer might find that it's running slowly. If you notice that the computer's performance has degraded when you use fast switching, log off to free up those resources.

Change Users

1. Click the Start button, and click Log Off to display the Log Off Windows dialog box.

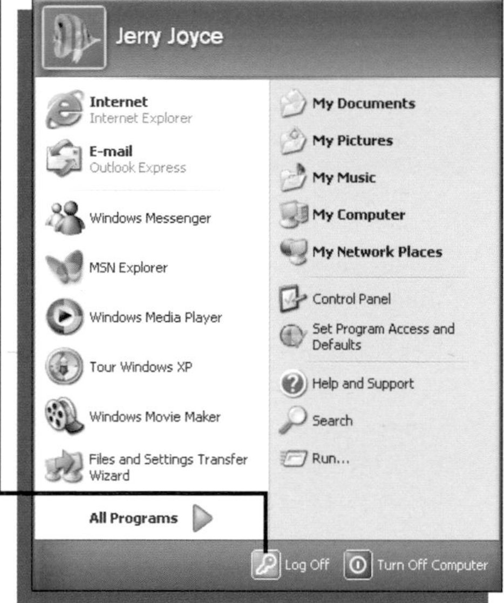

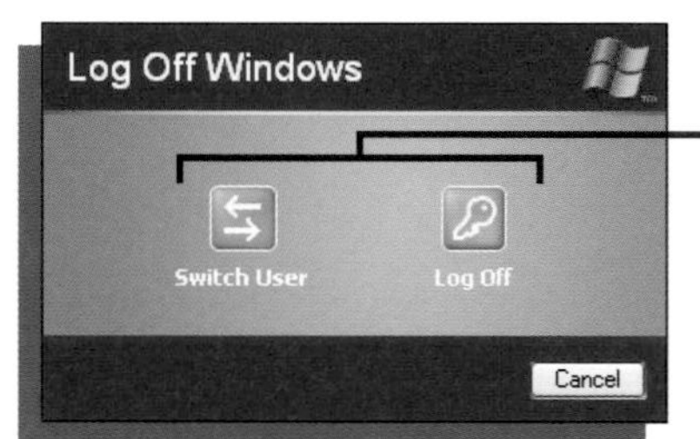

2. Click the action you want:
   - Switch User to suspend your use of the computer and allow someone else to log on to the computer and immediately be able to use his or her own Desktop configurations and other settings
   - Log Off to close all your running programs, save your settings, and sign yourself off the computer

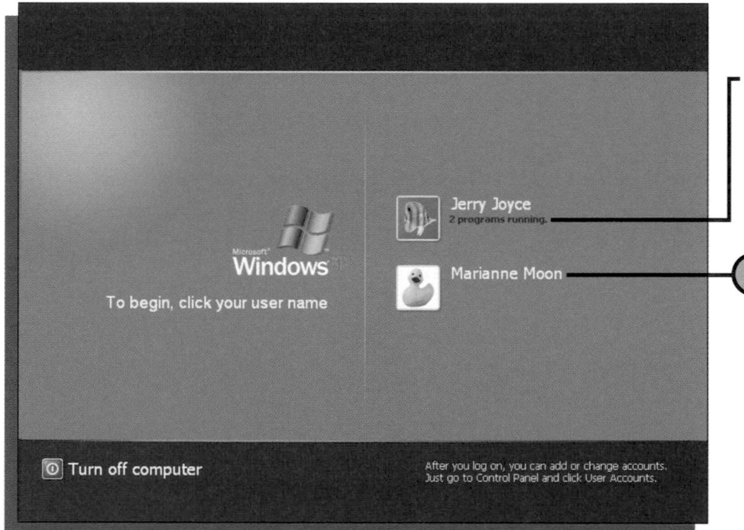

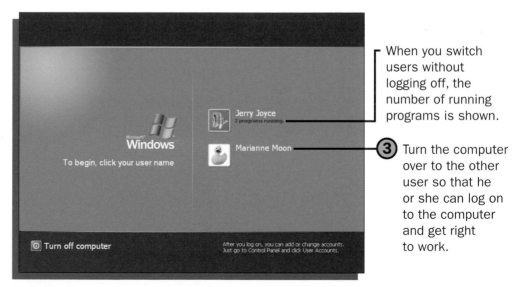

When you switch users without logging off, the number of running programs is shown.

3. Turn the computer over to the other user so that he or she can log on to the computer and get right to work.

Starting a Program

The real work of an operating system is to run software programs. Windows XP comes with a wide variety of programs, and you can install additional (and often more powerful) ones. Most programs are listed on the Start menu, but Windows XP gives you several ways to start your programs, so you can choose the way that's easiest for you or the one you like best.

Start a Program

 Do any of the following:

- Click the Start button, and choose a program from the Start menu.
- Click the Start button, point to All Programs, point to any relevant program groups to display additional submenus, and choose the program you want.
- Point to and then double-click the program icon on the Desktop.
- Open the My Computer folder, navigate to the folder that contains the program you want, and double-click the program.
- Open the My Computer folder, navigate to the folder that contains a file associated with the program, and double-click the file.
- Insert the CD that contains a program that's designed to run from the CD, and choose to run the program.
- Click the Start button, choose Run, type the full path and file name of the program, and click OK.

 Use the program, and close it when you've finished.

TIP: The programs listed in the table at the right are only some of the programs that come with Windows XP. You'll find descriptions of some of the other programs elsewhere in this book.

Frequently Used Windows XP Programs

Program	Purpose
Address Book	Stores names, addresses, and other contact information.
Calculator	Does arithmetic calculations and complex mathematical calculations.
Character Map	Inserts special characters from installed fonts.
Internet Explorer	Functions as a Web browser and an HTML document viewer.
Magnifier	Magnifies sections of the screen.
MSN Explorer	Provides a customized Web browser that works easily with MSN Web sites.
Narrator	Describes and reads aloud the screen contents.
Notepad	Creates, edits, and displays text documents.
On-Screen Keyboard	Allows keyboard input using the mouse or other pointing device.
Outlook Express	Provides e-mail, newsgroup, and directory services.
Paint	Creates and edits bitmap pictures; imports and edits scanned images and digital pictures.
Sound Recorder	Creates and plays digital sound files.
Windows Media Player	Plays sound, music, and video.
Windows Movie Maker	Converts, edits, organizes, and distributes video files.
WordPad	Creates, edits, and displays text, Rich Text Format, and Word documents.

Accessing Your Documents

The My Documents folder is a personal storage area where you can keep and access your documents. The My Computer folder is the gateway to your computer's contents, and it displays the icons that represent all your local storage areas: removable disk drives, hard disks, CD drives, and so on. From here you can venture as deep into the folder structure of your computer as you dare.

SEE ALSO: For information about displaying or hiding the My Documents folder, the My Computer icon, and a few other familiar icons that appeared on the Desktop in earlier versions of Windows, see "Customizing the Desktop" on pages 226–227.

Open My Documents

1 Click the Start button, and choose My Documents from the Start menu to open the My Documents window.
2 Click a file to select it.
3 Read about the tasks you can do with this file.
4 Click to see the details about the file.
5 Double-click a file to open it.
6 Use the scroll bars, if necessary, to view all the documents. Click the scroll arrows to scroll a small increment at a time, or drag the scroll box to scroll a greater distance.
7 Click the Close button when you've finished.
Scroll box
Scroll arrow
My Documents
File and Folder Tasks
Rename this file
Move this file
Copy this file
Publish this file to the Web
E-mail this file
Print this file
Delete this file
Other Places
Desktop
Shared Documents
My Computer
My Network Places
Details
Comments
Fax
My Music
My Pictures
My Received Files
My Stuff
My Videos
Events
Ideas
Info
More information
Notes
Problems
Proposal
Regulations
Shopping List
Status
Today
start

TIP: If you can't find the file you need in the My Documents folder, click a different location in the Other Places section of the window.

TIP: Each user of the computer (provided he or she logs on) has a separate My Documents folder, as well as other personalized settings. The My Documents folder is quickly accessible from the Start menu, but it's actually located in the Documents And Settings folder under the user's name.

Open Any Folder

1 Click the Start button, and choose My Computer from the Start menu to open the My Computer window.

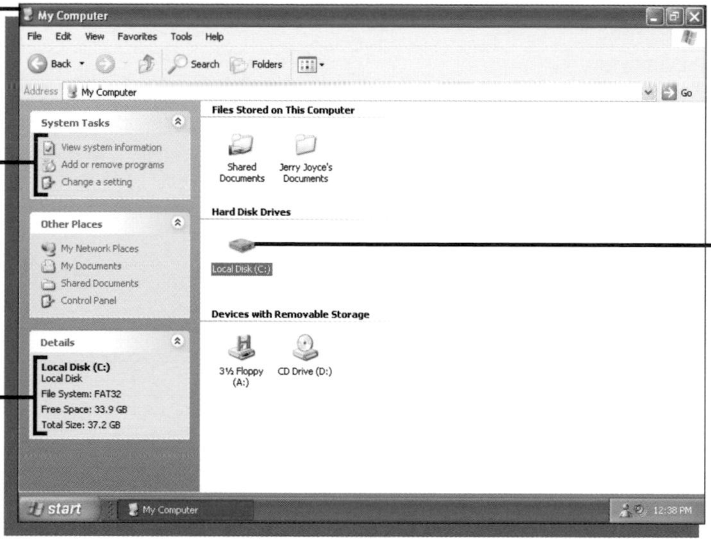

3 Read the information about the drive and the actions you can take.

SEE ALSO: For information about changing the way folders are displayed, see "Changing the Window View" on page 171 and "Windows Views" on page 172.

2 Click a drive icon to select it.

4 Double-click a drive icon to open a window for that drive.

5 Click the Back button to return to the previous window, the Forward button to move to a previously visited subfolder, or the Up button to move from a subfolder back to its parent folder.

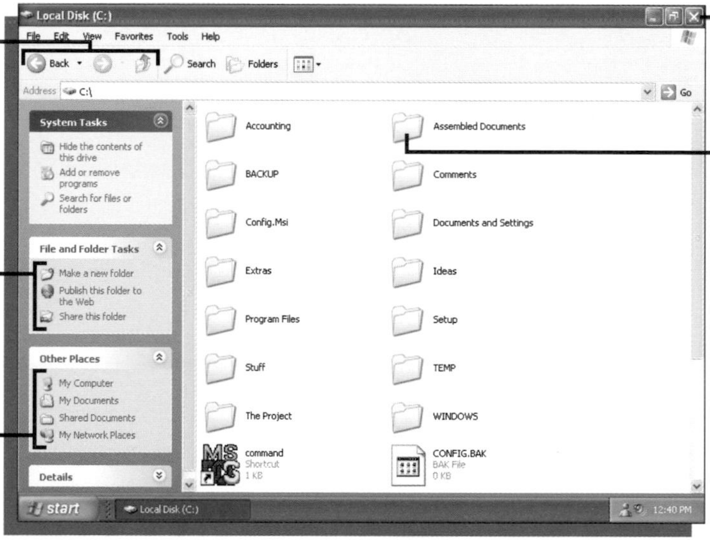

6 Select a folder or a file, and read about the tasks you can do with this folder or file.

7 Click a new destination if you want to work in a different folder.

9 Click the Close button when you've finished.

8 To open a folder, double-click it.

Switching Among Open Windows

Whatever your working style, it's inevitable that you'll end up with more than one window open on your computer—your My Documents window and your My Network Places window, perhaps, or a couple of program windows. Instead of closing one window to get to another, you can simply switch windows.

Select a Window

1. On the taskbar, click to switch to the window you want.

2. If Windows XP has grouped similar types of windows, click the button for the grouping, and then click the window you want.

TIP: If there isn't enough room on the taskbar to display a button for each open window, Windows XP groups similar types of windows under one button. To arrange all the windows in the group, right-click the button, and choose the arrangement you want from the shortcut menu that appears.

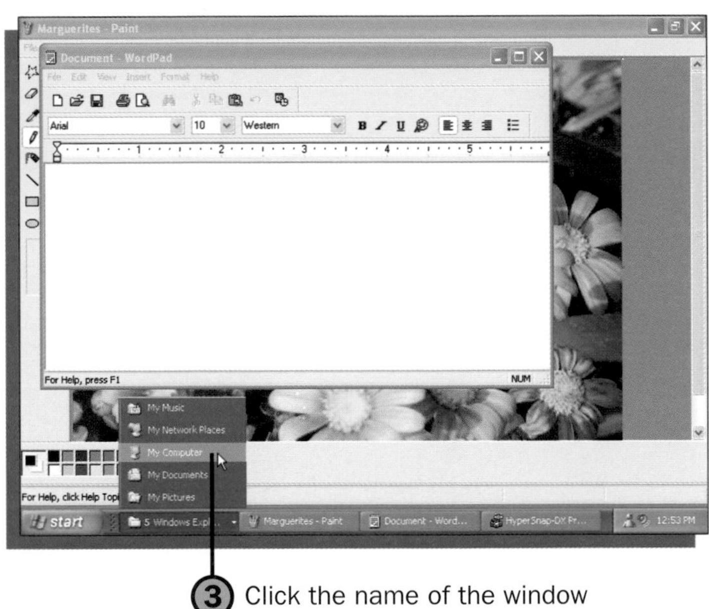

3. Click the name of the window to open the window.

TRY THIS: Hold down the Alt key and press the Tab key. Still holding down the Alt key, press the Tab key several times. Note that the selection cycles through all the open windows. When you release the Alt key, you switch to the window that was selected.

Mouse Maneuvers

Navigating with a mouse is like traveling in a helicopter: You can lift off from any spot and set down wherever you want. Using the keyboard is like taking the scenic route—you get to explore the road less traveled, and you might even come across features and techniques that are new to you. But to finish your tasks as quickly as possible—and to take advantage of some of the best features of Windows XP—give your mouse the job!

Before you fly off on your mouse wings, you might need some Mouse Basics. Here at Mouse School you'll learn to point, click, double-click, right-click, select, multiple-select, and drag with your mouse. Don't be too surprised if the mouse acts a bit differently from the way you expect it to. Windows XP gives you numerous options for customizing the way your mouse works, so be patient and experiment a bit. And read "Customizing Your Folders" on pages 236–237 for information about setting up Windows XP so that your mouse works the way you want it to.

Point: Move the mouse until the mouse pointer (either a small arrow-shaped pointer or a tiny hand) is pointing to the item you want.

Depending on your mouse-click settings, either you click an item to select it...

...or the item becomes selected when you simply point to it.

Click: Point to the item you want, and then quickly press down and release the left mouse button.

Double-click: Point to the item you want, and then quickly press down and release the left mouse button twice, being careful not to move the mouse between clicks.

Right-click: Point to the item you want, and then quickly press down and release the right mouse button.

Select: Point to an item, and click to select it. To select an icon when the system is set to open an item with a single click, point to the icon but don't click. A selected item is usually a different color from other similar items or is surrounded by a frame.

Multiple-select: To select a list of adjacent or sequential items, click the first item, hold down the Shift key, and click the last item. To select or deselect *nonadjacent* items, hold down the Ctrl key and click each item you want. (Not all windows and dialog boxes permit multiple selection.)

Drag: Select the item you want. Keeping the mouse pointer on the selected item, hold down the left mouse button and move the mouse until you've "dragged" the item to the desired location; then release the left mouse button.

Point to the item...

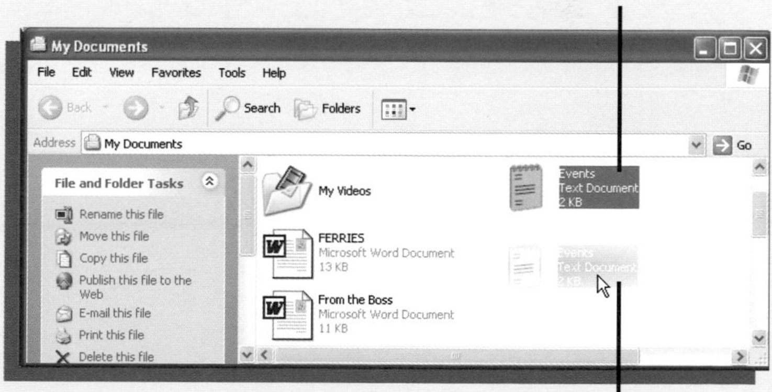

...and drag it into a new location.

Managing Windows

"Managing" a window means bossing it around: You can move it, change its size, and open and close it. Most programs are contained in windows. Although these windows might have some different features, most program windows have more similarities than differences.

Use the Buttons to Switch Between Sizes

The program's title bar

Buttons for switching between window sizes

TIP: To automatically arrange all the windows on your Desktop, right-click a blank spot on the taskbar, and choose the arrangement you want from the shortcut menu.

TRY THIS: Double-click the title bar of a maximized window to restore the window to its original size. Double-click the title bar again to return the window to its maximized size. Now press Alt+Spacebar to open the window's Control menu, and choose the action you want from the menu.

1. Click the Maximize button, and the window enlarges and fills the screen. (If the window is already maximized, you won't see the Maximize button.)
2. Click the Restore Down button, and the window gets smaller. (If the window is already restored, you won't see the Restore Down button.)
3. Click the Minimize button, and the window disappears but you can see its name on a button on the taskbar.
4. Click the window's name on the taskbar button, and the window zooms back to the size it was before you minimized it.

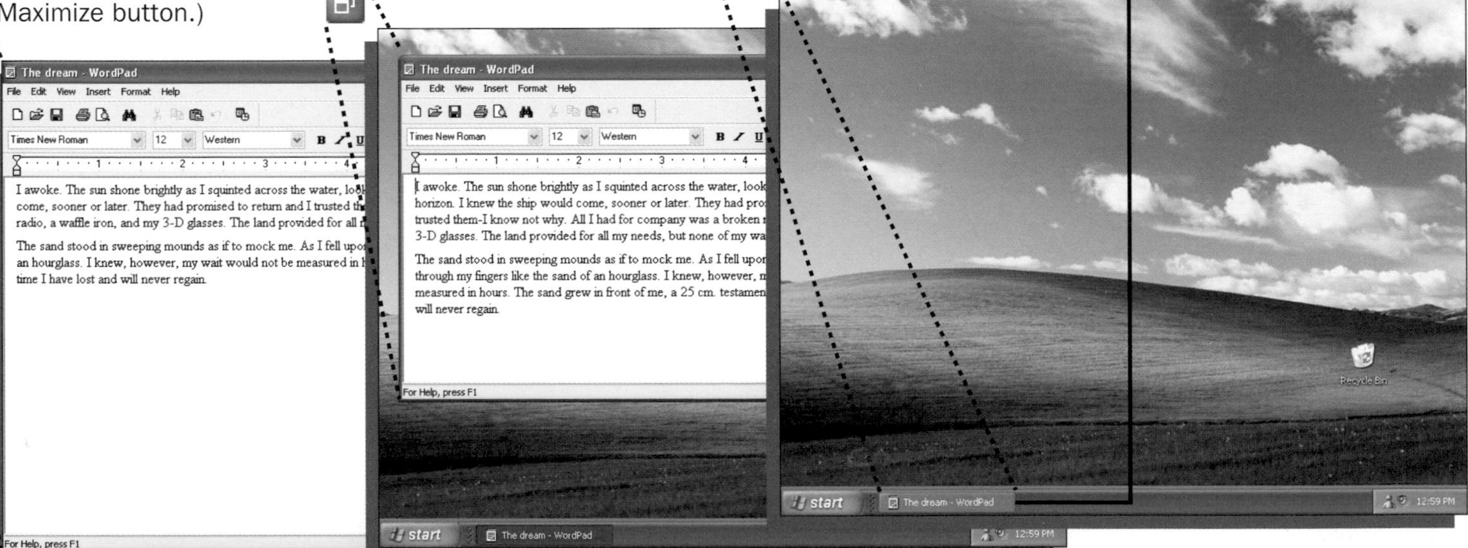

Use the Mouse to Resize a Window

1. Move the mouse over one of the borders of the window until the mouse pointer changes into a two-headed arrow. Drag the window border until the window is the size you want. The directions of the arrowheads show you the directions in which you can move the window border.

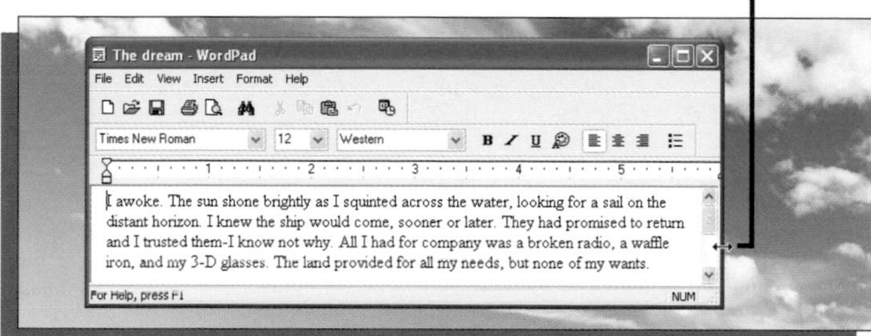

TRY THIS: Move your mouse over a side border, and drag the border to change the window's width. Now move your mouse over the bottom border, and drag the border to change the window's height. Finally, move your mouse over one of the window's corners to change the window's height and width.

TIP: To see the contents of a window when you move it rather than seeing a blank placeholder rectangle, right-click the Desktop, choose Properties from the shortcut menu, and, on the Appearances tab, click the Effects button. In the Effects dialog box, select the Show Window Contents While Dragging check box, and then click OK.

Move a Window

1. Point to the window's title bar.

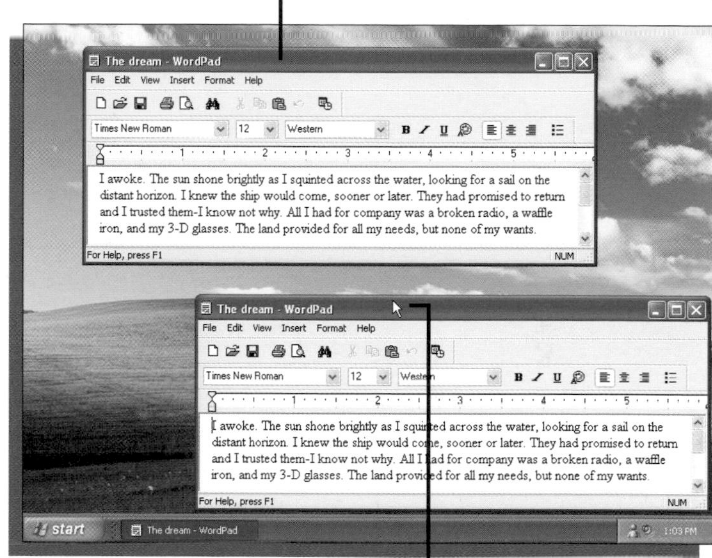

2. Drag the window to a new location.

SEE ALSO: For information about dragging items with the mouse, see "Mouse Maneuvers" on page 17.

TIP: You can't manually resize a maximized window, so if the window you want to resize is currently maximized, click the Restore Down button.

Getting Help

What are big and colorful; packed with information, procedures, shortcuts, and links to online information; and sadly underutilized? The Help programs! Of course, they couldn't possibly replace this book, but you can use them to find concise step-by-step procedures for diagnosing and overcoming problems, and to explore many aspects of managing Windows XP. There are three basic types of help: the Help And Support Center, Program Help, and dialog box Help.

Use the Help And Support Center

1. Click the Start button, and choose Help And Support to open the Help And Support Center.

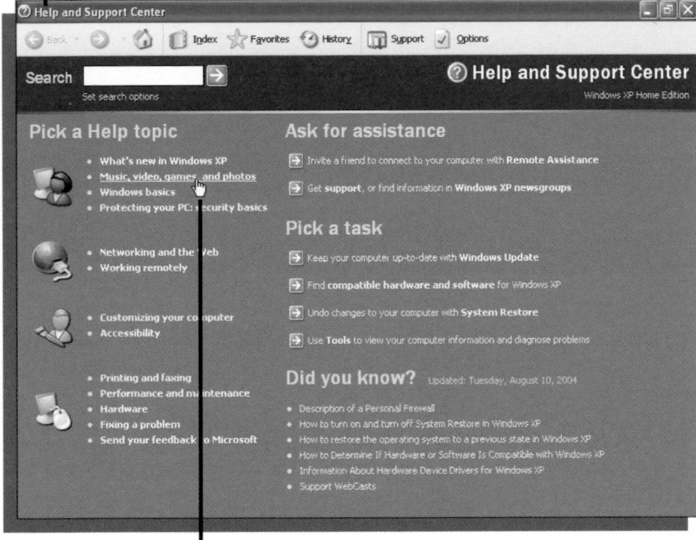

2. Click a link to the main topic of interest. If the item has subtopics, click the subtopic you want.

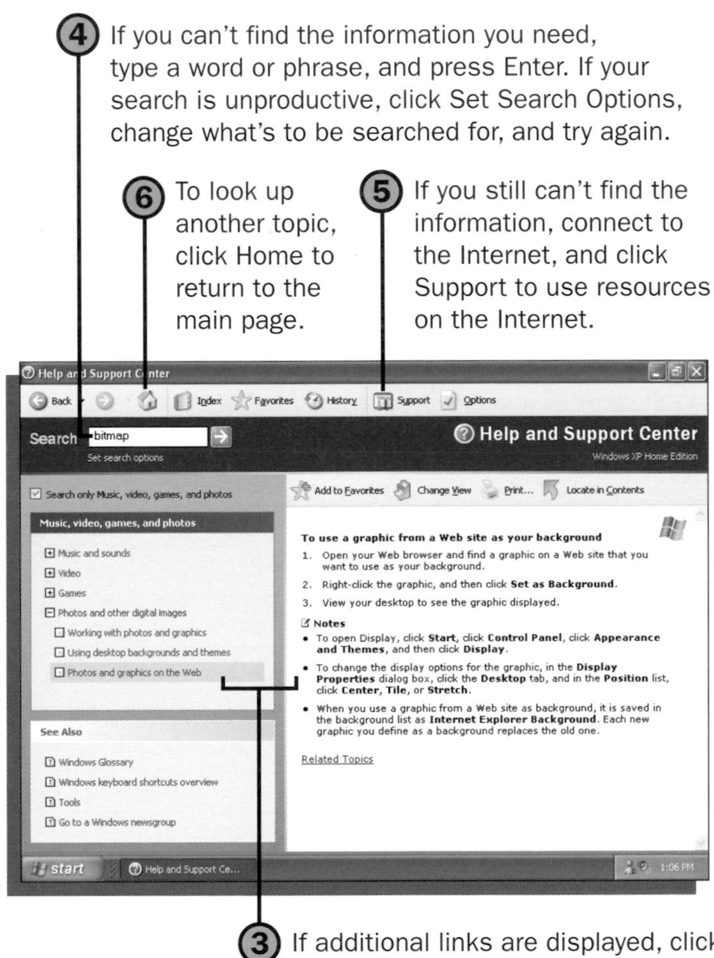

3. If additional links are displayed, click the link that best suits your needs, and then read the information.
4. If you can't find the information you need, type a word or phrase, and press Enter. If your search is unproductive, click Set Search Options, change what's to be searched for, and try again.
5. If you still can't find the information, connect to the Internet, and click Support to use resources on the Internet.
6. To look up another topic, click Home to return to the main page.

TIP: Once you've found the information you want to read as you step through procedures, click the Change View button to display only the relevant information and hide all the extra material.

Use Program Help

1. Choose Help Topics from the program's Help menu to open the Help program.
2. On the Contents tab, click the main topic of interest. Click a subtopic if necessary.
3. Read the information.
4. If you can't find the information you need, click the Index tab, and search for help using keywords.
5. Click the Close button when you've finished.

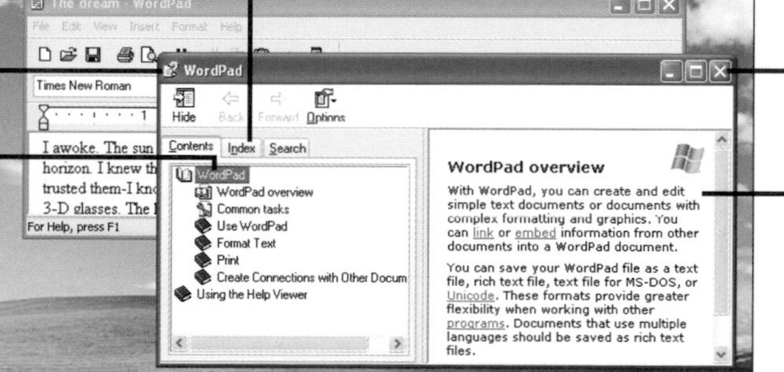

Use Dialog Box Help

1. In any Windows XP dialog box that contains a Help button, click the Help button.
2. Click the item you want information about.
3. Read the Help information, and then click anywhere to close Help.

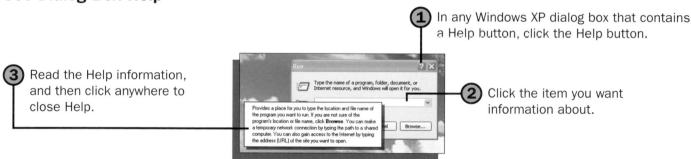

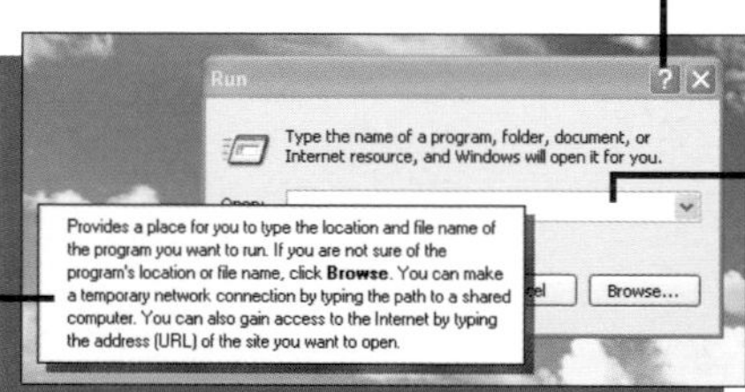

SEE ALSO: For information about getting online help from someone you hope will be knowledgeable about computers and programs, see "Helping Each Other" on pages 302–303.

TIP: To get a printed copy of a Help topic, click Print. To copy information, select the text, and press Ctrl+C. You can then press Ctrl+V to paste the copied text into a program such as WordPad.

Using Shortcut Menus for Quick Results

Windows XP and the programs that work with it were designed to be intuitive—that is, they anticipate what you're likely to want to do when you're working on a particular task, and they place the appropriate commands on a shortcut menu that you open by clicking the *right* mouse button. These shortcut menus are *dynamic,* which means they change depending on the task in progress.

TRY THIS: See what's on the shortcut menus. Right-click the Start button, and note the commands on the shortcut menu that appears. Now right-click a button on the taskbar, and then right-click a blank spot on the taskbar. Open the Start menu and right-click an item. Continue experimenting by right-clicking the Recycle Bin icon on the Desktop, other items on the Desktop, and various files and folders in folder windows. Amazing, isn't it?

Use a Shortcut Menu Command

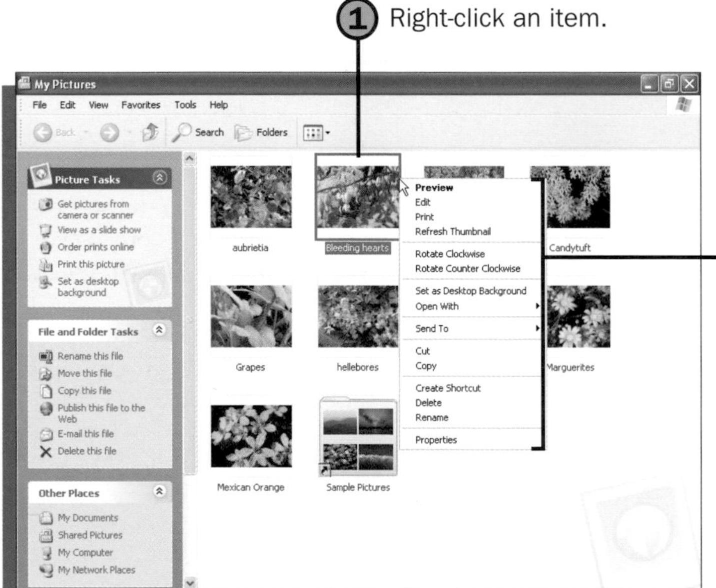

2 Choose a command from the shortcut menu to accomplish the task at hand. If the item or action you want isn't listed on the shortcut menu, do any of the following:

- From the shortcut menu, choose any items whose names have arrows next to them to see whether the item or action you want is on one of the shortcut menu's submenus.
- Check to be sure that you right-clicked the proper item.
- Check the program's documentation or Help files to verify that what you want to do can be accomplished from the item you right-clicked.

TIP: The tasks listed in a folder window are also dynamic, depending on the types of files in the folder, but they usually provide actions that are less specific than those listed on a shortcut menu.

TIP: If you're not sure how to accomplish what you want to do, right-click the item in question, and you'll usually see an appropriate command on the shortcut menu.

Running Programs and Playing Games

In this section

- Composing, Saving, Closing, and Opening a Document
- Copying Material Between Documents
- Inserting Special Characters
- Crunching Numbers
-  Having the Computer Wake You Up
- Running Commands
-  The Microsoft Plus! Packs
- Playing Games
- Running Older Programs
- Starting a Program when Windows Starts
- Changing the Way a Program Starts
- Quitting When You're Stuck

Getting to know the programs that come with Microsoft Windows XP is a bit like moving into new living quarters. Just as your new abode has the basics—stove, refrigerator, and (dare we say it?) windows—the Windows XP operating system comes with many basic accessories and tools. And just as you'll add all the accoutrements that transform empty rooms into a cozy home, you'll add programs to Windows XP to utilize its full potential as you work (and play).

But let's cover the basics first. There's WordPad, a handy little word processor; and Calculator, for scientific calculations as well as quick basic arithmetic. In this section, we'll concentrate on some everyday tasks: composing, saving, and printing a document; creating and editing text; copying items between documents that were created in different programs; and inserting characters such as © and é that don't exist on your keyboard. We'll also take a look at the Calculator and try out some different types of calculations. Finally, we'll discuss working at the command prompt, running MS-DOS programs, and what you can do to get out of trouble when a program isn't working properly.

This section wouldn't be complete without some information about the games that come with Windows XP and with the Windows XP Plus! packs. Whether you want to take a few minutes to work off some energy with a quick game of Pinball, lose yourself for an hour or two in a game of Solitaire, or go further afield and seek out players from around the world to join you in an international game of Backgammon or Checkers, Windows is ready to play!

Composing a Document

WordPad is a powerful little word processor with which you can create documents in Rich Text format, or as plain text or Unicode text documents. In most cases you'll want to create a document with formatting for a well-designed, professional look. Save the document as you create it, and print it when you've finished.

Create a Document

1. Start WordPad from the Accessories submenu of the Start menu. If WordPad is already running, click the New button on the toolbar, click Rich Text Document in the list, and click OK.

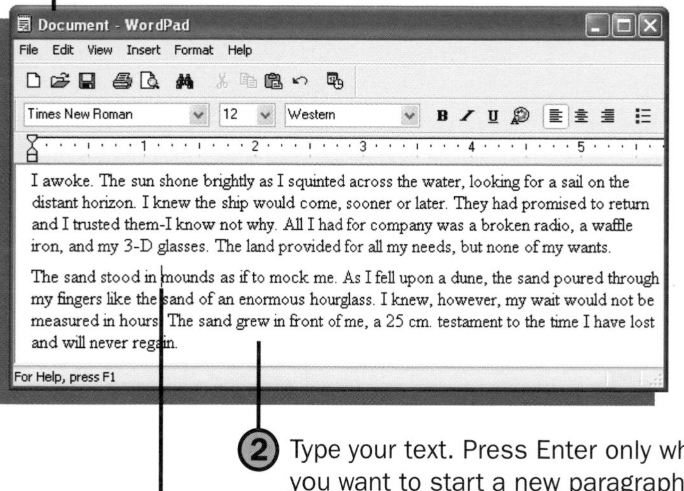

2. Type your text. Press Enter only when you want to start a new paragraph.
3. To edit the text, click in the document where you want to make the change. An insertion point indicates where your edit will be placed.

> I awoke. The sun shone brightly as I squinted across the water, looking for a sail on the distant horizon. I knew the ship would come, sooner or later. They had promised to return and I trusted them-I know not why. All I had for company was a broken radio, a waffle iron, and my 3-D glasses. The land provided for all my needs, but none of my wants.
>
> The sand stood in sweeping mounds as if to mock me. As I fell upon a dune, the sand poured through my fingers like the sand of an enormous hourglass. I knew, however, my wait would not be measured in hours. The sand grew in front of me, a 25 cm. testament to the time I have lost and will never regain.

4. To insert additional text into a paragraph you've already typed, click where you want to insert the new text, and type it. If the text you want to insert is stored on the Clipboard, click the Paste button on the toolbar instead of typing the text.

> I awoke. The sun shone brightly as I squinted across the water, looking for a sail on the distant horizon. I knew the ship would come, sooner or later. They had promised to return and I trusted them-I know not why. All I had for company was a broken radio, a waffle iron, and my 3-D glasses. The land provided for all my needs, but none of my wants.
>
> The sand stood in sweeping mounds as if to mock me. As I fell upon a dune, the sand poured through my fingers like the sand of an enormous hourglass. I knew, however, my wait would not be measured in hours. The sand grew in front of me, a 25 cm. testament to the time I have lost and will never regain.

5. To delete text, select it, and press Delete. To save the text for later use instead of deleting it, place it on the Clipboard by clicking the Cut button on the toolbar.

> I awoke. The sun shone brightly as I squinted across the water, looking for a sail on the distant horizon. I knew the ship would come, sooner or later. They had promised to return and I trusted them-I know not why. All I had for company was a broken radio, a waffle iron, and my 3-D glasses. The land provided for all my needs, but none of my wants.
>
> The sand stood in sweeping mounds as if to mock me. As I fell upon a dune, the sand poured through my fingers like the sand of an hourglass. I knew, however, my wait would not be measured in hours. The sand grew in front of me, a 25 cm. testament to the time I have lost and will never regain.

6. To replace existing text with different text, select the text, and then type the new text.

TIP: The Windows Clipboard is a temporary "holding area" for items you copy or cut.

Format the Document

1. Select the text to be formatted.
2. Specify the font, font size, and font script (the locale or type of font). Apply bold, italic, underlined, or color emphasis as desired.

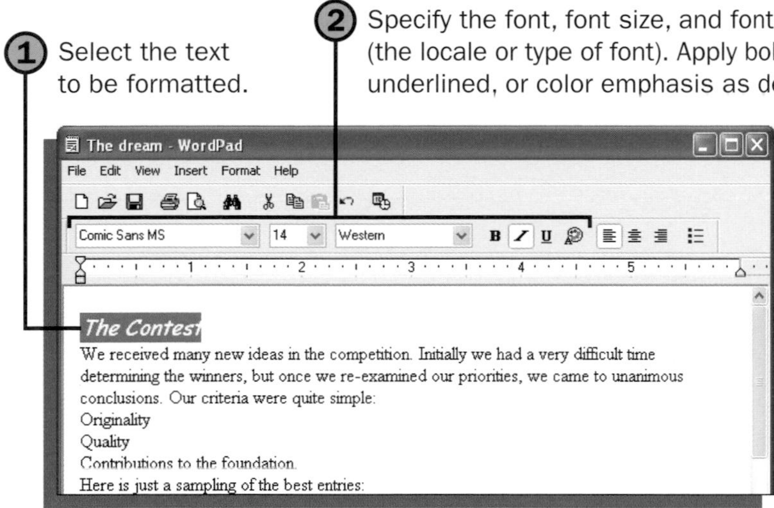

3. Click in the paragraph you want to format, or select all the paragraphs to which you want to apply the same formatting.
4. Use the Alignment buttons to align your text, or use the Bullets button to create a bulleted list.

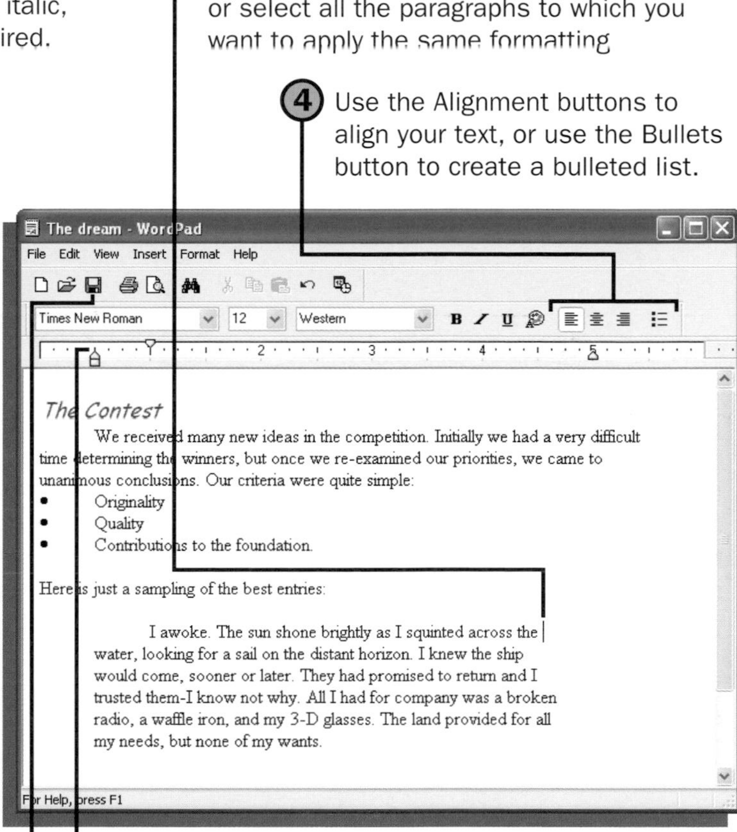

5. Drag the indent markers to set the left, right, and first-line indents. Click in the ruler to set a tab stop.
6. Save the document.

CAUTION: If you're planning to save your document as a Text Document (plain text), don't apply any formatting to it. If you do, all the formatting will be lost when you save the document.

TRY THIS: Select some text in a document, and choose Font from the Format menu. In the Font dialog box, specify a font, a font size, and any emphasis you want, and click OK. Now click in a paragraph, choose Paragraph from the Format menu, and use the Paragraph dialog box to set exact measurements for the paragraph indents you want. Click OK. Choose Tabs from the Format menu, and use the Tabs dialog box to set the exact position of any tabs you want in the paragraph. Click OK. Now move to the end of the paragraph, press Enter, and type some text. You'll see that all the paragraph formatting from the previous paragraph has been copied and applied to the new paragraph.

Saving, Closing, and Opening a Document

After you've created a document, you'll probably want to save it for later use. When you've finished using the program in which you created the document, close the program so that it isn't using space or taking power from your computer. Then, when you're ready to work on your document again, you can easily restart the program and open the document directly from the running program.

Save a Document

1. Click the Save button on the toolbar, or, if the toolbar isn't visible, choose Save from the File menu.
2. If you don't want to save the document to the default folder, specify a different drive or folder.

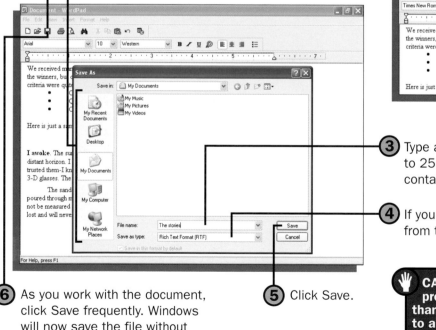

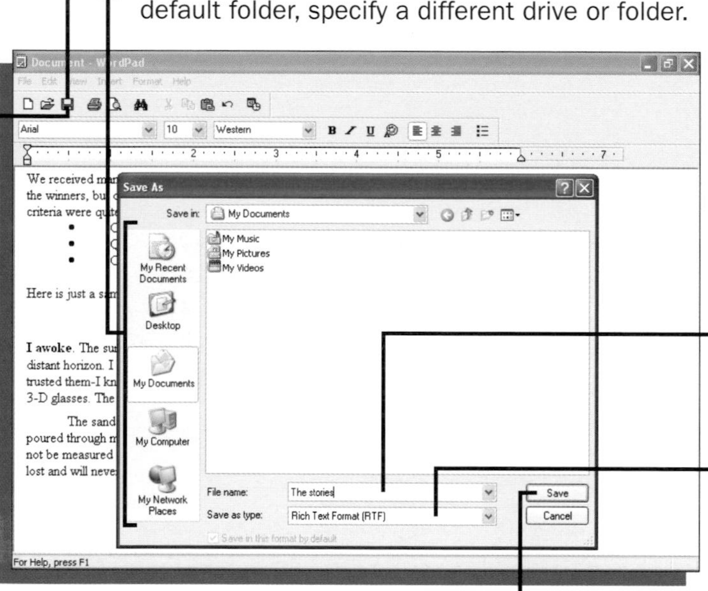

3. Type a name for the document. The name can be up to 255 characters long; it can contain spaces but can't contain the * : < > | " \ or / characters.
4. If you want to save the document in a different format from that of the default file format, select the format.
5. Click Save.
6. As you work with the document, click Save frequently. Windows will now save the file without displaying the Save As dialog box.

TIP: In many programs, you can press Ctrl+S to quickly save a document.

Close a Document

1. Click the Save button one last time to make sure that you've saved all changes in the document.
2. Click the Close button to end the program.

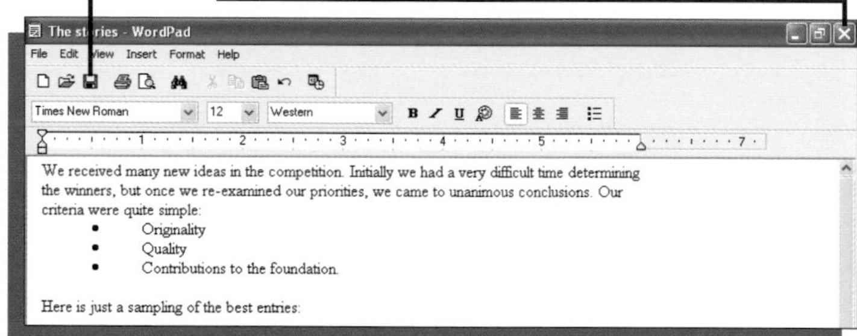

CAUTION: Long file names are often truncated by programs, so a descriptive short name is better than a long one. If you want to include the full path to a file, you can use the : and \ characters in the File Name box.

Open a Document

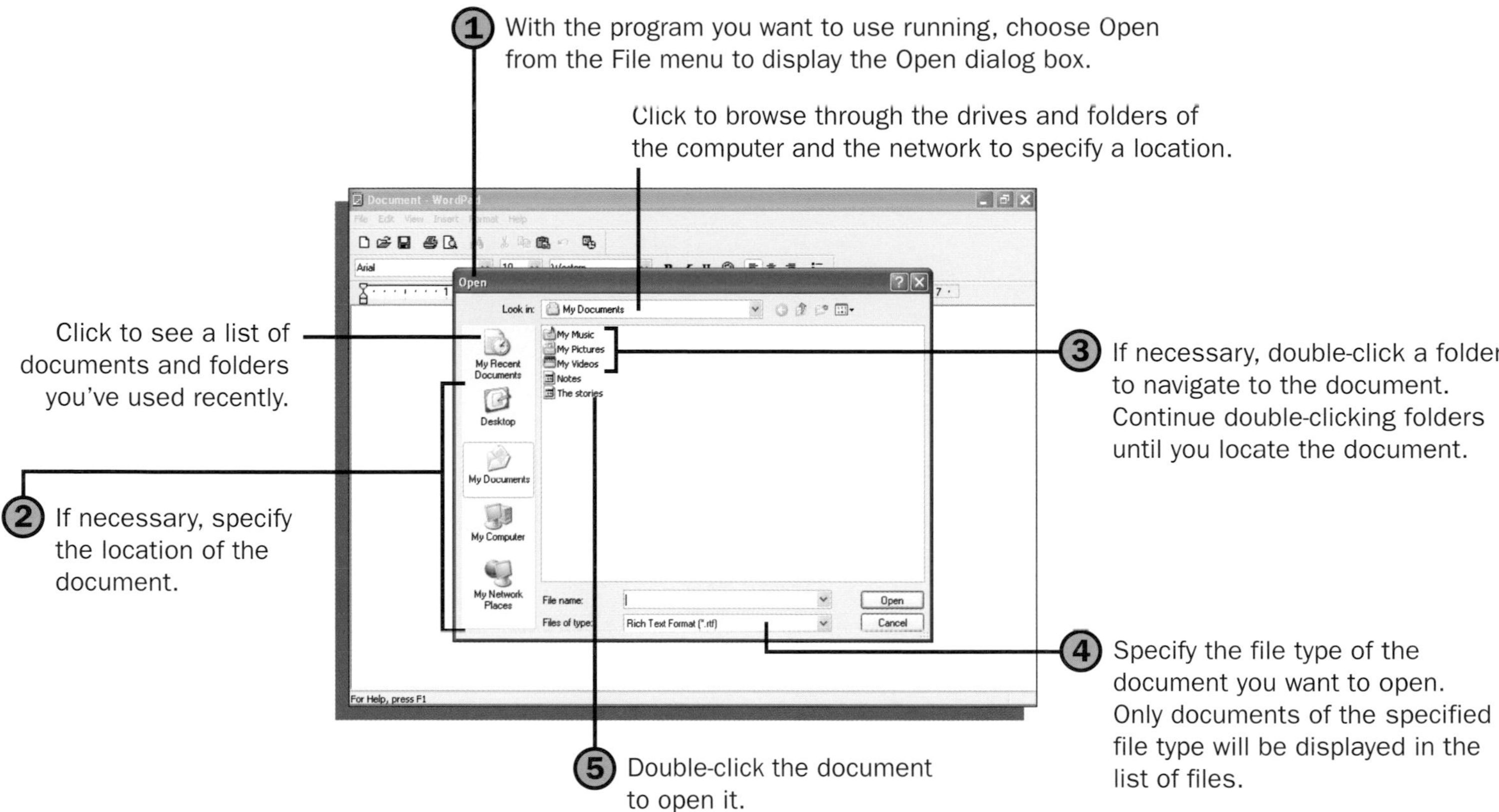
1 With the program you want to use running, choose Open from the File menu to display the Open dialog box.
Click to browse through the drives and folders of the computer and the network to specify a location.
Click to see a list of documents and folders you've used recently.
2 If necessary, specify the location of the document.
3 If necessary, double-click a folder to navigate to the document. Continue double-clicking folders until you locate the document.
4 Specify the file type of the document you want to open. Only documents of the specified file type will be displayed in the list of files.
5 Double-click the document to open it.
Open
Look in:
My Documents
My Music
My Pictures
My Videos
Notes
The stories
My Recent Documents
Desktop
My Documents
My Computer
My Network Places
File name:
Files of type:
Rich Text Format (*.rtf)
Open
Cancel
For Help, press F1

TRY THIS: Many programs can stay open for additional work even after you close the document you're working on. Open the File menu and look at the commands. If there's a Close command, click it to close the document without closing the program. If there's a New command but no Close command, choose New to see whether it closes the open document.

TIP: Most, but not all, programs use the Save As and Open dialog boxes just like the ones used by WordPad. If you have a program that uses its own style of dialog box, you'll probably need to consult the program's documentation if you need additional help.

Copying Material Between Documents

It's easy to copy material from a document that was created in one program to a document that was created in another program. The way you insert the material depends on what it is. If it's similar to and compatible with the receiving document—text that's being copied into a WordPad document, for example—you can usually insert it as is and can edit it in the receiving document's program. If the item is dissimilar—a sound clip, say, inserted into a WordPad document—either it's *encapsulated,* or isolated, as an object and can be edited in the originating program only, or you simply are not able to paste that item into your document.

Copy and Insert Material

1. In the source document, select the material you want to copy.
2. Choose Copy from the Edit menu. Windows places copied items on the Windows Clipboard. (You can copy only one item at a time, so always paste the Clipboard contents into your document before you copy anything else, or you'll lose whatever was on the Clipboard.)

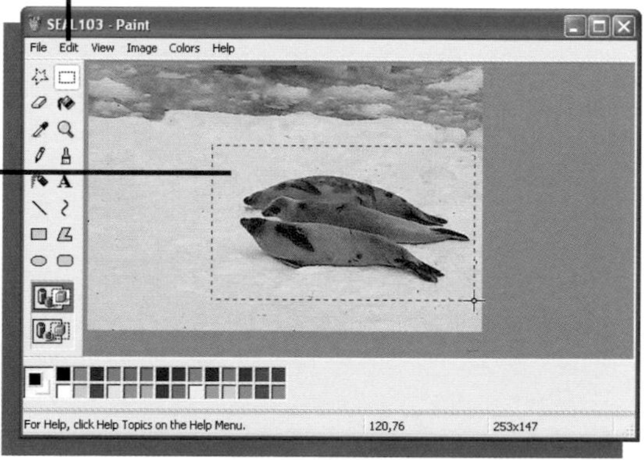

3. Switch to the destination document.
4. Click where you want to insert the material.
5. Click the Paste button or choose Paste from the Edit menu.

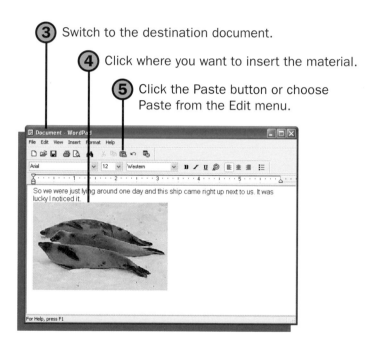

TIP: To insert the copied material in a different format, or as an icon for an online document, choose Paste Special from the Edit menu instead of choosing the Paste command, provided the command is available on the menu.

TIP: Some programs—those that are part of Microsoft Office, for example—have their own Clipboard, which allows you to store and retrieve multiple copied items from Office programs.

Dialog Box Decisions

You're going to be seeing a lot of *dialog boxes* as you use Windows XP, and if you're not familiar with them now, you soon will be. Dialog boxes appear when Windows XP or a program—WordPad, let's say—needs you to make one or more decisions about what you want to do. Sometimes all you have to do is click a Yes, a No, or an OK button; at other times, there'll be quite a few decisions to make in one dialog box. The Print dialog box, shown below, is typical of many dialog boxes and is one you'll probably be seeing frequently, so take a look at its components and the way they work.

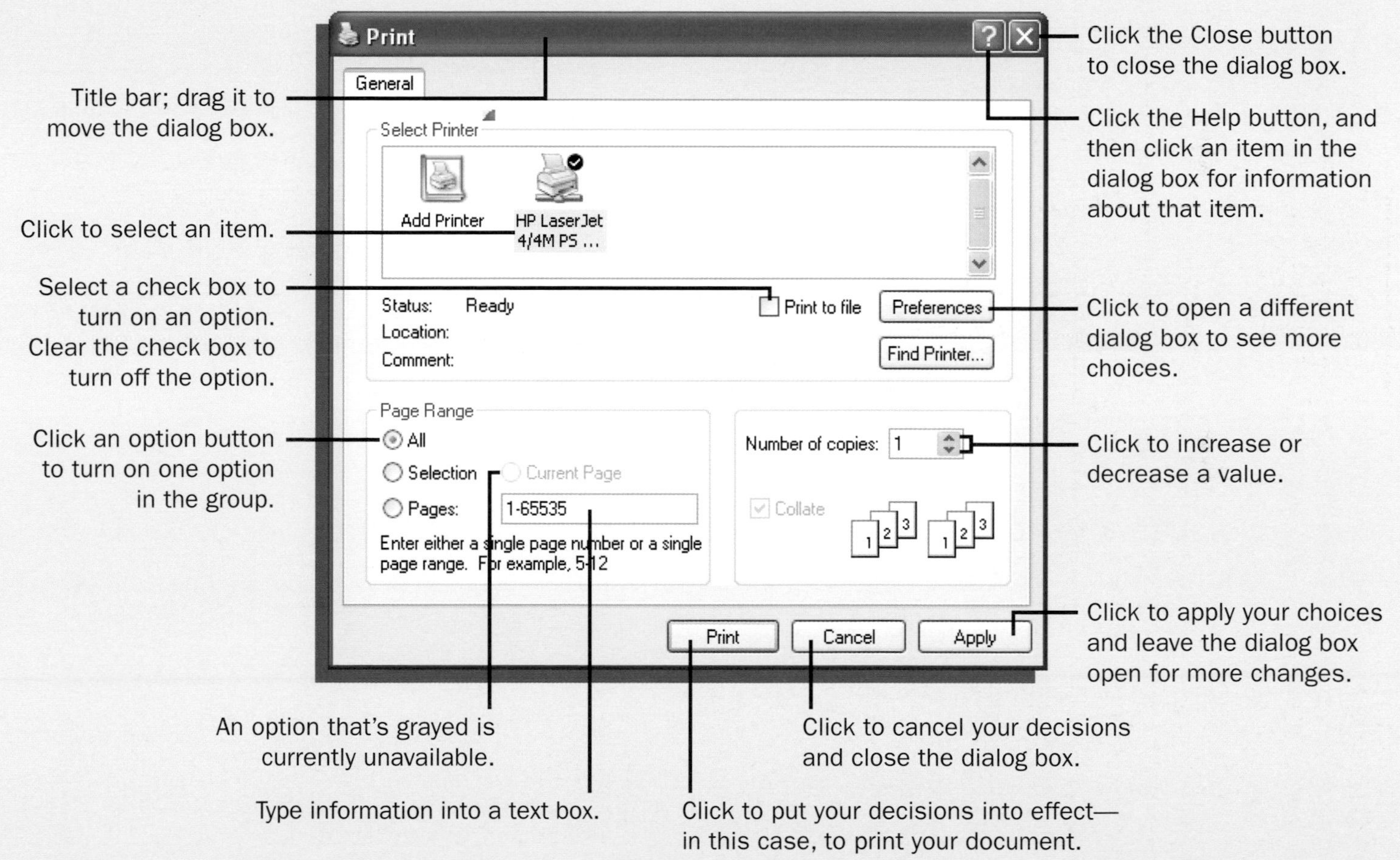

Print
General
Select Printer
Add Printer
HP LaserJet 4/4M PS ...
Status: Ready
Location:
Comment:
Print to file
Preferences
Find Printer...
Page Range
All
Selection
Current Page
Pages:
1-65535
Enter either a single page number or a single page range. For example, 5-12
Number of copies: 1
Collate
Print
Cancel
Apply
Title bar; drag it to move the dialog box.
Click to select an item.
Select a check box to turn on an option. Clear the check box to turn off the option.
Click an option button to turn on one option in the group.
Click the Close button to close the dialog box.
Click the Help button, and then click an item in the dialog box for information about that item.
Click to open a different dialog box to see more choices.
Click to increase or decrease a value.
Click to apply your choices and leave the dialog box open for more changes.
An option that's grayed is currently unavailable.
Type information into a text box.
Click to cancel your decisions and close the dialog box.
Click to put your decisions into effect—in this case, to print your document.

Inserting Special Characters

Windows XP provides a special accessory program called Character Map that lets you insert into your programs the characters and symbols that aren't available on your keyboard. Character Map displays all the characters that are available for each of the fonts on your computer.

Find and Insert a Character

1. Start Character Map from the System Tools submenu of the Start menu.
2. Specify a font.

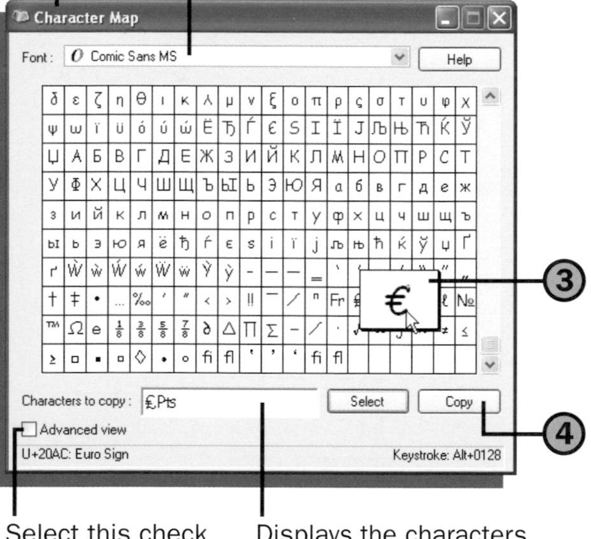

3. Double-click the character you want to insert. Double-click any other characters that you want to insert at the same time.
4. Click Copy to place the character or characters on the Clipboard.

Select this check box to use search features to locate a character.

Displays the characters you've selected to be copied to the Clipboard.

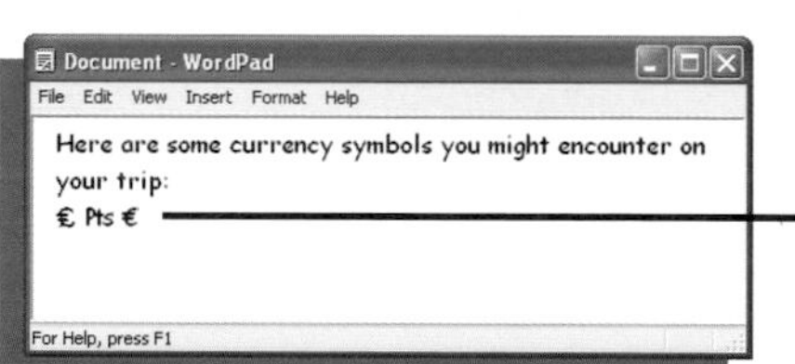

5. Switch to your program, click where you want to insert the character or characters, and press Ctrl+V (or choose Paste from the Edit menu) to paste the character or characters from the Clipboard into your document. Format and edit the inserted text as desired.

TIP: Click a character to see an enlarged view of it to ensure that you're selecting the correct character.

CAUTION: The Windows Clipboard is a temporary "holding area" for items you want to cut or copy and paste. The Clipboard can hold only one item at a time, so do your pasting immediately after you've done your copying.

SEE ALSO: **For information about installing Character Map if it isn't already installed, see "Adding or Removing Windows Components" on pages 210–211.**

TRY THIS: In Character Map, select a character you insert frequently, and note the keyboard shortcut for the character in the bottom right corner of the Character Map dialog box. Switch to the program into which you want to insert the character, hold down the Alt key, and use the numeric keypad to enter the numbers. Format the inserted character with a different font or font size if desired.

Crunching Numbers

Need to do a quick calculation but don't have enough fingers? Want to convert a decimal number into a hexadecimal or binary number? You can do these procedures, and even a few complex geometric and statistical calculations, with the Calculator.

> **TIP:** To determine the purpose of a key and to view its keyboard shortcut, right-click the key, and choose What's This? from the shortcut menu.

Use the Calculator

1. Start the Calculator from the Accessories submenu of the Start menu.
2. Either click the number buttons or type the numerals you want. Continue until you've entered the entire number.
3. Click a function.
4. Enter the next number.
5. When you've entered all the numbers, click the equal (=) button. Press Ctrl+C to copy the result if you want to paste it into your document.

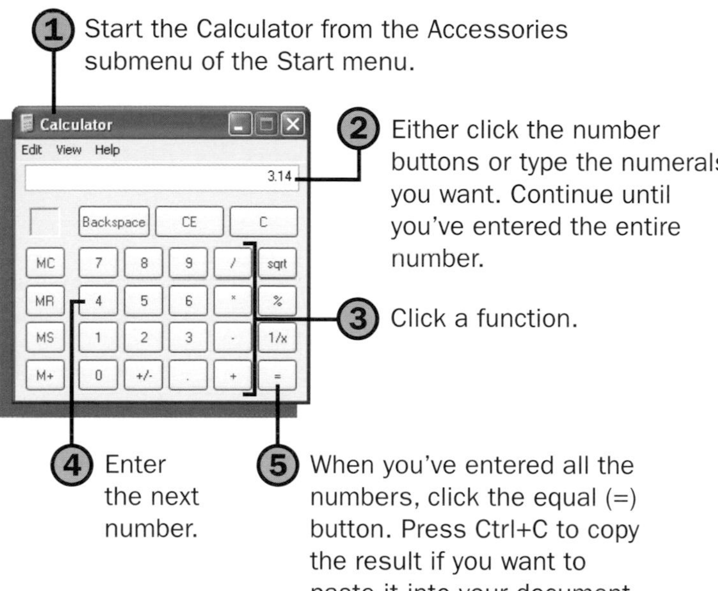

> **TIP:** To speed up your calculations, use the numeric keypad on your computer's keyboard, pressing the + – * / and Enter keys instead of clicking the corresponding buttons. Make sure, however, that the Num Lock key is turned on.

Make Complex Calculations

1. Choose Scientific from the View menu.
2. Choose a numbering system if you don't want to calculate using the standard decimal system.
3. Enter a value.
4. Use any of the function keys to calculate a new value.

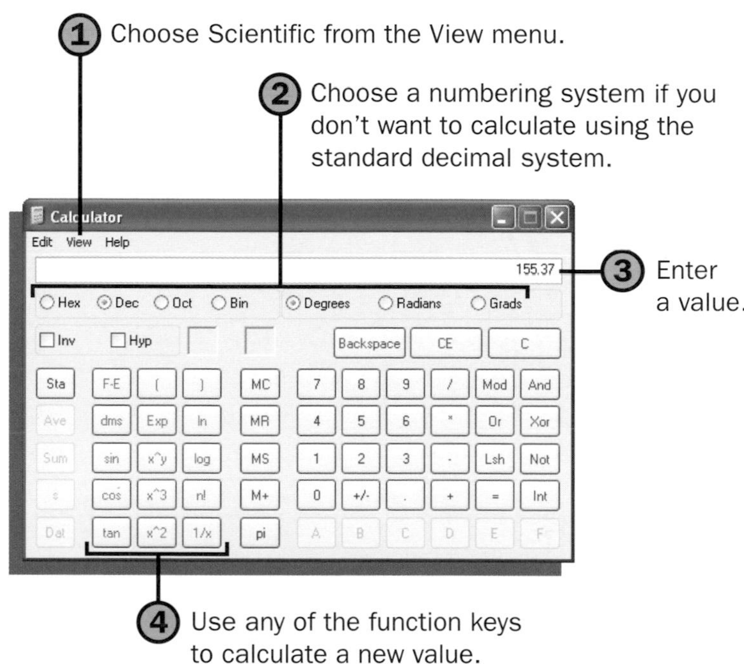

> **TRY THIS:** Enter a long number, and then choose Digit Grouping from the View menu. Note that the digits are grouped and separated by either a space, a comma, or a period, depending on the type of number as well as your regional settings.

Having the Computer Wake You Up ❂ NEW FEATURE

Is your work at the computer putting you to sleep? Or do you need an alarm at various times throughout the day to remind you that it's lunchtime, time for a meeting, or time to escape and go home? Either way, you can set your computer to wake you up or to alert you that it's time to do something specific. With the Microsoft Plus! Digital Media Edition installed on your computer, you can use the Plus! Alarm Clock to play your choice of music or sounds to wake you from your slumbers or daydreams.

TRY THIS: Set an alarm for the time you come home. Set the alarm to sound every day at a specific time if you arrive home at the same time each day, or create separate alarms if you return at variable times. Select a playlist you've created as the alarm sound. Now, provided your computer is running, you'll be welcomed home with your favorite music.

SEE ALSO: For information about creating a playlist, see "Arranging Your Media with Playlists" on pages 134–135.

Set the Alarm

1. Choose Plus! Alarm Clock from the Microsoft Plus! Digital Media submenu, and click the Create Alarm button to start the Create New Alarm Wizard.
2. Type a descriptive name for the alarm if you don't want to use the default name.
3. Specify at what intervals you want the alarm to sound.
4. Under Start Time, click the hour that's displayed to select it, and then use the scroll arrows to specify the hour you want. Then click the minutes, and use the scroll arrows to specify the minutes you want. Finally, click AM or PM, and use the scroll arrows to specify which one you want.
5. Select the setting you want for the alarm interval you chose. Each type of interval has different settings.
6. Under Start Date, click the down arrow, and choose the date for the first time the alarm will sound.
7. Click Next.
8. Specify how you want to display your media files, and then choose the media file you want as your alarm.
9. Click Next, verify that the settings are correct, and then click Finish to set the alarm.

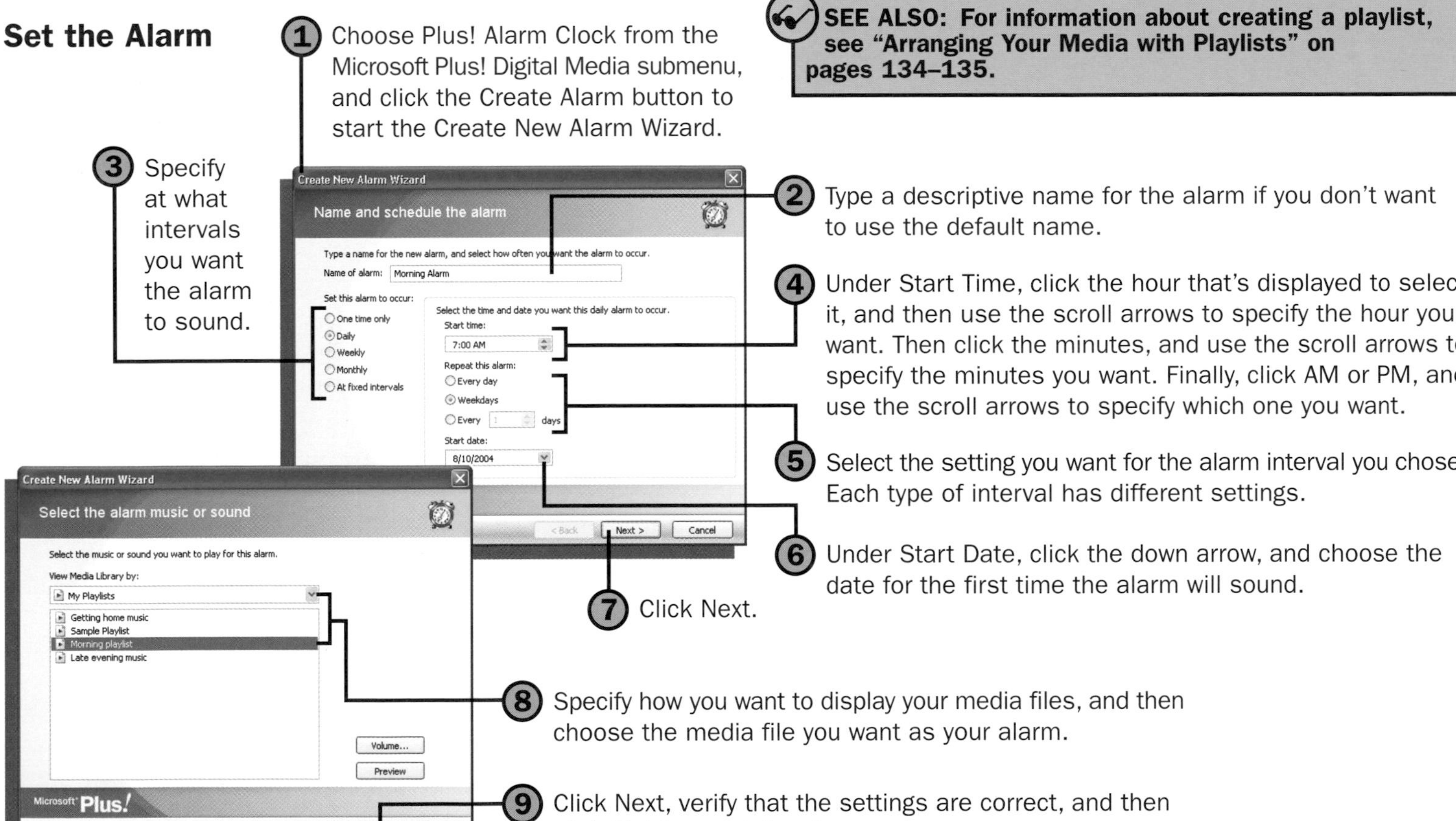

Shut Off the Alarm

TIP: To stop the Plus! Alarm Clock from running in the background, choose Exit from the File menu in the Alarm Clock window; or right-click the clock icon, and choose Exit from the shortcut menu that appears.

1. When the alarm starts and the Plus! Alarm Clock window appears, do any of the following:

- Click Snooze to temporarily turn off the alarm.
- Click Turn Off Ring to cancel the alarm until the next time it's scheduled to start.
- Click Change to start the Change Alarm Wizard if you want to modify any or all of the alarm settings.
- Close the window to use the snooze feature or turn off the alarm, depending on your settings.

Customize the Alarm

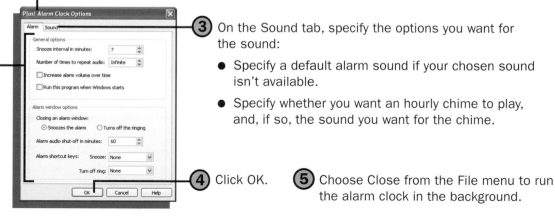

1. In the Plus! Alarm Clock window, choose Options from the Tools menu to display the Plus! Alarm Clock Options dialog box. If the Plus! Alarm Clock window isn't displayed, double-click the clock icon in the notification area of the taskbar to display it.

2. On the Alarm tab of the Options dialog box, modify the way the alarm works.

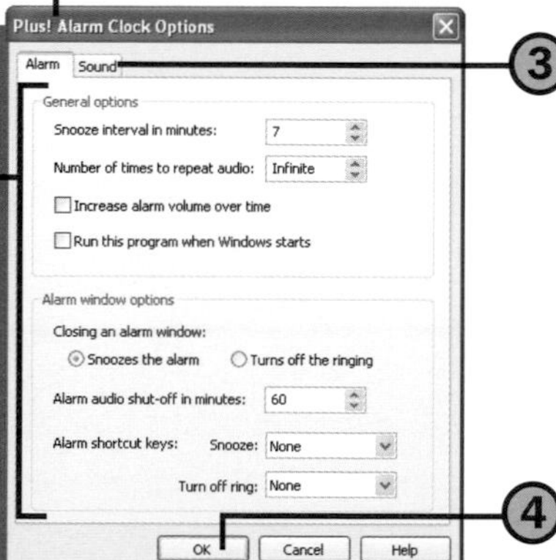

3. On the Sound tab, specify the options you want for the sound:

- Specify a default alarm sound if your chosen sound isn't available.
- Specify whether you want an hourly chime to play, and, if so, the sound you want for the chime.

4. Click OK.

5. Choose Close from the File menu to run the alarm clock in the background.

Running Commands

In Windows XP, the command prompt is the place where you can execute *command-line* instructions. Most of the commands are the old standard MS-DOS commands, some are enhancements of the MS-DOS commands, and others are commands that are unique to Windows XP. When you want or need to work from the command prompt, you can open a command prompt window and execute all your tasks there, including using the basic commands, starting a program, and even starting a program in a new window.

Run a Command

1. Open a command prompt window by choosing Command Prompt from the Accessories submenu of the Start menu.
2. At the prompt, type a command, including any *switches* and extra *parameters,* and press Enter.
3. Enter any additional commands you want to run.

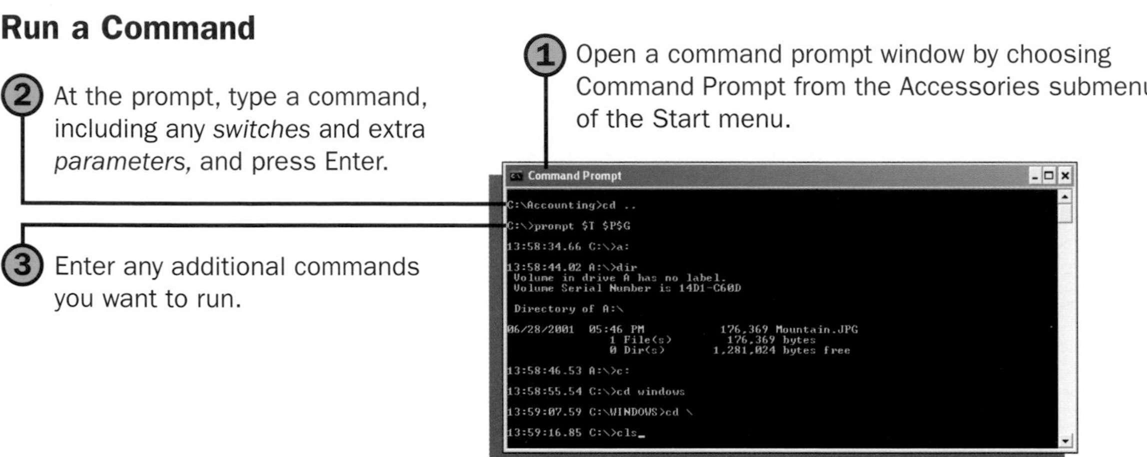
Command Prompt
C:\Accounting>cd ..
C:\>prompt $T PG
13:58:34.66 C:\>a:
13:58:44.02 A:\>dir
Volume in drive A has no label.
Volume Serial Number is 14D1-C60D
Directory of A:\
06/28/2001 05:46 PM 176,369 Mountain.JPG
1 File(s) 176,369 bytes
0 Dir(s) 1,281,024 bytes free
13:58:46.53 A:\>c:
13:58:55.54 C:\>cd windows
13:59:07.59 C:\WINDOWS>cd \
13:59:16.85 C:\>cls_

CAUTION: The command prompt is a powerful weapon that can disrupt your system, delete files, and create general havoc. Don't execute commands unless you know what they're designed for.

TIP: Many commands have switches that allow the use of extra parameters, giving you greater control of the command. A switch is the part of the command with the forward slash (/), followed by a letter, a number, or another instruction. A parameter is an additional instruction you provide, such as the file name or drive letter.

The Top 10 Command Prompt Commands

Command	Function
cd	Switches to the specified folder (or directory).
cls	Clears the screen.
copy	Copies the specified files or folders.
dir	Shows the contents of the current directory.
drive:	Switches to the specified drive (type the drive letter and a colon).
exit	Ends the session.
mem	Displays memory configuration.
path	Displays or sets the path the command searches.
prompt	Changes the information displayed at the prompt.
rename	Renames the specified file or files if the wildcard characters ? or * are used.

Find a Command

1. At the command prompt, type **help** and press Enter.
2. Review the list of commands.

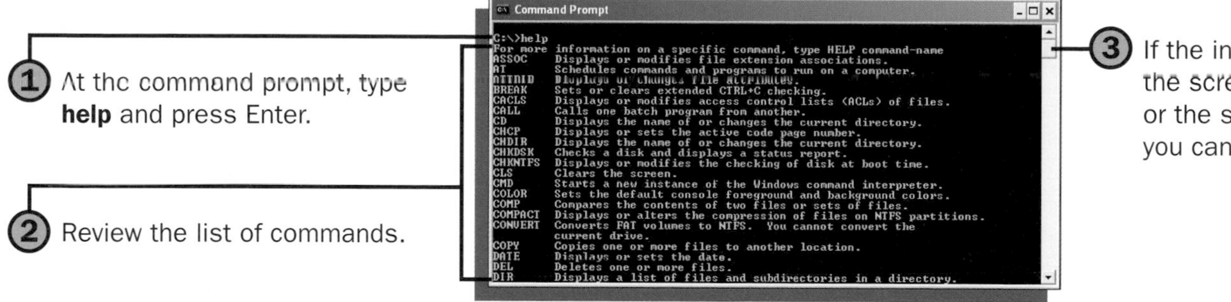

Command Prompt
CHDIR [/D] [drive:][path]
C:\>help
For more information on a specific command, type HELP command-name
ASSOC Displays or modifies file extension associations.
AT Schedules commands and programs to run on a computer.
BREAK Sets or clears extended CTRL+C checking.
CACLS Displays or modifies access control lists (ACLs) of files.
CALL Calls one batch program from another.
CD Displays the name of or changes the current directory.
CHCP Displays or sets the active code page number.
CHDIR Displays the name of or changes the current directory.
CHKDSK Checks a disk and displays a status report.
CHKNTFS Displays or modifies the checking of disk at boot time.
CLS Clears the screen.
CMD Starts a new instance of the Windows command interpreter.
COLOR Sets the default console foreground and background colors.
COMP Compares the contents of two files or sets of files.
COMPACT Displays or alters the compression of files on NTFS partitions.
CONVERT Converts FAT volumes to NTFS. You cannot convert the current drive.
COPY Copies one or more files to another location.
DATE Displays or sets the date.
DEL Deletes one or more files.
DIR Displays a list of files and subdirectories in a directory.

3. If the information scrolls off the screen, use the scroll bar or the scroll arrows so that you can see the entire list.

Get Information About a Command

1. Type a command followed by a space and **/?** and then press Enter to get information about the command.
2. Read the information.

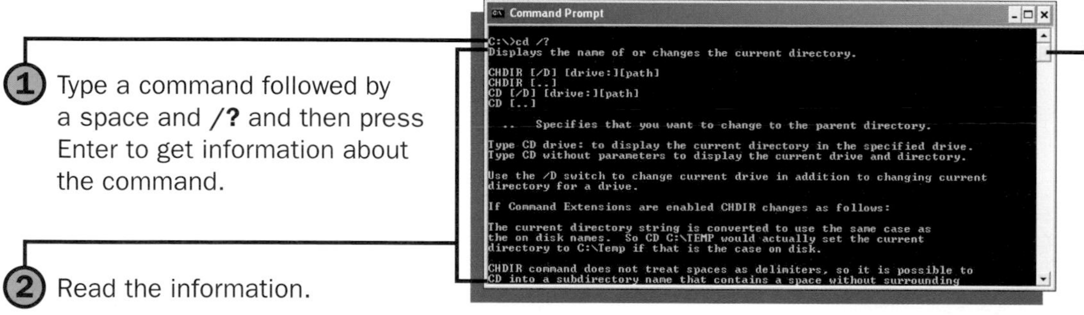

CD [/D] [drive:][path]

.. Specifies that you want to change to the parent directory.

If Command Extensions are enabled CHDIR changes as follows:
The current directory string is converted to use the same case as the on disk names. So CD C:\TEMP would actually set the current directory to C:\Temp if that is the case on disk.
CHDIR command does not treat spaces as delimiters, so it is possible to CD into a subdirectory name that contains a space without surrounding

3. If the information scrolls off the screen, use the scroll bar or the scroll arrows so that you can see the entire text.

TIP: To change some of the settings for the command prompt window—the font, the cursor size, or the colors, for example—right-click the window's title bar, and choose Properties from the shortcut menu.

TRY THIS: At the command prompt, type help > dosref.txt **and press Enter. Now use Notepad or WordPad to open the file *dosref.txt* that's stored on your hard disk (it's the folder that was active when you typed the command). The > symbol redirected the output from the screen to the file. You now have a reference for the commands, which you can easily print out.**

The Microsoft Plus! Packs NEW FEATURE

There are two versions of Microsoft Plus! for Windows XP: the Microsoft Plus! Standard Pack, which provides additional features for Windows Media Player and digital recording, games, themes, and screen savers; and the Plus! Digital Media Edition, which provides new tools for enjoying and working with your digital media, and generally making your computer come alive for parties and entertainment. The Plus! packs are separate products that you purchase in addition to Windows XP, so you'll need to decide whether you want one or both Plus! packs.

Microsoft Plus! Standard Pack

This pack includes:

- Voice control for Windows Media Player
- A converter to change MP3-format music files into the more compact Windows Media Audio (WMA) format
- A CD label maker to create labels, inserts, and booklets for the CDs you create
- Speaker profiles to enhance sound on certain brands of speakers
- A personal DJ program to create custom playlists from multiple sources
- Twelve Media Player skins to customize the look of Windows Media Player
- Three new 3-D visualizations that can be displayed while your music plays
- Three new games: Russian Squares, Labyrinth, and HyperBowl
- Four Themes to modify the look of your Windows environment
- Eight three-dimensional screen savers

Microsoft Plus! Digital Media Edition

This pack includes:

- An alarm clock that plays your music at preset times
- An analog recorder to capture music from records and tapes as digital music
- A converter to convert MP3, WAV, and WMA formats into the Windows Media format of your choice
- A CD label maker to create labels, inserts, and booklets for the CDs you create
- Electronic dancers who dance on your screen while your music plays
- A Windows Media skin that lets you quickly choose individual music files while limiting access to the rest of your computer
- Photo Story, which lets you assemble a photo show with narration, background music, and panning across the pictures
- A program for downloading and organizing your digital media and Internet files on a Pocket PC portable device

Note that the two products work a bit differently from each other. In the standard Plus! pack, you access all the programs from a window that opens. In the Digital Media Edition, you start all the programs from a submenu of the Start menu. The two Plus! packages do have some similarities, however: For example, any items that are additions to Media Player are integrated directly into Media Player, which means that if you have Plus! on your computer, the new skins will appear in the Skin Chooser section of Media Player. You can also download many more enhancements to both of the Plus! packs from the Microsoft Plus! Web site. Note, however, that without having either or both of the Plus! packs installed on your computer, you won't be able to install any of these downloads.

Playing FreeCell

FreeCell—a modified version of Solitaire—is a game you play by yourself. The entire deck is dealt, and, as in Solitaire, you arrange the cards by stacking them in descending order, alternating the red and black cards. Unlike the way you play Solitaire, the sequence of cards can begin anywhere in the stack. You can move a single card onto another card to add to the sequence of cards, or into one of the free cells at the top, or into a blank column after the column has been emptied of cards. You win by stacking all the cards by suit in ascending order.

Play FreeCell

1. Start FreeCell from the Games submenu of the Start menu, and choose New Game from the Game menu to start your game.

Free cells

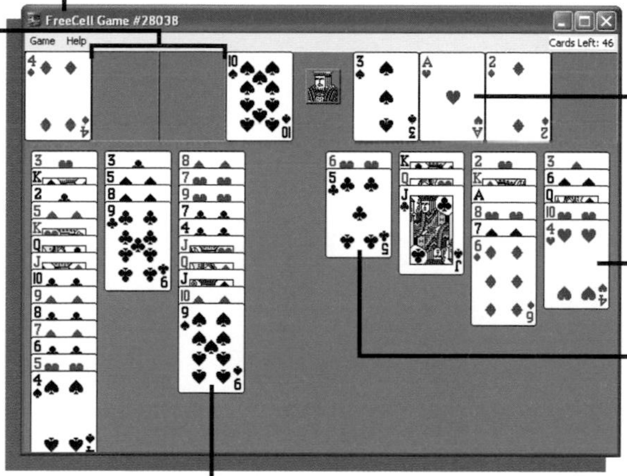

FreeCell Game #28038

Game Help

Cards Left: 46

2. When possible, move an Ace to the top of the window and stack the cards by suit in ascending order (FreeCell might do this for you automatically).
3. Click to select the card you want to move.
4. Click another card to move the selected card on top of it. (The cards must be stacked in alternating colors in descending numeric order.)
5. Continue stacking the cards, including moving cards into or from a free cell. You can also move one card or a series of cards into an empty column.
6. Repeat steps 2 through 5 until all the cards are stacked by suit.

TIP: If there are enough available free cells, you can move an entire series of cards from one column into another.

TIP: Try to free the Ace cards early in the game and to keep as many free cells and empty columns as possible.

TIP: To replay a specific game, note the game number on the title bar. When you're ready to replay the game, choose Select Game from the Game menu, enter the game number, and click OK.

Playing Hearts

You play Hearts against three hands controlled by the computer. The objective is to score the *fewest* points. For each trick you win, you're awarded one point for each heart and 13 points for the Queen of Spades. You must use the same suit that's played first unless you're void of that suit. You take the trick if you've played the highest card of the suit played.

Play Hearts

1. Start Hearts from the Games submenu of the Start menu.
2. Enter your playing name, and click OK.

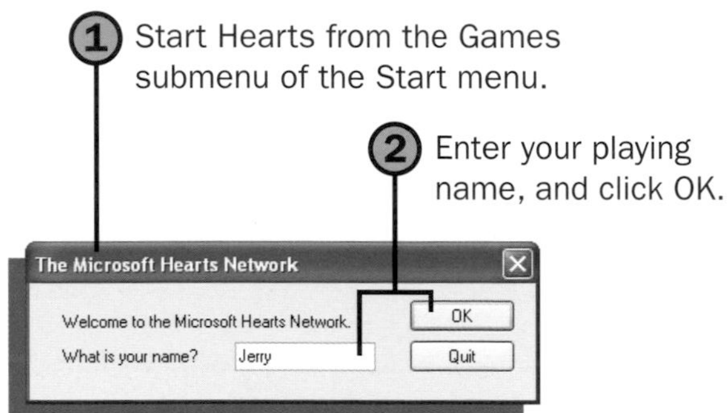

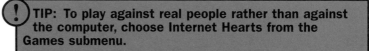

TIP: To play against real people rather than against the computer, choose Internet Hearts from the Games submenu.

TIP: Another scoring option is to "shoot the moon," whereby you collect all the points in one hand. If you succeed, each of the other players receives 26 points, and you receive zero points for the hand.

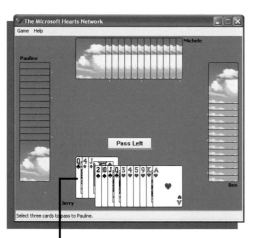

3. Click the cards to be passed, and click the Pass button. Click the OK button after you've received your cards.

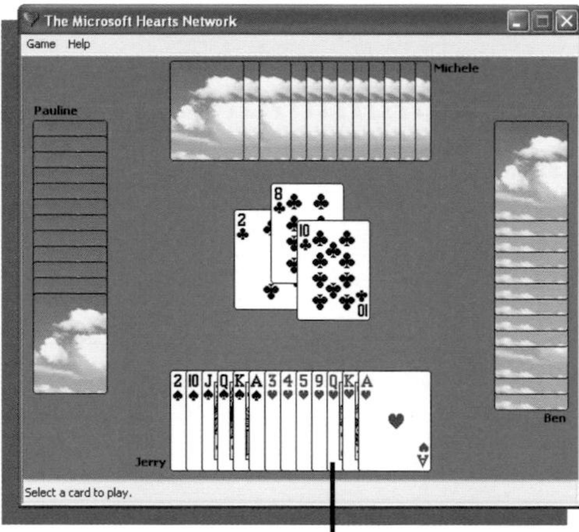

4. The Two of Clubs is automatically played to start the game. If you don't have the Two of Clubs, wait for your turn, and then click the card you want to play. Continue playing until the first player scores 100 or more points. The lowest score wins.

Playing HyperBowl ❂ NEW FEATURE

HyperBowl is a bowling game that comes with Microsoft Plus! You can play the game on a *Classic* bowling lane or on the *Pins Of Rome* lane, a winding and bumpy lane full of obstacles. The objective is to roll the ball down the lane and knock over as many pins as possible before your time limit expires. Scoring is done in the same way as in standard bowling.

TIP: The version of HyperBowl that comes with Microsoft Plus! offers only two bowling lanes and allows only one player at a time. However, you can purchase the full game to gain access to the other lanes and for multi-player support.

Go Bowling

1. Start the HyperBowl Plus! Edition game from the Games submenu of the Start menu. Wait for the game to fully load, and then move the mouse to start the game.

The clock shows how much time you have left (in seconds) to hit the pins.

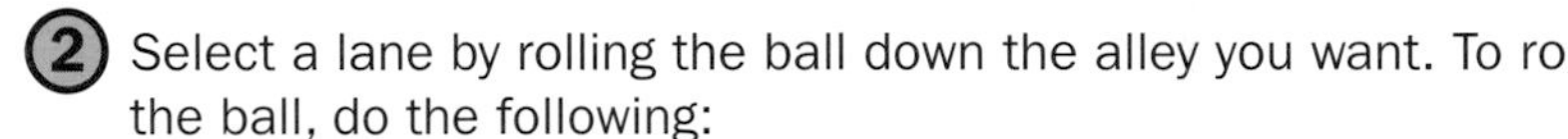

2. Select a lane by rolling the ball down the alley you want. To roll the ball, do the following:
   - Move the mouse (or trackball) forward (away from you) to roll the ball forward. The farther forward you push the mouse, the faster the ball rolls.
   - Move the mouse to the left to move the ball to the left, or to the right to move the ball to the right.
   - Move the mouse backward to slow the ball down.
3. Bowl your game, using the mouse to roll the ball and making sure the ball strikes the pins before your time runs out. Scoring is automatic.
   - In the Classic lane, bowl as you would in a regular bowling alley.
   - In the Pins Of Rome lane, navigate along the curvy and undulating lane, avoiding the urns to reach the pins.
4. After you've completed the game, wait for the final score to be displayed. You can then start a new game or press the Esc key and choose to quit HyperBowl.

Playing Labyrinth ⊕ NEW FEATURE

The Labyrinth Plus! Edition game that comes with Microsoft Plus! is a digital adaptation of the old wooden Labyrinth game that frustrated so many of us when we were younger. The digital version, of course, has many different options and designs, and it incorporates features that couldn't have been used in the old game. The object of the game is to move the ball though the maze by tilting the playing surface and trying to prevent the ball from falling into a hole. Not all the levels and mazes are available in the Plus! Edition. You can, however, download additional mazes. See Labyrinth Help for a link to upgrading the game.

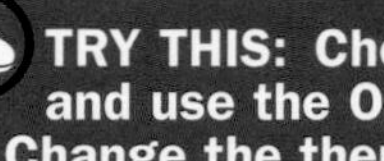

TRY THIS: Choose Options from the Main menu, and use the Options menu to customize the game: Change the theme, the appearance of the ball, the mouse sensitivity, the sound volume, and several other settings. Then play a game to see whether you like your settings.

CAUTION: Labyrinth sometimes freezes if you use the Alt+Tab key combination to switch windows. To avoid this problem, end your game before you switch windows.

Move Through the Maze

Start The Labyrinth Plus! Edition game from the Games submenu of the Start menu. Step through the menus to specify the game you want to play:

- From the Main menu that appears, choose Play.
- From the Play menu, choose to play the Arcade or the Race The Clock version of the game.
- On the Level menu, double-click the game level at which you want to play.

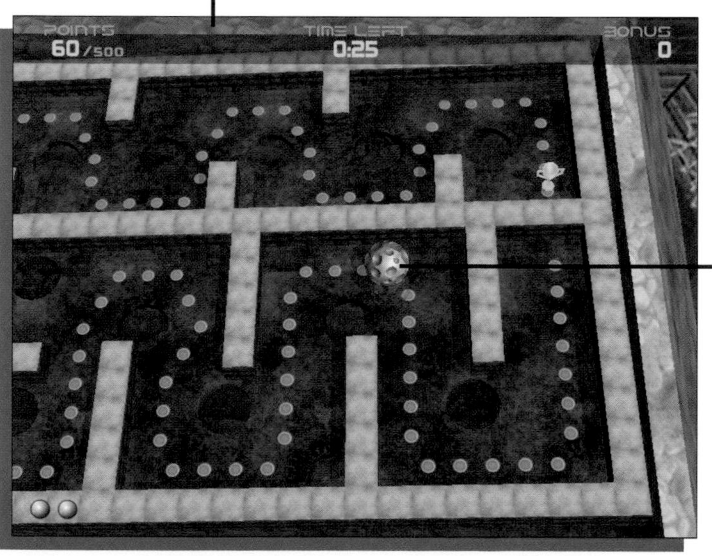

Use the mouse to tilt the game board and thus move the ball so that you can navigate through the maze, avoiding the holes and collecting points from hitting the other items displayed in the maze.

- Move the mouse to the left to raise the right side of the maze and move the ball to the left.
- Move the mouse to the right to raise the left side of the maze and move the ball to the right.
- Move the mouse forward to raise the near side of the maze and move the ball toward the back of the maze.
- Move the mouse backward to raise the far side of the maze and move the ball toward the front of the maze.

After you've completed the game, click a mouse button, and, from the menu that appears, choose a command to continue playing or to exit the game.

Playing Minesweeper

Minesweeper is a game you play against the computer. The goal is to uncover, in the shortest possible time, all the squares that don't contain mines. If you uncover a square that contains a mine, you lose. The key is to use the numbers in the uncovered squares to determine which adjacent squares contain the mines.

> **TIP:** The number in a square represents the total number of mines in adjacent squares—directly above, below, diagonal to, or to the left or right of the numbered square. Use several exposed numbers to figure out where the mines are.

Play Minesweeper

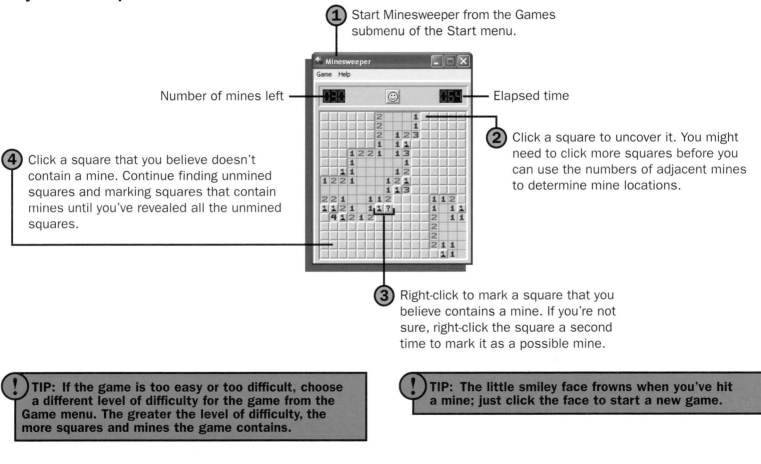

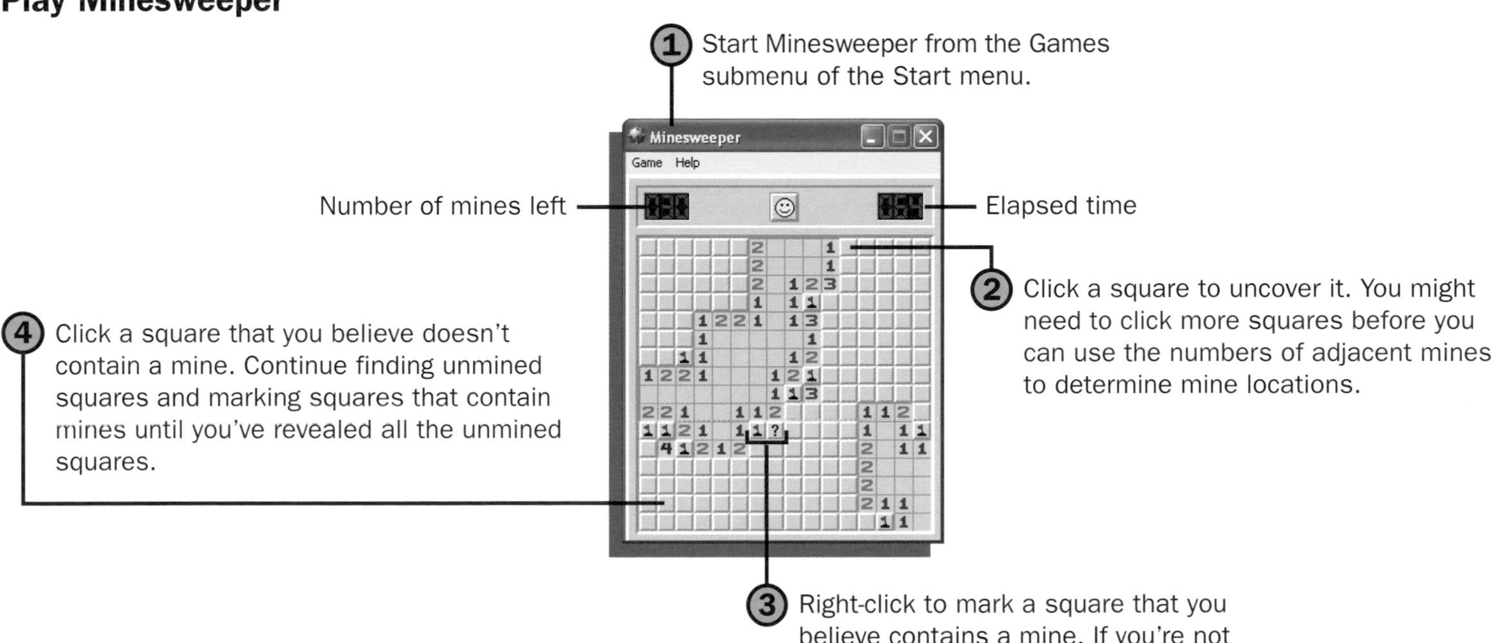

1. Start Minesweeper from the Games submenu of the Start menu.
2. Click a square to uncover it. You might need to click more squares before you can use the numbers of adjacent mines to determine mine locations.
3. Right-click to mark a square that you believe contains a mine. If you're not sure, right-click the square a second time to mark it as a possible mine.
4. Click a square that you believe doesn't contain a mine. Continue finding unmined squares and marking squares that contain mines until you've revealed all the unmined squares.

> **TIP:** If the game is too easy or too difficult, choose a different level of difficulty for the game from the Game menu. The greater the level of difficulty, the more squares and mines the game contains.

> **TIP:** The little smiley face frowns when you've hit a mine; just click the face to start a new game.

Playing Pinball

Pinball is a dazzling game with extensive sound effects. The object of the game is to keep each ball in play as long as possible while scoring the greatest number of points. Unlike most computer games, Pinball is played using the keyboard exclusively. You have three balls for the game unless you win extra balls, and you can advance through nine steps, or ranks, with each rank being more difficult to achieve and awarding a greater number of points.

Play Pinball

1. Start Pinball from the Games submenu of the Start menu.
2. On the Options menu, specify how many players are in the game, and whether you want to hear the pinball sounds or play background music.
3. Hold down the Spacebar and then release it to shoot the ball into play.
4. Use the keys as shown in the table to control the play.

CAUTION: Use the Nudge keys sparingly and very cautiously—it's quite easy to tilt the game.

TIP: We'd *never* endorse goofing off, but if you *should* just happen to be taking a little break and playing games instead of working, press the Esc key to mute the sounds and minimize the game if the wrong person gets too close to your computer.

Pinball Control Keys

Key	Function
Z	Left flipper and reentry lane lights
/ (forward slash)	Right flipper
X	Nudge from left
. (period)	Nudge from right
Up arrow key	Nudge from bottom
F2	New game
F3	Pause/resume
F4	Full screen/window

TIP: Press the F8 key to change which keys you want to use to control the game.

TIP: Pressing either flipper button changes which reentry lanes are lit.

Playing Russian Squares ⊕ NEW FEATURE

Russian Squares Plus! Edition is a game that comes with Microsoft Plus! It's a fast-moving matching game in which you move squares around so that whole rows or columns contain matching squares. Once a row or column matches, it disappears, and you get points. The catch is that you have very little time to accomplish your goal, and, if you run out of time, the game adds a new row or column, which messes up your almost completed row or column. After you've removed all the squares, you advance to a higher level where it's even more difficult to remove squares.

TIP: You can use the arrow keys on your keyboard to move the squares, but, once you get the feel of it, using the mouse is much quicker. If the mouse doesn't move the squares, choose Mouse from the Options menu.

TIP: If you have difficulty discerning the differences between squares, point to Themes on the Options menu, and choose Shapes from the submenu that appears.

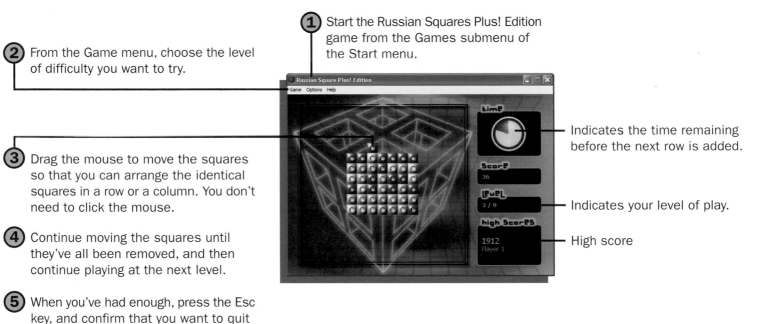

Play Russian Squares

1. Start the Russian Squares Plus! Edition game from the Games submenu of the Start menu.
2. From the Game menu, choose the level of difficulty you want to try.
3. Drag the mouse to move the squares so that you can arrange the identical squares in a row or a column. You don't need to click the mouse.
4. Continue moving the squares until they've all been removed, and then continue playing at the next level.
5. When you've had enough, press the Esc key, and confirm that you want to quit the game.

Indicates the time remaining before the next row is added.

Indicates your level of play.

High score

Playing Solitaire

Solitaire is a classic card game that, as its name implies, you play by yourself. The object is to reveal all the cards that are turned face down and eventually to arrange all the cards in four piles, with each pile being a single suit stacked in ascending order from Ace through King.

> **TIP:** To change the way a game is played—the number of cards drawn at one time, whether or not the game is timed, or the method of scoring—choose Options from the Game menu.

Play Solitaire

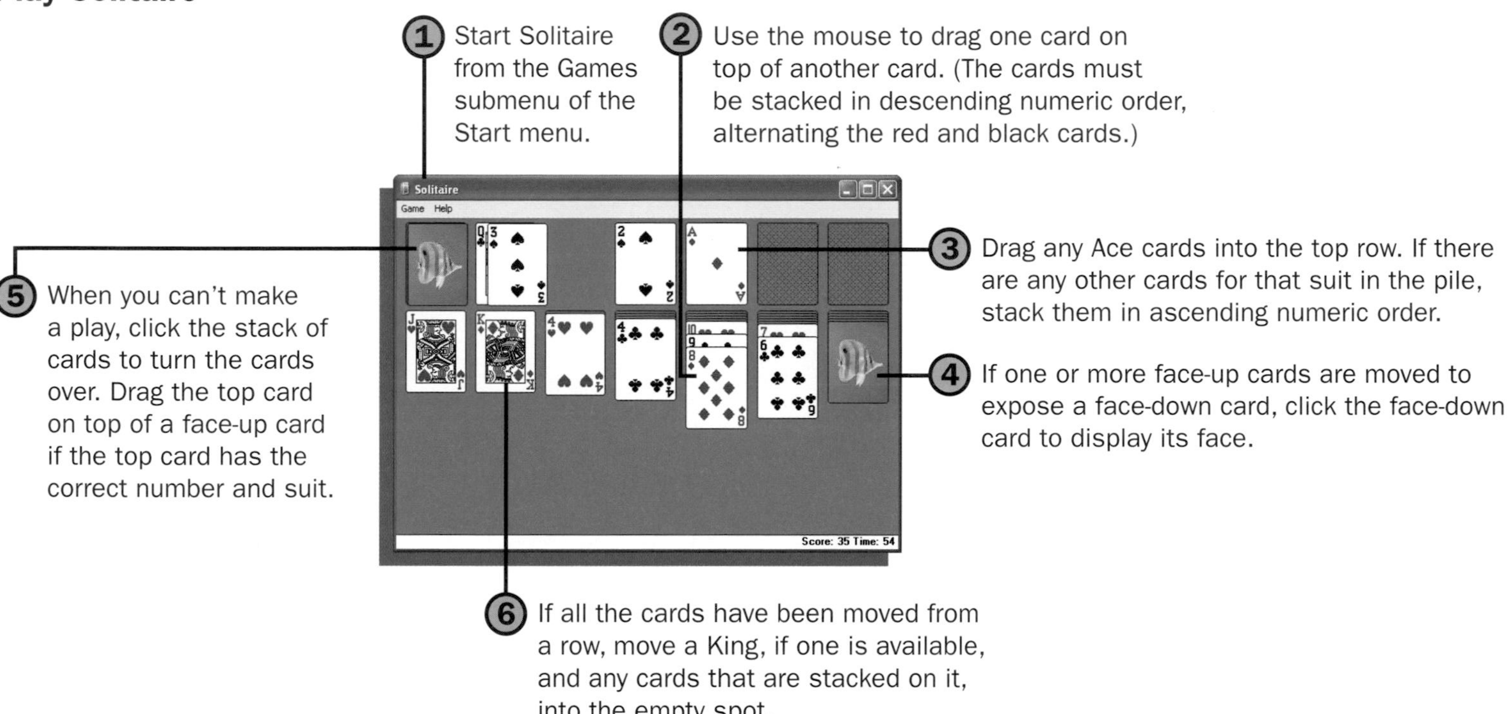

1. Start Solitaire from the Games submenu of the Start menu.
2. Use the mouse to drag one card on top of another card. (The cards must be stacked in descending numeric order, alternating the red and black cards.)
3. Drag any Ace cards into the top row. If there are any other cards for that suit in the pile, stack them in ascending numeric order.
4. If one or more face-up cards are moved to expose a face-down card, click the face-down card to display its face.
5. When you can't make a play, click the stack of cards to turn the cards over. Drag the top card on top of a face-up card if the top card has the correct number and suit.
6. If all the cards have been moved from a row, move a King, if one is available, and any cards that are stacked on it, into the empty spot.

> **TIP:** To change the pattern of the card backs, choose Deck from the Game menu.

> **SEE ALSO:** For information about other Solitaire card games, see "Playing FreeCell" on page 37 and "Playing Spider Solitaire" on the facing page.

Playing Spider Solitaire

Spider Solitaire is yet another version of Solitaire. Unlike the way you play other Solitaire games, the object is to stack the cards by suit in one column in descending order. When a series from King to Ace is complete, the cards are removed. The level of difficulty is determined by how many suits are used (one, two, or four).

> **TIP: To display possible moves, press the M key. Press it again to see another possible move.**

> **TIP: Choose Save This Game from the Game menu to save the game for later play.**

Play Spider Solitaire

1. Start Spider Solitaire from the Games submenu of the Start menu.

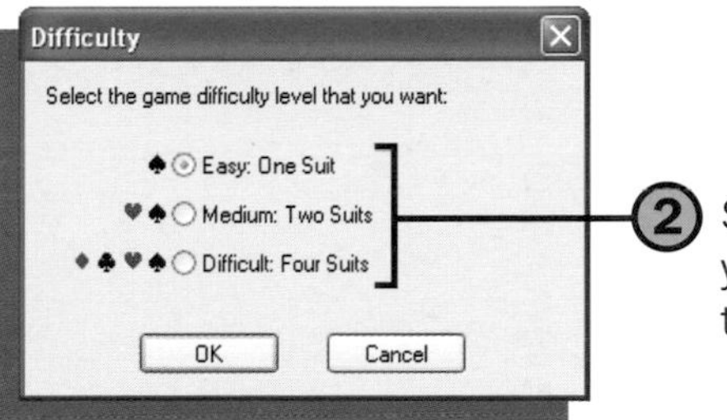

2. Specify how many suits you want to use, and then click OK.

3. Use the mouse to drag one card on top of another card. You can stack the cards in descending numeric order regardless of suit, but it's best to stack by suit.

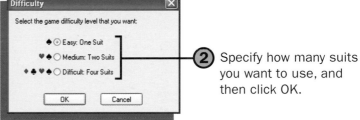

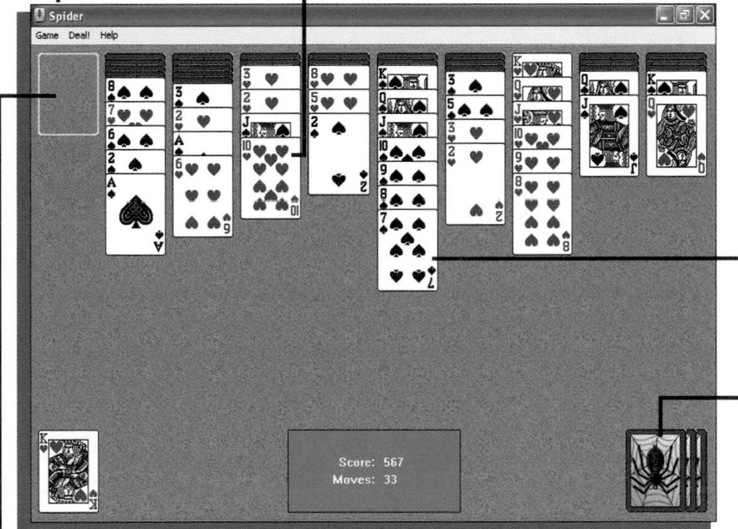

4. Drag a group of sequential cards of the same suit onto another card. (Only cards of the same suit can be moved as a group.)

5. If there's an empty column, move a card or a sequence of cards into the column.

6. If no moves are available, click the stacked cards to deal another round. (You can't deal if there's an empty column.) Continue playing until all the cards have been removed or until all the cards have been dealt and there are no longer any moves available.

Playing Games over the Internet

Windows XP provides five games—Backgammon, Checkers, Hearts, Reversi, and Spades—that are designed to be played against other players over the Internet. When you start a game and connect to the Internet, the game server will try to find players matched to your skill level and language. (You can't select the players or the locations of your opponents.) You can communicate with the other players by using the Chat feature.

TIP: To play additional types of games and to select specific individuals to be your opponents, connect to the Gaming Zone. You'll see the MSN Gaming Zone item on the Contents tab of the Help program in the game you're currently playing.

Play a Game

1. Start an Internet game from the Games submenu of the Start menu.

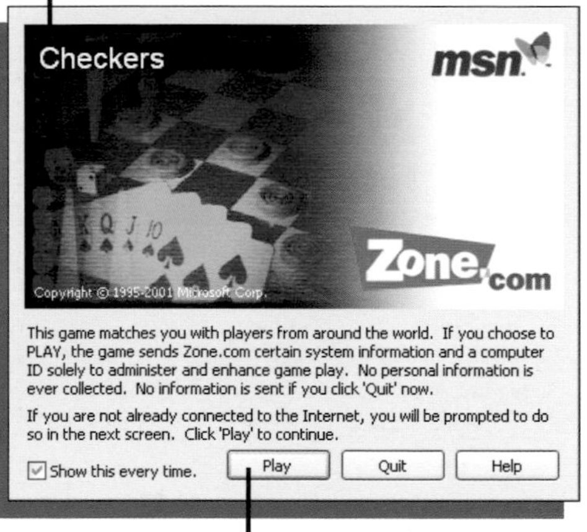

2. Click Play. If you're not already connected to the Internet, connect when prompted.

3. Click a message to send to your opponent.

4. Play the game and make your moves as prompted.

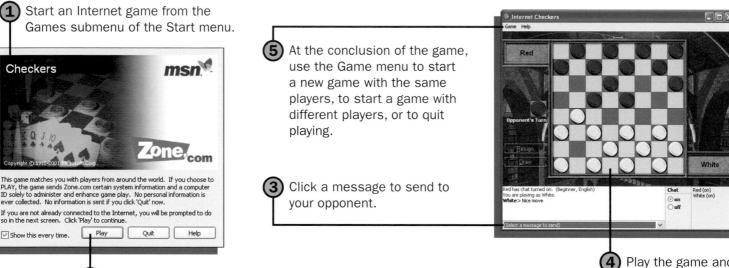

5. At the conclusion of the game, use the Game menu to start a new game with the same players, to start a game with different players, or to quit playing.

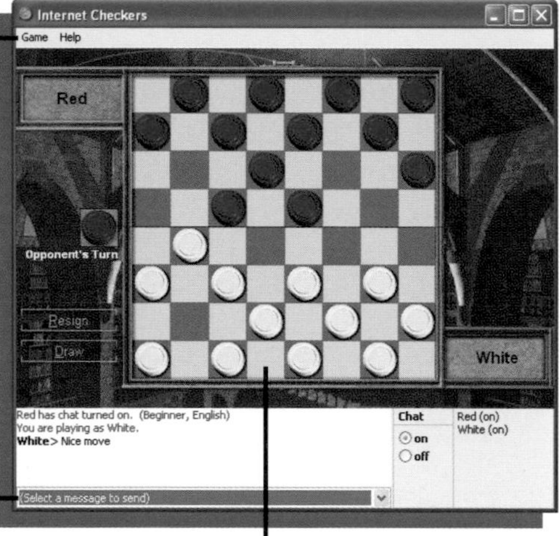

TIP: You can also play certain games over the Internet using Windows Messenger, provided you and your opponent both have the games installed.

SEE ALSO: For information about playing games over the Internet using Windows Messenger, see "Sending Instant Messages" on page 84.

Running Older Programs

Most programs work well with Windows XP. Some older ones, however, are designed exclusively for earlier versions of Windows, and don't work properly in Windows XP. However, Windows XP can get those programs to run by cleverly acting as though it were an earlier version of Windows.

TIP: If changing the compatibility mode or the display settings doesn't fix the problem, check with the manufacturer for updated drivers or other fixes.

Set the Compatibility

1. Open the Start menu, right-click the program you want to run, and choose Properties from the shortcut menu.

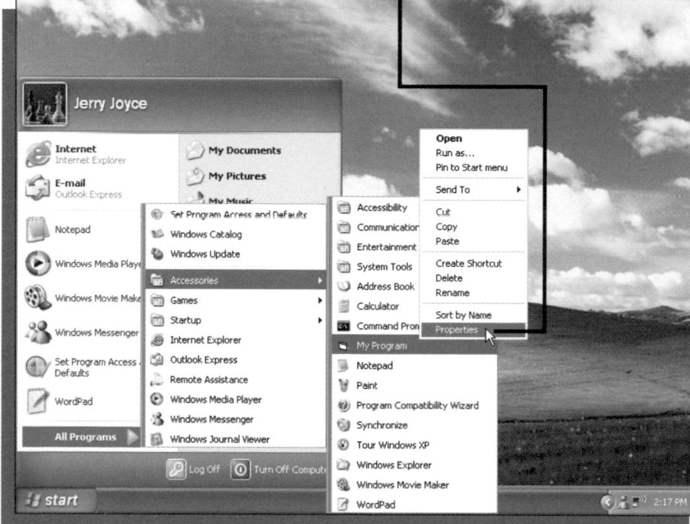

2. Select this check box to run the program in compatibility mode.
3. Specify the version of Windows the program was designed for.
4. Select the check boxes for applying the appropriate restrictions to the display and text services, based on the program's documentation and updated notes from the manufacturer.
5. Click OK. Try running the program. If it still doesn't run, open the Properties dialog box again and change the settings. Continue experimenting until you get the program to work.

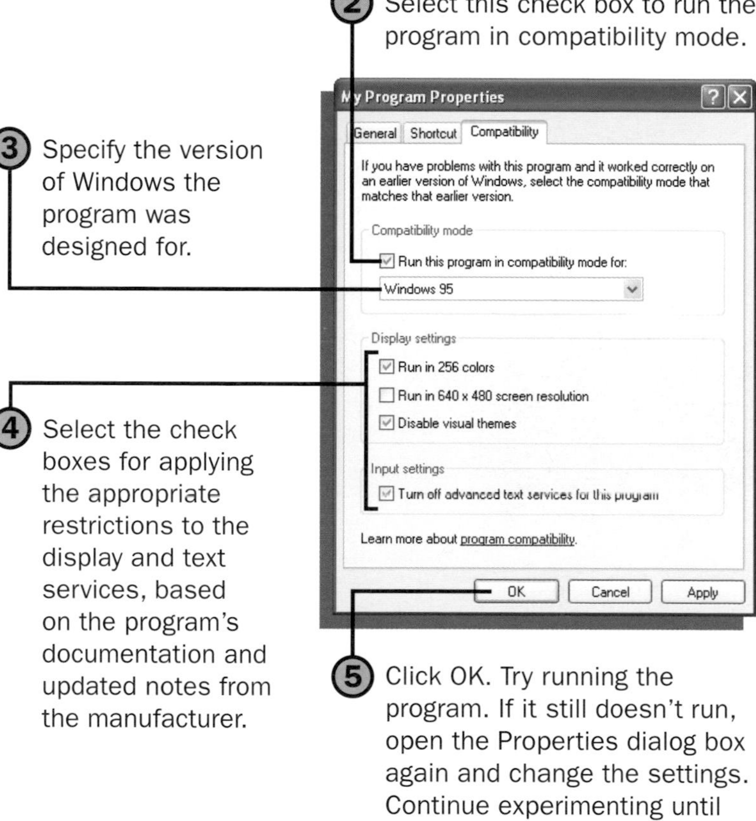

CAUTION: Windows XP will remember the compatibility settings between uses for programs that are installed on the computer's hard disk, but it won't remember the compatibility settings for programs that you run from a CD.

TIP: To learn more about compatibility modes, or to run the Program Compatibility Wizard, which can help you identify the settings you need, click the Program Compatibility link in the Properties dialog box.

Starting a Program When Windows Starts

If you always start your workday using the same program, you can have that program start when Windows XP starts. And if you use the same document each day, you can have that document start automatically in the program. Windows XP might take a little longer to load, but your program will be ready for you right away.

SEE ALSO: For information about adding programs or documents to the Start menu, see "Customizing the Start Menu" on pages 232–233.

Add a Program to the Startup Submenu

1. Point to All Programs on the Start menu, and move through the folders until you locate the program you want.

CAUTION: Some programs are automatically placed in the Startup folder when they're installed, so they always start when Windows XP starts. You can remove many of these programs if you don't want them to start automatically; however, some programs won't function properly without certain items in the Startup folder. If you want to remove a program from the Startup folder, drag it to the All Programs submenu, restart the computer, use the program, and check to verify that everything is working properly. If not, drag the program back to the Startup folder.

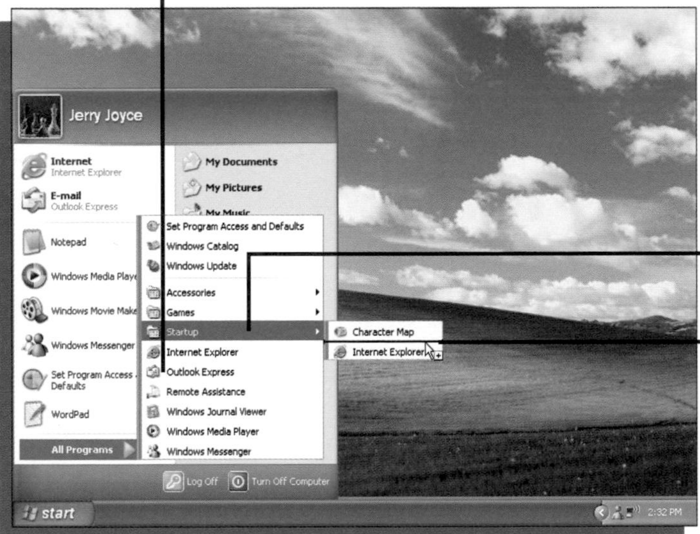

2. Hold down the Ctrl key and drag the program on top of the Startup item on the Programs submenu.
3. When the Startup submenu opens, drag the program onto the submenu. Release the mouse button and then the Ctrl key.
4. Open the Startup folder and verify that the program is on the Startup submenu. The next time Windows XP starts, the program will start.

TIP: The Startup folder isn't the only place from which a program starts automatically when Windows XP starts; some programs use the Registry settings to start automatically. The Startup folder, however, is the only location that you can easily modify.

TIP: To have a program start with a specific document loaded, place the document in the Startup folder. The document must be correctly associated with the program—that is, it must normally start in that program when you double-click the document.

Changing the Way a Program Starts

Many programs have special *command switches* that you can use to start the program or to modify the way it starts or runs. You can add these commands to the shortcut that starts the program, as well as specify the size of the window and even specify a keyboard shortcut that quickly switches to the program.

Modify the Shortcut

1. Locate the shortcut to the program (on the Start menu, on the Desktop, or in a folder). If there is no shortcut to the program or if you're not permitted to modify the existing shortcut, create a new one. Right-click the shortcut, and choose Properties from the shortcut menu.

2. Click the Shortcut tab.

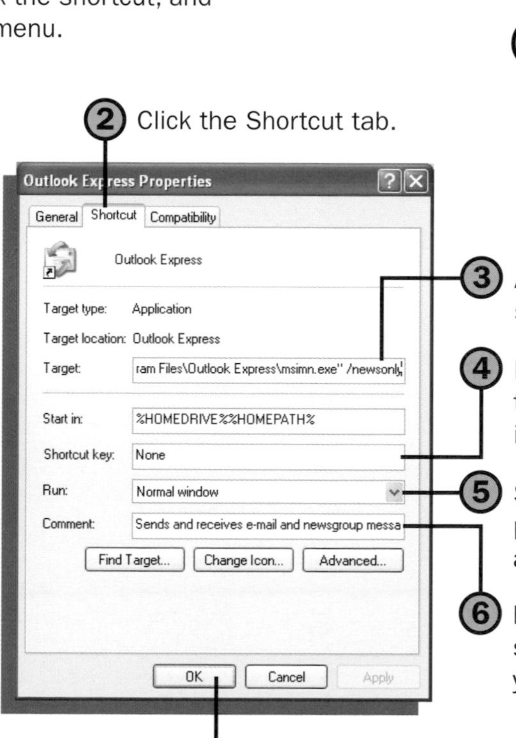

3. Add any special command switches, as specified in the program's documentation.
4. If you want to use a keyboard shortcut that switches to the running program, click in the box and press the key combination.
5. Specify whether you want to run the program in a normal, a maximized, or a minimized window.
6. Modify the comment to change the text shown in the pop-up description when you point to the shortcut.
7. Click OK.

TRY THIS: Click the Start button, point to All Programs, right-click Outlook Express on the menu that appears, and choose Properties from the shortcut menu. In the Target box on the Shortcut tab, type a space and then the command switch /newsonly **after the closing quotation marks, and click OK. Open the Start menu, point to All Programs, and choose Outlook Express to open Outlook Express as a news reader only. This is a useful way to connect to newsgroups if you use a program other than Outlook Express—Microsoft Outlook, for example—for your e-mail.**

SEE ALSO: For information about creating a shortcut, see "Creating Quick Access to a File or Folder" on page 179.

Quitting When You're Stuck

If a program isn't working properly and doesn't respond when you try to close it, Windows XP isolates the program so that it doesn't affect your other programs. Provided you're sure that the program really isn't working—as opposed to just taking a long time to do something—you can "end the task." When you use this option, you'll probably lose any unsaved work in the misbehaving program, and, if the problem persists, you might need to reinstall the program.

TIP: **If you can't end a specific program, press Ctrl+Alt+Delete to display the Task Manager. On the Applications tab of the Task Manager dialog box, click the offending program, and then click End Task. If that doesn't work, close all your other running programs, and choose Turn Off from the Shut Down menu in the Task Manager dialog box. If Windows XP is really misbehaving and still doesn't respond, your last resort is to turn off your computer.**

End the Task

1. When you're sure that the program has stopped working, click the Close button on the program's title bar. You might need to try this several times before you can get the program to respond to your click. Be patient!

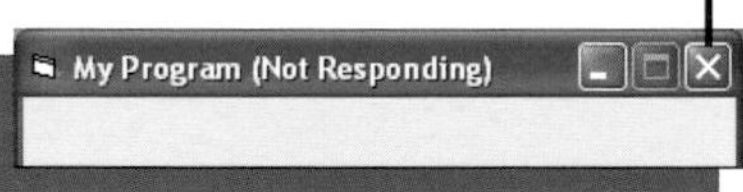

SEE ALSO: **For information about fixing configuration problems when you restart your computer, see "Starting Up When There's a Problem" on page 296.**

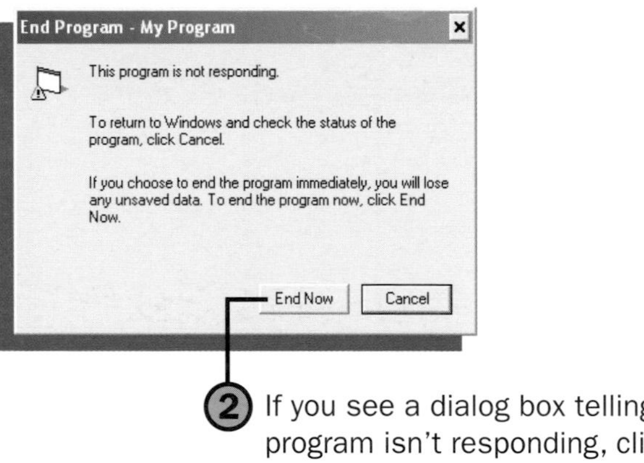

2. If you see a dialog box telling you the program isn't responding, click End Now.

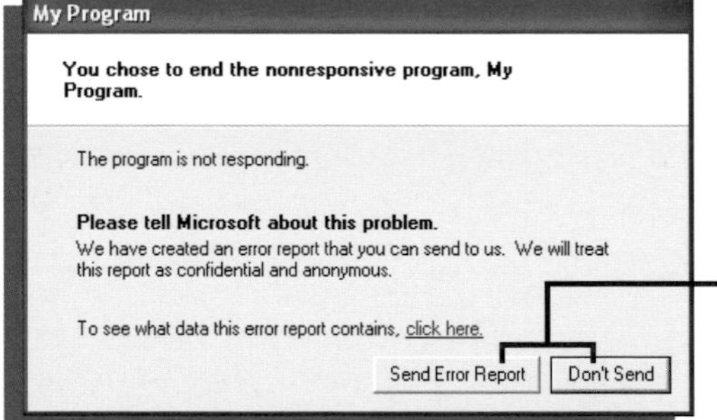

3. When a message appears, click Send Error Report to send technical data about the error over the Internet to Microsoft, or click Don't Send if you want to keep the problem to yourself.

Exploring the Internet

In this section

Whether you call it the Internet, the Net, or the Web, and whether you use it for business, homework, research, communicating, or shopping, the Web is probably already your window on the world. With that insight in mind, one of the goals of Microsoft Windows XP's designers was to enable you to move between the Web and your own computer in an almost effortless fashion.

If you know the address of the Web page or site you want, you can simply type the address in the Address Bar, and Microsoft Internet Explorer will find and display the page for you. If you don't know the address, you can use the Search feature to search the Internet to find the requested information. Once you've found the page, you can use the *hyperlinks* that you'll find on most pages to navigate from one page or site to another to obtain any additional information you need.

When you start Internet Explorer, it takes you to your *home page,* which is usually a page you've customized to display information that you want to see every day. However, if you want to designate another page as your home page or change some items on the existing home page, you can do so with a couple of mouse-clicks. If there's a page you want to revisit, you can add it to your Favorites list, and Internet Explorer will create a shortcut to that page for you. You can save a Web page and then send it, with all its formatting intact, to friends or colleagues. You can economize on connection charges by saving Web pages and viewing them off line, and you can even set up your computer so that those pages will be updated automatically whenever any of their content changes.

Finding a Web Page

You do most of your navigation on the Internet using the hyperlinks (also called *links* or *jumps*) that are located on Web pages. When you click a link, an Internet address is sent to your Web browser, which looks for the Web site and then displays the requested page. After you've located a Web page, you can explore further if you want. It's a bit like looking up a word in a dictionary and then looking up another word to expand your understanding of the first one.

TIP: If you start Internet Explorer from the Start menu, from your Desktop, or from the Quick Launch toolbar, Internet Explorer goes to the page you've designated as your home page. If you start Internet Explorer by clicking a link, choosing a menu command, or using an Internet address, Internet Explorer goes to that specific page and bypasses your home page.

SEE ALSO: For information about changing your home page, see "Setting Your Home Page" on the facing page.

For information about controlling and safeguarding your Internet connection, see "Protecting Personal Information on the Internet" on page 256 and "Restricting Internet Access" on page 259.

Explore

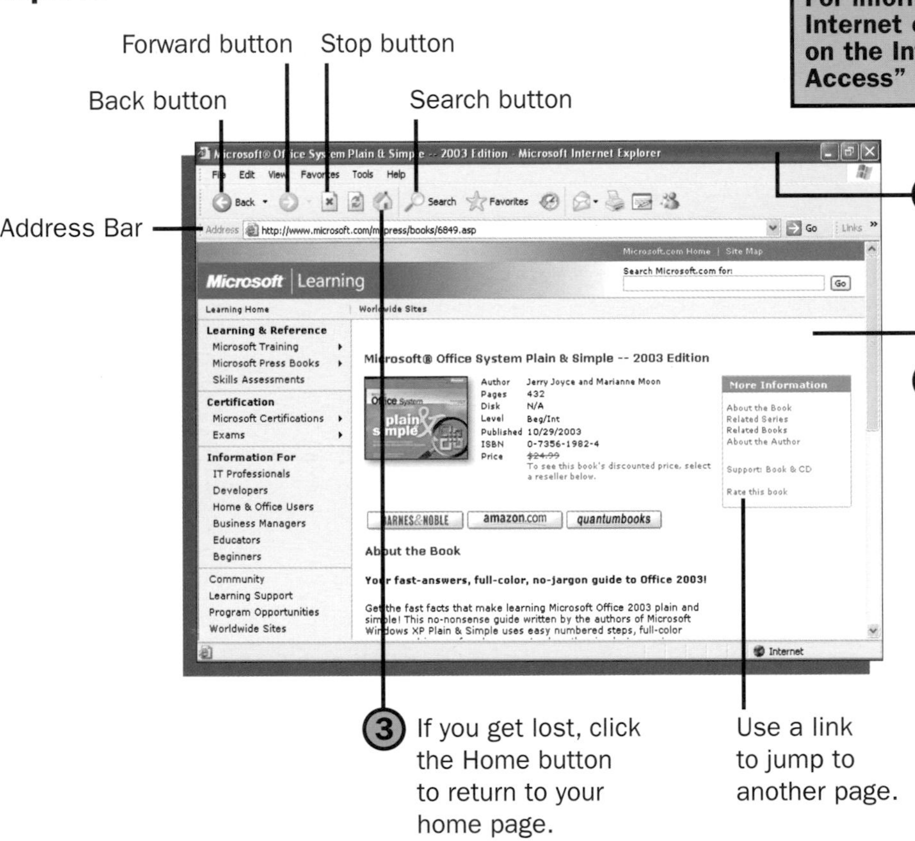

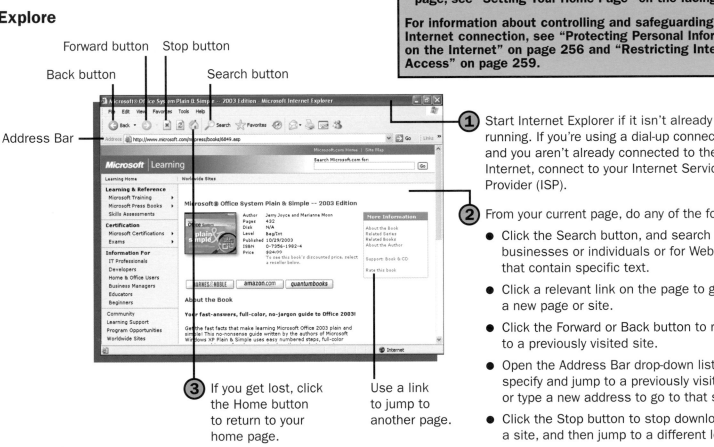

1. Start Internet Explorer if it isn't already running. If you're using a dial-up connection and you aren't already connected to the Internet, connect to your Internet Service Provider (ISP).
2. From your current page, do any of the following:
   - Click the Search button, and search for businesses or individuals or for Web pages that contain specific text.
   - Click a relevant link on the page to go to a new page or site.
   - Click the Forward or Back button to return to a previously visited site.
   - Open the Address Bar drop-down list to specify and jump to a previously visited site, or type a new address to go to that site.
   - Click the Stop button to stop downloading a site, and then jump to a different location.
3. If you get lost, click the Home button to return to your home page.

Use a link to jump to another page.

Setting Your Home Page

When you start Internet Explorer, you automatically go to your home page—a page that you might have customized or that contains the links and services you want. If you'd rather use a different home page, or if you want to reset the home page after a service or a program has changed it, you can designate a new home page with just a couple of mouse-clicks.

TIP: If a service provider or an installed program has made substantial changes to the way Internet Explorer looks and works, click the Restore Defaults button on the Advanced tab of the Internet Options dialog box to return Internet Explorer to its normal functionality.

Reset the Home Page

1. Use Internet Explorer to go to the page you want to use as your home page.

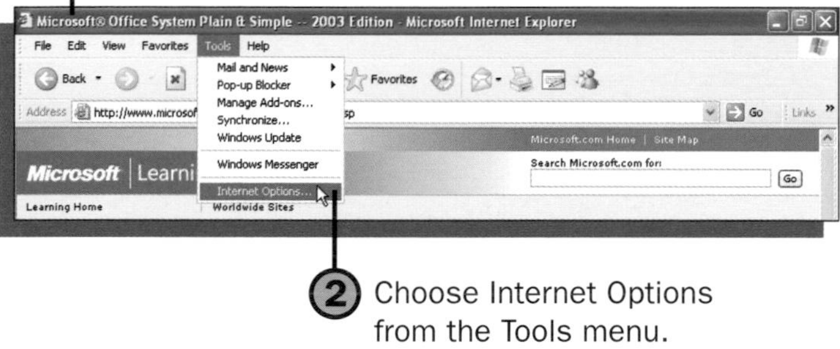

2. Choose Internet Options from the Tools menu.

3. Click Use Current.

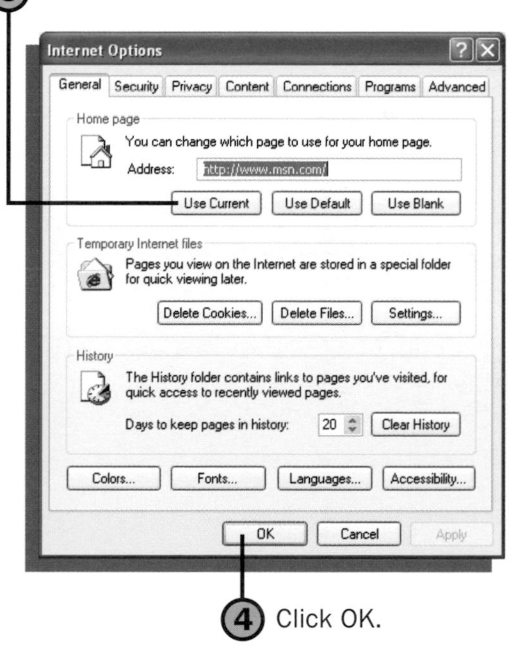

4. Click OK.

TIP: If you don't want anyone who uses your computer to review the Internet sites you've visited recently, click the Clear History button on the General tab of the Internet Options dialog box.

CAUTION: Some service providers don't allow you to change your home page. You're required to use the service's home page until you're properly logged on. If this is the case, your only recourse is to complain loudly to that service provider.

TIP: Web-page content changes frequently, so what you see on some of the Web pages shown in this book might look a bit different from what you see when you access those same pages on line.

Returning to Your Favorite Sites

When you find a good source of information or entertainment, you don't need to waste a lot of time searching for that site the next time you want to visit it. You can simply add the site to your Favorites list, and Internet Explorer will obligingly create a shortcut to the site for you. And when there are sites that you go to all the time, you can place them on your Links toolbar for even easier access.

Save a Location

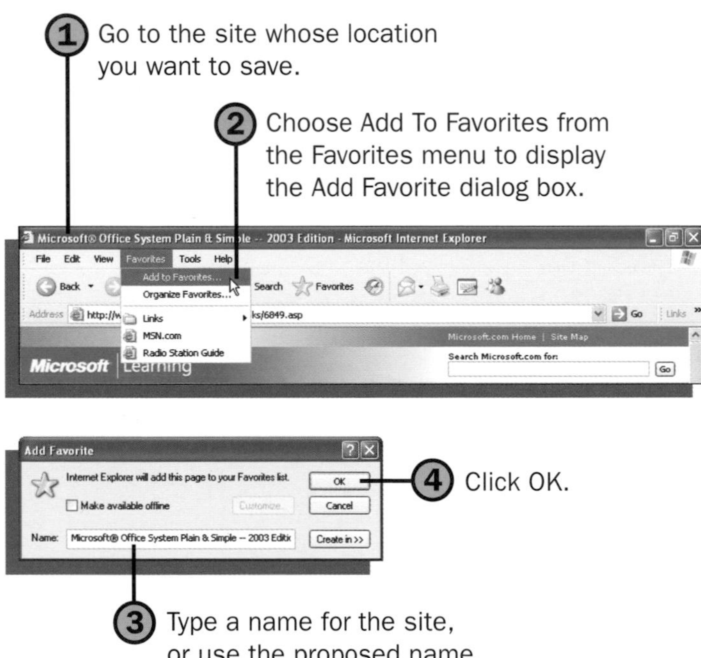

1. Go to the site whose location you want to save.
2. Choose Add To Favorites from the Favorites menu to display the Add Favorite dialog box.
3. Type a name for the site, or use the proposed name.
4. Click OK.

Return to a Location

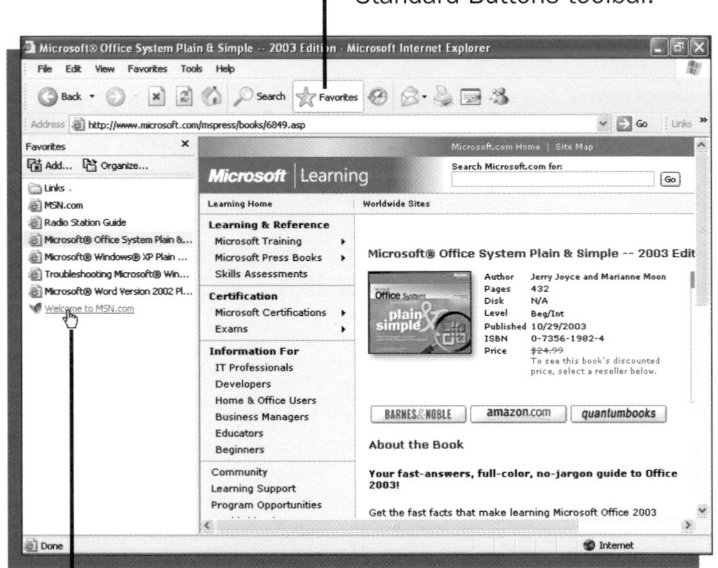

1. Click Favorites on the Standard Buttons toolbar.
2. In the Favorites Explorer Bar, click the name of the site you want to return to. If the site is contained in a subfolder, click the folder and then click the site.

TIP: If you'll be storing many different favorite locations, click the Create In button in the Add Favorite dialog box and create a file structure for your pages.

SEE ALSO: For information about working with toolbars, see "Navigating with Toolbars" on page 186 and "Displaying and Arranging the Toolbars" on page 231.

Access Your Frequently Visited Sites

1. Display both the Address and the Links toolbars.

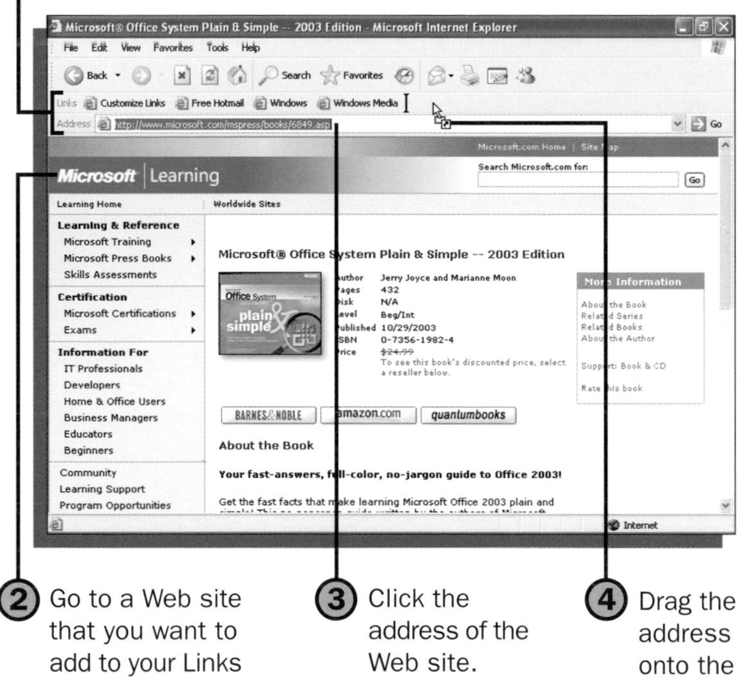

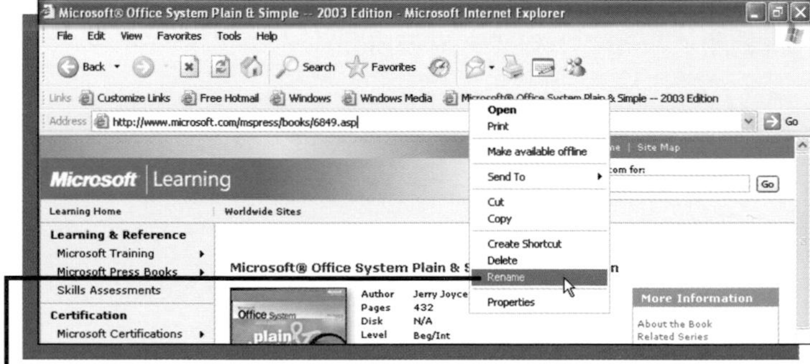

2. Go to a Web site that you want to add to your Links toolbar.
3. Click the address of the Web site.
4. Drag the address onto the Links toolbar.
5. Right-click the link on the Links toolbar, and choose Rename from the shortcut menu that appears. Type a short, friendly name for the Web site in the Rename dialog box, and click OK.
6. Repeat steps 2 through 5 to add other sites to your Links toolbar. If necessary, right-click any link you don't want, and choose Delete from the shortcut menu to customize the Links toolbar.

TRY THIS: Did you forget to save the location of a Web page that you want to return to? In Internet Explorer, click the History button on the Standard Buttons toolbar. In the History Explorer bar, search for the page you want by the time period in which you visited it. If the site is contained in a subfolder, click the folder to reveal the site. Click the site to return to it, and then add it to either the Favorites list or the Links toolbar.

TIP: If the Links toolbar isn't visible, point to Toolbars on the View menu, and choose Links from the submenu. If the Links toolbar is compressed, double-click it to expand it. If it won't expand, right-click it, and choose Lock The Toolbars from the shortcut menu.

Going to a Specific Web Page

If someone has given you an Internet address that isn't in one of the usual forms—for example, a hyperlink in an online document, in an e-mail message, or in another Web page—you can easily specify the address. You don't even need to go to your default home page but can simply jump to the destination. To do so, you use the Address toolbar in Internet Explorer, on the Windows taskbar, or in any folder window.

TRY THIS: Start typing an address for a Web page you visited recently. As you type, you'll notice that a list box appears containing proposed addresses. If the address you want is listed, use either the mouse to click the address or the down arrow key to select the address, and then press Enter. If no proposed addresses ever appear, in Internet Explorer, choose Internet Options from the Tools menu, click AutoComplete on the Content tab, and select the Web Addresses check box. Click OK twice, and then try typing the address again.

Specify an Address

1. In Internet Explorer, on the Windows taskbar, or in a folder window, display the Address toolbar if it isn't already displayed:
   - In Internet Explorer or in a folder window, point to Toolbars on the View menu, choose Address Bar from the submenu, and then click the current address.
   - Click a blank spot on the Windows taskbar, point to Toolbars on the shortcut menu that appears, and choose Address.

2. Click the current address in the Address toolbar to select the entire address.
3. Type the address with which you want to replace the current selected address. (You don't need to type the *http://www.* part of the address.)

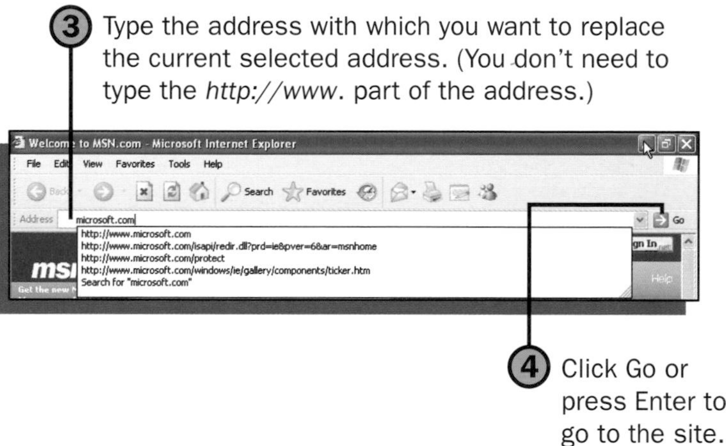

4. Click Go or press Enter to go to the site.

TIP: You can use the Address toolbar for more than just going to a Web page. You can also enter the address of a folder, a drive, or even another computer on your network.

SEE ALSO: For information about displaying the Address toolbar if it isn't visible or if it's compressed, see "Navigating with Toolbars" on page 186 and "Displaying and Arranging the Toolbars" on page 231.

Saving a Web Page

If a Web page contains important information that you know you'll want to refer to in the future, you can save the page on your computer. The way you save it, however, affects which information will be available when you open the saved page. After you've saved the Web page, you can send it to friends and colleagues if you want.

Save a Web Page

1. Start Internet Explorer if it isn't already running, and connect to the Internet if you aren't already connected. Go to the Web page you want to save.
2. Choose Save As from the File menu to display the Save Web Page dialog box. 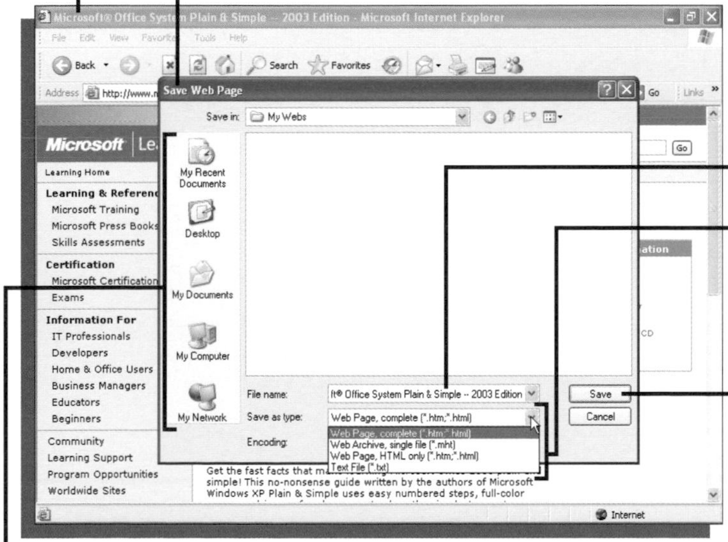
3. If you don't want to save the document to the default folder, specify a different location, drive, or folder.
4. Type a name for the file, or use the proposed name.
5. Click in the list to specify the way you want the Web page to be saved:
   - Web Page Complete to save the formatted text and layout and to place all the linked resources, such as pictures, in a separate folder
   - Web Archive, Single File to create a single archive file that contains all the elements of the Web page
   - Web Page, HTML Only to save the formatted text and layout but none of the linked items, such as pictures
   - Text File to save only the text
6. Click Save.

TIP: If you're planning to send a Web page to someone, save the page as a Web Archive so that the single file will contain all the elements of the Web page. The recipient will need to have Internet Explorer version 4 or later (or a similar browser) installed on his or her computer to be able to read a Web Archive file.

CAUTION: Sometimes, although certain items on a Web page appear to be text, they're actually graphics elements. This is usually the case when the designer of the page or site wanted to include some special formatting that couldn't be done with normal HTML formatting. If you save the page either as Web Page, HTML Only or as Text File, the information that has that type of special formatting won't be saved.

Viewing Web Pages Off Line

If you aren't always connected to the Internet, or if you simply want to economize on connection charges, you can store the Web pages you want and then read them off line at your leisure. And if there are Web sites that you visit frequently, you can set up your computer so that the stored Web pages will be updated, or *synchronized,* automatically when the information in them changes. That way, you'll always have the most recent version of the Web page.

Store a Web Page

1. Start Internet Explorer if it isn't already running, and connect to the Internet if you aren't already connected. Go to the Web page you want to store.
2. Choose Add To Favorites from the Favorites menu to display the Add Favorite dialog box.

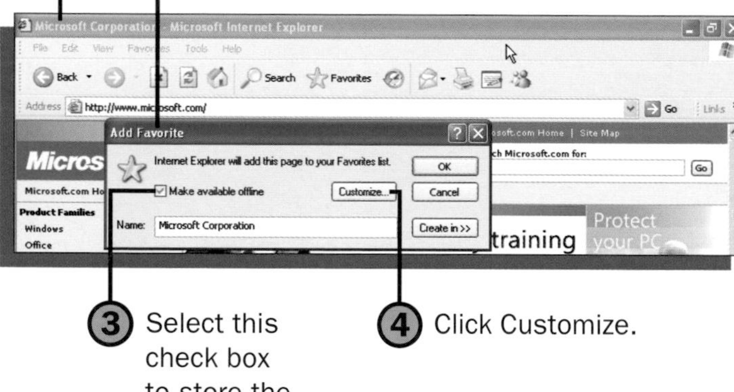

3. Select this check box to store the Web page.
4. Click Customize.

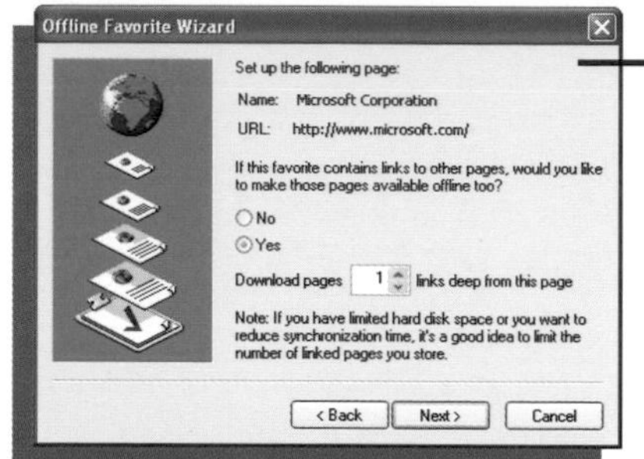

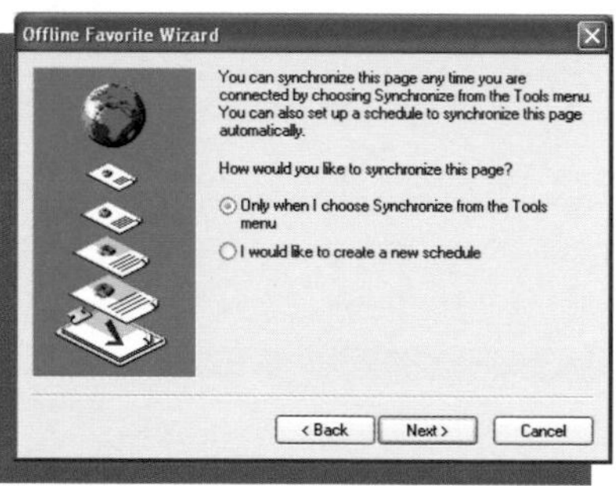

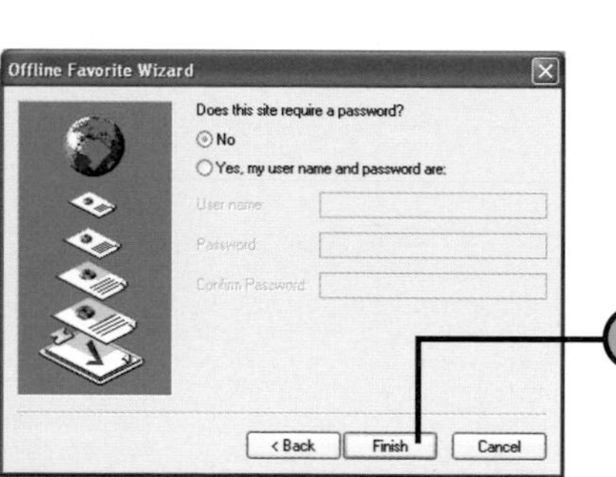

5. Step through the Offline Favorite Wizard, specifying whether
   - Pages linked to this page are also to be stored.
   - Web pages are to be updated manually or automatically, and, if automatically, specifying the schedule for updating.
   - A password is required, and, if so, specifying your user name and password.
6. Click Finish, and wait for the Web page or pages to be synchronized.
7. Repeat steps 2 through 6 for any other pages you want to view off line. Disconnect from Internet Explorer when you've finished.

SEE ALSO: For information about deleting all your offline files from your hard disk, see "Maintaining Your Hard Disk" on page 286.

View an Offline Web Page

1. With your computer *not* connected to the Internet, start Internet Explorer if it isn't already running. If the computer keeps trying to connect, choose Work Offline from the File menu.

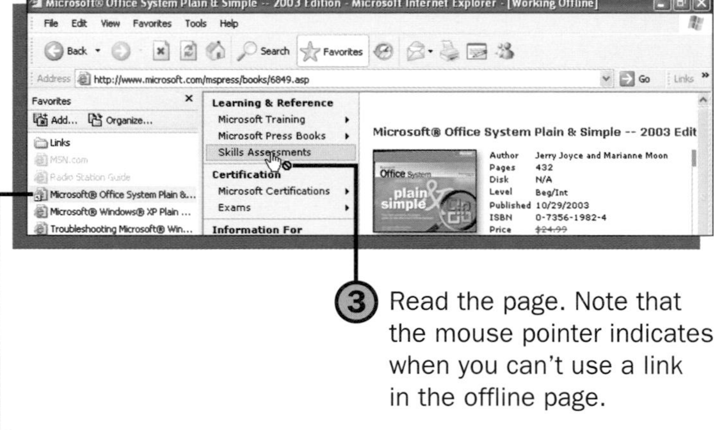

2. Open the Favorites menu or the Favorites Explorer pane, and click the Web page in the list. Note that files set for offline viewing display a different icon than do files available only while you're on line.

3. Read the page. Note that the mouse pointer indicates when you can't use a link in the offline page.

CAUTION: Offline Web pages use a large amount of disk space, especially if you choose to save pages that are linked to your main page. If your disk space is limited, be selective about the Web pages you store.

TIP: Even if you've set up your offline Web pages to be synchronized automatically, use the Synchronize command when you want to update a page manually.

Synchronize Your Offline Web Pages

1. Connect to the Internet if you aren't already connected.

2. Choose Synchronize from Internet Explorer's Tools menu or from the Accessories submenu of the Start menu to display the Items To Synchronize dialog box.

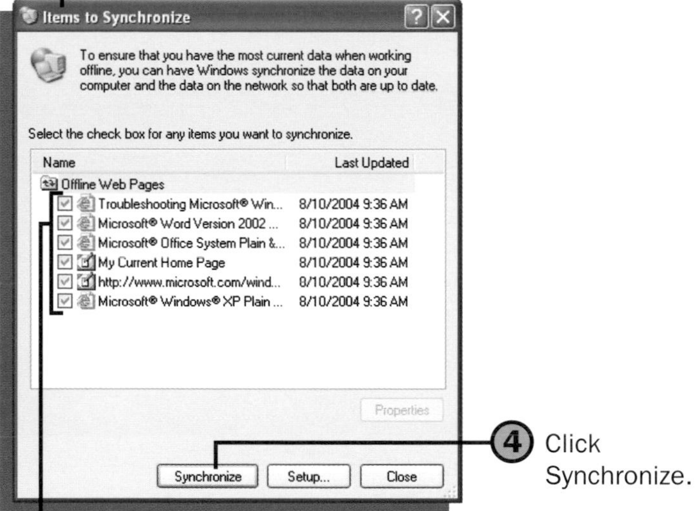

3. Select the check boxes (if they aren't already selected) for the Web pages you want to be automatically updated, and clear the check boxes for the Web pages you don't want to be updated.

4. Click Synchronize.

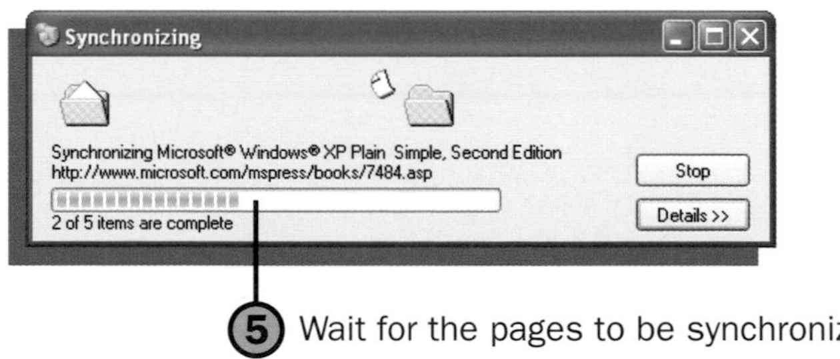

5. Wait for the pages to be synchronized.

Controlling Pop-Up Windows ❂ NEW FEATURE

Argh! Doesn't it drive you crazy when you go to a Web site, only to face a relentless barrage of pop-up windows that try to sell you a bunch of stuff you don't want? With Windows XP Service Pack 2 installed, you can tell Internet Explorer to pop those pop-up windows. However, if there are certain pop-up windows you want to look at, you can tell Internet Explorer to display them.

NEW FEATURE: The Pop-Up Manager can block all pop-up windows or only those from sites you don't trust, depending on your settings. Blocking pop-ups isn't just a convenience—pop-ups can be used to run malicious code or to steal personal information.

Use the Pop-Up Manager

1. In Internet Explorer, point to Pop-Up Manager on the Tools menu, and choose Block Pop-Up Windows from the submenu if this item isn't already checked.
2. In a Web site where a pop-up has been blocked, click the Information Bar.

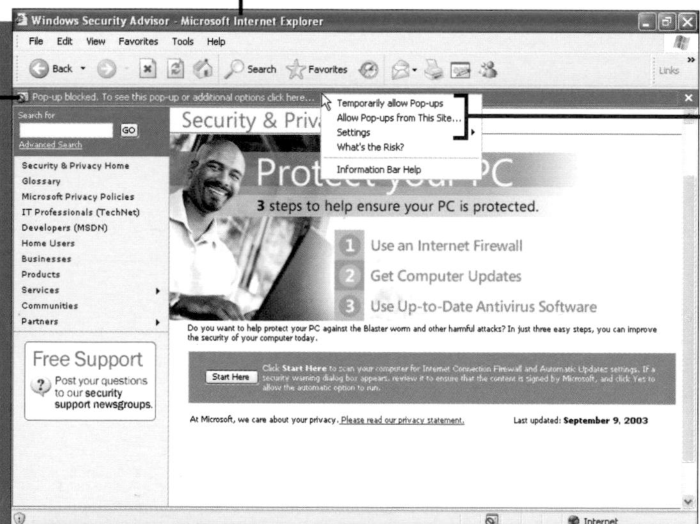

3. Select the item you want from the shortcut menu:
   - Temporarily Allow Pop-Ups to allow pop-ups from this Web site during this one visit
   - Allow Pop-Ups From This Site to add this site to your list of exceptions and always permit pop-ups from this site
   - Settings to turn off the Pop-Up Blocker, hide the Information Bar, manually add the addresses of sites that you'll allow to show pop-ups, or change the level (High, Medium, or Low) of the filtering of pop-ups

TIP: By default, the pop-up blocker is set to Medium filter level, which blocks pop-ups either when you click a link to open a pop-up window or when the Web site you're visiting is in the Internet Explorer Local Intranet or the Trusted Sites security zone. To block all pop-ups, point to Pop-Up Blocker on the Internet Explorer Tools menu, choose Pop-Up Blocker Settings from the submenu, and, in the Pop-Up Blocker Settings dialog box, select the High filter level.

CAUTION: The Information Bar appears when other security problems are encountered, such as when a Web page tries to download a file or an ActiveX control. To maintain security, make sure the Information Bar isn't turned off—and pay attention to the messages it contains.

Copying Material from a Web Page

Sometimes, although you might want to save one or two items from a Web page, you have no use for the entire page. It's a simple matter to save only the parts of the page you want.

CAUTION: When you copy material from a Web page, make sure that you're not violating any copyrights.

Save a Picture

1. Right-click the picture, and choose Save Picture As from the shortcut menu.

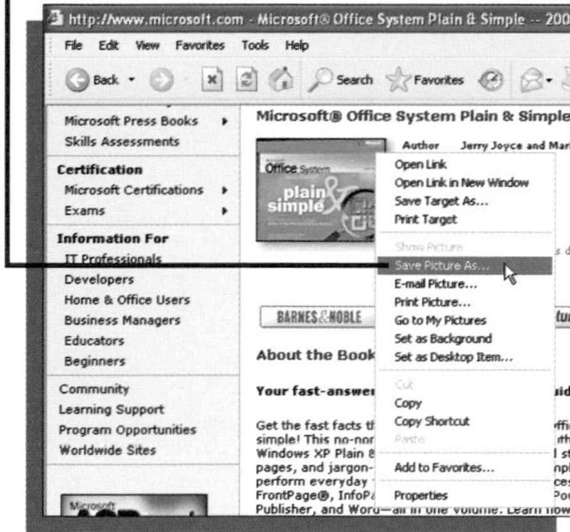

2. In the Save Picture dialog box that appears, save the picture in the folder and the format that you want, using a descriptive file name.

Save Some Text

1. Click at the beginning of the text you want to copy. You won't see an insertion point, but Internet Explorer is smart—it knows where you clicked.

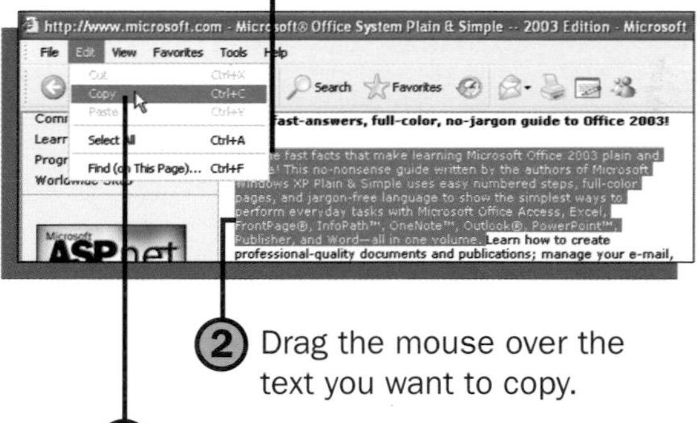

2. Drag the mouse over the text you want to copy.
3. Choose Copy from the Edit menu.
4. Switch to a word processing program such as WordPad, paste the text, and save the document.

TIP: Web pages are often constructed using tables and nested tables. If you try to copy text from a Web page but are unable to select only the material you want, here's what to do. Select the material you want, along with any other material that simultaneously becomes selected, copy it, and paste it into your word processing program. In that program, delete the superfluous content, and save the document. If you're using Microsoft Word as your word processor, choose the Paste Options command from the Edit menu to paste only the formatted text; that way, you won't have to delete pictures and other content you don't want.

Transferring Files with FTP

File Transfer Protocol, or FTP, is a standard way of transferring large files from one location to another. Although most FTP occurs automatically when you click a link on a Web page to download a file, there might be times when you'll need to go directly to an FTP site, browse through folders, and then download or upload files. Fortunately, Internet Explorer makes this as easy as working in any folder on your computer or network.

SEE ALSO: For additional information about FTP and other methods of transferring files, see "Transferring Files" on page 82.

CAUTION: User names and passwords are not secure when you're logging on to an FTP server, so make sure that you use a different user name and password from the one you use to log on to your computer.

Transfer Files

1. With Internet Explorer running and the Address toolbar visible, type the address of the FTP site, and press Enter. In most cases, the address is in the form *ftp://ftpsitename,* where *ftpsitename* is the full name of the FTP site—for example, *microsoft.com.*

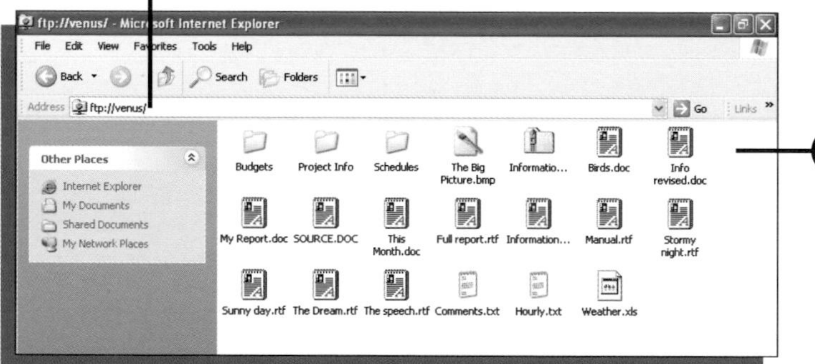

3. Use the FTP site as you would any other folder window: Double-click an item to open it, drag an item to a folder on your computer to download the file, or drag a file from a folder on your computer to the FTP site to upload the file.

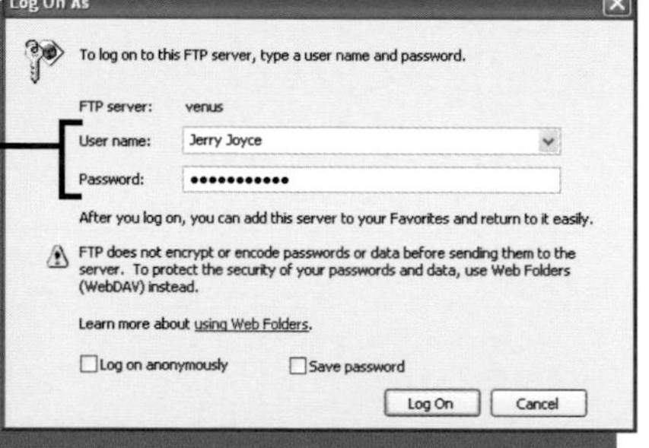

2. If you're required to log on to the site, enter the user name and password that were assigned to you by the administrator of the site, and click Log On. If the dialog box doesn't appear, right-click the window, and choose Login As to display the Log On As dialog box.

Finding Something on the Internet

To search for a specific item on the Internet—a list of sources where you can buy other *Plain & Simple* books, for example, or the menu and locator map for that new restaurant you want to try—you can jump right to a search page and set up your query. Once the results are displayed, you can jump to the page that contains the information you're looking for, and, if it's not what you want, you can try another page.

TIP: To change or eliminate the animated character in the Search Companion pane, use a different search engine, the Indexing Service, or the advanced search fields; then click Change Preferences in the Search Companion pane, and make your changes.

Search for an Item

1. Click the Start button, and choose Search from the Start menu to display the Search Results dialog box. Connect to the Internet if you aren't already connected.
2. Click Search The Internet.
3. Type the information you want to use as your search criterion, and press Enter.
4. Click to maximize the window if it isn't already maximized.
5. Click a link in the search results.
6. Conduct any other related actions you want.
7. Close the Search Companion when you've finished with the search results.

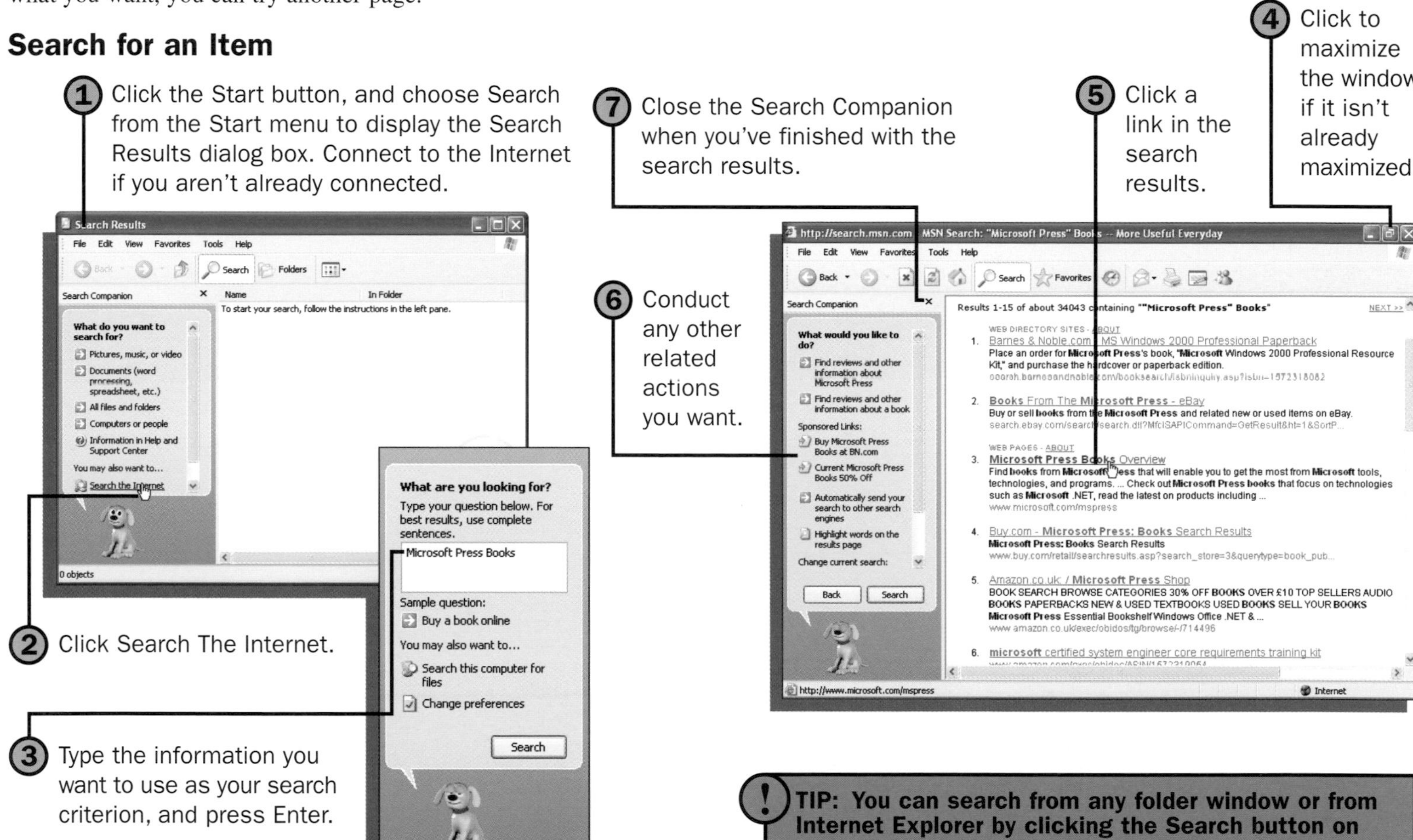

TIP: You can search from any folder window or from Internet Explorer by clicking the Search button on the Standard Buttons toolbar.

Transferring Your Settings

If you use more than one computer or more than one type of browser to explore the Internet, you don't need to duplicate your list of favorite Web sites, nor do you need to duplicate the registrations, sign-ins, and customizations for Web sites that usually keep that information stored as cookies on your computer. Instead, you can export your list of favorite sites and cookies from one computer or program and import them onto the other computer.

Save the Information

1. With Internet Explorer running, on the computer that contains the items you want to transfer, choose Import And Export from the File menu to start the Import/Export Wizard. Click Next to start the wizard.

2. Step through the wizard specifying
   - The location of your Favorites list (usually already selected for you).
   - That you want to export your Favorites list.
   - The location in which you want to save the file containing the information.

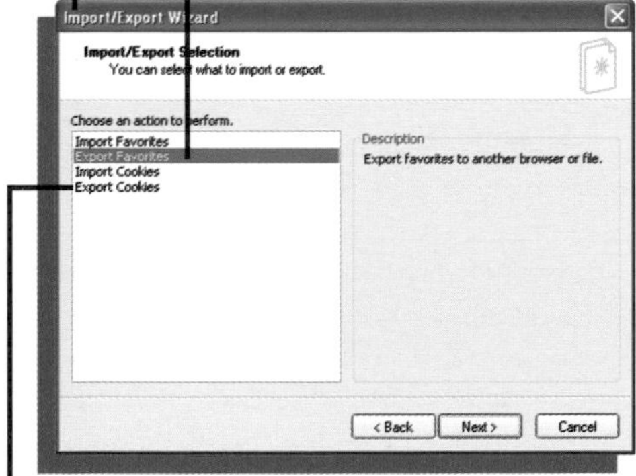

3. Use the wizard again to export the cookies if you want to transfer them too.

4. Transfer the files to a location that will be accessible by the other computer, such as a shared folder or removable storage—a disk or USB storage device, for example.

Transfer the Information

1. With Internet Explorer running, on the computer to which you want to transfer the information, choose Import And Export from the File menu to start the Import/Export Wizard. Click Next to start the wizard.

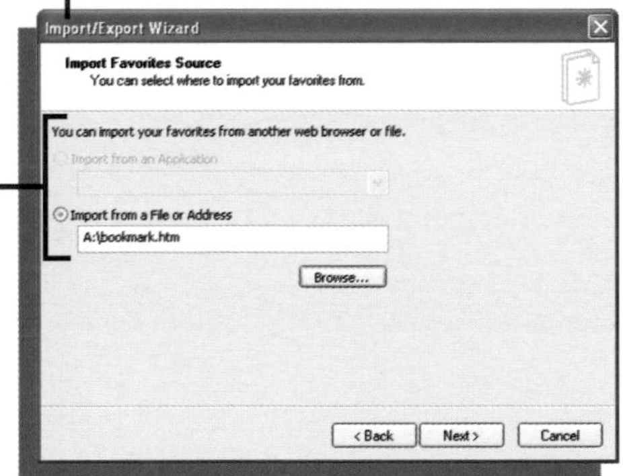

2. Step through the wizard specifying
   - That you want to import Favorites information.
   - The location of the file containing the information you previously exported.
   - The destination folder.

3. Repeat the wizard to import cookies if you previously exported them.

TIP: If you have more than one Internet browser on your computer, you can use the Import/Export Wizard to transfer Favorites (bookmarks) and cookie information directly between the browsers.

Communicating

In this section

The ability to communicate electronically is one of a computer's most used and most valued features. In this section, we'll discuss the tools that Microsoft Windows XP provides to enable you to reach out and connect with other people.

Microsoft Outlook Express helps you organize and customize your e-mail and does double duty as a news reader. It can complete an address from your Contacts list when you type only the first couple of letters of your contact's name, and it can automatically add a signature to your messages. You can format your e-mail messages with fonts and colors, and you can choose or create your own e-mail stationery. If you often send one message to the same group of people, you can combine all their addresses into a *group* so that you don't have to enter each individual's address. You can enclose files, or *attachments,* with your e-mail, and if an attached file exceeds the size that your mail system can handle, you can *compress* the file to make it smaller. If you're using a public computer, you can send and receive your e-mail using Microsoft Internet Explorer. There's also a great new security feature in Outlook Express that helps you limit e-mail snooping by spammers and mass mailers.

You can use Windows Messenger to exchange instant text messages or to conduct working sessions with up to five of your contacts whenever they're on line. If text messages aren't personal enough, you can have voice and video chats, provided your contacts are running Windows XP. In a Windows Messenger session, you can share programs, discuss documents on line, and transfer large files without compressing them.

Sending E-Mail

You don't have to address an envelope or trek to the mailbox on a cold, rainy day. All you do is select a name, create a message, and click a Send button. Outlook Express and your mail server do the rest. What could be more convenient?

Create a Message

1. Open Outlook Express from the Start menu. Click Create Mail. If you want to send a formatted message with a background and coordinated fonts and bullets, click the down arrow next to the button, and click the stationery you want to use.
2. Start typing the recipient's name. Press Enter when Outlook Express completes the name based on the names in your Contacts list, or continue typing if the proposed name is incorrect. To add more names, type a semicolon (;), and then start typing another recipient's name.
3. Press the Tab key to move to the CC field, and type the names of the people who are to receive a copy of the message. 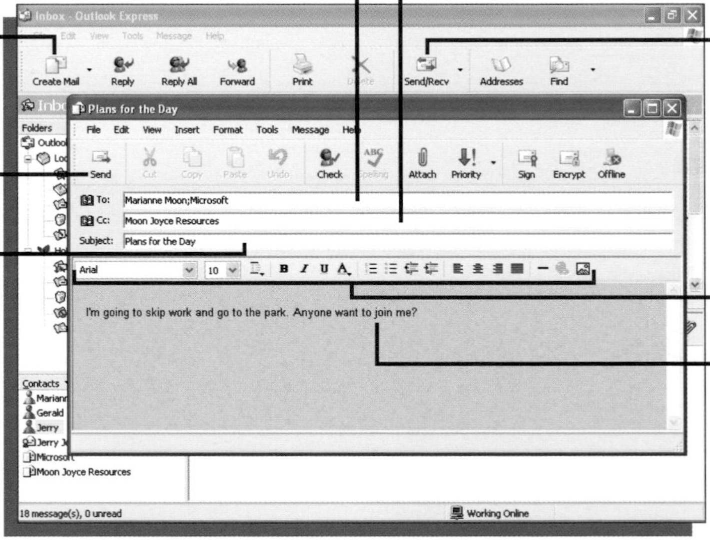
4. Press the Tab key to move to the Subject line, type a subject, and press Tab again to move into the message area.
5. Type your message. Use any of the formatting tools to format your message.
6. Click Send to send the message to your Outbox.
7. When you've composed all the messages you want to send, click Send/Recv to send the messages in the Outbox to your mail server.

Formatting tools

SEE ALSO: For information about adding formatting, pictures, or your signature, see "Designing Your Default Message" on page 70.

For information about setting up e-mail accounts in Outlook Express, see "Setting Up Outlook Express" on pages 216–217.

CAUTION: A formatted message uses HTML formatting. Use Plain Text formatting if you're not sure whether the recipient has a mail reader that supports HTML formatting. Messages using Plain Text formatting are smaller and will download faster over a slow Internet connection than will messages using HTML formatting, especially those that contain pictures.

Saving and Sending a Draft Message

You can't always complete an e-mail message without being interrupted by someone or something. Or perhaps you want to mull over what you've said for a while and make a few changes to the wording before you send the message. Fortunately, you can save your message in its incomplete form and then return to it when you're ready, finish it, and send it on its way.

Create a Draft

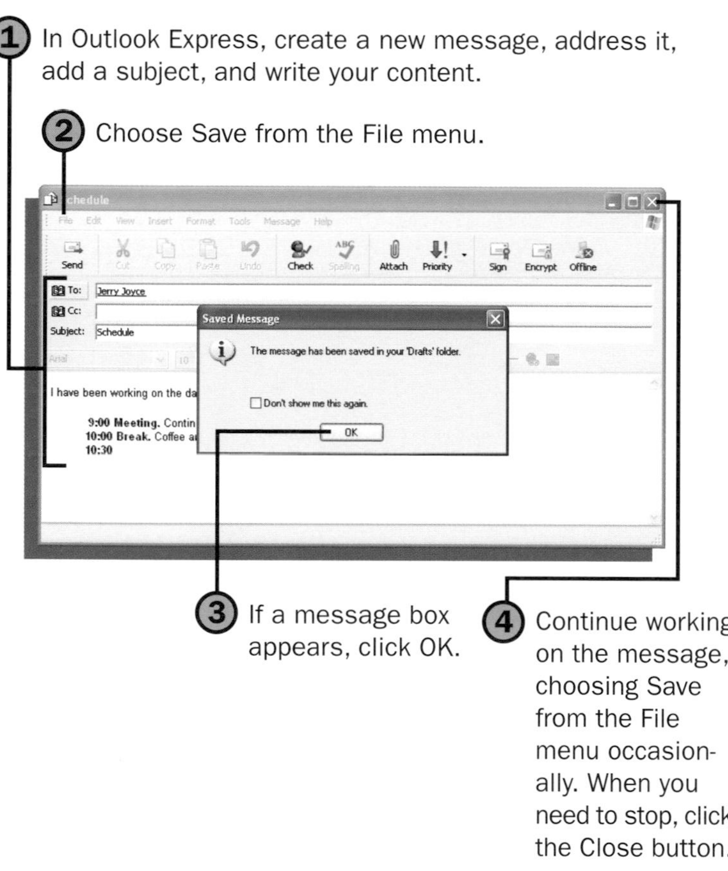

1. In Outlook Express, create a new message, address it, add a subject, and write your content.
2. Choose Save from the File menu.
3. If a message box appears, click OK.
4. Continue working on the message, choosing Save from the File menu occasionally. When you need to stop, click the Close button.

Send the Draft

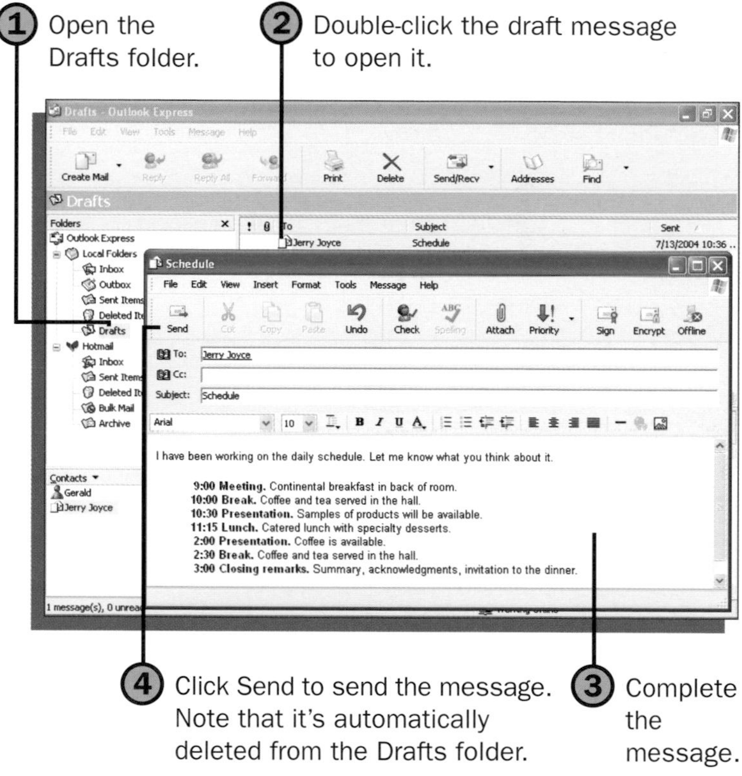

1. Open the Drafts folder.
2. Double-click the draft message to open it.
3. Complete the message.
4. Click Send to send the message. Note that it's automatically deleted from the Drafts folder.

TIP: Even if you're able to complete a lengthy message in one sitting, you'll probably want to save it occasionally just as a precaution. If you close a partially completed message without sending it, Outlook Express will ask you whether you want to save a draft.

Receiving and Reading E-Mail

Outlook Express lets you specify how frequently you want it to check for incoming e-mail, and it notifies you when you receive new mail. You can check your Inbox and see at a glance which messages have and haven't been read, or you can set the view to list unread messages only.

> **TIP:** When you start Outlook Express, it checks for your mail, and it checks periodically thereafter while it's running. To receive mail immediately when you don't want to wait for the system to check your mailbox for you, click the Send/Recv button. To change the frequency with which Outlook Express checks for mail, choose Options from the Tools menu, and change the settings on the General tab.

Read Your Messages

1. Click the Inbox for the mail service you want to view if it isn't the currently active folder.
2. On the View menu, specify how you want to view your messages:
   - Point to Current View, and choose the type of messages you want displayed.
   - Point to Sort By, and choose the way you want the messages to be ordered.
   - Choose Layout, specify whether and where you want the preview pane displayed, and click OK.
3. Click a message header, and read the message in the preview pane.
4. Double-click a message header to view the message in a separate window.

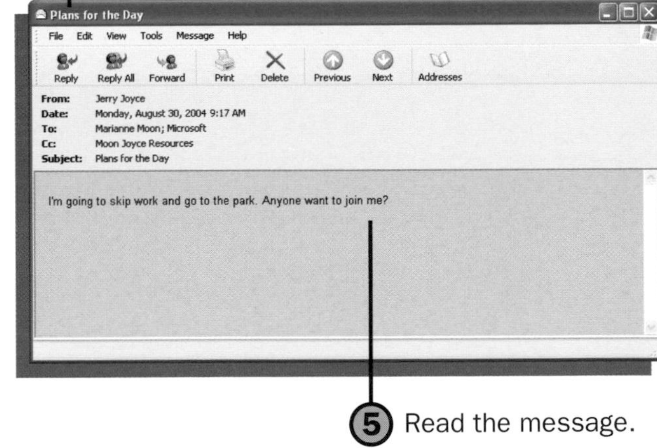

5. Read the message.

> **TRY THIS:** On the Read tab of the Options dialog box, click the Fonts button. Click a different font in the Proportional Font list and a different font size in the Font Size list, and click OK. Close the Options dialog box, and look at the messages in the preview pane.

Using E-Mail on a Public Computer

When you're away from your home computer—staying in a hotel, visiting a cybercafé, attending a conference, and so on—you can often use a public computer to access your e-mail. In order to do this, you must be able to access your e-mail account via the Web—using Internet Explorer instead of a dedicated mail program, for example. E-mail accounts such as Hotmail are designed for Web access, and many other types of accounts also support Web access together with their normal e-mail access.

TIP: If you sign in and accidentally tell Internet Explorer to remember your password, choose Internet Options from the Tools menu, and, on the Content tab, click the AutoComplete button. In the AutoComplete Settings dialog box, click the Clear Passwords button, confirm that you want to delete the password, and then click OK twice. By doing this, you prevent someone else from signing on to the computer using your stored password.

SEE ALSO: For information about connecting to a public wireless network, see "Connecting to a Wireless Network" on pages 204–205.

For information about increasing security when you use your own computer on a public network, see "Configuring the Windows Firewall" on pages 264–265.

Check the Mail

1. In Internet Explorer, type the name of the Web page of your e-mail server in the Address toolbar, and press Enter.

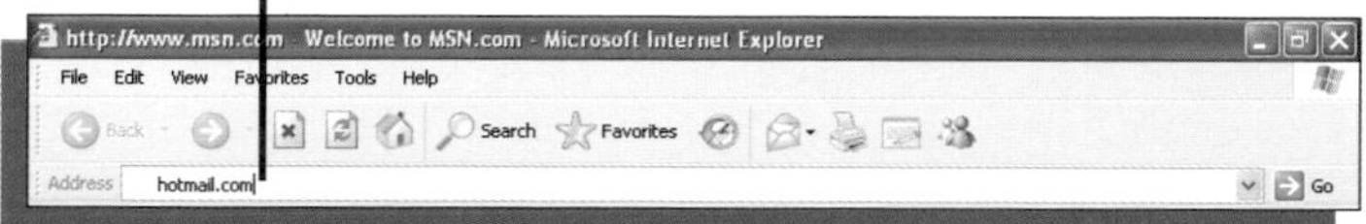

2. If you need to sign in using a .NET Passport, do the following:
   - Type your e-mail address.
   - Type your password.
   - If the check box for automatic sign-in is checked, clear it.
   - Select the check box that directs the system not to remember your e-mail address.
   - Click Sign In.

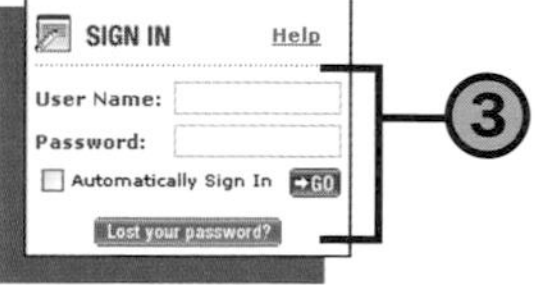

3. If you don't use a .NET passport to sign in, follow the directions to sign in. Make sure that you clear any check boxes so that your password and/or e-mail address won't be remembered.

4. Use your e-mail service as usual. When you've finished, sign out, and close Internet Explorer so that all items are deleted.

Designing Your Default Message

Why not let your computer do some of your work for you? When you design a default mail message, every new message that you start will look exactly the way you want, with all the elements in place—a specific background picture, your signature automatically inserted at the end of the message, a font that makes the message a little more "you," and so on.

TIP: If you know that a certain contact can receive only plain-text–formatted messages, right-click his or her name in your Contacts list, choose Properties from the shortcut menu, and, on the Name tab, select the Send E-Mail Using Plain Text Only check box. Click OK. To send a message in plain text only once, choose Plain Text from the Format menu when you compose the message.

Add a Signature

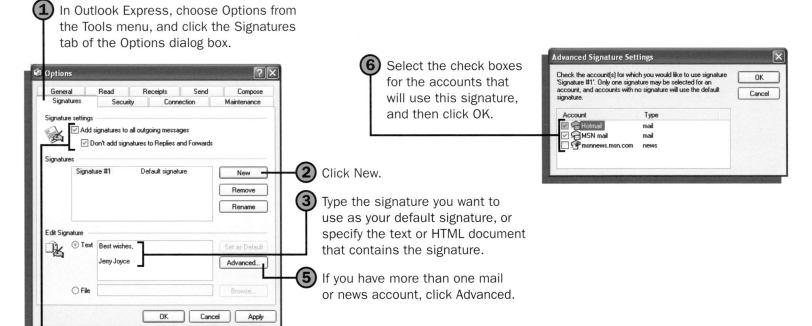

1. In Outlook Express, choose Options from the Tools menu, and click the Signatures tab of the Options dialog box.

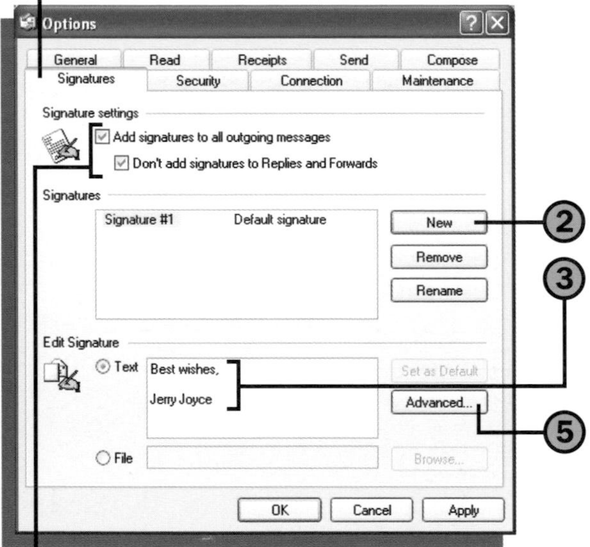

2. Click New.
3. Type the signature you want to use as your default signature, or specify the text or HTML document that contains the signature.
4. Specify whether you want the signature added automatically to all outgoing messages and whether or not you want it included in replies and forwarded messages.
5. If you have more than one mail or news account, click Advanced.
6. Select the check boxes for the accounts that will use this signature, and then click OK.

Advanced Signature Settings

Check the account(s) for which you would like to use signature 'Signature #1'. Only one signature may be selected for an account, and accounts with no signature will use the default signature.

Account	Type
Hotmail	mail
MSN mail	mail
msnnews.msn.com	news

OK

Cancel

TIP: If your message is in the HTML format, your signature file can be an HTML document too. If you enjoy experimenting with HTML, you can create anything from an attractive or ornate signature to a humorous or truly obnoxious one. The signature file, however, can't be any larger than 4 KB.

Specify Your Stationery

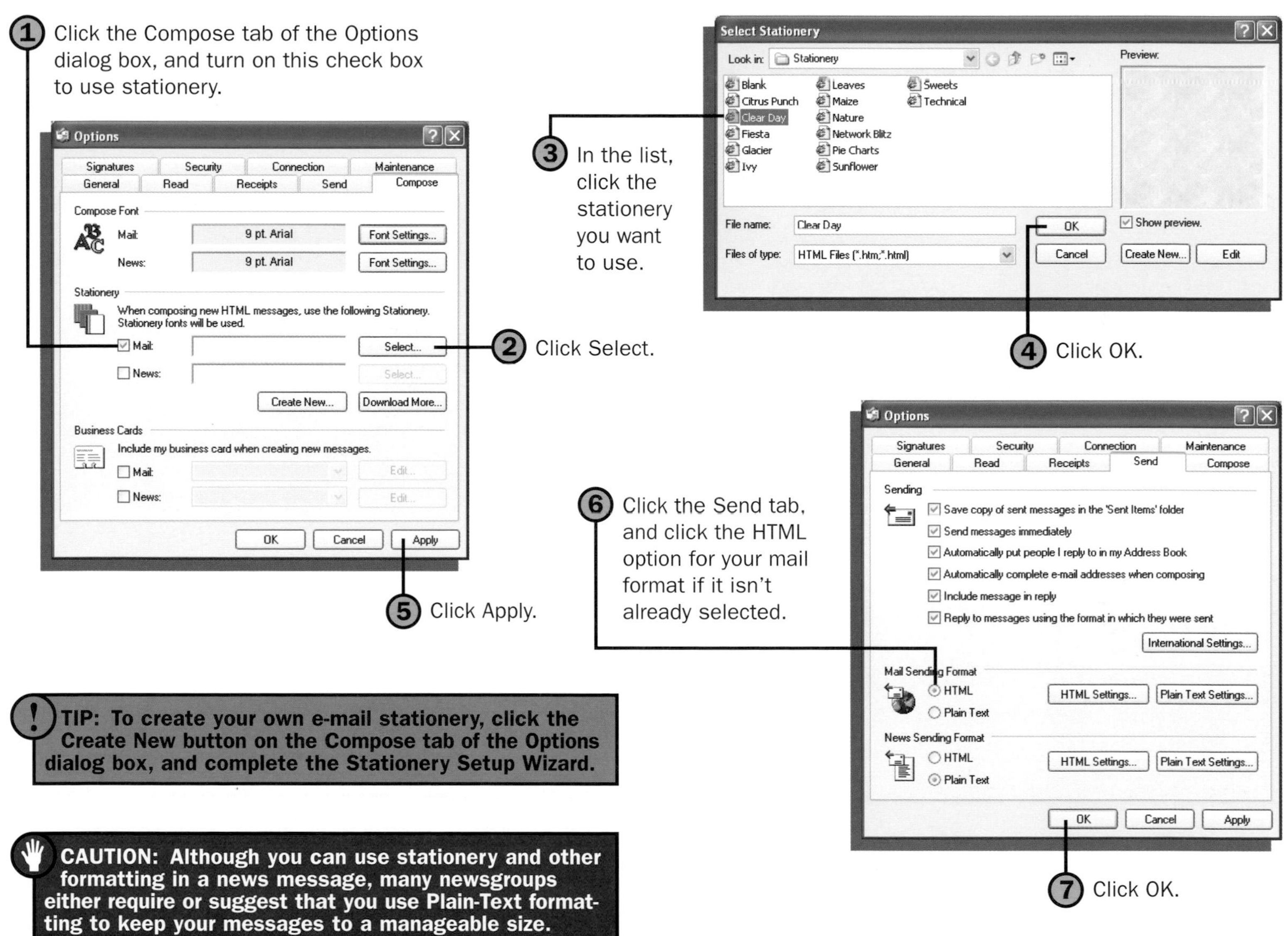

1. Click the Compose tab of the Options dialog box, and turn on this check box to use stationery.
2. Click Select.
3. In the list, click the stationery you want to use.
4. Click OK.
5. Click Apply.
6. Click the Send tab, and click the HTML option for your mail format if it isn't already selected.
7. Click OK.

TIP: To create your own e-mail stationery, click the Create New button on the Compose tab of the Options dialog box, and complete the Stationery Setup Wizard.

CAUTION: Although you can use stationery and other formatting in a news message, many newsgroups either require or suggest that you use Plain-Text formatting to keep your messages to a manageable size.

Sending or Receiving a File

A great way to share a file—a Microsoft Word document, a picture, or even an entire program—is to include it as part of an e-mail message. The file is kept as a separate part of the message—an *attachment*—that the recipient can save and open at any time.

TIP: Some mail systems can't accommodate attachments larger than about 1 MB, and some types of files can be corrupted when they're sent as attachments. In those cases, you can compress the file before you send it. To do so, send the file to a compressed folder, and then e-mail the compressed folder. You can also use other file-transfer methods such as those available through FTP services or Windows Messenger.

SEE ALSO: For information about other ways to transfer files, see "Transferring Files" on page 82.

For information about using compressed folders, see "Compressing Files" on pages 174–175.

Send a File by E-Mail

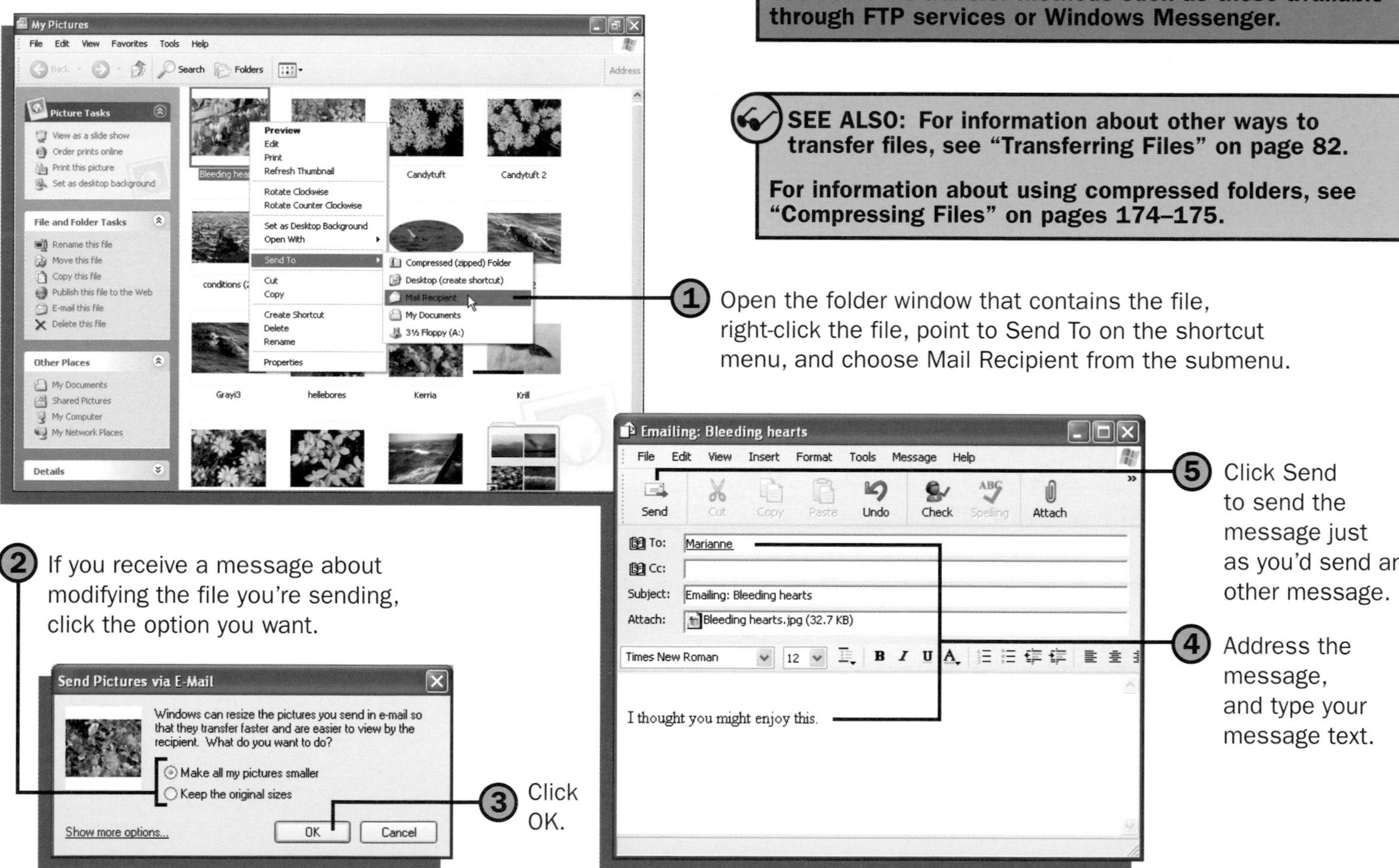

1. Open the folder window that contains the file, right-click the file, point to Send To on the shortcut menu, and choose Mail Recipient from the submenu.
2. If you receive a message about modifying the file you're sending, click the option you want.
3. Click OK.
4. Address the message, and type your message text.
5. Click Send to send the message just as you'd send any other message.

Receive an Attachment

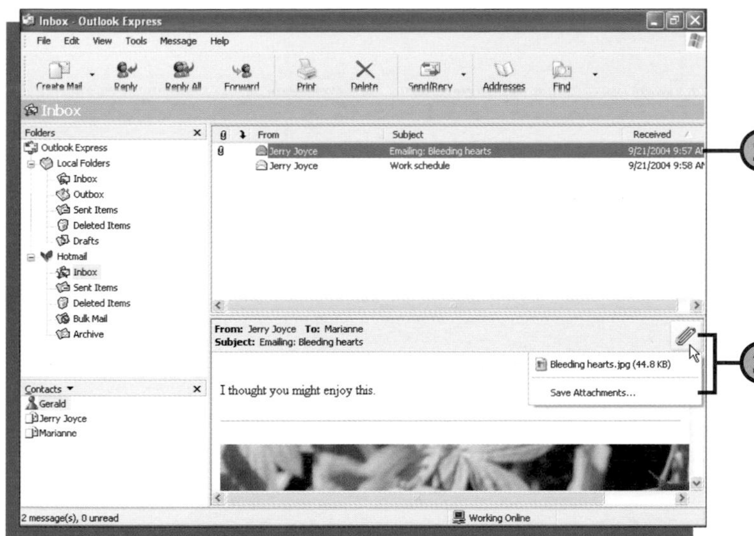

SEE ALSO: **For information about protecting yourself and others from e-mail viruses, see "Foiling E-Mail Viruses" on page 276.**

1. Select a message you've received that contains an attachment.
2. Click the Attachment icon, and, from the menu that appears, choose
   - The name of the file to open the file.
   - Save Attachments to save the file to disk without opening it.

CAUTION: **Viruses are often distributed in attached files. *Never* open an attachment you aren't expecting without first saving the attachment to disk and then using a virus-scanning program to inspect the file.**

TRY THIS: **Open a folder window, and select two or more files. Right-click one of the files, point to Send To on the shortcut menu, and choose Mail Recipient from the submenu. In your message, click the Attach button, and use the Insert Attachment dialog box to locate an additional file in a different folder. Select the file, and click Attach. You now have multiple files enclosed in a single message.**

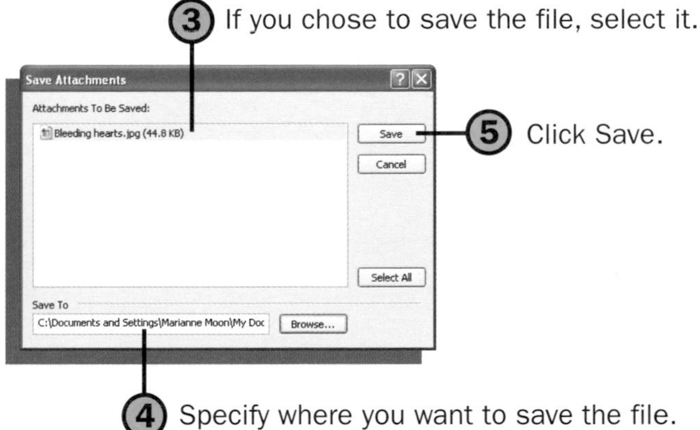

3. If you chose to save the file, select it.
4. Specify where you want to save the file.
5. Click Save.

Replying to or Forwarding a Message

When you receive an e-mail message that needs a reply or that you want to forward to someone else, all it takes is a click of a button to create a new message. But be careful when you use the Reply All button—your message could be received by a lot of people for whom it wasn't intended!

TIP: When you reply to a message that has an attached file, the attachment isn't included with your reply. When you forward a message, though, the attachment is included so that the recipient can open or save it.

Reply to or Forward a Message

1. Select the message header.
2. Click the appropriate button:
   - Reply to send your reply to the writer of the message only
   - Reply All to send your reply to the writer of the message and to everyone listed in the original message's To and CC lines
   - Forward to send a copy of the message to another recipient

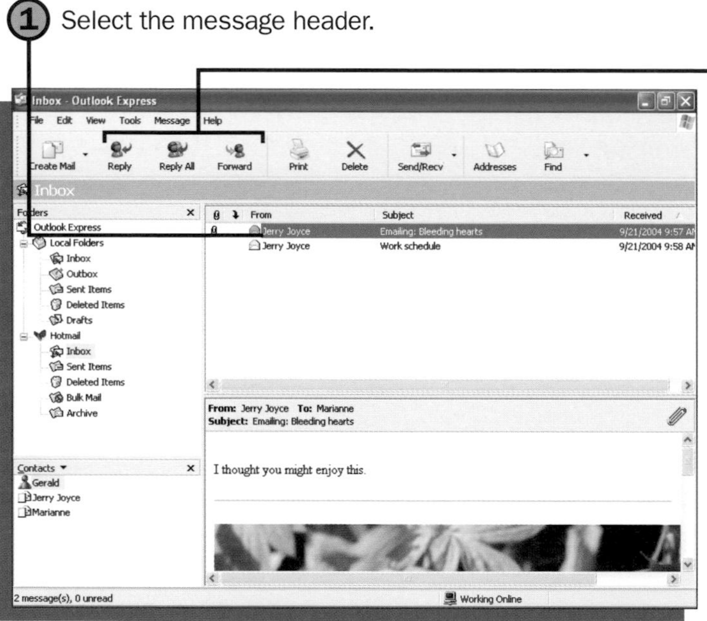

3. Add names to or delete names from the To and CC lines.

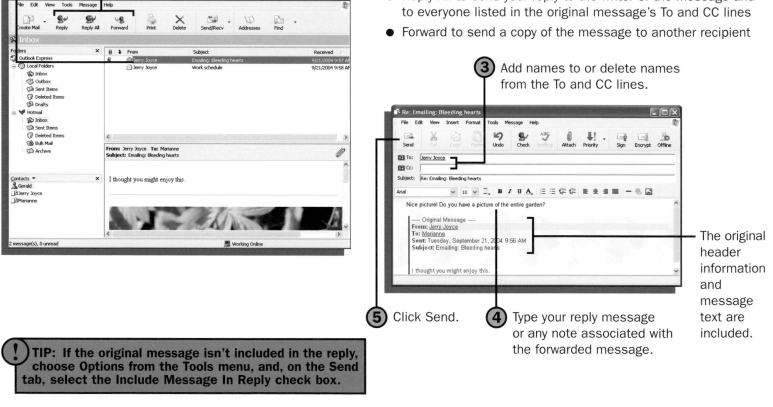

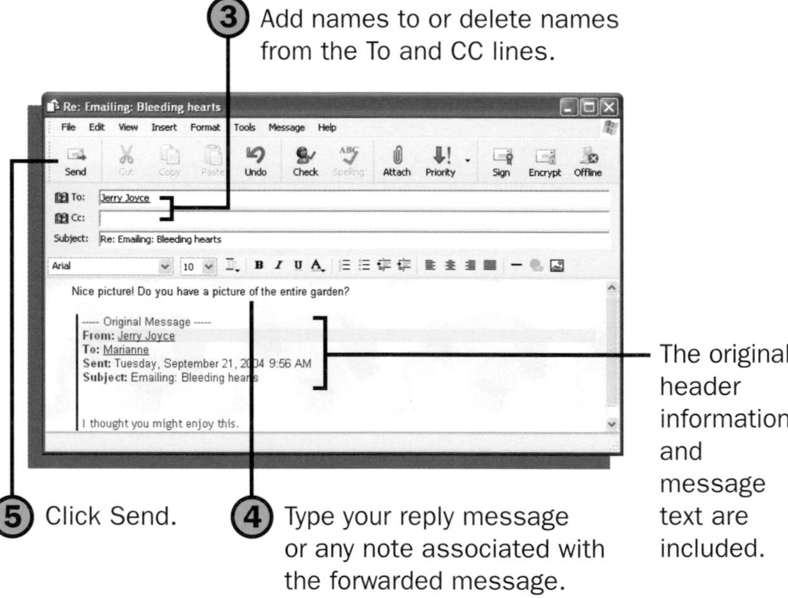

4. Type your reply message or any note associated with the forwarded message.
5. Click Send.

The original header information and message text are included.

TIP: If the original message isn't included in the reply, choose Options from the Tools menu, and, on the Send tab, select the Include Message In Reply check box.

Subscribing to Newsgroups

With so many newsgroups available, you'll probably want to be selective about the ones you review. You can do so in Outlook Express by *subscribing* to the newsgroups you like. Those newsgroups will appear in the message pane when you select the news server and will also appear on the Folders Bar, if it's displayed, when you expand the listing for a news server.

SEE ALSO: For information about setting up your news servers, see "Setting Up Outlook Express" on pages 216–217.

Specify Your Newsgroups

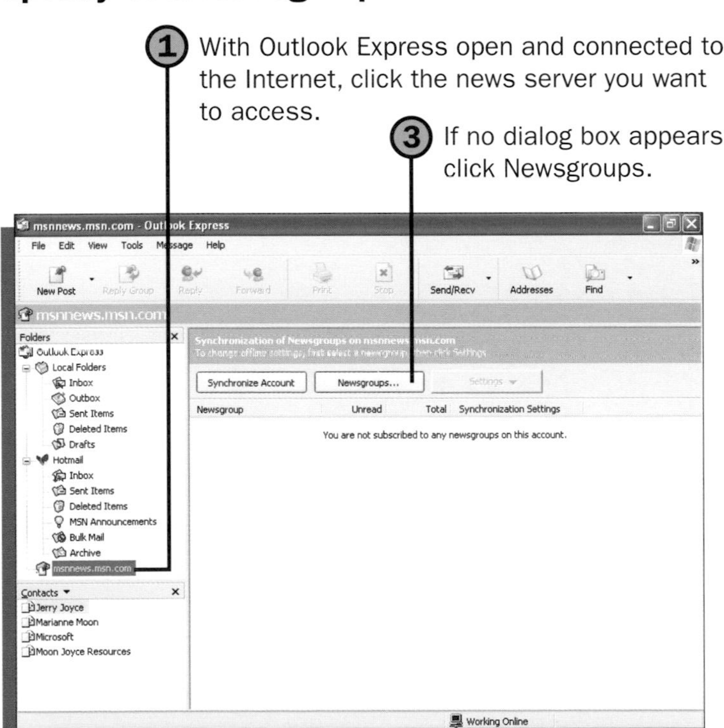

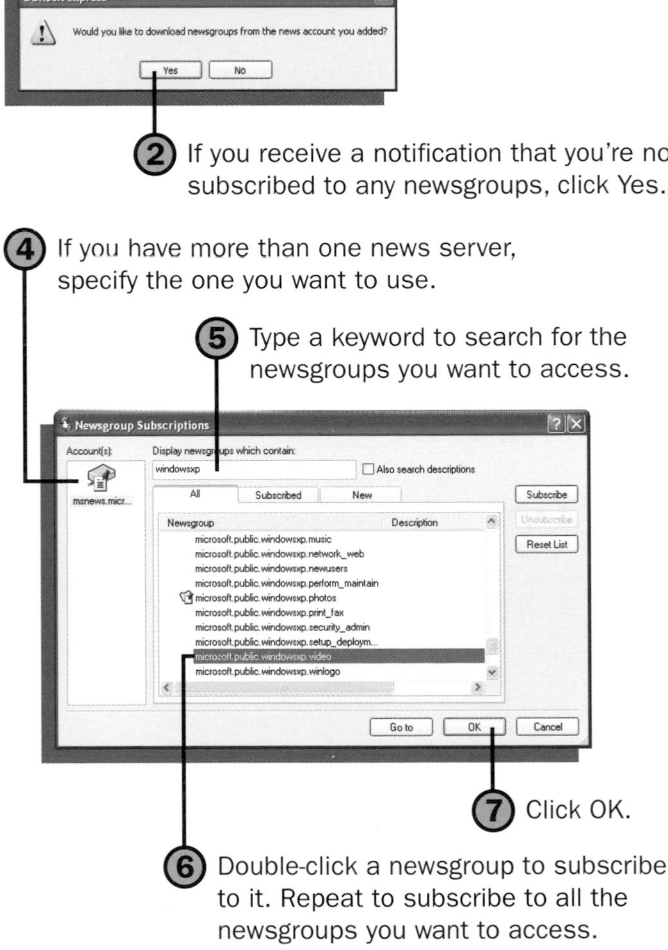

1. With Outlook Express open and connected to the Internet, click the news server you want to access.
2. If you receive a notification that you're not subscribed to any newsgroups, click Yes.
3. If no dialog box appears, click Newsgroups.
4. If you have more than one news server, specify the one you want to use.
5. Type a keyword to search for the newsgroups you want to access.
6. Double-click a newsgroup to subscribe to it. Repeat to subscribe to all the newsgroups you want to access.
7. Click OK.

TIP: To see the full names of the newsgroups, drag the boundary between the Newsgroup and Description labels to widen the Newsgroup area.

Reading and Writing the News

Reading and adding to the news—or the gossip, tirades, and misinformation that often pass for news in Internet newsgroups—is as simple as reading or sending your e-mail. All you need to do is specify a newsgroup and select a message, and then either read the message or click a button to respond to it.

TIP: A "thread" is a series of messages in which one person posts a message and other readers reply to the message and/or to the replies.

Select a Message

TIP: To open the news message in a separate window, double-click the message.

2. On the View menu, point to Current View, and choose the view you want:
   - Show All Messages to see everything
   - Hide Read Messages to display only the messages you haven't read
   - Show Downloaded Messages to see the messages you've downloaded
   - Hide Read Or Ignored Messages to display only the messages you haven't read or that haven't been marked to be ignored
   - Show Replies To My Messages to see responses to your messages

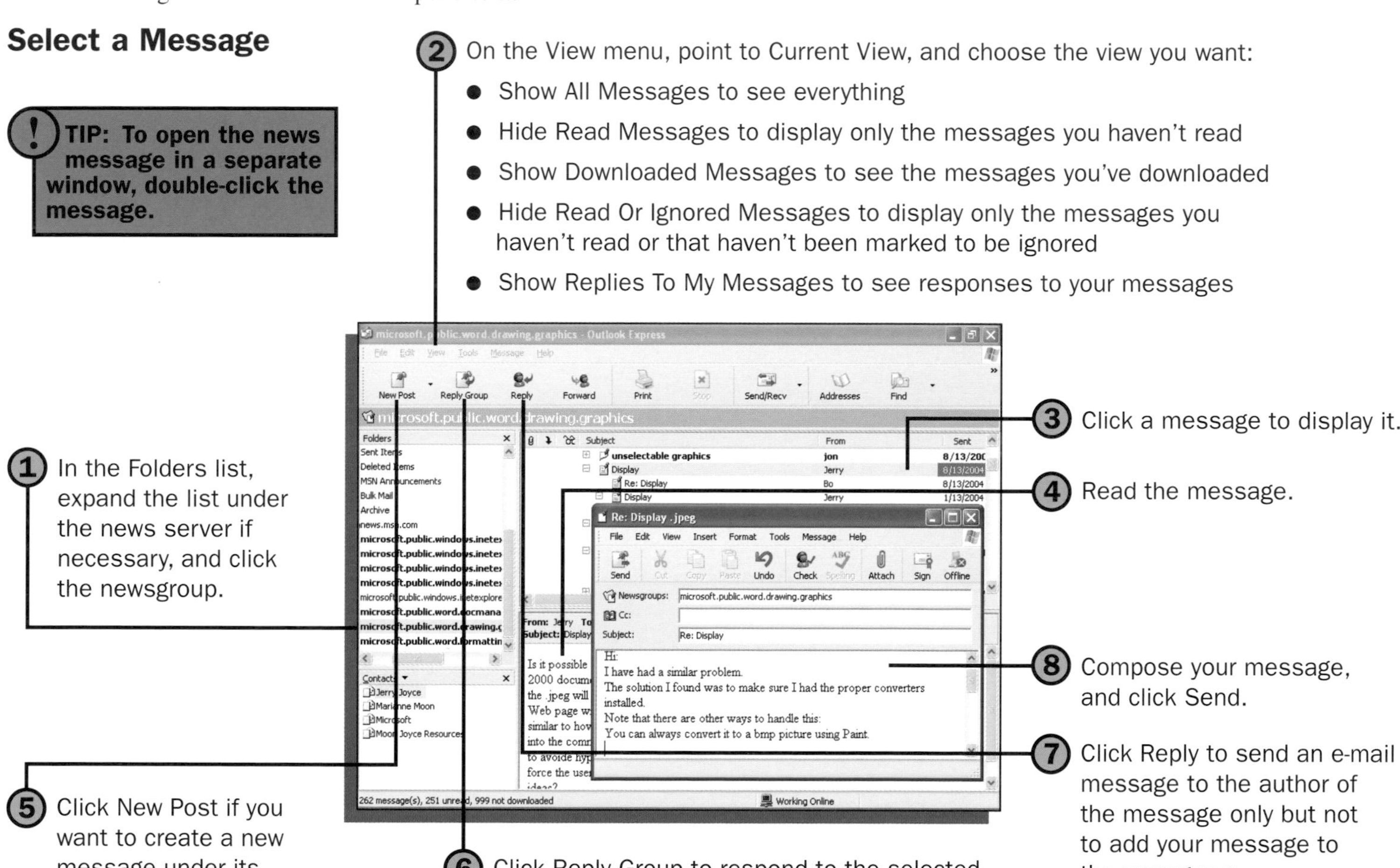

1. In the Folders list, expand the list under the news server if necessary, and click the newsgroup.
3. Click a message to display it.
4. Read the message.
5. Click New Post if you want to create a new message under its own topic (to start a new *thread*).
6. Click Reply Group to respond to the selected message and have your message added under that message (to add it to the thread).
7. Click Reply to send an e-mail message to the author of the message only but not to add your message to the newsgroup.
8. Compose your message, and click Send.

Reading E-Mail and News Off Line

If you aren't always connected to the mail and news servers, or if you want to economize on connection charges, you can download your e-mail and newsgroup messages, disconnect from the Internet, and then read the messages at your leisure. Any replies or new messages you compose will be stored in your Outbox until you reconnect.

Download the Messages

1. Click the mail or news service whose content you want to read off line.
2. Click Settings, and specify what you want to be downloaded.
3. Select the check boxes for the folders or groups you want to download. Clear the check boxes for those you don't want to download.
4. Click Synchronize Account. Connect to the Internet if you aren't already connected.

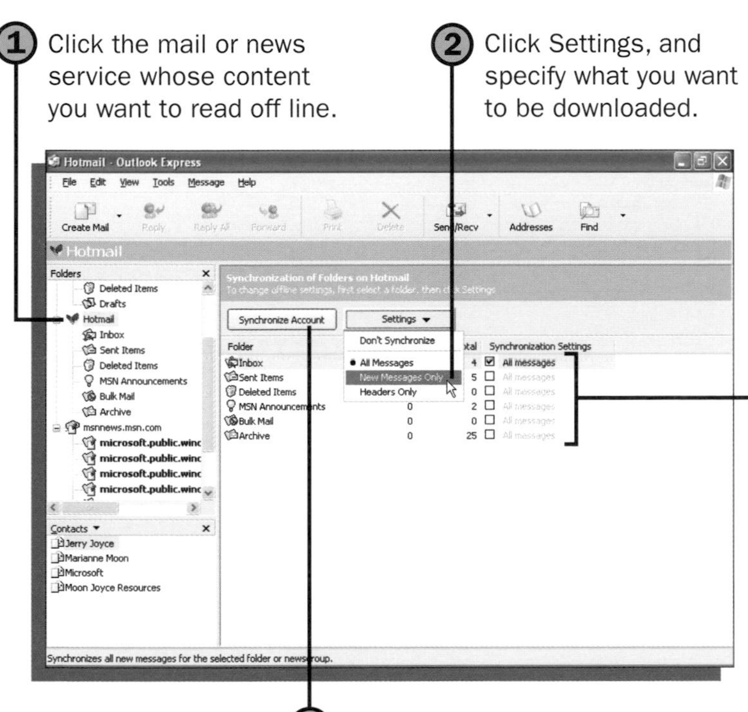

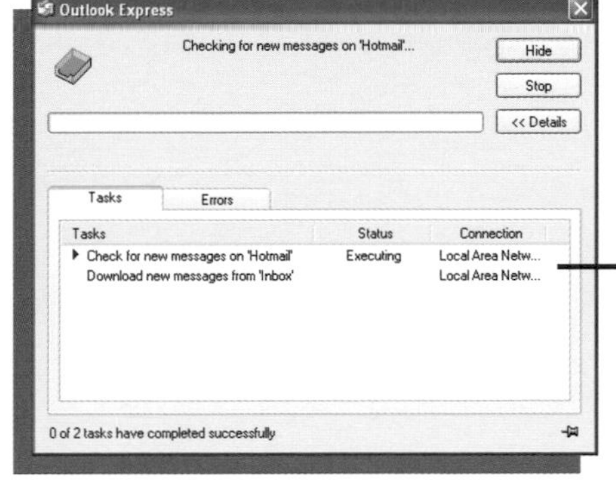

5. Wait for the messages to download, and then disconnect from the Internet.
6. Click a message to read it. If Outlook Express tries to reconnect, choose Work Offline from the File menu, and then click the message to read it.

TIP: Unless you've changed some settings, all your messages are automatically downloaded from a POP3 e-mail service. However, messages aren't routinely downloaded from an HTTP service (a Hotmail account, for example) or an IMAP service. Use the method described in the procedure on this page to download any messages from those mail services that you want to review off line.

Limiting E-Mail Snooping ⊕ NEW FEATURE

One of the most insidious ways mass mailers and spammers verify that your e-mail address is valid is to include a picture that they hope you'll download from a Web server. When your computer accesses the site that contains the picture, your e-mail address is automatically verified. You can guard against this invasion of your privacy by having Outlook Express prevent automatic downloading of pictures in all your mail.

Block the Pictures

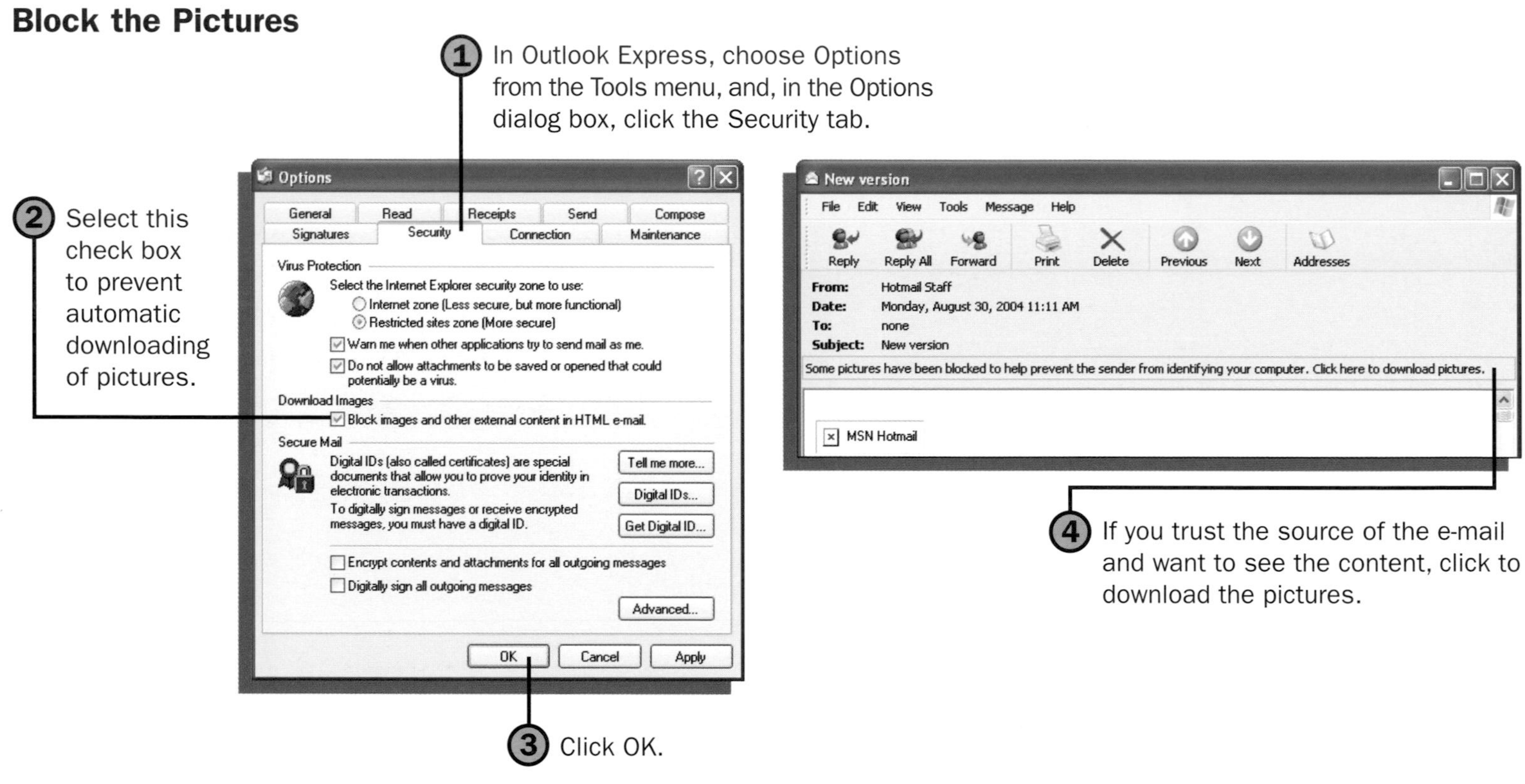

TIP: If you want to see the picture that has been blocked, click the link to it in the e-mail message.

Managing Your Messages

Why not let Outlook Express do some of the work of organizing your e-mail messages? By creating rules, you can tell Outlook Express how you want your messages to be treated, based on subject, content, e-mail addresses, or various other factors.

> **TIP: If a rule already exists, the Message Rules dialog box appears when you choose Message Rules from the Tools menu. Click New to display the New Mail Rules dialog box.**

> **TIP: Create news rules to organize your newsgroups, and create a Block Senders list to have mail automatically deleted when it comes from a specified e-mail address or domain.**

Create Your Rules

1. Point to Message Rules on the Tools menu, and choose Mail from the submenu to display the New Mail Rule dialog box.
2. Select the check box for each identifying condition.
3. Select the check box for each action to be executed when the identifying conditions are met.
4. Click a link to provide the specific information required to execute the rule.
5. Type a name for the rule.
6. Click OK.

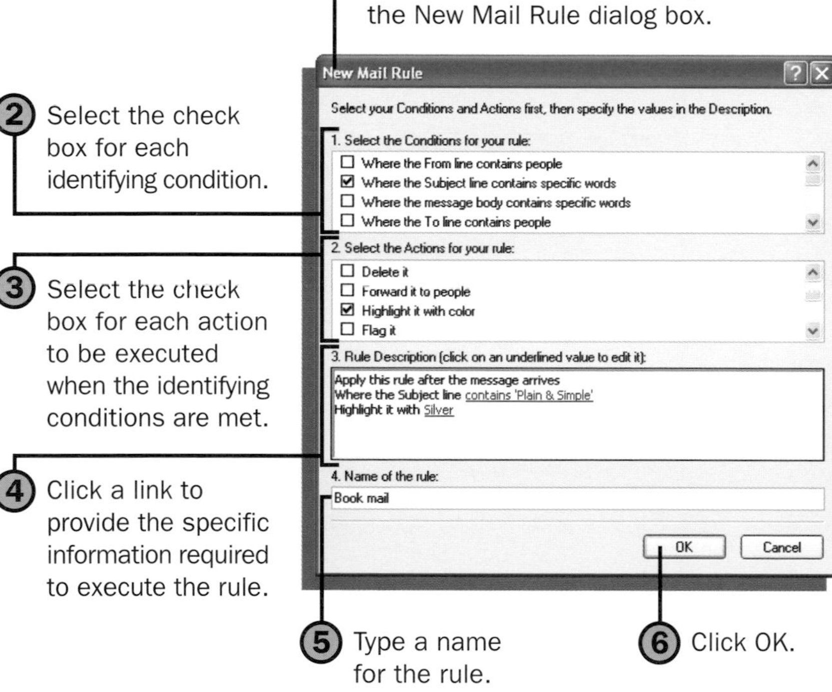

7. Click New, and repeat steps 2 through 6 to create additional rules.
8. Use the Move Up and Move Down buttons to change the order in which the rules are executed.
9. Click OK.

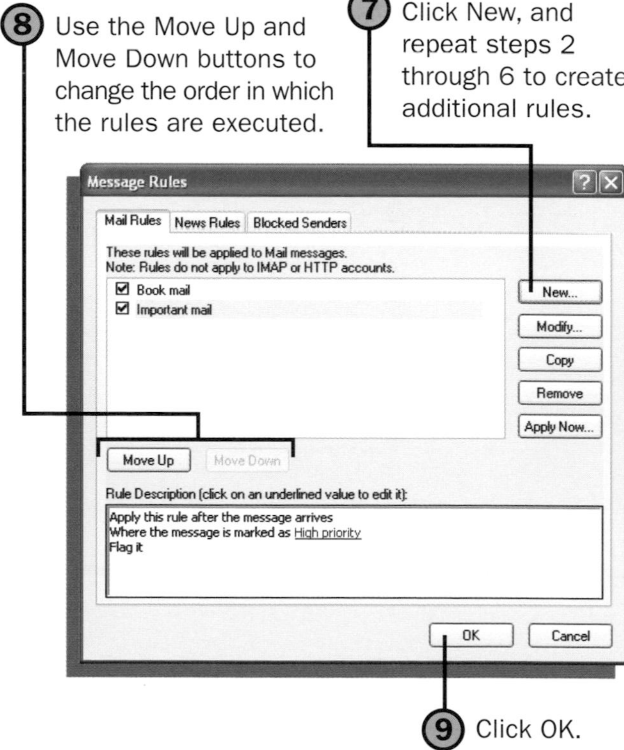

Managing Your E-Mail Contacts

When you're using e-mail, you don't need to type an address every time you send a message; you can retrieve addresses from your Contacts list. All the names shown in the Contacts list are actually stored in your Address Book, a separate program that works with Outlook Express and other programs. If you frequently send one message to the same group of people, you can gather all their addresses into a *group,* and then all you need to find and use is that one address item. It's a real time-saver.

Create a New Contact

1. In Outlook Express, point to New on the File menu, and choose Contact from the submenu to display the Properties dialog box.
2. On the various tabs of the Properties dialog box, enter the information you want to record.
3. Click OK.

TIP: To automatically add to your Address Book the addresses of all the people whose messages you reply to, choose Options from the Tools menu, and, on the Send tab, select the Automatically Put People I Reply To In My Address Book check box.

Add an Address from a Message

1. In the Inbox, right-click the message.

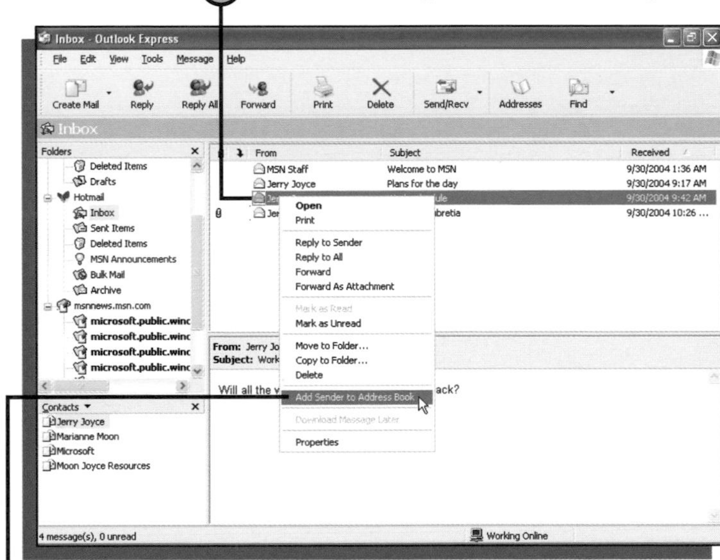

2. Choose Add Sender To Address Book from the shortcut menu. If the command is grayed (unavailable), connect to the Internet or to your mail server, click the message to download it, and then right-click it and choose the command again.

TIP: To add to your Address Book someone whose name is listed in the CC line of a message, double-click the message to open it in a separate window, and then right-click the name you want to add.

Create a Group

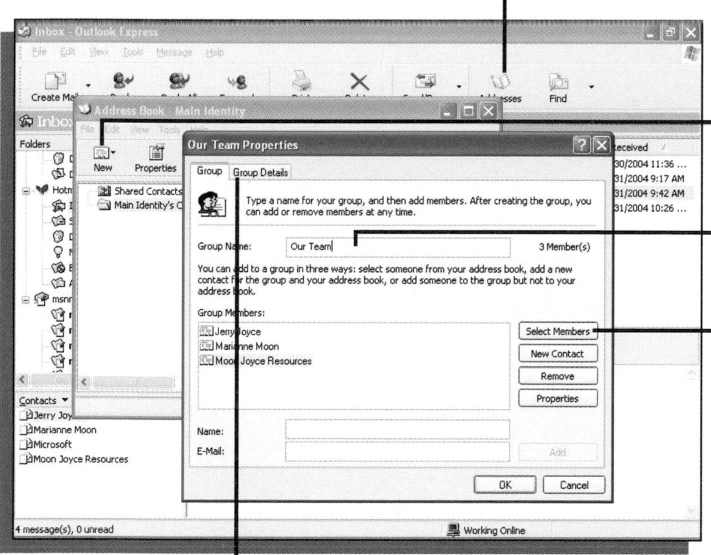

1. Click Addresses on the toolbar.
2. On the Address Book toolbar, click New, and choose New Group from the menu.
3. On the Group tab of the Properties dialog box, type a descriptive name, or *alias,* for the group.
4. Click Select Members.
5. Click the name of someone you want to include in the group.

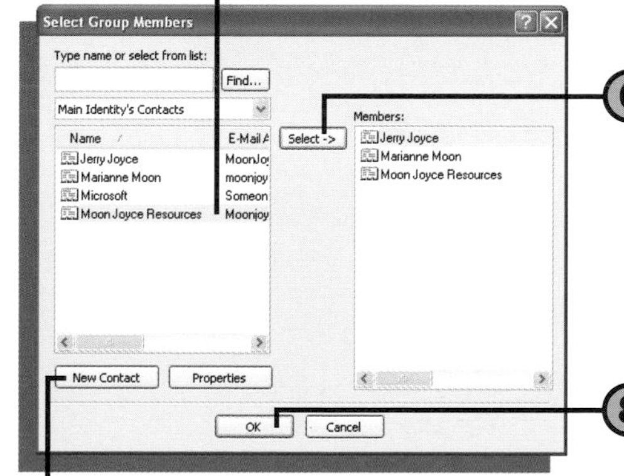

6. Click Select. Continue selecting members and clicking the Select button until the Members list is complete.
7. Use the New Contact button or the Name and Members boxes to add to the group any new members who aren't listed in your Address Book.
8. Click OK.
9. Add any further information to the Group Details tab, and click OK. Close the Address Book when you've finished.

TRY THIS: Create a group. Start a new e-mail message, and use the group name as the address in the To line. Send the message, and then look at that message in your Sent Items folder. Note that the address of each member of the group is listed.

TIP: You can collect addresses from address books from other computers, other programs, or other users by using the Import command on the File menu, by clicking the Find button on the address book's toolbar to use a directory service, or by opening and importing an electronic business card *(vCard)* that someone sent you. (A vCard, or virtual card, is a file that contains a single Address Book entry with contact information for an individual.)

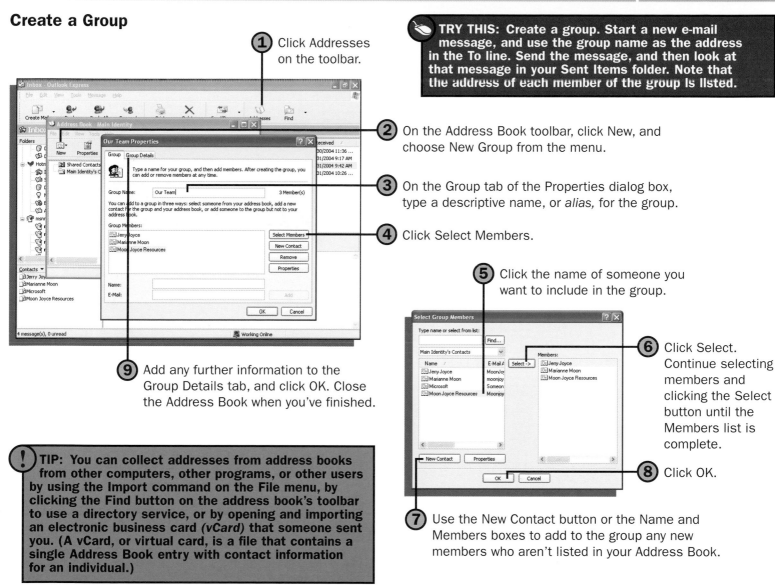

Transferring Files

In most cases, transferring files is a simple task: If you want to transfer a few small files, you can easily send them by e-mail or copy them to a removable disk. On a network, you can simply move the files to a shared folder. If you're not connected to a business network, you can connect using a dial-up server or a VPN (Virtual Private Network) connection over the Internet. However, if you need to transfer a number of large files but you don't have access to a network, there are several possible solutions. Listed below are additional methods for directly transferring files; you should find at least one among them that's appropriate for your situation. To find more information about any of these methods, look in the index of this book and/or search the Windows XP Help And Support Center.

Direct Network Connection: A direct network connection connects two computers with a special cable, using either the serial or parallel port on each computer or an infrared link. Once the computers are connected, you've established a network connection through which you have access to shared folders and files. However, this method works only with Windows-based computers.

HyperTerminal: HyperTerminal is a communications program that enables you to call and connect to another computer over a telephone line. The other computer must have a communications package (either HyperTerminal or a compatible program). You can select from a list of different standard transfer protocols. You can use HyperTerminal to connect to different types of computers and operating systems and to access Telnet computer services.

Windows Messenger: Send a file to or receive a file from any online contact. The recipient must agree to receive the file before you can send it.

Dial-Up Server: You can set up your own computer as a dial-up server so that other computers can call in to connect and establish a network link through which files can be transferred to and from the server.

FTP Transfer: You can use FTP (File Transfer Protocol) to transfer files to an FTP server over the Internet. In most cases you'll be able to use Internet Explorer to connect and manage files.

Windows XP also provides two invaluable tools to assist you in transferring files: the Compressed Folders feature and the Windows Briefcase.

Compressed Folders: The Compressed Folders feature reduces the size of the files it contains and keeps all the compressed files in one location. When you transfer a compressed folder, the receiving computer sees either a compressed folder (if the Compressed Folders feature is installed) or a ZIP-type file that can be opened using one of several third-party programs.

Windows Briefcase: The Windows Briefcase is a file-management tool. It helps you keep track of different versions of a file when the file has been edited on different computers. You copy files from your computer to the Briefcase and transfer the entire Briefcase to another computer, where the files can be edited and saved back into the Briefcase. When you return the Briefcase to your computer, the original files on your computer can be updated automatically.

Adding Online Contacts

Using Windows Messenger and a *Passport,* you can exchange instant messages with your designated contacts whenever they're on line. For you to be able to contact others, they must be in your Contacts list. You can add a person who has a Passport to your list, or you can send e-mail to someone who doesn't have a Passport to provide that person with information about obtaining a Passport and using the proper Windows Messenger software.

TIP: In most cases, when you set up Windows XP, you also set up your e-mail account and your Passport. If you didn't, however, or if you want to change your Passport, choose Control Panel from the Start menu, click User Accounts, and then click your user name.

TRY THIS: In Outlook Express, click the down arrow next to Contacts, choose New Online Contact from the menu, and add a new contact. Click an existing e-mail contact, open the Contacts menu again, and choose Set As Online Contact. Point to a contact's name and see whether that person is on line. If so, right-click the contact's name, and then choose Send Instant Message from the shortcut menu.

Add a Contact

1. Connect to the Internet if you aren't already connected.
2. Double-click the Windows Messenger icon in the notification area of the taskbar. If you don't see the icon, click the Start button, point to All Programs, and choose Windows Messenger from the submenu to open the Windows Messenger dialog box.

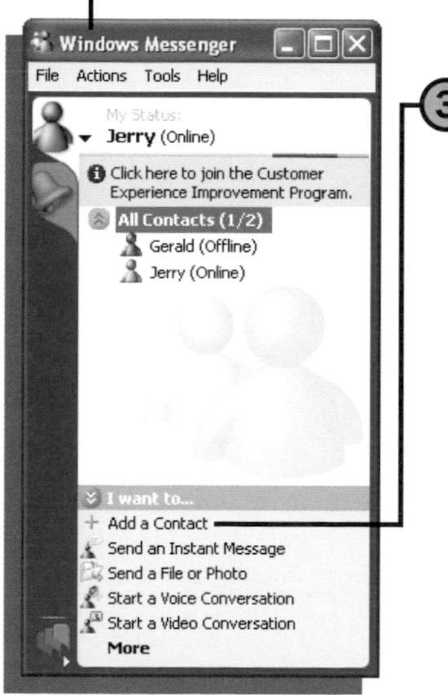

3. After you've logged on, click Add A Contact.

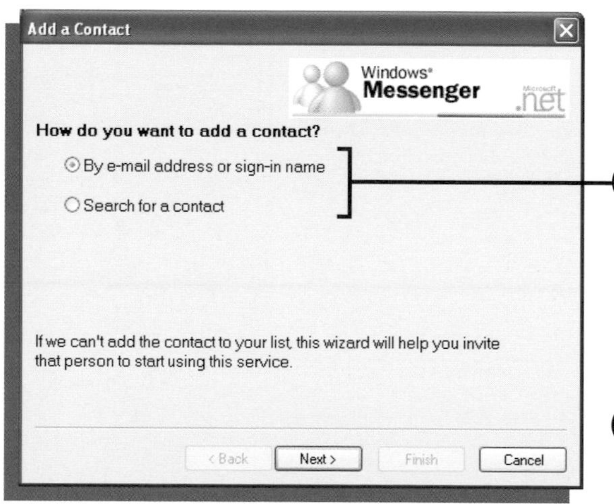

4. Step through the Add A Contact Wizard to add a contact. If the person you're adding doesn't have a Passport, or if you're not sure whether he or she has Windows Messenger installed, click the option to send an e-mail message explaining what's needed.
5. Wait for each person to accept your invitation to be an online contact.

Sending Instant Messages

Are you and your contacts ready for an online conversation? Each of your contacts must have a Passport and must have the Windows Messenger software installed. You can have as many as 75 different contacts and can include up to five people in a text conversation. Each message can contain up to 400 characters.

TIP: Instant messaging procedures and protocols change frequently. You'll probably need to upgrade the software periodically to maintain complete functionality.

TIP: You can play a game over the Internet with one of your contacts. Each of you must have the game installed on your computer, and the game must be designed for Internet play. To start a game, click the Invite button and invite your contact to play.

Have a Conversation On Line

1. Connect to the Internet if you aren't already connected.

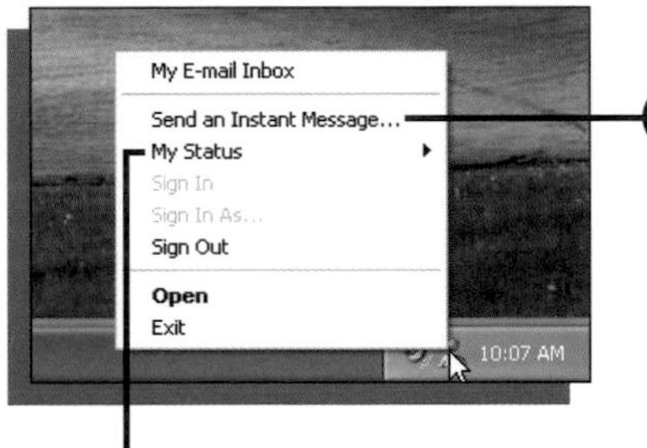

2. Click the Windows Messenger icon in the notification area of the taskbar. On the menu that appears, point to Send An Instant Message, and choose the person you want to connect to.

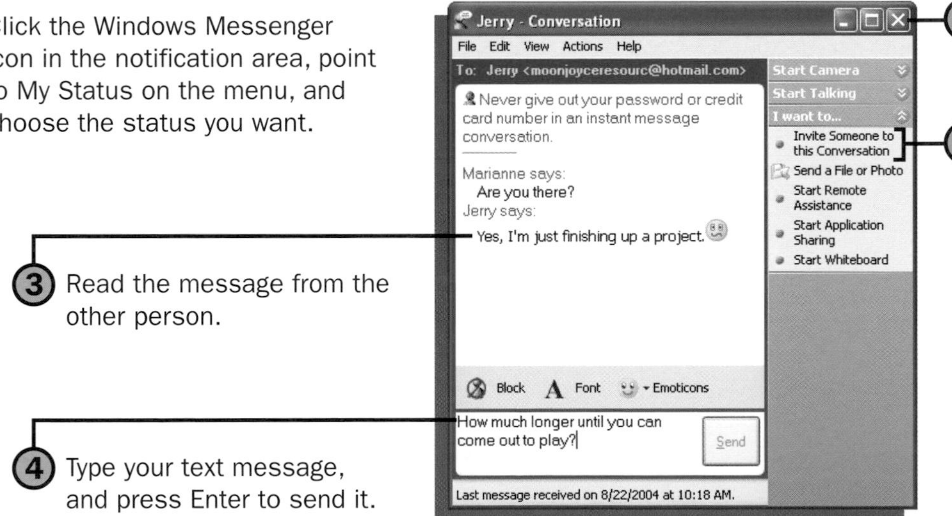

3. Read the message from the other person.
4. Type your text message, and press Enter to send it.
5. If you want another person to join the conversation, click Invite Someone To This Conversation, and choose that person's name from the submenu.
6. When the conversation is over, close the Conversation window.
7. Click the Windows Messenger icon in the notification area, point to My Status on the menu, and choose the status you want.

Having a Voice and Video Chat

If a text conversation is too antiquated or too impersonal for your taste, you can use both voice and video in your instant messages. If you and your contact are both using Windows Messenger on computers running Windows XP, and you both have the necessary sound systems and video cameras, having a voice and video chat is as simple as clicking a button.

Have a Chat

1. Connect to the Internet if you aren't already connected.
2. Click the Windows Messenger icon in the notification area of the taskbar. On the menu that appears, point to Send An Instant Message, and choose the person with whom you want to chat to open the Conversation dialog box.

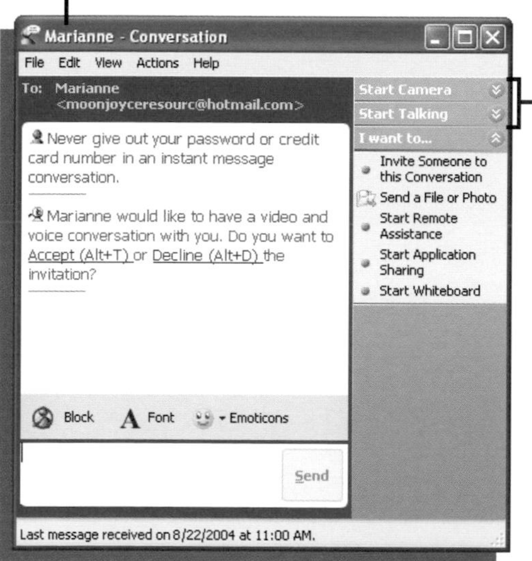

3. Do either of the following:
   - To have a video and voice conversation, click Start Camera, and wait for the other person to accept the invitation.
   - To have a voice-only conversation, click Start Talking, and wait for the other person to accept the invitation.

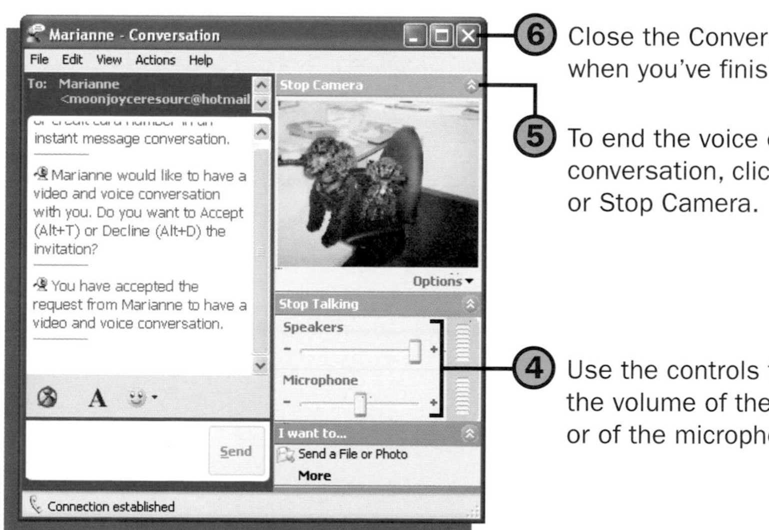

4. Use the controls to change the volume of the speakers or of the microphone.
5. To end the voice or video conversation, click Stop Talking or Stop Camera.
6. Close the Conversation window when you've finished.

> **TIP:** The first time you ran Windows Messenger, you should have stepped through the Audio And Tuning Wizard. If you find that your sound system needs some adjustment, close your conversation, double-click the Windows Messenger icon in the notification area of the taskbar, and, in the Windows Messenger window, choose Audio And Tuning Wizard from the Tools menu to retune your system.

Sharing Items with Your Contacts

If you need to display a program to one of your contacts, or if you want to allow the other person to use the program or to gain access to a folder on your computer, all you need to do is start a conversation, and then you can share the program or folder.

Share a Program or a Folder

1. On your computer, open the program, folder, or document you want to share.
2. Start a Windows Messenger conversation with the person with whom you want to share the item. Invite others into the conversation if you want.

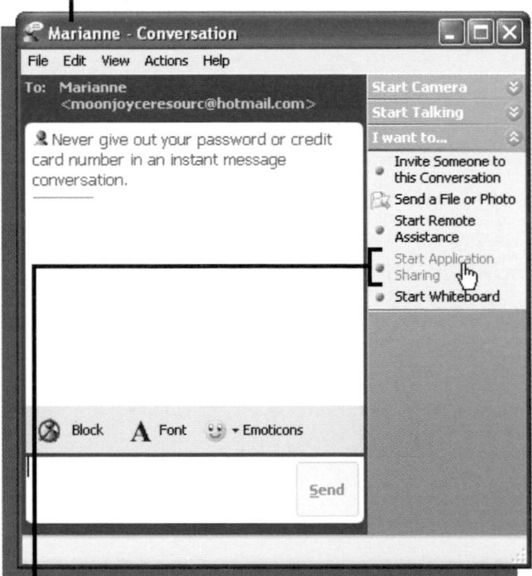

3. In the I Want To section, click Start Application Sharing. Wait for the other person to accept the invitation. If you're connected to more than one contact, you'll need to select the contact who is going to share the application. You can then share the application with other contacts.

CAUTION: If you share the Desktop and then allow the other person to control the Desktop or your shared programs, he or she will have full control of your computer and will be able to access anything from the Start menu. Even if you share only one program, the other person can make considerable modifications to your settings and files. Therefore, you should never leave your computer unattended when you're sharing items and you've given someone else control.

4. Select the item that's going to be shared.

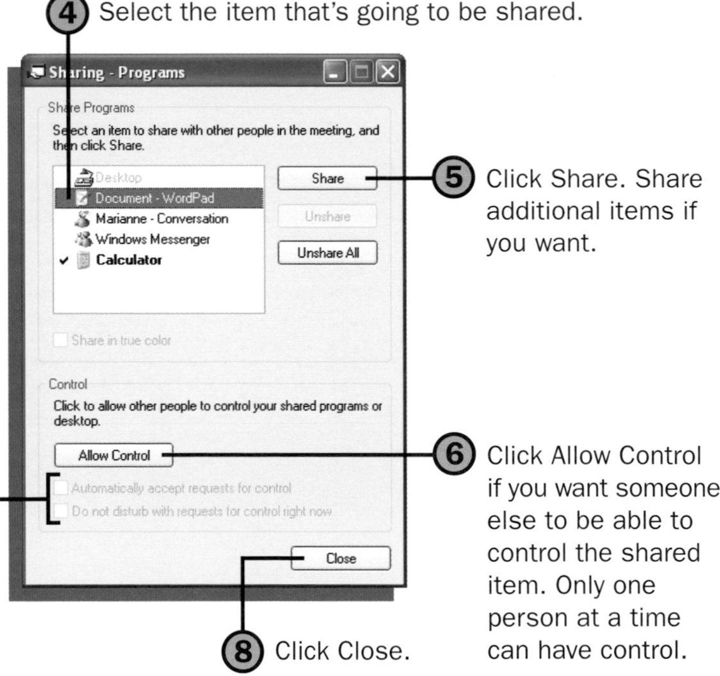

5. Click Share. Share additional items if you want.
6. Click Allow Control if you want someone else to be able to control the shared item. Only one person at a time can have control.
7. Select the check boxes for the type of control you want to allow.
8. Click Close.

SEE ALSO: For information about asking someone for help using remote assistance, see "Helping Each Other" on pages 302–303.

Use the Shared Item

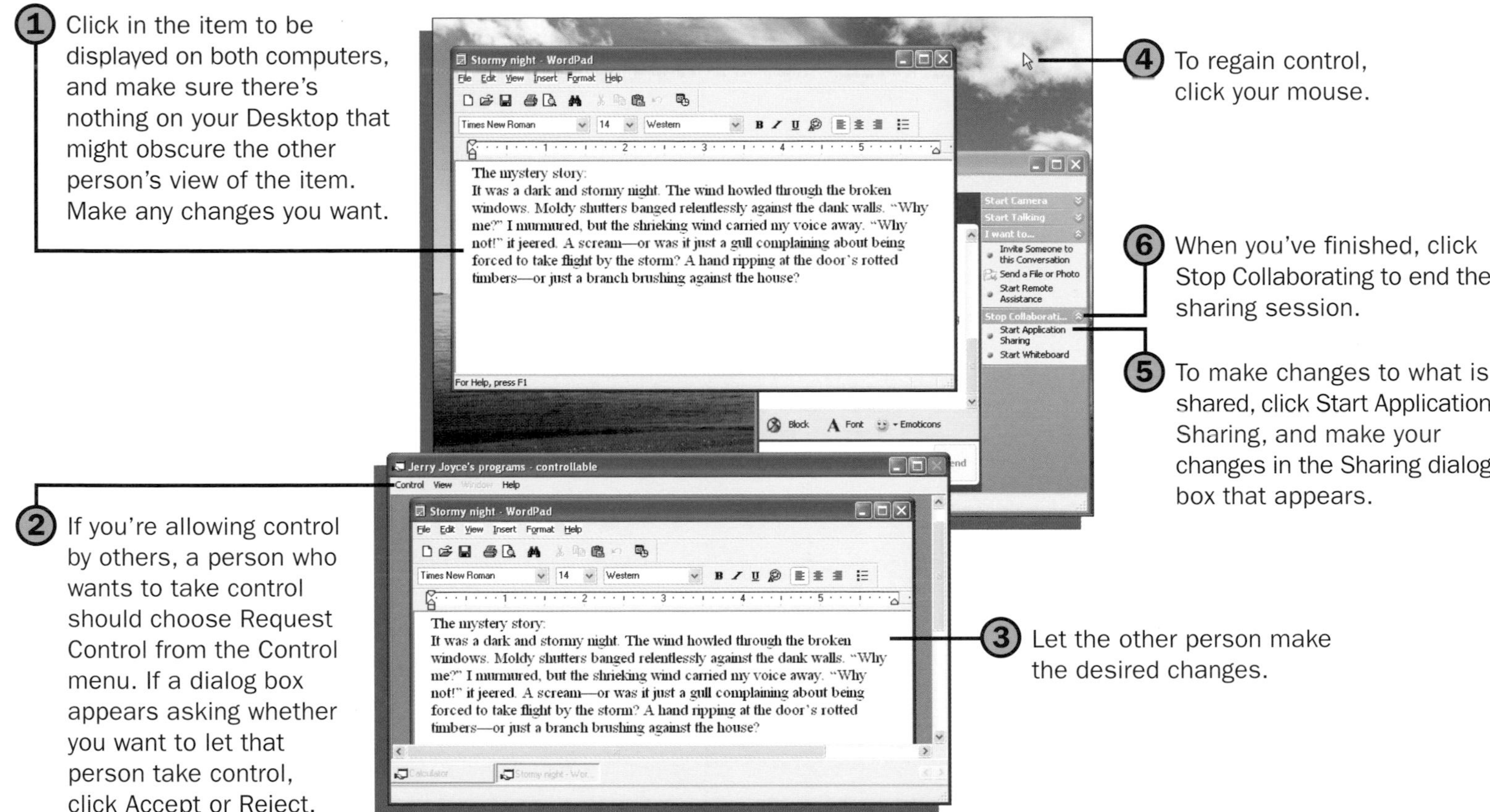

1. Click in the item to be displayed on both computers, and make sure there's nothing on your Desktop that might obscure the other person's view of the item. Make any changes you want.
2. If you're allowing control by others, a person who wants to take control should choose Request Control from the Control menu. If a dialog box appears asking whether you want to let that person take control, click Accept or Reject.
3. Let the other person make the desired changes.
4. To regain control, click your mouse.
5. To make changes to what is shared, click Start Application Sharing, and make your changes in the Sharing dialog box that appears.
6. When you've finished, click Stop Collaborating to end the sharing session.

TIP: Because of the resources that are required, if you're using video or voice conferencing, you can be connected to only one other contact. If you aren't using video or voice conferencing, you can share a program with up to five other people.

TIP: You can share and play certain games using Windows Messenger. In order for you to play a game, it must be installed on both computers and configured to be played over Windows Messenger. See the game's documentation for the proper settings.

Receiving Alerts ⊕ NEW FEATURE

You can receive updated information in Windows Messenger about a wide range of topics. When you customize your alerts, all you need to do is switch to the Alerts tab to receive your updated content.

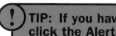

TIP: If you haven't signed up for any alerts, you can click the Alerts tab to sign up for the alerts you want.

Read Your Alerts

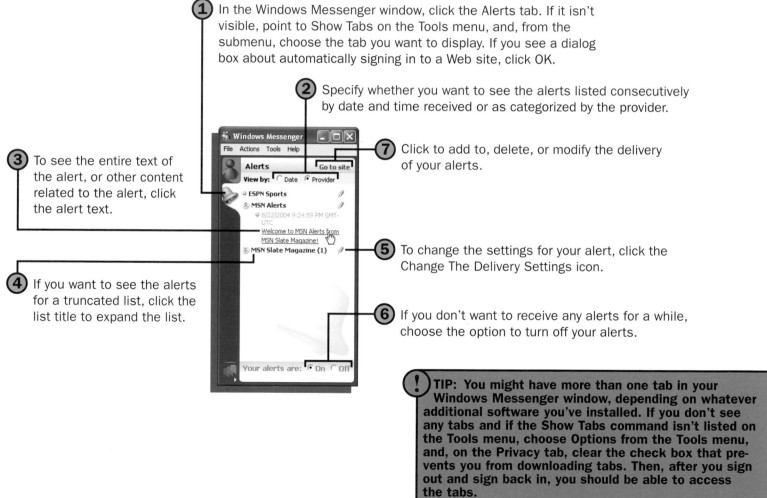

1. In the Windows Messenger window, click the Alerts tab. If it isn't visible, point to Show Tabs on the Tools menu, and, from the submenu, choose the tab you want to display. If you see a dialog box about automatically signing in to a Web site, click OK.
2. Specify whether you want to see the alerts listed consecutively by date and time received or as categorized by the provider.
3. To see the entire text of the alert, or other content related to the alert, click the alert text.
4. If you want to see the alerts for a truncated list, click the list title to expand the list.
5. To change the settings for your alert, click the Change The Delivery Settings icon.
6. If you don't want to receive any alerts for a while, choose the option to turn off your alerts.
7. Click to add to, delete, or modify the delivery of your alerts.

TIP: You might have more than one tab in your Windows Messenger window, depending on whatever additional software you've installed. If you don't see any tabs and if the Show Tabs command isn't listed on the Tools menu, choose Options from the Tools menu, and, on the Privacy tab, clear the check box that prevents you from downloading tabs. Then, after you sign out and sign back in, you should be able to access the tabs.

Sending a File by Windows Messenger

One of the easiest ways to transfer a file from one computer to another over the Internet is to use Windows Messenger, especially if you're sending a large file. When you send a file as an e-mail attachment you're often limited as to its size (usually it can be no larger than 1 MB), but when you use Windows Messenger there's no limitation on file size.

Send a File

1. Use Windows Messenger to connect to the person to whom you'll be sending the file.

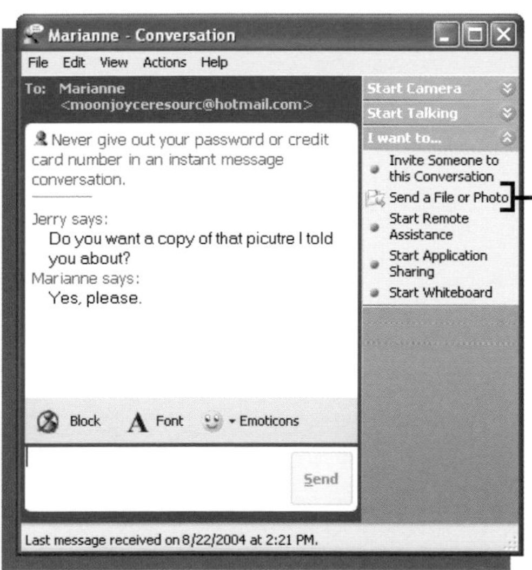

2. Click Send A File Or Photo. If you're connected to more than one person, select the recipient's name in the Send A File dialog box, and then click OK. (You can send a file to only one person at a time.)

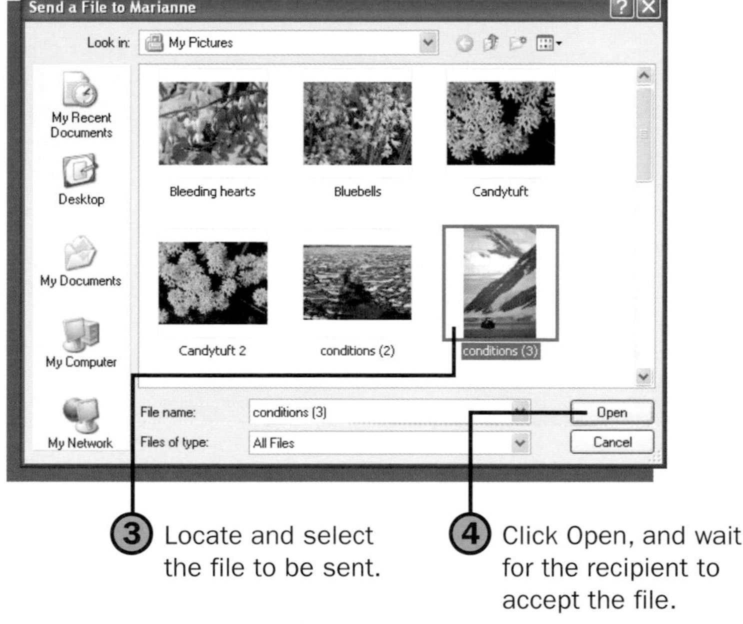

3. Locate and select the file to be sent.
4. Click Open, and wait for the recipient to accept the file.

CAUTION: If you receive a file but feel uncertain about its safety or its origin, don't click the link to the file in the Conversation window—that will open or run the file. Instead, choose Open Received Files from the File menu, and, when the folder opens, run a virus-scanning program to check the file.

TRY THIS: There's more than one way to send a file, and you don't need to start a conversation first. In the Windows Messenger window, right-click an online contact, choose Send A File Or Photo from the shortcut menu, and use the Select A File dialog box to select and send the file. Now choose Send A File Or Photo from the File menu, specify the address of the recipient on the Other tab of the Send A File dialog box, click OK, and send the file using the Select A File dialog box.

Formatting and Sending Your Message

When you use Windows Messenger to communicate with others, you can format your messages with the fonts and colors of your choice. You can also use *emoticons*—those little symbols that some people love and others just can't stand—instead of words.

TRY THIS: In your message, type a letter inside a pair of parentheses: (a), for example. Now do the same thing with numbers and the symbols above the numbers. See which ones create emoticons.

Format the Text

1. In your Conversation window, click Font to display the Change My Message Font dialog box.

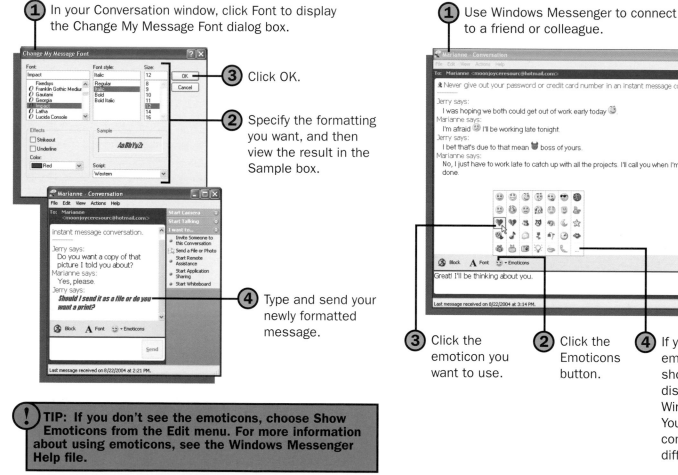

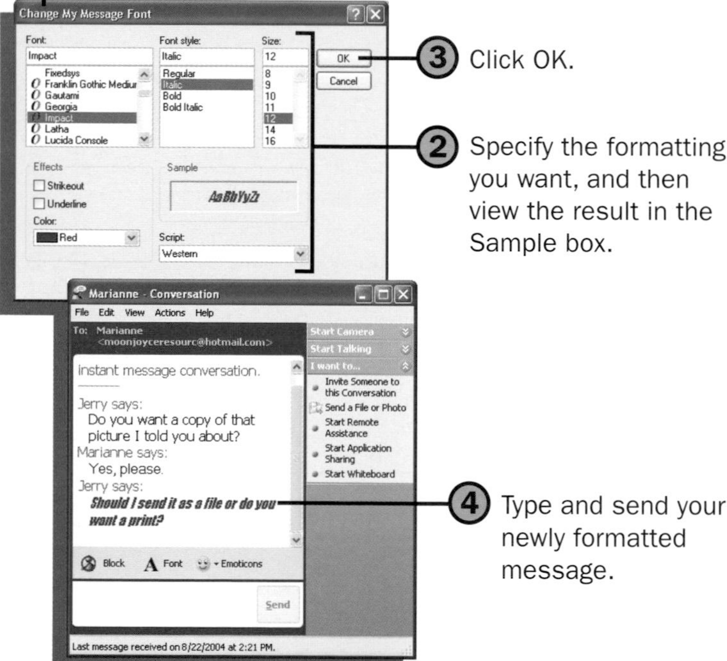

2. Specify the formatting you want, and then view the result in the Sample box.
3. Click OK.
4. Type and send your newly formatted message.

TIP: If you don't see the emoticons, choose Show Emoticons from the Edit menu. For more information about using emoticons, see the Windows Messenger Help file.

Use Emoticons

1. Use Windows Messenger to connect to a friend or colleague.

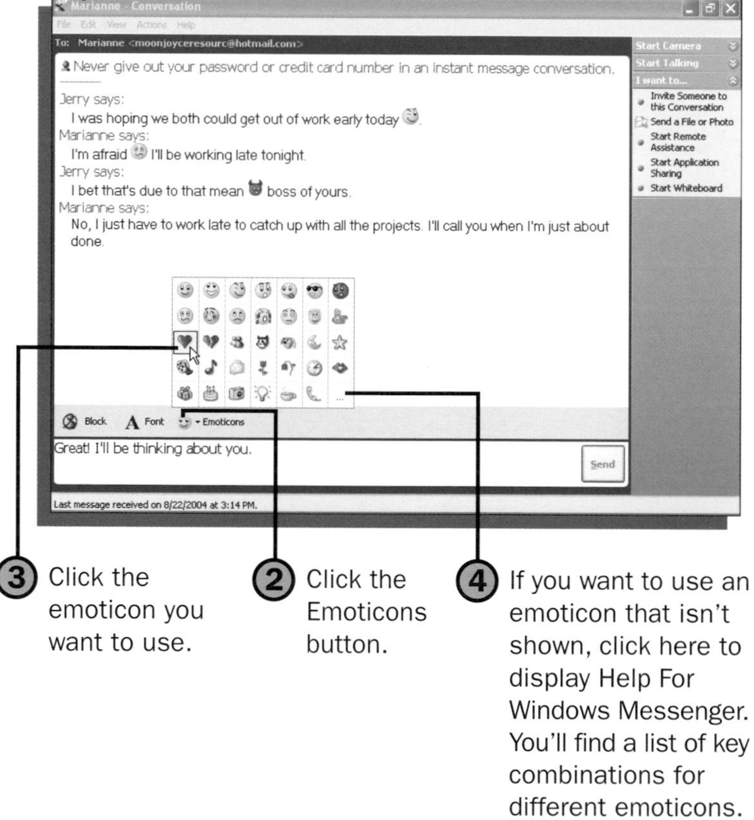

2. Click the Emoticons button.
3. Click the emoticon you want to use.
4. If you want to use an emoticon that isn't shown, click here to display Help For Windows Messenger. You'll find a list of key combinations for different emoticons.

Working with Pictures and Movies

In this section

Drawings and paintings, illustrations in magazines, photographs of people, pets, and places…we all love pictures. Whether you want to enliven your documents with original drawings or add family photographs to your e-mail or your Web page, Microsoft Windows XP provides the tools that will help you achieve professional-looking results.

You can create your own drawings or edit existing ones in the Paint program, using Paint's tools to create the effects you want. Even if you're not a great artist, it can be a lot of fun! However, you're not limited to Paint's *bitmap* images. Windows XP was designed to enable you to work confidently with digital images as well. With help from the Scanner And Camera Wizard, you can easily scan images directly into your computer or into any graphics program that's designed to accept scanned images. With a couple of mouse-clicks, you can also review, select, and download photographs from a digital camera into your computer. You can organize your pictures in the special pictures-friendly My Pictures folder that Windows XP provides, or you can create your own customized folders to house the picture-storage system that works best for you.

Another exciting tool that comes with Windows XP is Windows Movie Maker, which enables you to make great little movies from a variety of sources—you can use a digital video camera, a digital Web camera, existing video clips, or material from an analog video camera or from videotape or still pictures. You can edit your clips, create transitions between clips, and add an audio track, a musical soundtrack, background sounds, or a narration.

Drawing a Picture

If you're feeling artistic, you can create a picture in Paint. The Paint program comes with Windows XP and was designed to create and edit bitmap pictures in a variety of formats. Although you can print your picture if you want to, Paint pictures are usually inserted into other documents. You can also create a Paint picture and use it as the wallpaper for your Desktop.

TIP: A bitmap is just that: a map created from small dots, or *bits*. It's a lot like a piece of graph paper with some squares filled in and others left blank to create a picture. Different formats often have different amounts of information about the picture, and they store the information in different ways. The JPEG format, for example, generally reduces the size of a file, whereas a TIF-formatted file contains additional information and can produce a very high-quality picture.

Create a Picture

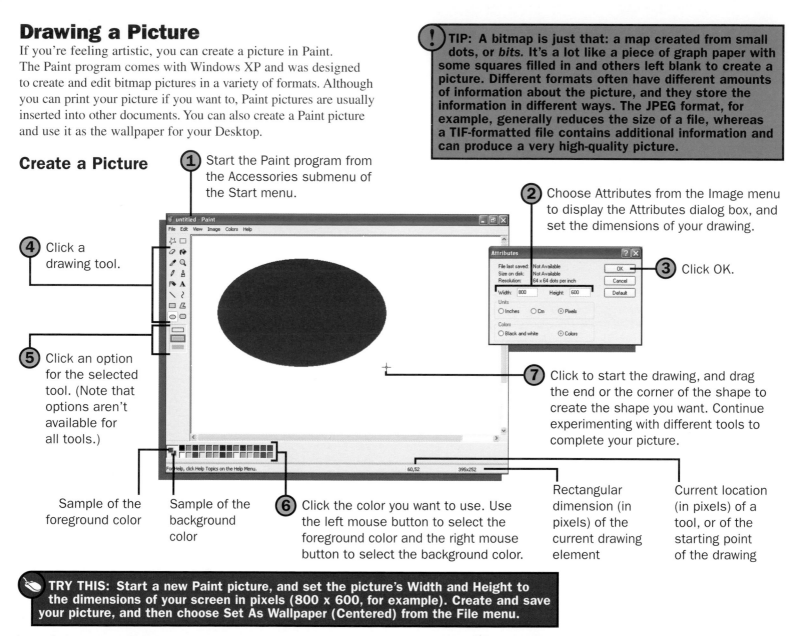

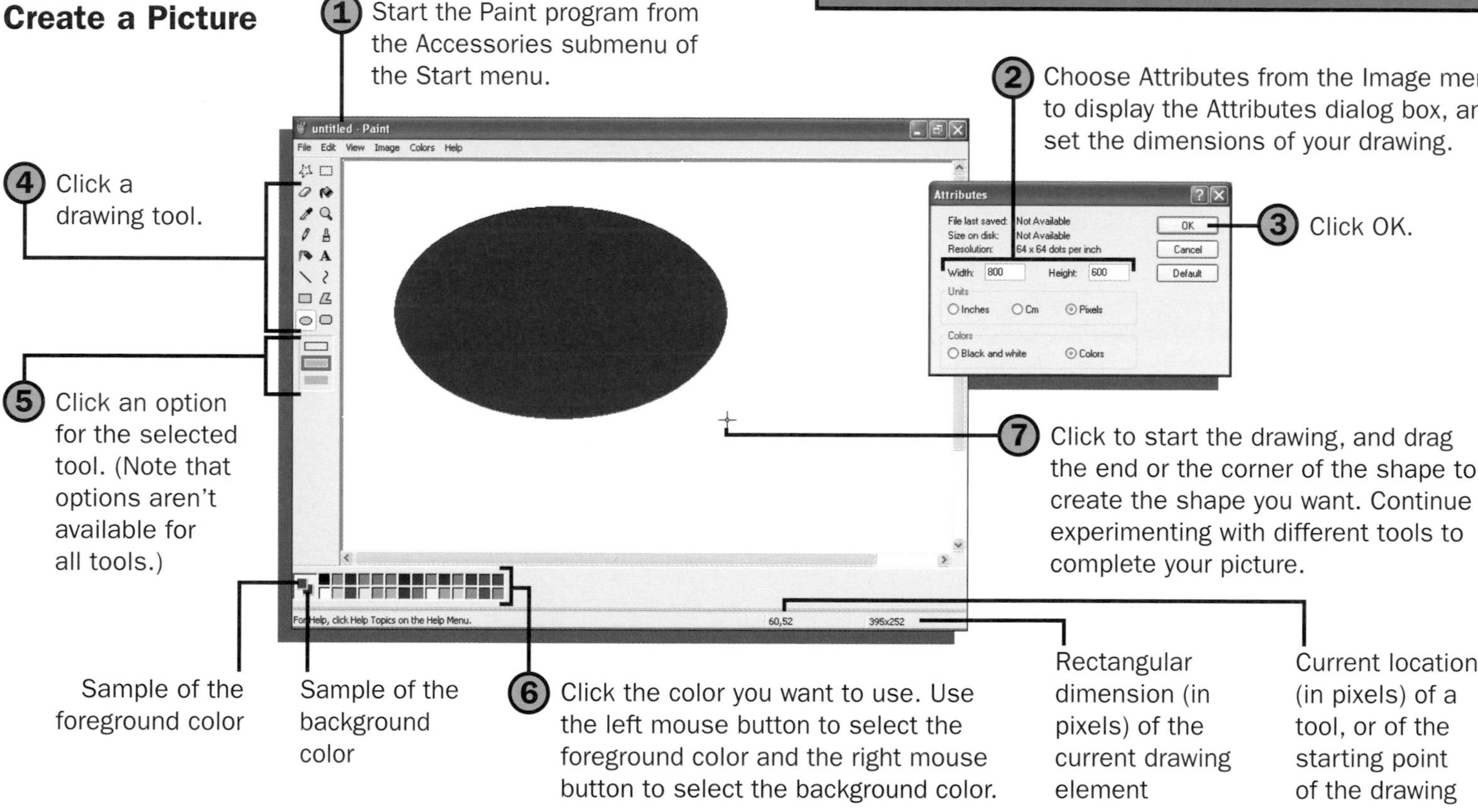
1 Start the Paint program from the Accessories submenu of the Start menu.
2 Choose Attributes from the Image menu to display the Attributes dialog box, and set the dimensions of your drawing.
3 Click OK.
4 Click a drawing tool.
5 Click an option for the selected tool. (Note that options aren't available for all tools.)
6 Click the color you want to use. Use the left mouse button to select the foreground color and the right mouse button to select the background color.
7 Click to start the drawing, and drag the end or the corner of the shape to create the shape you want. Continue experimenting with different tools to complete your picture.
Sample of the foreground color
Sample of the background color
Rectangular dimension (in pixels) of the current drawing element
Current location (in pixels) of a tool, or of the starting point of the drawing
untitled - Paint
File Edit View Image Colors Help
For Help, click Help Topics on the Help Menu.
60,52
395x252
Attributes
File last saved: Not Available
Size on disk: Not Available
Resolution: 64 x 64 dots per inch
OK
Cancel
Default
Width: 800
Height: 600
Units
Inches
Cm
Pixels
Colors
Black and white
Colors

TRY THIS: Start a new Paint picture, and set the picture's Width and Height to the dimensions of your screen in pixels (800 x 600, for example). Create and save your picture, and then choose Set As Wallpaper (Centered) from the File menu.

Use the Tools

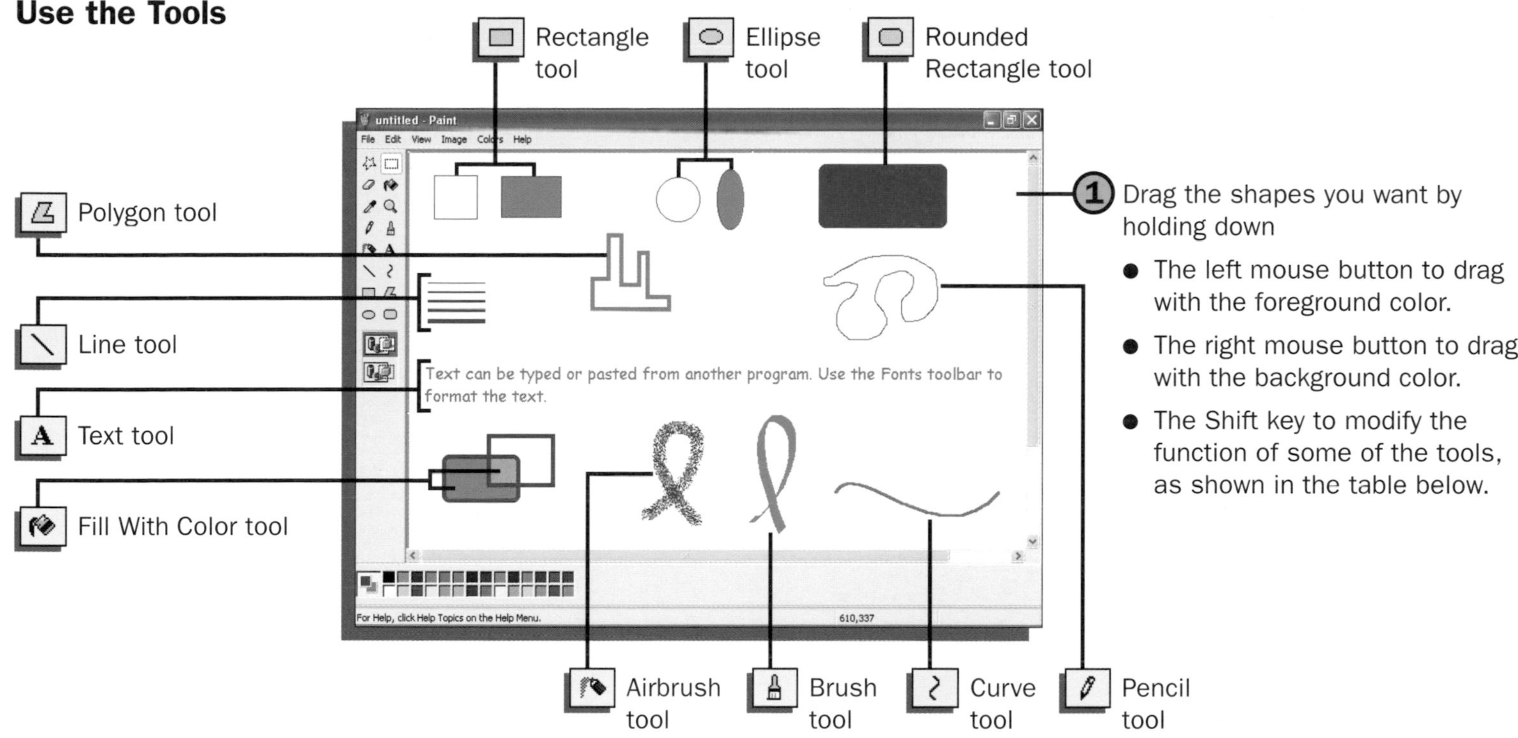

1. Drag the shapes you want by holding down
   - The left mouse button to drag with the foreground color.
   - The right mouse button to drag with the background color.
   - The Shift key to modify the function of some of the tools, as shown in the table below.

Change a Tool's Function with the Shift Key

Hold down the Shift key and	Result
The Ellipse tool	Creates a circle.
The Rectangle tool	Creates a square.
The Rounded Rectangle tool	Creates a square with rounded corners.
The Line tool	Draws a horizontal, vertical, or diagonal line.

SEE ALSO: For information about compressed folders, see "Compressing Files" on pages 174–175.

TIP: To add text to a picture, use the Text tool to draw a text box, and just start typing. As long as the text box is active, you can edit the text, change the font, and resize the text box. When you click outside the text box, the text is turned into a bitmap image that can be edited just like any other picture element.

TIP: A bitmap picture can create a very large file, depending on the resolution and color depth of your screen and the size and color depth at which you save the picture. You can substantially reduce the file size of a bitmap file (sometimes by more than 90 percent) by storing it in a compressed folder.

Editing a Picture

It's easy and fun to modify an existing bitmap picture to customize it, or to create a new picture using only part of the original picture. You can also modify the size or shape of part of the picture and can even create some special effects.

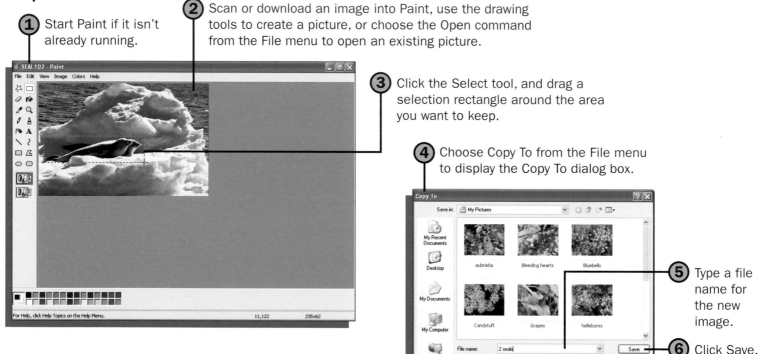

TIP: If you have a scanner or a digital camera set up on your computer, you can use the File menu to scan an image directly into Paint.

Crop a Picture

1. Start Paint if it isn't already running.
2. Scan or download an image into Paint, use the drawing tools to create a picture, or choose the Open command from the File menu to open an existing picture.

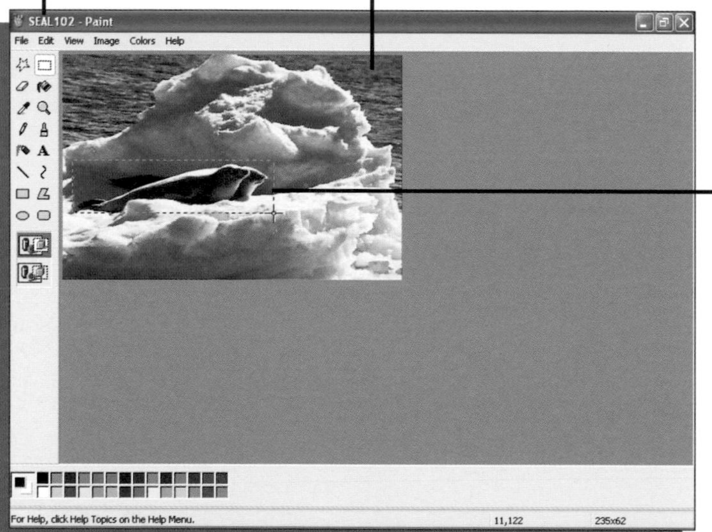

3. Click the Select tool, and drag a selection rectangle around the area you want to keep.
4. Choose Copy To from the File menu to display the Copy To dialog box.

5. Type a file name for the new image.
6. Click Save.

TRY THIS: Tweak your picture by clicking the Magnifier tool, selecting the 6x magnification level, and then using the Pencil tool to edit individual pixels, clicking the left mouse button for the foreground color and the right mouse button for the background color. Press Ctrl+G to display a grid identifying each pixel. Pres Ctrl+Page Up to return to Normal view.

TIP: You can save only the copied part of the picture as a bitmap (BMP) format. However, if you open the picture in Paint, you can then save it in a different format by choosing Save As from the File menu.

Modify a Picture's Size, Shape, or Color

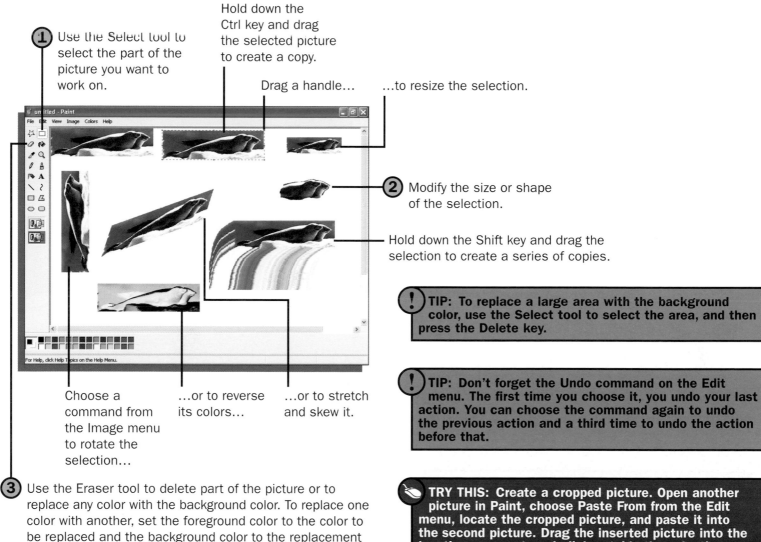

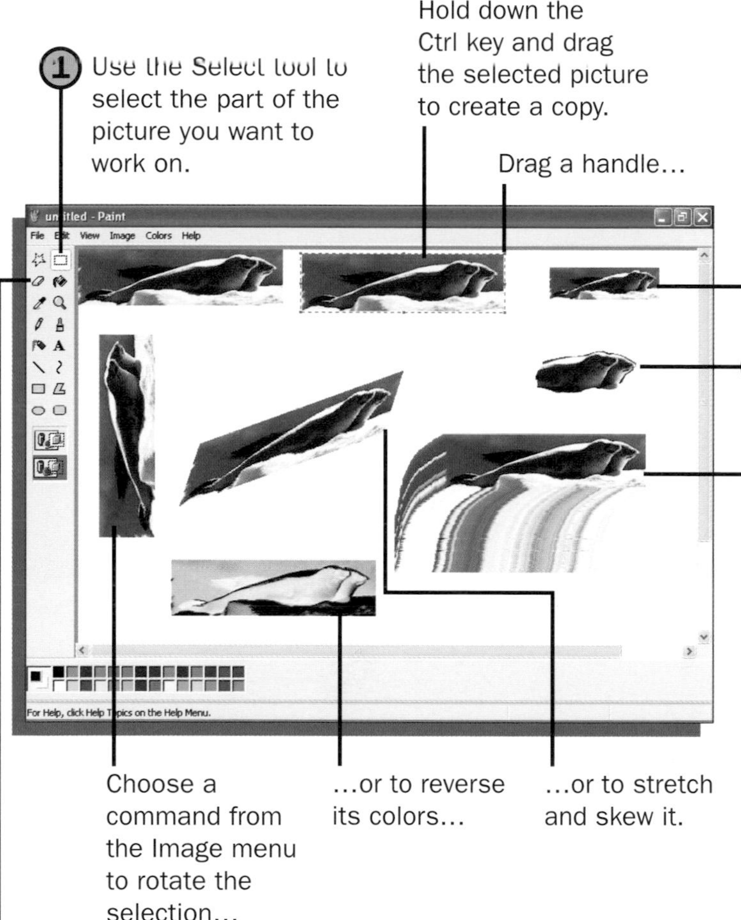

1. Use the Select tool to select the part of the picture you want to work on.

Hold down the Ctrl key and drag the selected picture to create a copy.

Drag a handle...

...to resize the selection.

2. Modify the size or shape of the selection.

Hold down the Shift key and drag the selection to create a series of copies.

Choose a command from the Image menu to rotate the selection...

...or to reverse its colors...

...or to stretch and skew it.

3. Use the Eraser tool to delete part of the picture or to replace any color with the background color. To replace one color with another, set the foreground color to the color to be replaced and the background color to the replacement color, and then hold down the right mouse button and drag the Eraser over the area whose color you want to replace.

TIP: To replace a large area with the background color, use the Select tool to select the area, and then press the Delete key.

TIP: Don't forget the Undo command on the Edit menu. The first time you choose it, you undo your last action. You can choose the command again to undo the previous action and a third time to undo the action before that.

TRY THIS: Create a cropped picture. Open another picture in Paint, choose Paste From from the Edit menu, locate the cropped picture, and paste it into the second picture. Drag the inserted picture into the location you want, and click outside the selection. Save the edited picture.

Scanning a Picture

A scanner is a great tool for digitizing images and making them available on your computer. Windows XP provides access to your scanner with the Scanner And Camera Wizard, which steps you through the process. The wizard adapts to the specific features of your scanner, so the options you see in the wizard might be different from those described here. If you want to scan using a specific program, you can tell Windows XP to bypass the wizard and to automatically start the program you want when you press the scanner button.

TIP: The Scanner And Camera Wizard will work only with scanners that use the Windows Image Acquisition (WIA) device drivers. If your scanner uses a TWAIN device driver, you'll need to use the software that came with the scanner to scan the images you want. Check the scanner's documentation to see what type of driver the scanner uses.

Set Up a Picture

1. Choose Scanner And Camera Wizard from the Accessories submenu of the Start menu, and, if the Select Device dialog box appears, double-click your scanner. In the Scanner And Camera Wizard, click Next to start the wizard.

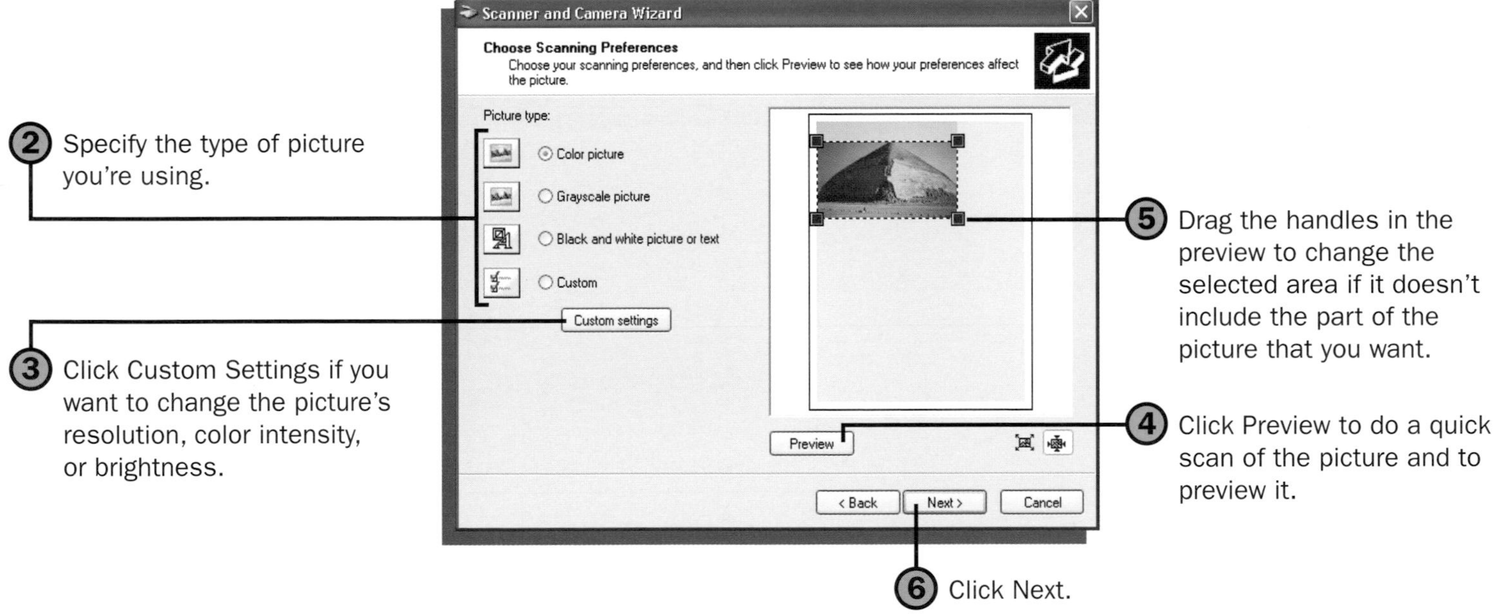

2. Specify the type of picture you're using.
3. Click Custom Settings if you want to change the picture's resolution, color intensity, or brightness.
4. Click Preview to do a quick scan of the picture and to preview it.
5. Drag the handles in the preview to change the selected area if it doesn't include the part of the picture that you want.
6. Click Next.

Scan the Picture

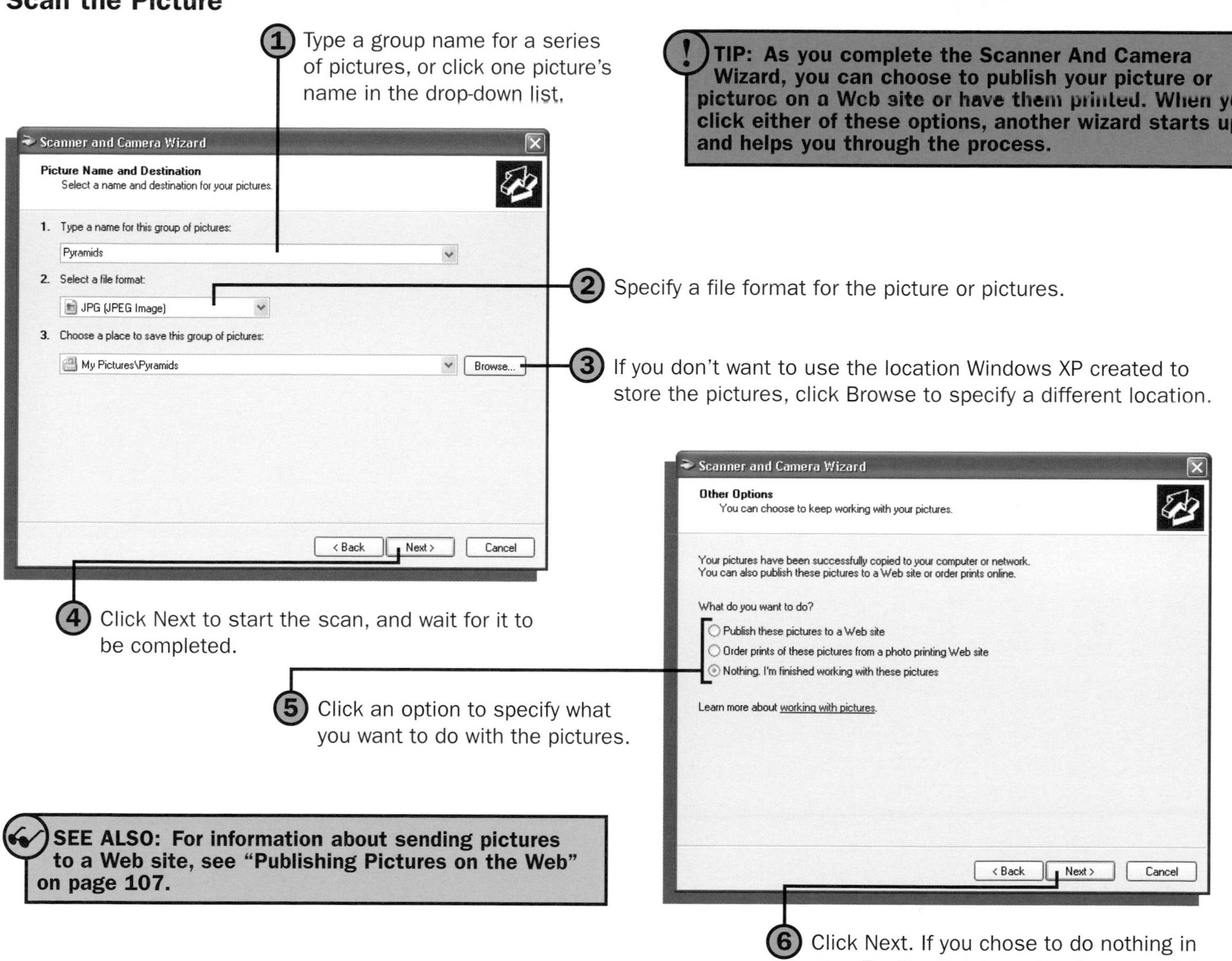
Scanner and Camera Wizard
Picture Name and Destination
Select a name and destination for your pictures.
1. Type a name for this group of pictures:
Pyramids
2. Select a file format:
JPG (JPEG Image)
3. Choose a place to save this group of pictures:
My Pictures\Pyramids
Browse...
< Back
Next >
Cancel
Scanner and Camera Wizard
Other Options
You can choose to keep working with your pictures.
Your pictures have been successfully copied to your computer or network.
You can also publish these pictures to a Web site or order prints online.
What do you want to do?
Publish these pictures to a Web site
Order prints of these pictures from a photo printing Web site
Nothing. I'm finished working with these pictures
Learn more about working with pictures.
< Back
Next >
Cancel

1. Type a group name for a series of pictures, or click one picture's name in the drop-down list.
2. Specify a file format for the picture or pictures.
3. If you don't want to use the location Windows XP created to store the pictures, click Browse to specify a different location.
4. Click Next to start the scan, and wait for it to be completed.
5. Click an option to specify what you want to do with the pictures.
6. Click Next. If you chose to do nothing in step 5, click Finish, and review your pictures.

TIP: As you complete the Scanner And Camera Wizard, you can choose to publish your picture or pictures on a Web site or have them printed. When you click either of these options, another wizard starts up and helps you through the process.

SEE ALSO: For information about sending pictures to a Web site, see "Publishing Pictures on the Web" on page 107.

Downloading Digital Camera Pictures

Once your digital camera is set up in Windows XP, the Scanner And Camera Wizard makes it easy for you to preview the pictures on your digital camera and to select the ones you want to download. You can also specify where you want the pictures to be stored, how they're to be named, and whether you want them to be deleted from your camera after you've downloaded them.

Download Pictures

1. Choose Scanner And Camera Wizard from the Accessories submenu of the Start menu, and, if the Select Device dialog box appears, double-click the name of your camera. In the Scanner And Camera Wizard, click Next to start the wizard. Wait while the thumbnail images are downloaded from your camera.

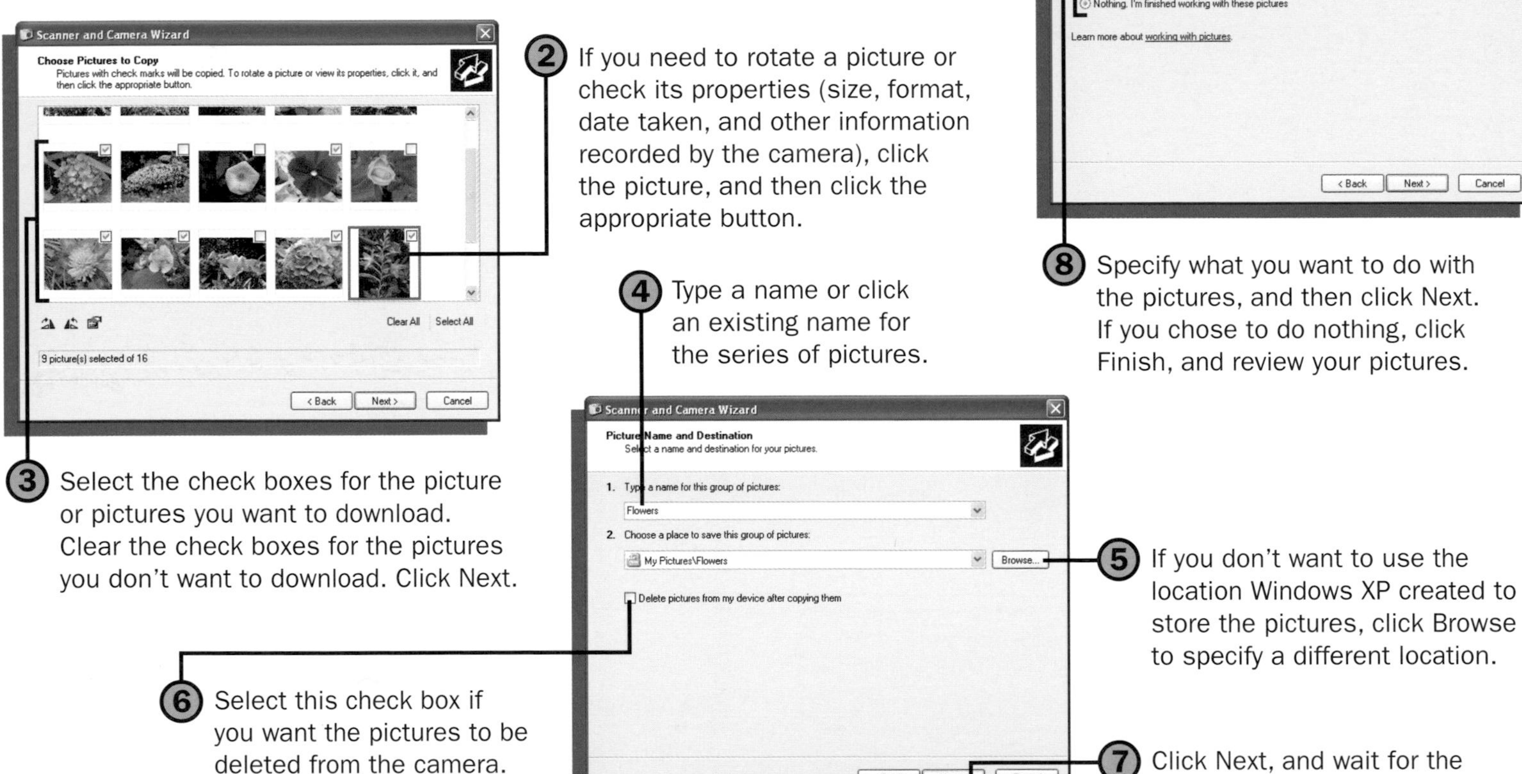
Scanner and Camera Wizard
Choose Pictures to Copy
Clear All
Select All
9 picture(s) selected of 16
< Back
Next >
Cancel
Picture Name and Destination
Select a name and destination for your pictures.
1. Type a name for this group of pictures:
Flowers
2. Choose a place to save this group of pictures:
My Pictures\Flowers
Browse...
Delete pictures from my device after copying them
Other Options
You can choose to keep working with your pictures.
Your pictures have been successfully copied to your computer or network.
You can also publish these pictures to a Web site or order prints online.
What do you want to do?
Publish these pictures to a Web site
Order prints of these pictures from a photo printing Web site
Nothing. I'm finished working with these pictures
Learn more about working with pictures.

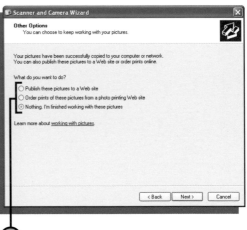

2. If you need to rotate a picture or check its properties (size, format, date taken, and other information recorded by the camera), click the picture, and then click the appropriate button.
3. Select the check boxes for the picture or pictures you want to download. Clear the check boxes for the pictures you don't want to download. Click Next.
4. Type a name or click an existing name for the series of pictures.
5. If you don't want to use the location Windows XP created to store the pictures, click Browse to specify a different location.
6. Select this check box if you want the pictures to be deleted from the camera.
7. Click Next, and wait for the pictures to be downloaded.
8. Specify what you want to do with the pictures, and then click Next. If you chose to do nothing, click Finish, and review your pictures.

Manage the Camera and the Pictures

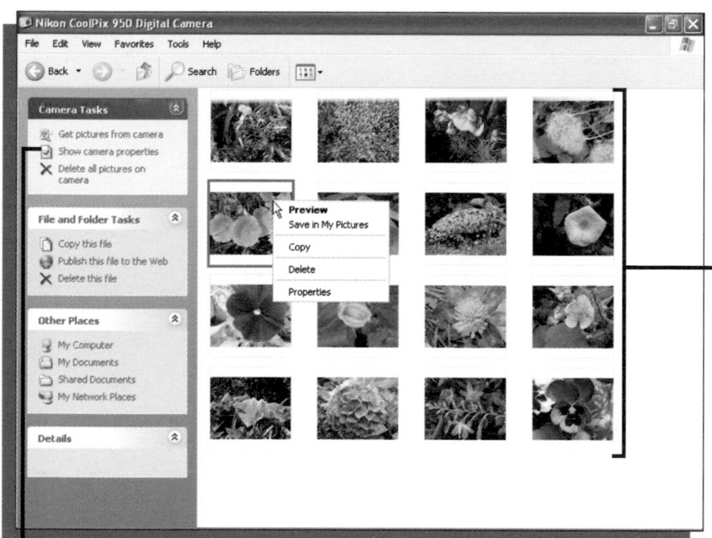

1. Choose My Computer from the Start menu, and, in the My Computer window, double-click the name of your camera. Wait for information, including thumbnails of the pictures, to be downloaded. Click a picture, and specify what you want to do with it:
   - Under File And Folder Tasks, click Publish This File To The Web to use the Web Publishing Wizard to place a picture on a Web site.
   - Under File And Folder Tasks, click Delete This File to delete a picture from the camera without downloading it.
   - Double-click a file to see a large preview of the picture. Use the tools in the Windows Picture And Fax Viewer, where the picture is displayed, to print, copy, or view the picture. Close the window when you've finished.
   - Right-click a picture, and choose Save In My Pictures from the shortcut menu to save the picture file to the My Pictures folder.
   - Under Camera Tasks, click Delete All Pictures On Camera to delete all the pictures in the camera without downloading them.
2. Click Show Camera Properties to see and modify the camera settings and to conduct a diagnostic test of the camera.

TIP: If Windows XP doesn't automatically set up the camera when it's first connected, use the manufacturer's setup disk to install it. You can also manually install your camera by clicking Printers And Other Hardware in the Control Panel and then clicking Scanners And Cameras. Use the Add An Imaging Device option in the Imaging Tasks section to install the camera.

SEE ALSO: For information about renaming files, see "Rename a File" and "Rename a Group of Files" on page 169.

CAUTION: Until you've completed the Scanner And Camera Wizard, only small thumbnail images of your pictures have been sent to your computer; the pictures themselves still reside only in your camera.

TIP: Switch to Details view to see the picture format, the date the picture was taken, and the size of the file. You'll see a preview of the selected picture in the Details part of the window.

Viewing Pictures

Windows XP provides a variety of ways to view your pictures so that you can decide which ones to keep, copy, print, or send to friends.

View All the Pictures

1. In the folder that contains the pictures, click the Views button, and click Filmstrip in the list if it isn't already selected.
2. Click a picture to see it in an enlarged size.

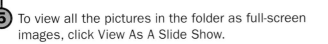

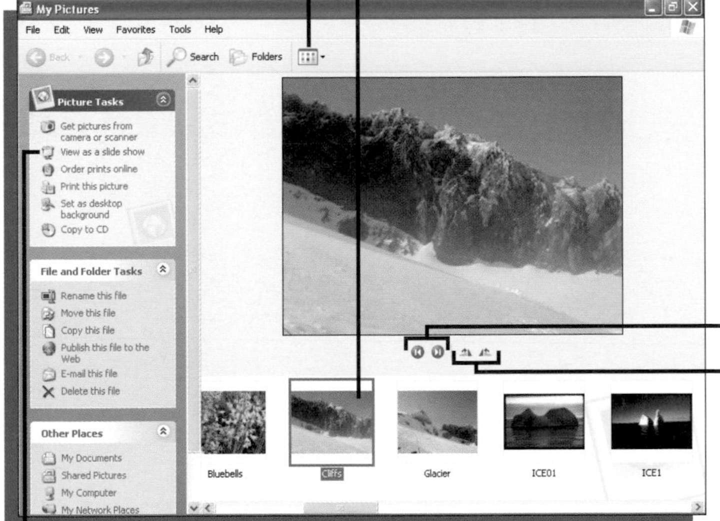

3. To view the pictures in sequence, click the Next Image button (or press the Right arrow key); to go through the pictures in reverse order, click the Previous Image button (or press the Left arrow key).
4. To rotate a picture, click the Rotate Clockwise or the Rotate Counterclockwise button.
5. To view all the pictures in the folder as full-screen images, click View As A Slide Show.
6. To advance a picture before it would normally advance, click anywhere in the picture.
7. To control the slide show, move the mouse to display the controls, and then use them to pause, advance, repeat, or end the slide show.

SEE ALSO: For information about e-mailing your pictures, see "Sending or Receiving a File" on pages 72–73.

For information about printing your pictures, see "Printing Your Photographs" on page 158.

Preview a Single Picture

1. In the folder window containing your pictures, double-click a picture to display it in the Windows Picture And Fax Viewer.
2. Use the controls on the toolbar to change the view of the picture; to rotate it; or to edit, copy, or print it.
3. Close the window when you've finished.

Display previous or next picture in folder.

Change size of displayed picture.

Show all pictures in a slide show.

Zoom in or out.

Rotate picture 90 degrees.

Delete picture.

Start Photo Printing Wizard.

Copy picture to a different location.

Open picture in editing program.

Get help.

TIP: Choose Tiles from the Views button to see a listing of your pictures that includes information about the dimensions of each picture (in pixels) and its file type. Choose Details from the Views button to see the size of the file, the date each picture was taken, and the date the file was last modified.

TIP: When you click the button on the Windows Picture And Fax Viewer toolbar that opens the picture for editing, the picture will open in Paint unless you have another picture-editing program installed.

TIP: When you're running your slide show, each picture is set to be displayed for five seconds. You can change the timing using the Tweak UI PowerToy.

SEE ALSO: For information about editing a picture in Paint, see "Editing a Picture" on page 94.

For information about displaying your pictures in different slide shows, see "Creating a Video Slide Show" on pages 102–103 and "Creating a Multimedia Screen Saver" on page 246.

For information about working with faxes, see "Sending a Fax" on page 160, "Receiving a Fax" on page 162, "Reviewing a Fax You've Received" on page 163, and "Viewing and Annotating a Fax" on page 164.

For information about using Tweak UI, see "Tweaking Your System" on pages 300–301.

Creating a Video Slide Show ❂ NEW FEATURE

Would you like to turn your pictures into an exciting video presentation that includes such professional effects as zooming in and out and panning across the pictures? And how about adding your own narrative and some background music? Don't worry—it's easier than it sounds. With Microsoft Plus! Digital Media Edition installed on your computer, you can use the Plus! Photo Story program to record a video slide show. You can even create a Video Compact Disc (VCD) of the slide show that can be played on most DVD players.

TIP: If you don't have Plus! Digital Media Edition, you can download a free simplified version of Plus! Photo Story 2 LE from the Microsoft Plus! Web page. This Photo Story 2 LE version does many of the same things as the full version; however, you won't be able to create a Video Compact Disc that can be played on a DVD player.

TIP: When you delete a picture, you're deleting only the copy of the picture in Photo Story, not the original picture. You can always click the Import Pictures button again to include additional pictures.

SEE ALSO: For information about using a slide show as a screen saver, see "Create a Custom Screen Saver" on page 245 and "Creating a Multimedia Screen Saver" on page 246.

Set Up the Story

1. Choose Plus! Photo Story from the Microsoft Plus! Digital Media Edition submenu of the Start menu. With Plus! Photo Story running, choose to begin a new story to move to the next page of the wizard.

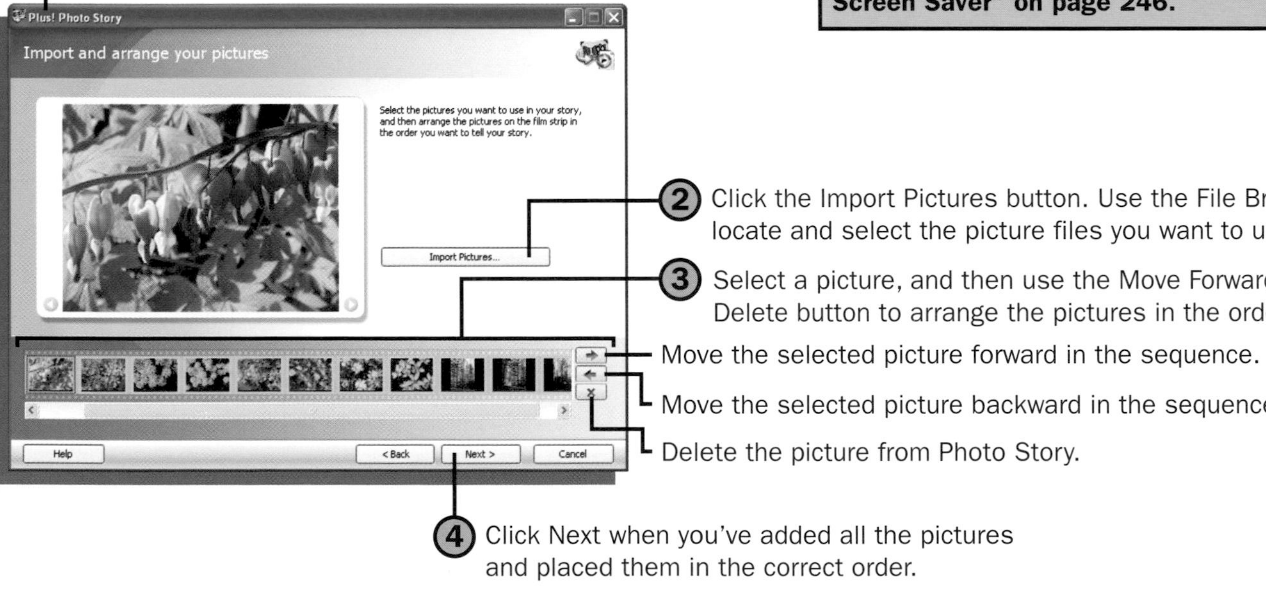

2. Click the Import Pictures button. Use the File Browser window to locate and select the picture files you want to use, and click OK.
3. Select a picture, and then use the Move Forward, Move Back, or Delete button to arrange the pictures in the order you want.

Move the selected picture forward in the sequence.

Move the selected picture backward in the sequence.

Delete the picture from Photo Story.

4. Click Next when you've added all the pictures and placed them in the correct order.

Record the Story

1. Click the Record button, and record the narration you want for the slide.

2. Move the mouse pointer over the sections of the slide that you want to emphasize through panning and zooming.

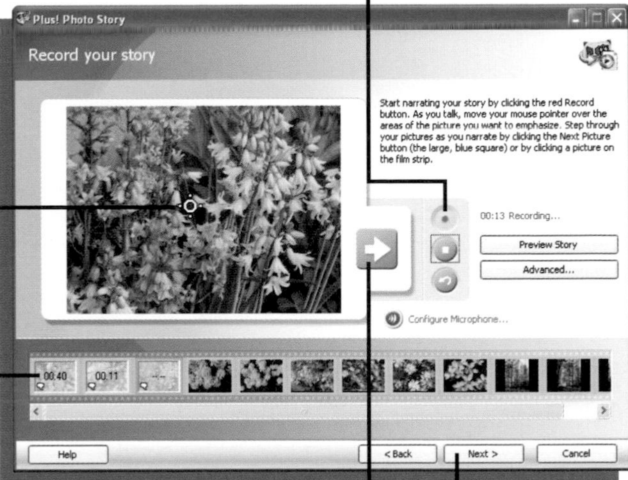

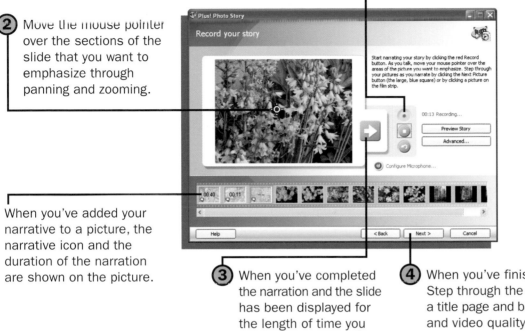

When you've added your narrative to a picture, the narrative icon and the duration of the narration are shown on the picture.

3. When you've completed the narration and the slide has been displayed for the length of time you want, click Next Picture.

4. When you've finished with all the slides, click Next. Step through the rest of the Photo Story Wizard to add a title page and background music, and to set the audio and video quality. Save both the Photo Story video and the project file.

TRY THIS: Click the first picture in the sequence, click the Record button, and record your narration. Click the Stop button. Click any of the other slides, click the Record button, and record the narration. Click Stop, click the Reset Picture button to delete the narration and timing for the picture, and then record a different narration.

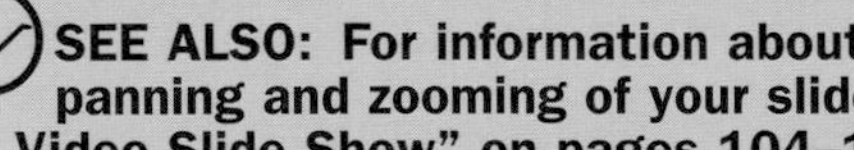

SEE ALSO: For information about customizing the panning and zooming of your slides, see "Editing Your Video Slide Show" on pages 104–105.

CAUTION: You must save the project file as well as the slide show if you want to edit the slide show using Plus! Photo Story.

Editing Your Video Slide Show ⊕ NEW FEATURE

When you create a video slide show using Plus! Photo Story, you'll probably want to put it together in segments and then do some editing: changing the order of the pictures, adding or deleting pictures, changing the way you zoom and pan, and tweaking the narration. You can easily fine-tune your slide show using this step-by-step process; just save the Photo Story project file, and then open it whenever you want to work on it.

CAUTION: When you use the Reset Picture button to reset a picture, be aware that you're also resetting the narration and deleting any custom zooming and panning.

TIP: To add special effects and custom transitions between the pictures, complete and save your video slide show, and then open it in Movie Maker 2 to modify it.

SEE ALSO: For information about adding transitions and special effects, see "Adding Transitions to Your Movie" on page 112 and "Using Video Effects" on page 113.

Edit the Story

1. Start Plus! Photo Story, and choose Edit A Photo Story in the first page of the Plus! Photo Story Wizard. In the Open dialog box that appears, double-click the Photo Story project you want to edit. In the Import And Arrange Your Pictures page of the wizard, click Import Pictures if you want to add more pictures to your story. Arrange the pictures in the order you want, and then click Next.

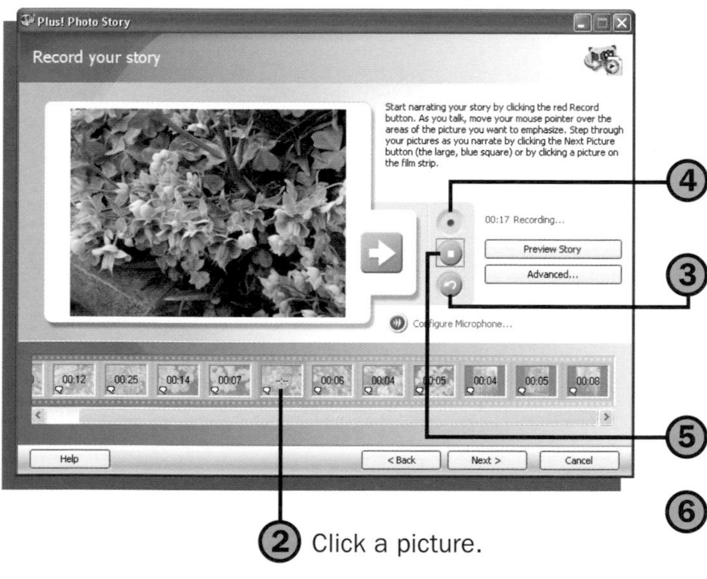

2. Click a picture.
3. If you want to change an existing narration by rerecording it, click the Reset Picture button, and, if you're asked, click Yes to confirm the resetting of the picture to delete the narration and any other custom settings.
4. Record the new narration for the selected picture.
5. Click Stop to end the recording.
6. Repeat steps 2 through 5 if you want to change the narration for any other pictures.

Customize a Picture

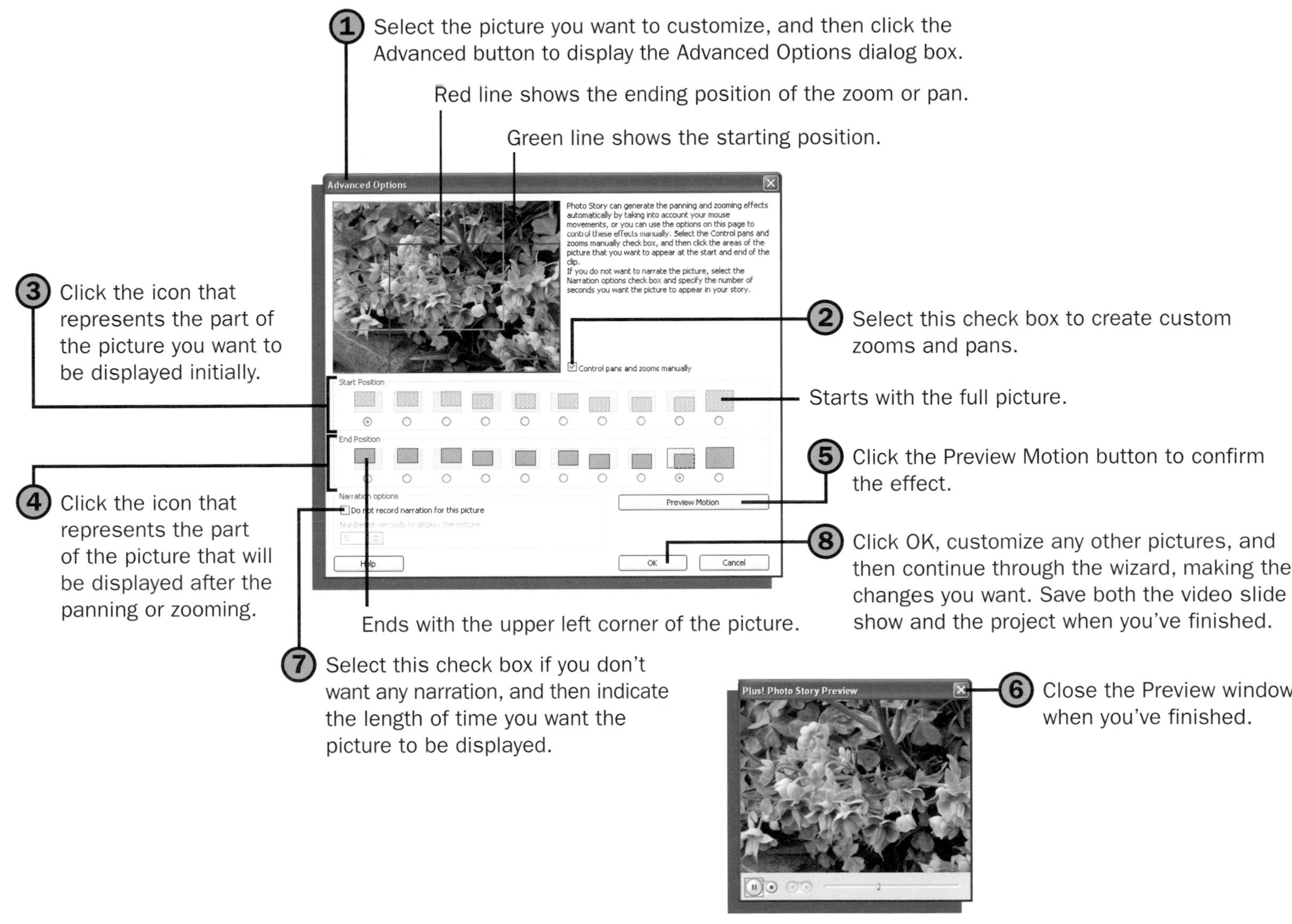

1. Select the picture you want to customize, and then click the Advanced button to display the Advanced Options dialog box.

Red line shows the ending position of the zoom or pan.

Green line shows the starting position.

2. Select this check box to create custom zooms and pans.

Starts with the full picture.

3. Click the icon that represents the part of the picture you want to be displayed initially.

4. Click the icon that represents the part of the picture that will be displayed after the panning or zooming.

Ends with the upper left corner of the picture.

5. Click the Preview Motion button to confirm the effect.

6. Close the Preview window when you've finished.

7. Select this check box if you don't want any narration, and then indicate the length of time you want the picture to be displayed.

8. Click OK, customize any other pictures, and then continue through the wizard, making the changes you want. Save both the video slide show and the project when you've finished.

Sharing Your Video Slide Show ⊛ NEW FEATURE

You've created your video slide show, so what's next? You want to be able to show it to an audience, of course! With Plus! Photo Story and a CD burner on your computer, you can create a Video Compact Disc (VCD) that can be played on a computer or on a DVD player attached to a television set.

Create Your VCD

1. With Plus! Photo Story running, either create your slide show or open an existing Photo Story project file. Step through the Plus! Photo Story Wizard until you reach the Completing Plus! Photo Story page of the wizard.
2. Click View Your Story to review the slide show. If necessary, use the Back button to make corrections, and then resave the story and the project file.
3. Click Create A Video CD Of Your Story.
4. Specify whether you want to include the Plus! Photo Story project file and the original picture files. Neither is required to play the VCD, but it's useful to include them if you plan to use the VCD to modify the slide show sometime in the future.
5. Select the recording device you want to use if you have more than one, as well as the recording speed and the number of copies you want to create.
6. Select the video format: NTSC for North and South America, Japan, and Korea; PAL for most of the rest of the world. Click the Help button if you need information about which format to use.
7. Click Create VCD, and wait for the disc to be created.
8. Exit Plus! Photo Story when you've finished.

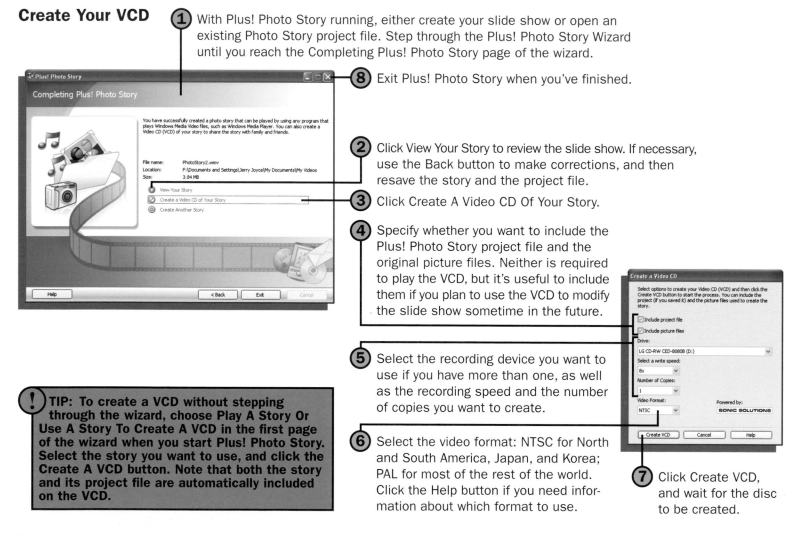

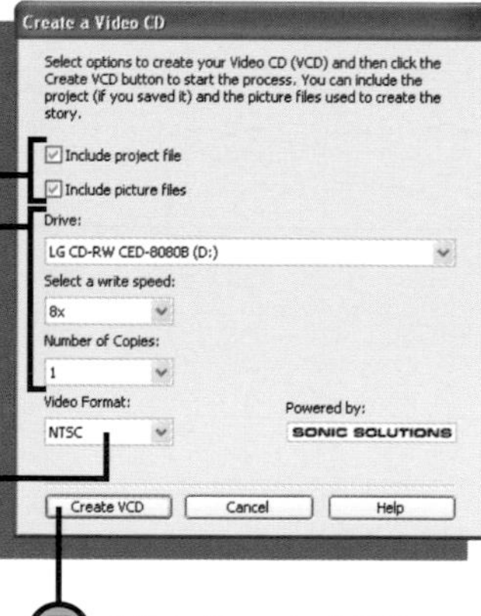

TIP: To create a VCD without stepping through the wizard, choose Play A Story Or Use A Story To Create A VCD in the first page of the wizard when you start Plus! Photo Story. Select the story you want to use, and click the Create A VCD button. Note that both the story and its project file are automatically included on the VCD.

Publishing Pictures on the Web

When you have some great pictures, you almost always want to share them with family, friends, or colleagues. One of the best ways to do this is to *publish* the pictures by putting them up on a Web site. Then you can let people know where to find the pictures so that they can view them at their leisure. Note that this procedure is based on using MSN (The Microsoft Network). If you're using another provider, the procedure might vary slightly.

Publish Your Pictures

1. In the folder that contains your pictures, select the picture you want to publish. If you want to publish multiple pictures, make sure they're all in the same folder (but you don't need to select them at this point).

2. Click Publish This File To The Web to start the Web Publishing Wizard, and click Next to start the wizard.

3. Select the check boxes for the pictures you want to publish, and clear the check boxes for the pictures you don't want to publish.

4. Click Next, and step through the wizard, providing the following information:
   - The service provider you want to use
   - Whether the pictures (and the folder containing the pictures) are to be available to the public or only to the people you specify
   - Whether you want to use an existing Web account or create a new one
   - The folder in which you want to store the pictures

5. Specify the resolution you want for the pictures. (The higher the resolution, the longer it will take for you to upload the pictures and for those who view them to download them.)

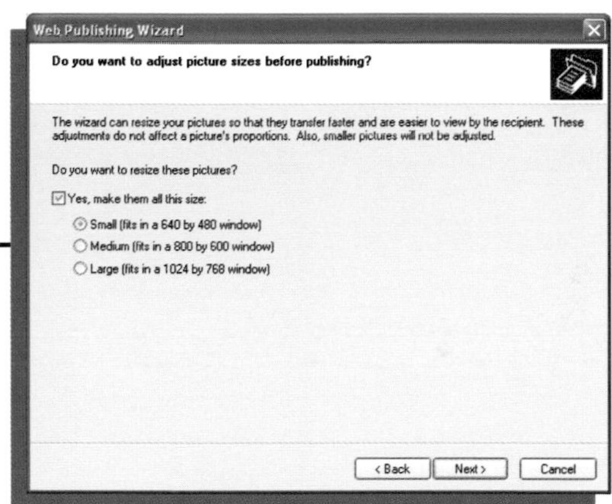

6. Click Next to upload the pictures, and then click Finish to complete the wizard.

Creating a Quick Movie ⊕ NEW FEATURE

You can quickly create a movie from a variety of video sources. Although you can manually create your movie by dividing an existing video clip into multiple clips and then adding transitions and titles, you'll find that it's much easier to leave such details to Movie Maker 2. Even if you really want to create a movie from scratch by yourself, it's a good idea to let Movie Maker create a quick movie first. That way, you'll get to see a first version of your movie, and that will probably give you some good insights into the best way to create your custom movie.

Preview Your Video Clips

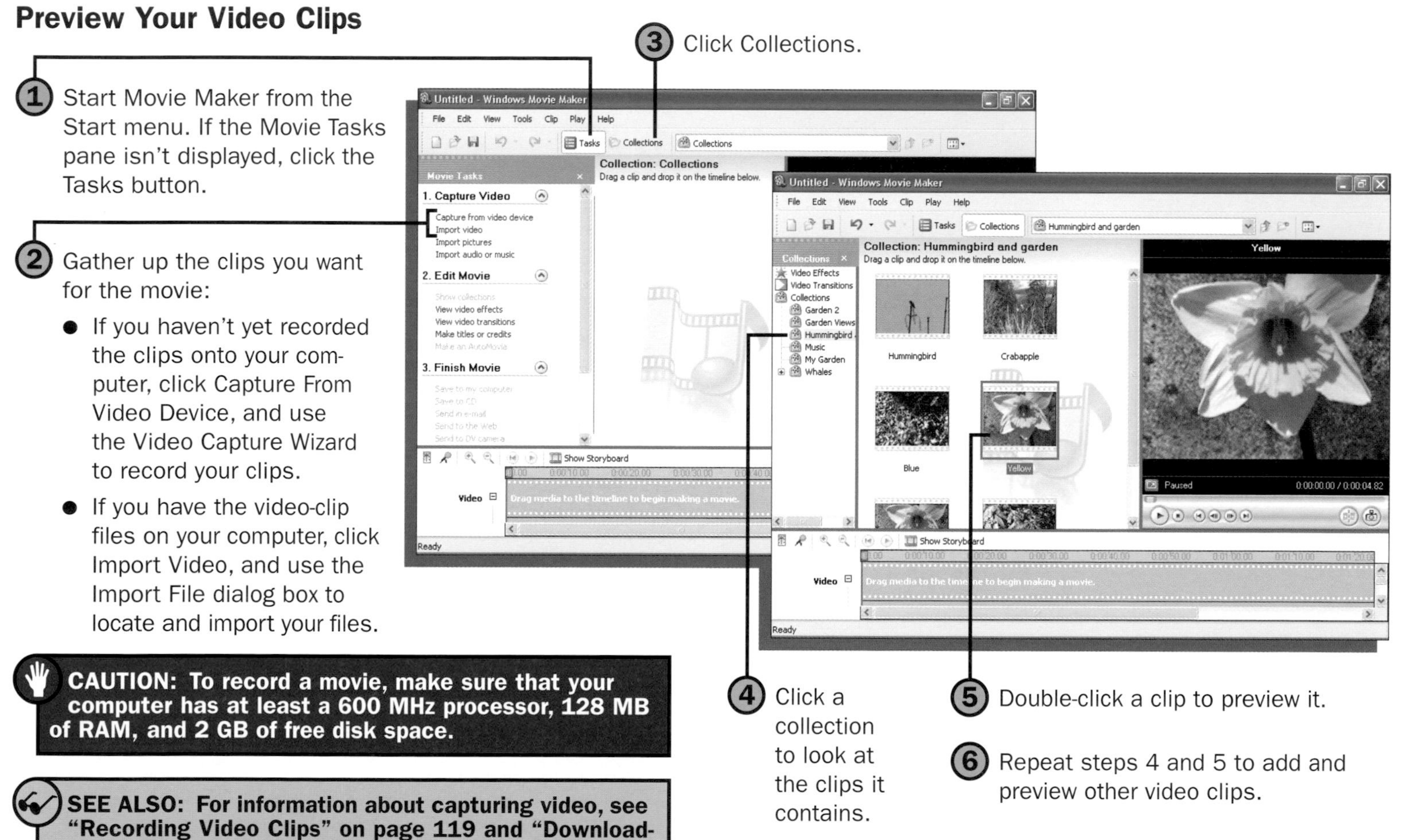

1. Start Movie Maker from the Start menu. If the Movie Tasks pane isn't displayed, click the Tasks button.
2. Gather up the clips you want for the movie:
   - If you haven't yet recorded the clips onto your computer, click Capture From Video Device, and use the Video Capture Wizard to record your clips.
   - If you have the video-clip files on your computer, click Import Video, and use the Import File dialog box to locate and import your files.
3. Click Collections.
4. Click a collection to look at the clips it contains.
5. Double-click a clip to preview it.
6. Repeat steps 4 and 5 to add and preview other video clips.

CAUTION: To record a movie, make sure that your computer has at least a 600 MHz processor, 128 MB of RAM, and 2 GB of free disk space.

SEE ALSO: For information about capturing video, see "Recording Video Clips" on page 119 and "Downloading a Video from a Digital Camera" on pages 120–121.

Create the Movie

1. Click the Tasks button if the Movie Tasks pane isn't displayed.

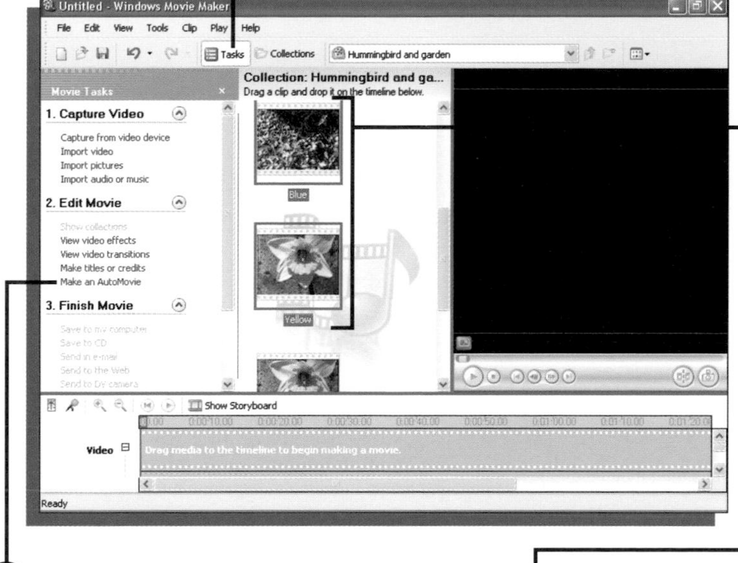

2. Hold down the Ctrl key, and click to select the video clips that you want to include in the movie.
3. Click Make An AutoMovie.
4. Select the movie style you want.
5. Click, and enter the title of your movie.
6. Click, and add audio or background music from a file.
7. Click, and wait for Movie Maker to create your movie.
8. Click Save, and save your video project.

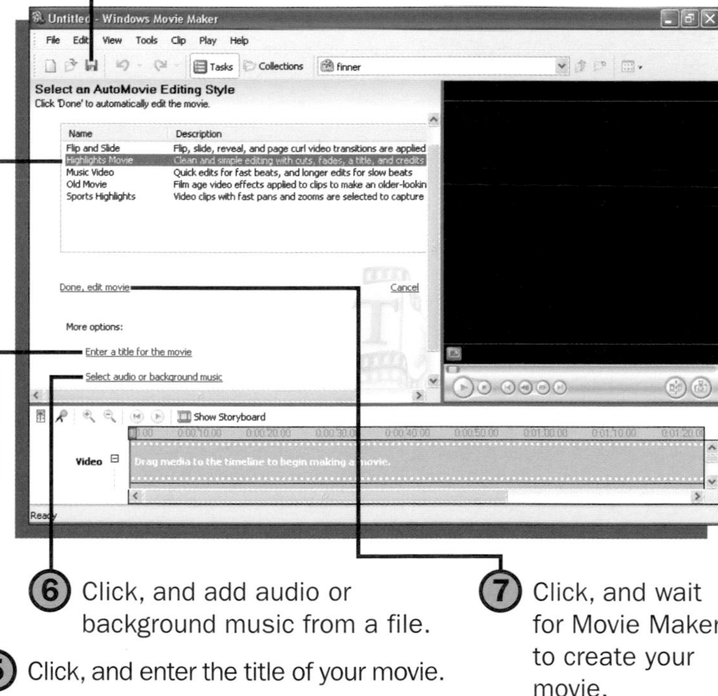

9. Choose the location in which you want to save the movie. Step through any wizards that appear, and provide the information requested.

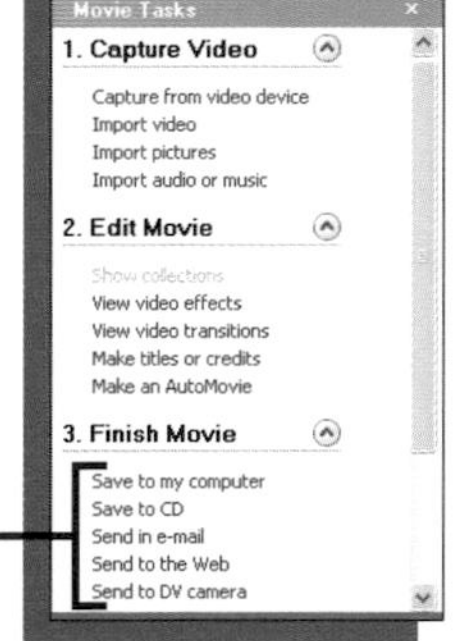

TRY THIS: Gather all your clips in one place. Right-click Collections in the Collections pane, choose New Collection from the shortcut menu, and name the new collection. Click a collection that contains a clip you want to put in a movie, hold down the Ctrl key, and drag the clip onto the new collection in the Collections pane. Click other collections, and drag any clips you want onto the new collection. Now click the new collection, and create a quick movie. Simple, isn't it?

Creating a Custom Movie

Using Movie Maker 2's AutoMovie feature is a quick and easy way to create a movie, but the result might not be exactly the movie you saw in your mind's eye. If you feel creative and want full control of the clips, the transitions, and the timing, you can create the movie step-by-step and customize it however you want.

> **SEE ALSO:** For information about adding video to your movie project, see "Creating a Quick Movie" on pages 108–109.
>
> For information about adding transitions, see "Adding Transitions to Your Movie" on page 112.
>
> For Information about adding video effects, see "Using Video Effects" on page 113.
>
> For Information about adding narration or a soundtrack to your movie, see "Adding Audio to Your Movie" on pages 116–117.

Set Up the Movie

1. Start Movie Maker from the Start menu. If the Movie Tasks pane isn't displayed, click the Tasks button.
2. Use the tasks in the Movie Tasks pane to capture or import your video clips into the project.

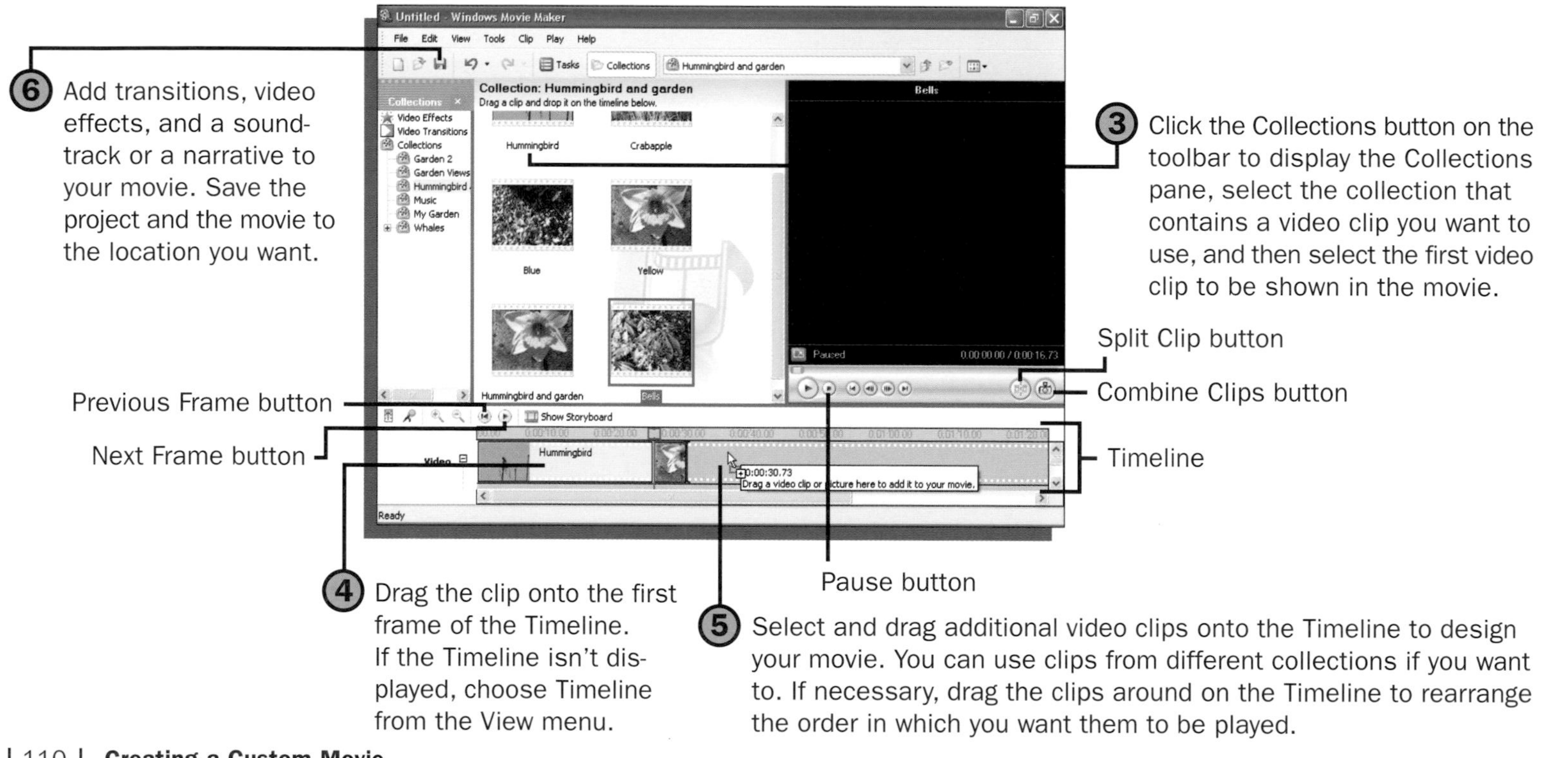

3. Click the Collections button on the toolbar to display the Collections pane, select the collection that contains a video clip you want to use, and then select the first video clip to be shown in the movie.
4. Drag the clip onto the first frame of the Timeline. If the Timeline isn't displayed, choose Timeline from the View menu.
5. Select and drag additional video clips onto the Timeline to design your movie. You can use clips from different collections if you want to. If necessary, drag the clips around on the Timeline to rearrange the order in which you want them to be played.
6. Add transitions, video effects, and a soundtrack or a narrative to your movie. Save the project and the movie to the location you want.

Splitting, Combining, and Trimming Clips

When you have an assortment of video clips, you might want to put only the first part of one particular clip in one part of your movie and then put the rest of that same clip in a different part of the movie. On the other hand, there might be a couple of clips that you'd prefer to treat as a single clip, or you might want to use only a portion of a clip. To do any of these maneuvers, you can split, combine, or trim existing clips.

TIP: When you trim a clip, the trimmed material is hidden in your project, not deleted from it. However, when you create your final movie file, the trimmed material isn't included.

TRY THIS: Click a clip in the Timeline, and then click the Play Timeline button. Click the Pause button when you reach the point at which you want to trim the clip, and choose Set Start Trim Point from the Clip menu to set the starting point for the clip, or choose Set End Trim Point from the Clip menu to set the end of the clip.

Customize Your Clips

1. Start Movie Maker 2, and open an existing Movie Maker project, or add video clips to a new project.

2. To separate a clip into two parts, double-click the clip to start playing it, and then click Pause to stop the play at approximately the point where you want to split the clip in two.

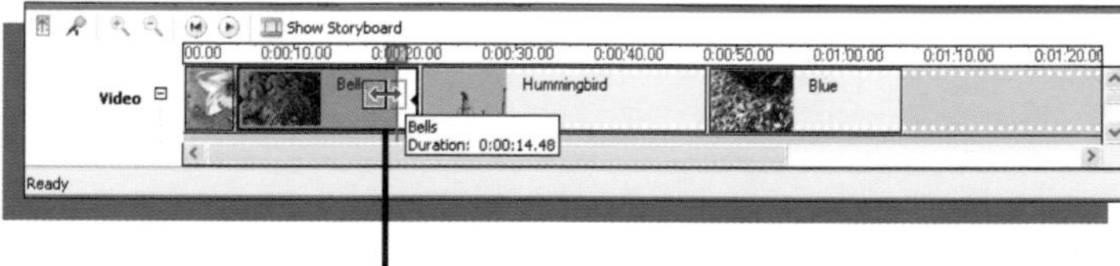

4. To combine clips, select two or more of the clips you want to combine, and then choose Combine from the Clip menu.

3. Use the Next Frame and the Previous Frame buttons to locate the exact frame, and then click the Split Clip button.

5. To trim a clip, with the Timeline displayed, click the clip you want to trim, and drag either the left or right side of the clip to trim it.

Adding Transitions to Your Movie ❁ NEW FEATURE

Most movies consist of multiple scenes. With each scene on a different video clip, you can add smooth transitions between scenes, just as the professionals do. For example, as you switch scenes, you can create the effect of turning a page, or you can have the current scene flip away and the next scene flip in. It's simple to do with Movie Maker 2's built-in transitions.

Add the Transitions

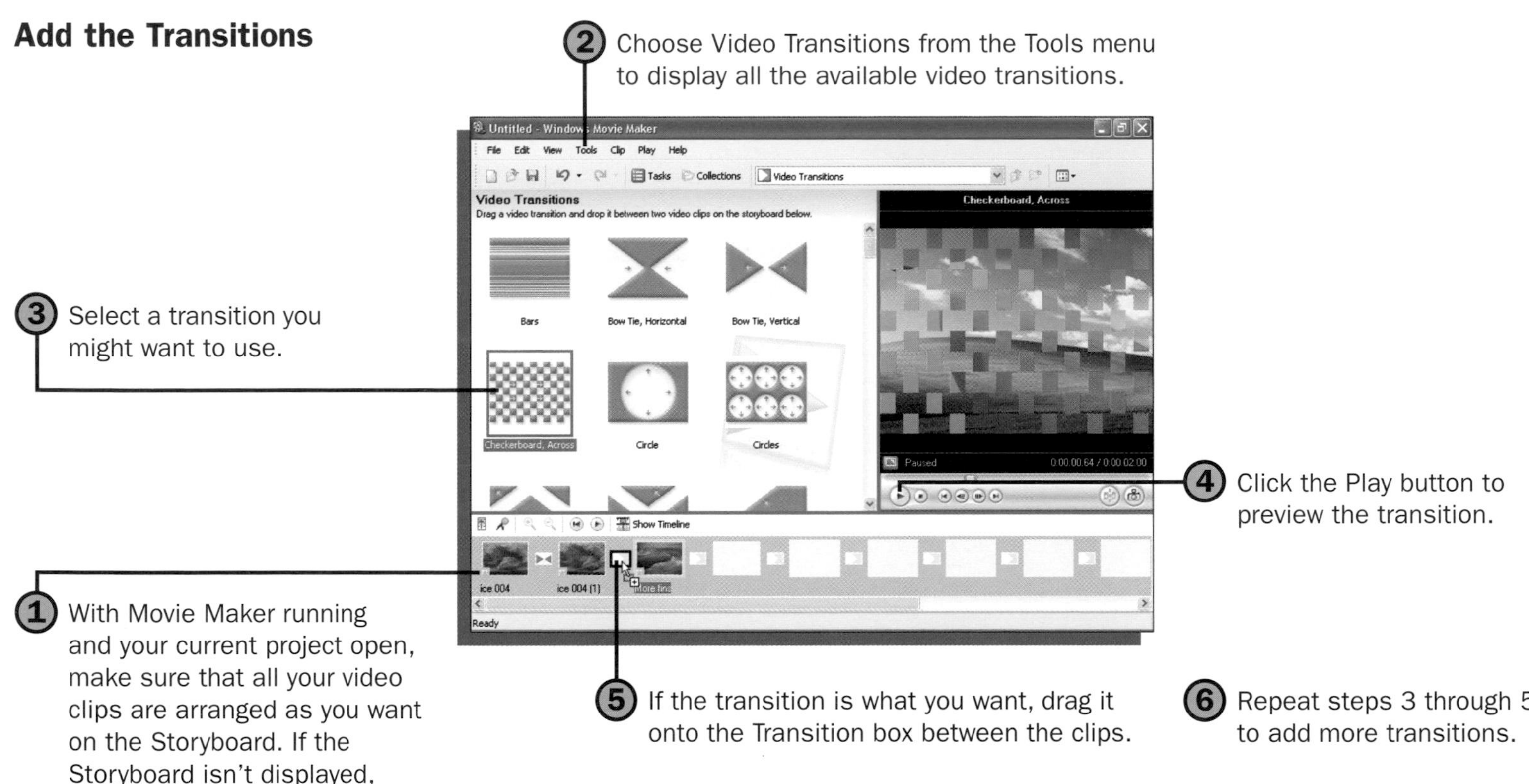

1. With Movie Maker running and your current project open, make sure that all your video clips are arranged as you want on the Storyboard. If the Storyboard isn't displayed, choose Storyboard from the View menu.
2. Choose Video Transitions from the Tools menu to display all the available video transitions.
3. Select a transition you might want to use.
4. Click the Play button to preview the transition.
5. If the transition is what you want, drag it onto the Transition box between the clips.
6. Repeat steps 3 through 5 to add more transitions.

TIP: When you create an AutoMovie, transitions between the clips are included automatically. You can change these transitions simply by dragging a different transition onto an existing one.

TIP: If you've installed Microsoft Plus! Digital Media Edition, you'll find many additional transitions, some with extremely dramatic effects.

SEE ALSO: For information about separating your scenes into different clips, see "Splitting, Combining, and Trimming Clips" on page 111.

Using Video Effects ⊕ NEW FEATURE

If you want something more interesting than just a plain old movie, you can get really creative with some special video effects. You can make your movie look like an old film, or you can add color effects that make it look as though it was filmed on another planet or in an alternate universe. All you have to do is add the effects you want while you're composing your movie in Movie Maker 2.

TRY THIS: Right-click the Video Effects box on a clip on the Storyboard, and choose Video Effects from the shortcut menu. In the dialog box that appears, add two or more effects, and click OK. Play the clip to see how the effects work. Repeat the process to remove any effect you don't want.

Add the Effects

1. With Movie Maker running and your current project open, make sure all your video clips are arranged as you want on the Storyboard. If the Storyboard isn't displayed, choose Storyboard from the View menu.
2. Choose Video Effects from the Tools menu to display all the available video effects.

3. Click the effect you want to use.
4. Click the Play button to preview the effect.
5. If you like the effect, drag it onto the Video Effects box on the video clip you want to apply it to.
6. Repeat steps 3 through 5 to add other video effects to other clips.

TIP: If you've installed Microsoft Plus! Digital Media Edition, you'll find many more video effects, including some really wild ones.

Adding Titles and Credits ⊕ NEW FEATURE

What's a movie without a title and credits? You might not need to acknowledge a gaffer, a best boy, drivers and caterers, and so on, but you can easily add a title, along with such credits as directing, filming, and writing.

TIP: The size of the font adjusts to fit the content of your title unless you specify a font size. If you do specify a font size, the text will use as many lines as necessary to include the whole title.

Add the Title

1. With your movie fully assembled in Movie Maker 2, choose Titles And Credits from the Tools menu to display the Titles And Credits options.
2. Choose where you want to add the title. If you want the title to precede a clip or to be on a clip, select the appropriate clip before clicking the title option you want.
3. Type the first line of the title.
4. If you want a second line of text, click in this area, and type the text.
5. Click to change the title animation, and select the animation you want for a one- or a two-line title.
6. Click to change the title font, color, and alignment, and specify whether you want to use large or small text.
7. Click to add the title.
8. Repeat steps 1 through 7 to add any other titles to your movie.

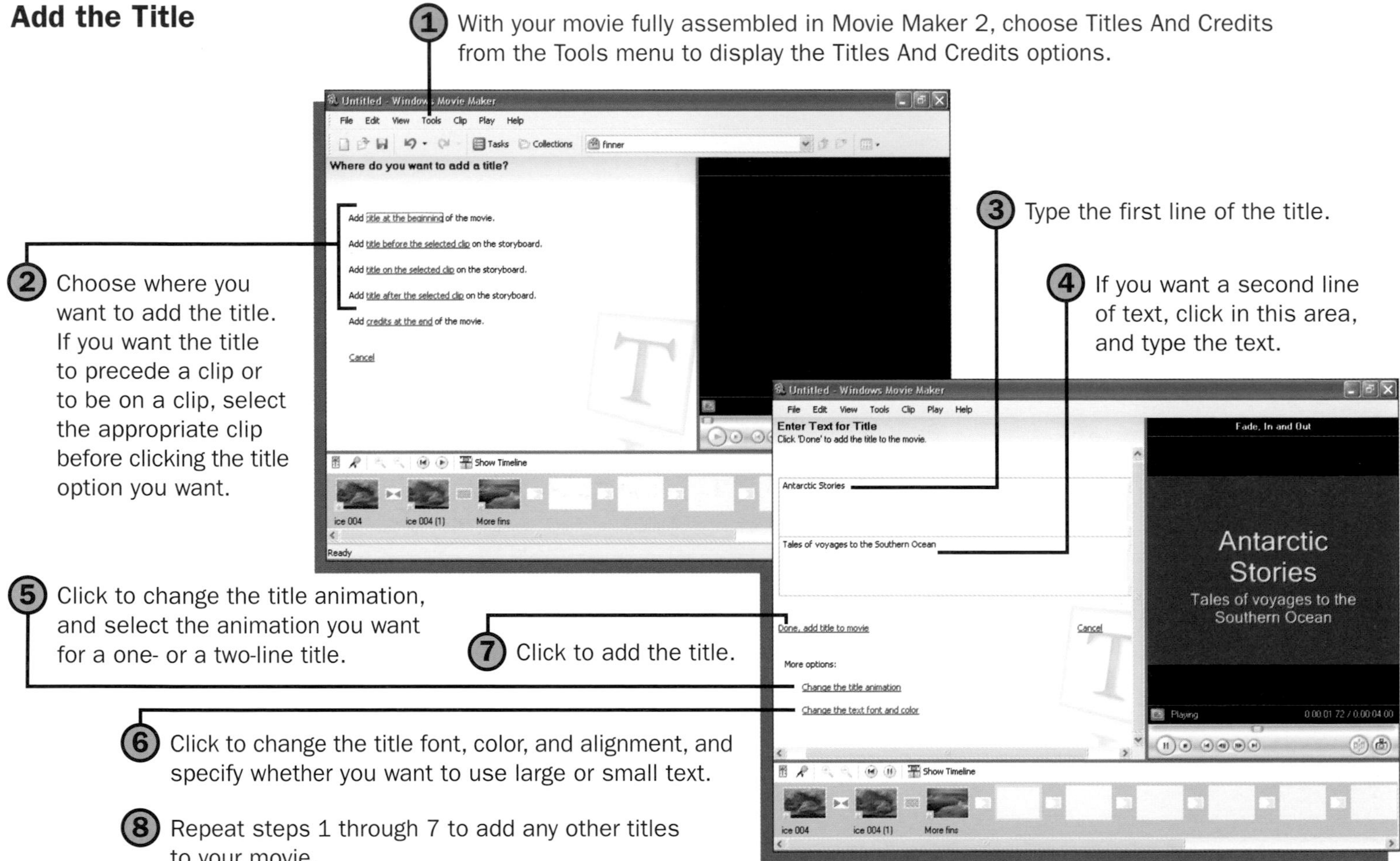
Untitled - Windows Movie Maker
File Edit View Tools Clip Play Help
Where do you want to add a title?
Add title at the beginning of the movie.
Add title before the selected clip on the storyboard.
Add title on the selected clip on the storyboard.
Add title after the selected clip on the storyboard.
Add credits at the end of the movie.
Cancel
Enter Text for Title
Click 'Done' to add the title to the movie.
Antarctic Stories
Tales of voyages to the Southern Ocean
Done, add title to movie
Cancel
More options:
Change the title animation
Change the text font and color
Fade, In and Out
Antarctic Stories
Tales of voyages to the Southern Ocean
Show Timeline
ice 004
ice 004 (1)
More fins

Add the Credits

1. Choose Titles And Credits from the Tools menu if the Titles And Credits options aren't displayed.

2. Click Add Credits At The End Of The Movie.

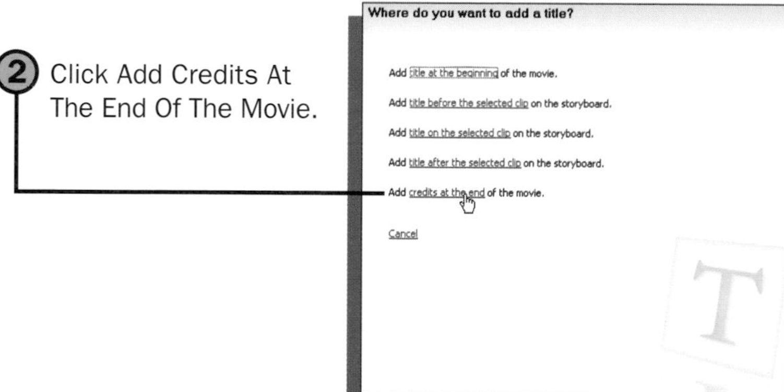
Where do you want to add a title?
Add title at the beginning of the movie.
Add title before the selected clip on the storyboard.
Add title on the selected clip on the storyboard.
Add title after the selected clip on the storyboard.
Add credits at the end of the movie.
Cancel

TIP: To edit an existing title or credit, double-click the clip containing the title or credit on the Storyboard or on the Timeline. If the title is on an existing video clip, double-click the title in the Title Overlay section of the Timeline. Make your changes, and then click Done.

TIP: To show the credits at the beginning of the movie, create the credits and add them to the end of the movie. Then drag the video clip containing the credits to the beginning of the movie.

3. Type **Credits** or any other title you want at the beginning of the credits. Press Tab to move to the next line.

4. Type the title of the specific credit, and press Tab to move to the next box.

5. Type the name of the person, company, or organization that receives the credit, and press Tab to move to the next line.

6. Repeat steps 4 and 5 until all the credits are complete.

8. Click to add the credits to the movie.

7. Click to change the animation or the font for the credits.

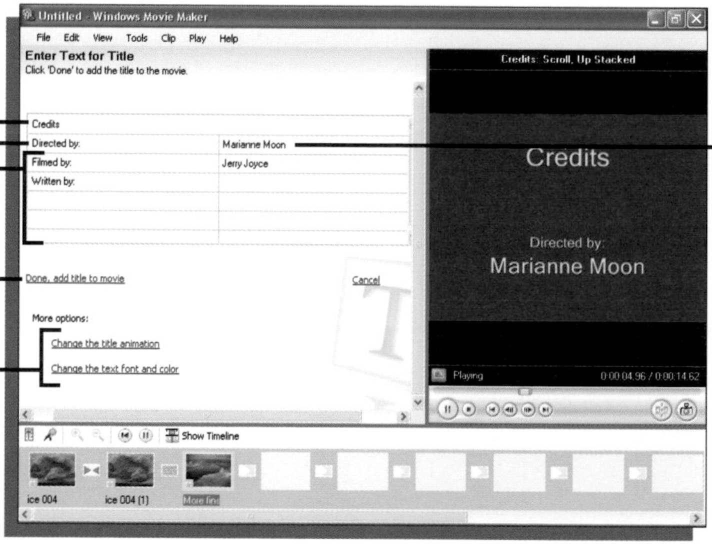

Adding Audio to Your Movie

When you record a movie with Movie Maker 2, any existing audio from your video clips will be included. You can also add a narration or a music soundtrack that will be integrated with the audio. If you didn't record an audio track when you originally recorded the video, however, and you want to add one now, or if you want to add a narration or a musical soundtrack to an existing movie, it's a simple process. A narration can either merge with the existing audio for the movie or completely replace it, whereas a soundtrack is always merged with any existing audio for the movie.

Create a Narration

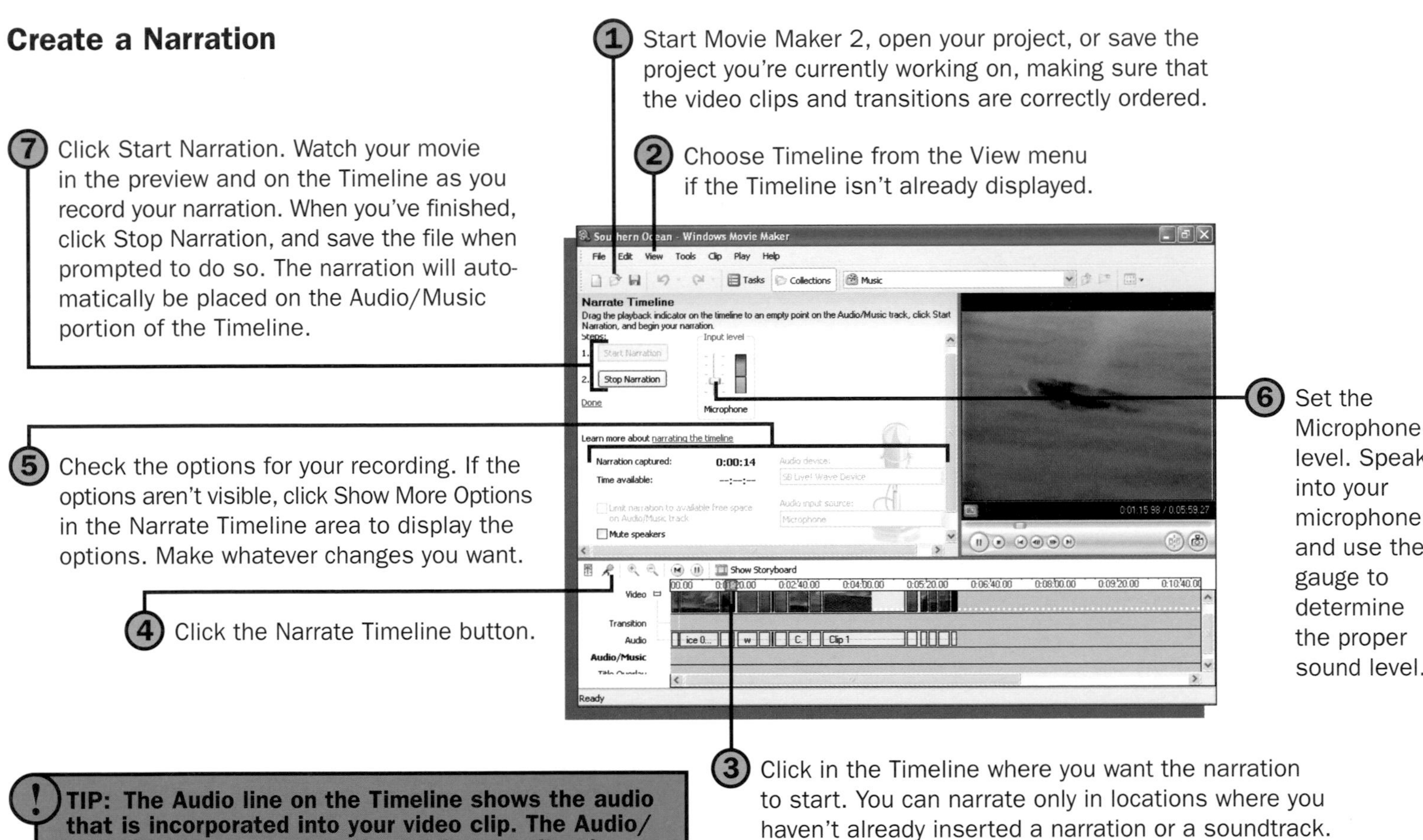

1. Start Movie Maker 2, open your project, or save the project you're currently working on, making sure that the video clips and transitions are correctly ordered.

2. Choose Timeline from the View menu if the Timeline isn't already displayed.

3. Click in the Timeline where you want the narration to start. You can narrate only in locations where you haven't already inserted a narration or a soundtrack.

4. Click the Narrate Timeline button.

5. Check the options for your recording. If the options aren't visible, click Show More Options in the Narrate Timeline area to display the options. Make whatever changes you want.

6. Set the Microphone level. Speak into your microphone, and use the gauge to determine the proper sound level.

7. Click Start Narration. Watch your movie in the preview and on the Timeline as you record your narration. When you've finished, click Stop Narration, and save the file when prompted to do so. The narration will automatically be placed on the Audio/Music portion of the Timeline.

TIP: The Audio line on the Timeline shows the audio that is incorporated into your video clip. The Audio/Music line shows the narration or the soundtrack. Items on the Audio/Music line can be cropped, moved, or deleted to customize your movie.

Add a Soundtrack

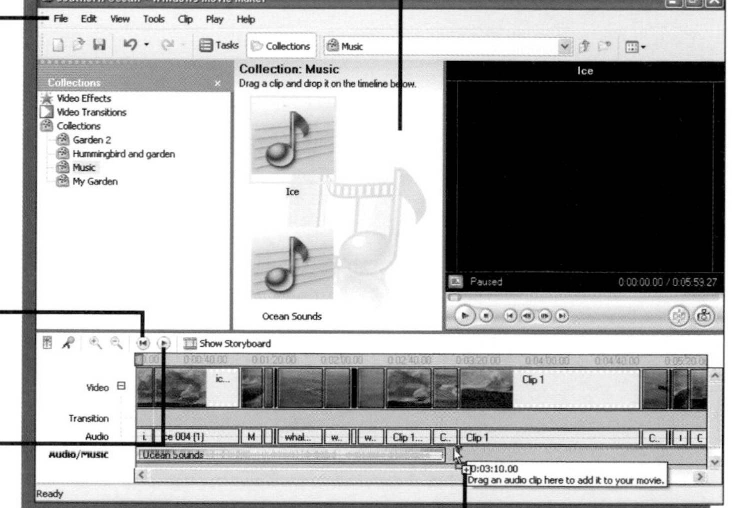

1. Create or import the audio files that you want to use for your soundtrack. The files need not be in Windows Media Format, but neither can they be protected media such as some CD music. You'll probably need to experiment to see which types of audio files you can use.
2. Drag a sound clip onto the Audio/Music line at the location (that is, the time) where you want the clip to be played during the movie. Add and position any other sound clips.
3. Click the Rewind Timeline button.
4. Click the Play Timeline button to preview your entire movie with your narration or soundtrack in place.
5. Save your project; then choose Save Movie File from the File menu, and save the movie in the location you want.

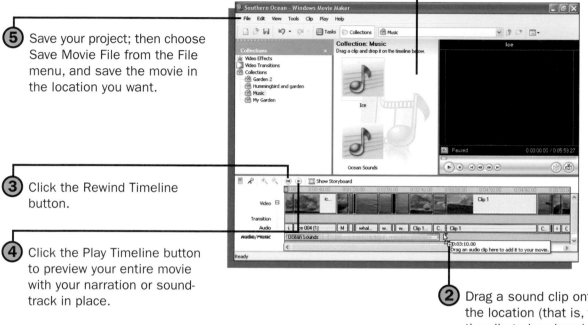

TIP: To eliminate any audio that was recorded with the video and to use only your own soundtrack, right-click the audio clip on the Audio line of the Timeline, and choose Mute from the shortcut menu.

CAUTION: If you're using music from a CD or another similar source for your soundtrack, be careful not to violate the copyright of the material.

SEE ALSO: For information about saving CD music to your hard drive in Windows Media Format, see "Copying CD Music" on pages 136–137.

For information about recording your own sound files, see "Creating a Sound File" on page 149.

Adding Slides to Your Movie

Your movie doesn't have to be all action. You can add digital pictures—photographs from a digital camera, for example—to your video clips to create title slides, or add still photographs to supplement the video clips. Or you can create a movie file using your still pictures and some music to produce a slide show with an accompanying soundtrack. You can also edit pictures or create them from scratch to add title slides for your movie.

SEE ALSO: For information about using Plus! Photo Story to easily create a slide show in which you can pan and zoom in or out on the pictures, see "Creating a Video Slide Show" on pages 102–103.

Add Slides

1. Start Movie Maker from the Start menu.
2. Click the Collections button if the Collections pane isn't displayed. If you want to use a separate Collections folder for your pictures, click the main Collections folder, choose New Collection Folder from the Tools menu, and name the new folder.
3. Click the Collections folder you want to contain your pictures, and choose Import Into Collections from the File menu. In the Import File dialog box that appears, locate and select the files you want, and click Import.
4. Choose Options from the View menu to display the Options dialog box, and, on the Advanced tab, specify the length of time you want each picture to be displayed. Click OK.
5. Drag the pictures onto the Storyboard in the sequence in which you want them displayed. Add any transitions and/or video effects you want. Use the Timeline view to add any audio or to modify the length of time an individual picture is displayed.
6. Click Save Movie when you've finished.

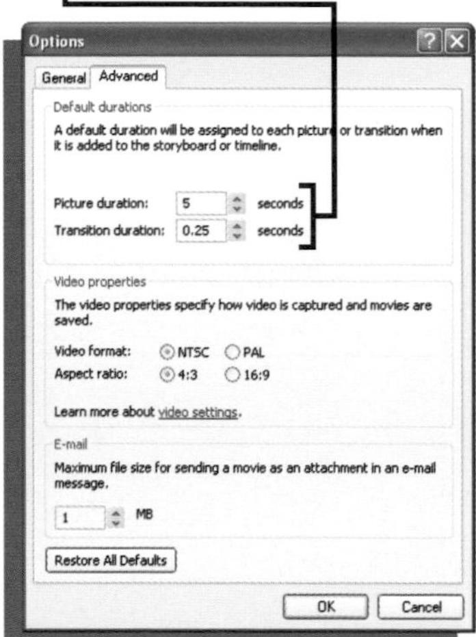

Recording Video Clips

With Windows Movie Maker 2, you can create a digital video file directly from a video camera, from a video recorder, or from a TV broadcast—provided you have the proper equipment. To record from an analog camera or a video recorder, you'll need a video-capture card. To record from a TV station, you'll need a TV tuner card on your computer, or you'll need to wire your TV or video recorder to the video-capture card on your computer. If you're using a digital Web camera, all you have to do is hook the camera directly to your computer.

SEE ALSO: For information about downloading a recorded video file from a digital video camera, see "Downloading a Video from a Digital Camera" on pages 120–121.

TIP: There are a couple of ways to download video directly from a video camera, depending on your camera's configuration. If you're using a USB connection, use the method described on this page. If you're downloading using an IEEE 1394 (FireWire) connection, you can automatically download an entire tape or can control the camera from your computer while downloading selected clips.

Record the Video

1. Start Movie Maker from the Start menu. Click Tasks if the Movie Tasks pane isn't displayed.
2. Click Capture From Video Device to start the Video Capture Wizard. Step through the first three screens of the wizard, specifying
   - The video device you want to use.
   - The name and location of the video file.
   - The video format for the file.

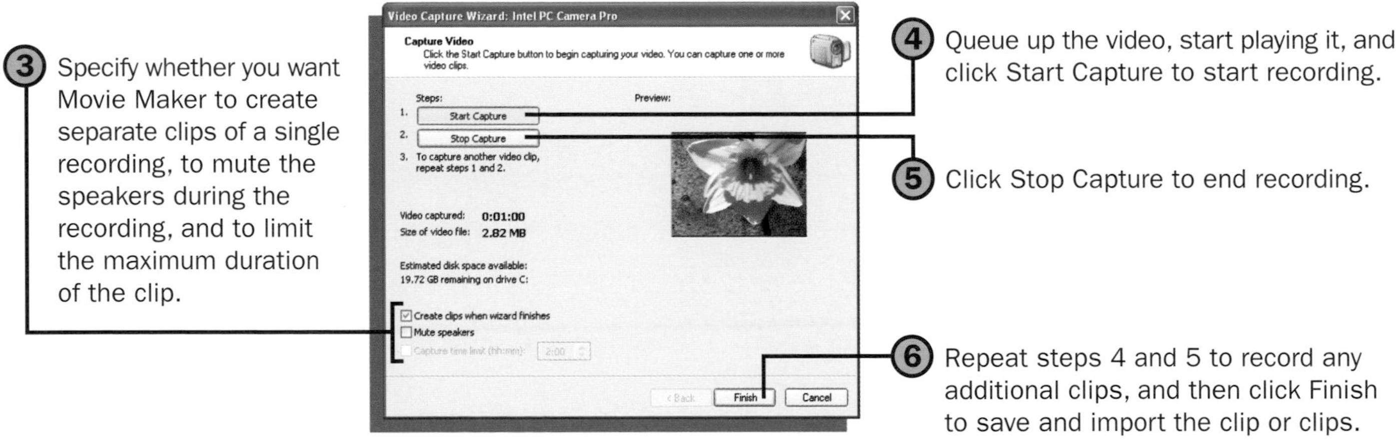

3. Specify whether you want Movie Maker to create separate clips of a single recording, to mute the speakers during the recording, and to limit the maximum duration of the clip.
4. Queue up the video, start playing it, and click Start Capture to start recording.
5. Click Stop Capture to end recording.
6. Repeat steps 4 and 5 to record any additional clips, and then click Finish to save and import the clip or clips.

Downloading a Video from a Digital Camera

If your digital video camera is attached to your computer using an IEEE 1394 (FireWire) connection, you can use Movie Maker to download all or part of a recorded video file directly into Movie Maker 2.

Download the Video

1. With your camera attached to the computer, turned on, and set to play recorded video, start Movie Maker from the Start menu. Click Tasks if the Movie Tasks pane isn't displayed. In the Movie Tasks pane, click Capture From A Video Source to start the Video Capture Wizard.

2. Step through the wizard, specifying
   - The digital video camera you're using.
   - The name and location of the video file.
   - The video settings. Choose Digital Device Format (DV-AVI) if you want to record your movie back to your digital camera.

TIP: Even if your camera's format isn't supported by Movie Maker, you might still be able to use Movie Maker to edit the video. Use the software that came with the camera to download the video, and check to see whether the supporting software will convert the video to the AVI or DV-AVI format, which you can then import. Another method is to set up the camera as though it were playing the video on an analog television, and then use a video-capture card to import the video onto your computer. However, you'll lose some quality with this method.

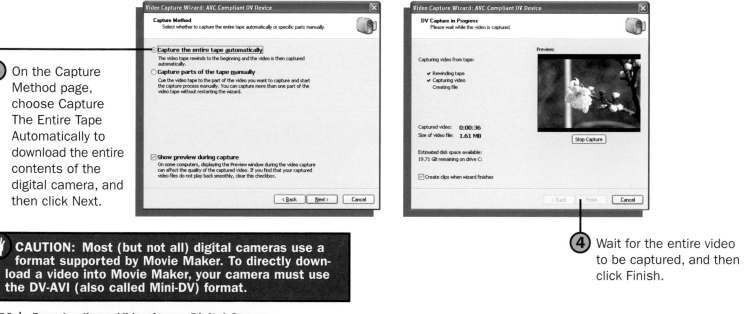

3. On the Capture Method page, choose Capture The Entire Tape Automatically to download the entire contents of the digital camera, and then click Next.

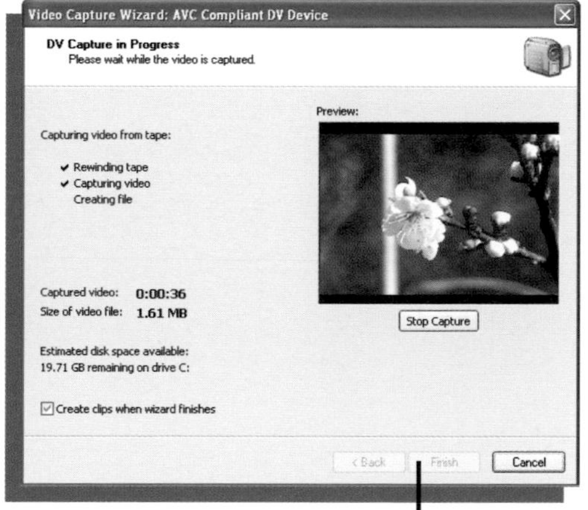

4. Wait for the entire video to be captured, and then click Finish.

CAUTION: Most (but not all) digital cameras use a format supported by Movie Maker. To directly download a video into Movie Maker, your camera must use the DV-AVI (also called Mini-DV) format.

Download Selected Clips

1. With Movie Maker running, and with your camera attached to your computer, turned on, and set to play recorded video, start the Video Capture Wizard. Step through the wizard, specifying the camera, the video file name, and the video setting.

2. On the Capture Method page of the wizard, click the Capture Parts Of the Tape Manually option, and then click Next.

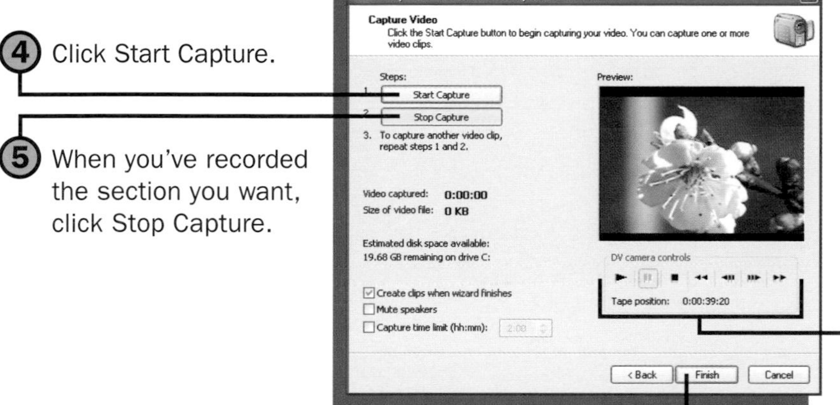

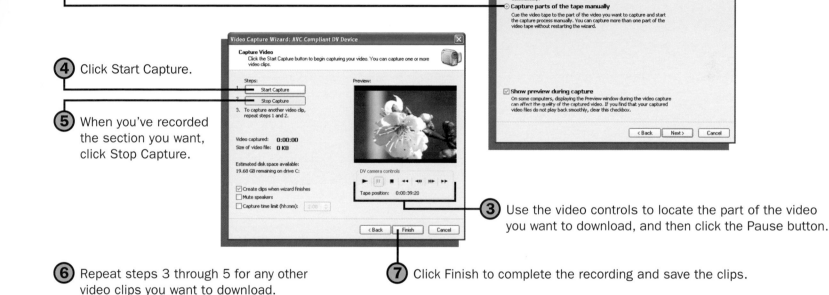

3. Use the video controls to locate the part of the video you want to download, and then click the Pause button.

4. Click Start Capture.

5. When you've recorded the section you want, click Stop Capture.

6. Repeat steps 3 through 5 for any other video clips you want to download.

7. Click Finish to complete the recording and save the clips.

Making Movies That People Actually Enjoy

We all love our own home movies, and, because we're usually reliving happy times when we watch them, we're tolerant of their flaws. Before we ask anyone else to watch a home movie, though, we should improve it as much as possible so that the members of our captive audience actually enjoy the show rather than trying to hide their yawning boredom. The trick, of course, is to use good camera skills so that you avoid the most common problems: panning and zooming too fast or too slowly, jittery pictures, bad lighting, and poorly composed images. However, once you've recorded your movie, there are several ways you can improve it if you need to.

Edit Your Movie

Even world-famous directors and experienced camera operators don't make a perfect movie as they're filming it. That's where the movie editor comes in!

Take out the trash. Don't use any material of inferior quality. You might love a clip that brings back fond memories even though Uncle David's head is cut off, but your audience won't love it. Delete the substandard material by splitting the clip, separating the quality from the trash, and using only the best clips.

Rearrange the content. You don't have to keep your movie's scenes in the order in which they were shot. Rearrange them based on subject matter or to produce a more logical sequence of events. Pay attention to continuity—for example, don't jump from a glimpse of Auntie Mimi presiding over a sunny picnic to an unrelated shot of her on a rainy day inside just because there wasn't enough footage of the picnic.

Tighten up the scenes. When you review the assembled movie and find that a scene runs too long, crop it down to prevent your audience's attention from wandering. Crop the beginning or the end of a clip by setting crop marks in the clip.

Control narrations and soundtracks. These elements can add a great deal of sophistication to a movie, but you need to insert them carefully. The sound content must be closely coordinated with the video action, and the sound quality and volume should add to rather than distract from the subject matter of the movie. If you're going to add a narration, write a script first, and rehearse it as often as you need to while you're previewing the movie. When you're sure the narration works, use a good-quality microphone to record it. Whether you're using a narration or a soundtrack, adjust the volume so that it doesn't get lost among the background sounds or blast your viewers out of their seats.

Check with the reviewers. Don't trust yourself to be objective about your movie. Before you distribute it, ask at least one person whose opinion you value to review the movie and to give you some constructive criticism. Then, if you need to, you can go back and make some tweaks to produce a movie that will leave your audience eager to watch your next extravaganza.

Make It Available

The size of your movie dictates the way you're going to distribute it. You shouldn't expect people to receive a huge video file by e-mail or to wait forever as they download it from the Web.

Use the appropriate quality. In a video file, the quality of the video is directly proportional to the file size. When you're ready to distribute your movie, you can save it specifically for the way you're going to use it. Movie Maker provides different ways to save your movie, each using a default video quality that's optimized for a specific use, thus creating a file whose size is appropriate for that particular use. This gives you the ability to create several versions of your movie, each optimized for a specific purpose.

Post it on the Web. You can use a Web service to publish your movie on the Web so that other people can play it directly from the Web site. To post your video on one of these services, in Movie Maker, click Send To The Web, and step through the Save Movie Wizard. In the wizard, you choose the quality of the movie based on the connection speed that you and others will use to access the movie.

E-mail it. To save the movie in a quality and file size appropriate for e-mailing, choose Send In E-Mail from the Movie Tasks pane of Movie Maker. As you step through the Save Movie Wizard, you can also save the completed movie file to your computer so that you can e-mail it to other people at a later date without having to step through the Save Movie Wizard again. When you've completed the wizard, your movie will be enclosed in an e-mail message, ready to be addressed and sent.

Put it on a CD. If you want to save and distribute your movie in a high-quality format, you can put it on a CD—provided, of course, that you have a CD recorder on your computer. To do so, choose Save To CD from the Movie Tasks pane of Movie Maker. Although you should be able to play the movie from the CD on another computer, you might not be able to play it using a DVD player attached to a television, unlike the video slide shows you can create with Plus! Photo Story. To show a movie created with Movie Maker, you need to have a DVD player that incorporates HIGHMAT, a fairly new technology that allows the DVD player to properly communicate with the CD. Check your DVD player for the HIGHMAT logo. To put your movie on a DVD, you'll need to use a third-party DVD movie-editing program. Create your movie in Movie Maker, and save it in the DV-AVI format. Then import the file into your DVD movie-editing program, and use that program to create your DVD. To do this, you'll need a large amount of free disk space on your computer to store the DV-AVI file. You'll be able to play the DVD on any computer with a DVD drive; however, to play it on a DVD attached to a TV you'll need a DVD player that can read DVD-R discs.

Send it back to your digital camera. If you have a digital camera connected to your computer using an IEEE 1394 (FireWire) connection, you can send the movie back to your camera for playback using the camera. To do so, choose Send To DV Camera from the Movie Tasks pane of Movie Maker, and step through the Save Movie Wizard. The movie will be saved in the DV-AVI format. Note, however, that this format creates files that are substantially larger than other formats and that need large quantities of temporary space on your computer's hard disk.

Know the format. Your movies are usually automatically saved in Windows Media Format (WMV), which dramatically reduces file size compared with other video formats. If you need to use a different format, however, you do have some choices. When you save the movie to your computer using the Save Movie Wizard, you can choose to use the DV-AVI format that's standard to digital cameras, or the high-quality video that's used for standard television recordings. The high-quality video format can be in either the NTSC or PAL format, depending on where the movie will be played (NTSC for North and South America, Japan, and Korea; PAL for most of the rest of the world). To switch between NTSC and PAL formats, choose Options from Movie Maker's Tools menu, and, on the Advanced tab of the Options dialog box, select your video format. On the same tab, you can also change the aspect ratio of the image to match the aspect ratio of the playback system. Windows Media Format files require Windows Media Player, so verify that whoever is going to view your video has that player installed.

Playing a DVD

You can play DVDs on your Windows Media Player, provided you have a DVD drive and a DVD decoder installed on your computer. When you play the DVD, you can change speeds and can show subtitles and captions. With some DVDs, you can even show different camera angles.

Set the Defaults

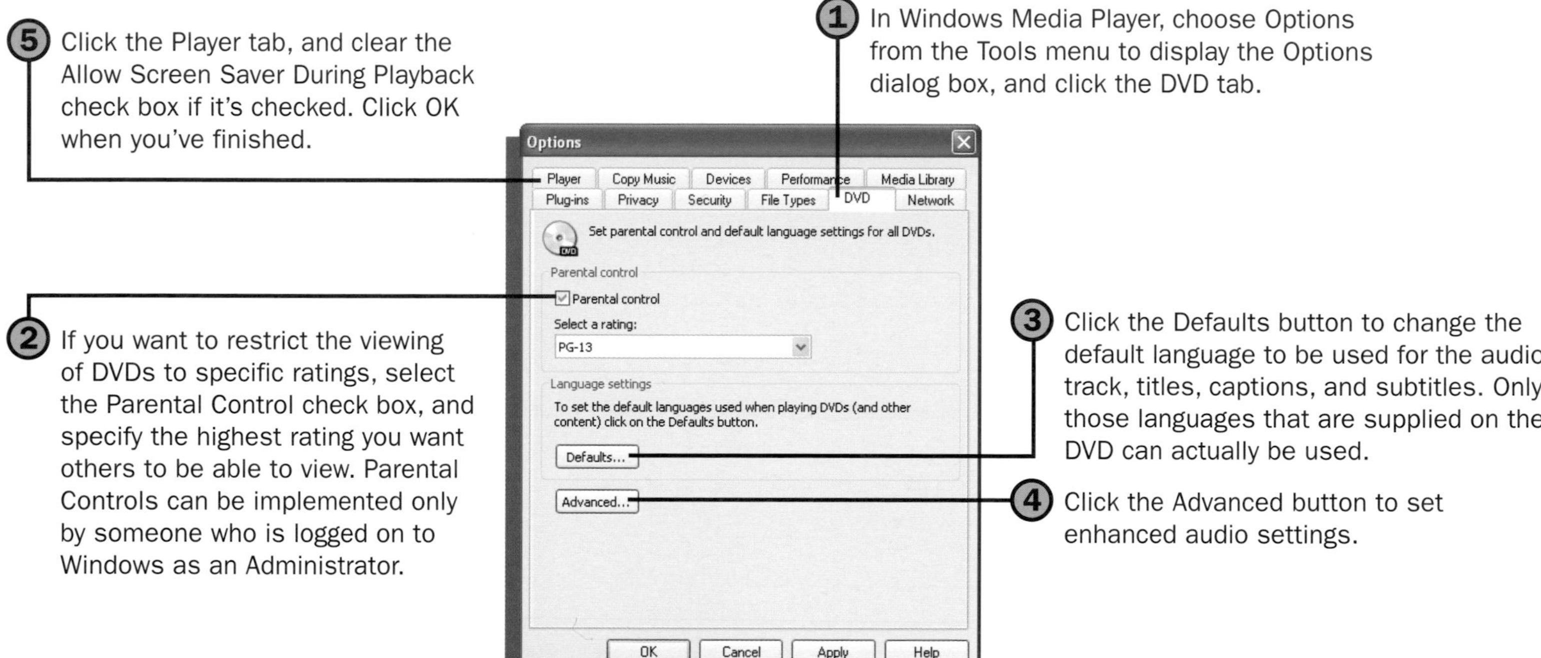

1. In Windows Media Player, choose Options from the Tools menu to display the Options dialog box, and click the DVD tab.
2. If you want to restrict the viewing of DVDs to specific ratings, select the Parental Control check box, and specify the highest rating you want others to be able to view. Parental Controls can be implemented only by someone who is logged on to Windows as an Administrator.
3. Click the Defaults button to change the default language to be used for the audio track, titles, captions, and subtitles. Only those languages that are supplied on the DVD can actually be used.
4. Click the Advanced button to set enhanced audio settings.
5. Click the Player tab, and clear the Allow Screen Saver During Playback check box if it's checked. Click OK when you've finished.

TIP: If you don't see any DVD commands on your menus or if there is no DVD tab in the Options dialog box, it means that Windows Media has not detected a DVD decoder. If a DVD player came with your DVD drive, make sure that it and its supporting software are installed, which should install the decoder. To purchase a DVD decoder on line, point to Plug-Ins on the View menu, and choose Download Plug-Ins from the submenu.

TIP: If the menus aren't visible, click the Show Menu Bar button at the top left of the full-size Media Player.

Customize the Play

1. Insert the DVD into your DVD drive. If the disc doesn't automatically start playing, point to DVD, VCD Or CD Audio on the Play menu, and, from the submenu, choose the drive that contains the DVD.

SEE ALSO: For information about adjusting the playback speed, see "Controlling Video Playback" on page 126.

2. Choose the language and captions you want from the Play menu. The submenus will display only the options available on the disc. Point to
   - Captions And Subtitles, and choose the language and type of caption or subtitle you want from the submenu.
   - Audio And Language Tracks, and choose the language you want to use from the submenu.

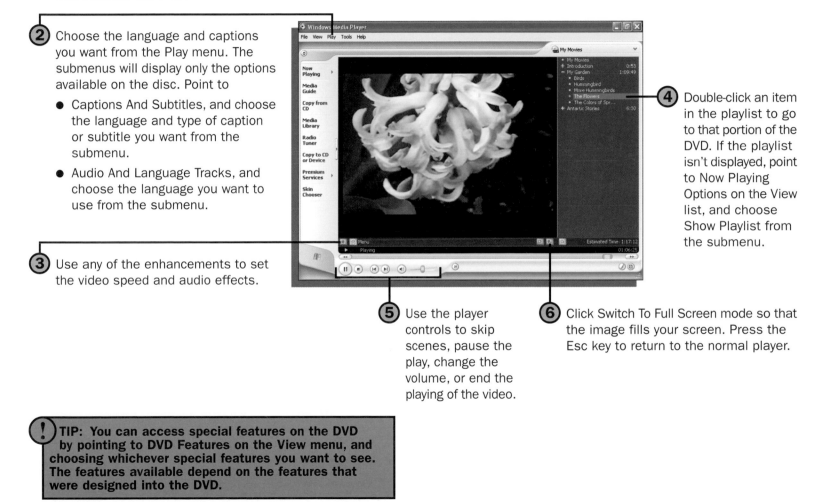

3. Use any of the enhancements to set the video speed and audio effects.

4. Double-click an item in the playlist to go to that portion of the DVD. If the playlist isn't displayed, point to Now Playing Options on the View list, and choose Show Playlist from the submenu.

5. Use the player controls to skip scenes, pause the play, change the volume, or end the playing of the video.

6. Click Switch To Full Screen mode so that the image fills your screen. Press the Esc key to return to the normal player.

TIP: You can access special features on the DVD by pointing to DVD Features on the View menu, and choosing whichever special features you want to see. The features available depend on the features that were designed into the DVD.

Controlling Video Playback

Watching video, whether it's streaming video from the Web or video files on your computer, is fairly straightforward. All you need to do is click the link on the Web page for the streaming video or choose the video from your Media Library, and then watch it on the Now Playing tab of Windows Media Player. However, you can also control the speed of the video playback and can even examine it frame by frame.

Adjust the Playback

1. With your video playing, keep clicking the Next Controls or the Previous Controls button until the Video Settings controls are displayed.
2. Use the sliders to adjust the hue, brightness, saturation, and contrast of the video.
3. Click to specify the size of the video image.
4. Keep clicking the Next Controls or the Previous Controls button until the Play Speed Settings controls are displayed.
5. Drag the slider to set the speed of the playback. The green area shows the range of available speeds.

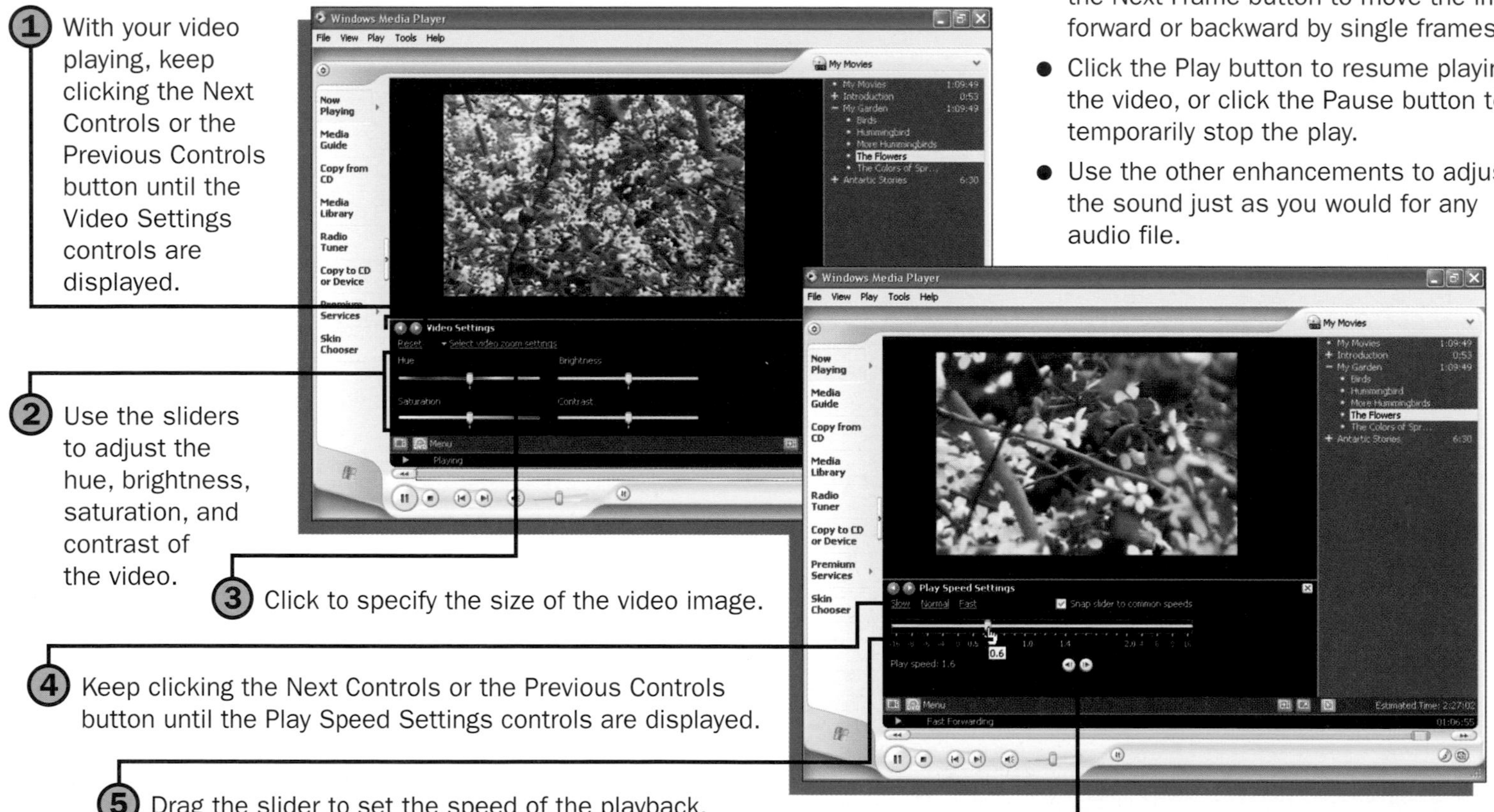

TIP: If you don't see any enhancements, point to Enhancements on the View menu, and choose Show Enhancements from the submenu.

6. Use the controls to modify the playback, as follows:
   - Click the Next Frame button to pause the video. Click the Previous Frame or the Next Frame button to move the image forward or backward by single frames.
   - Click the Play button to resume playing the video, or click the Pause button to temporarily stop the play.
   - Use the other enhancements to adjust the sound just as you would for any audio file.

Next Frame and Previous Frame buttons

Working with Music, Voice, and Sounds

In this section

If you like music, you'll *love* Microsoft Windows Media Player. You can use Media Player to download from the Internet all sorts of information about your favorite albums or performers, to play music tracks, and to copy individual pieces of music or entire CDs to your computer. You can arrange the media you want to play, regardless of format—songs, video clips, and so on—in the order you want in a customized *playlist.* If your computer is equipped with a CD recorder, you can record individual tracks to create your own CD, and if you've installed one of the Microsoft Plus! packs on your computer, you'll be able to create CD labels, inserts, and booklets. If you like to take your music with you, just transfer it from Media Player to your MP3 or other portable player. Having a party? Set up Media Player with music, visualizations, and running text. If you have old LPs or cassette tapes that you want to convert into digital format, you can easily do so provided you've installed the Plus! Digital Media Edition on your computer. You can even use your own voice commands to control Media Player, and you can choose among dozens of cool designs to outfit Media Player with a new *skin* to transform its appearance.

Microsoft Windows XP also provides a program called Narrator that actually reads aloud to you. Provided your computer has a sound system, Narrator can describe items on your screen and can read blocks of text to you. You can adjust the speed, volume, and pitch of Narrator's voice for your individual listening pleasure. Last but not least, would you like to have people dancing all over your computer screen? Read on....

What Is Media Player?

Windows Media Player is a multifaceted tool that you can have fun with in a variety of ways: You can use it to play music CDs, to copy music from CDs onto your computer, to download music from the Internet, to create your own music CDs, to watch streaming video that's being sent from the Internet or over a network, to organize your digital music collection, and to listen to a radio program that's being broadcast over the Internet. Depending on the types of media you play, you have numerous options for enhancing or modifying the way those media are played. You can, for example, change the stereo balance, add special effects, tweak the color of a video, and much more.

Note that Windows Media Player is frequently updated and improved, so the player you have might look a bit different from the one shown here. The basic way in which Media Player works, however, remains the same, so you should find all the features we discuss here in any updated version of Media Player.

Interact with what's currently playing: Watch a video or visualizations that go with the music, and control the sound and video quality.

Connect to the *WindowsMedia.com* Web site for downloads and samples.

Copy music from a CD onto your computer.

See a list of all the music and videos on your computer.

Connect to radio stations that broadcast over the Internet.

Copy music from your computer onto a CD or portable device.

Access services that charge for streaming media and file downloads.

Select a shape for your Media Player.

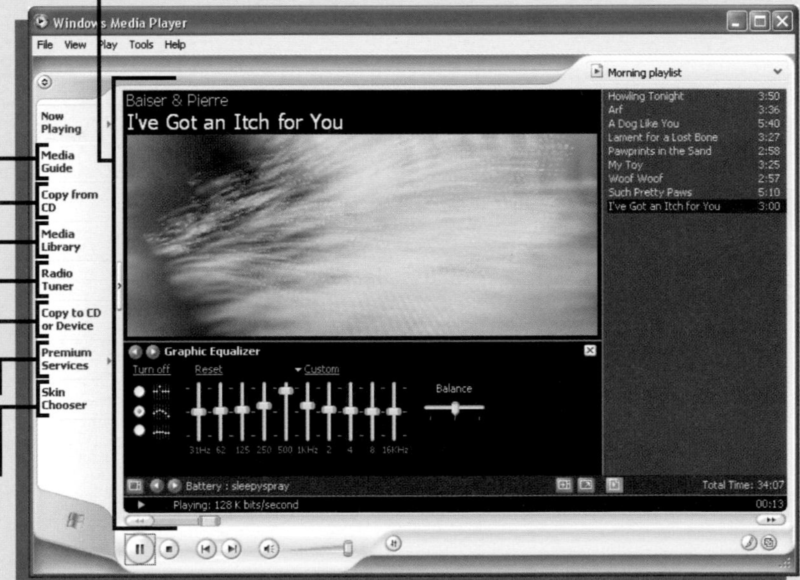

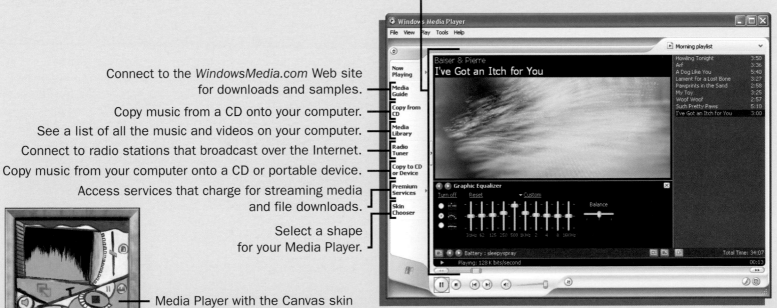

Media Player with the Canvas skin

Playing a Music CD

Playing a CD is as simple as putting the CD into the drive and waiting for Windows Media Player to start playing the music. However, Media Player can also provide additional information from the Internet about the music and the performer. With or without this additional information, you can control and customize the way the music is played.

SEE ALSO: For information about choosing which media files to play if Media Player is already running, see "Playing Any Media File" on pages 132–133.

For information about making Media Player the default player for CDs and other media, see "Setting Your Default Programs" on pages 212–213.

Play a CD

1. Insert the CD into your computer's CD drive, and wait for Media Player to start. If the CD is already in the drive, choose My Computer from the Windows Start menu, and double-click the CD drive.
2. Click to display the menu bar if it isn't already displayed.
3. Click the Now Playing tab if it isn't already displayed.
4. If the information you want to see about the album isn't displayed, point to Now Playing Options on the View menu, and choose one of the following from the submenu:
   - Show Title to display the title information above any visualization you've displayed
   - Show Media Information to display available information about the CD
   - Show Playlist to display a list of the songs in their playing order and with their playing times
5. Click the Now Playing Options button, point to a category on the menu that appears, and choose the item you want to display:
   - Visualizations to choose the image displayed
   - Info Center View to connect to Web content about the CD
   - Plug-Ins to use features that have been added to Media Player
   - Enhancements to set color, sound, and video, and to access hyperlinks to the music for e-mailing

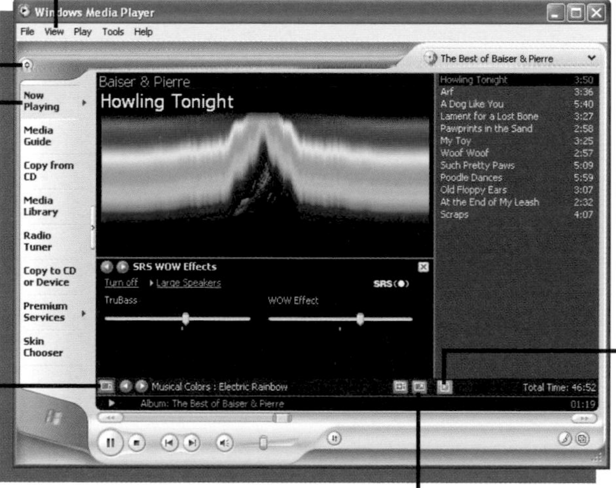

Click if you want Media Player use the full screen. Press the Esc key to return to normal size.

Downloading Music Information

To get the names of all the tracks on a CD, as well as lots of additional data about the album, and/or to get information about the music files that you've stored on your computer, you can let Media Player connect to the Internet, search for a Web page about the album or music file, and then download the information. Once you've downloaded it, the information is stored on your computer and is always available.

CAUTION: Seeking information comes with a price, and that price can be a loss of some privacy. Even if you don't send any personal information, your computer's IP address—a unique number that identifies you for this session only—and possibly the make of your computer are usually sent automatically. If you select the option in the Options dialog box to send a unique player ID to content providers, a static number that specifically identifies you to your enhanced-content service provider is sent for billing and tracking data.

Set Up Automatic Downloading

1. In Media Player, choose Options from the Tools menu to display the Options dialog box, and click the Privacy tab. 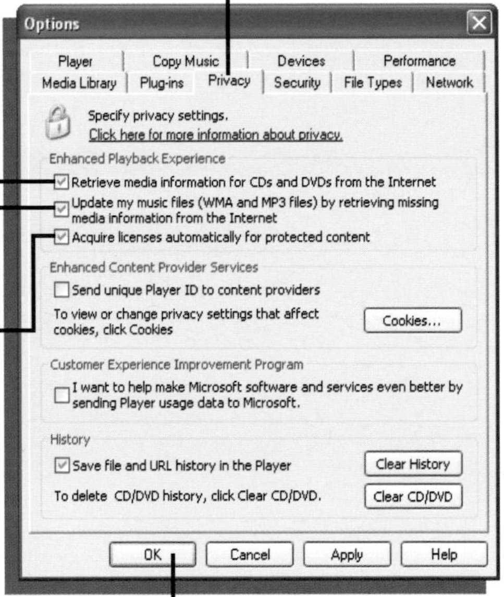
2. Select this check box to retrieve data about the album.
3. Select this check box to retrieve data about the music files on your computer.
4. Select this check box to download licenses you need in order to download or copy any protected music files.
5. Click OK.
6. If you aren't connected to the Internet, connect, play your music, and wait for the information to be downloaded.

Options

Player | Copy Music | Devices | Performance
Media Library | Plug-ins | Privacy | Security | File Types | Network

Specify privacy settings.
Click here for more information about privacy.

Enhanced Playback Experience
Retrieve media information for CDs and DVDs from the Internet
Update my music files (WMA and MP3 files) by retrieving missing media information from the Internet
Acquire licenses automatically for protected content

Enhanced Content Provider Services
Send unique Player ID to content providers
To view or change privacy settings that affect cookies, click Cookies
Cookies...

Customer Experience Improvement Program
I want to help make Microsoft software and services even better by sending Player usage data to Microsoft.

History
Save file and URL history in the Player
Clear History
To delete CD/DVD history, click Clear CD/DVD.
Clear CD/DVD

OK | Cancel | Apply | Help

Changing Media Player's Skin

You can change Media Player's appearance by viewing it in Full Mode or Skin Mode, and by changing its skin. Skins are designs that alter the appearance—but not the functionality—of Media Player. You use skins only when Media Player is in Skin Mode, but it's quick and easy to switch between the two modes whenever you want.

SEE ALSO: For information about displaying Media Player's controls as a toolbar on the Windows taskbar when Media Player is minimized, see "Displaying and Arranging the Toolbars" on page 231.

Change Its Skin

1. If Media Player isn't already running, start it from the All Programs submenu of the Start menu.
2. Click the Skin Chooser tab.
3. Click a design in the list.
4. Click Apply Skin.

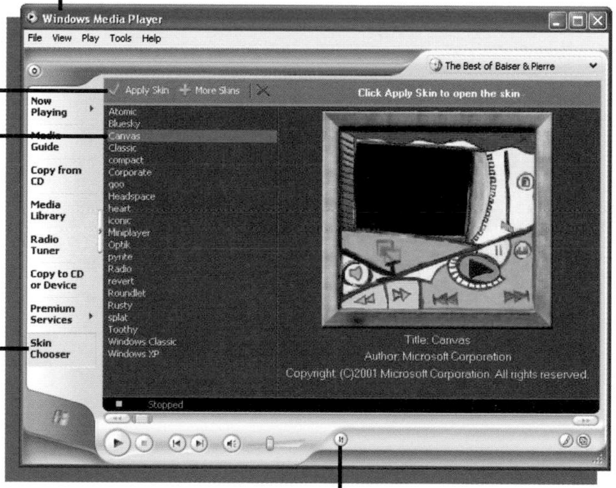

Switch To Skin Mode button.

5. Use the controls to play the media.
6. To return to the normal display, click the Return To Full Mode button. If you click the Switch To Skin Mode button while Media Player is in Full Mode, you'll be switched back to Skin Mode and the previously selected skin.

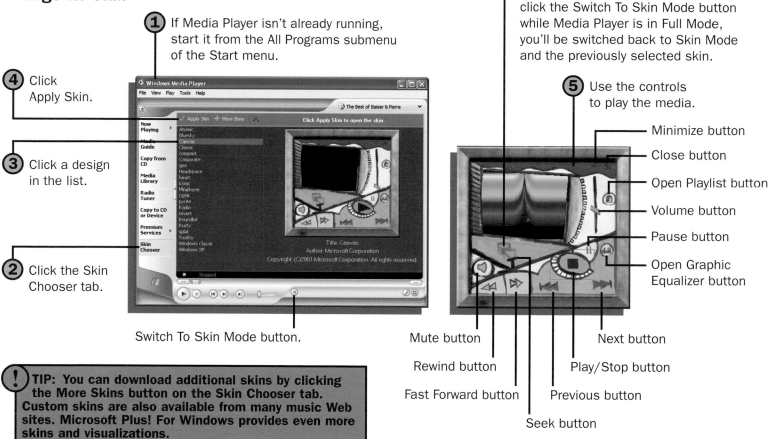

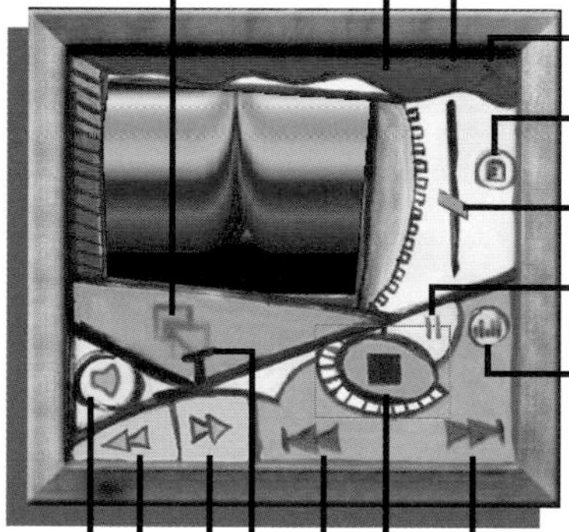

Minimize button
Close button
Open Playlist button
Volume button
Pause button
Open Graphic Equalizer button
Mute button
Rewind button
Fast Forward button
Seek button
Previous button
Play/Stop button
Next button

TIP: You can download additional skins by clicking the More Skins button on the Skin Chooser tab. Custom skins are also available from many music Web sites. Microsoft Plus! For Windows provides even more skins and visualizations.

Playing Any Media File

Media Player makes it easy to play your music or videos, and gives you several ways to do it. The basis for most organization in Media Player is the *playlist,* which is a selection of your media that you can organize any way you want. You can also access your music based on categories such as artist, album title, or genre. If you want to play a specific file or a selection of files that isn't included in your playlist, you can either start a playlist from a specific file or add files to a temporary playlist to play a series of the music you want.

TIP: To add to the Media Library every track that you play, regardless of its location, choose Options from the Tools menu, and, on the Player tab, select the check boxes for adding items that you've played. Click OK. To manually add an item, click the Add To Library button on the Media Library tab, and choose what you want to add from the menu.

Start Playing

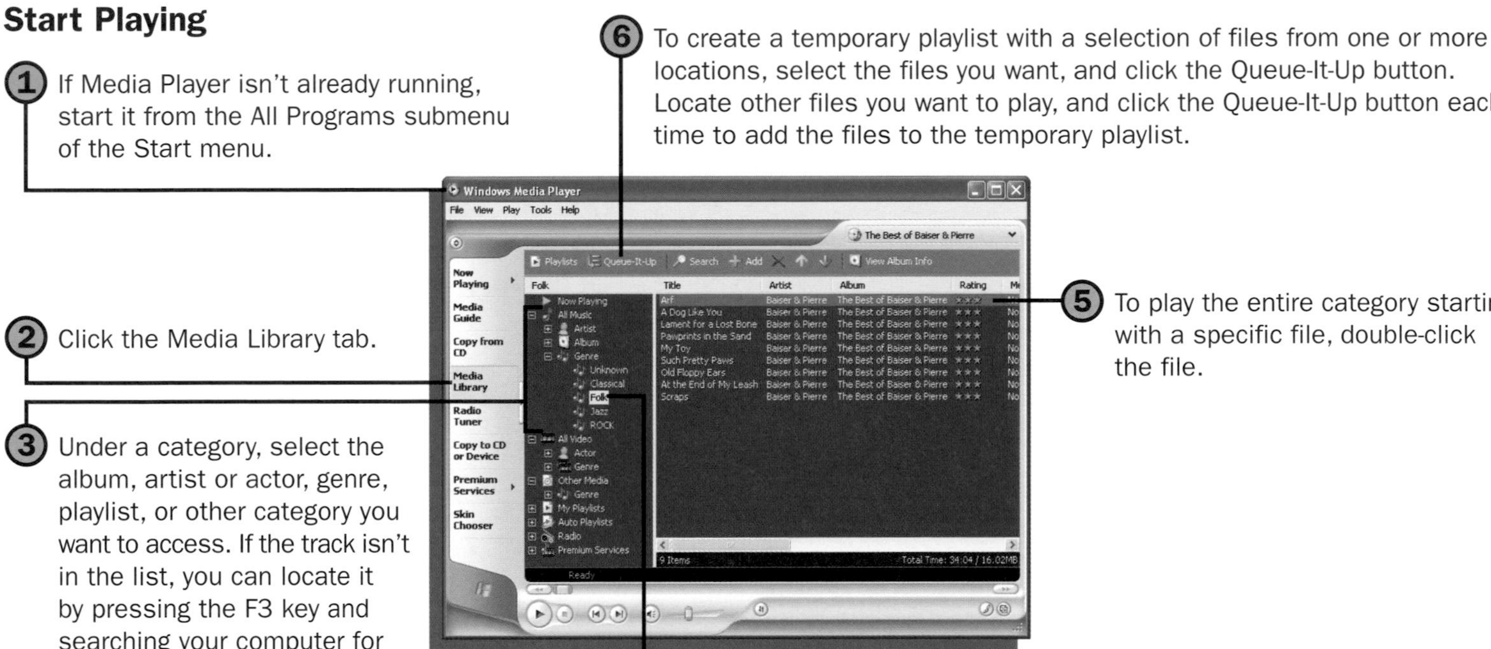

1. If Media Player isn't already running, start it from the All Programs submenu of the Start menu.
2. Click the Media Library tab.
3. Under a category, select the album, artist or actor, genre, playlist, or other category you want to access. If the track isn't in the list, you can locate it by pressing the F3 key and searching your computer for all media files.
4. To play the entire contents of the selection, double-click the category.
5. To play the entire category starting with a specific file, double-click the file.
6. To create a temporary playlist with a selection of files from one or more locations, select the files you want, and click the Queue-It-Up button. Locate other files you want to play, and click the Queue-It-Up button each time to add the files to the temporary playlist.

SEE ALSO: For information about creating a personal playlist that programs the items to be played, see "Arranging Your Media with Playlists" on pages 134–135.

Change the Play Order

1 Click the Now Playing tab if it isn't already displayed.

2 If the Playlist isn't displayed, point to Now Playing Options on the View menu, and choose Show Playlist from the submenu.

3 To jump to a specific file, double-click the file name in the playlist.

4 To change the order of the files in a playlist, click a file, and drag it to a new location.

5 To play the files in the playlist in a random order, click the Turn Shuffle On button. Click the button again to turn off the shuffle mode.

6 To select a different playlist or another category, click the down arrow at the left of the Now Playing box, and choose a category form the drop-down list.

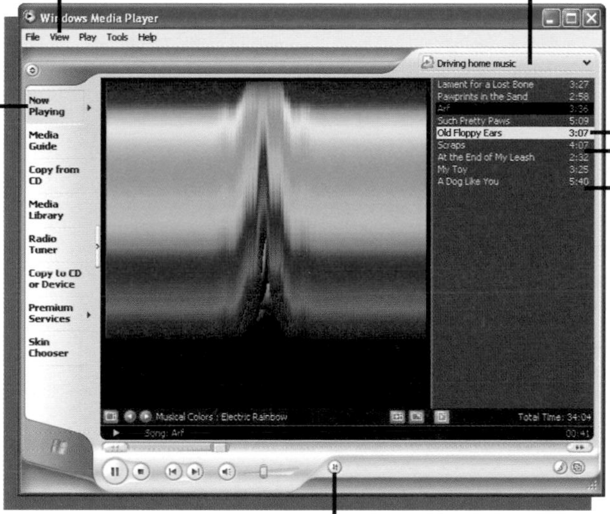

TIP: Windows Media Player can play music and video files that are stored in various formats; however, it doesn't play every format. Media Player must have the proper decoder to be able to play a specific format. To see a current list of the types of files that Media Player can play without needing an additional decoder, choose Options from the Tools menu, and, on the File Types tab of the Options dialog box, click the relevant categories to display a list of the file extensions, which indicate the types of files Media Player can play.

Arranging Your Media with Playlists

When you've amassed a large number of media files, it can be difficult to keep track of them and even more difficult to figure out how to organize them. Media Player comes to your rescue with two tools that can relieve your frustration: Playlists to help you go through your files and decide which items you want to group together; and Auto Playlists, with which Media Player assembles various playlists depending on the criteria you specify.

TRY THIS: Choose My Music from the Windows Start menu, locate a track you want to add to your playlist, right-click the track, and choose Add To Playlist from the shortcut menu. Click the playlist, and then click OK.

Create a Playlist

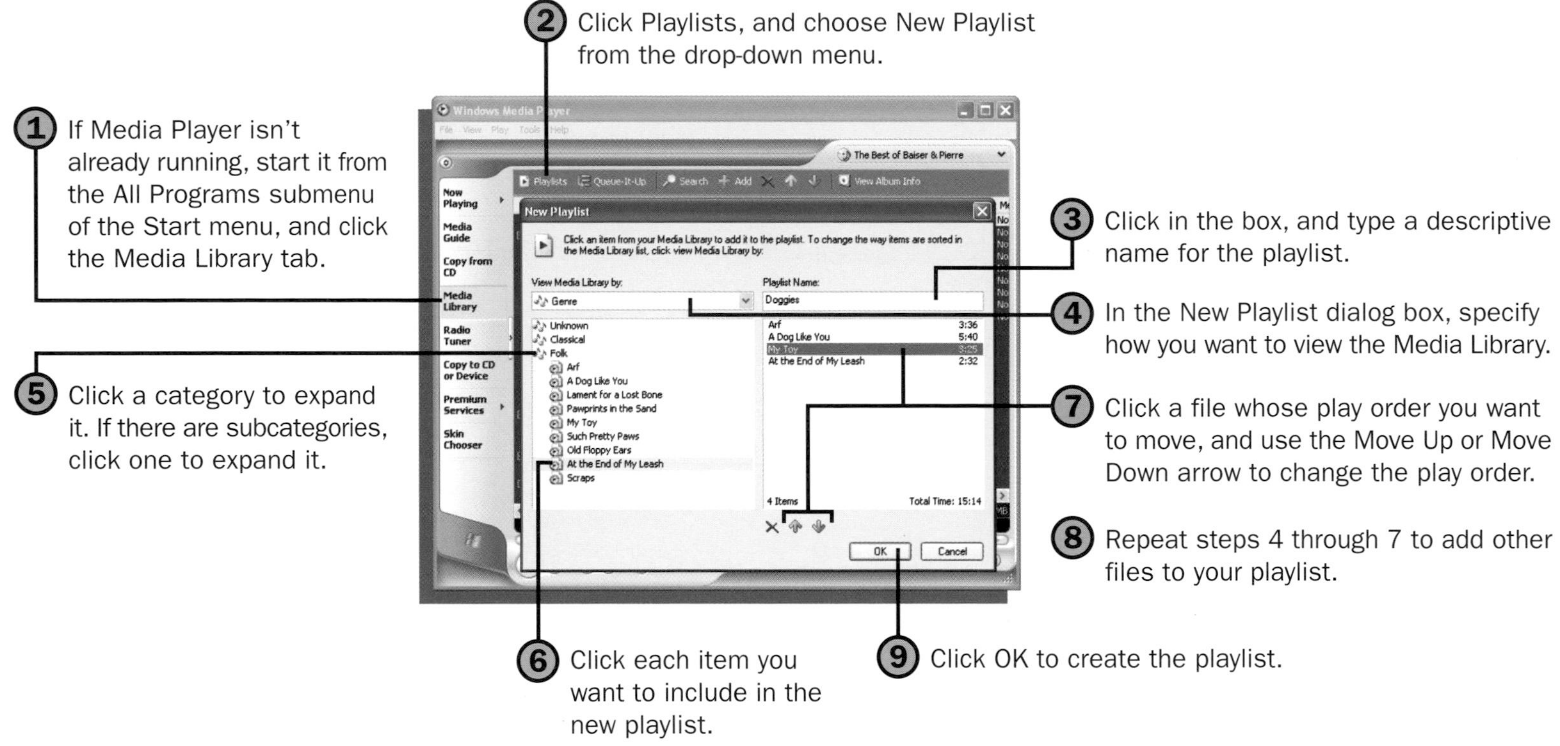

1 If Media Player isn't already running, start it from the All Programs submenu of the Start menu, and click the Media Library tab.
2 Click Playlists, and choose New Playlist from the drop-down menu.
3 Click in the box, and type a descriptive name for the playlist.
4 In the New Playlist dialog box, specify how you want to view the Media Library.
5 Click a category to expand it. If there are subcategories, click one to expand it.
6 Click each item you want to include in the new playlist.
7 Click a file whose play order you want to move, and use the Move Up or Move Down arrow to change the play order.
8 Repeat steps 4 through 7 to add other files to your playlist.
9 Click OK to create the playlist.

Create an Auto Playlist

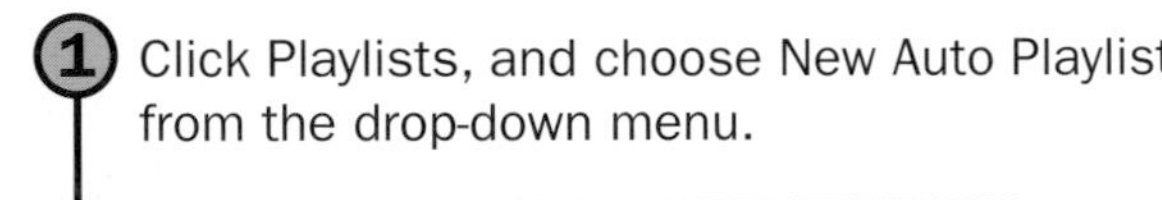

1. Click Playlists, and choose New Auto Playlist from the drop-down menu. 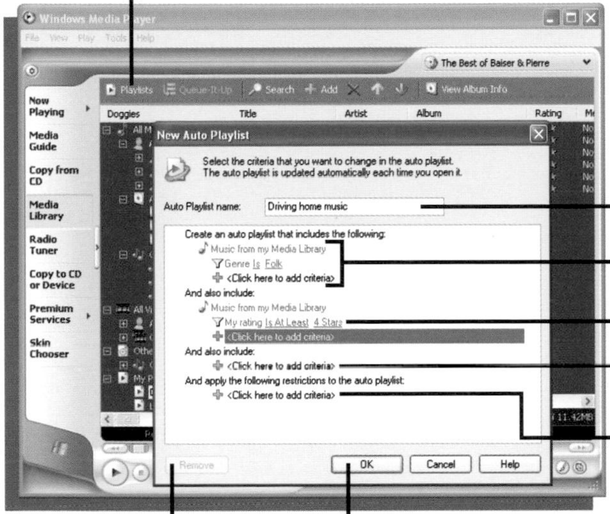
2. Type a name for the playlist.
3. Click to specify the criteria you want to use to assemble the playlist.
4. Click each underlined item to specify conditions for the criterion.
5. Click to add other criteria.
6. Click to add limitations to the criteria you've added to the list.
7. If you added an item that you've now decided you don't want to use, click the item, and then click Remove.
8. Click OK to create your list.

TIP: If you have a Microsoft Plus! pack installed on your computer, you can use Plus! Personal DJ to easily create custom playlists.

TIP: Windows Media Player also creates Auto Playlists all by itself, based on the way you listen to the music in your Media Library, on whether you have rated the music, and on various other features of the music.

TRY THIS: With the Media Library displayed, double-click the Auto Playlists category to expand the list of Auto Playlists. Click the 4 And 5 Star Rated Auto Playlist to see which music is rated so highly. Click the Fresh Tracks—Yet To Be Rated Auto Playlist to see which items you've downloaded but haven't played yet.

Copying CD Music

Instead of playing a different CD every time you want to hear a particular song or piece of music, you can copy individual tunes or entire CDs onto your computer's hard disk; then you can play the saved music in any order you like. When you copy the music, it's saved in Windows Media Format, which takes about half as much space as the original CD format and which allows you to transfer the music to another device—a portable player or a hand-held computer, for example. You can also record the saved music onto a CD if your computer is equipped with a CD recorder.

Copy the Music

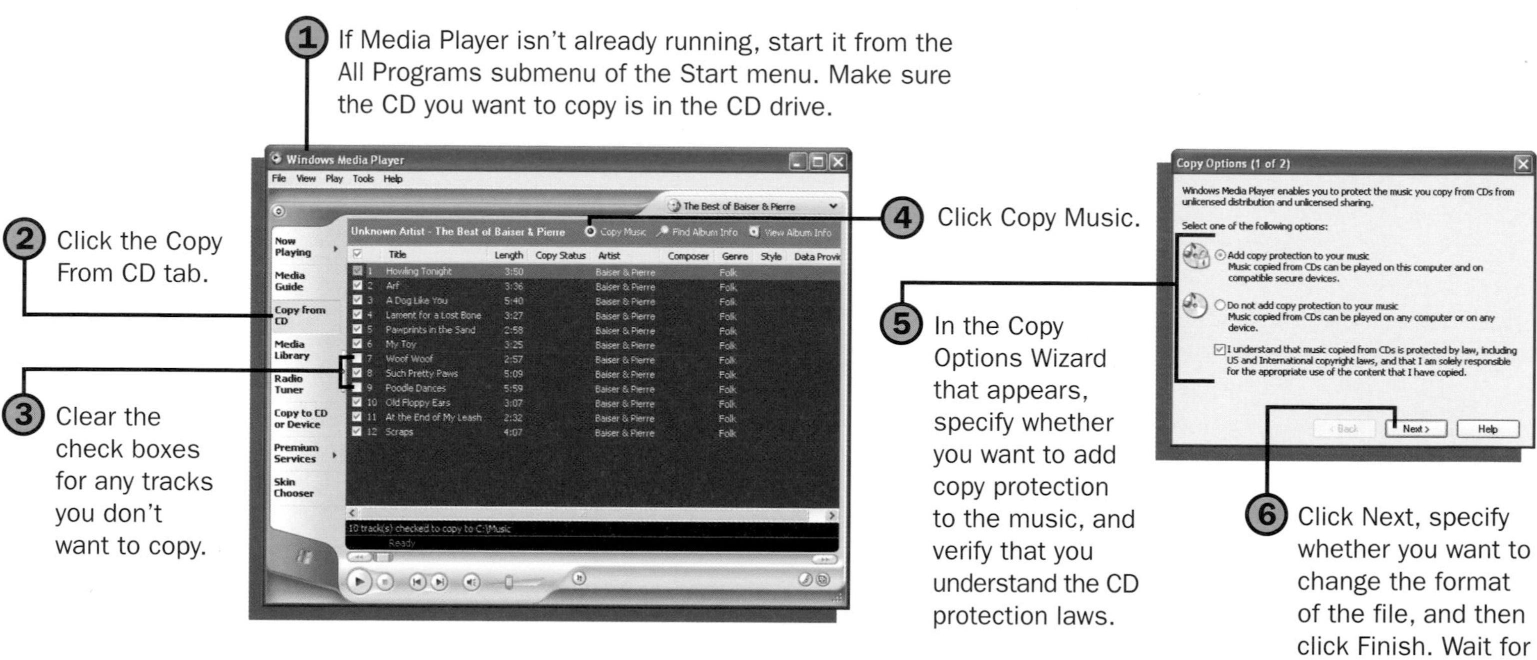

1. If Media Player isn't already running, start it from the All Programs submenu of the Start menu. Make sure the CD you want to copy is in the CD drive.
2. Click the Copy From CD tab.
3. Clear the check boxes for any tracks you don't want to copy.
4. Click Copy Music.
5. In the Copy Options Wizard that appears, specify whether you want to add copy protection to the music, and verify that you understand the CD protection laws.
6. Click Next, specify whether you want to change the format of the file, and then click Finish. Wait for the selected tracks to be copied.

TIP: If you didn't download the names of the tracks before getting ready to copy them, make sure that you're connected to the Internet, and then click the Find Album Info button to search the Internet for all the details.

SEE ALSO: For information about setting Media Player to download album information, see "Downloading Music Information" on page 130.

Create a Music CD

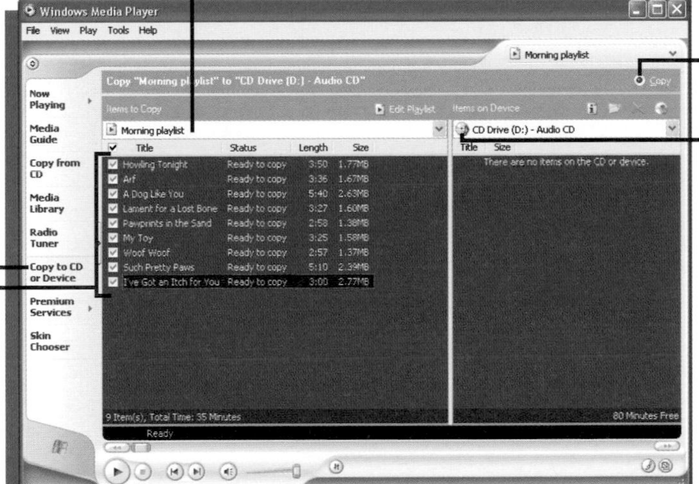

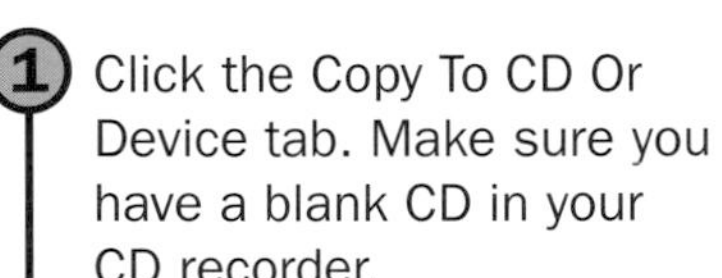

1. Click the Copy To CD Or Device tab. Make sure you have a blank CD in your CD recorder.

2. Select the music genre, album, playlist, or track that contains the music to be copied.

3. Select the check boxes for the tracks you want to copy, and clear the check boxes for the tracks you don't want to copy.

4. Select the format for the recording. If you have more than one recording device, select the device and the format.

5. Click the Copy Music button (the button changes to Cancel as soon as you start copying), and wait for the files to be converted and copied.

SEE ALSO: **For information about creating playlists so that you can record CDs from a variety of sources, see "Arranging Your Media with Playlists" on pages 134–135.**

For information about copying music to a portable device, see "Transferring Music to a Portable Device" on page 139.

TIP: **Media Player copies the files in Windows Media format, but be aware that some stereo systems and car CD players don't support this format. However, the CD should be playable on another computer that has Media Player installed. Additionally, the HIGHMAT (High Performance Media Access Technology) format can be read by many of the newer CD players. HIGHMAT is a new standard designed to enable the playing of CDs on any playback system that incorporates the HIGHMAT standard.**

Labeling Your CDs ⊛ NEW FEATURE

If you've installed either Microsoft Plus! or Microsoft Plus! Digital Media Edition on your computer, you have a program for creating great-looking CD labels, inserts, and booklets. (You'll need to buy the labels before you can print them, of course, and you can either buy special blank inserts and booklets or use standard paper and trim it to size.) You'll be amazed at the ease with which you can create artistic labels that make your recorded CDs look spectacular. And, best of all, the program takes the information from your playlist and automatically includes it on your label, insert, or booklet.

Create the Labels

1. Start the Plus! CD Label Maker program, and step through the first three parts of the wizard, specifying
   - The playlist on your computer or on an existing CD.
   - The template you want to use. Be sure to select the correct template for the type of item you want to create and for the type of labels you're using. If there's more than one label per page, specify which label you want to print.

3. If you're creating an insert or a booklet, click the appropriate tabs for designing each element.

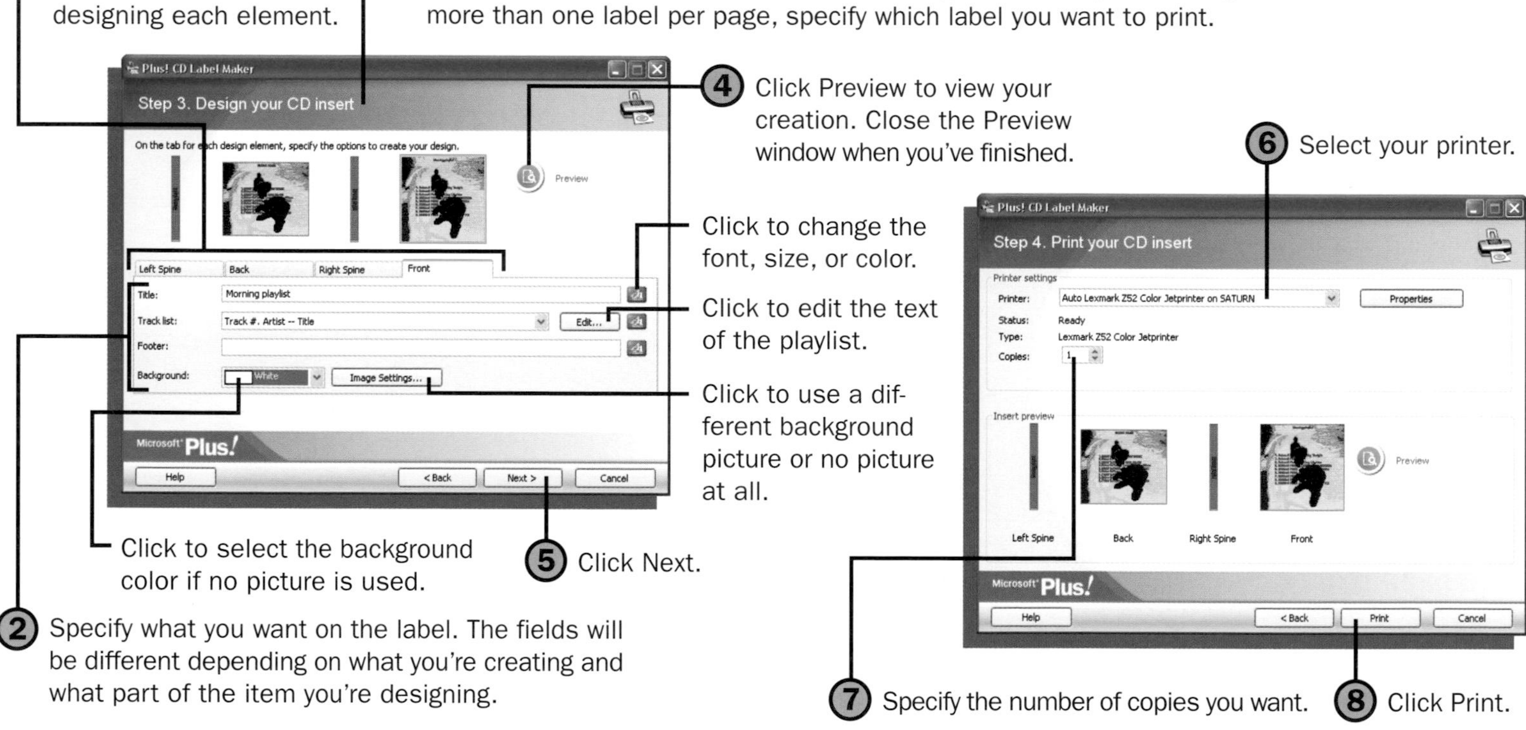

4. Click Preview to view your creation. Close the Preview window when you've finished.

Click to change the font, size, or color.

Click to edit the text of the playlist.

Click to use a different background picture or no picture at all.

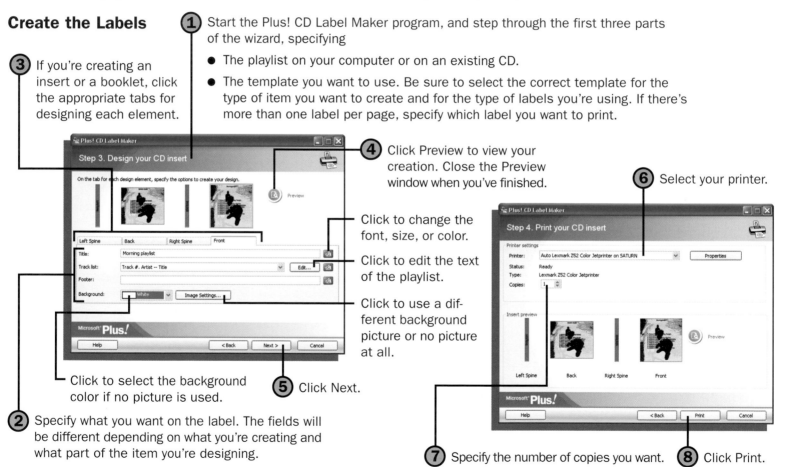

Click to select the background color if no picture is used.

5. Click Next.

2. Specify what you want on the label. The fields will be different depending on what you're creating and what part of the item you're designing.

6. Select your printer.

7. Specify the number of copies you want.

8. Click Print.

Transferring Music to a Portable Device

You don't need to lug those bulky CDs or tapes with you to listen to your favorite music when you're on the go. If you have a portable digital music player (often called an MP3 player), you can simply transfer the music you want from Windows Media Player to your handy little portable device, and you're all set!

TIP: Different players have different capabilities. Some players can use only MP3-formats; others can use both MP3 and Windows Media Format (WMA). Check the player's documentation before you download all your files.

TIP: Visit the Microsoft Plus! Digital Media Edition Web site and download the Plus! PowerToy: Plus! Portable Audio Device program. It can help you manage your files on the portable device.

Manage the Music

1. With the portable device properly installed on your computer, turned on, and attached to your computer, start Windows Media Player if it isn't already running, and click the Copy To CD Or Device tab.
2. Click the down arrow to open the Item To Copy drop-down list, and select the playlist or other source of the music you want to copy.
3. Click the down arrow in the Items On Device drop-down list, and choose your audio device.
4. Select the items you want to copy and clear the items you don't want to copy.
5. Click Copy.

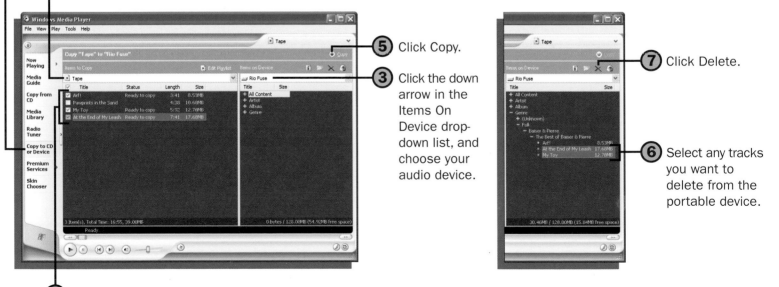

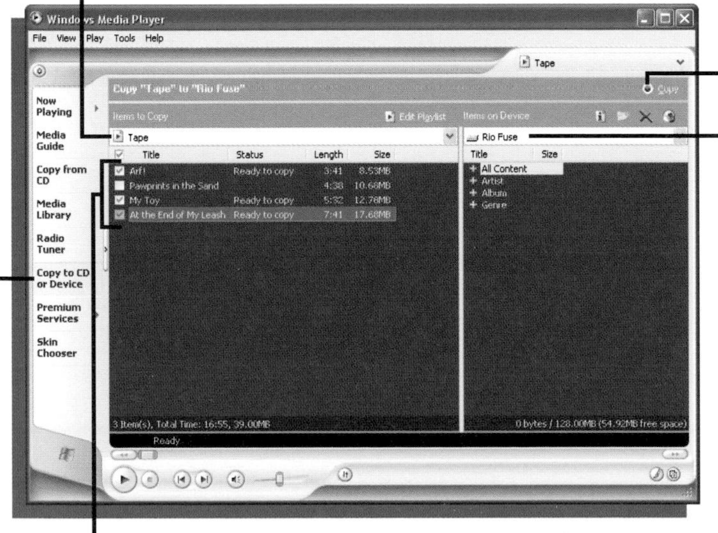

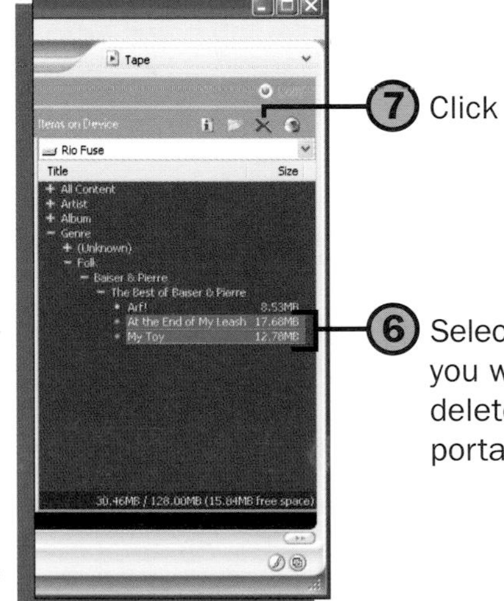

6. Select any tracks you want to delete from the portable device.
7. Click Delete.

Playing Music for a Party ⊛ NEW FEATURE

If you have Microsoft Plus! Digital Media Edition installed on your computer, you can prevent your guests from accessing or changing any files on your computer while Media Player is providing entertainment at your party. All you need to do is set up your music, turn on your security, and let the party begin. Whenever you need full access to the computer, simply quit Party Mode and log back on to your computer.

Set the Party Mode

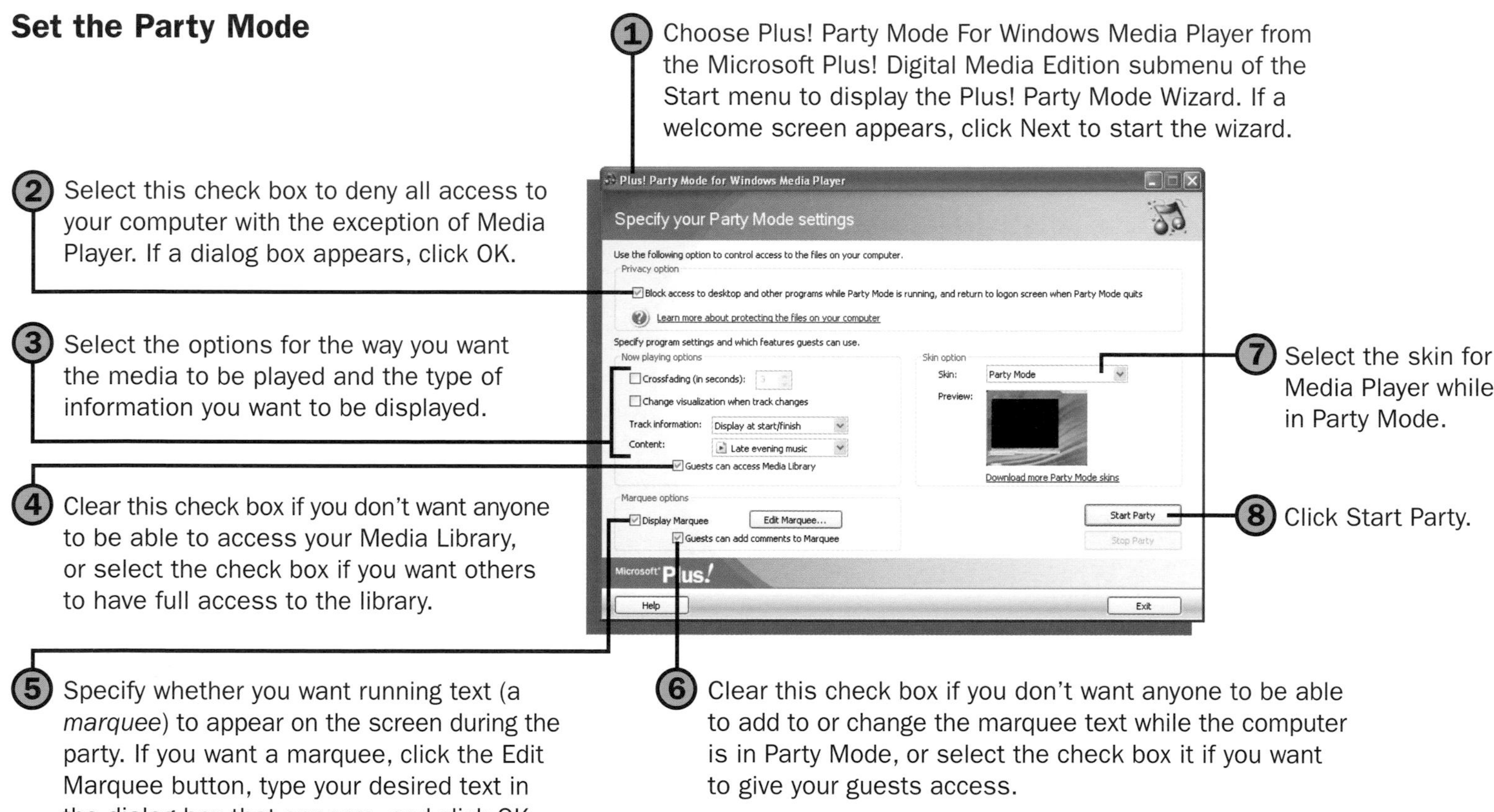

1. Choose Plus! Party Mode For Windows Media Player from the Microsoft Plus! Digital Media Edition submenu of the Start menu to display the Plus! Party Mode Wizard. If a welcome screen appears, click Next to start the wizard.
2. Select this check box to deny all access to your computer with the exception of Media Player. If a dialog box appears, click OK.
3. Select the options for the way you want the media to be played and the type of information you want to be displayed.
4. Clear this check box if you don't want anyone to be able to access your Media Library, or select the check box if you want others to have full access to the library.
5. Specify whether you want running text (a *marquee*) to appear on the screen during the party. If you want a marquee, click the Edit Marquee button, type your desired text in the dialog box that appears, and click OK.
6. Clear this check box if you don't want anyone to be able to add to or change the marquee text while the computer is in Party Mode, or select the check box it if you want to give your guests access.
7. Select the skin for Media Player while in Party Mode.
8. Click Start Party.

Party!

1. Click the Play button to play the media, or click the Pause button to temporarily stop the play.

2. Use the Visualization buttons to change the visualizations if you specified this option.

3. Click to display the playlist.

6. Click to stop Party Mode and show the Windows Log On screen. Log on to the computer, take care of whatever you have to do, and then use the Party Mode Wizard to resume the party or to end it.

5. Click to open the editor to add a comment to the marquee text or to edit the existing marquee text.

4. Click to show the marquee.

TIP: When you select a skin in Party Mode, you'll notice that the skins listed are not the same as those available in the normal Media Player mode. The Party Mode skins are designed to be displayed only in full screen to protect your computer from intrusion. Click the Download More Party Mode Skins link to get additional skins from Microsoft to enhance your party.

TRY THIS: Check the documentation that came with your computer's graphics card to see whether the card can be connected to your TV set. If so, hook it up, start Party Mode, and enjoy great visual effects for your party. Of course, you'll need to use your computer to control Media Player.

TIP: Like the regular skins, each Party Mode skin has a different appearance and places its controls in a different location. You might need to do a little exploring with each different skin to figure out how to control Media Player.

Converting Music Formats ⊕ NEW FEATURE

With either Microsoft Plus! or Microsoft Plus! Digital Media Edition installed on your computer, you can easily convert MP3 and wave (WAV) music and sound files to Windows Media Format (WMA). Why would you do this? The answer is that the WMA format is far more efficient than the other formats in storing your music, and it creates a much smaller file without compromising the quality of the sound. You can also use the Audio Converter program to change the file size of existing WMA files.

Find the Files

TIP: Although their interfaces are slightly different, the two converters work in a similar manner. The graphics on this page show the converter that comes with the Plus! Digital Media Edition.

1. Start the Microsoft Plus! Audio Converter from the Microsoft Plus! Digital Media Edition submenu of the Start menu, or start the Plus! MP3 Audio Converter from the Microsoft Plus! window.

2. Specify whether you want to convert all the files in a single folder, or discrete files that you select from different folders, and then click Next.

3. If you chose to convert all the files in a folder, specify the following, and then click Next:
   - The location of the folder containing all the files
   - The types of files to be searched for
   - Whether you want to exclude certain small files from conversion, and, if so, the minimum file size to be converted

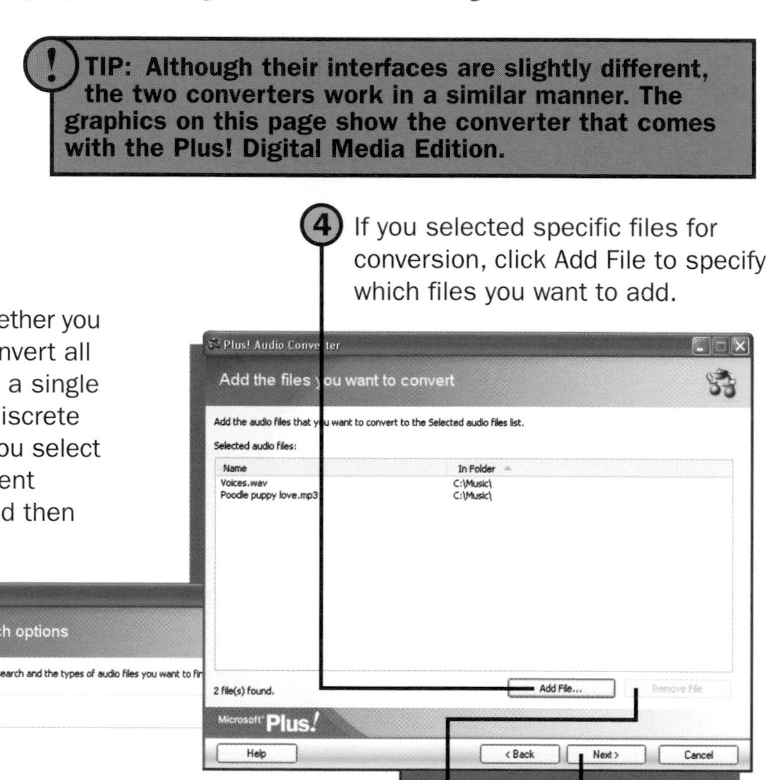

4. If you selected specific files for conversion, click Add File to specify which files you want to add.

5. If you chose to convert an entire folder, select any files you want to remove, and click Remove File.

6. Click Next.

Convert the Files

1. Select the Windows Media format to be used (available only in the Plus! Digital Media Edition version of the Plus! Audio Converter):
   - Windows Media Audio to use a constant bit rate. This might cause variations in the quality of the recording throughout the entire file.
   - Windows Media Audio (Variable Bit Rate) to allow the converter to vary the bit rate throughout the recording to gain consistent quality throughout the file.
   - Windows Media Audio Lossless for a file with no compression, which guarantees the highest quality but produces a large file.
   - MP3 to convert to MP3 format. You must have a third-party CODEC installed for this option to be available.
2. Specify the quality of the recording by specifying the bit rate or range of bit rates.
3. Select this check box if you want the volume of all your converted files to be consistent.
4. Specify where you want to store your converted files.
5. Specify what you want to do if the file has already been converted.
6. Select this check box if you want to add the converted file to the Windows Media Player Media Library.
7. Click Next.

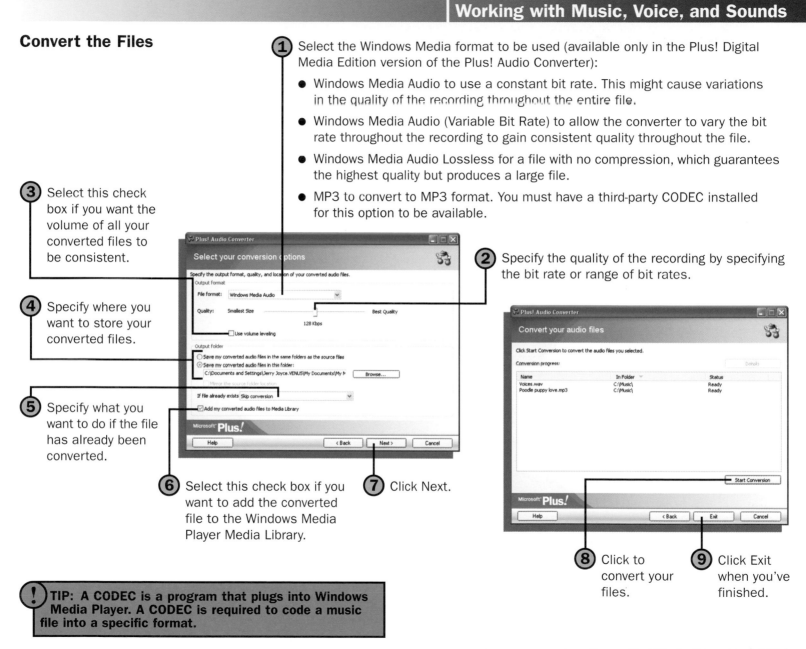

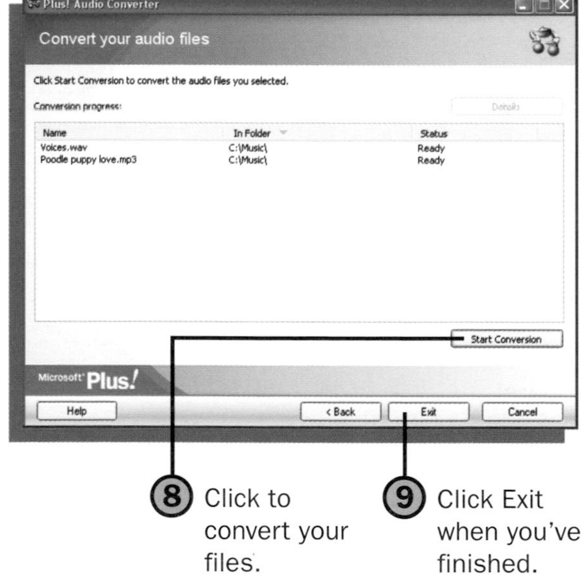

8. Click to convert your files.
9. Click Exit when you've finished.

TIP: A CODEC is a program that plugs into Windows Media Player. A CODEC is required to code a music file into a specific format.

Recording Analog Music ⊛ NEW FEATURE

Remember LPs and cassette tapes? When you use the Analog Recorder that comes with Microsoft Plus! Digital Media Edition, you can convert your old records and tapes into a digital format that you can play from your computer or other player. It might be a bit tricky to get the wiring just right for what you want to do—you'll need to use special connectors to get your analog player (tape player, amplifier, and so on) wired to the Line-In connection of your computer's sound card. Once you've got the wiring taken care of, though, recording your music is easy.

> **TIP: The connector you need depends on your analog player's output. In most cases, you'll need a cable with two RCA-type plugs at one end to connect to the analog player, and a mini-plug (3.5 mm or 1/8 inch) to connect to your sound card. Most computer stores can provide you with this cable.**

Record Your Music

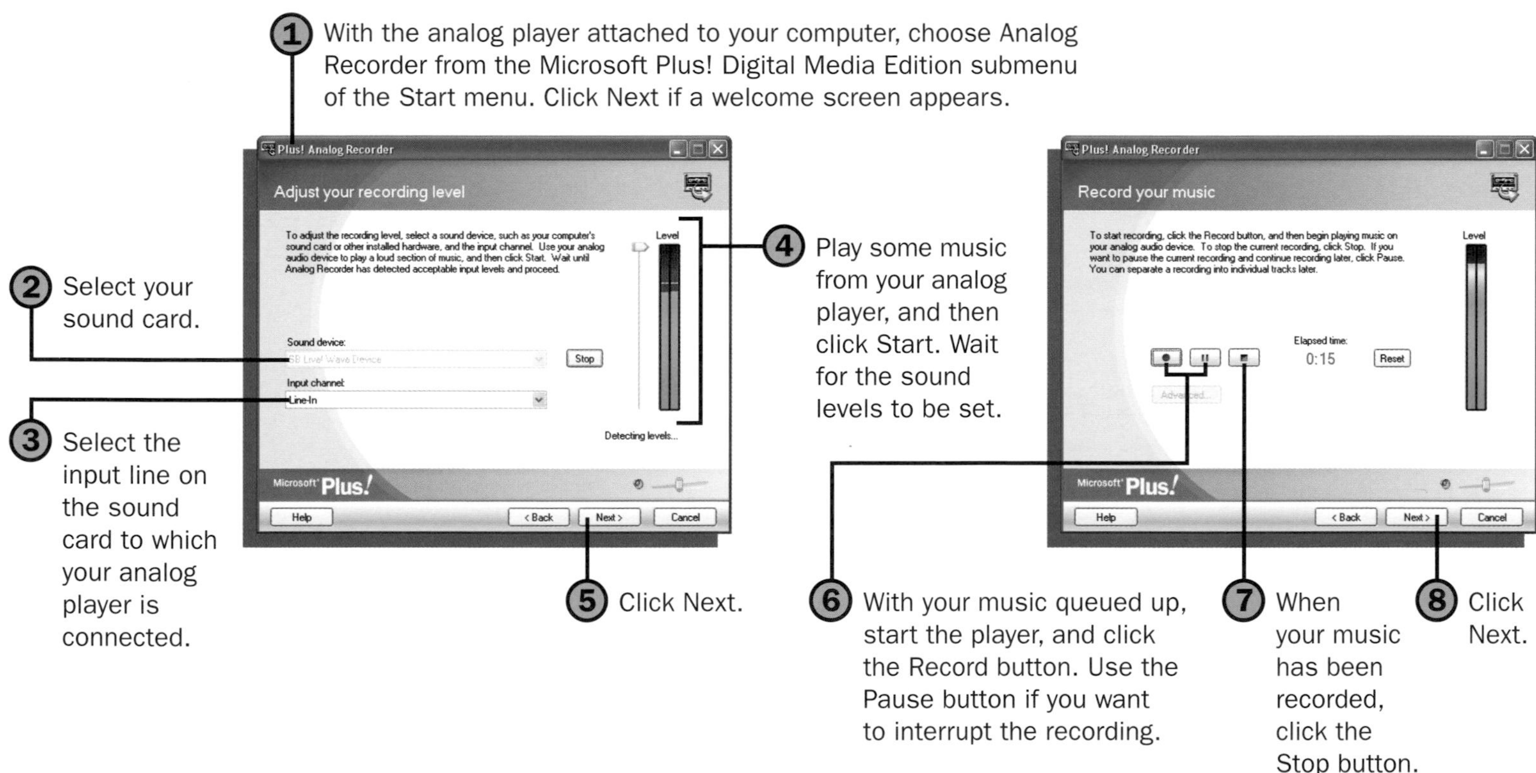

1 With the analog player attached to your computer, choose Analog Recorder from the Microsoft Plus! Digital Media Edition submenu of the Start menu. Click Next if a welcome screen appears.
2 Select your sound card.
3 Select the input line on the sound card to which your analog player is connected.
4 Play some music from your analog player, and then click Start. Wait for the sound levels to be set.
5 Click Next.
6 With your music queued up, start the player, and click the Record button. Use the Pause button if you want to interrupt the recording.
7 When your music has been recorded, click the Stop button.
8 Click Next.
Plus! Analog Recorder
Adjust your recording level
Sound device:
Input channel:
Line-In
Stop
Level
Detecting levels...
Help
< Back
Next >
Cancel
Record your music
Elapsed time:
0:15
Reset

Save the Tracks

1. Double-click a track to preview it.
2. Modify the track if necessary, as follows:
   - If one track contains two or more songs, use the slider to locate the areas between the songs, and click the Split Track button to create separate tracks.
   - If one song was split into two tracks, select the tracks, and click the Combine Tracks button.

Combine Tracks button

Split Track button

3. Select a track, and enter the track and album information. Repeat for the other tracks.

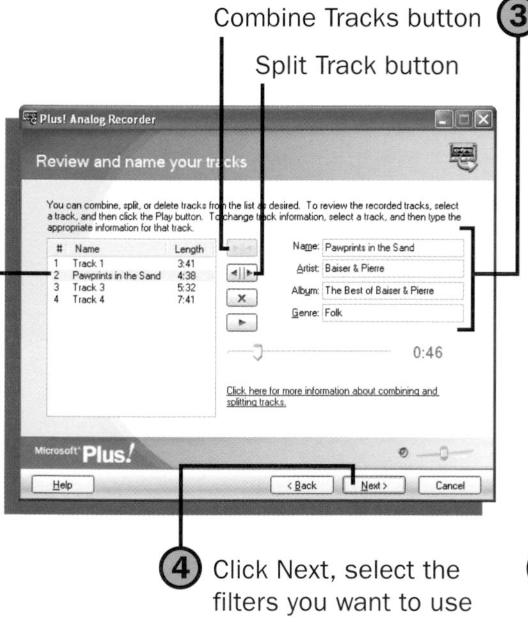

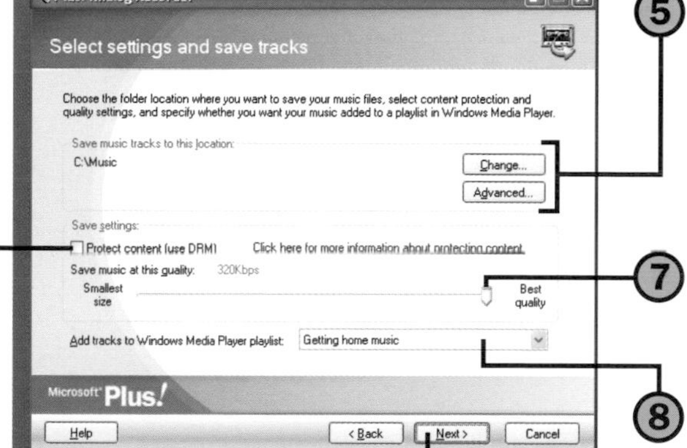

4. Click Next, select the filters you want to use to improve the quality of the recording, and click Next again.
5. Click the Change button to specify where you want to save your music files. Click the Advanced button if you want to change the way files are named and stored.
6. Select this check box to use Digital Rights Management and require a license for the music to be copied.
7. Select the quality, and thus the file size, for the recording.
8. Specify whether you want the file to be added to a Windows Media Player playlist, and, if so, which playlist.
9. Click Next, and step through the remainder of the wizard to save your files.

Talking to Media Player

With Microsoft Plus! Voice Command For Windows Media Player, you can use voice commands to control Media Player instead of using your mouse or keyboard. When it's running, Media Player will recognize specific commands that you use to control the media you play and to change Media Player's appearance.

TRY THIS: Start and set up Voice Command. Click the Voice Command icon on the taskbar, and choose Plus! Voice Command On from the menu that appears to make sure the feature is turned on. Into your microphone, say, "Media Player, view Skin Mode." Now play some music, and control it using phrases such as "Media Player, next" and "Media Player, repeat." If you've selected an alternative call sign, use it instead of saying "Media Player."

Set It Up

1. Choose Microsoft Plus! from the Start menu, and, in the Digital Media section, click the Start button under Plus! Voice Command For Windows Media Player. If this is the first time you're using Plus! Voice Command, specify whether you want Plus! Speech Command to be your only speech command tool. Then step through the Plus! Voice Command For Windows Media Player Wizard to set up your microphone, to learn how to use voice recognition, and to teach the program to recognize your speech patterns.
2. Click the Plus! Voice Command For Windows Media Player icon in the notification area of the taskbar, and choose Options from the menu that appears to display the Plus! Voice Command For Windows Media Player Options dialog box.

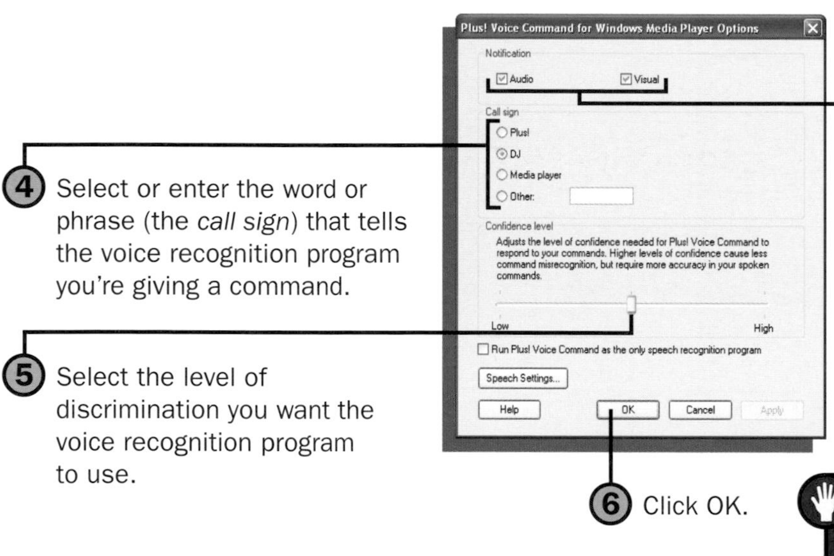

3. Select the type of feedback you want to verify that your commands are interpreted correctly.
4. Select or enter the word or phrase (the *call sign*) that tells the voice recognition program you're giving a command.
5. Select the level of discrimination you want the voice recognition program to use.
6. Click OK.
7. Use a command to control the player, remembering to preface the command with the call sign.
8. When you want Voice Command to stop running, click the Plus! Voice Command For Windows Media Player icon on the taskbar, and choose Exit from the menu that appears.

CAUTION: Plus! Voice Command was designed for an earlier version of Media Player 9, so you might find that some commands produce quirky results. Check the Microsoft Plus! Web site for updates and information.

Adding Dancers to Your Desktop ❂ NEW FEATURE

Is your computer environment too serious, too boring, too static? If you want to, you can liven it up considerably with some high-energy dancers who'll entertain you as they whirl and prance around on your screen. With Microsoft Plus! Digital Media Edition, you can choose from an assortment of dancers—human and otherwise—with or without accompanying music.

> **TIP:** If a dancer is in your way, just drag him, her, or it to another location on your screen. You can also right-click the dancer to access the same menu that you open by clicking the Plus! Dancer icon.

> **TIP:** There are many more dancers available for free download, and they come in different sizes.

Add Dancers

1. Choose Plus! Dancers from the Microsoft Plus! Digital Media Edition submenu of the Start menu.

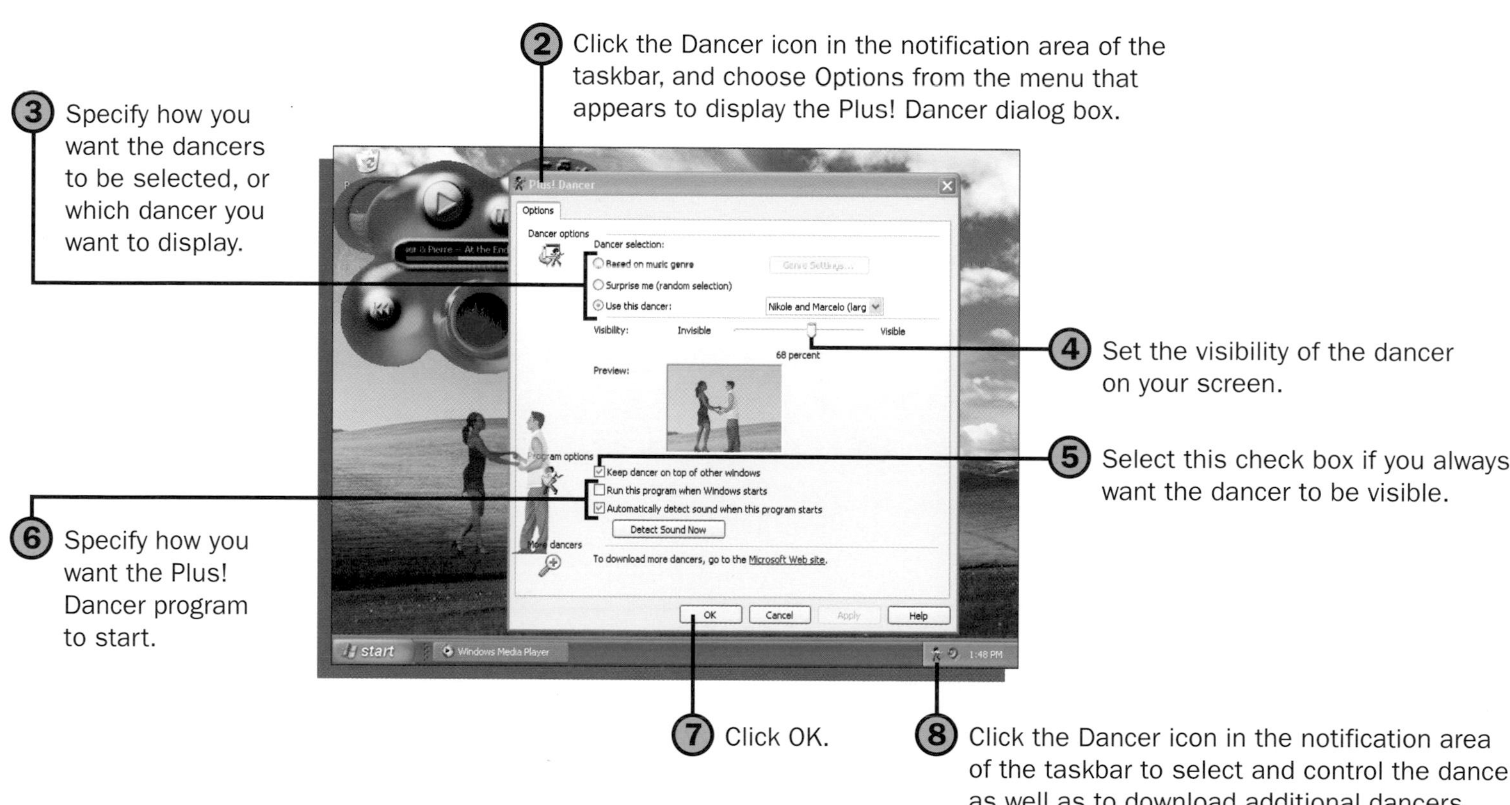

2. Click the Dancer icon in the notification area of the taskbar, and choose Options from the menu that appears to display the Plus! Dancer dialog box.
3. Specify how you want the dancers to be selected, or which dancer you want to display.
4. Set the visibility of the dancer on your screen.
5. Select this check box if you always want the dancer to be visible.
6. Specify how you want the Plus! Dancer program to start.
7. Click OK.
8. Click the Dancer icon in the notification area of the taskbar to select and control the dancer, as well as to download additional dancers.

Letting Your Computer Do the Talking

Windows XP provides a program called Narrator that actually speaks to you! Narrator can describe aloud the items that are currently displayed on your screen, and it can even read long blocks of text. Narrator has some limitations, but it can be very useful in the right circumstances. Of course, for Narrator to work, your computer must have a sound system.

TIP: Some programs, such as Microsoft Office 2003, have much greater voice capabilities than Narrator, including full voice recognition. If you have installed any such programs, you might find different settings for Narrator from those described here. To view all the settings, open the Control Panel from the Start menu; click the Sounds, Speech, And Audio Devices category; and then click the Speech icon.

Listen to Narrator

1. Choose Narrator from the Accessibilities submenu of the Start menu to display the Narrator dialog box. If you see an introductory dialog box, click OK.
2. Select this check box to have Narrator describe aloud all the elements in the active window, the items on the Desktop, and so on. 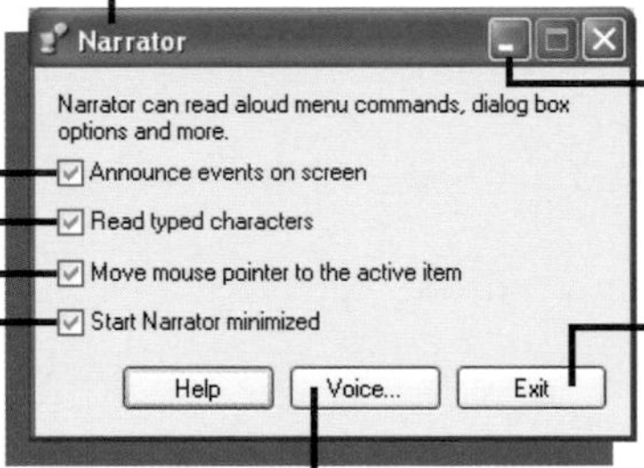
3. Select this check box to have Narrator read aloud any editable text, such as text in a WordPad document.
4. Select this check box to have the mouse pointer move automatically to the item that's active or currently selected.
5. Select this check box to have the Narrator dialog box minimized and out of the way when you start Narrator.
6. Click Voice to open the Voice Settings dialog box.
7. Adjust the reading speed, volume, and pitch of Narrator's voice. Click OK when you've finished. 
8. Click the Minimize button when you've adjusted all the settings to your satisfaction.
9. To close Narrator, click its button on the taskbar to restore it if you've minimized it, and then click Exit.

Narrator

Narrator can read aloud menu commands, dialog box options and more.

- Announce events on screen
- Read typed characters
- Move mouse pointer to the active item
- Start Narrator minimized

Help | Voice... | Exit

Voice Settings

Voice: Microsoft Sam

Speed: 5

Volume: 5

Pitch: 5

OK | Cancel

TRY THIS: Start Narrator, and select the Read Typed Characters check box. Open an existing WordPad document, preferably one that contains a lot of text. Listen as Narrator reads the text. Switch to various other programs to determine which ones Narrator can or can't read from.

Creating a Sound File

You usually use a sound file to record or play a short, simple sound—a beep or a bark, an occasional musical chord or two, or even a short message. Windows XP and many programs use sound files (called WAV files) to mark an event—starting up, for example—or to record a short message, such as an audio comment. Using Sound Recorder and a microphone or some other input device, you can record and play your own sound files, each of which can be up to 60 seconds long.

TIP: To reduce the size of a sound file, save the file, choose Properties from the File menu, and choose a format that will compress the sound file. Different formats are designed for different purposes, so take a look at the Sound Recorder Help file if you need information about the various formats.

Record Sounds

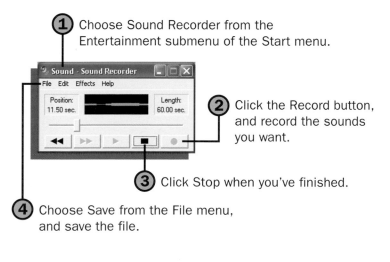

1. Choose Sound Recorder from the Entertainment submenu of the Start menu.

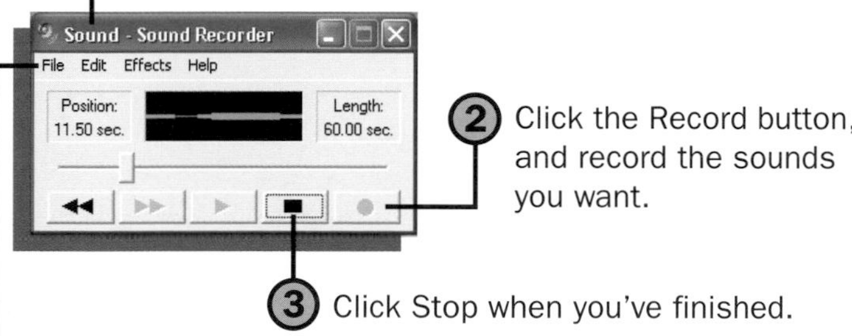

2. Click the Record button, and record the sounds you want.
3. Click Stop when you've finished.
4. Choose Save from the File menu, and save the file.

TIP: The Stop button is grayed and inactive until you start recording.

SEE ALSO: For information about setting the recording levels for different input devices, see "Set the Recording Volume" on page 151.

Add Sounds and Effects

1. Move the slider to the location in the sound file where you want to add an existing sound file.
2. From the Edit menu, choose Insert File to add a file and to record over any existing sound, or choose Mix With File to merge a file with any existing sound. Use either the Insert File or the Merge With File dialog box to locate the file you want, and click Open.

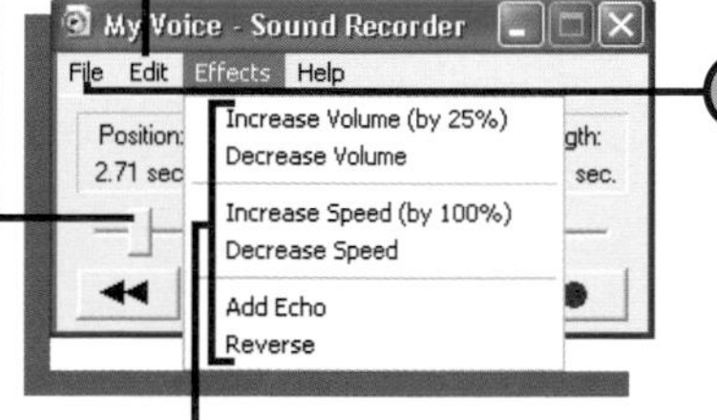

3. From the Effects menu, choose the type of effect you want to add to the entire sound file:
   - Increase Volume or Decrease Volume to change the volume of the recorded file
   - Increase Speed or Decrease Speed to speed up or slow down the recording
   - Add Echo to add an echo to the recording
   - Reverse to have the recording play backward
4. Choose Save from the File menu.

Controlling the Volume

If the sound your computer emits to signal an event—the logon or logoff sound, for example—is an earsplitting assault, relief in the form of adjusting the volume is just a click away. You can also use the volume control to keep your music and other sounds muted so that you don't disturb other people, or, when you're the only person around, you can crank up the sound level and blast away! You can also control the volume levels when you're using a microphone or any input line and can select the best settings for your speakers. Although many programs have individual controls, you can use the volume control to set all your sound levels.

TIP: If the Volume icon doesn't appear on the taskbar, choose Control Panel from the Start menu, and click the Sounds, Speech, And Audio Devices category. Click the Adjust The System Volume task, and, on the Volume tab, select the Place Volume Icon In The Taskbar check box. Click OK. If the icon still doesn't appear on the taskbar, your sound system might not work with this control. Instead, use the controls on the Volume tab of the Sounds And Audio Devices Properties dialog box.

Set the Master Volume Level

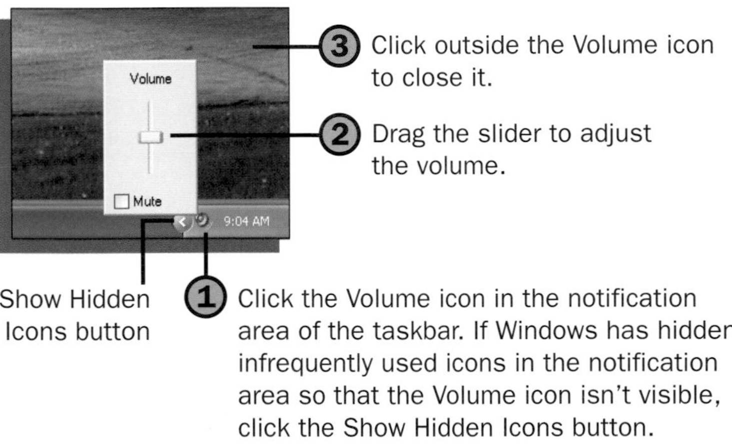

1. Click the Volume icon in the notification area of the taskbar. If Windows has hidden infrequently used icons in the notification area so that the Volume icon isn't visible, click the Show Hidden Icons button.
2. Drag the slider to adjust the volume.
3. Click outside the Volume icon to close it.

Show Hidden Icons button

TIP: If you're using a device that isn't listed in the volume control, choose Properties from the Options menu, and select the check box for the device. To see any available advanced settings, including tone settings, and using only digital sound output, choose Advanced Options from the Options menu, and then click any Advanced button that you see in the volume control.

Set the Volume for Individual Devices

1. Double-click the Volume icon on the taskbar.
2. Adjust the settings for the device or devices whose volume you want to adjust, and then use the device or devices to check the sound level.

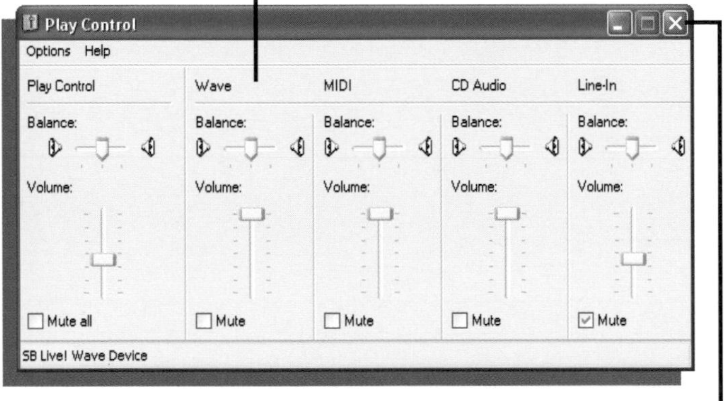

3. When the adjustments are correct, close the volume control.

Set the Recording Volume

1. Double-click the Volume icon on the taskbar.
2. Choose Properties from the Options menu to display the Properties dialog box, and click the Recording option.
3. Select the check boxes for the devices to be displayed in the recording control, and clear the check boxes for the devices you don't want displayed. Click OK.

CAUTION: Before you spend a lot of time trying to tweak your volume settings, make sure that you have the correct settings for your speakers. To see whether the speakers have been set up with the correct configuration, choose Control Panel from the Start menu, and click the Sounds, Speech, And Audio Devices category. Click the Change The Speaker Settings task. Under Speaker Settings, click Advanced, and then specify the correct speaker configuration in the list. Click OK, click the Speaker Volume button, adjust the speakers, and then click OK in the Speaker Volume dialog box and again in the Sound And Audio Devices Properties dialog box.

4. Adjust the settings for the device or devices whose recording volume you want to adjust, and then use the device or devices to check the sound level.

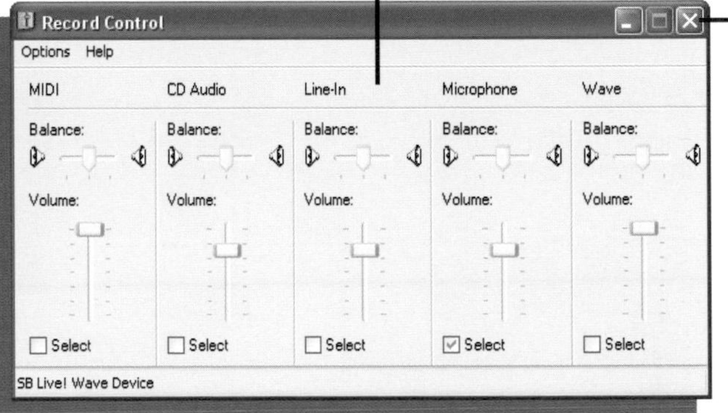

5. When the adjustments are correct, close the recording control.

TIP: The items listed in the Show The Following Volume Controls list in the Properties dialog box depend on your computer's sound system and on the equipment installed on the computer.

Associating a Sound with an Event

If you want to hear audio cues for events in Windows XP—the closing of a program or the arrival of new mail, for example—you can assign sounds to these events. Windows XP comes with a variety of predesigned sound schemes that you can use, or you can create your own customized audio cues.

TIP: Put any WAV audio files that you want to use for events into the Media folder (you'll find it in the Windows folder), and the files will appear in the Sounds list, so you won't need to use the Browse button to locate them.

Use an Existing Sound Scheme

1. Open the Control Panel, click the Sounds, Speech, And Audio Devices category, and then click the Change The Sound Scheme task to display the Sounds And Audio Devices Properties dialog box.

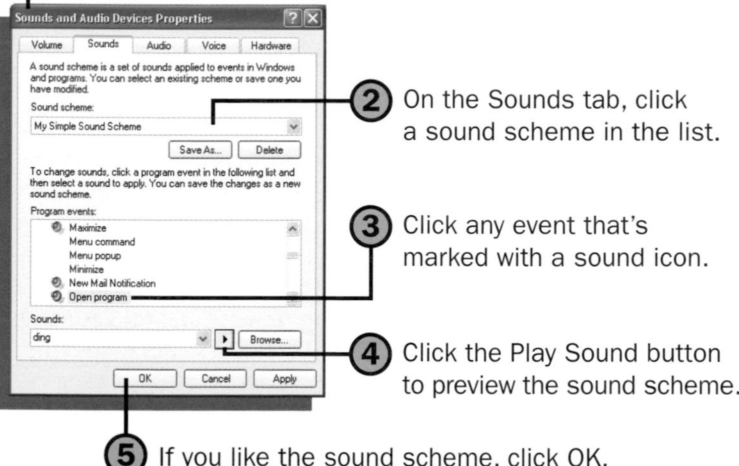

2. On the Sounds tab, click a sound scheme in the list.
3. Click any event that's marked with a sound icon.
4. Click the Play Sound button to preview the sound scheme.
5. If you like the sound scheme, click OK.

TIP: You might or might not have numerous sound schemes available, depending on what other software you've installed, whether the computer was upgraded from a previous version of Windows, or whether someone else has created sound schemes. If you have only the one default Windows scheme, why not create a sound scheme of your own?

Create a Sound Scheme

1. If the Sounds And Audio Devices Properties dialog box isn't displayed, open it from the Control Panel.
2. On the Sounds tab, click an event to which you want to assign a sound.

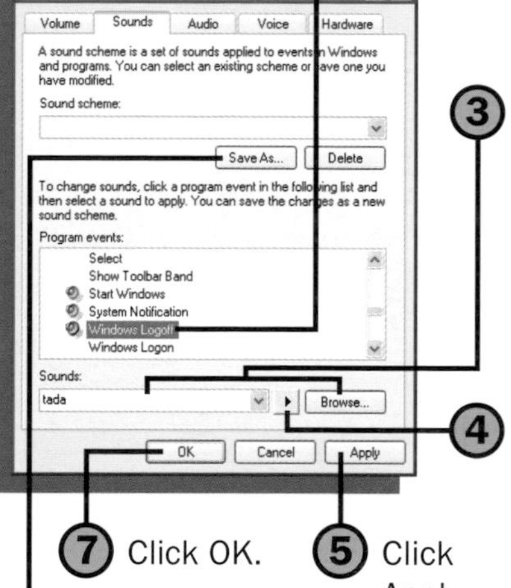

3. Click a sound in the Sounds list, or use the Browse button to find a sound in another folder. Click None in the Sounds list to remove a sound from an event.
4. Use the Play Sound button to preview the sound. Continue to select events and assign the sounds you want.
5. Click Apply.
6. Click Save As, enter a name for the sound scheme you've created, and click OK.
7. Click OK.

8 Printing and Faxing

In this section

If, as many people do, you feel a bit daunted by the printing process because of previous unpleasant experiences with uncooperative printers, the first part of this section of the book will guide you painlessly through the printing maze.

If you have more than one printer, we'll show you how to designate one printer as your *default* printer, and how to *target* another printer when you don't want to—or can't—use the default printer. We'll also show you how to check the progress of your print jobs in the print queue. We know you'll welcome a great feature in Microsoft Windows XP—a wizard that makes it really easy to print your photographs. With just a few clicks, you can choose the sizes, the number of copies, and the orientation you want for your pictures, and then you can just sit back and let Windows do the work. And if you've ever printed a Web page and been unhappily surprised by the chaotic result, you'll appreciate the ability Microsoft Internet Explorer gives you to easily print readable Web pages.

The second part of this section of the book is all about faxes and faxing. Provided you have a fax modem, you can use Fax Service to send and receive faxes using your computer rather than a separate fax machine. You can set up your computer to receive faxes automatically, or—if you have a single phone line that you use for both fax and voice—you can specify which calls you want to receive as faxes and which you want to answer yourself. And you can either set up your computer to automatically print incoming faxes, or you can help save the environment by reading your faxes on line.

Printing from a Program

In most programs, you can print a document on any printer that's installed on your computer or shared over a network. By using the Print dialog box, you can specify which printer to use and can customize the way your document is printed.

SEE ALSO: For information about setting a printer as the default printer, see "Specifying a Default Printer" on page 156.

Print a Document

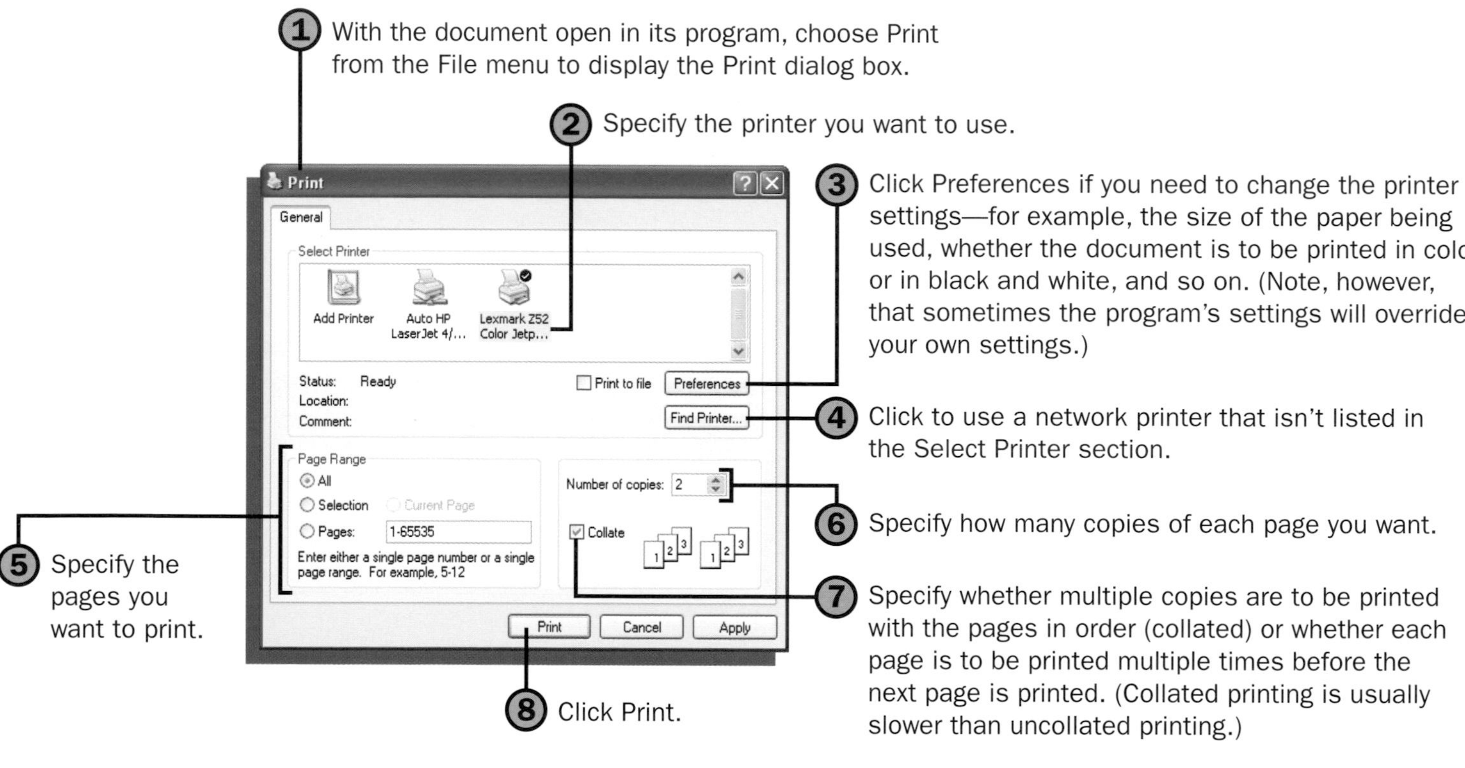

1. With the document open in its program, choose Print from the File menu to display the Print dialog box.
2. Specify the printer you want to use.
3. Click Preferences if you need to change the printer settings—for example, the size of the paper being used, whether the document is to be printed in color or in black and white, and so on. (Note, however, that sometimes the program's settings will override your own settings.)
4. Click to use a network printer that isn't listed in the Select Printer section.
5. Specify the pages you want to print.
6. Specify how many copies of each page you want.
7. Specify whether multiple copies are to be printed with the pages in order (collated) or whether each page is to be printed multiple times before the next page is printed. (Collated printing is usually slower than uncollated printing.)
8. Click Print.

TIP: The Selection option in the Page Range section of the Print dialog box tells the printer to print the text or the item that's currently selected in the document. The Current Page option tells the printer to print the page that contains the insertion point.

TIP: If the Print command on the File menu isn't followed by an ellipsis (...), the Print dialog box probably won't be displayed, and the document will be printed on the default printer using the default settings.

Printing a Document

When you want to print a document or a group of documents, you can print directly from Windows XP without having to start the program in which the document was created; that program, however, must be installed on your computer. It's a great convenience to be able to quickly send several documents to your printer and then walk away while Windows XP does all the work.

Print a Document Using the Default Printer

1. Open the folder that contains the items you want to print, and select the document or documents.

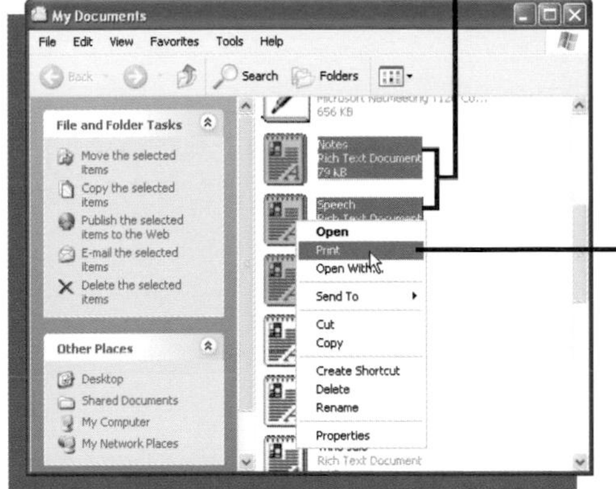

2. Right-click a selected document, and choose Print from the shortcut menu.

TIP: Some programs require the use of the system default printer. To print documents that were created in any of those programs, you'll either have to use the default printer or have Windows XP switch the default-printer designation to the printer you want to use.

SEE ALSO: For information about setting a printer as the default printer, see "Specifying a Default Printer" on page 156.

Print a Document Using a Specific Printer

1. Choose Control Panel from the Start menu, click the Printers And Other Hardware category, and then click the View Installed Printers Or Fax Printers task to open the Printers And Faxes folder.

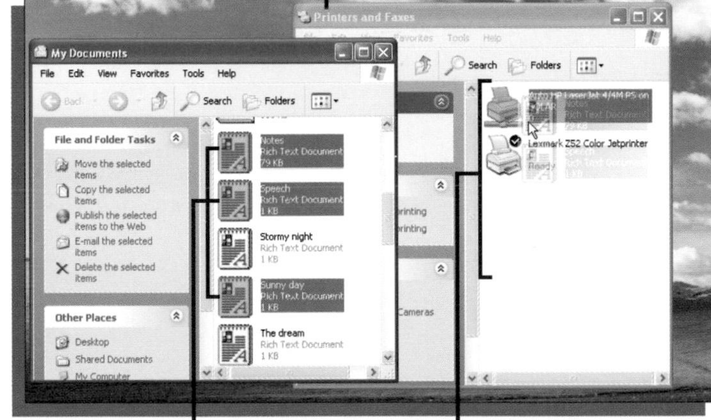

2. Select the document or documents you want to print.
3. Drag the selected document or documents into the Printers And Faxes folder and onto the printer you want to use.

Specifying a Default Printer

Some programs are set up to print only on the system default printer. Other programs are set up to print on the system default printer but allow you to *target,* or change to, a different printer. If several printers are available, you can designate any one of them as your default printer.

Change the Default

1. Choose Control Panel from the Start menu, click the Printers And Other Hardware category, and then click the View Installed Printers Or Fax Printers task to open the Printers And Faxes folder.
2. Right-click the printer you want to use as the default printer.
3. Choose Set As Default Printer from the shortcut menu.
4. Close the Printers folder when you've finished.

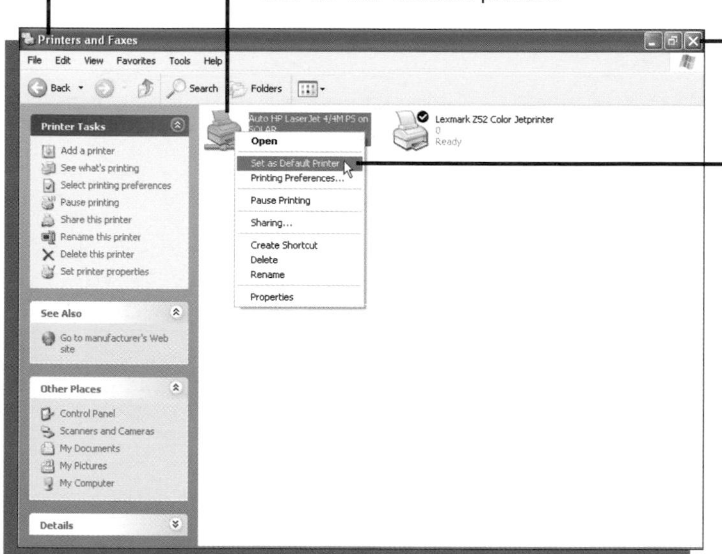

TIP: If there's a check mark next to the printer icon, the printer you've chosen has already been designated as the default printer.

SEE ALSO: For information about printing on different printers, see "Printing from a Program" on page 154 and "Printing a Document" on page 155.

For information about adding access to the Printer And Faxes folder from the Start menu, see "Customizing the Start Menu" on pages 232–233.

CAUTION: If you have both a printer and Fax Service installed on your computer, make sure that the Fax printer isn't designated as your default printer. If it is, documents that you want to print might seem to have disappeared. (It's easy to accidentally set the Fax printer as the default when you delete an existing printer before you install a new one.)

Controlling Your Printing

When you send your documents to be printed, each print job is *queued,* or lined up, in the order in which it's received by the print server. You can see the progress of your print job in the queue, and you can temporarily suspend the printing of your document or even remove it from the queue if you want.

View the Queue

1. Choose Control Panel from the Start menu, click the Printers And Other Hardware category, and then click the View Installed Printers Or Fax Printers task to open the Printers And Faxes folder.

2. Double-click the printer you're using to open the print queue for that printer.

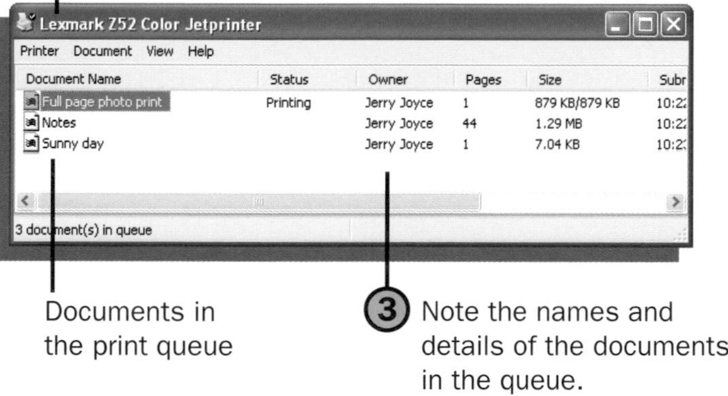

Documents in the print queue

3. Note the names and details of the documents in the queue.

TIP: To temporarily stop the printer from printing all the documents in the print queue, choose Pause Printing from the Printer menu. To cancel the printing of all the documents in the print queue, choose Cancel All Documents from the Printer menu.

TIP: Even after you've paused or canceled a print job, the printer might continue to print a page or two because those pages are already stored in the printer.

Stop the Presses

1. Right-click the name of your document.

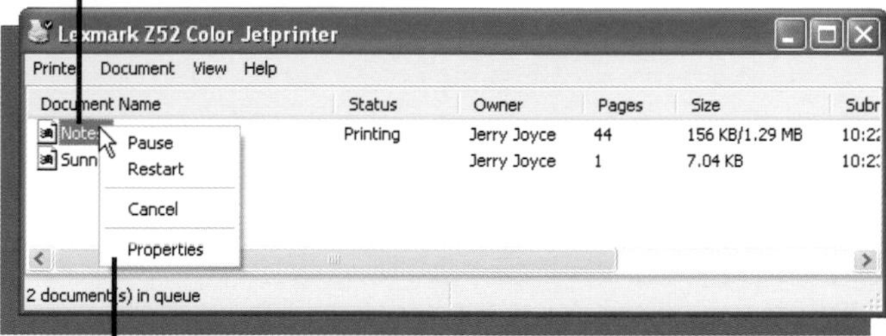

2. Choose the action you want from the shortcut menu:
   - Pause to temporarily stop your document from printing
   - Resume to resume printing after the document printing has been paused (note that Resume appears on the menu after you've chosen Pause)
   - Restart to restart printing the document from the beginning after the document printing has been paused
   - Cancel to delete the document from the print queue

Printing Your Photographs

Printing your photographs used to be quite a challenge—depending on their format and resolution, your pictures might be printed in different sizes or in different orientations on the page. Windows XP now makes your life a lot easier by providing a wizard that lets you lay out the pictures just as you want them so that you get exactly the desired results every time.

Print the Pictures

1. Select the photograph you want to print. If you want to print multiple photos, make sure they're all in the same folder. However, you don't need to select them at this point.
2. Click Print This Picture to display the Photo Printing Wizard, and then click Next to start the wizard.

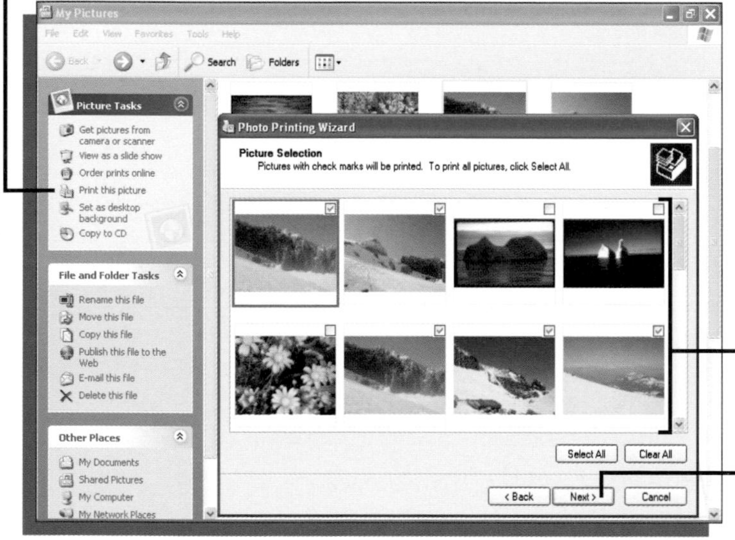

3. Select the check boxes for the photos you want to print and clear any check boxes that are already selected for the photos you don't want to print.
4. Click Next. On the Printing Options page of the wizard, specify the printer and printing preferences you want to use, and click Next again.

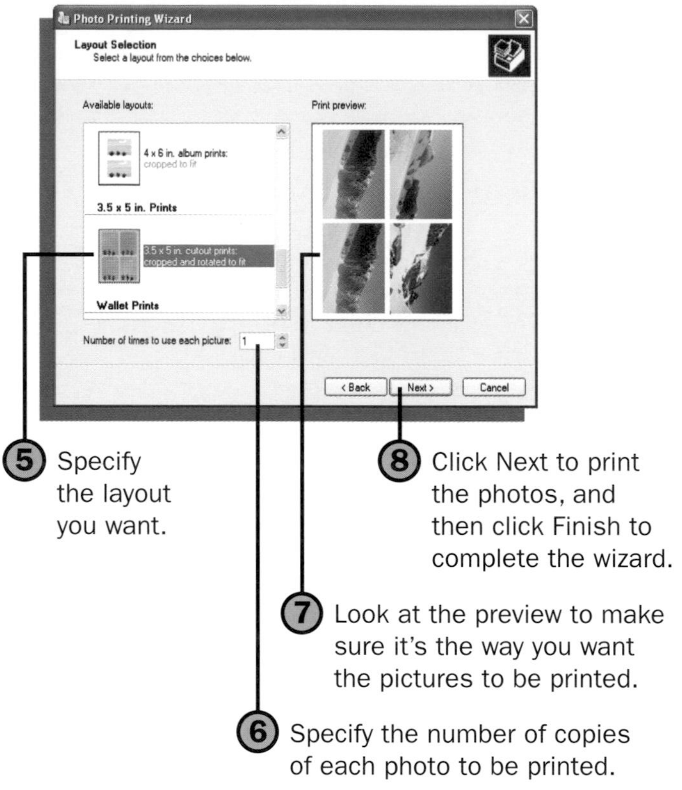

5. Specify the layout you want.
6. Specify the number of copies of each photo to be printed.
7. Look at the preview to make sure it's the way you want the pictures to be printed.
8. Click Next to print the photos, and then click Finish to complete the wizard.

SEE ALSO: For information about previewing your pictures, see "Viewing Pictures" on pages 100–101.

Printing Web Pages

If you've ever visited a Web page whose content you found so interesting or informative that you wanted to print it out for yourself or for someone else to read, the printed result might have been less than satisfactory—odd-looking pages filled with cut-off text, for example, and an indecipherable hodgepodge of disconnected graphics, tables, frames, and text. However, using Internet Explorer, you can now convert Web pages into a printable form. All you need to do is specify how you want the pages to be set up, take a quick look at the layout to make sure it includes the items you want to print, and then print the pages.

Check the Layout

1. With the Web page you want to print displayed in Internet Explorer, choose Print Preview from the File menu. Examine the page to make sure the layout is suitable for printing and that the information in the header and footer is what you want displayed.
2. To print more than one page, click the Next Page button to see the additional page or pages.

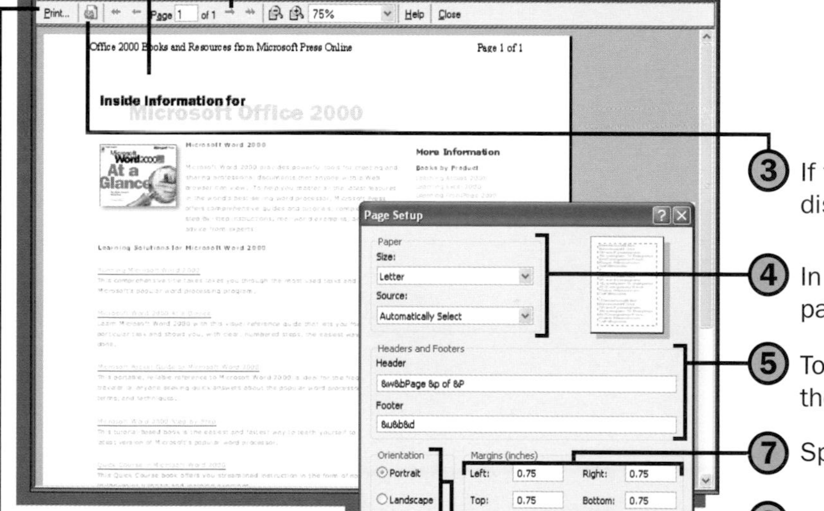

3. If there's any truncated text, or if you want to change what's displayed in the header or footer, click the Page Setup button.
4. In the Page Setup dialog box that appears, specify the page size.
5. To change the contents of the header or footer, use the codes in the table on this page.
6. Specify whether you want the page to be printed in portrait (longer than wide) or landscape (wider than long) orientation.
7. Specify different margins if necessary.
8. Click OK.
9. Examine the layout based on your changes, and then click Print to print the Web page.

Header and Footer Codes

Code	Result
&b *any text*	Right-aligns text.
&b *any text* &b	Centers text.
&d or &D	Inserts short date or long date.
&p	Inserts page number.
&P	Inserts total number of pages.
&t or &T	Inserts time in 12-hour or 24-hour format.
&u	Inserts Web page address.
&w	Inserts window title.

Sending a Fax

With Fax Service installed, you can send a fax directly from your computer, whether it's a single-page fax with notes or a fax with several pages. To send only a few quick notes, simply enter them on a cover page. If you're sending a multiple-page document, you can decide whether or not to include a cover page.

SEE ALSO: For information about reviewing faxes you've sent and faxes that you've scheduled for later transmission, see "Reviewing a Fax You've Received" on page 163.

For information about setting up your fax, see "Setting Up for Faxing" on page 218.

Fax a Single-Page Note

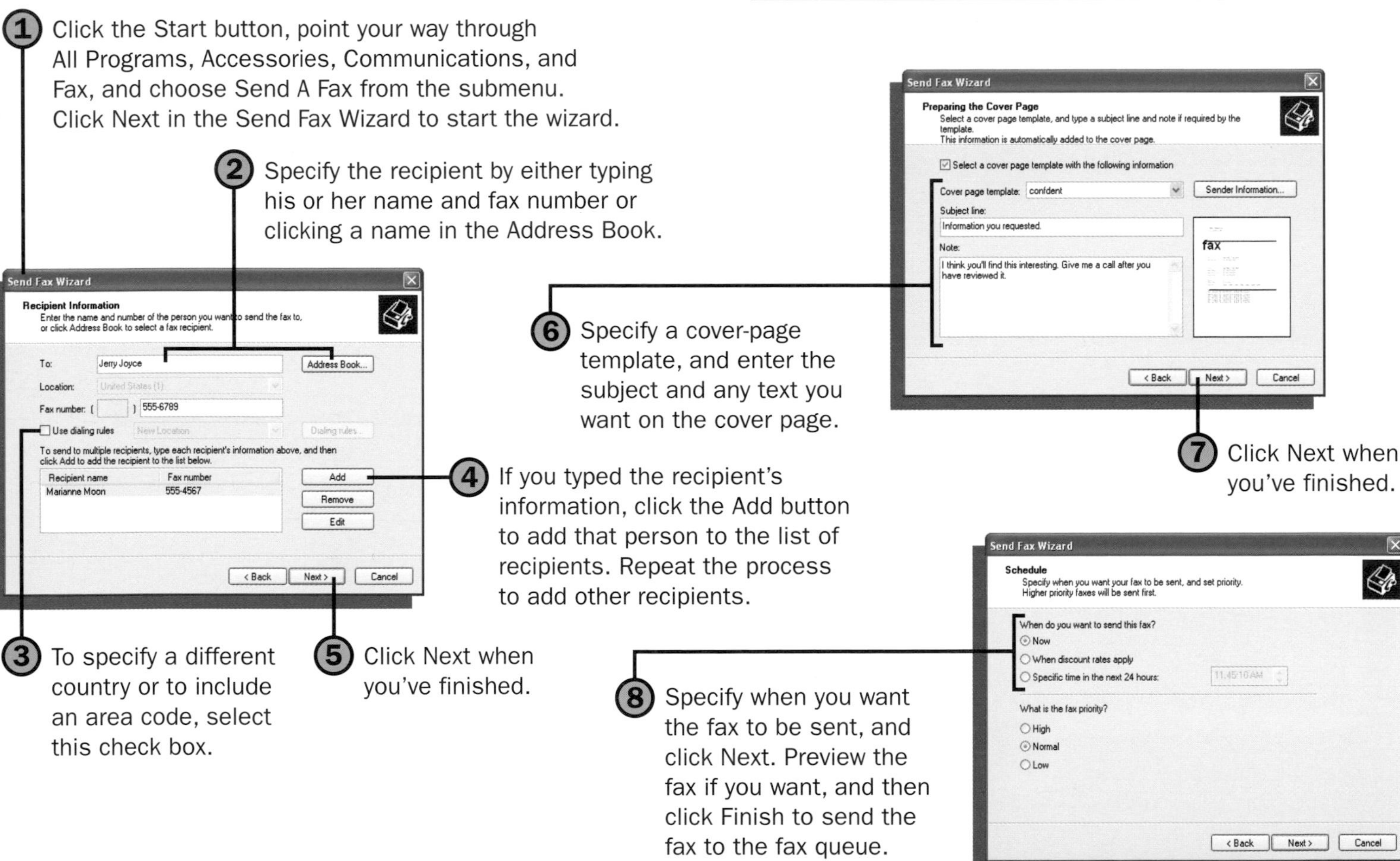

1. Click the Start button, point your way through All Programs, Accessories, Communications, and Fax, and choose Send A Fax from the submenu. Click Next in the Send Fax Wizard to start the wizard.
2. Specify the recipient by either typing his or her name and fax number or clicking a name in the Address Book.
3. To specify a different country or to include an area code, select this check box.
4. If you typed the recipient's information, click the Add button to add that person to the list of recipients. Repeat the process to add other recipients.
5. Click Next when you've finished.
6. Specify a cover-page template, and enter the subject and any text you want on the cover page.
7. Click Next when you've finished.
8. Specify when you want the fax to be sent, and click Next. Preview the fax if you want, and then click Finish to send the fax to the fax queue.

Fax a Document

1. Open or create the document in its program.
2. Choose Print from the File menu to display the Print dialog box.

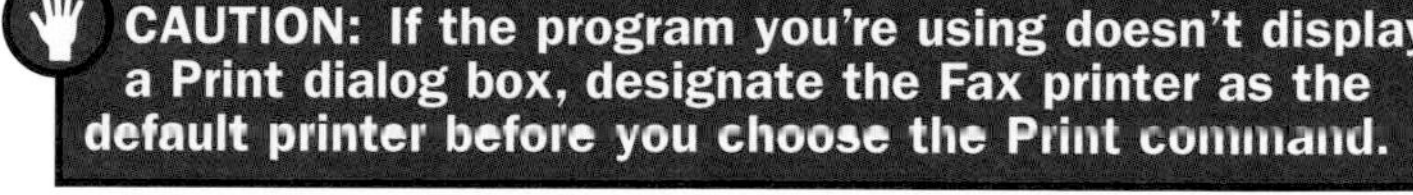

CAUTION: If the program you're using doesn't display a Print dialog box, designate the Fax printer as the default printer before you choose the Print command.

SEE ALSO: For information about setting a default printer, see "Specifying a Default Printer" on page 156.

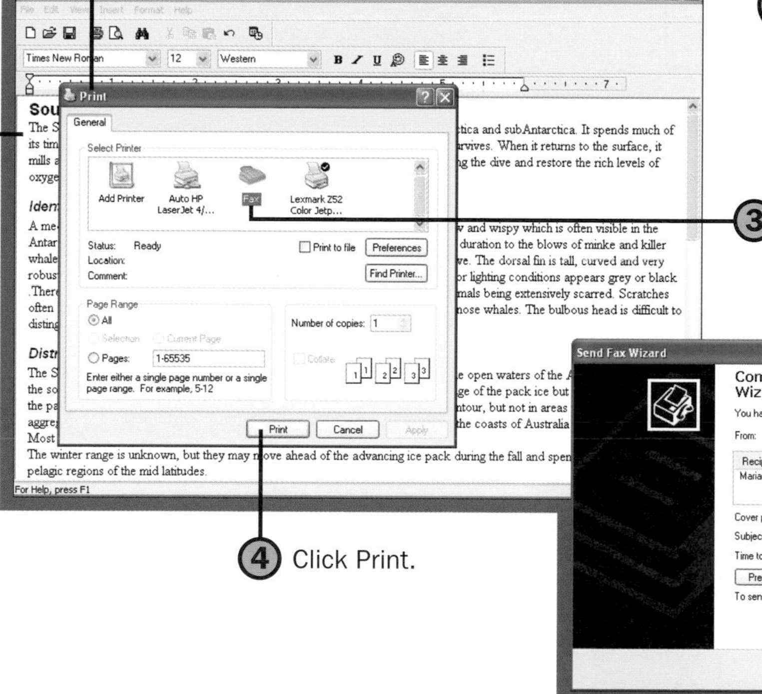

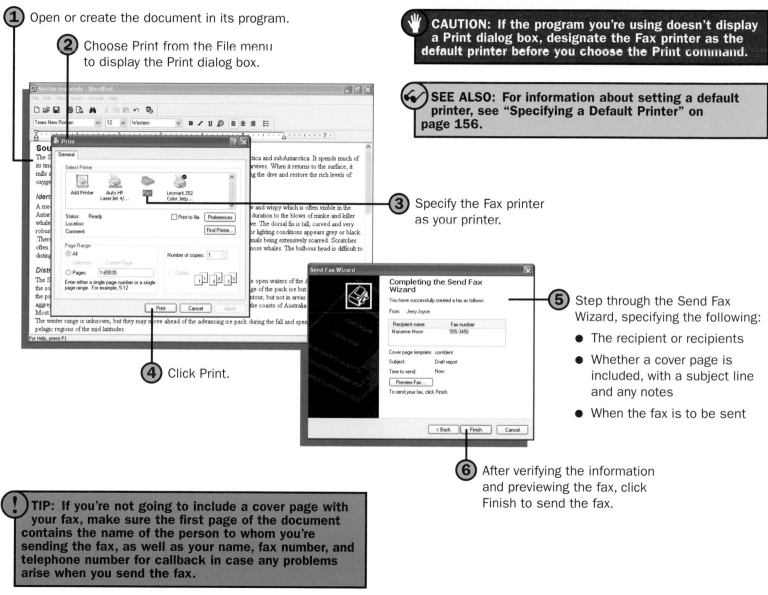

3. Specify the Fax printer as your printer.
4. Click Print.
5. Step through the Send Fax Wizard, specifying the following:
   - The recipient or recipients
   - Whether a cover page is included, with a subject line and any notes
   - When the fax is to be sent
6. After verifying the information and previewing the fax, click Finish to send the fax.

TIP: If you're not going to include a cover page with your fax, make sure the first page of the document contains the name of the person to whom you're sending the fax, as well as your name, fax number, and telephone number for callback in case any problems arise when you send the fax.

Receiving a Fax

If you have a phone line dedicated to your computer and you set it to automatically receive faxes, all you have to do is review your received faxes. However, if you use your phone line for both voice and fax calls, you'll probably have your computer set up to receive faxes only when you tell it to do so.

SEE ALSO: **For information about setting your computer to receive faxes either manually or automatically, see "Setting Up for Faxing" on page 218.**

Receive a Fax Manually

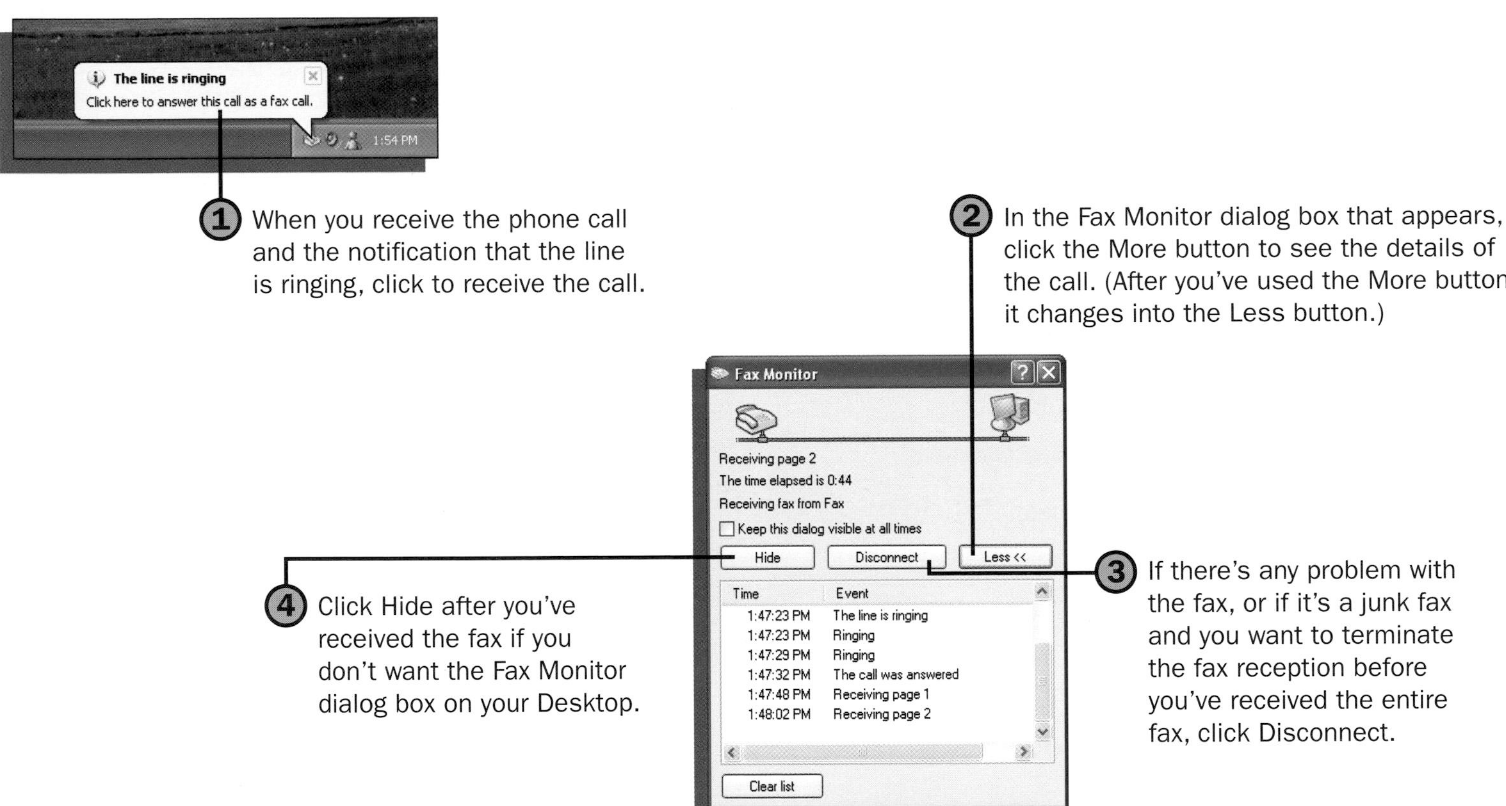

1. When you receive the phone call and the notification that the line is ringing, click to receive the call.
2. In the Fax Monitor dialog box that appears, click the More button to see the details of the call. (After you've used the More button, it changes into the Less button.)
3. If there's any problem with the fax, or if it's a junk fax and you want to terminate the fax reception before you've received the entire fax, click Disconnect.
4. Click Hide after you've received the fax if you don't want the Fax Monitor dialog box on your Desktop.

Reviewing a Fax You've Received

After you receive a fax, you might want to review it, print it, save it, or send it to someone else. To review a fax, you use the Fax Console. You can also use the Fax Console to review faxes that you've sent, faxes that have yet to be sent, or a fax that you're currently receiving.

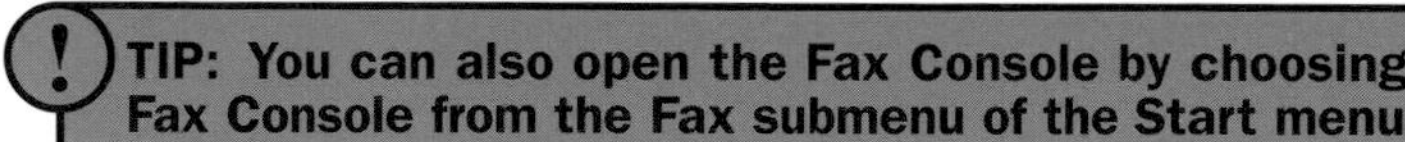

TIP: You can also open the Fax Console by choosing Fax Console from the Fax submenu of the Start menu.

Read a Fax

1. Click the New Fax Received icon.
2. Click Inbox if it isn't already selected.
3. Review the details of the received faxes.
4. Click a fax to select it, and then click the appropriate button:
   - View to see the fax on the screen
   - Print to send the fax to your printer
   - Save As to save the fax to a folder as a TIF-format fax
   - Mail To to include the fax as an attachment in an e-mail message

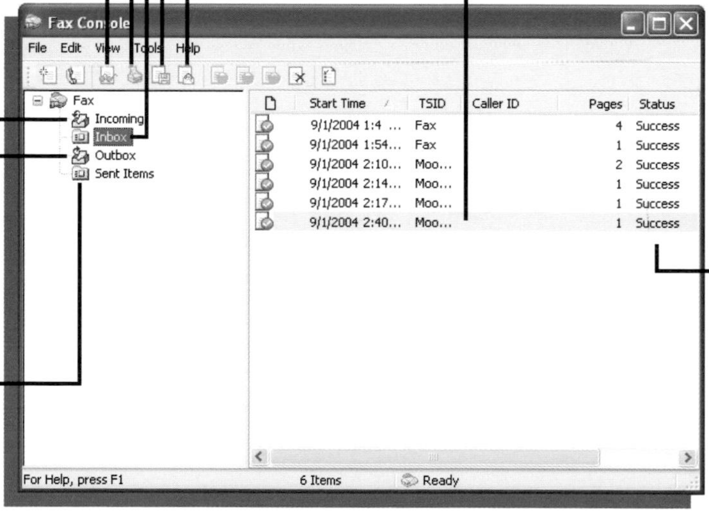

Print button

Save As button

View button

Mail To button

5. Click Incoming to review the status of a fax that's currently being received.
6. Click Outbox to review any faxes scheduled to be sent at a later time. To suspend or cancel the transmission of a fax, click the fax, and then click either the Pause button or the Delete button.
7. Click Sent Items to see the faxes you've sent. Click a fax in the list, and use the appropriate button to view, print, save, or e-mail the fax.

Viewing and Annotating a Fax

Save a tree—read your faxes on line! To do so, use the Windows Picture And Fax Viewer to read the fax, and even to annotate it with your comments, doodles, or whatever else you want to add.

TIP: If you have a mouse with a wheel, rotating the wheel when you're using the Windows Picture And Fax Viewer changes the magnification of the image instead of scrolling the page as it does in many other programs.

View a Fax

1. If the Fax Console isn't already open, display it by choosing Fax Console from the Fax submenu of the Start menu.
2. Double-click the fax to be viewed.
3. Use the buttons in the Windows Picture And Fax Viewer to view the fax.

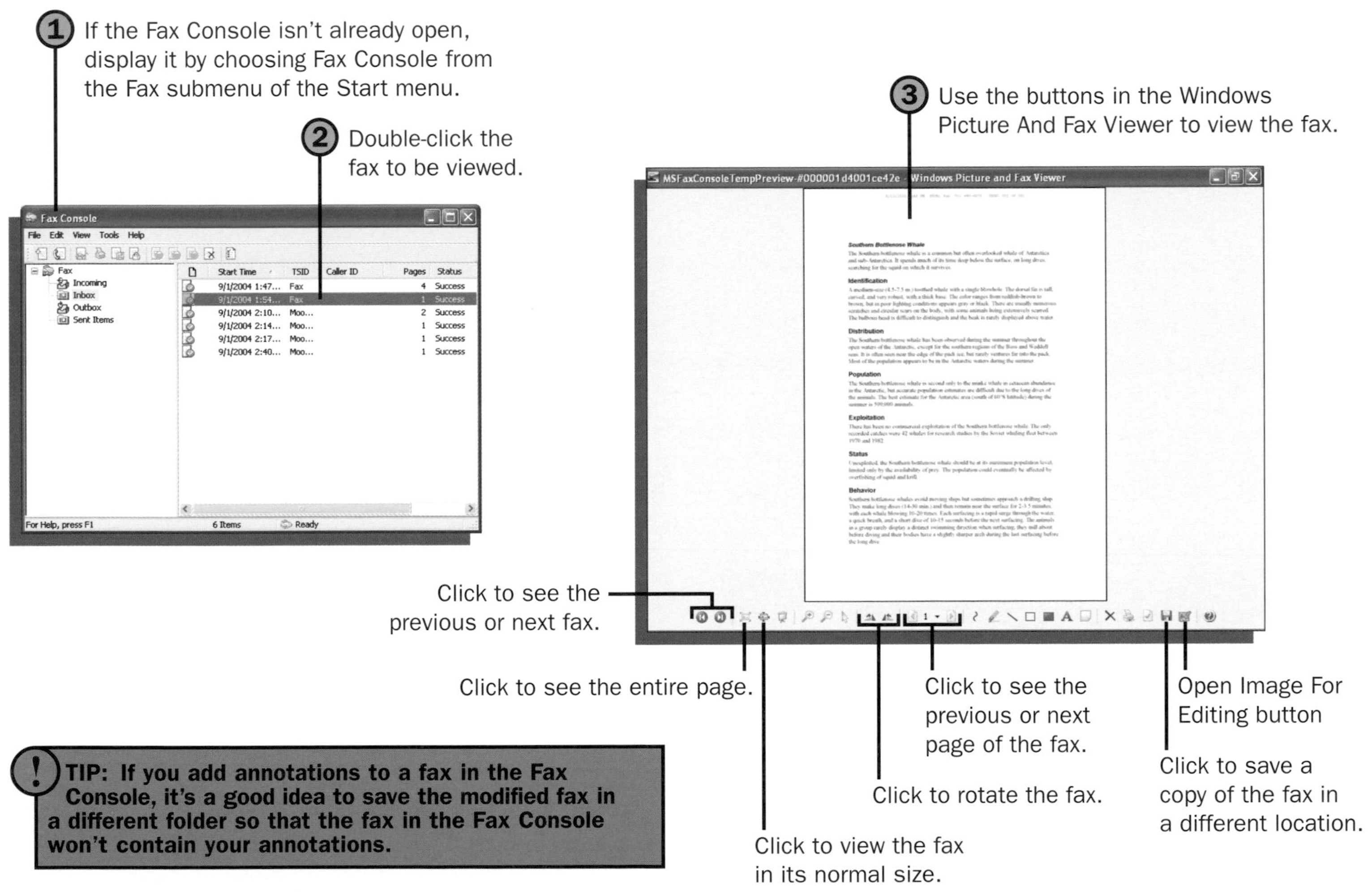

Click to see the previous or next fax.
Click to see the entire page.
Click to view the fax in its normal size.
Click to rotate the fax.
Click to see the previous or next page of the fax.
Open Image For Editing button
Click to save a copy of the fax in a different location.

TIP: If you add annotations to a fax in the Fax Console, it's a good idea to save the modified fax in a different folder so that the fax in the Fax Console won't contain your annotations.

Annotate the Fax

1. Use the appropriate annotation tool to mark up the fax:
   - Freehand to draw a line in any shape
   - Highlight to create a rectangular highlight
   - Straight Line to draw a straight line
   - Frame to draw a rectangular border around an area
   - Solid Rectangle to draw a filled rectangle that obscures anything under it
   - Attached Note to create a text box in which to enter a comment

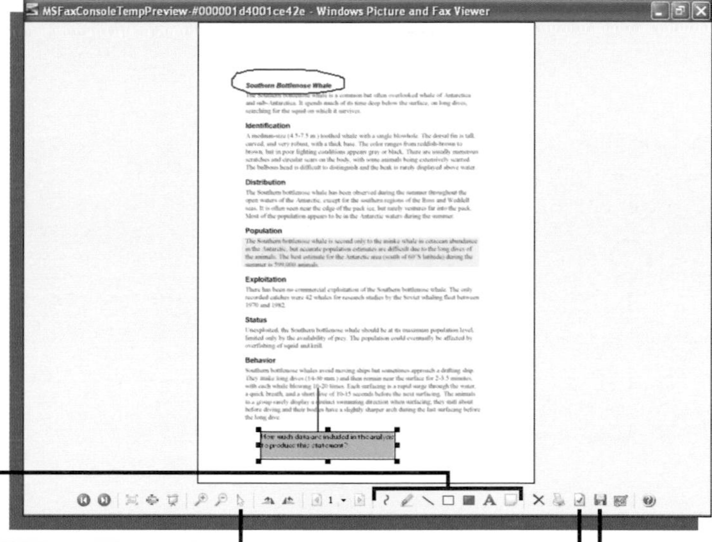

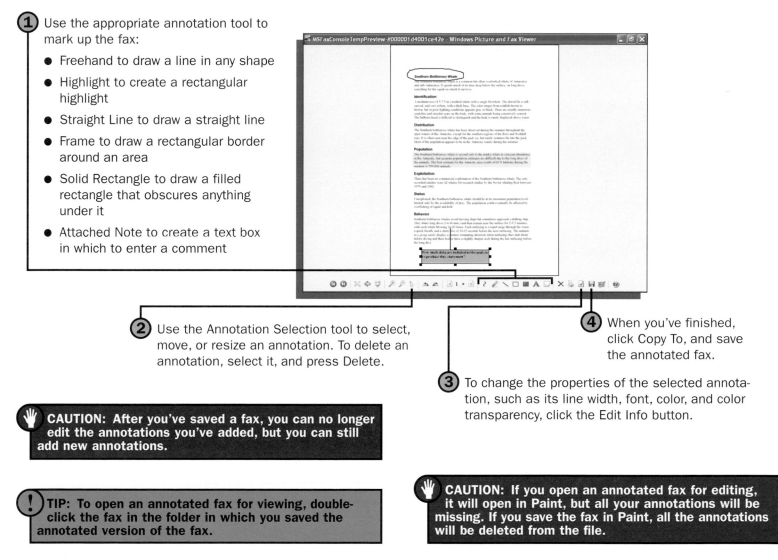

2. Use the Annotation Selection tool to select, move, or resize an annotation. To delete an annotation, select it, and press Delete.

3. To change the properties of the selected annotation, such as its line width, font, color, and color transparency, click the Edit Info button.

4. When you've finished, click Copy To, and save the annotated fax.

CAUTION: After you've saved a fax, you can no longer edit the annotations you've added, but you can still add new annotations.

TIP: To open an annotated fax for viewing, double-click the fax in the folder in which you saved the annotated version of the fax.

CAUTION: If you open an annotated fax for editing, it will open in Paint, but all your annotations will be missing. If you save the fax in Paint, all the annotations will be deleted from the file.

Creating a Fax Cover Page

Whenever you send a fax, it's good practice to include a cover page that contains information about the recipient and the sender, as well as the number of pages being sent. You can use the standard cover pages that Fax Service provides, or you can create your own cover page that contains the information you want in the design of your choice. The easiest way to create your own cover page is to start with one of the existing cover pages that Fax Service supplies, and then modify the page to your own use.

Create a Cover Page

1. If the Fax Console isn't already open, choose Fax Console from the Fax submenu of the Start menu. Choose Personal Cover Pages from the Tools menu to open the Personal Cover Pages dialog box.

TIP: To modify an existing personal cover page, select it in the Personal Cover Pages dialog box, and click Open.

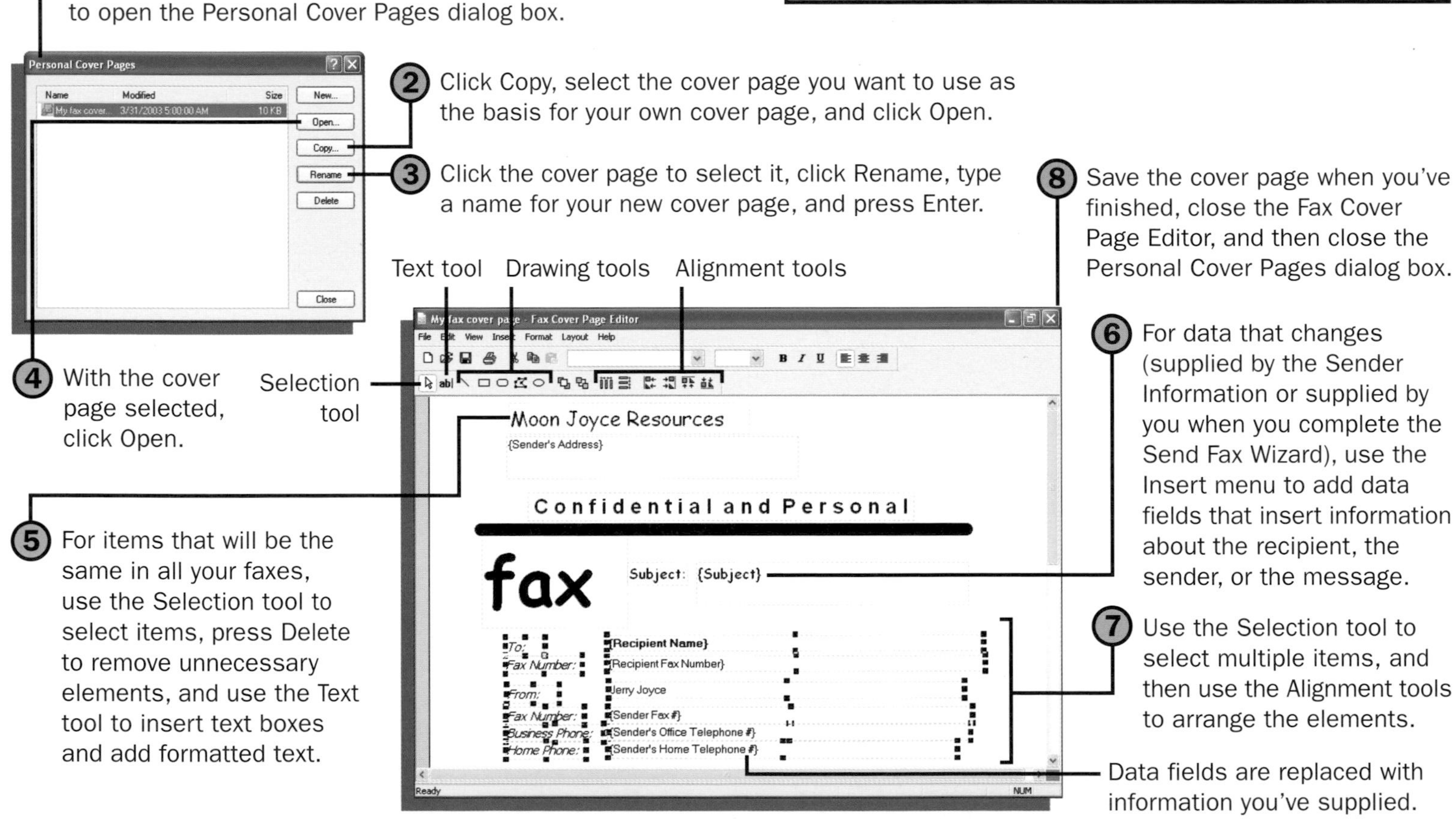

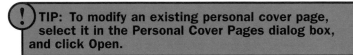

2. Click Copy, select the cover page you want to use as the basis for your own cover page, and click Open.
3. Click the cover page to select it, click Rename, type a name for your new cover page, and press Enter.
4. With the cover page selected, click Open.
5. For items that will be the same in all your faxes, use the Selection tool to select items, press Delete to remove unnecessary elements, and use the Text tool to insert text boxes and add formatted text.
6. For data that changes (supplied by the Sender Information or supplied by you when you complete the Send Fax Wizard), use the Insert menu to add data fields that insert information about the recipient, the sender, or the message.
7. Use the Selection tool to select multiple items, and then use the Alignment tools to arrange the elements.
8. Save the cover page when you've finished, close the Fax Cover Page Editor, and then close the Personal Cover Pages dialog box.

Managing Files and Folders

In this section

We all know that to work productively, with minimal stress and frustration, we must *get organized!* That's where Microsoft Windows XP comes in. It supplies the framework—a basic file structure of drives and some ready-made folders, which you can use as is if it works for you. If not, you can create your own file- and folder-management system. Organize the files within the folders—alphabetically or by size, type, date, and so on. Move, copy, and rename files or groups of files. If you delete a file or folder by mistake, you can easily recover it. If you want the people who share the computer with you to have access to certain files and folders, you can put those items in folders that are designed to be shared. You can change the appearance of the windows in which you view your documents and folders, and, depending on the information you need, you can view them in any of six different views.

The Desktop is the place to put the files, folders, and other items you use every day, just as you do on a real desktop. To have immediate access to a report you're preparing or a performance review you're struggling with, put either the document itself or a shortcut to it on the Desktop.

You can transfer files or back up crucial information by copying the material onto removable disks—floppy disks or ZIP-type disks, for example. If you have a CD recorder installed on your computer, you can put the material on CDs—the CD Writing Wizard walks you helpfully through the process. Finally, we'll talk about the toolbars, which you use to navigate your way through the information on your computer, your intranet if you have one, and the Internet.

Organizing Your Files

If you have a limited number of files, you can easily keep them all in a single folder, such as the My Documents folder. However, if you have many files, or files dealing with different projects, you'll probably want to organize them by placing them in individual folders. If a file doesn't have a suitably descriptive name, you can change it to one that's more useful, and if there's a group of related files, you can rename each file in the group with the same group name followed by consecutive numbering—for example, *stories*, *stories(1)*, *stories(2)*, and so on.

Move or Copy a File

1. Open the window containing the file or files you want to move or copy.
2. Select the file or files to be moved or copied.
3. Click Move The Selected Items or Copy The Selected Items (or Move This File or Copy This File if you've selected only one file).

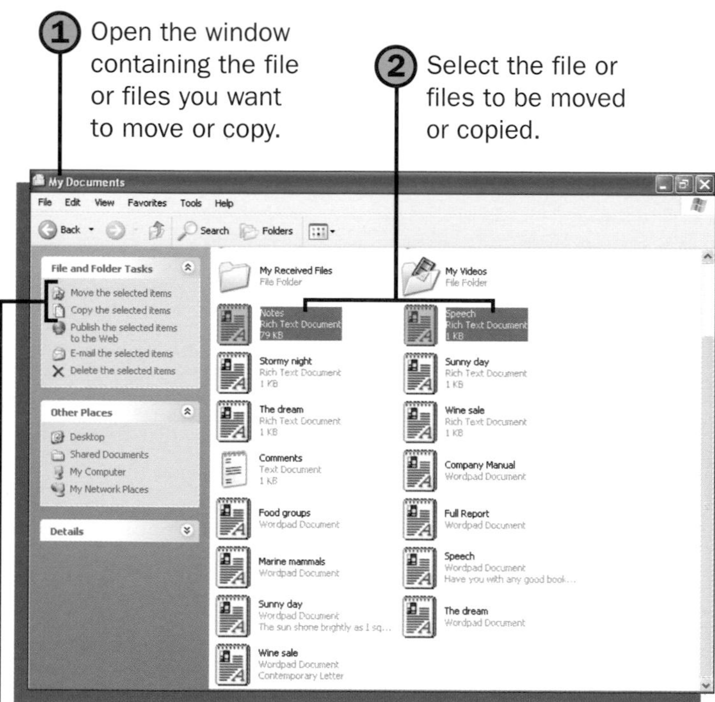

TIP: In previous versions of Windows, you moved or copied files either by dragging them into a different window, or by using the Folders button in a folder window to show all the folders on the computer or in a network location and then dragging the files into one of those folders. You can still use either of these methods to move or copy files, but it's much easier to click the Move or Copy task.

TIP: To select a series of adjacent files, click the first file, hold down the Shift key, and click the last file in the group. To select nonadjacent files, hold down the Ctrl key as you click each file to be selected.

4. In the Move Items or the Copy Items dialog box, expand the listing by clicking plus signs until the destination folder is displayed. Click the destination folder.
5. If you want to create a new folder for the file or files, click Make New Folder.
6. Click Move or Copy to move or copy the file or files.

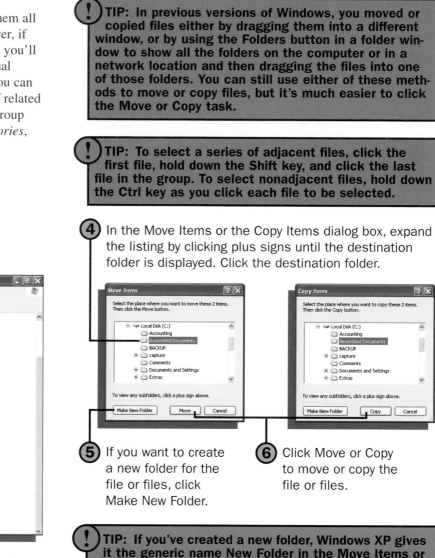

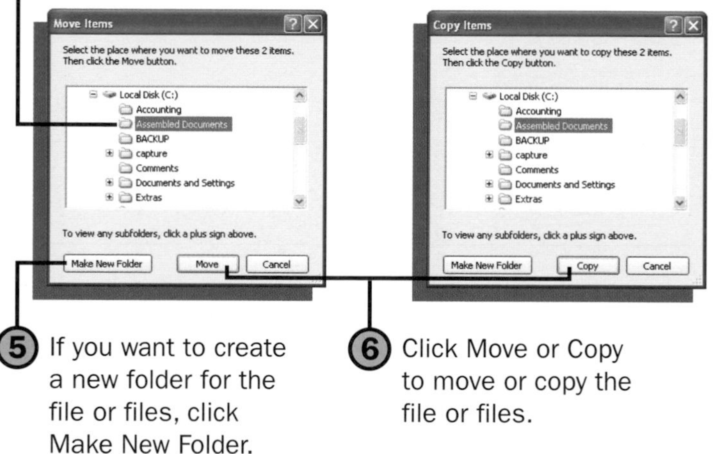

TIP: If you've created a new folder, Windows XP gives it the generic name New Folder in the Move Items or Copy Items dialog box. You'll want to rename the folder, using the same technique you use to rename a file.

Rename a File

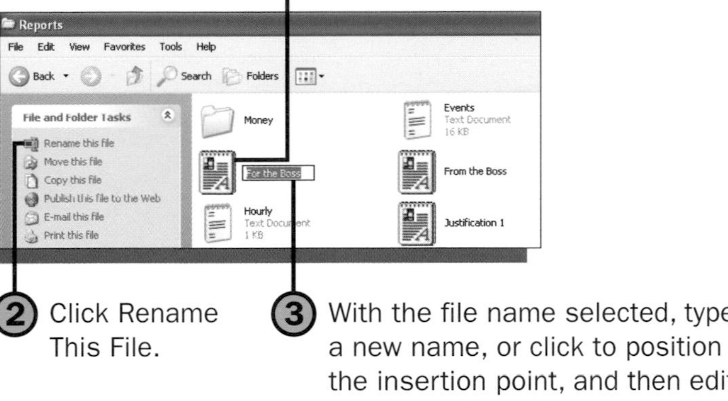

1. Click the file to select it.
2. Click Rename This File.
3. With the file name selected, type a new name, or click to position the insertion point, and then edit the name. Press Enter when the name is correct.

CAUTION: File names (or folder names) can be as long as 255 characters, but, because a long name is often truncated by a program, a descriptive short name is a better choice. You can use spaces and underscores in names, but you can't use the * : < > | ? " \ or / characters. If there's a file extension (up to three characters following the period at the end of the file name), don't change or delete it. Windows XP uses that extension to identify the type of file.

TIP: To delete a file or a group of files, select the file or group of files, and press the Delete key.

Rename a Group of Files

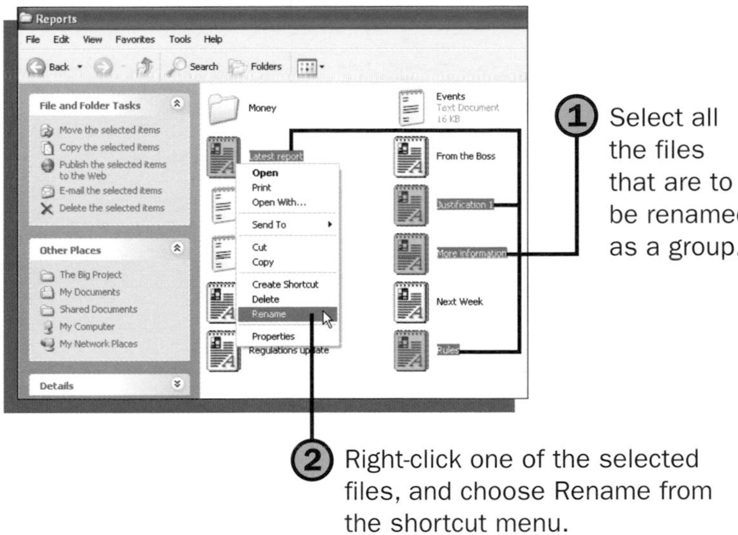

1. Select all the files that are to be renamed as a group.
2. Right-click one of the selected files, and choose Rename from the shortcut menu.

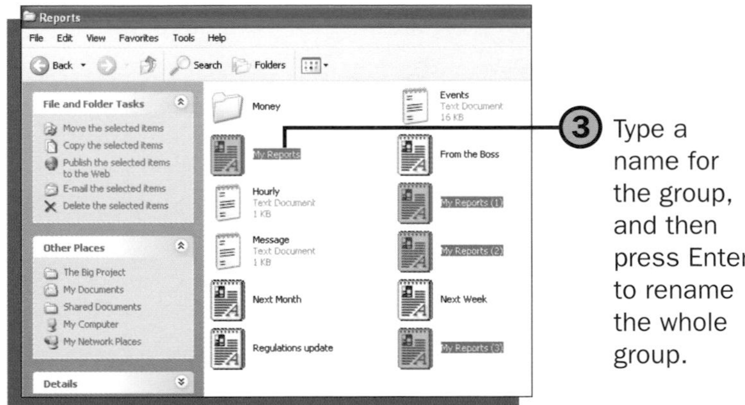

3. Type a name for the group, and then press Enter to rename the whole group.

Recovering a Deleted Item

If you accidentally delete a file, folder, or shortcut from your computer's hard disk, you can quickly recover the item either by undoing your action immediately or by restoring the deleted item from the Recycle Bin. The Recycle Bin holds all the files you've deleted from your hard disk(s) until you empty the bin or until it gets so full that the oldest files are deleted automatically.

Undo a Deletion

1. Point to a blank spot on the Desktop or to a blank part of any folder window, and right-click.
2. Choose Undo Delete from the shortcut menu.

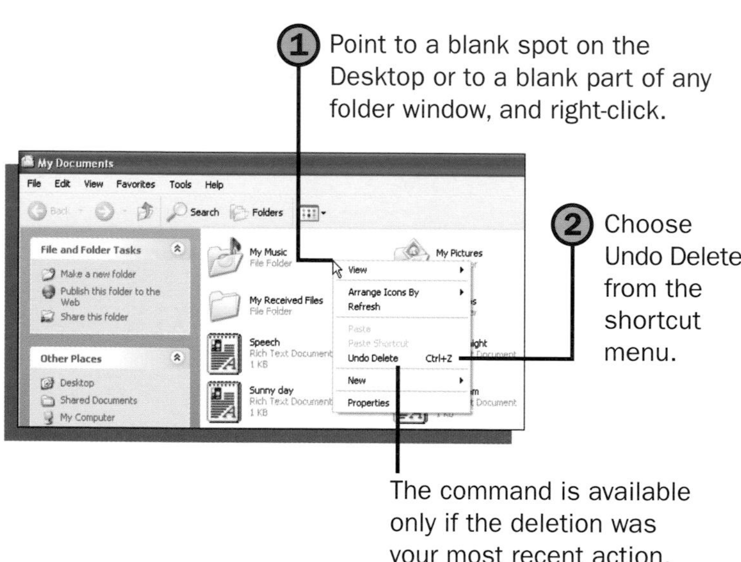

The command is available only if the deletion was your most recent action.

TIP: Windows XP remembers as many as three of your most recent actions, so if you executed an action after you deleted something, undo the action first, and then undo the deletion.

TIP: When you've deleted a folder, you have to restore the entire folder. You can't open a deleted folder in the Recycle Bin and restore selected files.

Restore an Item

1. Double-click the Recycle Bin icon on the Desktop to open the Recycle Bin window.
2. Select the item or items to be recovered.

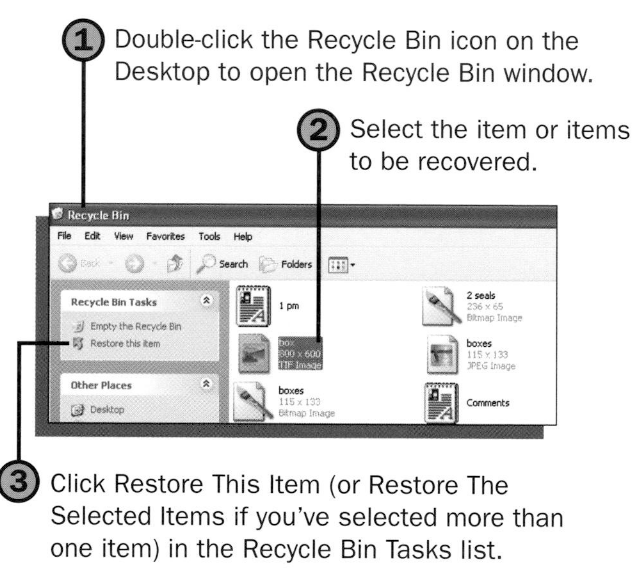

3. Click Restore This Item (or Restore The Selected Items if you've selected more than one item) in the Recycle Bin Tasks list.

CAUTION: You can't recover any files that you've deleted from a removable disk, so be careful! Once they're gone, they're gone forever.

Changing the Window View

You can change the appearance of the windows that contain your files and folders so that the information is presented in the way that's the most useful for you.

Choose a View

1. In the window whose view you want to change, click the Views button.
2. Click the view you want to use.

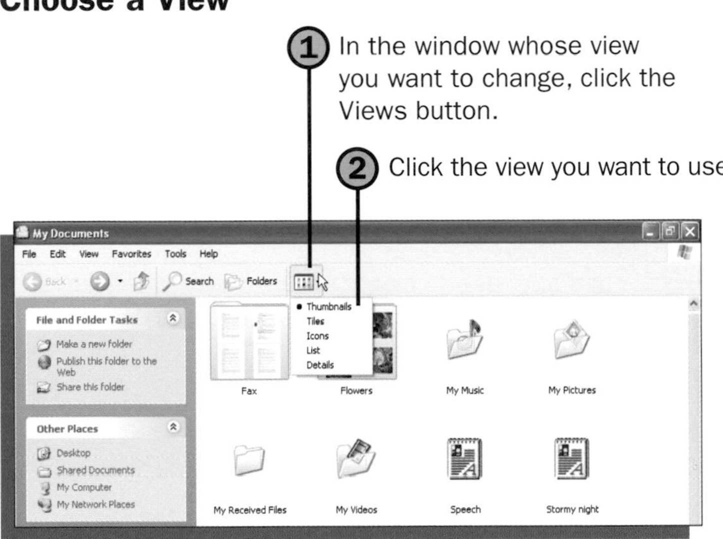

SEE ALSO: For information about the different views, see "Windows Views" on page 172.

For information about changing the look and type of information displayed, see "Customizing Your Folders" on pages 236–237.

Arrange the Information

1. Point to Arrange Icons By on the View menu, and choose the type of item by which you want to sort the listing.

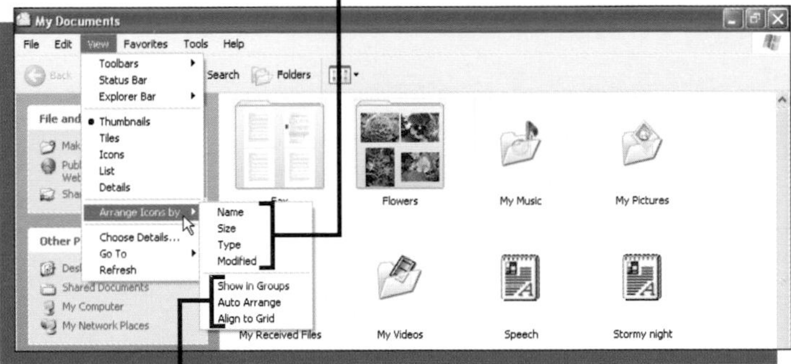

2. Point to Arrange Icons By on the View menu again, and choose one of the following options from the submenu:
   - Show In Groups to group items (folders, files, and so on) under classifications based on the item by which the list is sorted
   - Auto Arrange to have icons automatically repositioned to fill any gaps in the arrangement
   - Align To Grid to have icons snap to an invisible grid so that they line up with each other even though the alignment might leave gaps in the arrangement
3. If you want to use an additional option, point to Arrange Icons By again, and choose the additional option. (Note that not all options are available for all views.)

Windows Views

Windows XP can display the contents of a folder window in one of six available views, and you can modify each view in several ways. You can choose the view you want from the View menu, or you can click the Views button on the Standard Buttons toolbar. Then you use the View menu to change the way the items are arranged. You'll probably want to experiment to see which view is best suited for your work and for the contents of the folder. For example, you might want to use Icons view in a folder that contains only a few files of different types, Details view when you're looking for files that were created on a specific date, Thumbnails view when you're managing pictures, and Filmstrip view when you're reviewing the pictures.

The six views are described on these two pages.

Filmstrip: Displays a large preview of the selected picture file, together with thumbnail views of all the files and subfolders in the folder. This view is available only for folders that have been set up for pictures.

Thumbnails: Displays a miniature representation of the file or folder. If the file is a picture, the picture is displayed. If you've saved a preview of the file, the preview is usually displayed. For a folder that has been customized to use an identifying picture, or for a folder that contains multiple pictures, the identifying picture or the first few pictures contained in the folder are displayed. If no picture or preview is available for the file or folder, an icon is displayed.

Tiles: Displays large icons with information about the file next to each icon. The information that's displayed changes depending on which property (date or size, for example) you've used to arrange the icons.

Filmstrip view

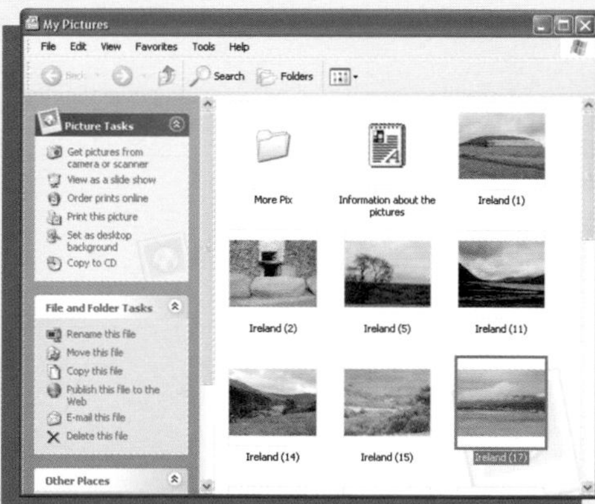

Thumbnails view

Tiles view

Icons: Displays icons that indicate whether each item represented is a folder or a file. The name of the item is listed below the icon.

List: Displays small icons representing folders and files in a vertical listing that can snake through multiple columns. The name of the item is listed next to the icon. Note that in List view you can't arrange the items in groups.

Details: Displays small icons in a single-column list that shows the name of the item and includes details such as size, type, and date.

Once you've chosen the view you want, Windows XP offers more options. In each view, you can arrange the way the files are sorted—for example, you can arrange them in order by name, size, file type, or date. If you prefer, you can arrange the files in groups, based on the way they were sorted—for example, if you've sorted the files by size, you can then group them according to their relative sizes in subgroups of tiny, small, medium, or large files. In all views, you choose the arrangement you want from the View menu. In Details view, you can also click the title of a column to sort by that column.

Windows XP doesn't stop there, of course. You can change the look of each icon in the folder, or add a picture to the folder itself. By defining the types of files that will be stored in a folder, you can customize the way the folder is set up and what tools you'll have available. You'll find more information about customizing folders in "Customizing Your Folders" on pages 236–237.

Icons view

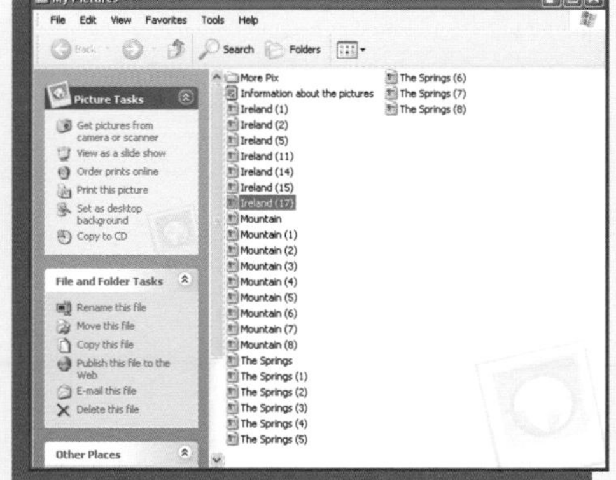

List view

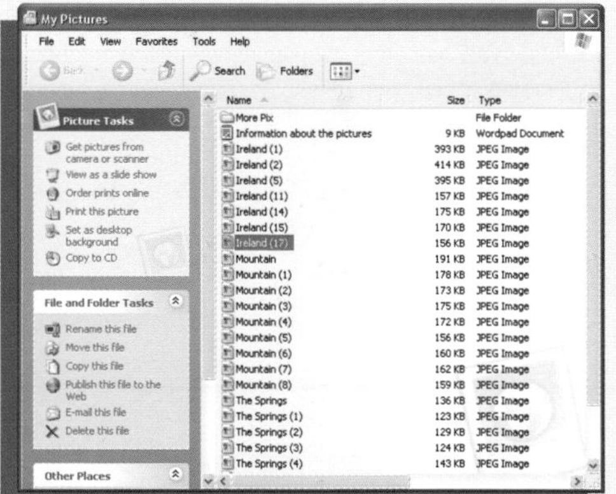

Details view

Compressing Files

Compressed folders are special folders that use compression software to decrease the sizes of the files they contain. Compressed folders are useful for reducing the file size of standard documents and programs, but they're invaluable when you're storing large graphics files such as bitmaps or when you're transferring large files by e-mail.

SEE ALSO: **For information about encrypting compressed folders for increased security, see "Protecting Your Files with a Password" on page 253.**

For more information about compressing an entire drive, or compressing an existing folder using the NTFS file system, see "Compressing a Drive or a Folder" on pages 284–285.

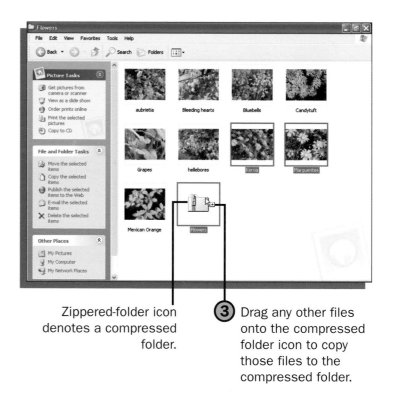

Create a Compressed Folder

1. Select the file or files to be copied to a compressed folder.

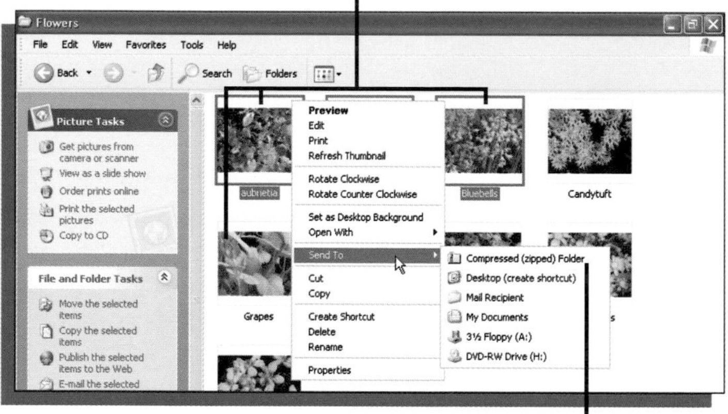

2. Right-click one of the selected files, point to Send To on the shortcut menu, and choose Compressed (Zipped) Folder from the submenu. Rename the compressed folder if necessary.

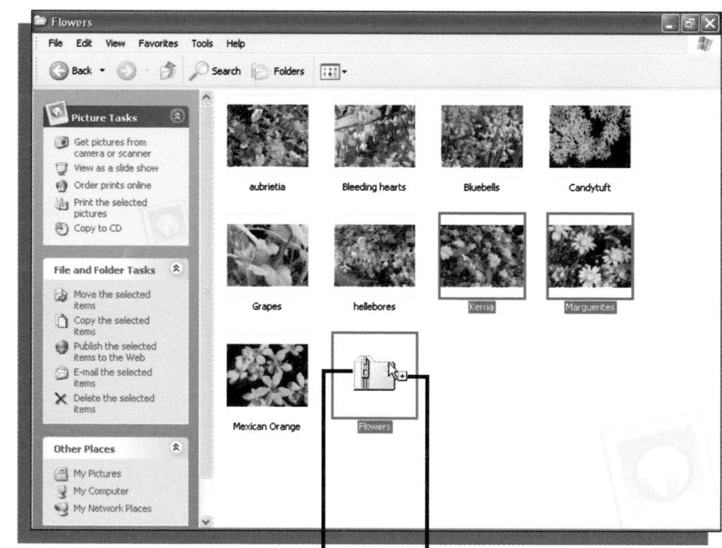

Zippered-folder icon denotes a compressed folder.

3. Drag any other files onto the compressed folder icon to copy those files to the compressed folder.

TIP: **A compressed folder is compatible with file-compression programs that support the ZIP file format.**

Use a Compressed File

1 Double-click the compressed folder to open it.

2 Double-click an item in the folder to open it in its associated program. If the item is a program, double-click it to run it. (Note, though, that not all files and programs will function properly from the compressed folder.)

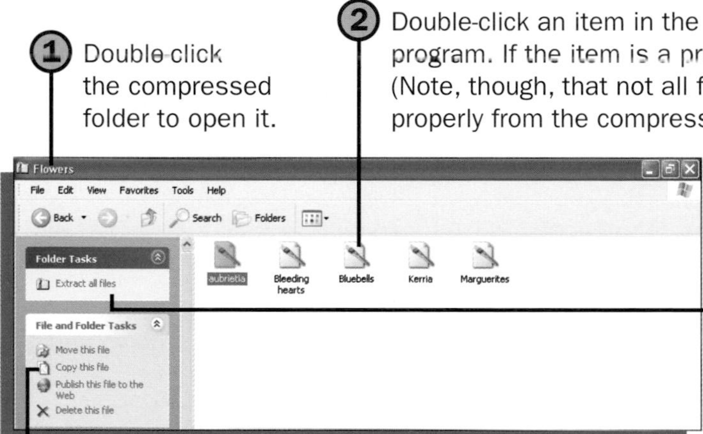

4 To decompress all the files in the folder and copy them to another folder, click Extract All Files.

3 To decompress a single file, select it, click Copy This File, and specify which folder you want the file to be copied to.

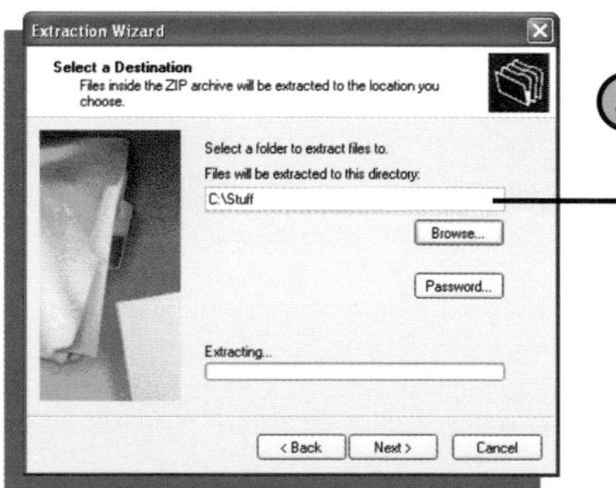

5 Step through the Extraction Wizard, specifying where the files are to be extracted, or copied, to.

TRY THIS: Compress a large file (or a group of files) by placing it in a compressed folder. Click the compressed-folder icon, and click E-Mail This File in the File And Folder Tasks list. Send the folder, which is now listed as a ZIP-type file, to the person who needs it. If the recipient's operating system isn't equipped with the compressed-folders feature, he or she will need to use a third-party compression program that uses ZIP-type compressed files to open the files.

CAUTION: Compressed folders preserve the contents of most files, but it's possible that you could lose some data when you're using certain file formats. It's wise to test your file format in a compressed folder before you move valuable files into that folder.

Adding Files and Folders to the Desktop

The Windows XP Desktop is more than just a place for pictures and icons. You can use the Desktop to store frequently used files and folders for quick access, or to store parts of files for later use.

Add a File

1. Open the folder window that contains the file you want to put on the Desktop.

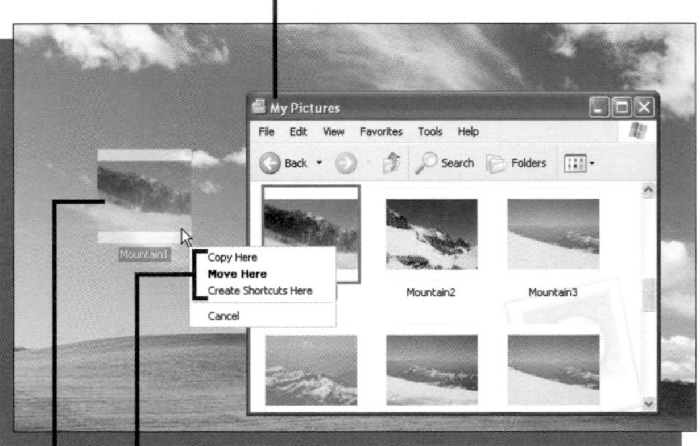

2. Hold down the *right* mouse button and drag the document onto the Desktop.
3. From the shortcut menu that appears, choose either to copy or move the file onto the Desktop, or to create a shortcut to the document.

Add a Folder

1. Right-click a blank spot on the Desktop.
2. Point to New on the shortcut menu, and choose Folder from the submenu.

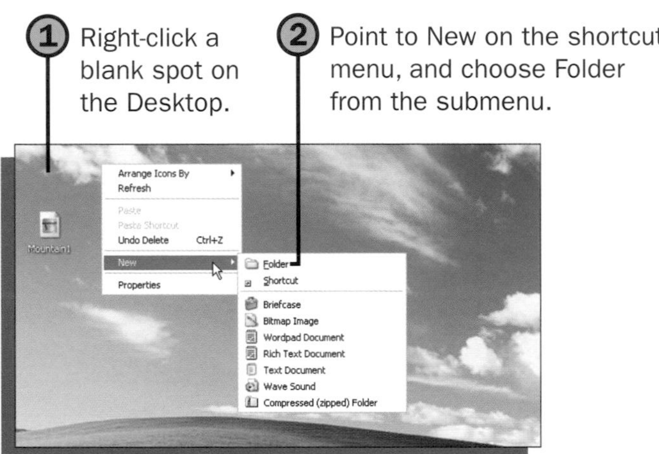

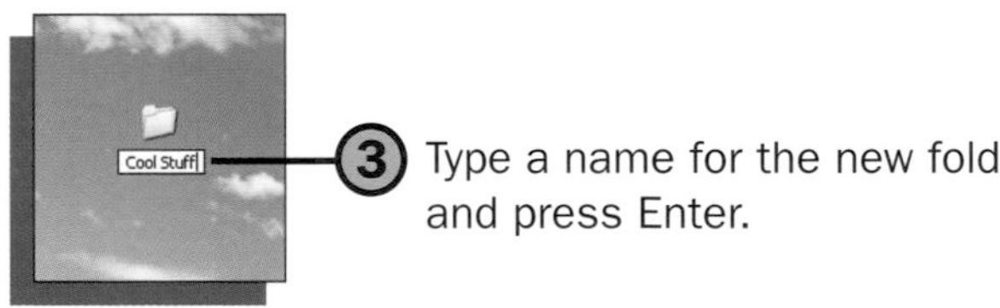

3. Type a name for the new folder, and press Enter.

SEE ALSO: For information about accessing documents from a toolbar, see "Navigating with Toolbars" on page 186.

For information about displaying or hiding the standard icons (such as My Computer) on the Desktop, see "Customizing the Desktop" on pages 226–227.

TIP: Items that you've placed on the Desktop are actually stored in the Documents And Settings folder under your name.

Save a File to the Desktop

1. Create a file in your program.
2. Choose Save from the File menu to display the Save As dialog box.
3. Click Desktop. If Desktop isn't listed in the program's Save As dialog box, click Desktop in the Save In drop-down list.
4. Type a name for the file.
5. Click Save.

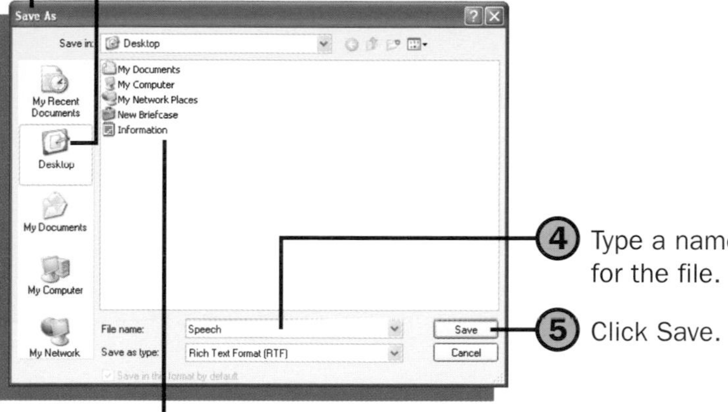

Files of the same type are listed so that you can avoid using an existing name (and thus replacing an existing file).

TRY THIS: Start WordPad, and type some text. Select the text and drag it onto the Desktop. Start a new document in WordPad, type some text, and then drag the WordPad scrap from the Desktop into the WordPad document.

Save Part of a File to the Desktop

1. Select the part of the file you want to save.

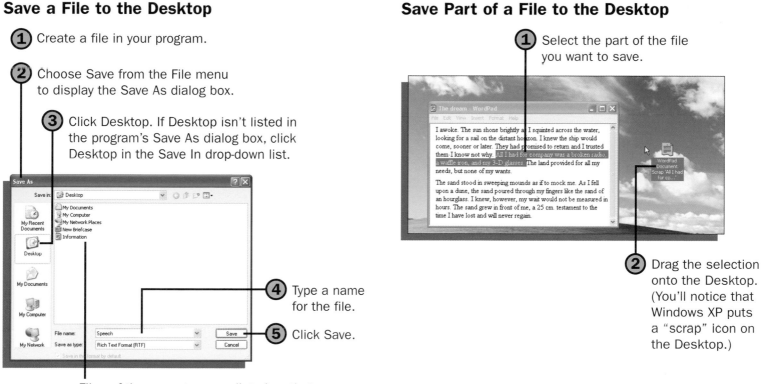

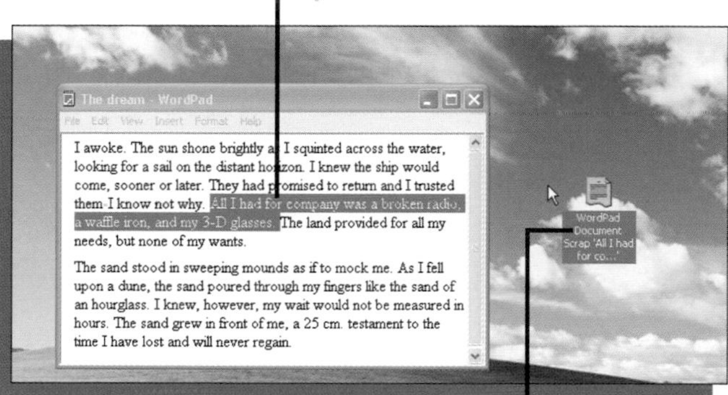

2. Drag the selection onto the Desktop. (You'll notice that Windows XP puts a "scrap" icon on the Desktop.)

TIP: If the program you're using doesn't support dragging and dropping, and you want to save a section of text as a scrap on the Desktop, copy the selected text, right-click a blank spot on the Desktop, and choose Paste from the shortcut menu.

TIP: Scraps can also be stored in folders, so you can organize them just as you can any other files.

Sharing Files with Other Users

Each user of your computer has his or her own set of folders in which to keep documents, music, and so on. If you want the other people who use your computer to have access to certain files, you can place those files in special folders that are designed specifically for sharing. If you're connected to a network, the files in these folders are also available to other people on the network.

TIP: If you open a folder that doesn't show a Shared Documents item in the Other Places list, but you want to copy a file from the folder to the Shared Documents folder, click the Folders button on the Standard Buttons toolbar, and drag the file onto the Shared Documents folder shown in that list.

Share a File

1. Open the folder that contains the file or files you want to share.

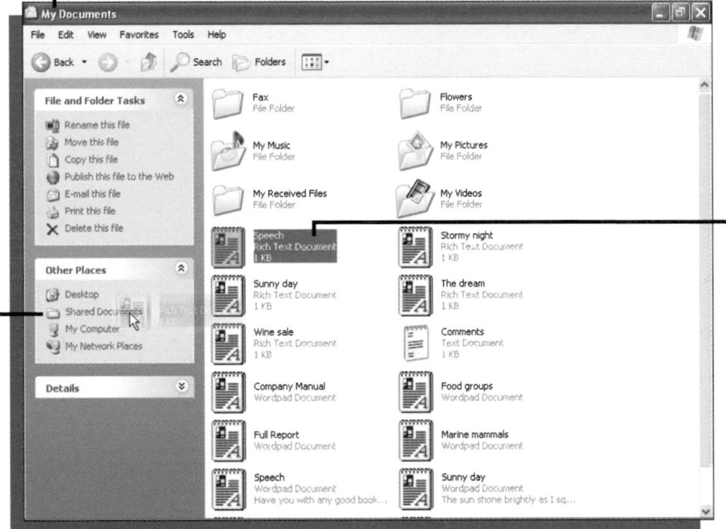

2. Select the file. If you want to share several files, select all of them.

3. Drag the file or files onto the Shared Documents item. Anyone who uses the computer can now access the file or files in the Shared Documents folder.

TRY THIS: Select a file, click the Copy This File task in the File And Folder Tasks list, select the Shared Documents folder in the Copy Items dialog box, and click Copy. The file has now been copied instead of moved.

SEE ALSO: For information about making your folders private so that other users of your computer can't access them, see "Keeping Your Files Private" on page 248.

Creating Quick Access to a File or Folder

If you use a particular file or folder frequently, you can access it quickly by placing a shortcut to it on the Desktop, on the Start menu, or just about anywhere you want. A shortcut to a document opens the document in its default program; a shortcut to a program file starts the program; a shortcut to a folder opens the folder in a window.

Create a Shortcut to a File or Folder

1. Open a window that contains the file or folder.

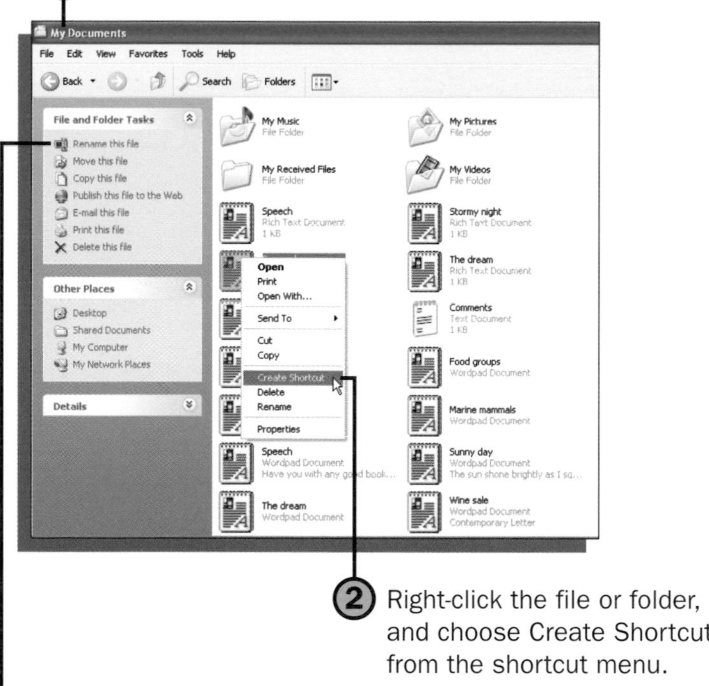

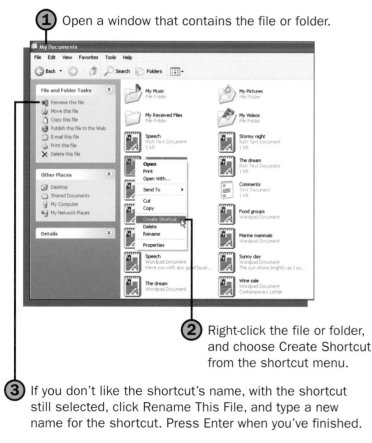

2. Right-click the file or folder, and choose Create Shortcut from the shortcut menu.
3. If you don't like the shortcut's name, with the shortcut still selected, click Rename This File, and type a new name for the shortcut. Press Enter when you've finished.

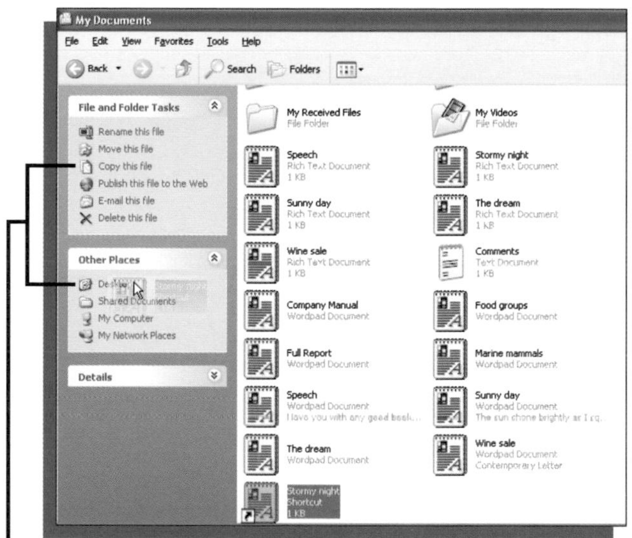

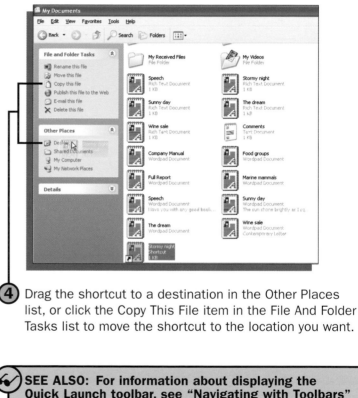

4. Drag the shortcut to a destination in the Other Places list, or click the Copy This File item in the File And Folder Tasks list to move the shortcut to the location you want.

SEE ALSO: For information about displaying the Quick Launch toolbar, see "Navigating with Toolbars" on page 186.

For information about adding items to the Start menu, see "Customizing the Start Menu" on pages 232–233.

Copying Files from and to a Removable Disk

A quick and easy way to transfer files is to put them on a floppy disk, a USB storage device, or some other type of removable disk. When you receive a removable disk, you can copy the files from it to your computer. When you want to give some files to a friend or coworker, you can copy the files onto a disk for that person.

You can also use a removable disk to back up and save your critical files in case you accidentally delete a file from your computer, or to safeguard against losing files because of a power failure or some other problem with your computer.

Copy Files from a Disk

1. Insert the disk into the drive. If a window displaying the disk contents doesn't open, choose My Computer from the Start menu to display the My Computer window, and then double-click the drive to open a folder window for the drive.
2. Select a file (or a group of files).

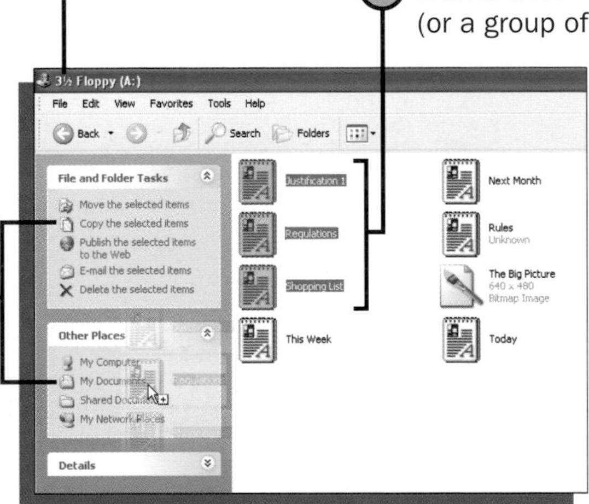

3. Drag the selection to a destination in the Other Places list to copy the file or files to that destination. If the destination you want isn't listed, click Copy The Selected Items to copy the file to the destination you want.

Copy Files to a Disk

1. With the removable disk in its drive, locate and select the file or files you want to copy to the removable disk.

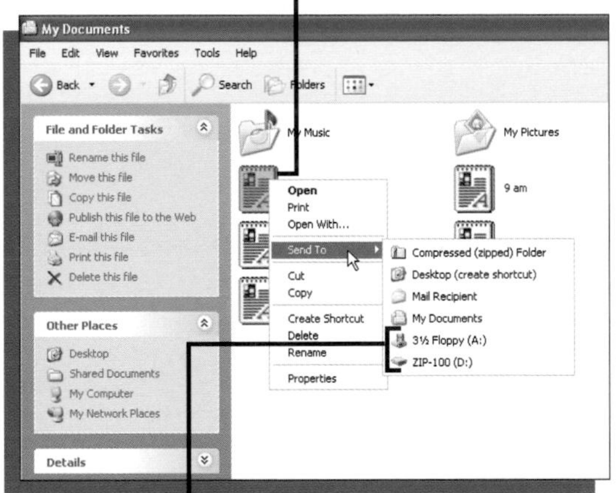

2. Right-click one of the selected files, point to Send To on the shortcut menu, and choose the removable disk from the submenu. Wait for all the selected files to be copied.

CAUTION: To avoid system problems when you're removing any disk other than a floppy disk, in the My Computer folder window, select the disk, and click the Eject This Disk task. To remove a USB drive, click the Safely Remove Hardware icon on the Windows taskbar.

Managing a Removable Disk

Removable disks are invaluable items, but they do require some management. When you want to copy several items onto a disk, you need to monitor how much space is available on the disk, especially if you use the small-capacity 3½-inch disks. If you frequently reuse your removable disks, you might also find it necessary to occasionally format a disk. (Formatting a disk removes all the files from the disk and resets the disk's filing system so that it's prepared for new content.)

Check the Amount of Space on a Disk

1. With the disk in the drive, choose My Computer from the Start menu to display the My Computer folder window.
2. Right-click the drive, and choose Properties from the shortcut menu to display the disk's Properties dialog box.

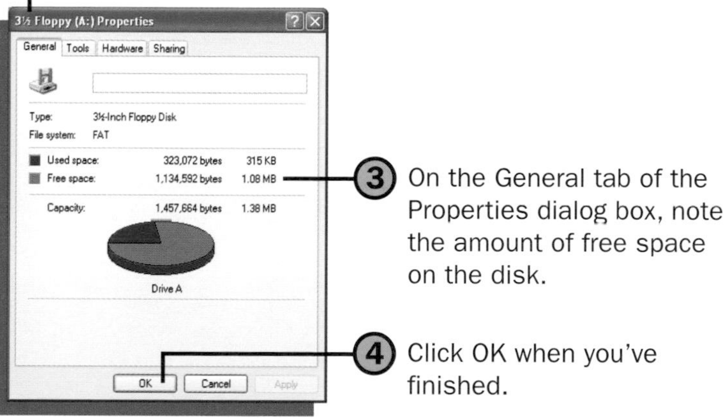

3. On the General tab of the Properties dialog box, note the amount of free space on the disk.
4. Click OK when you've finished.

CAUTION: When you either format a removable disk or delete files from it, the files are permanently deleted and can't be recovered from the Recycle Bin.

SEE ALSO: For information about safely removing a USB disk-storage device, see "Preventing Hardware Problems" on page 287.

Format a Disk

1. If you're certain the disk doesn't contain any files that you'll need again, in the My Computer folder window, right-click the drive, and choose Format from the shortcut menu to display the Format dialog box.

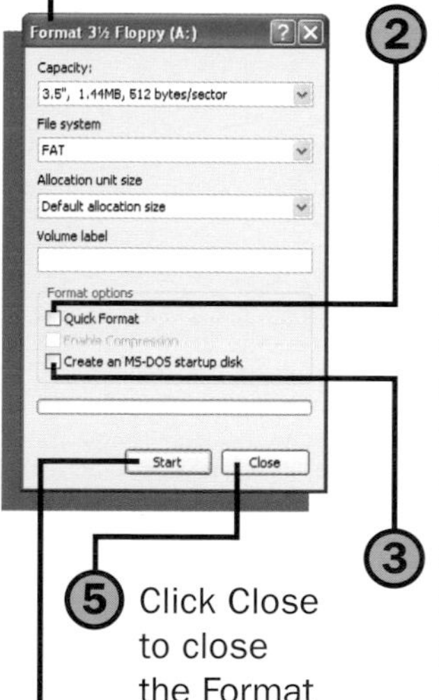

2. Select this check box to quickly remove the listings of files (but not the content of the files, which is overwritten by the new files) from the disk and to free up the entire disk for new files. Clear the check box to fully remove all the old files for added security or if you run into a problem with the current disk formatting—for example, if you can't format the disk using quick formatting.
3. Select this check box if you want to use a floppy disk to start up your computer and to run it using MS-DOS. (This option applies to floppy disks only.)
4. Click Start, and then click OK when you're warned about erasing all items on the disk. Wait for the disk to be formatted. Click OK when the formatting has been completed.
5. Click Close to close the Format dialog box.

Copying Files to a CD

If you have a CD recorder (sometimes called a CD burner) installed on your computer, you can copy your files to a CD for safe storage or easy distribution. To do so, you copy all the files you want to include on the CD into a temporary storage area, and then, after all the files are assembled, you copy them from the temporary storage area to the CD. You can continue copying files to the CD until it's full.

Gather and Copy Your Files and Folders

1. Using My Computer, My Documents, or any other folder window, locate and select the file or files and/or the folder or folders you want to copy.

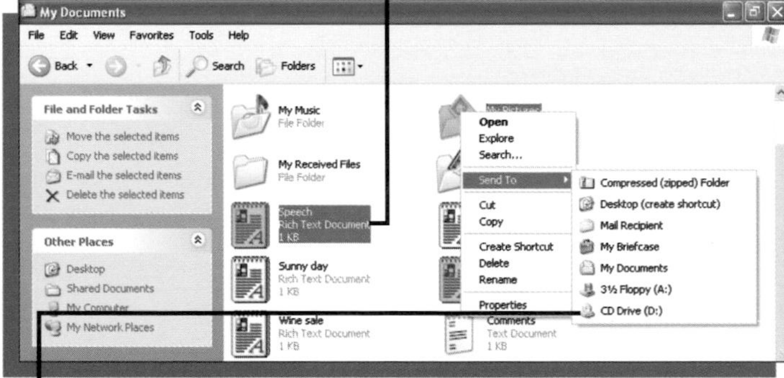

2. Right-click one of the selected items, point to Send To on the shortcut menu, and choose your CD drive. Repeat for other files and folders from different locations to gather all the items you want to copy into one temporary storage area.

TIP: If you're copying pictures from the My Pictures folder (or from any folder that's been set up to store pictures), click Copy To CD in the Picture Tasks list to copy the files you want to copy to the CD. To copy the entire folder, make sure that no pictures are selected, and then click Copy All Items To CD in the Picture Tasks list.

Organize the CD

1. In the My Computer folder window, double-click your CD drive to display the folder window for the drive.

2. Review the files that you've gathered to be copied to the CD.
3. If you want to organize some of the files by placing them in a folder, click Make A New Folder, name the folder, and then drag the files into the folder.

Create the CD

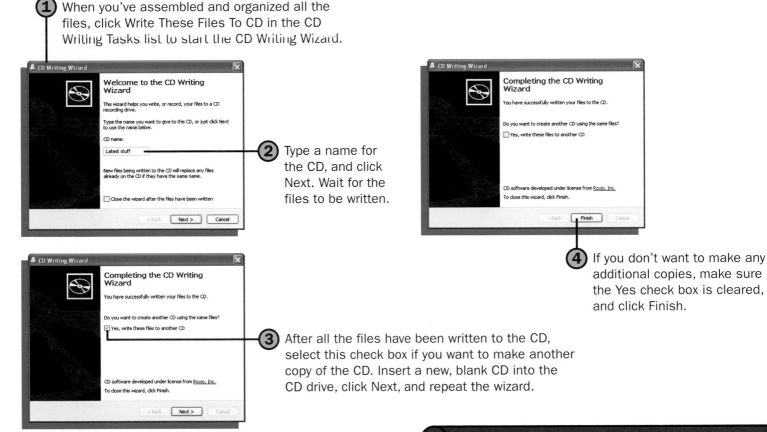

1. When you've assembled and organized all the files, click Write These Files To CD in the CD Writing Tasks list to start the CD Writing Wizard.

2. Type a name for the CD, and click Next. Wait for the files to be written.

3. After all the files have been written to the CD, select this check box if you want to make another copy of the CD. Insert a new, blank CD into the CD drive, click Next, and repeat the wizard.

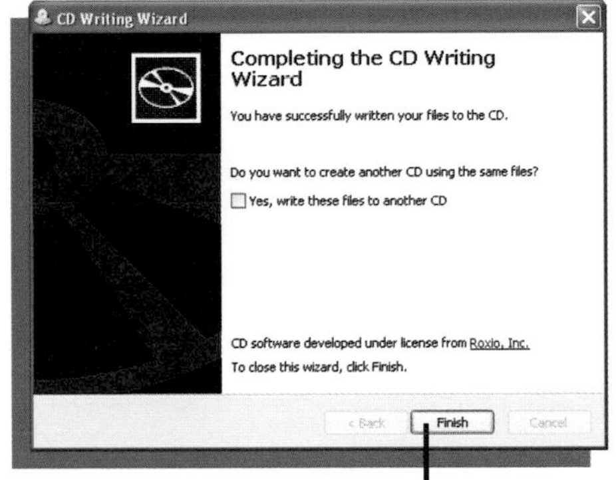

4. If you don't want to make any additional copies, make sure the Yes check box is cleared, and click Finish.

SEE ALSO: For information about creating music CDs, see "Copying CD Music" on page 136.

For information about creating labels for your CD, see "Labeling Your CDs" on page 138.

TRY THIS: In the CD Drive window, press Ctrl+A to select everything. Right-click any of the selected items, and choose Properties from the shortcut menu. Note the number of files and folders, and especially the size of all the items on the disk. Click OK. The combined size of all the files should give you a good idea as to whether or not all your files will fit on the CD.

Finding a File

If you don't remember the exact name or location of a file, tell Windows XP what you do remember—for example, the document type, all or part of its name, when it was last modified, the drive or the computer where it resides—and then let Windows XP do the searching for you.

TIP: You can also search for a document by clicking the Search button in any folder window. Unless you change the search area, the search will be limited to the current folder and any subfolders it contains.

Find a File

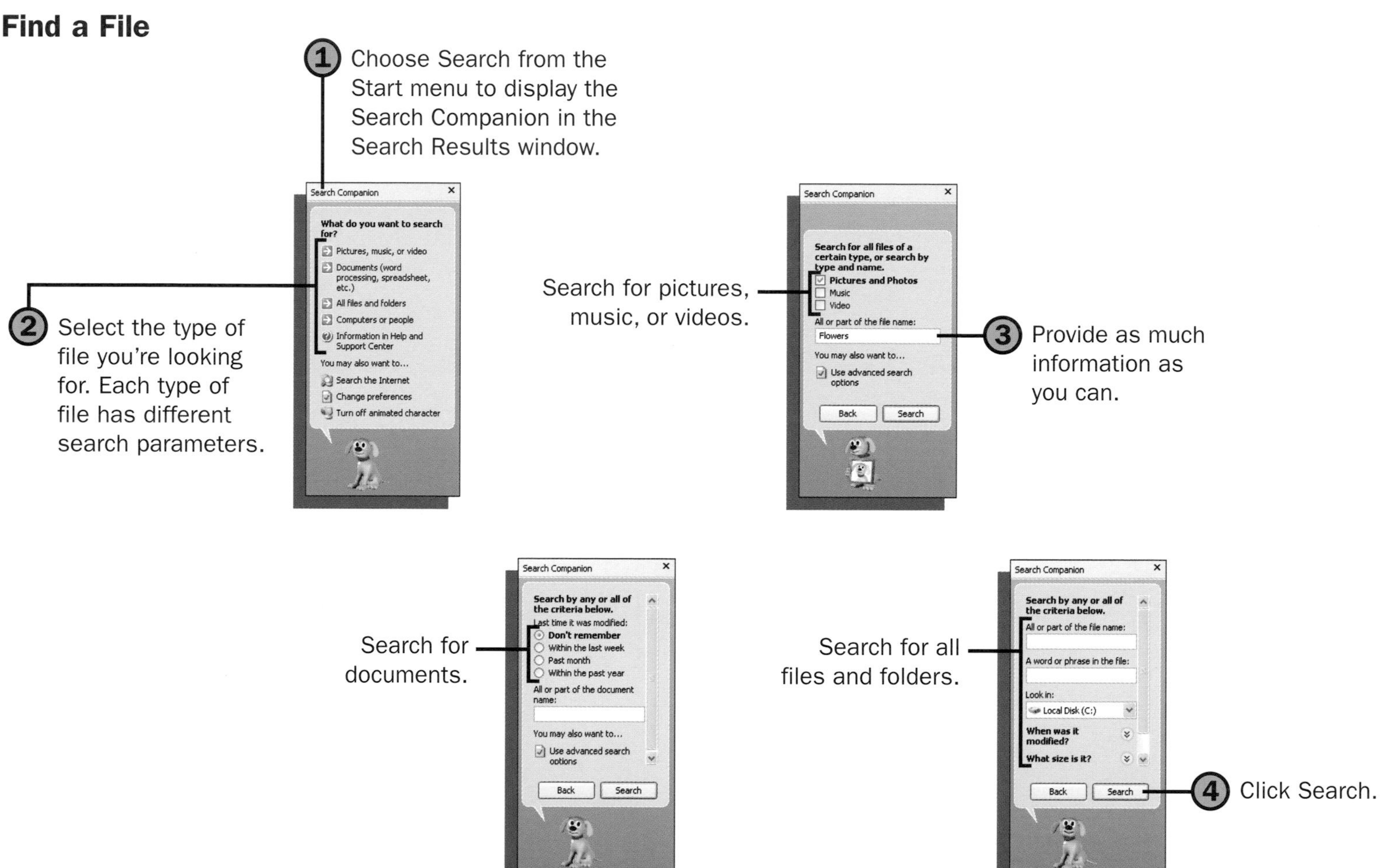

Use the Results

1 Review the results of the search.

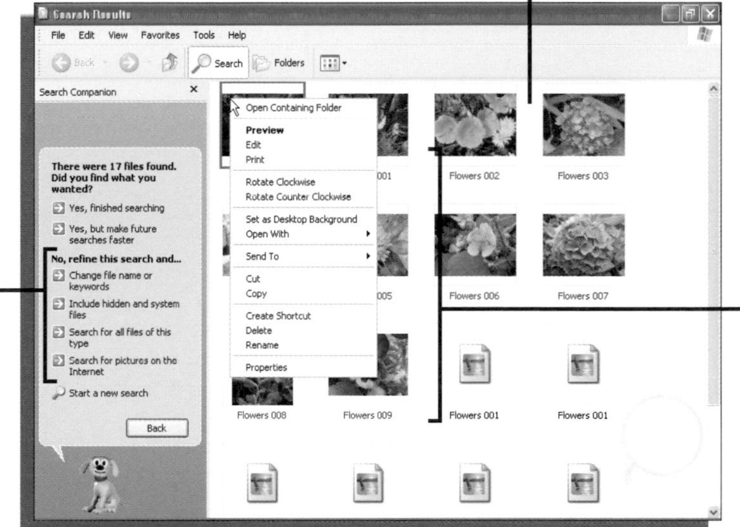

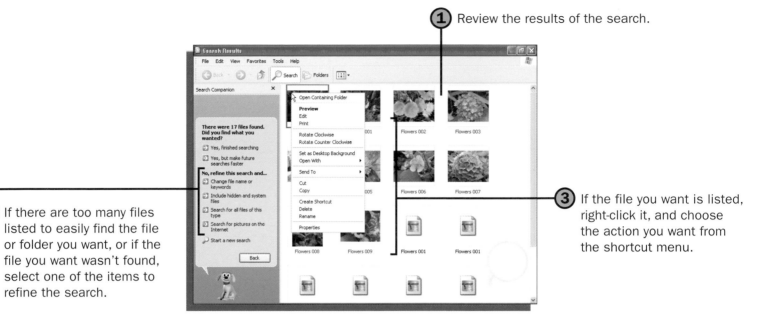

2 If there are too many files listed to easily find the file or folder you want, or if the file you want wasn't found, select one of the items to refine the search.

3 If the file you want is listed, right-click it, and choose the action you want from the shortcut menu.

TIP: If you find yourself searching frequently, you can have Windows XP conduct a faster and more extensive search by using the Indexing Services. To enable the Indexing Services, instead of choosing the type of file in the Search Companion area, click Change Preferences, and then click With Indexing Services. The Indexing Services feature speeds up a search, but, because it frequently needs to update the index of all your files whenever you make changes to the contents of the hard disk, it might slow down your computer's normal operating speed.

TIP: If you're not sure whether a file is the one you want, point to the file, and read the information in the pop-up description that appears. If you want more information, right-click the file, and choose Properties from the shortcut menu.

Navigating with Toolbars

There are six toolbars associated with the Windows XP taskbar, and they provide access to programs, folders, and documents as well as to Internet and intranet sites.

Display a Toolbar

1. Right-click a blank spot on the taskbar.
2. Point to Toolbars on the shortcut menu, and choose the toolbar you want to display. (A toolbar with a check mark next to its name is one that's already displayed.)
3. Double-click the toolbar if it isn't already expanded.
4. If the toolbar doesn't expand, right-click a blank spot on the taskbar, choose Lock The Taskbar from the shortcut menu, and repeat step 3.

SEE ALSO: For information about creating your own toolbars and modifying the toolbars in folder windows, see "Displaying and Arranging the Toolbars" on page 229.

The Taskbar's Toolbars

Toolbar	Function
Address	Opens the item when you specify its address. The address can be the path and the file or folder name, a program name, a computer on the network, or even the Internet address of a Web page.
Desktop	Provides quick access to the icons, files, folders, and shortcuts on the Desktop.
Language Bar	Switches input languages if Windows has been configured to use more than one language.
Links	Links you to the same locations that are shown on the Internet Explorer Links toolbar.
Quick Launch	Launches Internet Explorer, Outlook Express, and Windows Media Player, or minimizes all the windows on the Desktop.
Windows Media Player	Provides control for operating Windows Media Player when Media Player is minimized.

See All the Buttons

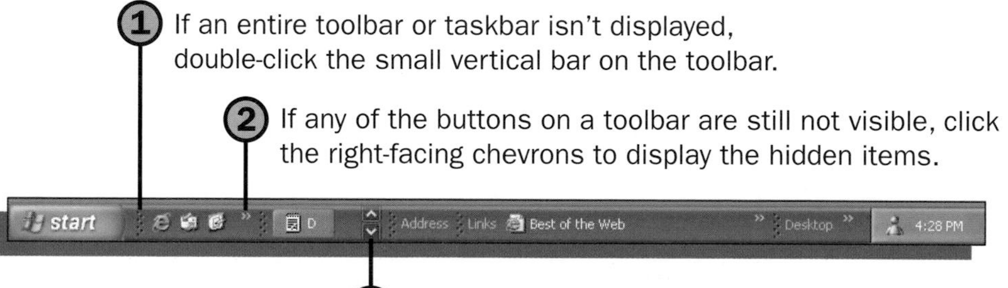

1. If an entire toolbar or taskbar isn't displayed, double-click the small vertical bar on the toolbar.
2. If any of the buttons on a toolbar are still not visible, click the right-facing chevrons to display the hidden items.
3. If all the buttons on the taskbar are still not visible, use the up or down arrow to scroll through all the items.

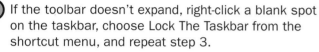

10 Networking

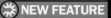

In this section

Networking—once a requirement only in large corporations—is now almost a necessity in a multi-computer household, a home office, or a small business. With two or more computers connected, you can access files and folders on other computers that have been set up for sharing, and you can share the files and folders on your computer with other people. (And if there are items to which you want to limit other people's access—your private files, for example—you can do so.) But that's not all—a network also enables you to share printers, to share an Internet connection, and to communicate over the network using Windows Messenger (see "Sending Instant Messages" on page 84) or, alternatively, NetMeeting, which we'll discuss in this section. One of the nice things about NetMeeting is that you don't have to be connected to the Internet to have a conversation or a quick meeting with a friend or coworker.

Windows XP also makes it easy for you to telecommute—the Remote Desktop Connection allows you to sit at your home computer and actually work on the Desktop of your office computer, provided your office computer is running Windows XP Professional or Windows XP Server. It's a great way to get some of your work done from the comfort of your home. If you need to gain access to your office network from your home computer, you can do so via a remote connection: by dialing up a network server, for example, or using the Internet to create a VPN (Virtual Private Network), which ensures a secure connection to another computer. We'll also show you how simple it is to connect to a wireless network, whether you're in a small coffee shop or a big conference center.

Exploring Your Network

Windows XP automatically searches for the shared folders, printers, and whatever other items are shared on your network's computers. You can also open a window to all the shared folders on a specific computer, or you can connect to a computer that's in a different workgroup.

Connect to a Shared Folder

1. Choose My Network Places from the Start menu to open the My Network Places window.
2. Double-click a shared folder to access its contents.

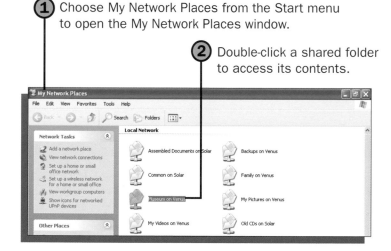

NEW FEATURE: The Show Icons For Networked UPnP Devices item in the Network Tasks area is a security enhancement installed with Service Pack 2. It's designed to avoid security vulnerabilities in Universal Plug and Play software. Click this task to install support software and allow access to any UPnP devices on your network.

TIP: If you've set up your network but you don't see My Network Places on the Start menu, choose My Computer from the Start menu, and click My Network Places in the Other Places list. Close the window. My Network Places should now be listed on the Start menu.

Connect to a Computer

1. In the My Network Places window, click View Workgroup Computers.

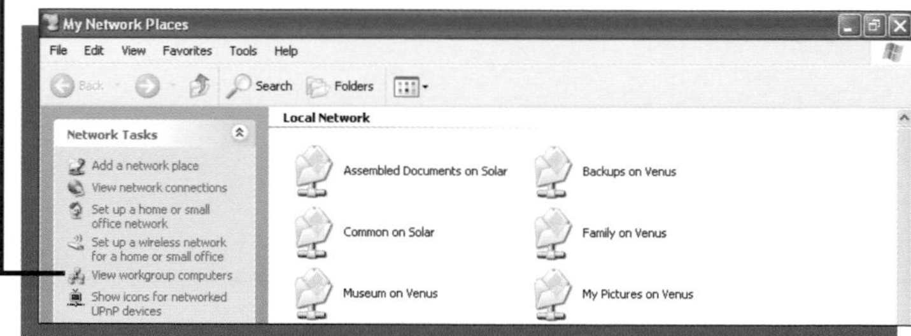

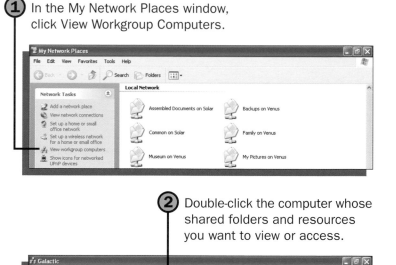

2. Double-click the computer whose shared folders and resources you want to view or access.

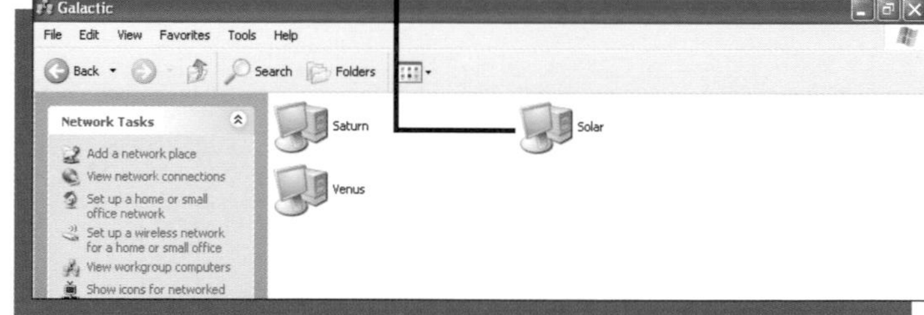

Connect to a Computer in a Different Workgroup

1. In the My Network Places window, click View Workgroup Computers if your workgroup computers aren't already displayed.
2. Click the Up button on the Standard toolbar to view all the workgroups on your network.
3. Double-click the workgroup you want to access.

TIP: If a Connect To dialog box appears when you try to access a computer or folder, enter the valid user name and password required to access the computer.

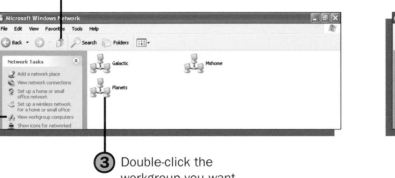

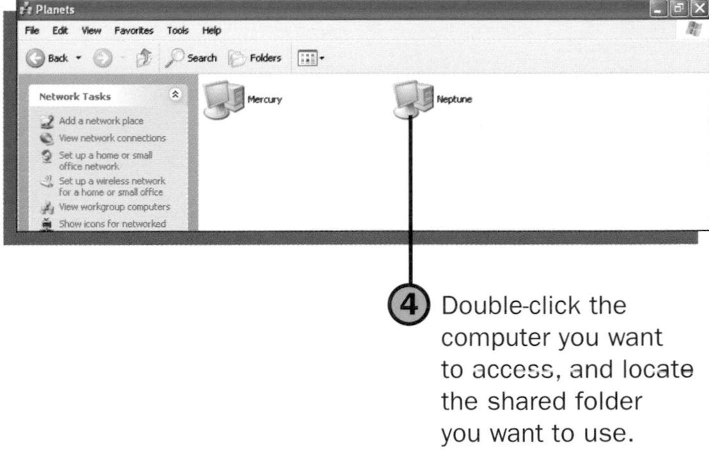

4. Double-click the computer you want to access, and locate the shared folder you want to use.

TIP: To see the folders and other resources that are being shared by your computer over the network, look at the list of workgroup computers, and then double-click your own computer's name in the list. Review the shared folders and their contents. Only shared items are displayed.

SEE ALSO: For information about setting up your network, see "Setting Up a Network" on pages 220–221.

For more information about working with restricted access to network features, see "Creating Custom Access Across the Firewall" on pages 266–267.

For information about how and why these security features are implemented, see "Maintaining High Security with Service Pack 2" on pages 260–261.

Sharing Items over the Network

Once you've set up your network, you can share all the documents that are stored in the Shared Documents folder. If this folder contains any subfolders, you can share their contents too. You can also designate which folders and printers on your computer you want to share with other network users.

Share a File

1. Use My Computer to locate the file you want to share.

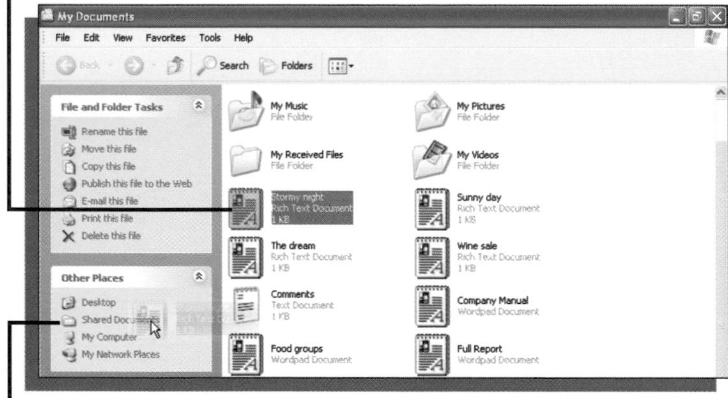

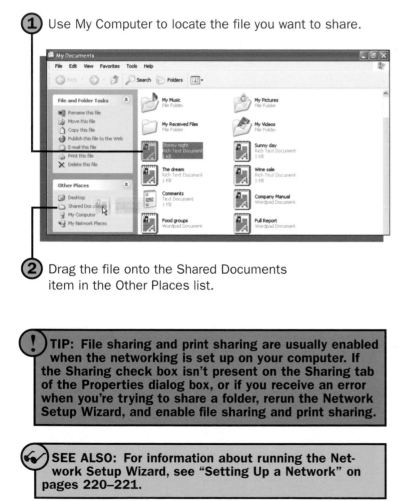

2. Drag the file onto the Shared Documents item in the Other Places list.

TIP: File sharing and print sharing are usually enabled when the networking is set up on your computer. If the Sharing check box isn't present on the Sharing tab of the Properties dialog box, or if you receive an error when you're trying to share a folder, rerun the Network Setup Wizard, and enable file sharing and print sharing.

SEE ALSO: For information about running the Network Setup Wizard, see "Setting Up a Network" on pages 220–221.

Share a Folder

1. Use My Computer to open the drive or folder containing the folder you want to share.
2. Right-click the folder you want to share, and choose Sharing And Security from the shortcut menu to display the folder's Properties dialog box.

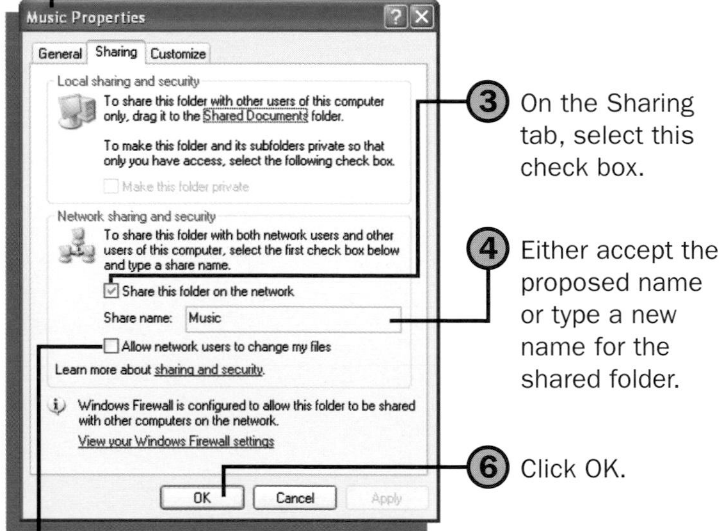

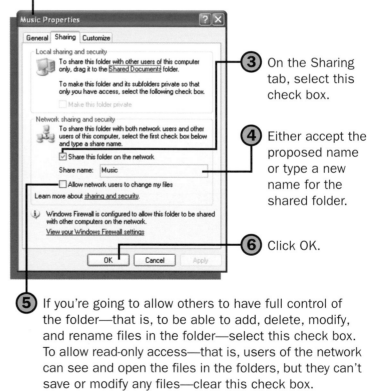

3. On the Sharing tab, select this check box.
4. Either accept the proposed name or type a new name for the shared folder.
5. If you're going to allow others to have full control of the folder—that is, to be able to add, delete, modify, and rename files in the folder—select this check box. To allow read-only access—that is, users of the network can see and open the files in the folders, but they can't save or modify any files—clear this check box.
6. Click OK.

Share a Printer

1. Choose Control Panel from the Start menu, click the Printers And Other Hardware category, and click the View Installed Printers Or Fax Printers task. Right-click the printer to be shared, and choose Sharing from the shortcut menu to display the printer's Properties dialog box.

2. On the Sharing tab, click the Share This Printer option.

3. Either accept the proposed name or type a new name for the shared printer.

4. If there are computers on your network that use an operating system other than Windows XP or Windows 2000, and if those computers will be using your printer, click Additional Drivers.

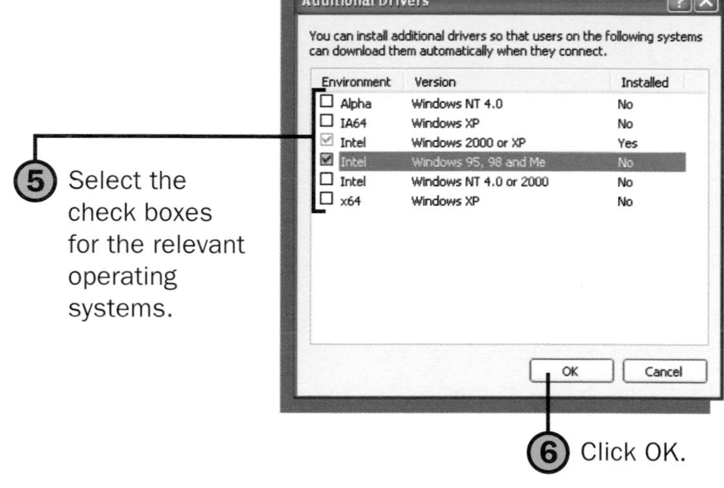

5. Select the check boxes for the relevant operating systems.

6. Click OK.

7. If prompted, insert the Windows XP CD into your computer's CD drive, and click OK. Wait for the drivers to be installed. Click OK in the Additional Drivers dialog box, and click OK in the printer's Properties dialog box.

TIP: If you want to limit your shared printer's availability, click the Advanced tab of the printer's Properties dialog box, and set the times during which the printer will be available.

About Networks

A network, whether it's large or small, gives you the ability to connect computers so that they can communicate with each other. Windows XP Home Edition is designed for a small network (a *peer-to-peer network*), where all the computers communicate directly with each other. To work on a larger network (a *client-server network*), where communication between computers is routed through a server, you'll need to use Windows XP Professional. On a home network, one of your computers (or a router, if installed) acts as a *server,* or *host,* on your peer-to-peer network. The host does two things: It assigns each computer on your network a unique identifying number (an IP address), and it coordinates traffic to the Internet through its shared Internet connection. Other than providing those services, the host computer is just like all the other computers on your network.

On a small network, the organizational unit is the workgroup. Members of the same workgroup can easily access shared files, printers, and other resources. In most cases, working on a home network will be easiest if all the computers are members of the same workgroup. Even if you have separate workgroups, however, you can still access the same resources, although it might take a little bit of extra work the first time you try it. Windows XP has a special tool called a *netcrawler* that inspects the network and finds all the shared resources. If you have different workgroups, the list of shared resources on the other workgroups might not always be current.

Computers can be connected to a network in a variety of ways: by direct connections with cables, with wires that go through network hubs, with connections through your power or phone lines, or even without any wires at all. With so many options, setting up a network can be a simple job or a truly miserable experience. Some connections use "standard" network software and settings; others require special software and configurations. If you're installing a network from a network installation kit, the kit should include all the instructions and software you'll need to get the network set up. If you're simply installing a network card in each computer, and Windows XP doesn't detect and set up each newly installed network card, use the setup CD or disk to install each card. If you don't have a setup program, run the Add New Hardware Wizard from the Control Panel. For more information, see "Adding Hardware" on page 222.

Windows XP also has a special tool for dealing with different types of network configurations on a single network. If, for example, you have one computer that has a wireless network connection to a couple of computers and also has a different network connection using cables to a couple more computers, Windows XP can connect these two networks by installing a *bridge* on the first computer to provide a connection to both networks.

When Windows XP is installed, network software (called the *TCP/IP protocol*) is installed too. This software enables you to communicate over the Internet and on your own network. With standard network configurations, and on special networks where the software drivers are already installed, Windows XP is almost ready to run. Before you use the network, though, you'll need to run the Network Setup Wizard to identify your computer to the network and to specify the types of access you want over the network. You'll also need to specify whether you want to share your Internet connection or any of your files. If you're creating a new network, you'll need to run the wizard on each computer so that the proper settings and software are installed on each machine. Once the network is set up, you'll find that sharing resources is easy and convenient.

Creating a Connection to a Network Folder

If you frequently use one particular folder on the network, you can access that folder quickly by assigning a drive letter to it. By doing so, you will not only gain quick access to the folder from My Computer but will also be able to access the folder in programs that don't let you browse My Network Places to find a file.

TRY THIS: Create a network drive. Open My Computer, and verify that the drive is listed in that window. Start a program, use the drive to open or save a file, and then close the program. Right-click My Computer, and choose Disconnect from the shortcut menu to delete the drive assignment.

Assign a Drive

1. Choose My Network Places from the Start menu.
2. Click View Workgroup Computers in the Network Tasks list.
3. Double-click the computer that contains the shared folder.

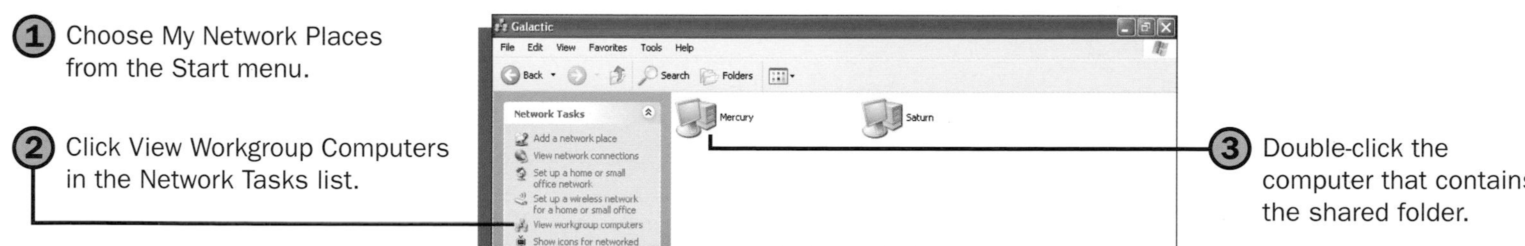

4. Right-click the folder, and choose Map Network Drive from the shortcut menu.

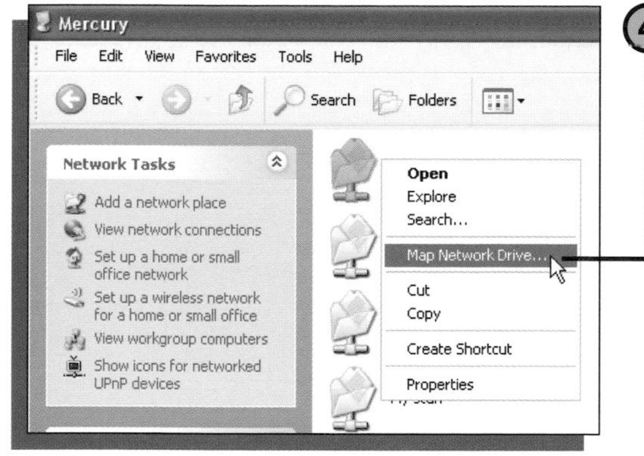

5. In the Map Network Drive dialog box, click a drive letter for this folder.
6. Clear this check box if you want to use the drive assignment during this session only, or keep the check box selected if you want to reestablish this drive assignment each time the computer is started.
7. Click Finish.

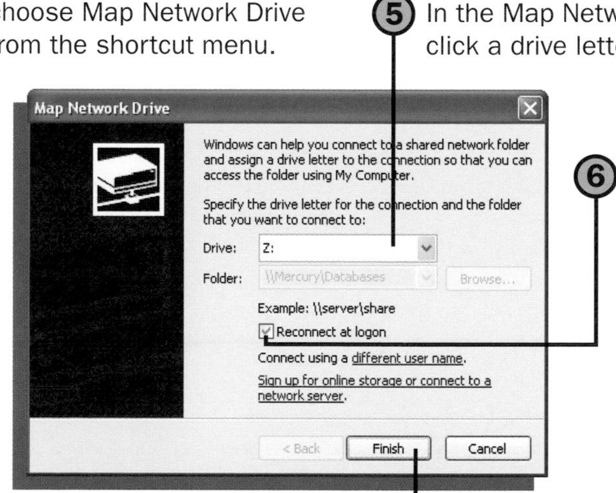

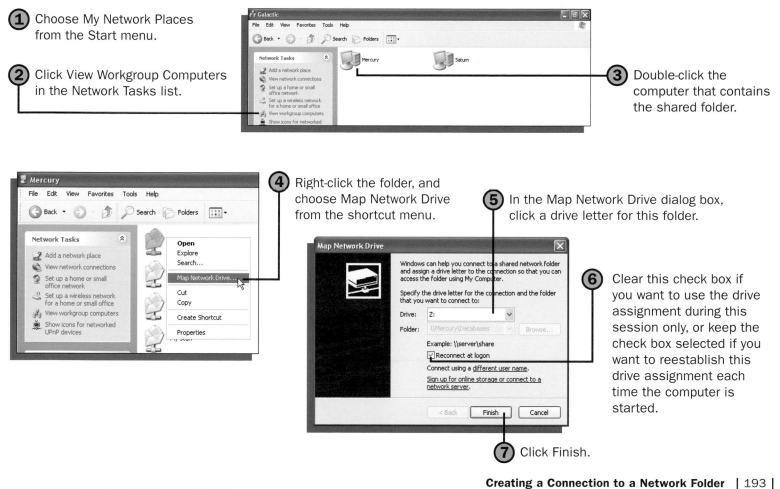

Controlling a Shared Dial-Up Internet Connection

When a network is set up to share a dial-up connection to the Internet, the connection can be left open even when no one is using it. However, if you're concerned about tying up the phone line or if you want to economize on the phone or ISP connection charges, you can have the connection end automatically when no one is using it. Alternatively, you can manually end the connection from your computer even if the phone line isn't connected to your computer.

Configure the Connection

1. On the computer that's hosting the Internet connection, choose My Network Places from the Start menu, and click View Network Connections in the Network Tasks list. Click the Internet connection you use, and click Change Setting Of This Connection in the Network Tasks list to display the connection's Properties dialog box.

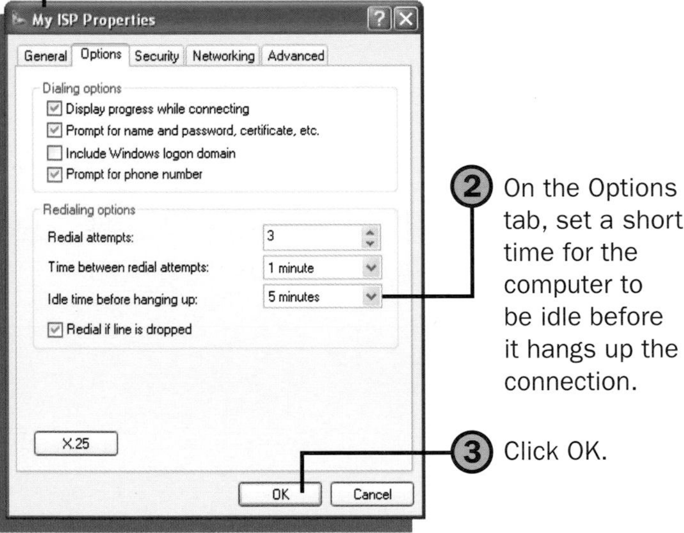

2. On the Options tab, set a short time for the computer to be idle before it hangs up the connection.
3. Click OK.

End the Connection

1. On the computer that's using the Internet connection over the network, choose My Network Places from the Start menu, and click View Network Connections in the Network Tasks list to display the Network Connections dialog box.
2. Click the Internet connection you're using to select it.

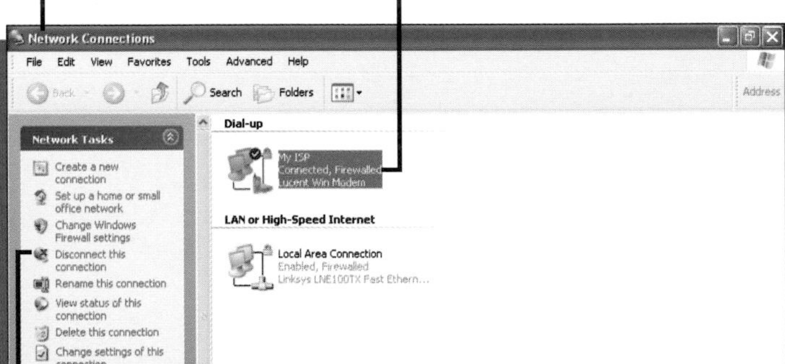

3. Click Disconnect This Connection.

TRY THIS: To set up your computer to quickly hang up the connection over the network, right-click the connection in the Network Connections window, and choose Properties from the shortcut menu. Select the Show Icon In Notification Area When Connected check box to show an icon in the notification area of the taskbar, and click OK. To disconnect, click the icon, and then click Disconnect in the Status dialog box that appears.

Communicating over the Network

Windows Messenger is a great way to communicate over the Internet, but you can use it over your network only if you're connected to the Internet or to a network that's running Microsoft Office Live Communications Server 2003 or Microsoft Exchange 2000 Server. Fortunately, there's a Windows XP feature called NetMeeting that provides similar functionality over your network without tying up—or being slowed down by—your connection to the Internet.

Start NetMeeting

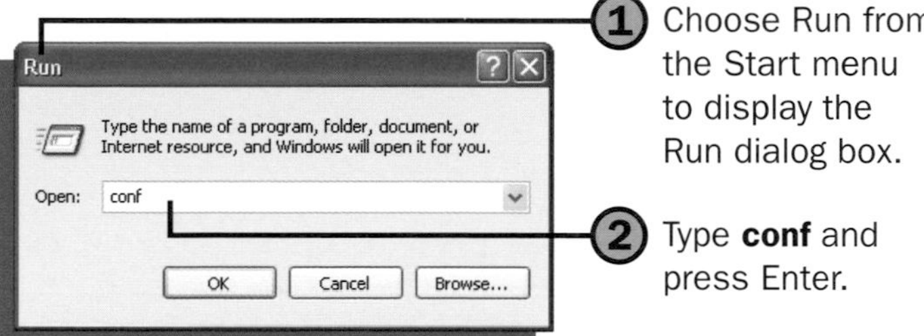

1. Choose Run from the Start menu to display the Run dialog box.
2. Type **conf** and press Enter.

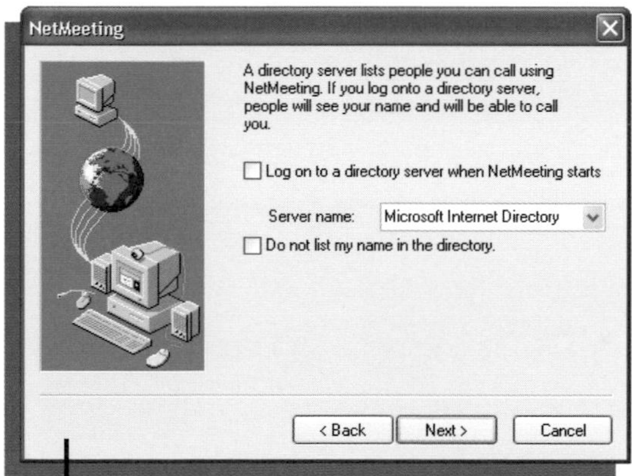

3. If you haven't used NetMeeting before, step though the NetMeeting Setup Wizard. Make sure that you choose not to connect to the Internet directory unless you're planning to use NetMeeting over the Internet as well as on your network.

Connect to a Computer

1. With NetMeeting running on both computers, type the name of the computer you're calling, and press Enter. Wait for the other person to answer your call.

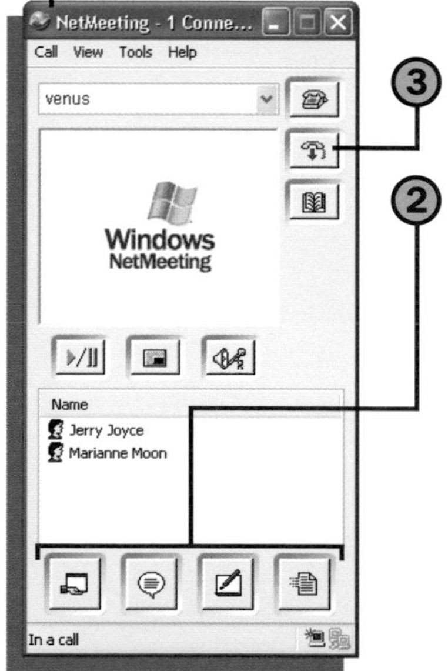

3. Click the End Call button when you've finished.
2. Use the tools to conduct your conversation or meeting, as follows:
   - Share Program to display and share a running program with other people
   - Chat to exchange text messages
   - Whiteboard to share illustrations
   - Transfer Files to exchange files

TIP: NetMeeting has been replaced by Windows Messenger for most uses, but the tools in the two features are very similar. However, you can't use Windows Messenger without being connected to the Internet, and, because NetMeeting allows video from only one computer, you can't have a two-way video session in NetMeeting as you can in Windows Messenger.

Controlling a Computer on Your Network

Do you want to gain full access to one computer from another over your network? By sharing a computer's Desktop using NetMeeting, you can access and run programs, reorganize files, and so on—all from the other computer's Desktop.

SEE ALSO: For information about using Desktop Sharing with a computer that's running Windows XP Professional, see "Controlling a Computer at Your Workplace" on pages 198–199.

For information about opening ports, see "Creating Custom Access Across the Firewall" on pages 266–267.

Share the Desktop

1. On the other computer on the network (the one you want to control), choose Run from the Start menu, type **conf** and press Enter to start NetMeeting.
2. From the Tools menu, choose Remote Desktop Sharing.
3. Step through the Remote Desktop Sharing Wizard. Be sure to set up a password-protected screen saver when you're prompted to do so.

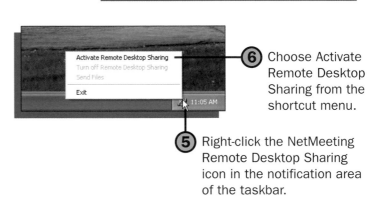

4. Close NetMeeting when you've finished.
5. Right-click the NetMeeting Remote Desktop Sharing icon in the notification area of the taskbar.
6. Choose Activate Remote Desktop Sharing from the shortcut menu.

TIP: Desktop Sharing is automatically blocked by the Windows Firewall. For access through the firewall, you must manually open ports 522, 389, 1503, 1720, and 1731 on both computers. When you've finished, make sure that you close these ports by clearing their check boxes on the Exceptions tab of the Windows Firewall dialog box. A less secure method is to disable the Windows Firewall on both computers.

Connect to the Computer

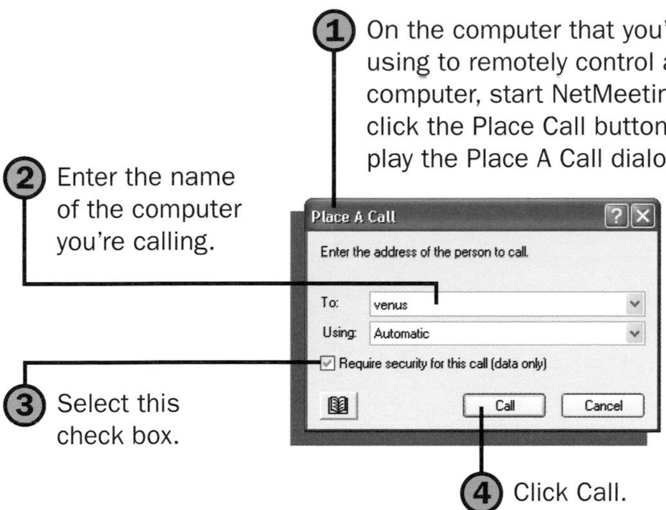

1. On the computer that you'll be using to remotely control another computer, start NetMeeting, and click the Place Call button to display the Place A Call dialog box.
2. Enter the name of the computer you're calling.
3. Select this check box.
4. Click Call.

TIP: Using a password-protected screen saver prevents other people from using your computer when it's unattended.

5. Enter your password when prompted, and click OK.
6. Work from the Desktop of the computer you're controlling remotely.
7. Click the End Call button in NetMeeting when you've finished.

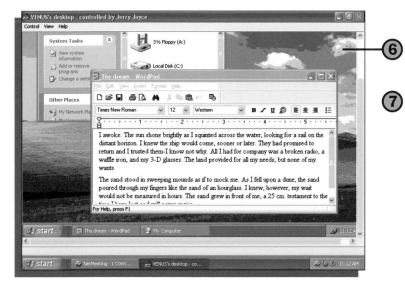

TIP: To temporarily deactivate Remote Desktop Sharing on your computer, right-click the NetMeeting Remote Desktop Sharing icon on the taskbar, and choose Turn Off Remote Sharing from the shortcut menu. To permanently remove Remote Desktop Sharing, start NetMeeting, choose Remote Desktop Sharing from the Tools menu, and clear the Enable Remote Desktop Sharing On This Computer check box.

Controlling a Computer at Your Workplace

Wouldn't it be great to sit at your home computer—wearing your pajamas and slippers if you want—and actually be able to use your computer at work? If your work computer is running Windows XP Professional or Windows XP Server, you can use the Remote Desktop Connection to take control of your work computer and get your work done just as if you were sitting in your office. However, you can't use Remote Desktop Connection to remotely control a computer running Windows XP Home.

TIP: **The computer you're connecting to must be configured to allow the Remote Desktop Connection, and the user name with which you log on must be authorized to create the Remote Desktop Connection. If you're the authorized user, you can't connect with a blank password—you must have a valid password.**

TIP: **Windows Firewall might block the Remote Desktop Connection unless you specify Remote Desktop as an exception to the firewall.**

Connect to the Computer

1. Use your usual method to connect to your office network.
2. Choose Remote Desktop Connection from the Communications submenu of the Start menu to display the Remote Desktop Connection dialog box.

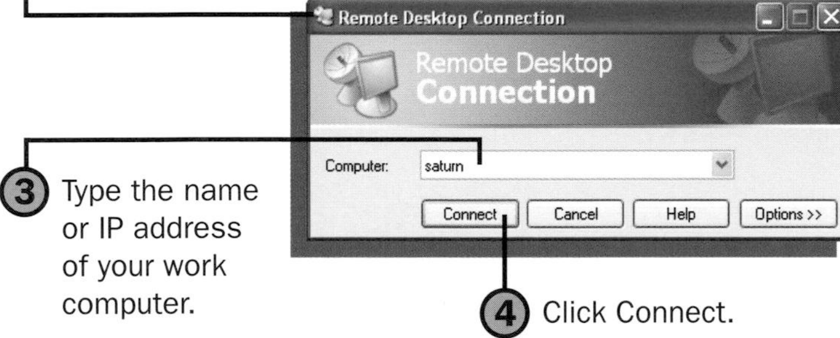

3. Type the name or IP address of your work computer.
4. Click Connect.

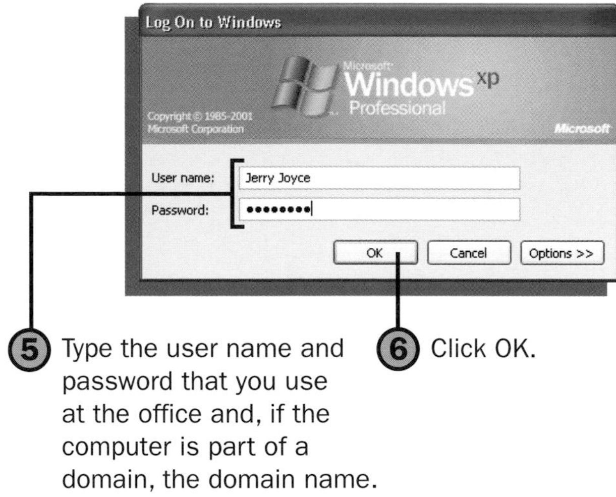

5. Type the user name and password that you use at the office and, if the computer is part of a domain, the domain name.
6. Click OK.

TIP: **If you're running Windows XP Professional, you can enable the Remote Desktop Connection by choosing the Performance And Maintenance category in the Control Panel, clicking the System Control Panel icon, and, on the Remote tab of the System Properties dialog box, selecting the check box to enable remote access to the computer.**

SEE ALSO: **For information about configuring Windows Firewall, see "Creating Custom Access Across the Firewall" on pages 266–267.**

Control the Computer

1. Use the remote Desktop of your work computer just as if you were sitting at your desk in the office.
2. Click to resize the remote Desktop. 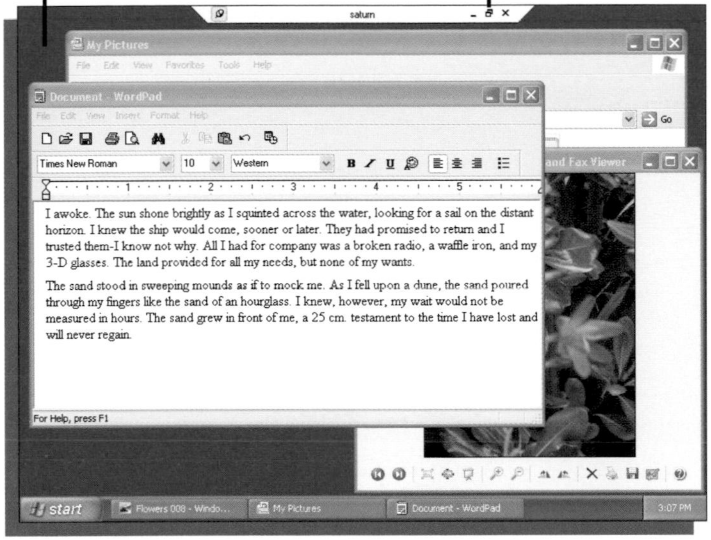
3. Switch between programs on your home computer and your work computer. You can copy and paste items, such as text or graphics, between programs, regardless of which computer each program is on.

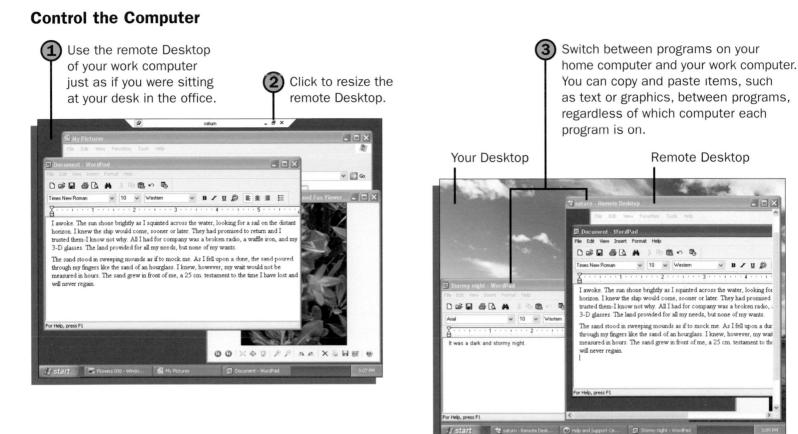

Your Desktop

Remote Desktop

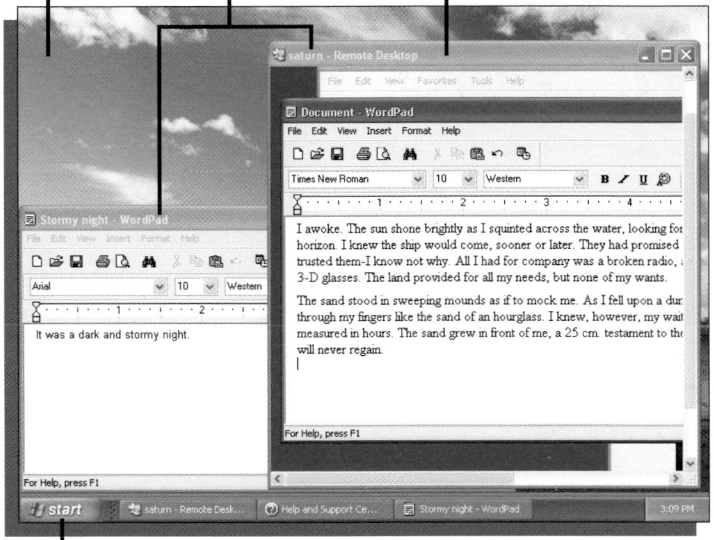

4. When you've finished, open the Start menu, and choose to log off or disconnect.

CAUTION: If someone else is logged on to the remote computer when you log on, the other person will be logged off, which could possibly cause some loss of data.

Connecting to a Network Using a Modem

If you want to connect to a business network over a phone line, you can use Dial-Up Networking to make the connection and to log on to the company's network. You'll be required to establish an account that lets you access resources on the network, and you'll need the proper permissions to connect. Be sure to get all the information you need from the company's network administrator before you connect. Every company has its own security settings and policies, so you'll need those details for the proper configuration.

CAUTION: If you choose to save your user name and password so that anyone can use them, you're leaving the network vulnerable to unauthorized access and possible damage, all in your name. To protect access, save the name only for yourself, and use a password when you first log on to your computer. Also make sure that your computer is free of viruses. When you connect directly to a large network, your computer is probably the weakest link in the network's security.

Create the Dial-Up Connection

1. Choose New Connection Wizard from the Communications submenu of the Start menu, and click Next to start the wizard.

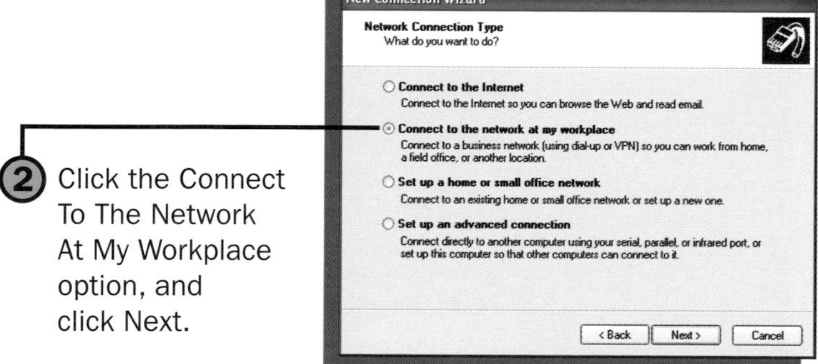

2. Click the Connect To The Network At My Workplace option, and click Next.

3. Click the Dial-Up Connection option, and click Next.

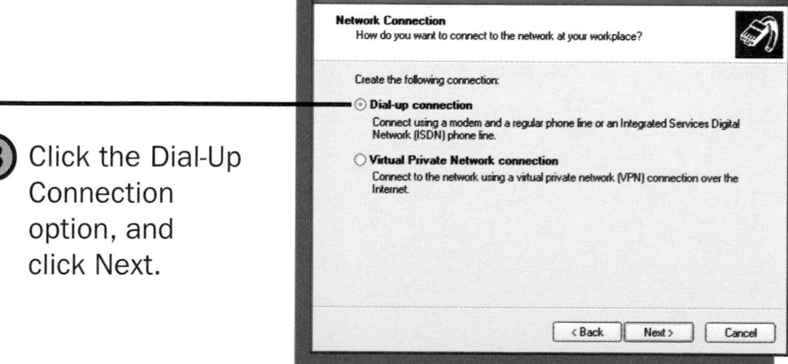

4. Type a name for the connection, and click Next.

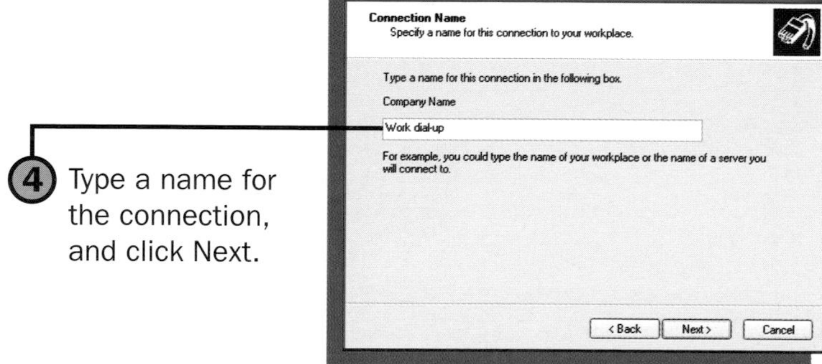

5. Type the phone number for calling the network, and click Next. Click Finish to create the connection.

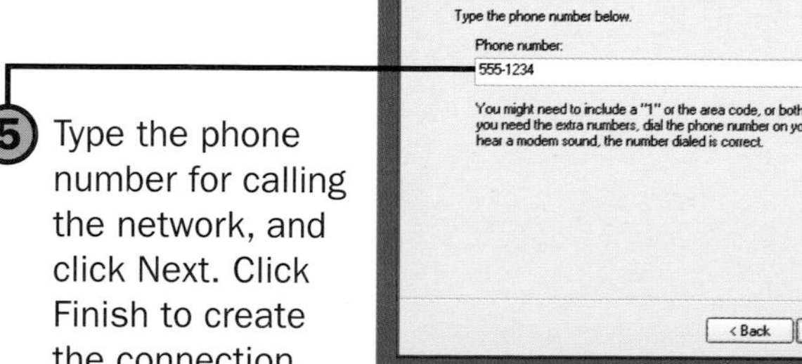

Connect

1. Point to Connect To on the Start menu, and choose the connection to your work computer from the submenu to display the Connect dialog box.

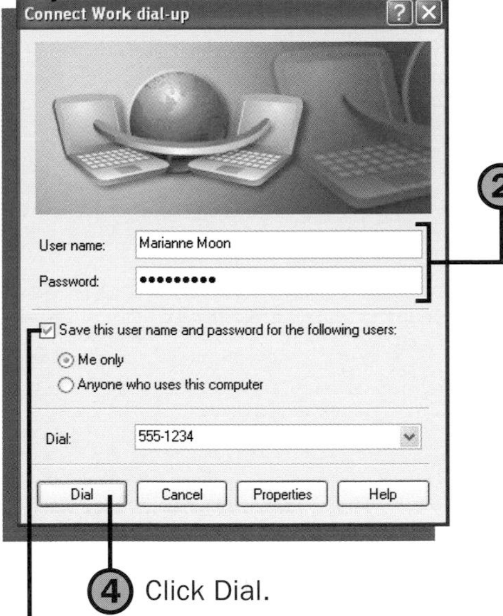

2. Enter your assigned user name and password to connect to the remote network.
3. If you don't want to enter your user name and password each time you connect, select this check box, and then click the Me Only option. To save the information so that anyone who uses the computer can use your name and password, click the Anyone Who Uses This Computer option.
4. Click Dial.

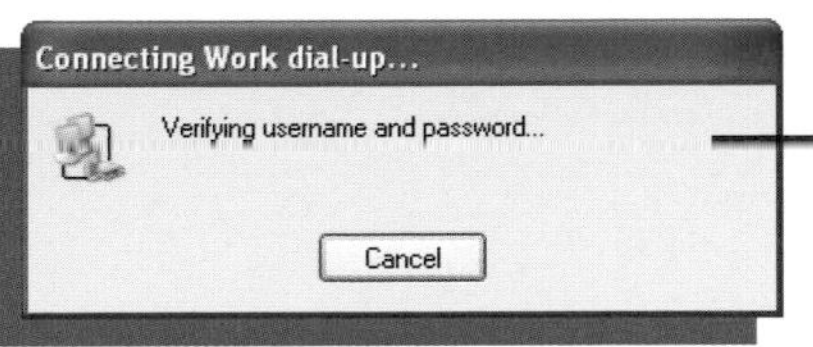

5. Wait to be connected, and then use the connection just as you use any network connection.

6. When you've finished, click the connection icon in the notification area of the task bar to display the Status dialog box. Click Disconnect.

TIP: What you're able to do on the network depends on the design of the system you're connected to. If you run into any problems accessing the resources you need, contact the network administrator for advice.

TIP: If you need to make the connection through an operator, click View Network Connections in the Network Tasks list in My Network Places, select the connection, and choose Operator-Assisted Dialing from the Advanced menu.

Connecting to a Network over the Internet

To connect to your network over the Internet, you can use a VPN (Virtual Private Network), which provides a secure connection between your computer and the network. The computer you connect to must be configured as a VPN server and must be connected to the Internet. Before you connect, verify that you have the correct name of the host computer and the correct user name and password that have been assigned to you.

Create the VPN Connection

1. Choose New Connection Wizard from the Communications submenu of the Start menu, and click Next to start the wizard.

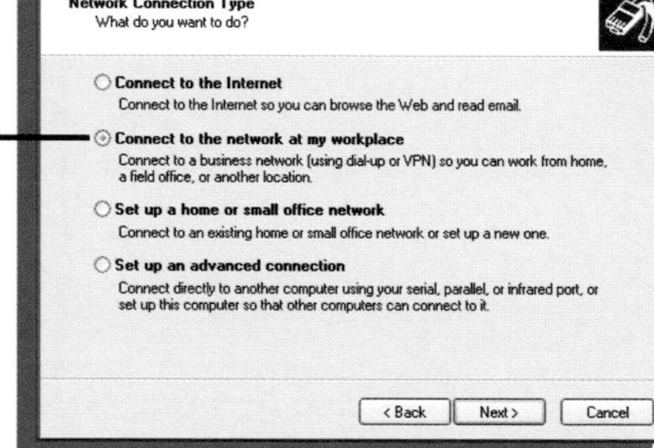

2. Click the Connect To The Network At My Workplace option, and click Next.

3. Click the Virtual Private Network Connection option, and click Next.

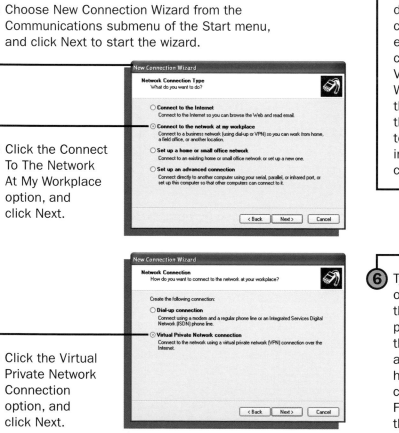

4. Type a name for the connection, and click Next.

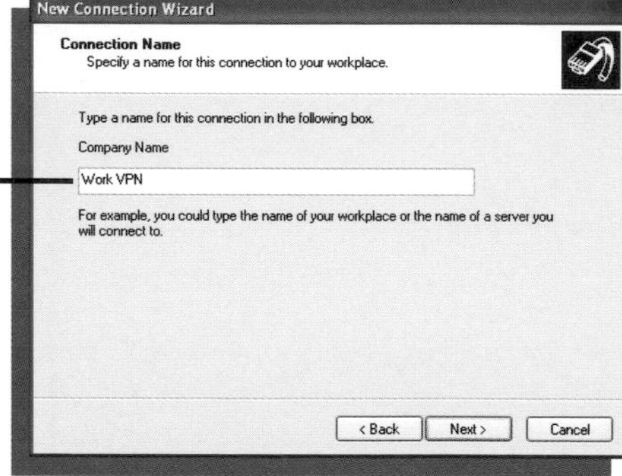

5. Specify whether or not you want Windows XP to dial the Internet connection whenever you want to connect to the VPN. If you want Windows XP to do the dialing, click the connection to the Internet in the list, and click Next.

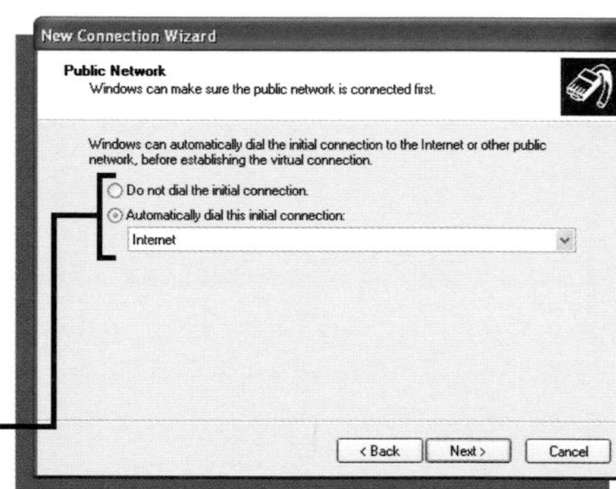

6. Type the host name or the IP address that you were provided with by the person who administers the host computer, and click Next. Click Finish to create the connection.

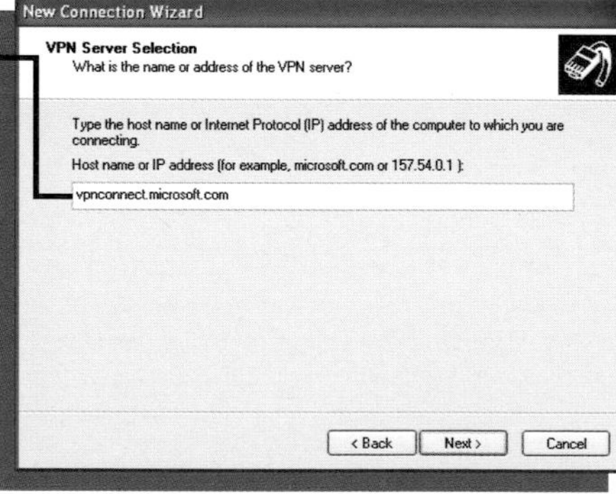

Connect

1. If you chose not to have your Internet connection made automatically when the VPN connection is made, and if you're not currently connected, connect to the Internet. Point to Connect To on the Start menu, and choose the connection to your work computer from the submenu to display the Connect dialog box.

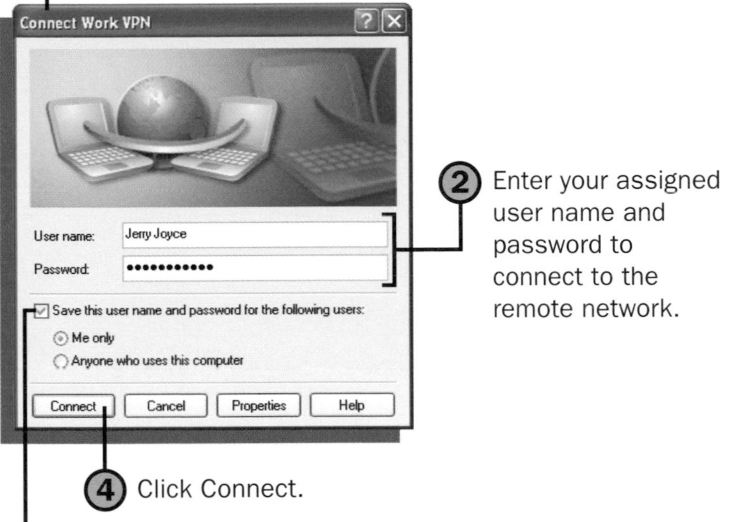

2. Enter your assigned user name and password to connect to the remote network.
3. If you don't want to enter your user name and password each time you connect, select this check box, and then click the Me Only option. To save the information so that anyone who uses the computer can use your name and password, click the Anyone Who Uses This Computer option.
4. Click Connect.

5. Wait for the connection to be established, and then use it just as you use any other network connection.

6. When you've finished, click the connection icon for the VPN in the notification area of the taskbar to display the Status dialog box. Click Disconnect.

TIP: Sometimes the configuration used by an ISP (Internet Service Provider) can interfere when you're creating a VPN connection. If you encounter any problems, check with your ISP to determine whether you need to change any of your settings.

TIP: Although a VPN connection provides a direct and secure connection to the network, you're still subject to all the slowdowns that you might experience whenever you use the Internet, including a slow connection to your service provider, slow performance by your service provider, a general slowdown of the Internet, and poor performance from the VPN server. If you're planning to transfer large files, be prepared to wait!

Connecting to a Wireless Network ❂ NEW FEATURE

The world is bristling with wireless networks, many of which are available to you—provided, of course, that you have a portable computer with a wireless network adapter, and that you know how to connect. You'll find that many of these "Wi-Fi hotspots," whether they're in small coffee shops or large conference centers, provide free access to the Internet and/or the ability to communicate with other computers on the same network. However, in airports and in some of the big coffee chains, you'll often have to pay a fee to access a wireless network. Then all you need to do is turn on your computer and connect to the network you want.

SEE ALSO: For information about setting up a password for your computer, see "Setting Your Password" on page 250.

For information about increasing firewall security for use with public wireless networks, see "Configuring the Windows Firewall" on pages 264–265.

For information about setting up a secure wireless network, see "Securing Your Wireless Network" on pages 274–275.

Connect to an Open-Access Network

1. In an area where you expect a wireless network to be present, turn on your computer with the wireless network adapter installed.

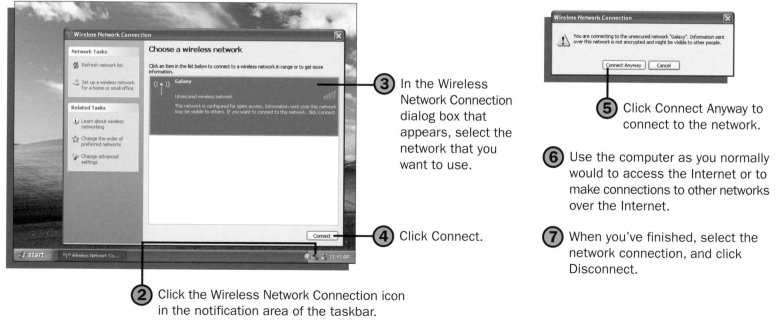

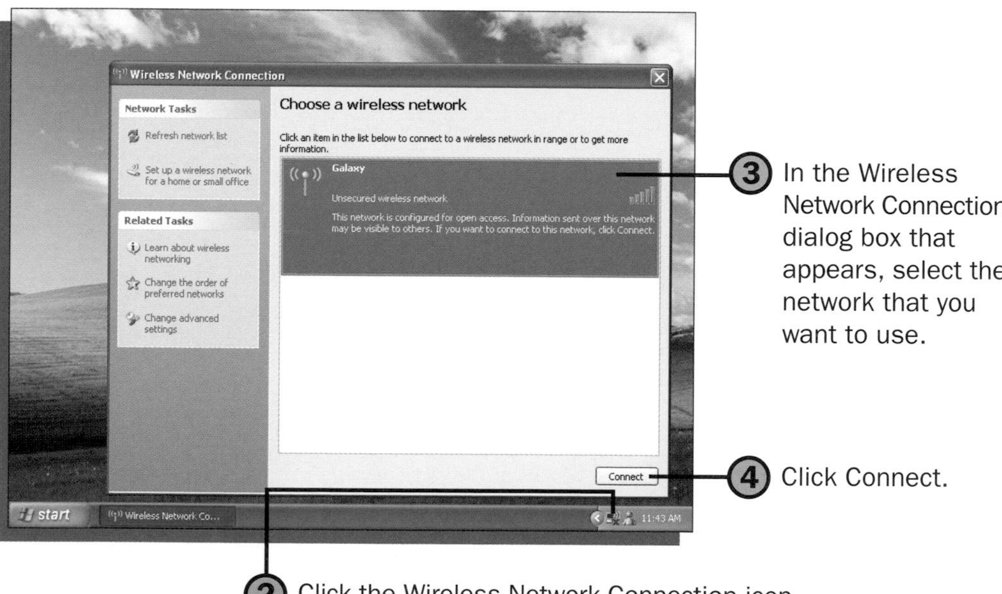

2. Click the Wireless Network Connection icon in the notification area of the taskbar.
3. In the Wireless Network Connection dialog box that appears, select the network that you want to use.
4. Click Connect.

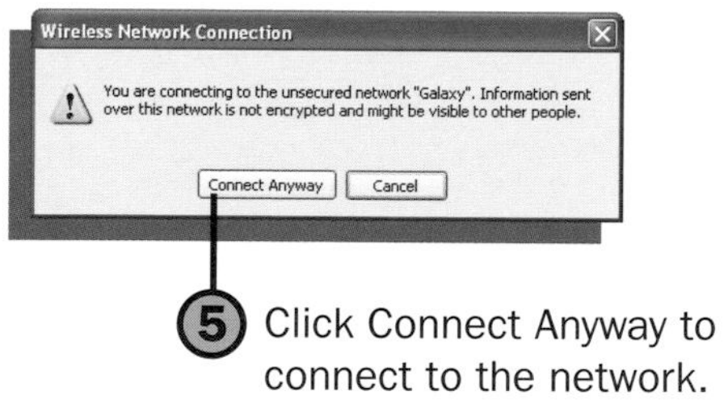

5. Click Connect Anyway to connect to the network.
6. Use the computer as you normally would to access the Internet or to make connections to other networks over the Internet.
7. When you've finished, select the network connection, and click Disconnect.

Connect to a Secure Network

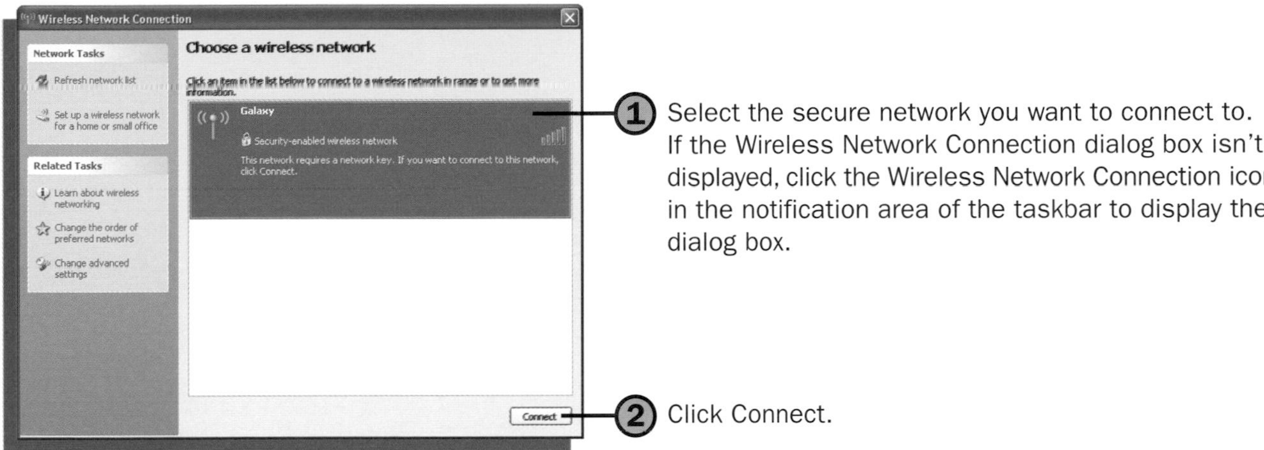

1. Select the secure network you want to connect to. If the Wireless Network Connection dialog box isn't displayed, click the Wireless Network Connection icon in the notification area of the taskbar to display the dialog box.
2. Click Connect.

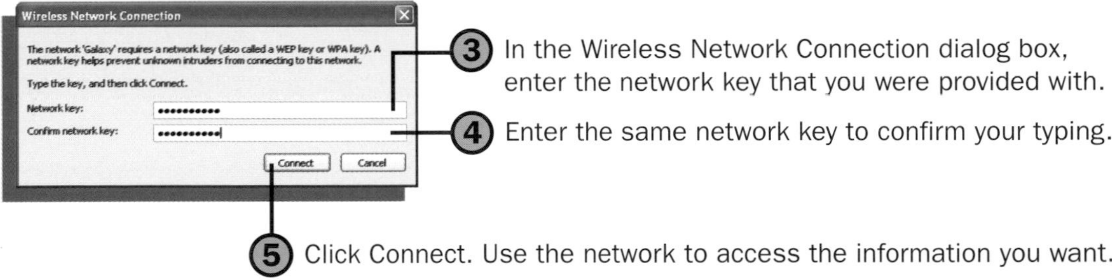

3. In the Wireless Network Connection dialog box, enter the network key that you were provided with.
4. Enter the same network key to confirm your typing.
5. Click Connect. Use the network to access the information you want.
6. If the Wireless Network Connection dialog box isn't open when you've finished, double-click the Wireless Network Connection icon in the notification area of the taskbar. In the Wireless Network Connection dialog box, click Disconnect (the Connect button changes to the Disconnect button when you're connected to the network).

CAUTION: Any files that are stored in shared folders can be accessed by other users of the network. Make sure that you require a password to access your computer so that full authentication is needed to access your files.

Connecting to Your Computer from Another Location

If you want to connect to your own computer from another computer and establish a network connection so that you can transfer or use files, you can turn your computer into a small version of a dial-up network server. To do so, you create an incoming connection and allow only authorized users to connect to your computer.

Create an Incoming Connection

1. Choose New Connection Wizard from the Communications submenu of the Start menu, and click Next to start the wizard.

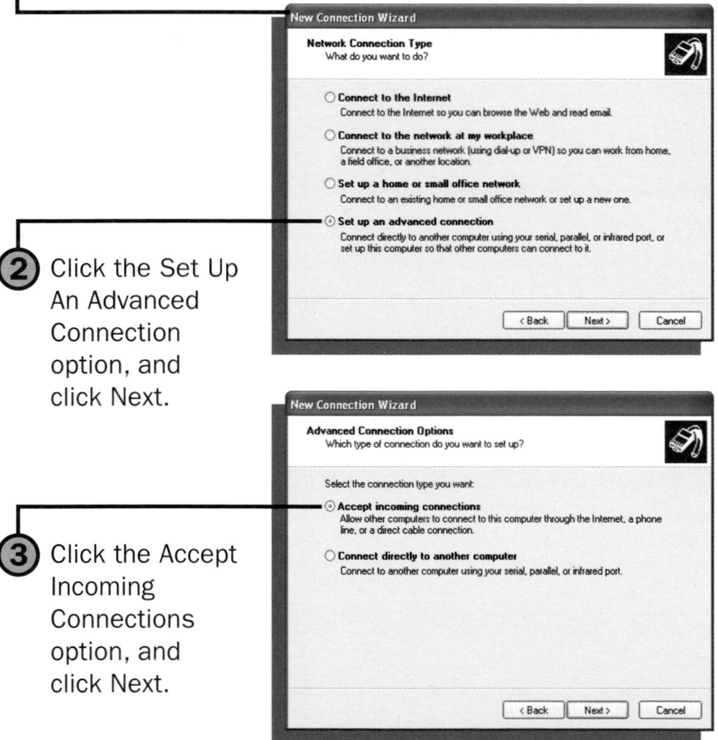

2. Click the Set Up An Advanced Connection option, and click Next.
3. Click the Accept Incoming Connections option, and click Next.

4. Specify the device (usually your modem) that you'll be using, and click Next.

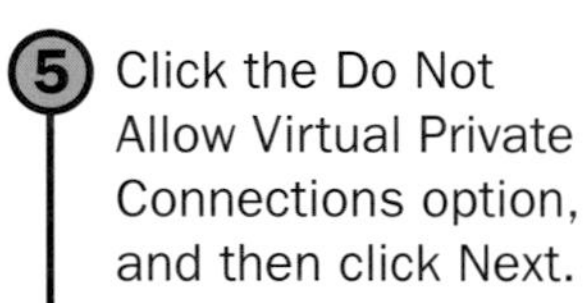

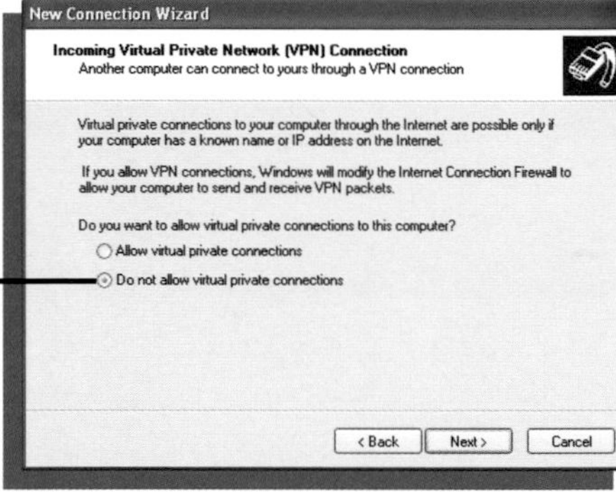

5. Click the Do Not Allow Virtual Private Connections option, and then click Next.
6. Select the check boxes for the users who are allowed access to your computer. (Only authorized users of the computer can connect.)

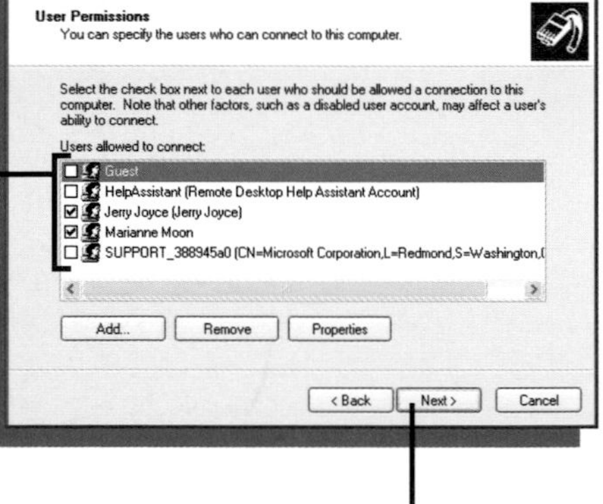

7. Click Next, click Next again in the Network Software page of the wizard, and click Finish to create the incoming connection.

Setting Up

In this section

One of the things that usually takes all the fun out of buying a new computer is having to set up all over again the files and settings that took such a long time to get exactly right on your old computer. Well, we have good news for you! You can transfer your files and settings easily and quickly with the help of a wizard that walks you through the process. If you choose to transfer the information over your network, you provide a few pieces of information and type a password, and the transfer happens automatically. If you use disks to transfer the information, just follow the instructions on the screen until the transfer is complete.

True to this section's title, you'll also find information about setting up dial-up Internet access so that you can explore the far reaches of the Web's vastness; setting up Outlook Express for sending and receiving e-mail messages, as well as for subscribing to newsgroups; setting up Fax Service so that you can send and receive faxes directly through your computer; setting up a printer that's attached to your computer; and setting up a network.

In addition, in this section we'll talk about adding or removing Microsoft Windows XP components or parts thereof, installing software programs, and adding hardware devices to your computer.

If these all sound like daunting tasks, rest assured that they're not. With the instructions on the pages that follow, and with help from the wonderful wizards of Microsoft, you'll sail right through them.

Transferring Files and Settings

If you said "bye-bye" to your old computer and went out and bought a new super-duper computer loaded with Windows XP, you'll be glad to know that you can transfer your files and all sorts of settings from the old computer to the new one. You don't have to set everything up again! You can transfer your settings, including those for Outlook Express, Internet Explorer, and your dial-up connections, by running the Files And Settings Transfer Wizard on both your old and new computers.

Set Up the Computers

1. On the new computer, choose the Files And Settings Transfer Wizard from the System Tools submenu of the Start menu.

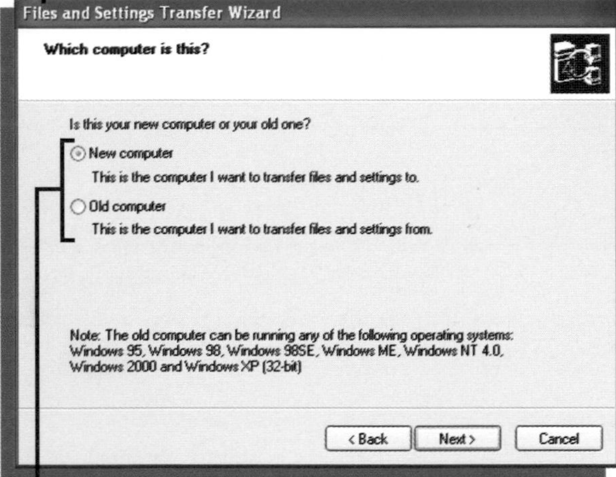

2. On the new computer, step through the beginning part of the wizard, completing the information below, and then stopping when the wizard tells you to stop. Specify that
   - This is the new computer.
   - You're going to use the Windows XP CD on the old computer. If you don't have the CD, use the option to create a copy of the wizard on a floppy disk.

3. On the old computer, insert the Windows XP CD, and, when it starts, choose Perform Additional Tasks from the menu that appears. On the next menu, choose Transfer Files And Settings to start the Files And Settings Transfer Wizard. Step through the wizard, specifying
   - That this is the old computer.
   - Whether you're going to transfer the file using a serial transfer cable, your network (which is the easiest way), a multitude of floppy disks, or a removable drive or network drive.

TIP: The network-connection option is available only when both computers are running the Files And Settings Transfer Wizard and when both computers are properly connected to your network.

Transfer the Information

1. On the old computer, specify whether you want to copy files, settings, or both, and whether you want to select which files and settings are to be copied.

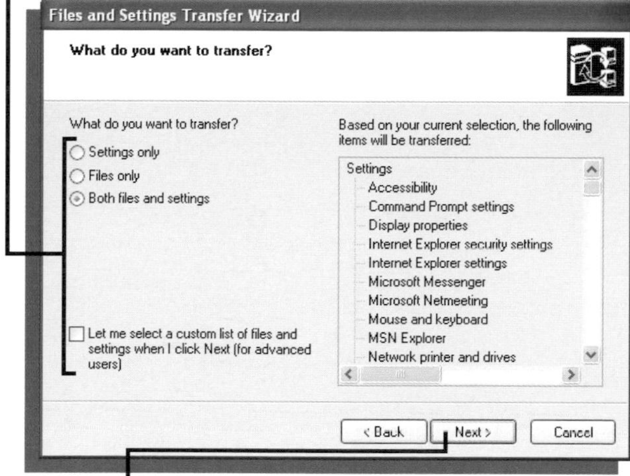

2. Click Next. If you're using disks, follow the instructions on the screen, and switch disks when prompted to do so.

TIP: If you're using a serial transfer cable, you'll need to establish the connection on both computers before you start gathering information from your old computer. Follow the directions in the wizard to establish the connection.

TIP: Some files and settings can't be transferred. After you've completed the transfer procedure but before you click Finish, note any comments about files or settings that weren't transferred successfully.

3. If you're transferring the information over your network, write down the password that's displayed on the new computer, type it in the Password dialog box on the old computer, and click OK. The transfer will take place automatically.

4. If you're using disks, on the new computer, click Next. Click the Floppy Drive Or Other Removable Media option, and click Next. Follow the instructions on the screen to switch disks.

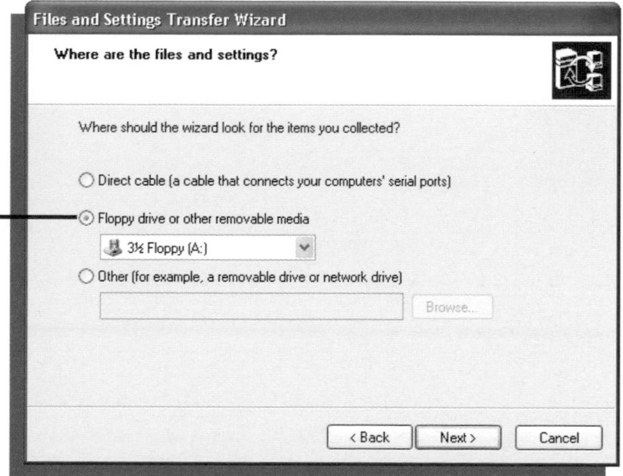

5. Click Finish when the transfer is complete.

Adding or Removing Windows Components

When Windows XP is installed on your computer, some—but not all—of its components are included in the installation. If any components you need haven't been installed, you can add them, and, by the same token, if there are components you never use, you can remove them from your system to save disk space.

TIP: A shaded check box indicates that only some of the items in the group will be installed. Use the Details button to modify which items are to be installed.

Add or Remove a Component Group

1. Save any documents you're working on, and close all your running programs.
2. Choose Control Panel from the Start menu, and click the Add Or Remove Programs category to display the Add Or Remove Programs dialog box.
3. Click Add/Remove Windows Components to start the Windows Components Wizard.
4. On the Windows Components page of the wizard, clear a check box to remove an entire component, or select a check box to add all the items in a component group.

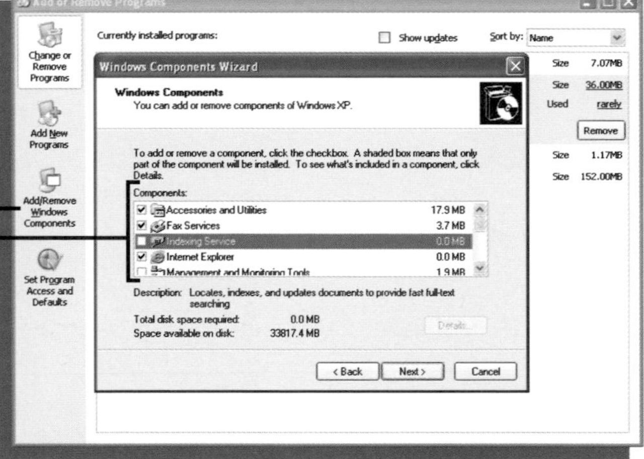

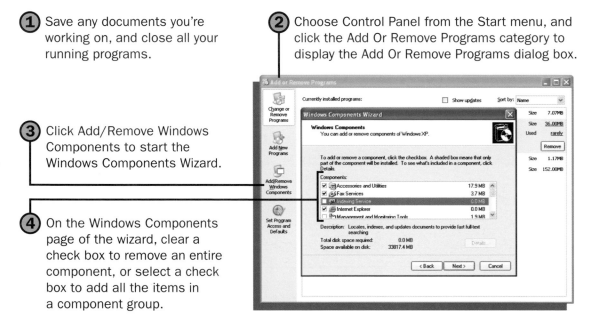

SEE ALSO: For information about updating existing Windows components or adding components that have recently been released, see "Updating Your System" on page 290.

TIP: You can install additional components and utilities from other sources. On the Windows XP CD, in the Valueadd folder, you'll find the Setup program for Windows Backup—a program for backing up and safeguarding your files. If you buy Microsoft Plus! For Windows XP, you'll find that it contains numerous additional components and utilities. And you can find many other items at the Windows Update Web site.

Add or Remove an Item in a Component Group

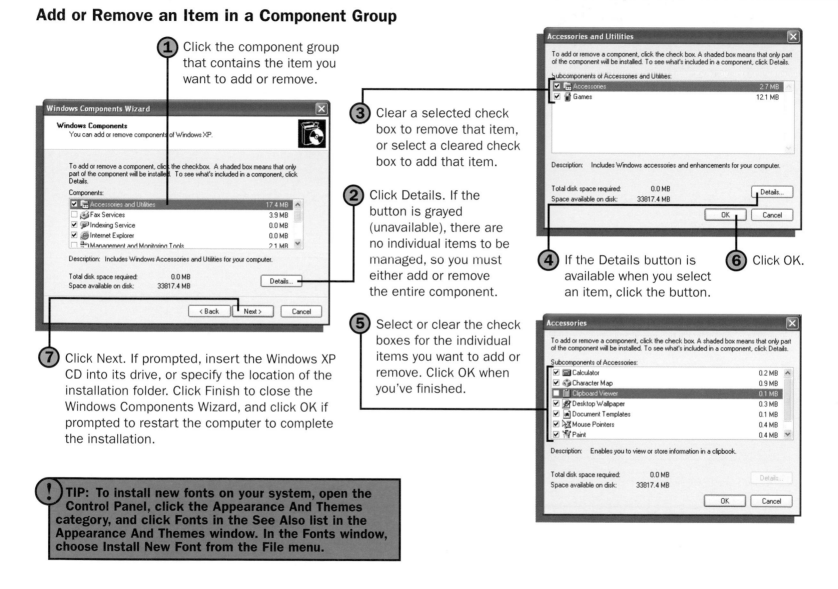

1. Click the component group that contains the item you want to add or remove.

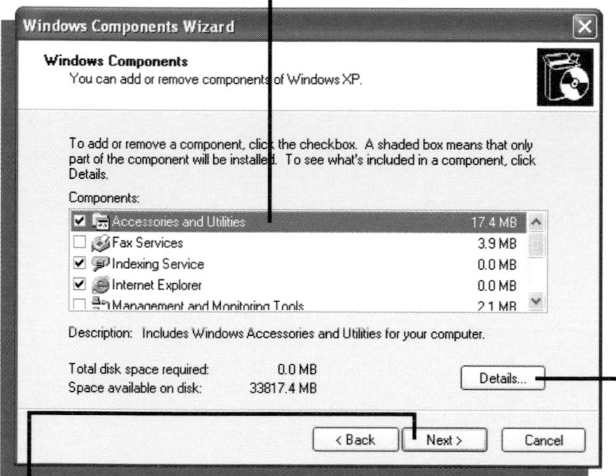

2. Click Details. If the button is grayed (unavailable), there are no individual items to be managed, so you must either add or remove the entire component.
3. Clear a selected check box to remove that item, or select a cleared check box to add that item.

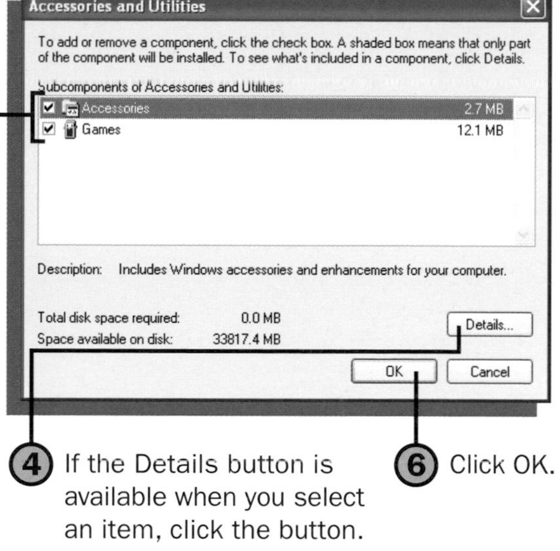

4. If the Details button is available when you select an item, click the button.
5. Select or clear the check boxes for the individual items you want to add or remove. Click OK when you've finished.

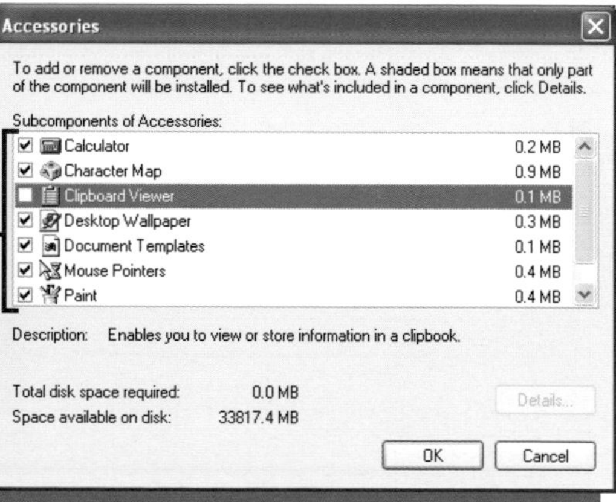

6. Click OK.
7. Click Next. If prompted, insert the Windows XP CD into its drive, or specify the location of the installation folder. Click Finish to close the Windows Components Wizard, and click OK if prompted to restart the computer to complete the installation.

TIP: To install new fonts on your system, open the Control Panel, click the Appearance And Themes category, and click Fonts in the See Also list in the Appearance And Themes window. In the Fonts window, choose Install New Font from the File menu.

Setting Your Default Programs ⊕ NEW FEATURE

When you set up Windows XP, certain programs are designated as the default programs for specific tasks: Outlook Express for your e-mail, for example; Internet Explorer for Web browsing; Windows Media Player for playing videos and digital music; and Windows Messenger for instant messaging. However, if there are other programs you want to use instead, you can set them as your default programs.

TIP: Programs that have previously been used or associated with the type of file selected are shown on the Open With submenu. Choosing a program from that submenu will open a file in that program but won't make the program the default program for that type of file.

Set a Program to Always Open a File

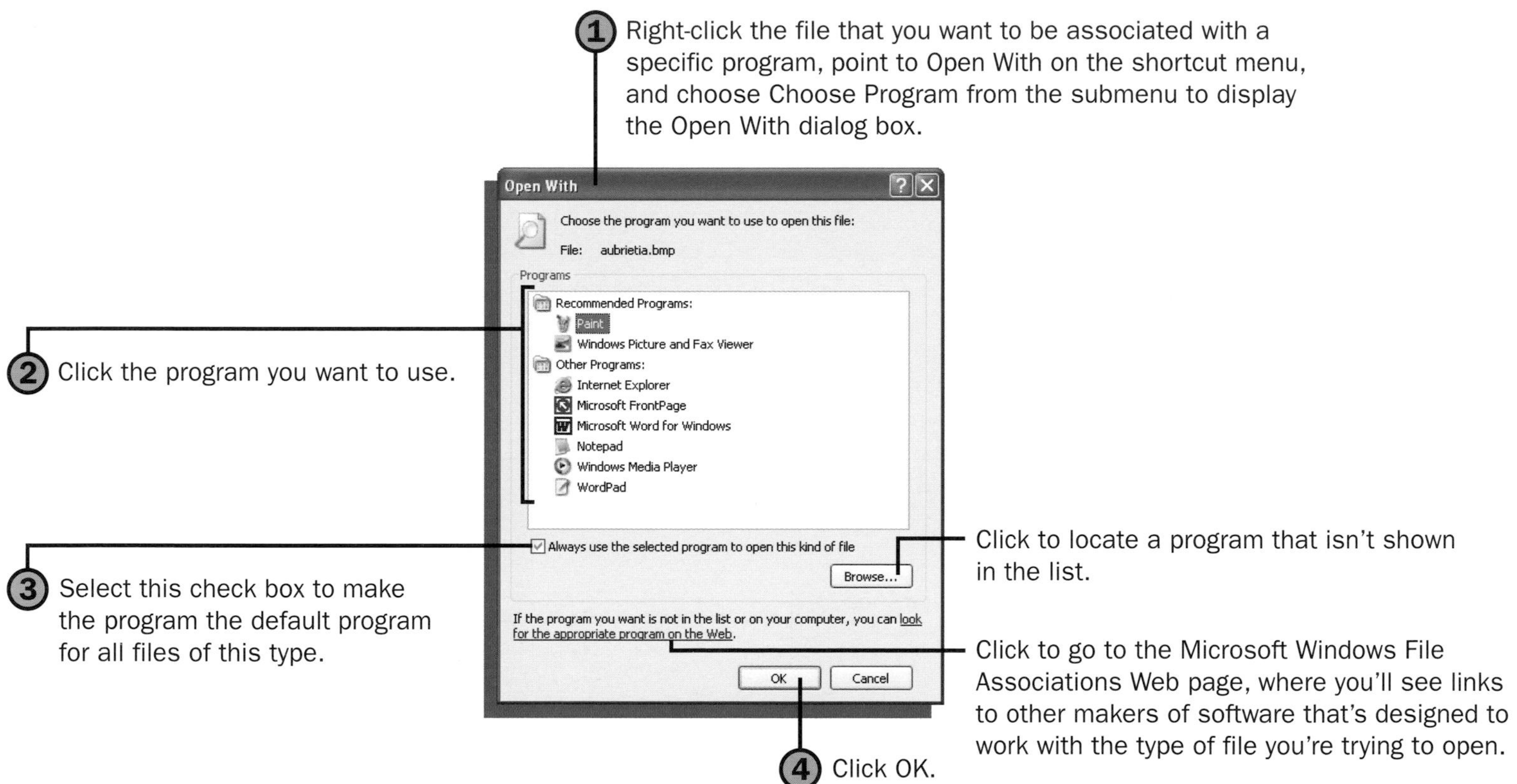

1 Right-click the file that you want to be associated with a specific program, point to Open With on the shortcut menu, and choose Choose Program from the submenu to display the Open With dialog box.
Open With
Choose the program you want to use to open this file:
File: aubrietia.bmp
Programs
Recommended Programs:
Paint
Windows Picture and Fax Viewer
Other Programs:
Internet Explorer
Microsoft FrontPage
Microsoft Word for Windows
Notepad
Windows Media Player
WordPad
Always use the selected program to open this kind of file
Browse...
If the program you want is not in the list or on your computer, you can look for the appropriate program on the Web.
OK
Cancel
2 Click the program you want to use.
3 Select this check box to make the program the default program for all files of this type.
Click to locate a program that isn't shown in the list.
Click to go to the Microsoft Windows File Associations Web page, where you'll see links to other makers of software that's designed to work with the type of file you're trying to open.
4 Click OK.

Set the System Defaults

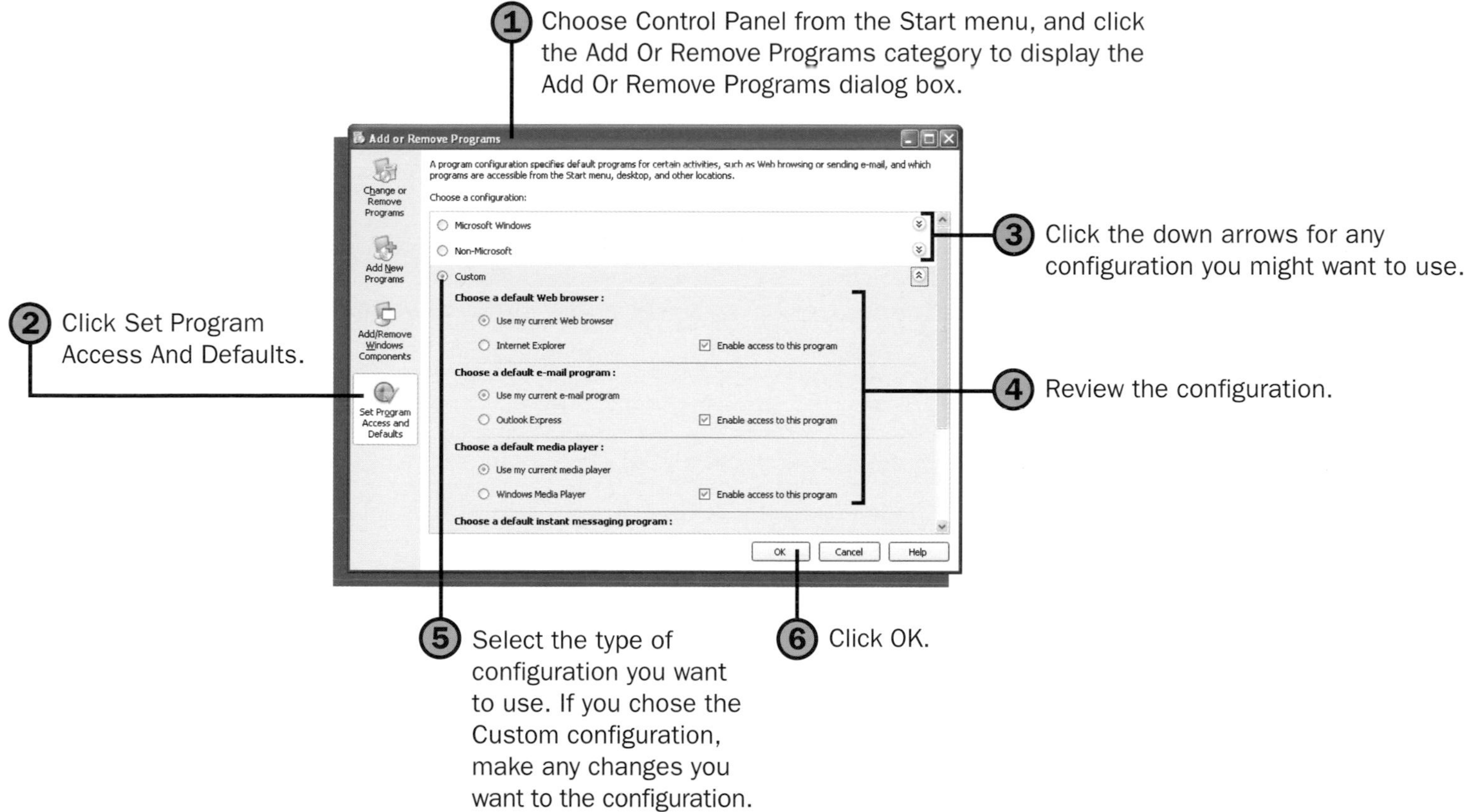

1. Choose Control Panel from the Start menu, and click the Add Or Remove Programs category to display the Add Or Remove Programs dialog box.
2. Click Set Program Access And Defaults.
3. Click the down arrows for any configuration you might want to use.
4. Review the configuration.
5. Select the type of configuration you want to use. If you chose the Custom configuration, make any changes you want to the configuration.
6. Click OK.

NEW FEATURE: The Set Program Access And Defaults tool makes it easy to use whatever program you want. By setting a program as the default, you ensure that the program will automatically open whenever you need it—when you double-click a music file, your default music player opens, when you choose to send a file via e-mail, your default e-mail program opens.

TIP: When you initially install certain programs, they'll automatically set themselves as the default programs for some files. If there's a program you want to use but it isn't set as your default program, use the procedure on the facing page to designate it as the default program before you use the Set Program Access And Defaults settings.

Installing a Software Program

Almost every software program contains its own installation program, which copies the required files to the computer's hard disk and tells Windows XP which files are installed, where they are, and what they do.

TIP: You can also install a program by double-clicking its *setup.exe* or *install.exe* program in a folder window.

TIP: Some programs are only partially installed until you use them for the first time. When you first choose one of these programs from the Start menu, you'll be asked whether you want to install it. You'll see this request if you chose Install On First Use when you installed the program.

Install a Program

1. Close all your running programs. If you're installing from a CD, insert the CD into its drive, follow the instructions that appear on the screen, and skip steps 2 through 5.
2. If the CD didn't start, or if you're installing from a different drive or from a network location, choose Control Panel from the Start menu, and click the Add Or Remove Programs category to display the Add Or Remove Programs dialog box.

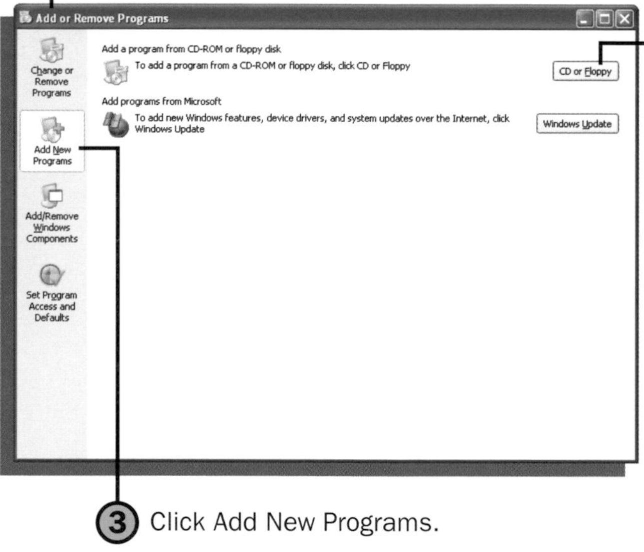

3. Click Add New Programs.
4. Click CD Or Floppy. If you are installing from a CD or disk, place it in to its drive. Click Next.
5. If the Setup or installation program is found, click Finish. If not, click Browse, locate the Setup or installation program on a different drive or in a network folder, and click Finish.

6. Follow the Setup or installation program's instructions, and close the Add Or Remove Programs dialog box when the installation is complete.

Setting Up Dial-Up Internet Access

Many ISPs (Internet Service Providers) supply installation CDs or other setup disks, and all you have to do is insert the CD or the disks into the appropriate drive and follow the instructions on the screen. However, if you don't have the installation materials, you can easily set up your connection manually.

Set Up a Connection

1. Choose New Connection Wizard from the Communications submenu of the Start menu, and click Next to start the wizard.
2. Click the Connect To The Internet option, and click Next.
3. Click the Set Up My Connection Manually option, and click Next.

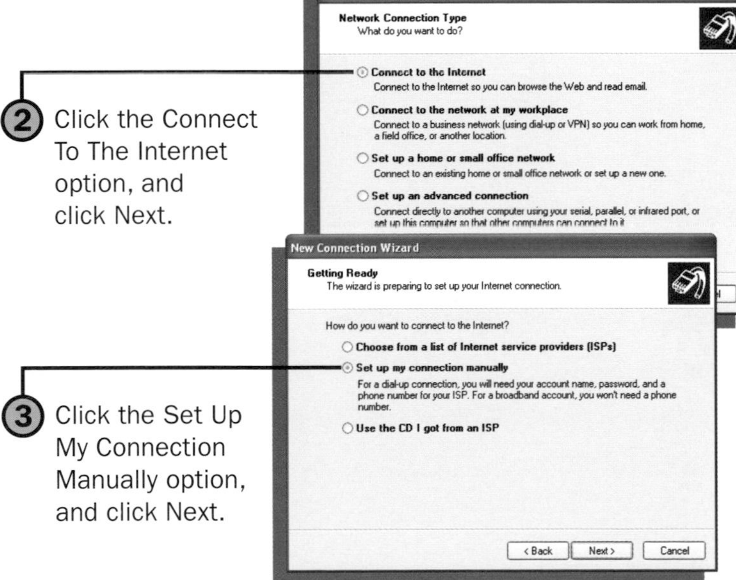

4. Click the Connect Using A Dial-Up Modem option, and click Next.

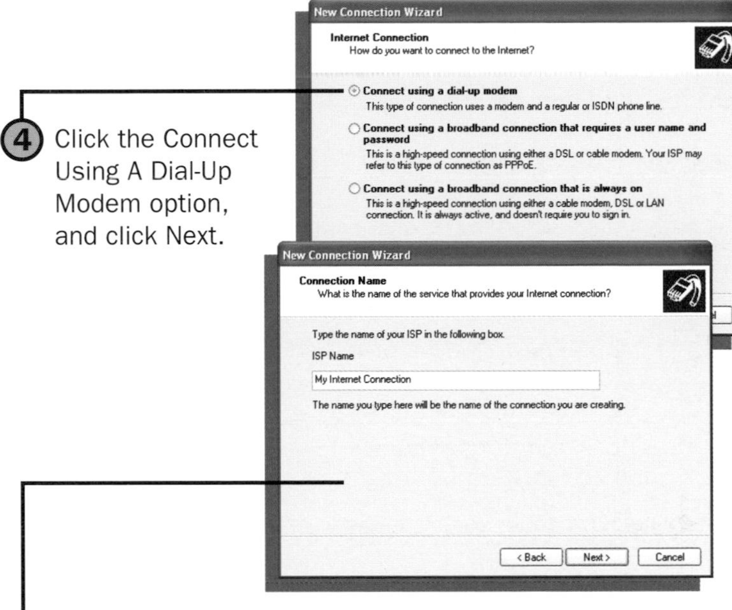

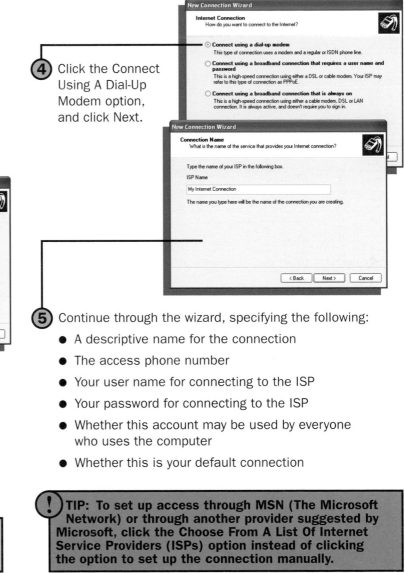

5. Continue through the wizard, specifying the following:
   - A descriptive name for the connection
   - The access phone number
   - Your user name for connecting to the ISP
   - Your password for connecting to the ISP
   - Whether this account may be used by everyone who uses the computer
   - Whether this is your default connection

SEE ALSO: For information about using a firewall to protect your Internet access, see "Configuring the Windows Firewall" on pages 264–265.

TIP: To set up access through MSN (The Microsoft Network) or through another provider suggested by Microsoft, click the Choose From A List Of Internet Service Providers (ISPs) option instead of clicking the option to set up the connection manually.

Setting Up Outlook Express

When you first set up Windows XP, you probably set up your e-mail account at the same time. However, if you didn't set up the account, or if you want to add newsgroups or another e-mail account, you can easily make changes to the Outlook Express setup.

TIP: In case you're wondering, POP3 is Post Office Protocol 3, IMAP is Internet Message Access Protocol, HTTP is Hypertext Transfer Protocol, and NNTP is Network News Transfer Protocol.

Set Up Your E-Mail Account

1. Choose Outlook Express from the Start menu. If this is the first time you've started Outlook Express, the Internet Connection Wizard will start.

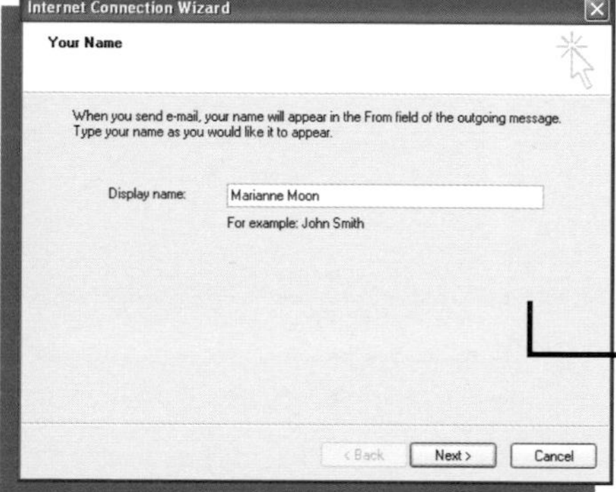

Internet Connection Wizard
Your Name
When you send e-mail, your name will appear in the From field of the outgoing message. Type your name as you would like it to appear.
Display name:
Marianne Moon
For example: John Smith
< Back
Next >
Cancel

Internet Connection Wizard
Internet E-mail Address
Your e-mail address is the address other people use to send e-mail messages to you.
E-mail address:
moonjoyceresourc@hotmail.com
For example: someone@microsoft.com
< Back
Next >
Cancel

2. Step through the wizard, specifying the following:
   - Your name as you want it displayed in your e-mail
   - Your e-mail address
   - The type of incoming mail server (HTTP, POP3, or IMAP)
   - The addresses of the incoming and outgoing e-mail servers, if they haven't already been supplied
   - Your e-mail account name (usually the same as your e-mail address) and your password
   - Whether your e-mail provider requires you to log on using Secure Password Authentication

SEE ALSO: For information about transferring your Outlook Express settings and messages from another computer, see "Transferring Files and Settings" on pages 208–209.

For information about creating an Internet connection to your ISP (Internet Service Provider), see "Setting Up Dial-Up Internet Access" on page 215.

Add an Account

1. In Outlook Express, choose Accounts from the Tools menu to display the Internet Accounts dialog box.

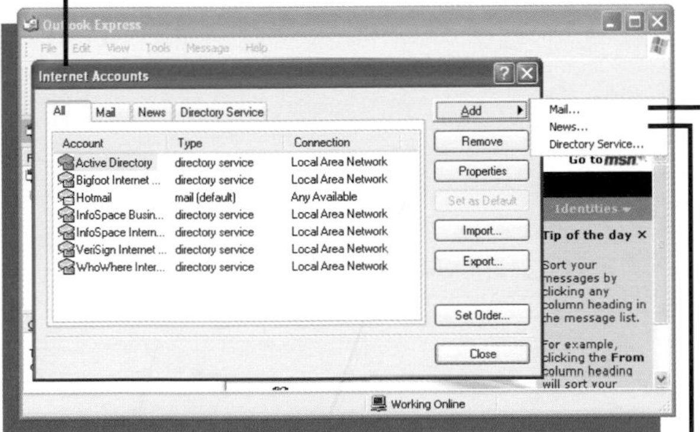

2. Click Add, and choose Mail from the submenu that appears. Step through the Internet Connection Wizard to add the e-mail account.

3. Click Add again, and choose News from the submenu to start the Internet Connection Wizard. Step through the wizard, specifying the following:
   - Your name as you want it to appear in the newsgroups
   - Your e-mail address
   - The address of the news server
   - Whether you need to log on to use the server, and, if so, your logon name and password

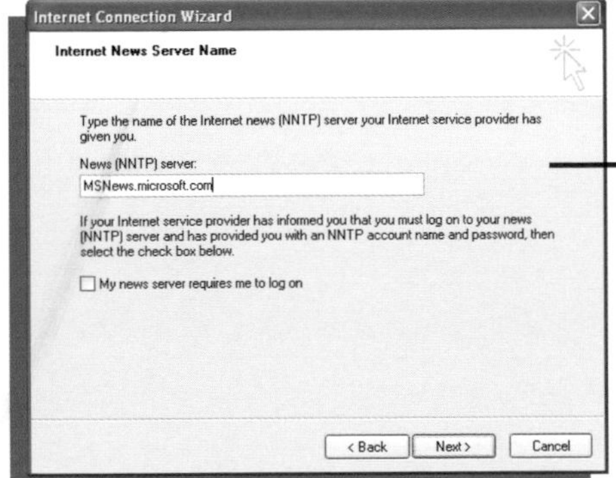

SEE ALSO: For information about using Outlook Express, see "Sending E-Mail" on page 66 and "Subscribing to Newsgroups" on page 75.

TIP: Gather up all your account information from your ISP before you set up the e-mail account. Mail protocols and server names can be complex and confusing.

Setting Up for Faxing

If your computer has a fax modem, you can use Fax Service, which allows you to send and receive faxes through your computer. Before you can use Fax Service, you'll need to provide some personal information that can be used on the fax cover page. You'll also need to enter your identification number for Fax Service and set options for the way you want your faxes to be sent and received.

Set the Options

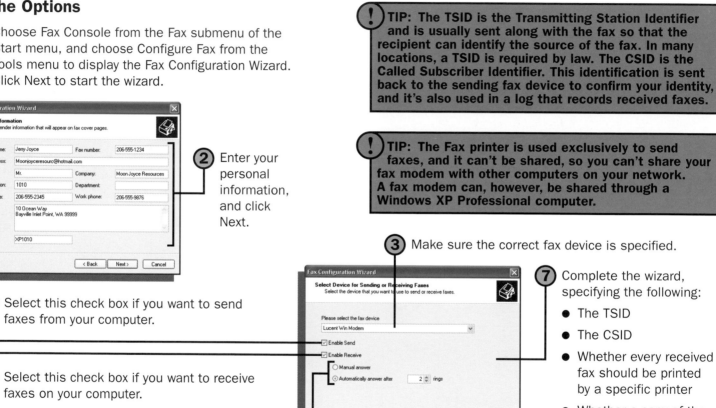

1. Choose Fax Console from the Fax submenu of the Start menu, and choose Configure Fax from the Tools menu to display the Fax Configuration Wizard. Click Next to start the wizard.

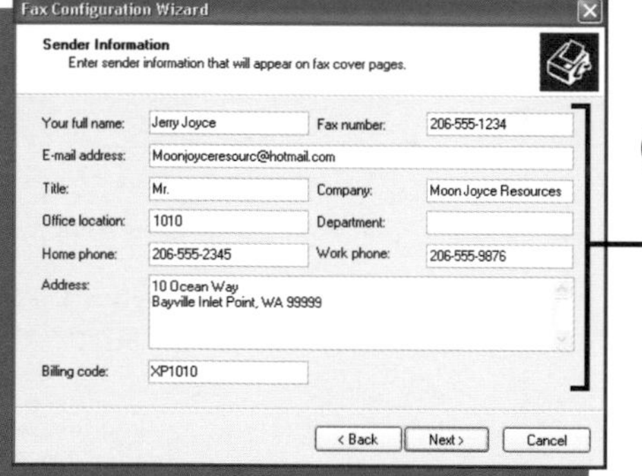

2. Enter your personal information, and click Next.

> **TIP:** The TSID is the Transmitting Station Identifier and is usually sent along with the fax so that the recipient can identify the source of the fax. In many locations, a TSID is required by law. The CSID is the Called Subscriber Identifier. This identification is sent back to the sending fax device to confirm your identity, and it's also used in a log that records received faxes.

> **TIP:** The Fax printer is used exclusively to send faxes, and it can't be shared, so you can't share your fax modem with other computers on your network. A fax modem can, however, be shared through a Windows XP Professional computer.

3. Make sure the correct fax device is specified.
4. Select this check box if you want to send faxes from your computer.
5. Select this check box if you want to receive faxes on your computer.
6. If you want to receive faxes, click an option to specify whether the faxes are to be received manually or automatically. If you specify automatic receiving, designate the number of rings before the modem answers the call.
7. Complete the wizard, specifying the following:
   - The TSID
   - The CSID
   - Whether every received fax should be printed by a specific printer
   - Whether a copy of the fax is to be stored in a specific folder

SEE ALSO: For information about installing Fax Service if it isn't already installed, see "Adding or Removing Windows Components" on pages 210–211.

Setting Up a Printer

Windows XP might or might not detect your printer, depending on how and to what the printer is attached. Windows should detect and install any printer that's attached to your computer's USB (Universal Serial Bus) or infrared port. If the printer is attached to a parallel or serial port, however, Windows might not have detected the printer when it was installed, so you'll need tell Windows about it yourself.

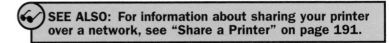

SEE ALSO: For information about sharing your printer over a network, see "Share a Printer" on page 191.

Set Up a Printer

1. If the printer came with an installation disk that's designed to work with Windows XP, follow the directions that came with the printer to run the installation program. The printer should then be installed correctly.

2. If you don't have an installation disk, with the printer connected and turned on, choose Control Panel from the Start menu, click the Printers And Other Hardware category, and click the Add A Printer task. Click Next to start the Add Printer Wizard.

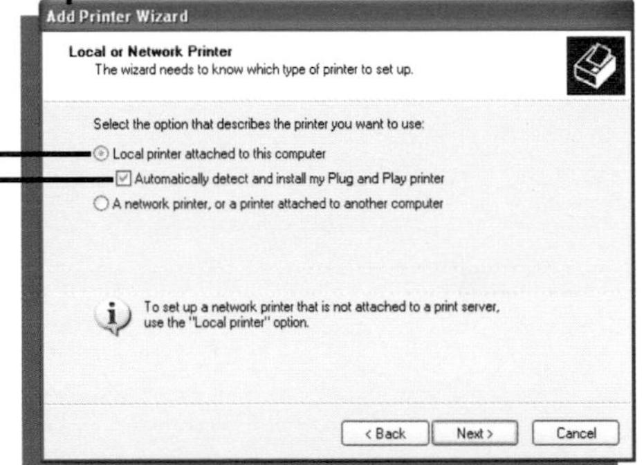

3. Click the Local Printer Attached To This Computer option.

4. Select this check box to have Windows XP look for the printer, and then click Next. If Windows doesn't detect the printer, click Next.

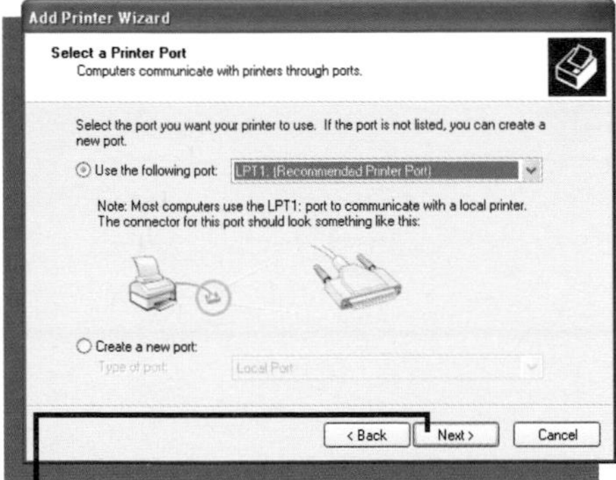

5. In the list, click the port to which the printer is connected, and click Next.

6. Do one of the following:
   - Select the manufacturer and model of the printer.
   - Click Have Disk if you have a disk or a download of the required files.
   - Click Windows Update to download new printer installation files.

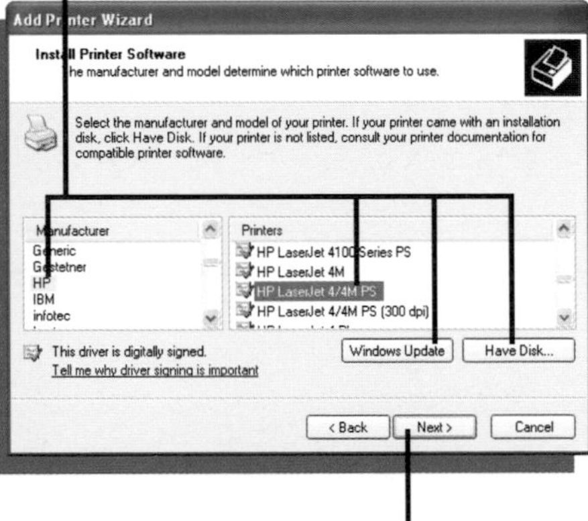

7. Click Next, and complete the wizard, specifying the following:
   - A name for the printer
   - Whether this is your default printer
   - Whether the printer is to be shared on your network, and, if so, the name it will display to the other computers
   - Whether you want to print a test page to verify the setup

Setting Up a Network

If your network hasn't already been set up, you can configure it easily. To do so, you first have to set up one of the computers as the network *host.* Then you configure the other computers on your network to be *clients* of the host. There are two different types of network configurations: one in which you use one of your computers to host the network and connect to the Internet, and the other in which you use a router that hosts the network and connects to the Internet. When you use a computer as the host, you first set up the host computer and then add the other computers as network clients. In a network with a router, all the computers are network clients.

Set Up the Host Computer

TIP: Be sure to set up your Internet connection on the host computer before you set up the network. Verify that all the computers that will be on the network have the proper network cards and cables and are turned on and operating correctly.

1. With all your network connections in place and all the computers turned on, on the computer that will host your network, choose Network Setup Wizard from the Communications submenu of the Start menu, and click Next to start the wizard.

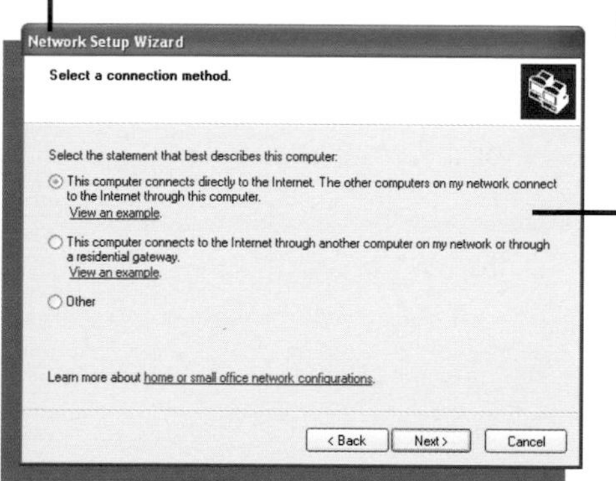

2. Step through the wizard, specifying the following:
   - That this computer connects directly to the Internet
   - The connection you'll use to connect to the Internet
   - A friendly description of the computer and a name for the computer
   - A name for your workgroup
   - Whether you want to allow sharing of files and printers on your computer over the network

3. After confirming the configuration and clicking Next, wait for the computer to do a preliminary search of the network to identify the computers and shared items that are available.

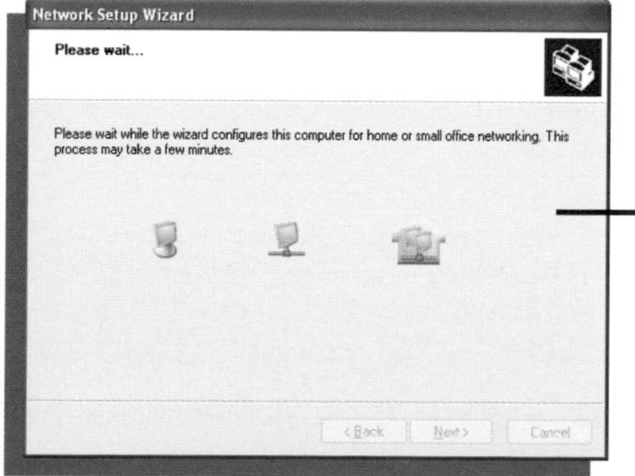

4. If a computer that will be part of the network isn't running Windows XP, do either of the following:
   - Click the Create A Network Setup Disk option if you don't have a Windows XP CD.
   - Click the Use My Windows XP CD option.

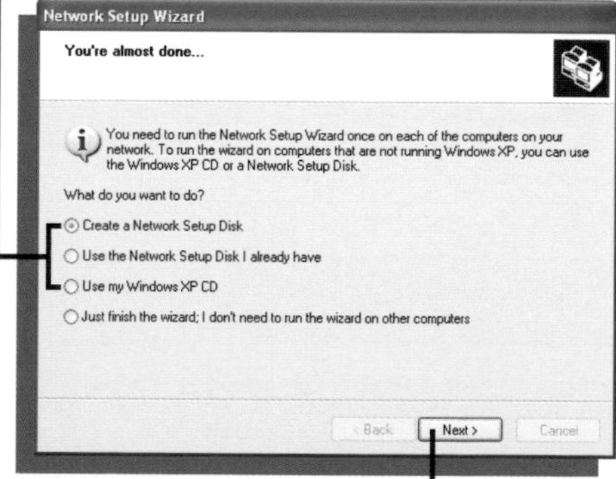

5. Click Next, and follow the instructions to complete the wizard.

Set Up a Network Client

1. Choose Network Setup Wizard from the Communications submenu of the Start menu, and click Next to start the wizard.

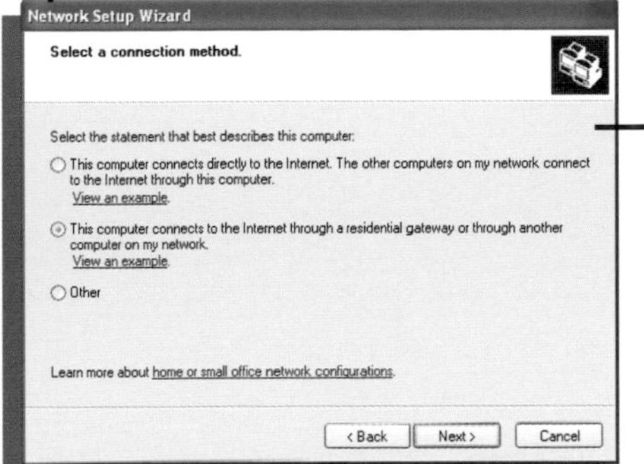

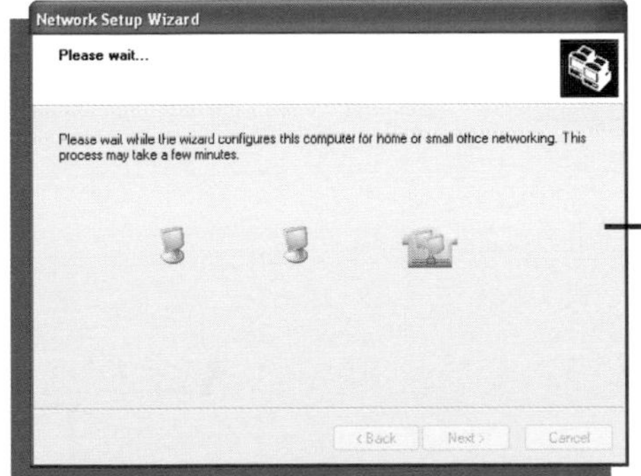

CAUTION: A network can have only one host. If you're adding a computer that's running Windows XP, and you want that computer to host an existing network that uses ICS (Internet Connection Sharing), you must disable ICS before you can set up your Windows XP computer as the host.

2. If the computer isn't running Windows XP, insert the Windows XP CD and, when the CD starts, choose Perform Additional Tasks from the menu that appears. From the next menu, choose Set Up A Home Or Small Office Network.

3. Step through the wizard, specifying the following:
   - That this computer connects to the Internet through another computer or through a residential gateway
   - A friendly description of the computer and a name for the computer
   - A name for your workgroup
   - Whether you want to allow sharing of files and printers on your computer over the network

4. After confirming the configuration and clicking Next, wait for the computer to search your network, and then complete the wizard.

TIP: If you aren't using the Windows XP CD, and if you created a setup disk, place the disk in the client computer's disk drive, choose Run from the Start menu, type a:netsetup **and press Enter.**

SEE ALSO: For information about setting up a wireless network that uses high security to prevent outside intrusion, see "Securing Your Wireless Network" on pages 274–275.

Adding Hardware

In most cases, when you install a piece of hardware, Windows XP detects it, configures it, and installs the necessary software drivers. Sometimes, however, Windows doesn't detect the hardware device, which means that you'll have to install it manually. When a device isn't detected, it's usually because Windows doesn't have the necessary software drivers, so you'll need to obtain that software from the manufacturer before you can install the device. If the hardware came with an installation CD, use it to install the hardware. If you don't have an installation CD, use the Add Hardware Wizard to install the hardware.

Set Up the Hardware

1. If the hardware has been properly installed on the computer but Windows XP doesn't recognize it, shut down Windows and then restart it to see whether Windows has detected the hardware now.
2. If Windows still hasn't detected the hardware, open the Control Panel, and click Printers And Other Hardware. Click Add Hardware in the See Also list to display the Add Hardware Wizard. Click Next to start the wizard.
3. Click the Yes, I Have Already Connected The Hardware option, and click Next.

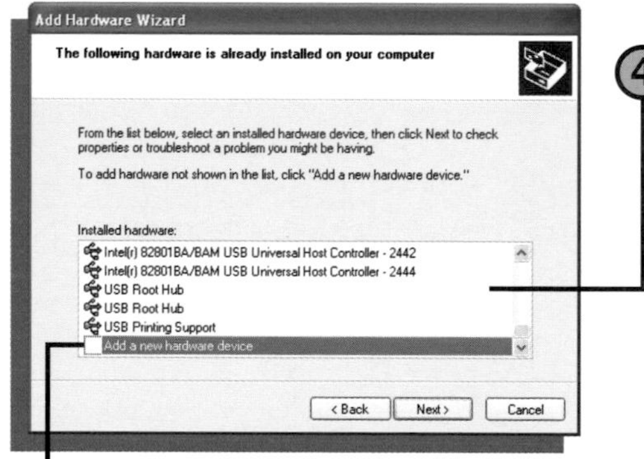

4. Review the list of installed items. If your hardware is listed, it has already been installed, but there might be a problem. Double-click the item to see whether there's any troubleshooting information about it and to complete the wizard.
5. If your hardware isn't listed, double-click Add A New Hardware Device. Click the Search For And Install The Hardware Automatically option, and click Next. If the hardware is detected, Windows should install it for you.

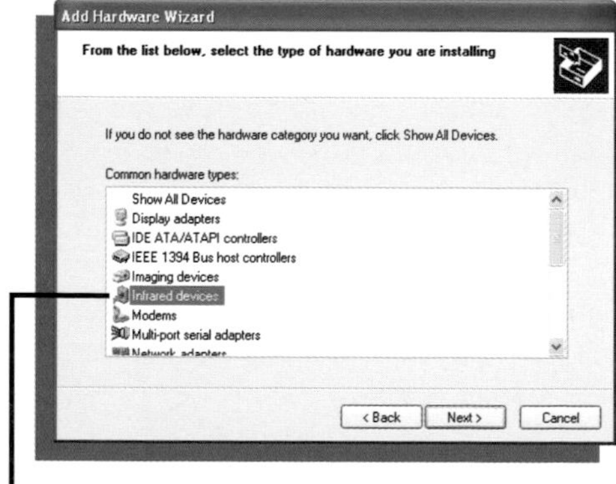

6. If Windows doesn't detect the hardware, click Next, and double-click the type of device.

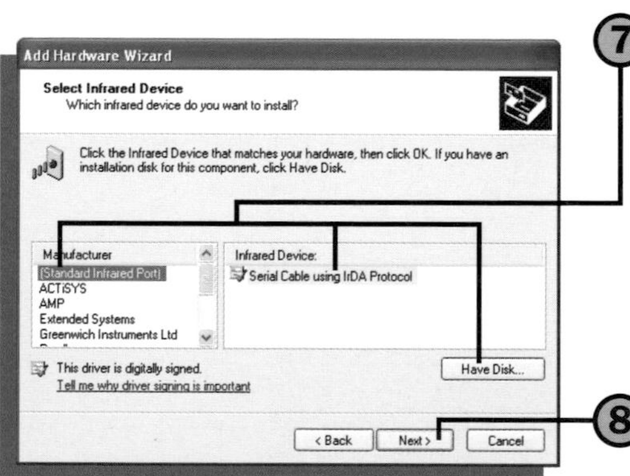

7. Do either of the following:
   - Click the manufacturer and model.
   - Click Have Disk if you have a disk or a download of the required files. Use the Browse button to locate the files, and click OK.
8. Click Next, and complete the wizard.

Customizing

In this section

With Microsoft Windows XP installed, you can customize just about everything on your computer to make it look and work exactly the way you want it to. If the new look of Windows XP doesn't appeal to you, you can revert to the classic Windows interface, design your own look with elements from both styles, or change the look to that of a Web page. You can customize your Desktop with a color, a picture, or Web content that can be updated on a specific schedule. You can change the size and color of almost everything; set items to open with one click instead of two; and rearrange or hide the taskbar, toolbars, Start menu, and Desktop items. You can even customize your little friend the mouse.

You can use a single window in which to open all your folders, or use a separate window for each folder if you prefer; you can choose the details—date, author, and so on—that you want to be shown in your folder windows; and you can customize your folder windows with colors and pictures. You can change the way you log on for increased security, change the picture that Windows assigns to your user account, and even change the way a CD starts, depending on its content.

If you have any problems with your vision, hearing, or manual dexterity—or if you simply want to try a different way of working—you can use some innovative tools: press key combinations one key at a time instead of simultaneously, use high-contrast color schemes or the Magnifier tool for better visibility, control mouse movements with the numeric keypad on your keyboard, specify visual cues to replace the computer's beeps, or type your text on the On-Screen Keyboard.

Changing the Overall Look

If Windows XP's interface doesn't appeal to you, you can change whatever you don't like about it—the colors, the fonts, and so on. If you yearn for the familiarity of the old classic Windows look, a few mouse-clicks do away with the new and bring back the old. Can't decide? How about a combination of the old and the new, or a design of your own?

TIP: Your Theme list might contain a variety of different themes, depending on whether you installed Windows XP as an upgrade, whether you installed one of the Microsoft Plus! For Windows XP packs, or whether you downloaded themes. To download themes, choose More Themes Online from the Theme list.

Switch to the Classic Windows Look

SEE ALSO: For information about the Microsoft Plus! packs, see "The Microsoft Plus! Packs" on page 36.

1. Right-click a blank spot on the Desktop, and choose Properties from the shortcut menu to display the Display Properties dialog box.
2. Click the Themes tab.
3. Click the down arrow in the Theme box, and click Windows Classic in the list.
4. Click Apply, and wait for the theme to be applied.

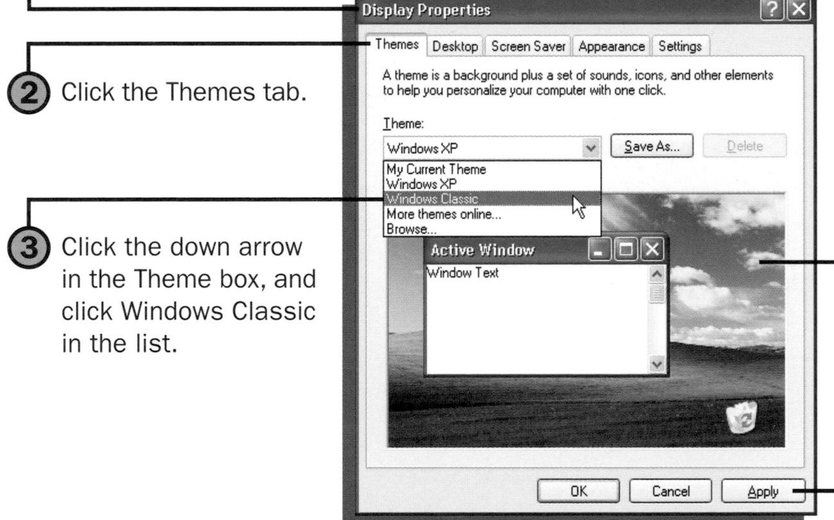

Preview of the Desktop and window appearance of the currently selected theme

CAUTION: If you modify a theme and then choose another theme, you'll lose all your changes. To preserve your changes, click the Save As button on the Themes tab, type a name for your theme, and click Save.

TIP: To return to the original Windows XP look after you've made changes, click Windows XP in the Theme list.

Customize the Look

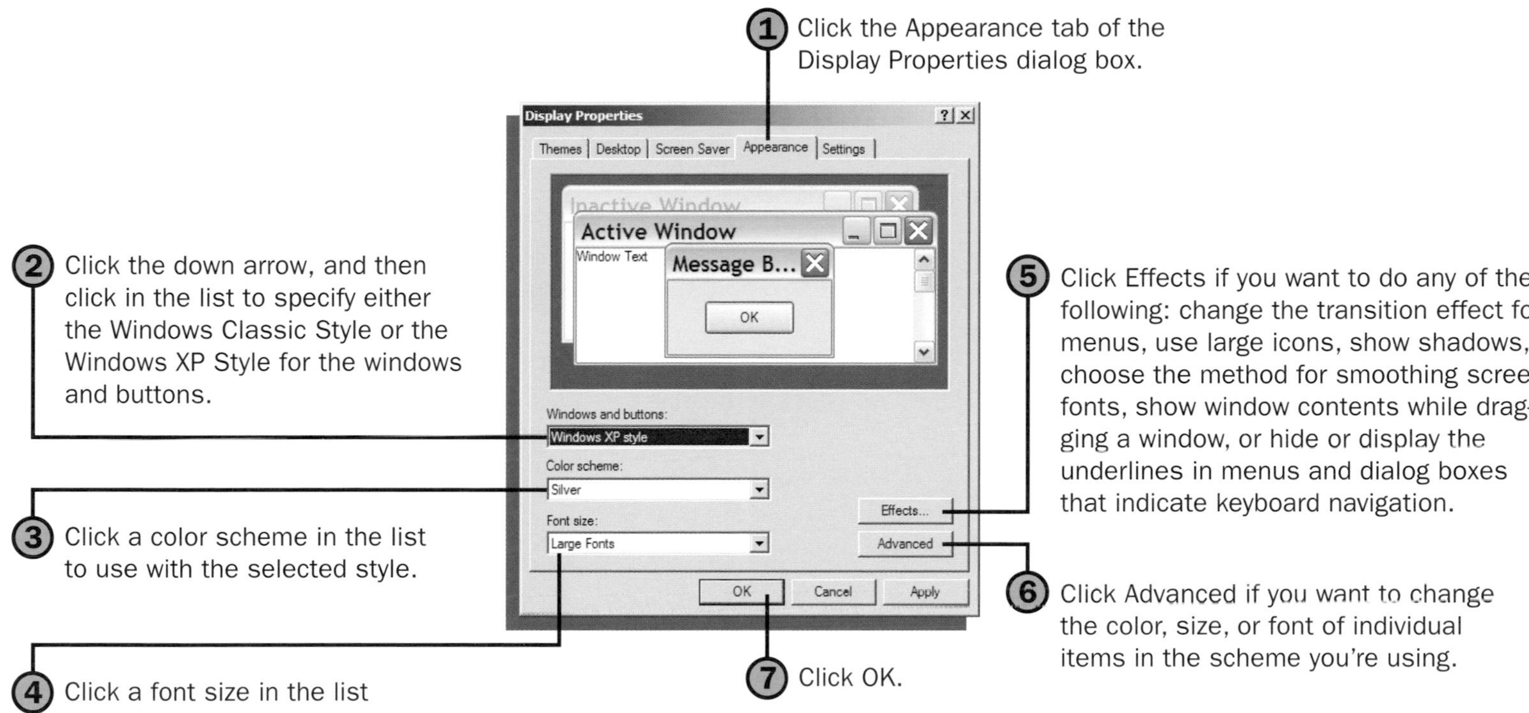

1. Click the Appearance tab of the Display Properties dialog box.
2. Click the down arrow, and then click in the list to specify either the Windows Classic Style or the Windows XP Style for the windows and buttons.
3. Click a color scheme in the list to use with the selected style.
4. Click a font size in the list to apply to the text.
5. Click Effects if you want to do any of the following: change the transition effect for menus, use large icons, show shadows, choose the method for smoothing screen fonts, show window contents while dragging a window, or hide or display the underlines in menus and dialog boxes that indicate keyboard navigation.
6. Click Advanced if you want to change the color, size, or font of individual items in the scheme you're using.
7. Click OK.

TIP: The ClearType option in the Effects dialog box smoothes the edges of screen fonts and can dramatically improve the readability of text on a flat screen, such as that of a portable computer. The ClearType option might not work quite as well on a standard CRT monitor.

SEE ALSO: For information about switching the Start menu to the classic Windows layout, see "Customizing the Start Menu" on pages 232–233.

Customizing the Desktop

Your physical desktop—whether it's oak, glass, or some sort of composite—always looks the same (assuming it's visible under that pile of paper in your "paperless office"). Your Windows XP Desktop, on the other hand, can change dramatically. You can paint it any color you want, and it can display a picture. You can hide all the standard Desktop icons or display the ones you need. Keep experimenting until you find the look you like.

Use a Background Color

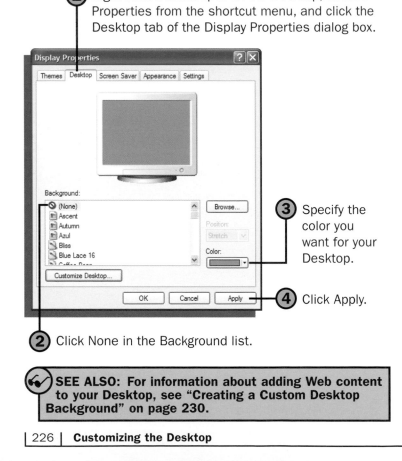

1. Right-click a blank spot on the Desktop, choose Properties from the shortcut menu, and click the Desktop tab of the Display Properties dialog box.

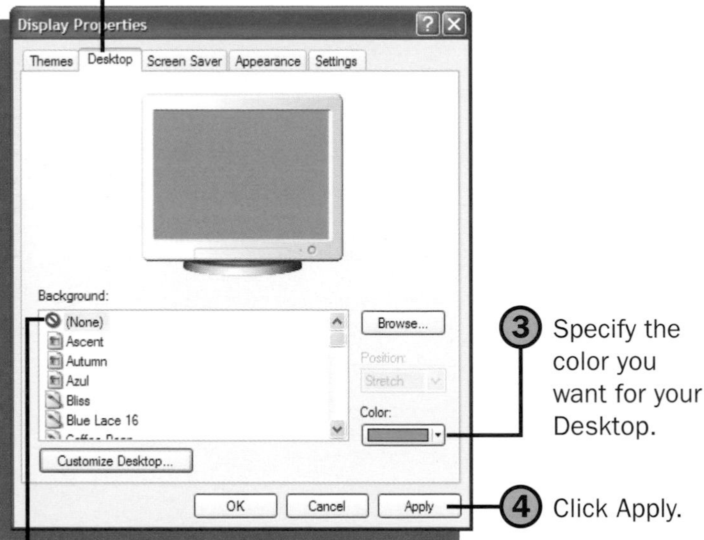

2. Click None in the Background list.
3. Specify the color you want for your Desktop.
4. Click Apply.

SEE ALSO: For information about adding Web content to your Desktop, see "Creating a Custom Desktop Background" on page 230.

TIP: If you add Web content to your Desktop, your Desktop icons will use the background color as the background for their text. If no Web content is displayed, the background for the text is transparent.

Use a Picture

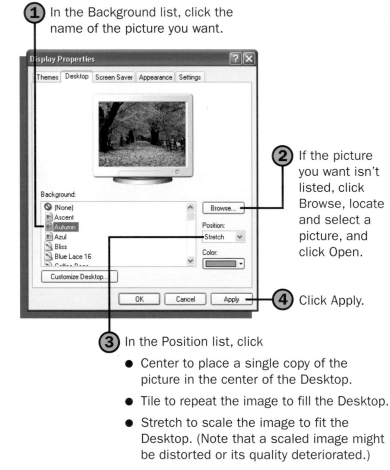

1. In the Background list, click the name of the picture you want.

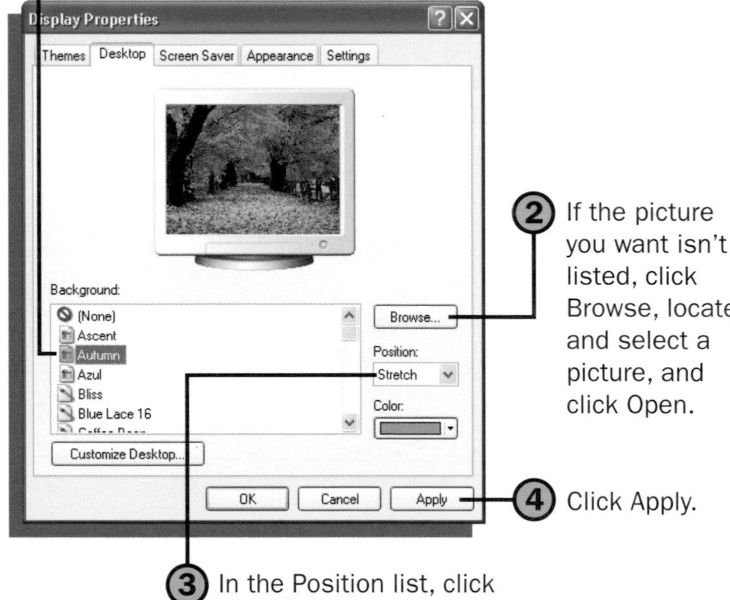

2. If the picture you want isn't listed, click Browse, locate and select a picture, and click Open.
3. In the Position list, click
   - Center to place a single copy of the picture in the center of the Desktop.
   - Tile to repeat the image to fill the Desktop.
   - Stretch to scale the image to fit the Desktop. (Note that a scaled image might be distorted or its quality deteriorated.)
4. Click Apply.

Display and Customize the Desktop Icons

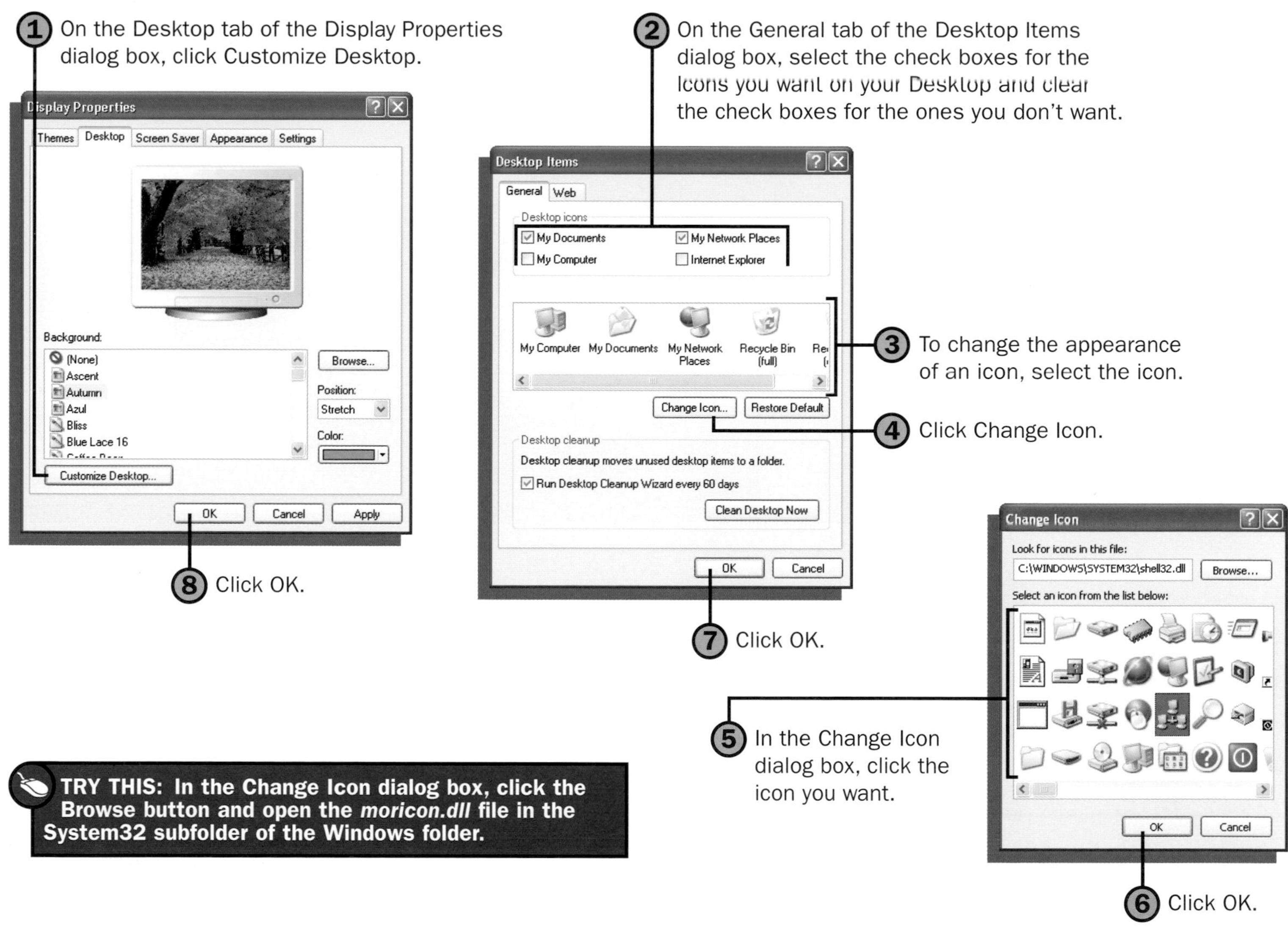

1. On the Desktop tab of the Display Properties dialog box, click Customize Desktop.
2. On the General tab of the Desktop Items dialog box, select the check boxes for the icons you want on your Desktop and clear the check boxes for the ones you don't want.
3. To change the appearance of an icon, select the icon.
4. Click Change Icon.
5. In the Change Icon dialog box, click the icon you want.
6. Click OK.
7. Click OK.
8. Click OK.

TRY THIS: In the Change Icon dialog box, click the Browse button and open the *moricon.dll* file in the System32 subfolder of the Windows folder.

Customizing Your Mouse

You're probably on pretty friendly terms with your mouse, but haven't you sometimes wished that you could build a better mouse? If your mouse's occasional disobedience is a source of frustration, you can lay down the law and tell that critter how to behave, and then you'll live together happily ever after.

SEE ALSO: For information about changing pointer appearances by applying a theme, see "Changing the Overall Look" on pages 224–225.

Set the Buttons

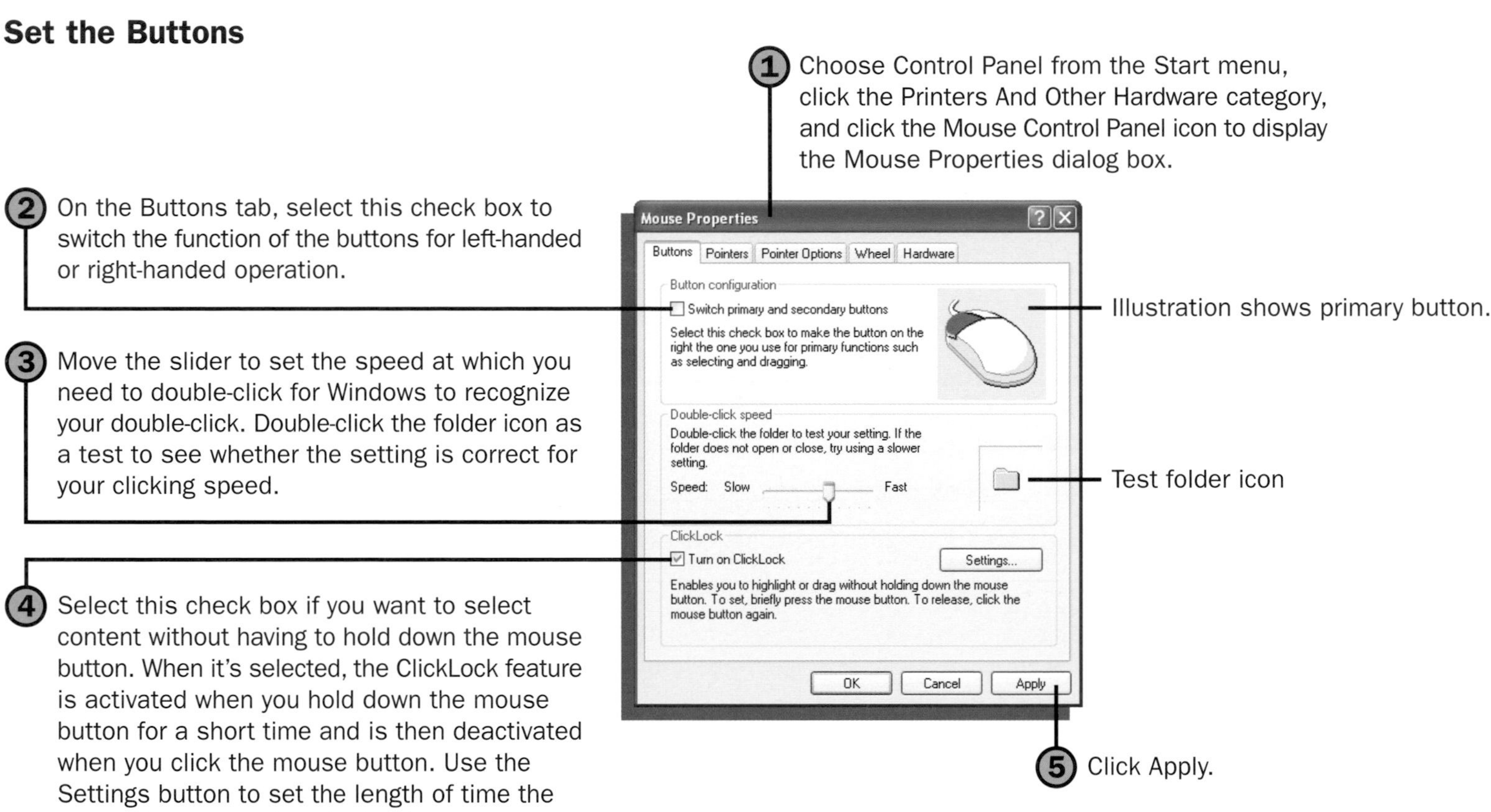

1. Choose Control Panel from the Start menu, click the Printers And Other Hardware category, and click the Mouse Control Panel icon to display the Mouse Properties dialog box.
2. On the Buttons tab, select this check box to switch the function of the buttons for left-handed or right-handed operation.
3. Move the slider to set the speed at which you need to double-click for Windows to recognize your double-click. Double-click the folder icon as a test to see whether the setting is correct for your clicking speed.
4. Select this check box if you want to select content without having to hold down the mouse button. When it's selected, the ClickLock feature is activated when you hold down the mouse button for a short time and is then deactivated when you click the mouse button. Use the Settings button to set the length of time the mouse button needs to be held down to activate ClickLock.
5. Click Apply.

Illustration shows primary button.

Test folder icon

Set the Mouse Pointer

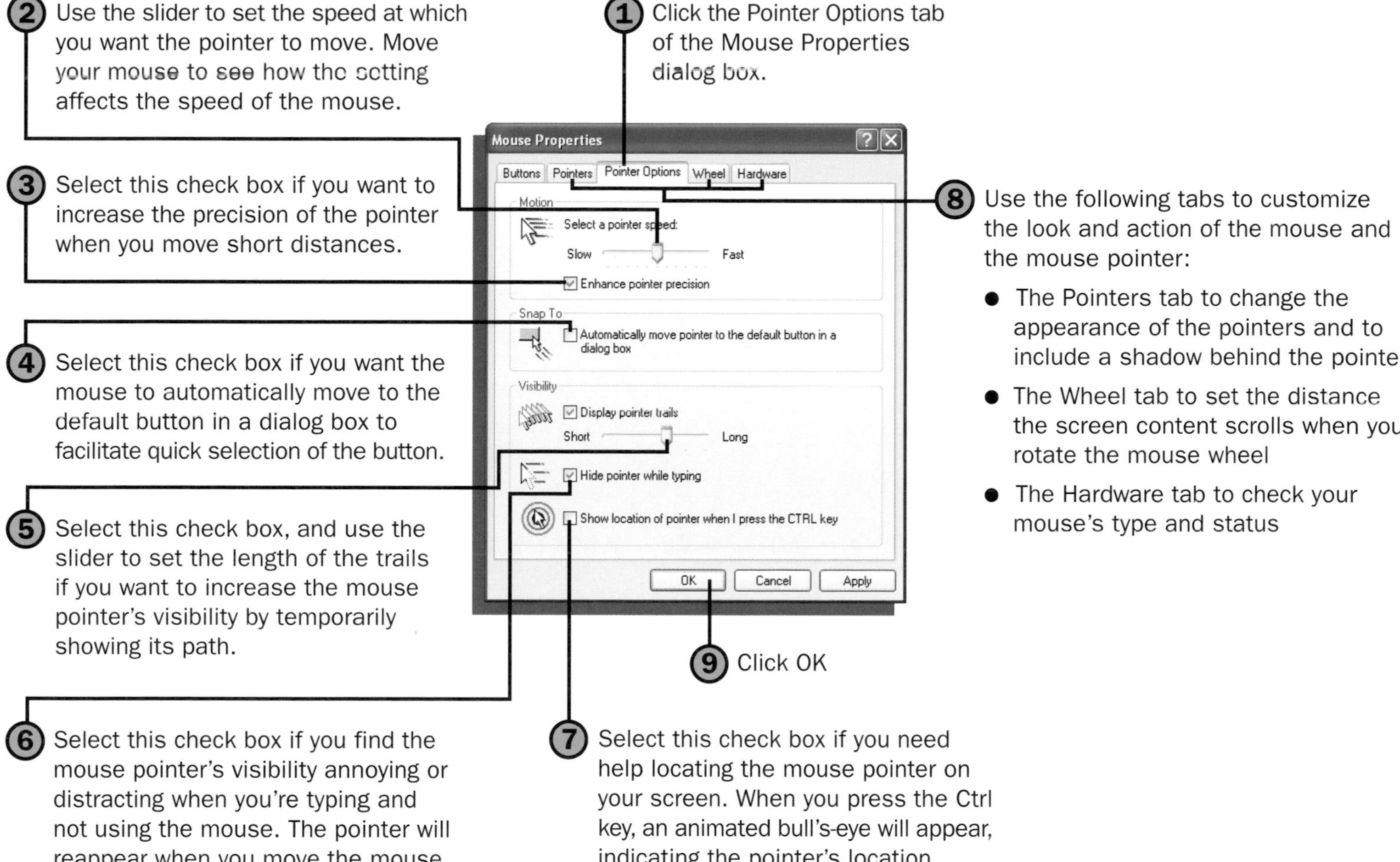

1. Click the Pointer Options tab of the Mouse Properties dialog box.
2. Use the slider to set the speed at which you want the pointer to move. Move your mouse to see how the setting affects the speed of the mouse.
3. Select this check box if you want to increase the precision of the pointer when you move short distances.
4. Select this check box if you want the mouse to automatically move to the default button in a dialog box to facilitate quick selection of the button.
5. Select this check box, and use the slider to set the length of the trails if you want to increase the mouse pointer's visibility by temporarily showing its path.
6. Select this check box if you find the mouse pointer's visibility annoying or distracting when you're typing and not using the mouse. The pointer will reappear when you move the mouse.
7. Select this check box if you need help locating the mouse pointer on your screen. When you press the Ctrl key, an animated bull's-eye will appear, indicating the pointer's location.
8. Use the following tabs to customize the look and action of the mouse and the mouse pointer:
   - The Pointers tab to change the appearance of the pointers and to include a shadow behind the pointer
   - The Wheel tab to set the distance the screen content scrolls when you rotate the mouse wheel
   - The Hardware tab to check your mouse's type and status
9. Click OK

Creating a Custom Desktop Background

You can place photographs, Web content, and various other items on your Desktop. Although any windows you use will always be on top of this content, they're still active, so you can move and resize the items, or have Web pages update on a preset schedule.

Add Web Content

1. Right-click a blank spot on the Desktop, choose Properties from the shortcut menu, and, on the Desktop tab of the Display Properties dialog box, click the Customize Desktop button.

2. On the Web tab of the Desktop Items dialog box, click New.

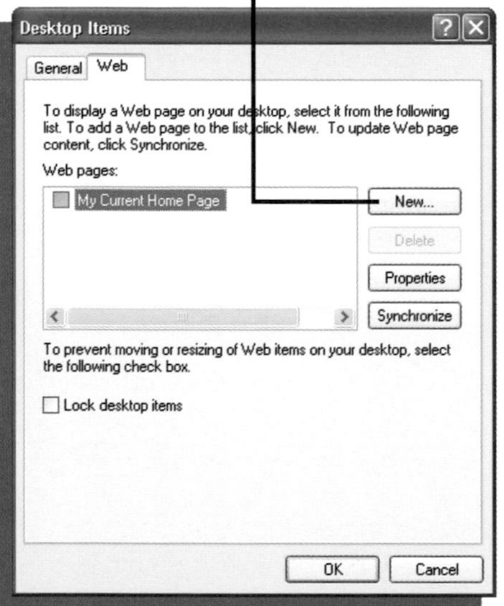

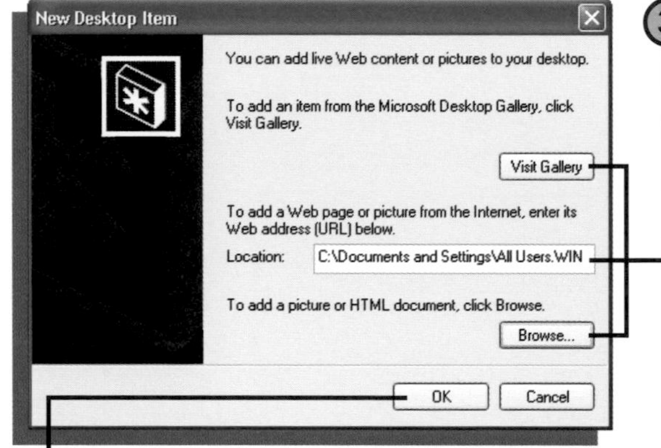

3. In the list, click the item you want to add, or specify its source:
   - Click Visit Gallery to download free Web components.
   - Type or paste the address of a Web site in the Location box.
   - Click Browse, and locate pictures, HTML documents, or offline Web pages that you've saved on your computer.

4. Click OK, and then click OK again to close the Display Properties dialog box.

5. Move the mouse pointer over an item until the title bar appears. Drag the title bar to move the item, or drag an edge to resize it.

Displaying and Arranging the Toolbars

The taskbar and the toolbars are indispensable tools for working efficiently in Windows XP. If you want, you can rearrange them so that they're tailored even more closely to your working style. For example, you can change the size of a toolbar or the taskbar, and you can "dock" either of them at any of the four sides of your screen. You can also "float" the toolbars—but not the taskbar—anywhere on your Desktop.

TIP: The New Toolbar command creates a toolbar that displays the contents of the folder you specify.

Display a Toolbar

1. Right-click a blank spot on the taskbar, and, if there's a check mark next to the Lock The Taskbar command on the shortcut menu, click the command to unlock the taskbar.

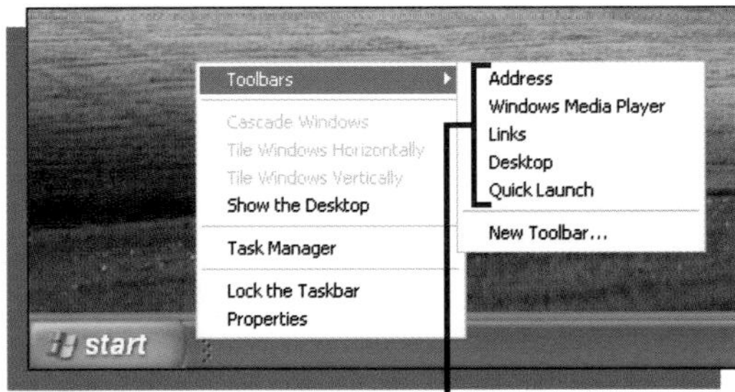

2. Right-click a blank spot on the taskbar, point to Toolbars on the shortcut menu, and choose the toolbar you want to display.

Move It

1. Drag a toolbar onto the Desktop and then to any of the four sides of the screen to dock it there. Drag the inside border of the toolbar to resize it.

2. Point to the name of the toolbar, and drag it onto the Desktop to create a floating toolbar. Drag a border of the toolbar to resize the toolbar.

Customizing the Start Menu

The Start menu is your main resource for organizing your programs, files, and so on, and getting your work done in Windows XP. You can customize the Start menu in several ways: You can change its new Windows XP look so that it looks like the Start menu in previous versions of Windows; you can modify the way items are displayed on the Start menu and its various submenus; and you can add items to or delete items from the main part of the Start menu and from the All Programs submenus.

Choose and Customize the Style

1. Right-click the Start button, and choose Properties from the shortcut menu to display the Taskbar And Start Menu Properties dialog box.

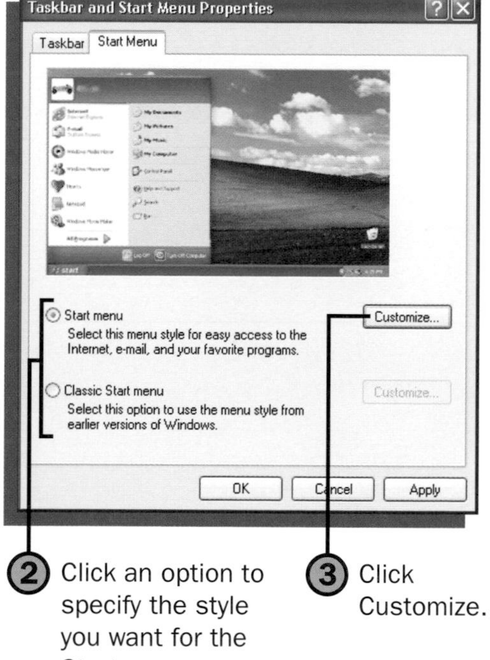

2. Click an option to specify the style you want for the Start menu.
3. Click Customize.
4. Specify whether you want to see large or small icons on the Start menu.

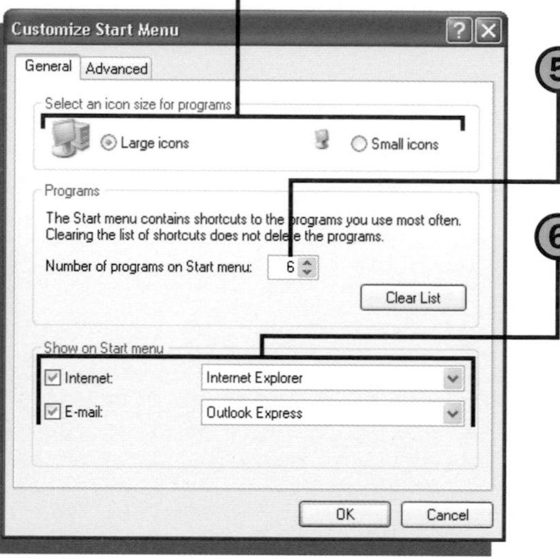

5. Specify how many recently used programs you want listed.
6. Select the check boxes if you want your Internet browser and e-mail program listed, and, if so, specify the programs.
7. On the Advanced tab, select this check box if you want submenus to open when you point to them (rather than when you click them).
8. Select this check box if you want newly installed programs to be highlighted on the Start menu.
9. Select check boxes and click options to specify whether and how various items are to be included on the Start menu.
10. Select this check box if you want an item with a submenu that lists your most recently used documents to be displayed.
11. Click OK, and then click OK again to close the Taskbar And Start Menu Properties dialog box.

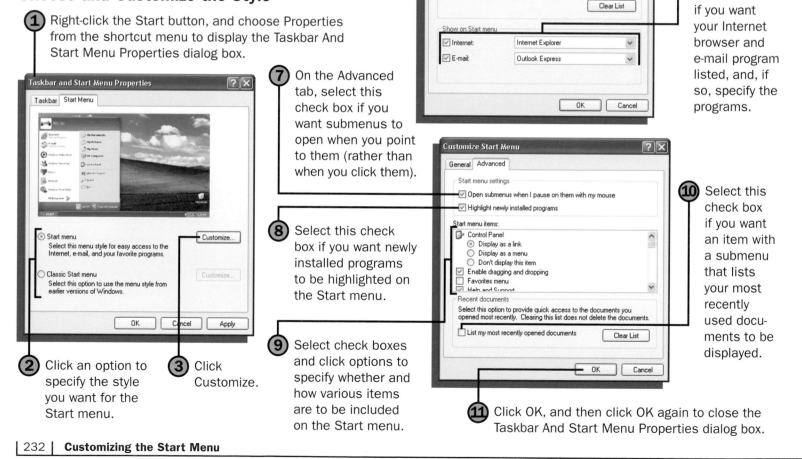

Add or Remove a Start Menu Program

1. Open the Start menu, locate the program you want to add (from one of the All Programs submenus or from a folder), and right-click it.

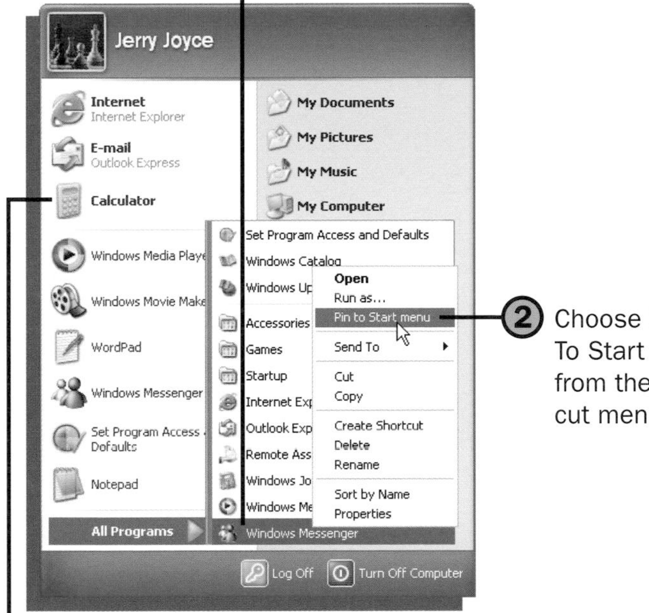

2. Choose Pin To Start Menu from the shortcut menu.

3. Right-click a program that has been "pinned" to the Start menu, and choose Unpin From Start Menu from the shortcut menu to remove the program.

TRY THIS: Drag a shortcut onto a submenu of the All Programs menu. Right-click the shortcut, and rename it. Drag any other items you want onto the submenu. Right-click anywhere in a submenu, and choose Sort By Name to organize that submenu.

TIP: To delete an item from a submenu of the Start menu, right-click the item, and choose Delete from the shortcut menu.

Add a Shortcut to an Item to the Start Menu

1. Locate the item, right-click it, point to Send To on the shortcut menu, and choose Desktop to create a shortcut on the Desktop to the item.

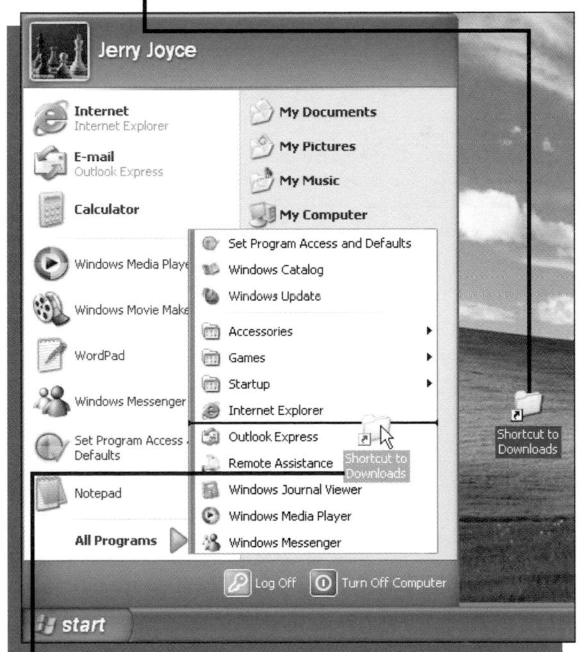

2. Drag the shortcut from the Desktop onto the Start button, and, when the Start menu opens, drag the shortcut to the location you want.

Customizing the Taskbar

The taskbar is a really handy navigation device, and you can make it even more efficient by customizing it to your work habits. You can specify which items are displayed on it and how they're displayed, and you can even hide the taskbar when you aren't using it and have it reappear when you need it.

TIP: As more and more programs place icons in the notification area of the taskbar, it's often difficult to find the ones you need and use. Hiding the inactive icons makes the ones you use easy to find. Anytime you need to access one of the hidden icons, just click the Show Hidden Icons button at the left of the notification area.

Customize the Taskbar

1. Right-click a blank spot on the taskbar, and choose Properties from the shortcut menu to display the Taskbar And Start Menu Properties dialog box.
2. Select this check box to prevent the taskbar from being moved to a new location or to prevent toolbars from being resized.
3. Select this check box to hide the taskbar when you're not using it. The taskbar will reappear when you move the mouse to whichever edge of the screen contains the taskbar.
4. Select this check box to prevent other windows from obscuring the taskbar.
5. Select this check box to have similar items grouped on one button when the taskbar is crowded.
6. Select this check box to display the Quick Launch toolbar.
7. Select this check box to have the clock appear in the notification area of the taskbar.
8. Select this check box to hide seldom-used icons in the notification area of the taskbar.
9. Click Customize to specify which icons are always displayed, which are never displayed, and which are hidden when inactive.
10. Click OK.

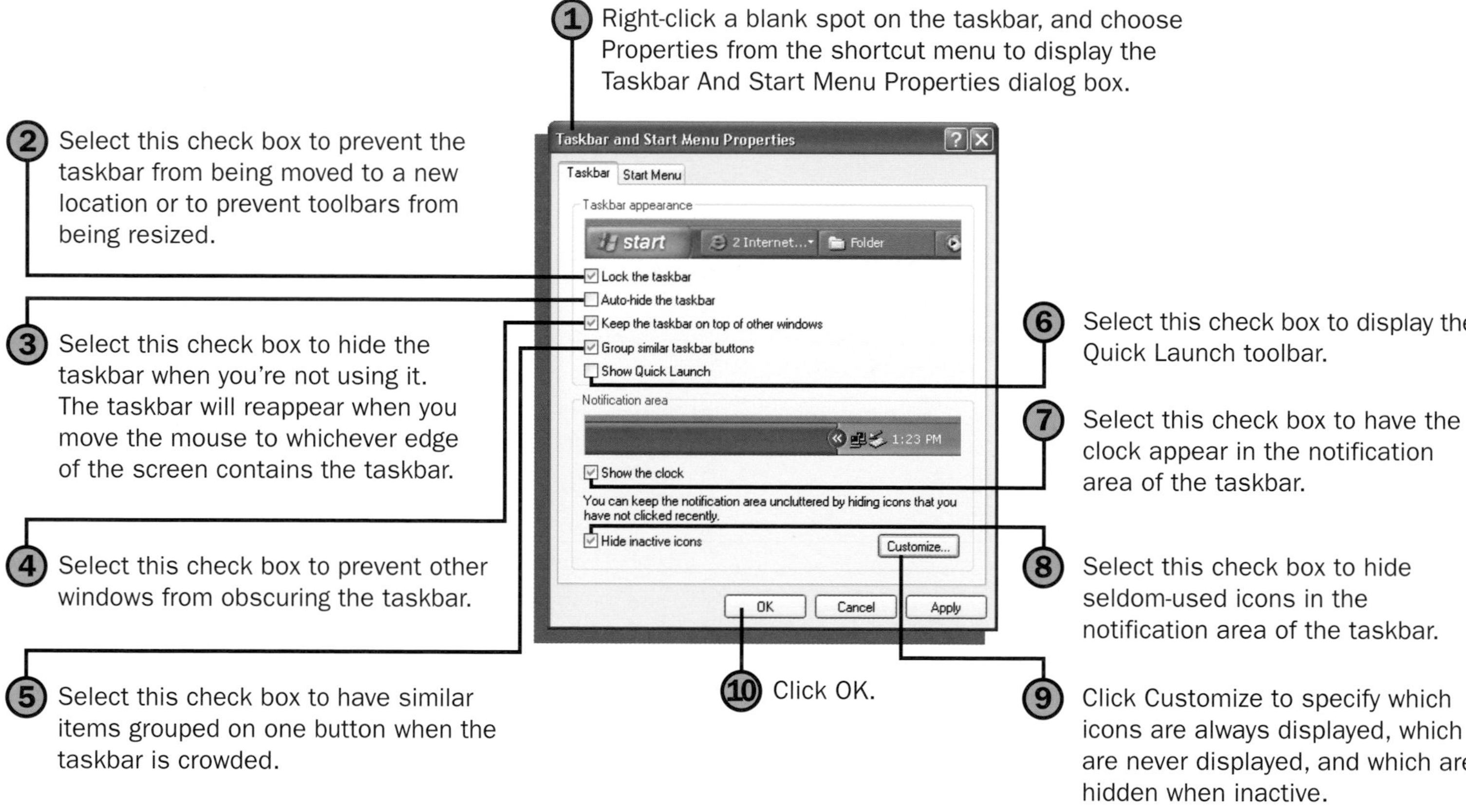

Changing the Logon

The standard—and the simplest—way to log on to Windows XP is to click your name on the Welcome screen, and, if you've set up a password, to type your password. If you're a traditionalist and/or if you want to boost the security of your system, you can switch to the traditional logon—that is, you type both your user name and your password. When you choose to use the traditional logon, though, you disable Fast User Switching (the ability to allow someone else to log on to your computer without your having to log off).

Change to the Traditional Logon

1. Choose Control Panel from the Start menu, click the User Accounts category, and then click the Change The Way Users Log On Or Off task to display the User Accounts window.
2. Clear this check box.

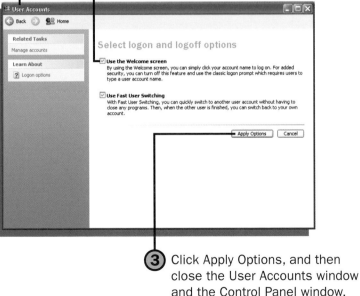

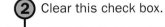

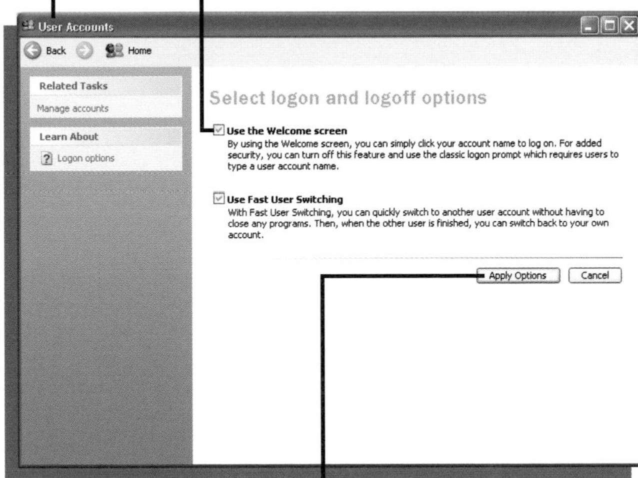

3. Click Apply Options, and then close the User Accounts window and the Control Panel window.

Log On

1. Choose Log Off from the Start menu, and confirm that you do want to log off.
2. In the Log On To Windows dialog box that appears, type your user name if it isn't already displayed.

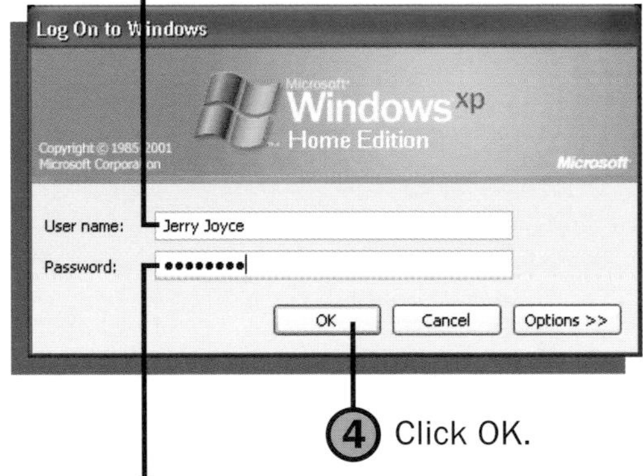

3. Type your password. If you haven't created a password, leave the box blank.
4. Click OK.

CAUTION: As you should always do whenever you're making systemwide changes, verify that you're the only person who's currently logged on to the computer.

Customizing Your Folders

Working in Windows XP means that you work with folders. To adapt the folders to your working style, you can customize them so that they look and work in exactly the way you like. Some of the changes you make apply to all your folders and other changes apply to the single folder that's open. In some cases, you can first apply the changes to a single folder and then, if you want, apply them to all your folders.

TIP: To learn more about the function of each option on the View tab, click the Help button at the top right of the dialog box, and then click the option.

TRY THIS: To apply the same view to all your folders, select a view from the Views button, choose Folder Options from the Tools menu, and, on the View tab, click the Apply To All Folders button. Click OK.

Change the Way All the Folders Work

1. Choose My Computer from the Start menu, and choose Folder Options from the Tools menu to display the Folder Options dialog box.

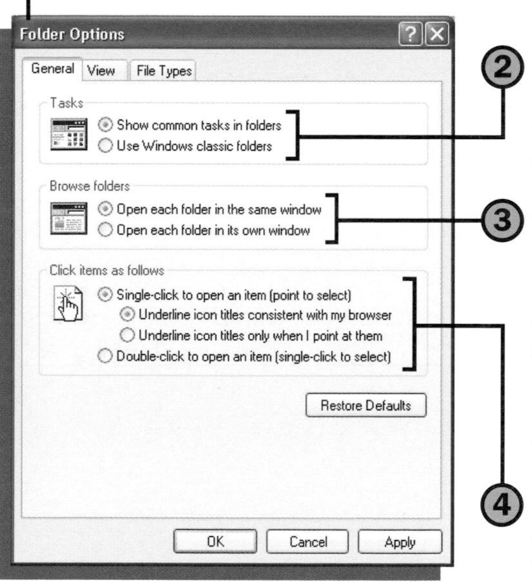

2. Click the first option to have frequently used tasks displayed on the left side of the folder. Click the second option to have only the contents of the folder displayed.
3. Click the first option if you want all your folders to open in the same window—that is, when you open one folder from another folder, the second folder's content replaces that of the first folder in the window. Click the second option if you want to use a separate window for each folder that you open.
4. Click the first option if you want to click only once to open an item in a folder. Click the second option if you want to double-click to open an item. If you chose the first option, specify how you want the icon text to be underlined.
5. Click the View tab.

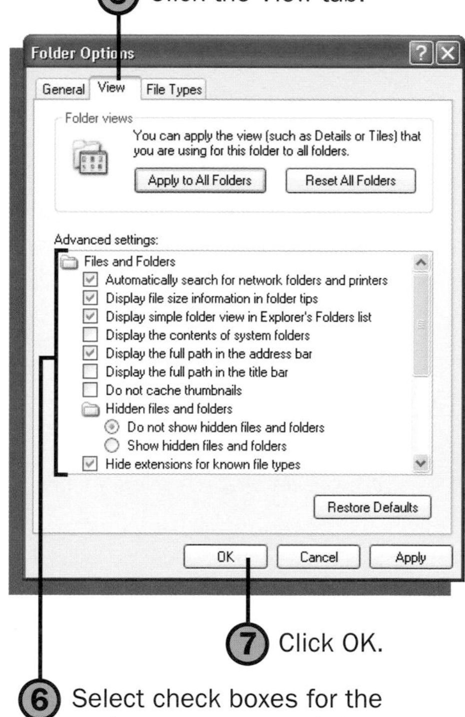

6. Select check boxes for the options you want and clear check boxes for the options you don't want.
7. Click OK.

Change the Look of a Folder

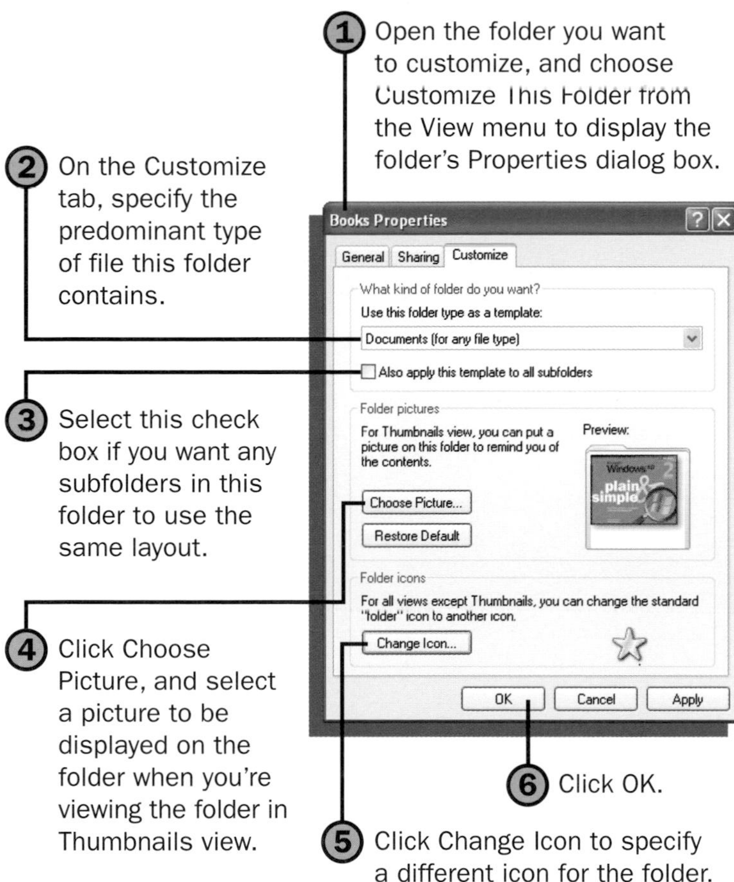

1. Open the folder you want to customize, and choose Customize This Folder from the View menu to display the folder's Properties dialog box.
2. On the Customize tab, specify the predominant type of file this folder contains.
3. Select this check box if you want any subfolders in this folder to use the same layout.
4. Click Choose Picture, and select a picture to be displayed on the folder when you're viewing the folder in Thumbnails view.
5. Click Change Icon to specify a different icon for the folder.
6. Click OK.

Change the Content That's Shown

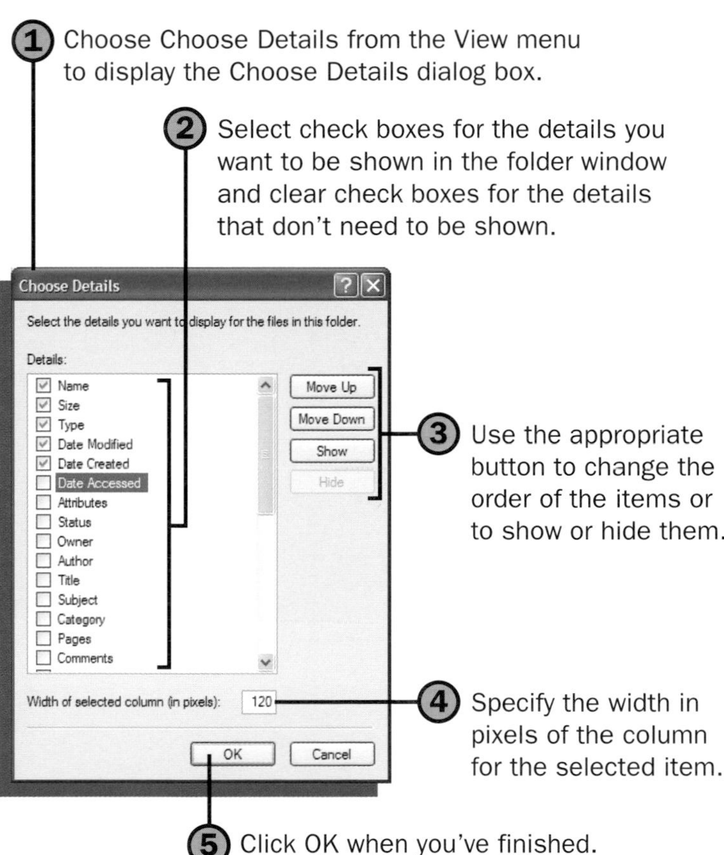

1. Choose Choose Details from the View menu to display the Choose Details dialog box.
2. Select check boxes for the details you want to be shown in the folder window and clear check boxes for the details that don't need to be shown.
3. Use the appropriate button to change the order of the items or to show or hide them.
4. Specify the width in pixels of the column for the selected item.
5. Click OK when you've finished.

Changing the Way a CD Starts

When you insert a CD into your computer's CD drive, Windows detects the type of content on the CD—music or pictures, for example. Then Windows either asks you what you want to do with the CD or starts doing something without asking you, such as playing the music. If you want to make the decisions, you can let Windows know just how you want it to handle the various types of content on your CDs.

Set the AutoPlay

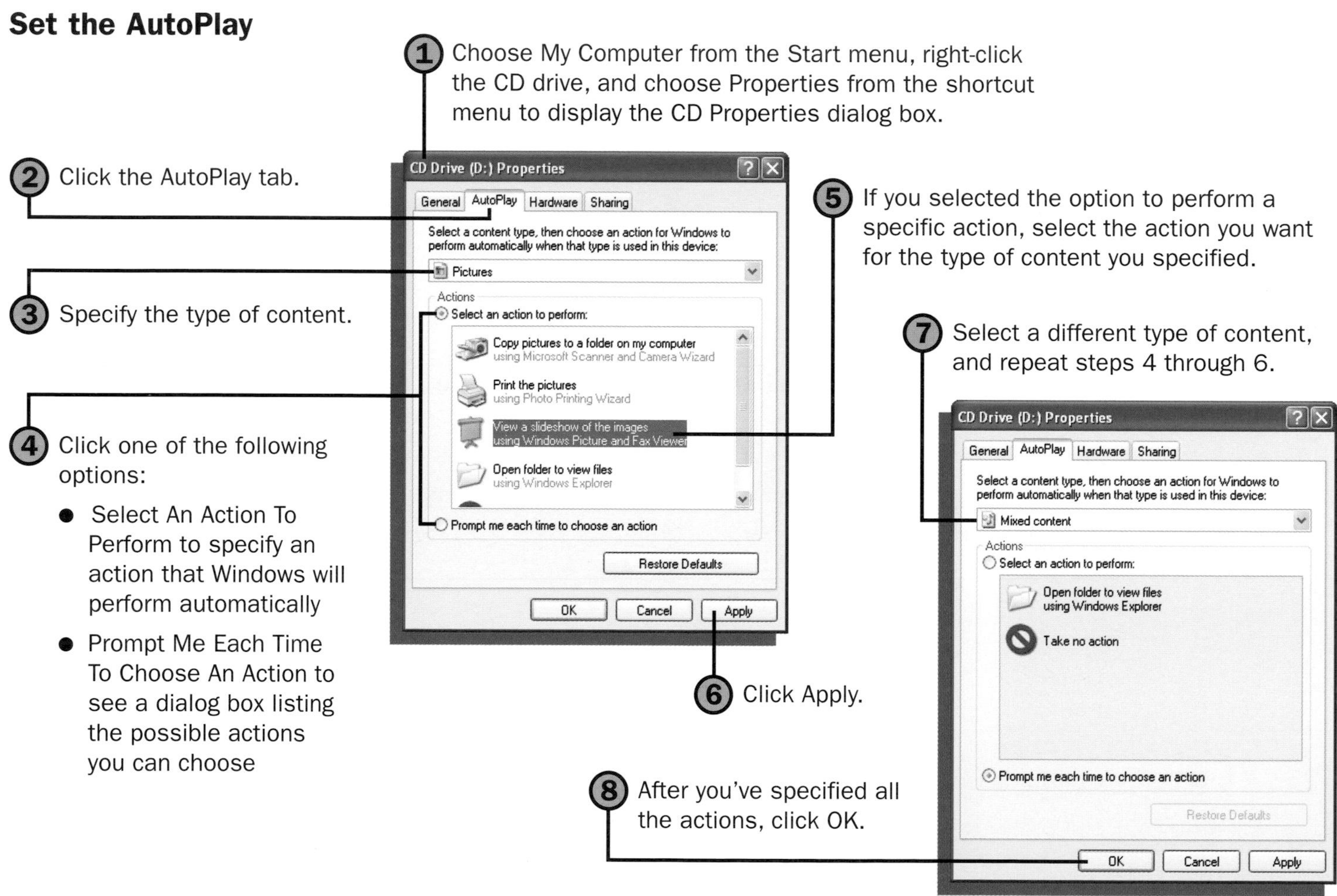

1 Choose My Computer from the Start menu, right-click the CD drive, and choose Properties from the shortcut menu to display the CD Properties dialog box.
2 Click the AutoPlay tab.
3 Specify the type of content.
4 Click one of the following options:
• Select An Action To Perform to specify an action that Windows will perform automatically
• Prompt Me Each Time To Choose An Action to see a dialog box listing the possible actions you can choose
5 If you selected the option to perform a specific action, select the action you want for the type of content you specified.
6 Click Apply.
7 Select a different type of content, and repeat steps 4 through 6.
8 After you've specified all the actions, click OK.
CD Drive (D:) Properties
General
AutoPlay
Hardware
Sharing
Select a content type, then choose an action for Windows to perform automatically when that type is used in this device:
Pictures
Actions
Select an action to perform:
Copy pictures to a folder on my computer using Microsoft Scanner and Camera Wizard
Print the pictures using Photo Printing Wizard
View a slideshow of the images using Windows Picture and Fax Viewer
Open folder to view files using Windows Explorer
Prompt me each time to choose an action
Restore Defaults
OK
Cancel
Apply
CD Drive (D:) Properties
Mixed content
Open folder to view files using Windows Explorer
Take no action
Prompt me each time to choose an action
Restore Defaults
OK
Cancel
Apply

Changing Your Account Picture

Windows XP arbitrarily assigns your user account a picture, which seems to show up all the time. When your computer is set to use the Welcome screen, you see the picture when you log on or switch users, and there it is again every time you open the Start menu. If you don't like the picture or if you feel that it has no relevance to you, and if you have a picture that's just right, you can change the picture.

TIP: The space where the user account picture goes is designed for a square picture, so, if your picture isn't square, you might want to crop it in Paint or in another photo-editing program to eliminate any blank space.

Change Your Picture

1. Click the Start button to open the Start menu, and click your account picture.

2. In the User Accounts window that appears, click the picture you want to use.

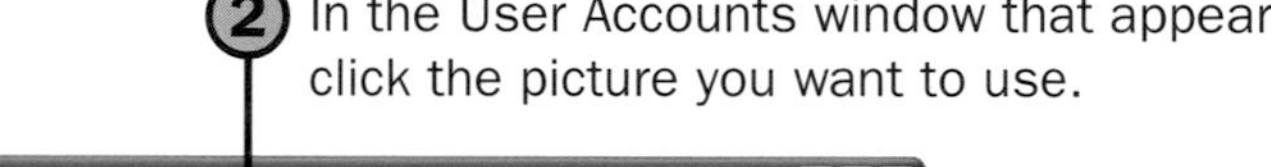

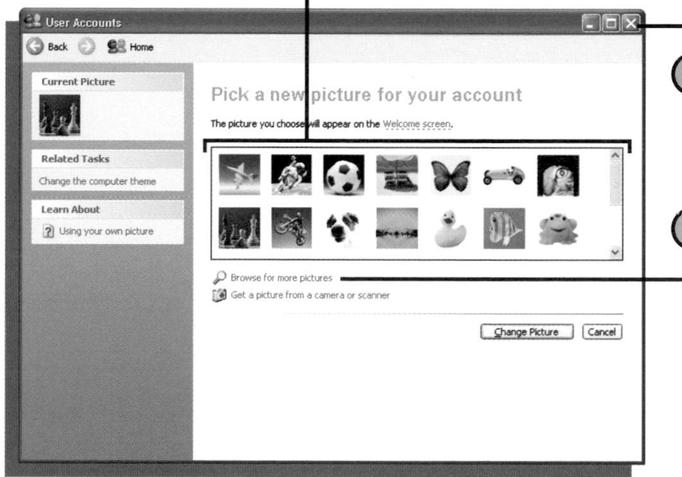

3. If you don't like any of the pictures, click Browse For More Pictures, locate and select the picture you want, and click Open.
4. Close the User Accounts window when you've finished.

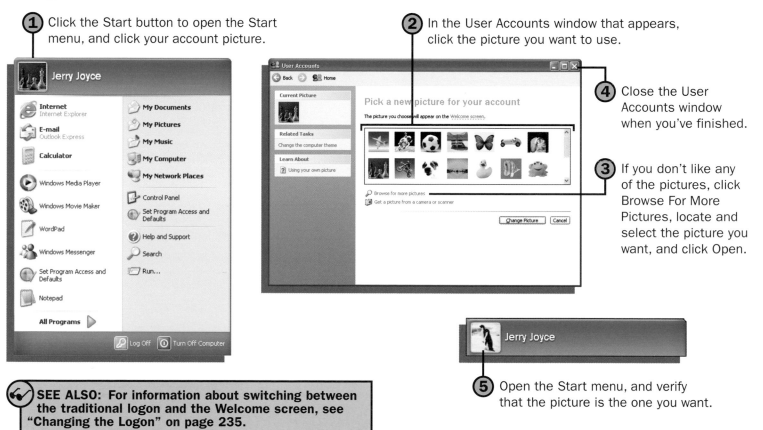

5. Open the Start menu, and verify that the picture is the one you want.

SEE ALSO: For information about switching between the traditional logon and the Welcome screen, see "Changing the Logon" on page 235.

Using Alternative Ways of Working

Windows XP provides several tools that let you change the way you enter information into, or receive information from, the computer. These tools—although designed primarily for people who experience difficulty when typing, using the mouse, seeing details on the screen, or hearing sounds—can be used by anyone who'd like to try some different ways of working on the computer. For example, you can use the keyboard to execute mouse actions, or use the mouse or another pointing device for keyboard input. Some other tools that can help you customize keyboard input are described in the table below.

Set the Options

1. Choose Control Panel from the Start menu, click the Accessibility Options category, and click Accessibility Options to display the Accessibility Properties dialog box.
2. On the various tabs of the dialog box, select the check boxes for the options you want to use, as described in the table. Click the Settings button for each option you selected, and specify how you want the option to function. Click OK.
3. On the General tab, specify whether you want the features you selected to be turned off after the computer has been idle for a set period of time, whether you want a warning message or a sound to be used when a feature is turned on or off, and whether you want the settings to be available when you log on and whenever any new users of the computer log on.
4. Click OK to close the dialog box.

TIP: You can use the Accessibility Wizard on the Accessibility submenu of the Start menu to provide a quick way to set up several tools at one time and to help you identify which tools you might want to use.

Alternative Input Options

Feature	What it does
StickyKeys	Sets key combinations with the Alt, Ctrl, and Shift keys to be pressable one key at a time.
FilterKeys	Ignores repeated characters or too-rapid key presses.
ToggleKeys	Makes different sounds when you turn the Caps Lock, Num Lock, or Scroll Lock key on or off.
SoundSentry	Flashes a specified screen component when the system beeps.
ShowSounds	Displays text instead of sounds for programs that support this feature.
High Contrast	Sets the color scheme for Windows XP to High Contrast to improve the visibility of components.
Cursor Blink Rate	Sets the speed at which the cursor (the insertion point in WordPad, for example) blinks.
Cursor Width	Sets the width of the cursor in programs.
MouseKeys	Sets the numeric keypad to control mouse movements.
SerialKey devices	Provides support for alternative input devices.

Use More Tools

1. On your keyboard, press the Windows key + U (or point to Accessories on the Start menu, point to the Accessibility submenu, and then choose Utilities Manager) to display the Utility Manager and to start Narrator.
2. Click the program you want to run.
3. Click Start to start the program.
4. Select or clear the check boxes to specify how you want the program to start.
5. Click another program and start it and/or set its options.
6. Click OK.

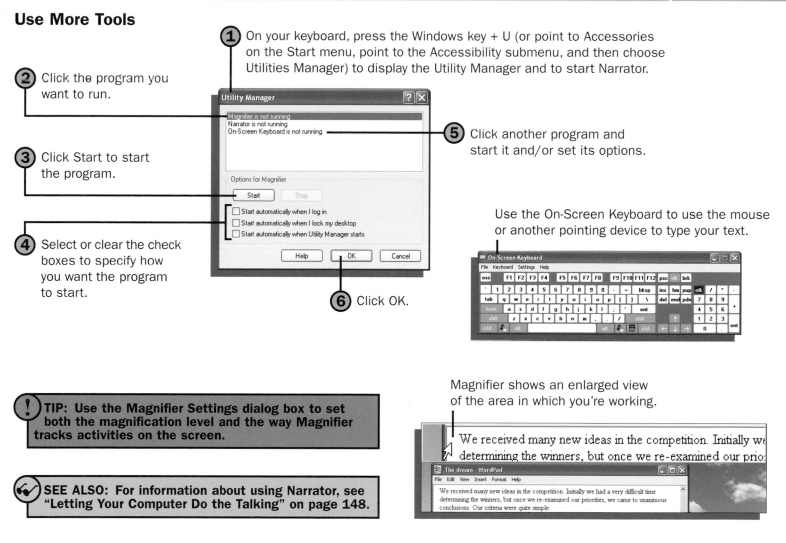

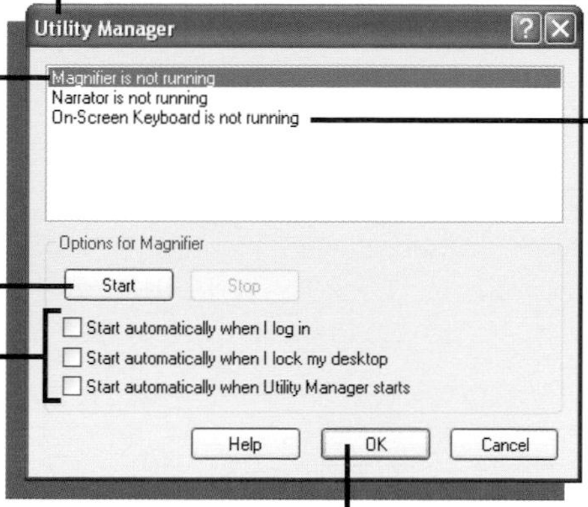

Use the On-Screen Keyboard to use the mouse or another pointing device to type your text.

Magnifier shows an enlarged view of the area in which you're working.

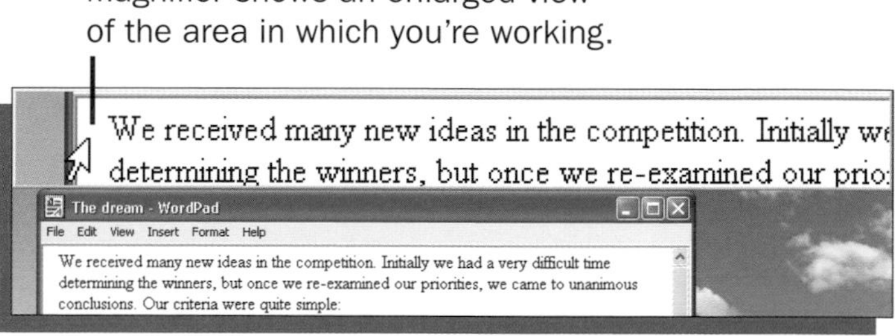

We received many new ideas in the competition. Initially we
determining the winners, but once we re-examined our prio
The dream - WordPad
File Edit View Insert Format Help
We received many new ideas in the competition. Initially we had a very difficult time
determining the winners, but once we re-examined our priorities, we came to unanimous
conclusions. Our criteria were quite simple:

TIP: Use the Magnifier Settings dialog box to set both the magnification level and the way Magnifier tracks activities on the screen.

SEE ALSO: For information about using Narrator, see "Letting Your Computer Do the Talking" on page 148.

Working in a Different Part of the World

If you're working in, or producing documents for use in, a region or country other than the one for which your computer was configured, you can change the default region and have Windows XP adjust the numbering, currency, time, and date schemes used by your programs. If you're working in a different language, you can switch the layout of your keyboard to conform to that language.

TIP: If you want to use more than one regional setting on your computer, you can add additional languages as shown on the facing page. When you switch the input language using the Language bar or a key combination, the regional settings also change.

Change the Default Region

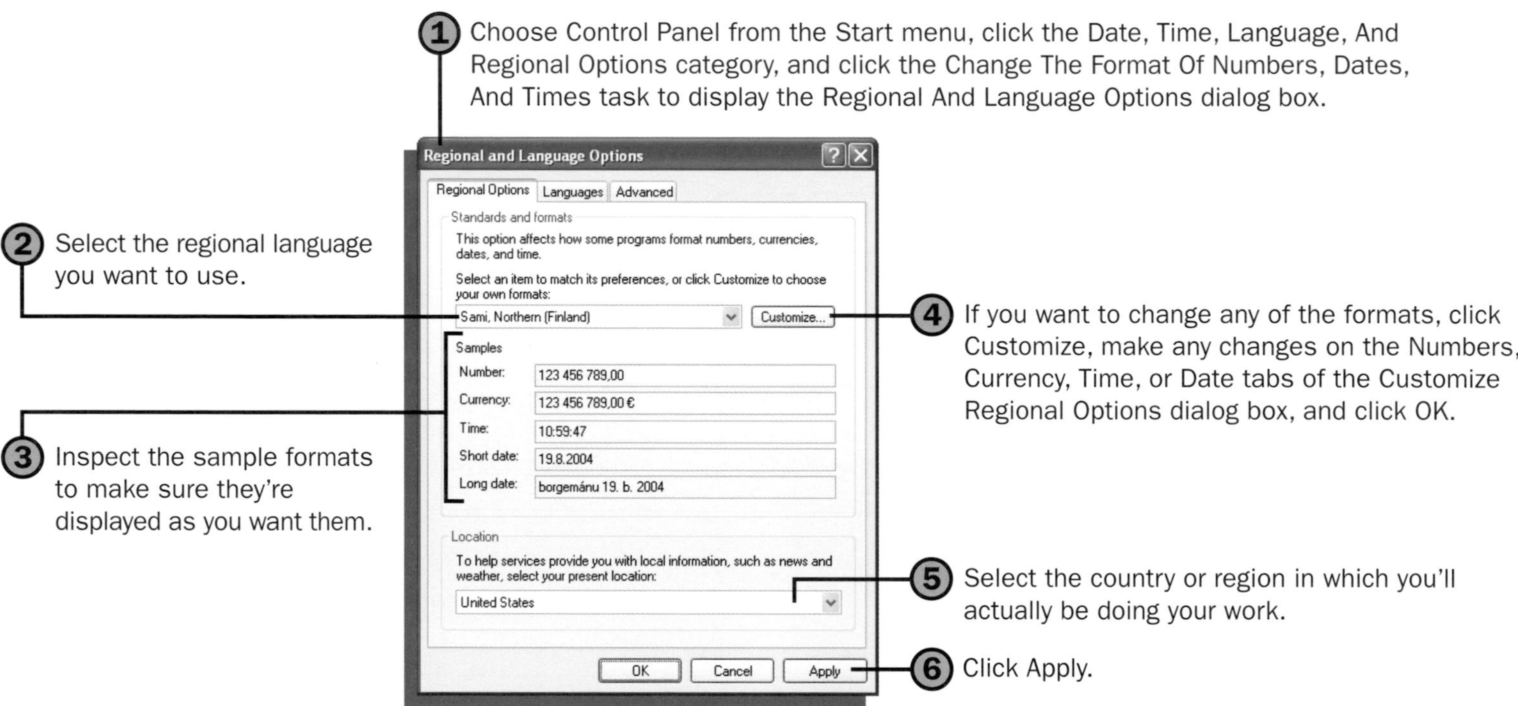

1 Choose Control Panel from the Start menu, click the Date, Time, Language, And Regional Options category, and click the Change The Format Of Numbers, Dates, And Times task to display the Regional And Language Options dialog box.
2 Select the regional language you want to use.
3 Inspect the sample formats to make sure they're displayed as you want them.
4 If you want to change any of the formats, click Customize, make any changes on the Numbers, Currency, Time, or Date tabs of the Customize Regional Options dialog box, and click OK.
5 Select the country or region in which you'll actually be doing your work.
6 Click Apply.
Regional and Language Options
Regional Options
Languages
Advanced
Standards and formats
This option affects how some programs format numbers, currencies, dates, and time.
Select an item to match its preferences, or click Customize to choose your own formats:
Sami, Northern (Finland)
Customize...
Samples
Number: 123 456 789,00
Currency: 123 456 789,00 €
Time: 10:59:47
Short date: 19.8.2004
Long date: borgemánu 19. b. 2004
Location
To help services provide you with local information, such as news and weather, select your present location:
United States
OK
Cancel
Apply

SEE ALSO: For information about using the On-Screen Keyboard, see "Using Alternative Ways of Working" on pages 240–241.

TIP: When you switch regions, languages, and keyboard settings, the On-Screen Keyboard changes to show the selected keyboard structure. Use this keyboard if you don't have a keyboard configured for the region and language you're using.

Add Language Support

1. On the Languages tab of the Regional And Language Options dialog box, click the Details button to display the Text Services And Input Languages dialog box.

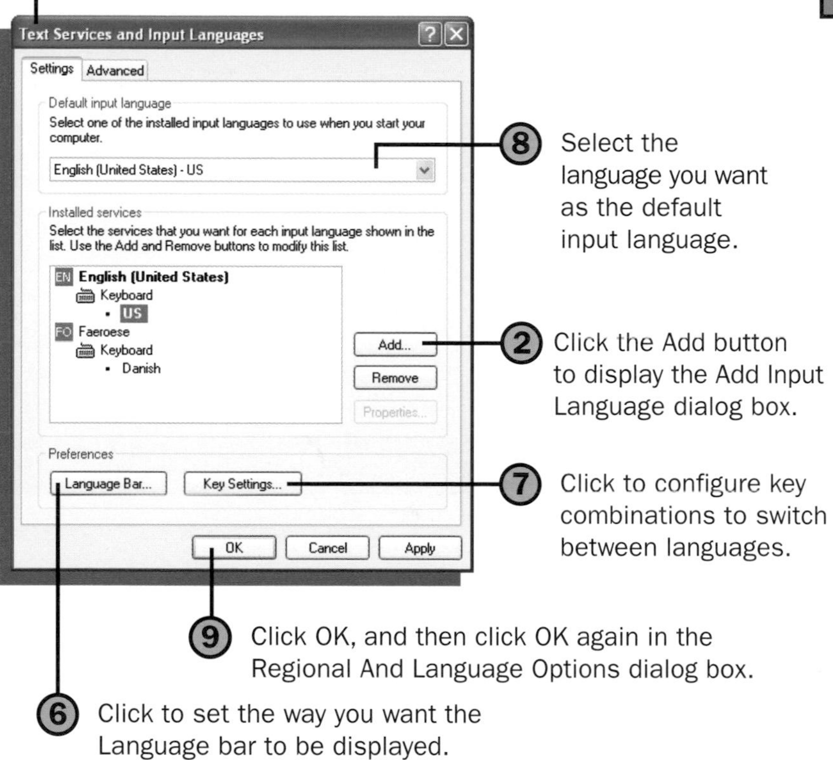

2. Click the Add button to display the Add Input Language dialog box.

3. Select the language you want.

4. Select the keyboard layout you want.

5. Click OK.

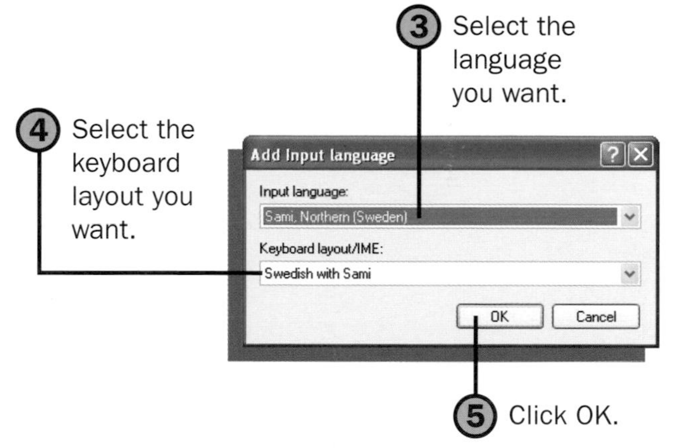

6. Click to set the way you want the Language bar to be displayed.

7. Click to configure key combinations to switch between languages.

8. Select the language you want as the default input language.

9. Click OK, and then click OK again in the Regional And Language Options dialog box.

TIP: The Text Services And Input Languages dialog box also lists all special text services, including speech recognition, that have been installed by other programs, such as Microsoft Office 2003.

TIP: The Language bar appears as part of the Windows taskbar and can be moved just like any other toolbar. Use it if you want to switch your input language and keyboard setup.

Using a Screen Saver

When you work at a computer, it's good for your eyes—and for your mental health—to take a break and look at something different once in a while. If you work with other people, you might not want them to be able to read your screen—albeit unintentionally—any time your computer is unattended. A screen saver can provide a nice little respite from your work as well as some privacy. To prevent anyone from using your computer—but still allow network access to it—when you're away from your desk, you can use the password option. You'll need to enter the password to end the screen saver when you're ready to get back to work.

Choose a Screen Saver

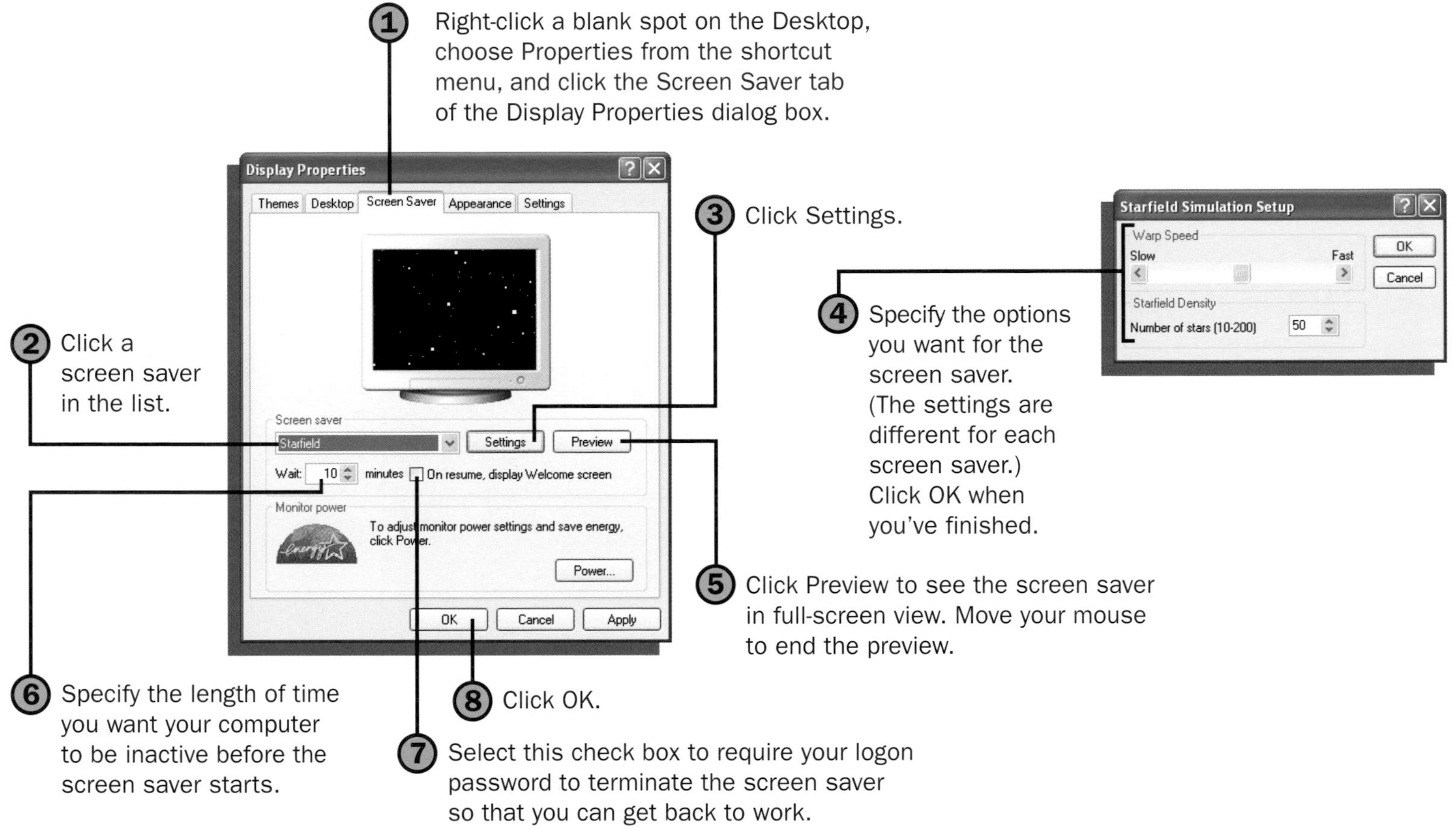

1. Right-click a blank spot on the Desktop, choose Properties from the shortcut menu, and click the Screen Saver tab of the Display Properties dialog box.
2. Click a screen saver in the list.
3. Click Settings.
4. Specify the options you want for the screen saver. (The settings are different for each screen saver.) Click OK when you've finished.
5. Click Preview to see the screen saver in full-screen view. Move your mouse to end the preview.
6. Specify the length of time you want your computer to be inactive before the screen saver starts.
7. Select this check box to require your logon password to terminate the screen saver so that you can get back to work.
8. Click OK.

Create a Custom Screen Saver

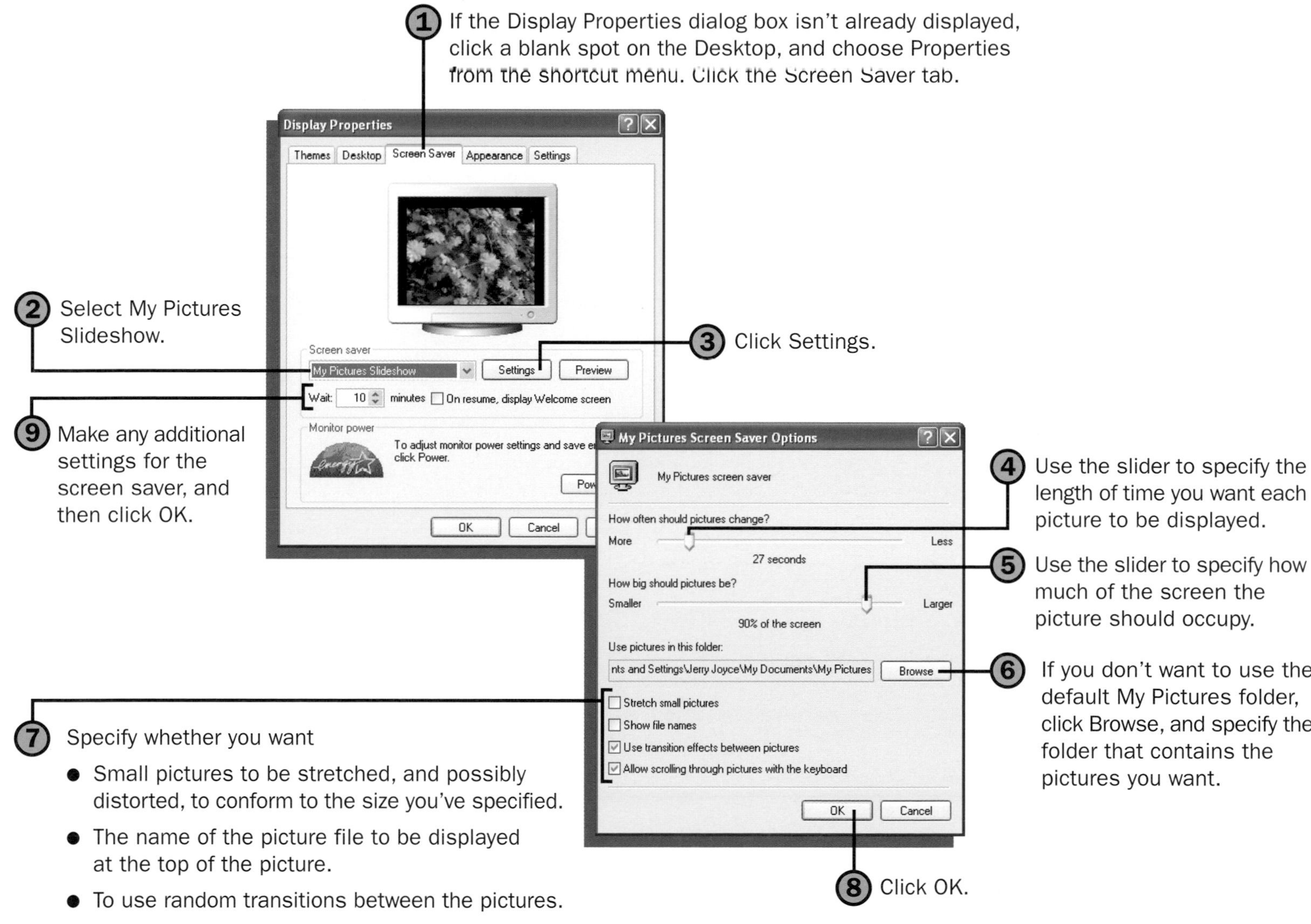

1. If the Display Properties dialog box isn't already displayed, click a blank spot on the Desktop, and choose Properties from the shortcut menu. Click the Screen Saver tab.
2. Select My Pictures Slideshow.
3. Click Settings.
4. Use the slider to specify the length of time you want each picture to be displayed.
5. Use the slider to specify how much of the screen the picture should occupy.
6. If you don't want to use the default My Pictures folder, click Browse, and specify the folder that contains the pictures you want.
7. Specify whether you want
   - Small pictures to be stretched, and possibly distorted, to conform to the size you've specified.
   - The name of the picture file to be displayed at the top of the picture.
   - To use random transitions between the pictures.
   - To be able to advance to the next or the previous picture by using the left or right arrow key.
8. Click OK.
9. Make any additional settings for the screen saver, and then click OK.

Creating a Multimedia Screen Saver ⊕ NEW FEATURE

If you have the Microsoft Plus! Digital Media Edition pack installed on your computer, you can create a screen saver that not only displays your pictures in a variety of ways but whose pictures are accompanied by the music of your choice.

SEE ALSO: For information about Microsoft Plus!, see "The Microsoft Plus! Packs" on page 36.

For information about creating playlists, see "Arranging Your Media with Playlists" on pages 134–135.

Create Your Screen-Saver Slide Show

1. Click a blank spot on the Desktop, choose Properties from the shortcut menu, and click the Screen Saver tab of the Display Properties dialog box. Choose Plus! My Pictures from the Screen Saver drop-down list, and then click the Settings button to display the Plus! My Pictures Settings dialog box.
2. Use the Browse button to select the folder containing the pictures you want, or use the Customize button to create a collection of pictures from different locations.
3. Select this check box if you want the pictures to appear in random order rather than in their current order in the folder or collection you're using.
4. Use the slider to set the interval at which the pictures change.
5. Select the style in which the pictures will be displayed.
6. Select the playlist for the music you want to accompany your screen-saver slide show.
7. Select this check box if you want the music tracks to be played in random order.
8. Click OK, make any other settings you want in the Display Properties dialog box, and click OK.

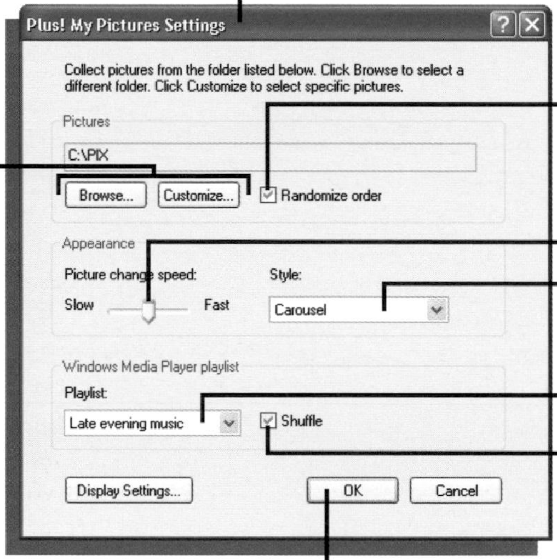

13 Maintaining Security

In days of old, only the administrators of large corporate networks had to worry about computer security. These days, with the proliferation of computer viruses, constant connections to the Internet, home networks, and sophisticated hacking techniques used by an ever-growing cadre of snoops and pranksters, everyone should be vigilant. In this section you'll find valuable information about the ways you can protect your files, your privacy on the Internet, and so on. If other people use your computer, you can protect your sensitive files from prying eyes by restricting *user rights,* by creating a password that protects the computer from unauthorized access, or by placing sensitive material in a compressed and *encrypted* folder. You can even lock your computer.

When you visit an Internet site that requests personal information, you can restrict the amount of information you provide by creating a special profile for that purpose. You can also control "cookies," those little files that Web sites use to keep track of your visits and preferences and that compile a lot of personal information about you. We'll also show you how to configure the Windows Firewall to create a high level of security. If several people use your computer (especially if any are children), you can use Content Advisor to restrict access to Internet sites that contain material you consider inappropriate. If you're setting up a wireless network, you can add security to prevent unauthorized access to the network. To monitor your overall security, check in periodically with the new Security Center, to verify that your firewall, virus protection, and software updates are working hard to protect you.

Keeping Your Files Private

If other people use your computer, they can normally gain access to any of your files, including those in your My Documents folder. If your computer uses NTFS (the NT file system), however, you can keep your files private so that only you can access them when you log on to the computer.

SEE ALSO: For information about NTFS, see "Know Your Rights, Know Your Format" on the facing page.

For information about creating a password, see "Setting Your Password" on page 250.

Keep the My Documents Folder Private

CAUTION: When you keep your My Documents folder private, you're also keeping all its subfolders private, including the My Music, My Pictures, Desktop, and Favorites subfolders. If you want to share any files from these folders, move them into the Shared Documents folder.

1. Choose My Computer from the Start menu to open the My Computer window.

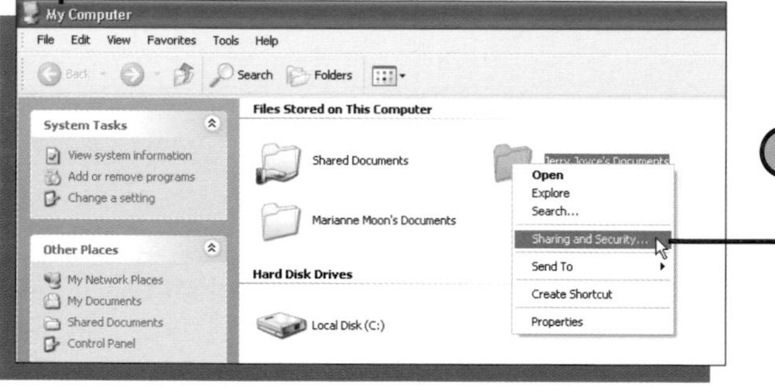

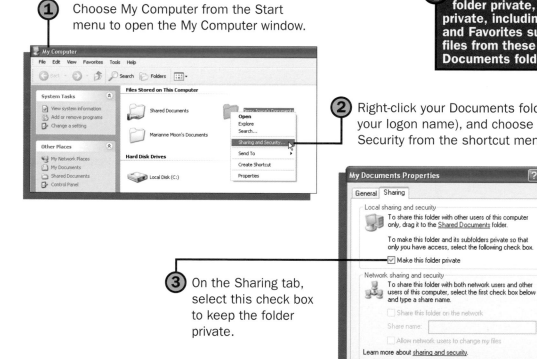

2. Right-click your Documents folder (it shows your logon name), and choose Sharing And Security from the shortcut menu.

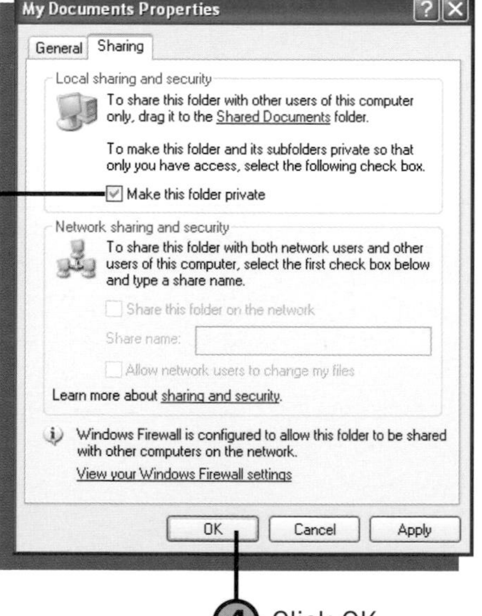

3. On the Sharing tab, select this check box to keep the folder private.
4. Click OK.

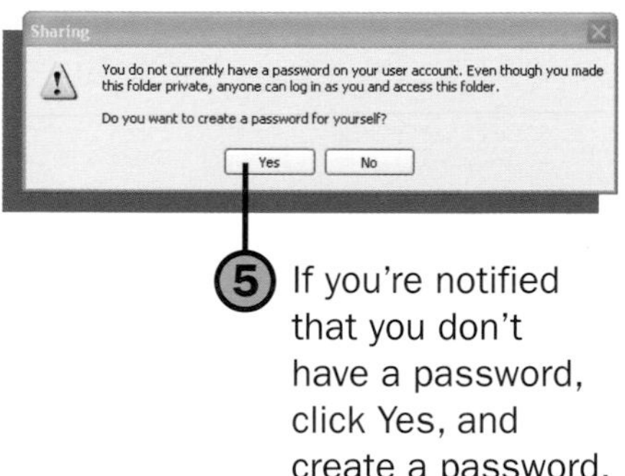

5. If you're notified that you don't have a password, click Yes, and create a password.

Know Your Rights, Know Your Format

Microsoft Windows XP provides several tools to help you effectively maintain security on your computer system. One of the principal ways to maintain security is to assign specific rights to each user of the computer. These rights can range from simply being allowed to use the computer all the way up to having permission to make changes to the entire system. You assign user rights by assigning individual users to the appropriate group. Another way to maintain security is to use the built-in security of the NTFS file system, which provides extra security in Windows NT–based operating systems but isn't available in the Windows 95, Windows 98, or Windows Me (Millennium Edition) operating system. Your computer might or might not be using the NTFS system.

User Groups

What you're allowed to do on your computer depends on the user group of which you're a member—the Administrators group, the Limited group, or the Guest group. You can tell which group you've been assigned to by choosing Control Panel from the Start menu and clicking the User Accounts category.

Administrators have full control of the computer and can make any changes to the system, including adding or removing software, changing user accounts, and even modifying the Windows XP configuration. Members of the Administrators group are trusted to be able to use and modify the computer and its programs without causing problems.

Limited users can do most things that don't affect the overall setup of the computer, such as run programs, use and create files, and install some programs. Members of the Limited group can't install any program that accesses the Windows Registry, and can't add or remove users or make substantial changes to Windows. Members of the Limited group might find that some older programs that weren't designed for use with Windows XP might not work correctly.

Guest users are people who don't have a user account on the computer. By logging on as a member of the Guest group, a user can work on the computer without being able to modify another user's settings. Guest users are quite limited in what they can do—they can run existing programs but can't install new programs or make any changes to Windows. By default, the Guest account is inactive and must be activated before it can be used. There is only one Guest account on the computer.

File Systems

The NTFS system provides extra security for your files. Some of this security is hidden, so you can't see it, but you can use it to keep your files private. Unless you're using NTFS, anyone who works on the computer can open the Documents And Settings folder and can access each user's My Documents folder, which is stored in the user's profile. If you're using NTFS, and your security settings are in place, you can access your My Documents folder only when you're logged on. NTFS isn't compatible with most other operating systems, however, so if your computer is running more than one operating system, you'll probably want to use the FAT or FAT32 file system instead of NTFS.

To see whether your computer uses NTFS, open My Computer, and click the hard disk. In the Details section of the window, you'll see the file system that's being used. If the computer has more than one hard disk, click each one and note the file system. For information about converting the hard disk to NTFS, see "Changing the Disk Format" on page 283.

Setting Your Password

Unless you create a password that allows you to gain entry to your user account, anyone can log on to your computer and access your files. If you want to protect the computer from unauthorized access, create a password that's easy for you to remember and difficult for others to guess.

Create a Password

1. Choose Control Panel from the Start menu, click the User Accounts category, and click your account to display the User Accounts window.
2. In the User Accounts window, click Create A Password.
3. Type your password, and then type it again to confirm that you didn't make a typing error.
4. Type a hint that will remind you, but no one else, of your password.
5. Click Create Password.

CAUTION: Passwords are *case-sensitive*—that is, *MyPASSWORD* and *mypassword* are two different passwords. Make sure that you remember and use the correct capitalization. If you have a problem logging on with your password, make sure the Caps Lock feature isn't turned on.

TIP: Windows will ask you whether you want to make your files private only if your computer uses NTFS and if you haven't already made the files private.

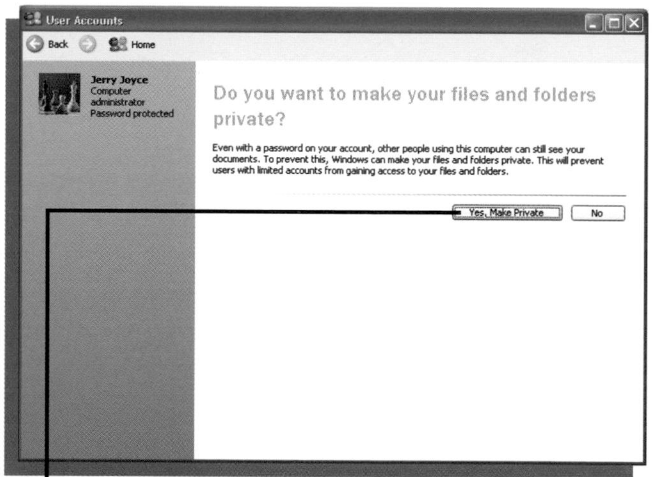

User Accounts
Back
Home
Jerry Joyce
Computer administrator
Password protected
Do you want to make your files and folders private?
Even with a password on your account, other people using this computer can still see your documents. To prevent this, Windows can make your files and folders private. This will prevent users with limited accounts from gaining access to your files and folders.
Yes, Make Private
No

6. If Windows asks you whether you want to make your files private, click Yes, Make Private if you want to prevent access by anyone other than yourself to all the files in the My Documents folder and its subfolders.

SEE ALSO: For information about changing a password, see "Changing Your Password" on the facing page and "Resetting Your Password" on page 252.

Changing Your Password

One of the best ways to prevent others from using your account is to change your password occasionally—especially if you've given it to someone or you suspect that someone might have guessed it or watched you type it. When you do change your password, create one that can't be easily guessed (don't use "password" or your well-known nickname, for example), and try to incorporate both uppercase and lowercase letters as well as one or two numbers. Of course, don't make the password so complicated that you can't remember it!

Change Your Password

1. Choose Control Panel from the Start menu, click the User Accounts category, and click your account to display the User Accounts window.
2. Click Change My Password.
3. Type your current password.

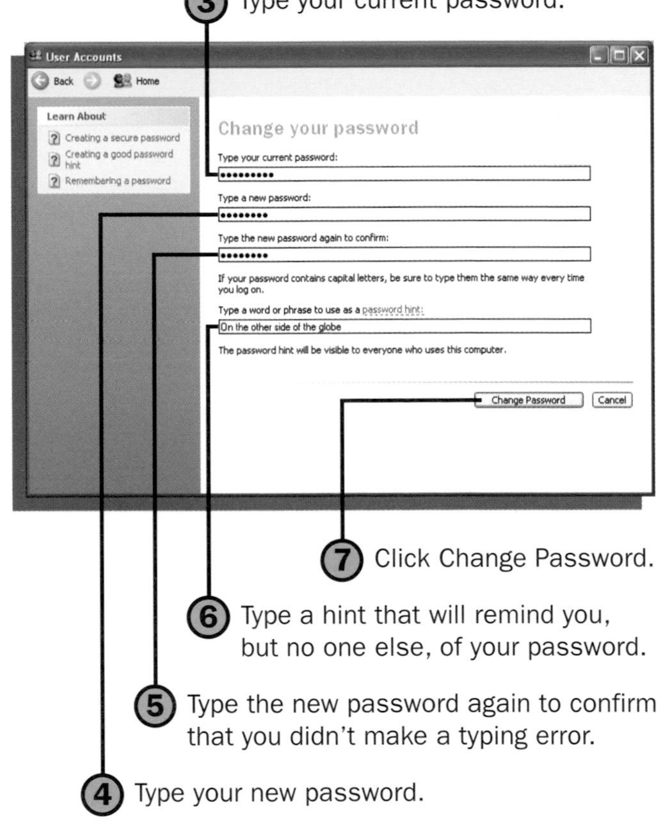
User Accounts
Back
Home
Learn About
Creating a secure password
Creating a good password hint
Remembering a password
Change your password
Type your current password:
Type a new password:
Type the new password again to confirm:
If your password contains capital letters, be sure to type them the same way every time you log on.
Type a word or phrase to use as a password hint:
On the other side of the globe
The password hint will be visible to everyone who uses this computer.
Change Password
Cancel

7. Click Change Password.
6. Type a hint that will remind you, but no one else, of your password.
5. Type the new password again to confirm that you didn't make a typing error.
4. Type your new password.

Resetting Your Password

Few things are more maddening than trying repeatedly to log on, only to realize that you've forgotten your password! If this happens, you have two choices: You can reset the password (or, if you're a member of the Limited group, you can ask an Administrator to reset it for you), which means that you'll lose all your settings and any security credentials and certificates; or you can use your Password Reset disk to log on and reset your password *and* save all your settings and credentials. The latter is obviously the better choice, so you should create a Password Reset disk while you still remember your password.

Create a Password Reset Disk

1. Choose Control Panel from the Start menu, click the User Accounts category, and click your account.
2. Click Prevent A Forgotten Password in the Related Tasks list in the User Accounts window to start the Forgotten Password Wizard.

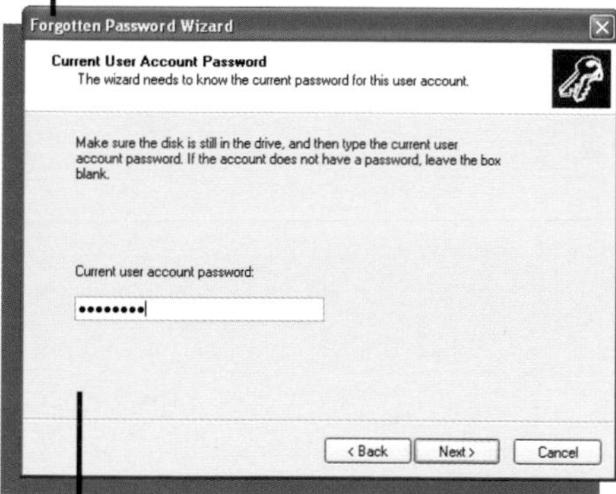

3. Step through the wizard, inserting a blank floppy disk in the drive and entering your current password when prompted. When you've completed the wizard, remove the disk, label it as your Password Reset disk, and store it in a secure location.

Reset Your Password

1. Click here to see your password hint. Enter the password if the hint did its job.

2. If you still don't remember the password, click here, and, in the pop-up box that appears, click Use Your Password Reset Disk.

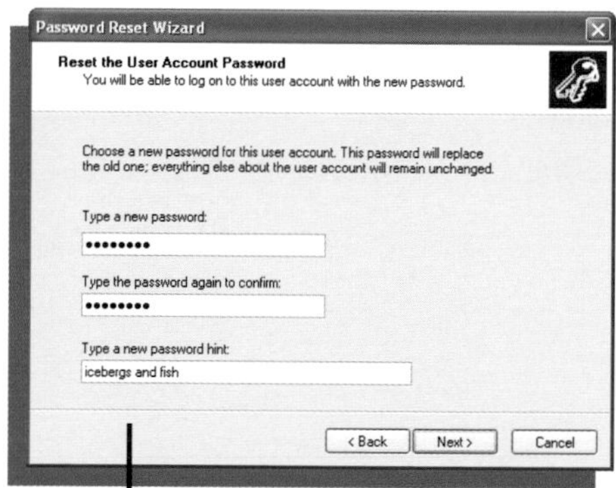

3. Step through the Password Reset Wizard, inserting your Password Reset disk into the drive. When prompted, type a new password and a new (and better!) password hint.

4. After completing the wizard, type your new password, and press Enter.

Protecting Your Files with a Password

If your files contain sensitive information that you want to protect from prying eyes, place the files in a compressed folder, and create a password. Then, regardless of where those files are located—on your computer, in a shared folder on a network, or on a floppy disk that you lost somewhere—they can be opened and viewed only by you or by someone who knows that password.

TIP: The encryption—that is, the scrambling of text to make it unreadable—of your files can't be cracked unless you're a very sophisticated cryptologist, so make sure you don't forget the password.

Encrypt a Compressed Folder

1. Create and open a new compressed folder. Copy your sensitive files into the folder.
2. Choose Add A Password from the File menu to display the Add Password dialog box.
3. Enter a password. (The password is case-sensitive, so remember your combination of uppercase and lowercase letters.)
4. Reenter the password.
5. Click OK.
6. Close the compressed folder.
7. When you want to access the files, double-click the compressed folder to open it, double-click a file, and enter the password when prompted.

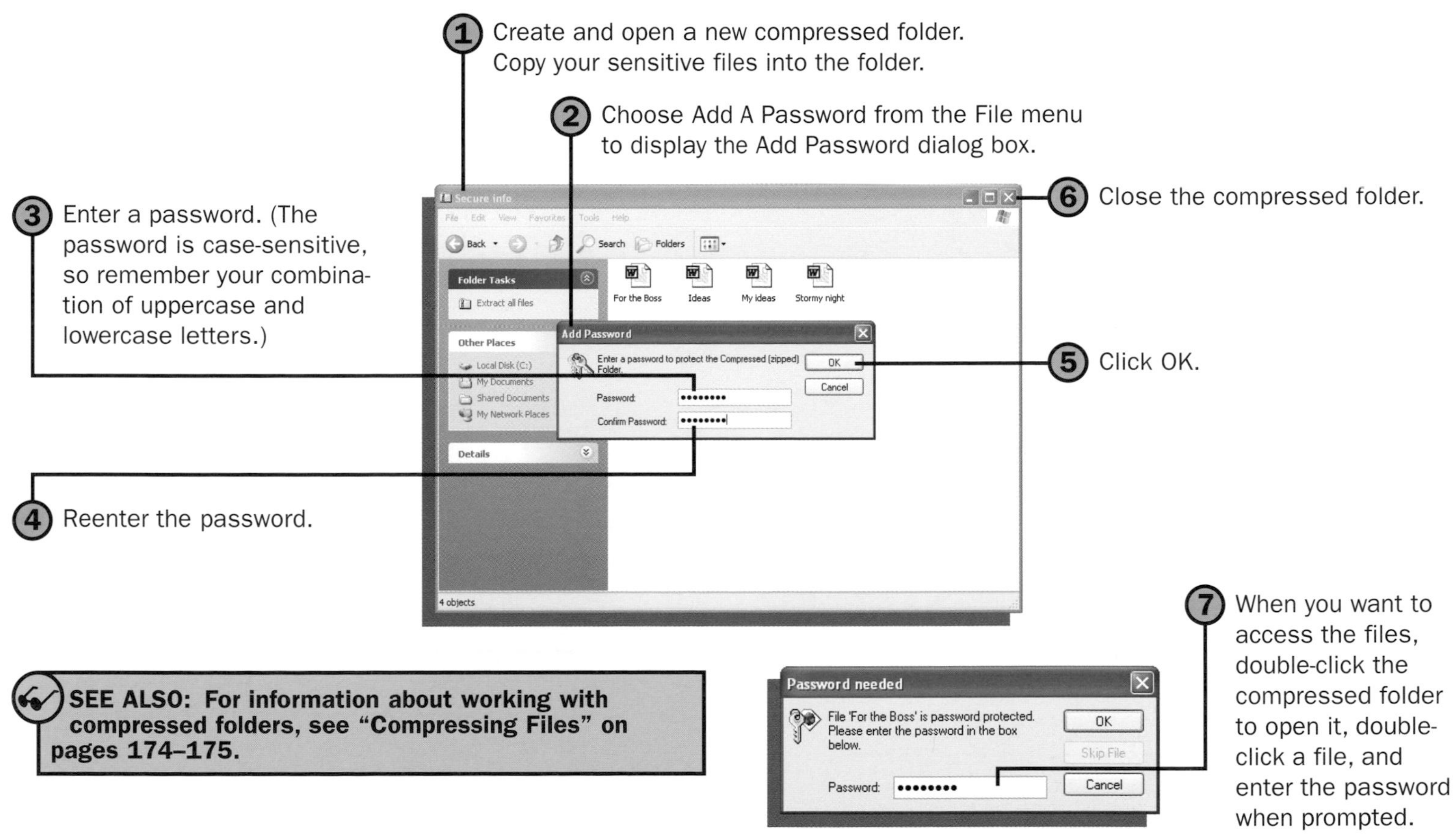

SEE ALSO: For information about working with compressed folders, see "Compressing Files" on pages 174–175.

Restricting User Rights

One of the surest ways to protect your computer from either malicious or accidental damage is to be extremely cautious when you're deciding on the select few who are responsible enough to be allowed full access to the computer. If you're the least bit uncertain, you can always assign people to the Limited group or ask them to log on as Guest users.

Change the Type of Access

1. Choose Control Panel from the Start menu, click the User Accounts category, and click the account you want to change to display the User Accounts window.
2. In the User Accounts window, click the Change The Account Type task.
3. Click the Limited option.

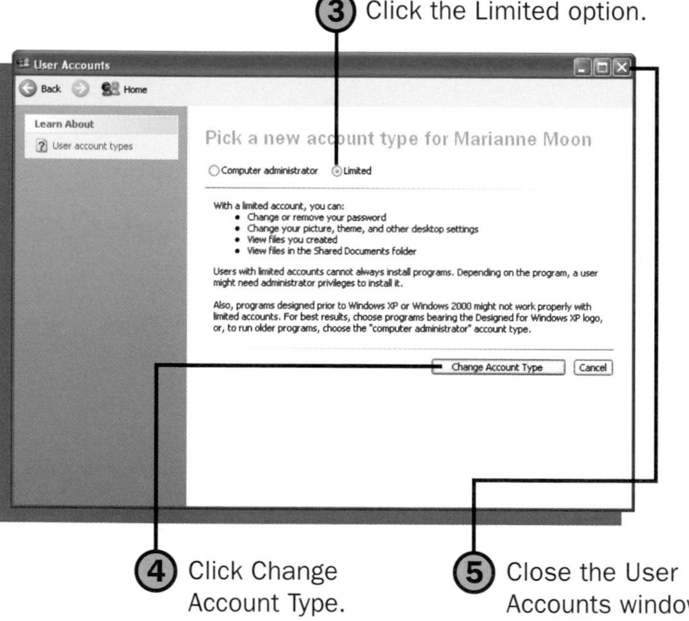

4. Click Change Account Type.
5. Close the User Accounts window.

CAUTION: Make sure that every member of the Administrators group uses a password to log on. Otherwise, a member of the Limited group could use an Administrators account to make changes (and could even change his or her account to that of an Administrator).

Use the Guest Account

1. If the Guest account isn't listed on the Welcome screen when you first log on (or when you choose Switch Users from the Start menu), click the User Accounts category in the Control Panel, and click the Guest account.
2. Click Turn On The Guest Account.

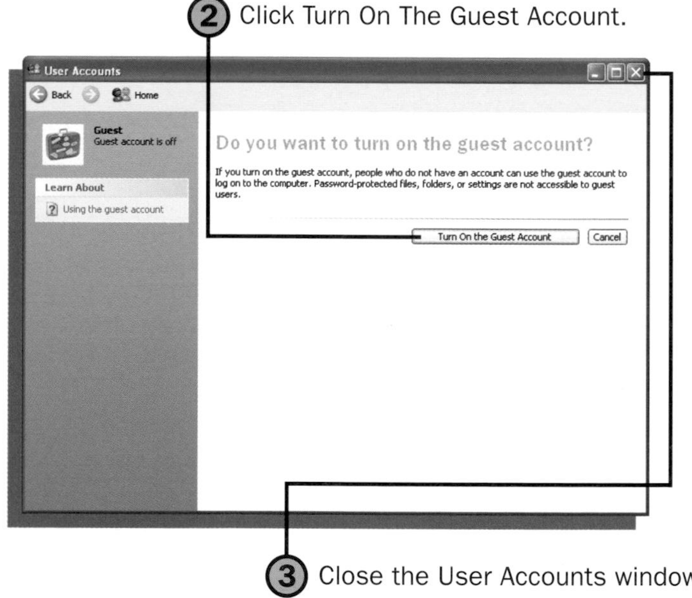

3. Close the User Accounts window.
4. To use the Guest account, click Guest when you log on. (You can't have a password with the Guest account.)

Locking Your Computer

If you leave your computer unattended for a while, you can lock it so that even though the programs that were running will continue to run, no one can access the computer using your name. Exactly what happens depends on whether or not you have Fast User Switching enabled.

TIP: **Fast User Switching is the tool that allows another user to log on to your computer without your having to log off. To enable or disable Fast User Switching, open the Control Panel, click the User Accounts category, and click the Change The Way Users Log On Or Off task.**

Lock the Computer

1. On your keyboard, press the Windows key + L.

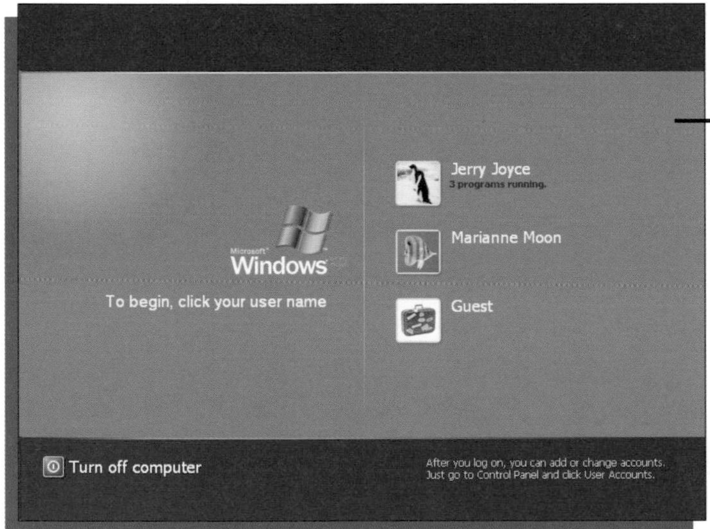

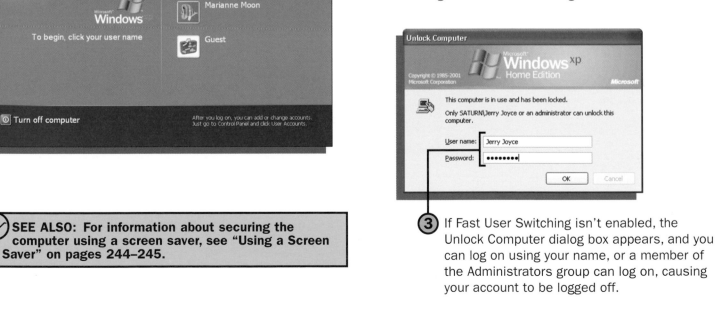

2. If Fast User Switching is enabled, you'll see the same window that appears when you choose to switch users, and you or another user can log on or resume working.

3. If Fast User Switching isn't enabled, the Unlock Computer dialog box appears, and you can log on using your name, or a member of the Administrators group can log on, causing your account to be logged off.

SEE ALSO: **For information about securing the computer using a screen saver, see "Using a Screen Saver" on pages 244–245.**

Protecting Personal Information on the Internet

Some Web sites that you visit ask you to provide information, such as your name and e-mail address. Others are less direct; they use *cookies*—little text files that are written by the Web site and stored on your computer—to track your activities. Despite their friendly name, cookies can be insidious invasions of your privacy, often using the material they gather for advertising, demographic data, and so on. You can set up Internet Explorer to limit the amount of information you reveal when you're on the Internet.

Set Your Profile

1. Start Internet Explorer if it isn't already running, choose Internet Options from the Tools menu, and then click the Content tab of the Internet Options dialog box.

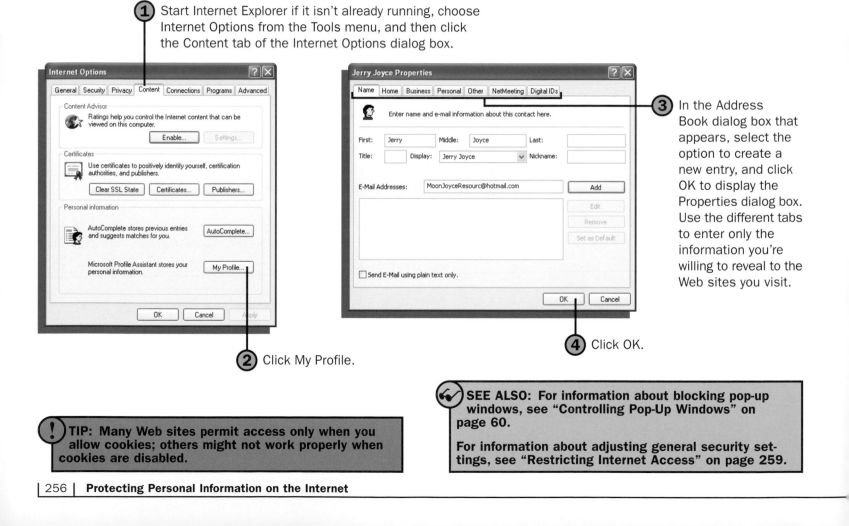

2. Click My Profile.

3. In the Address Book dialog box that appears, select the option to create a new entry, and click OK to display the Properties dialog box. Use the different tabs to enter only the information you're willing to reveal to the Web sites you visit.

4. Click OK.

TIP: Many Web sites permit access only when you allow cookies; others might not work properly when cookies are disabled.

SEE ALSO: For information about blocking pop-up windows, see "Controlling Pop-Up Windows" on page 60.

For information about adjusting general security settings, see "Restricting Internet Access" on page 259.

Control Those Cookies

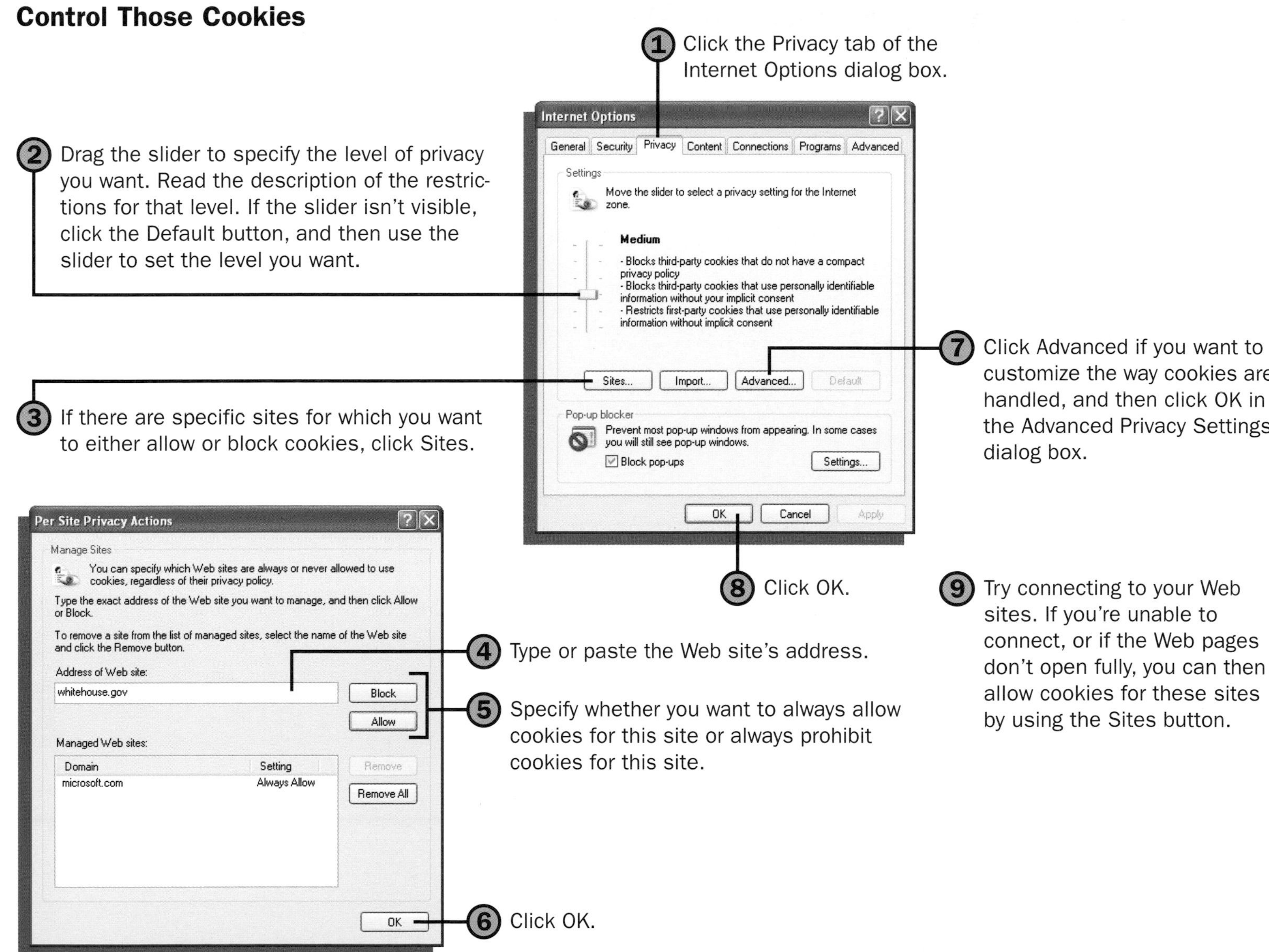

1. Click the Privacy tab of the Internet Options dialog box.
2. Drag the slider to specify the level of privacy you want. Read the description of the restrictions for that level. If the slider isn't visible, click the Default button, and then use the slider to set the level you want.
3. If there are specific sites for which you want to either allow or block cookies, click Sites.
4. Type or paste the Web site's address.
5. Specify whether you want to always allow cookies for this site or always prohibit cookies for this site.
6. Click OK.
7. Click Advanced if you want to customize the way cookies are handled, and then click OK in the Advanced Privacy Settings dialog box.
8. Click OK.
9. Try connecting to your Web sites. If you're unable to connect, or if the Web pages don't open fully, you can then allow cookies for these sites by using the Sites button.

Setting Internet Explorer Security

Although most Web sites pose little security threat to your computer, some sites are designed with malicious intentions. To protect yourself from these sites, as well as to allow access to additional features for sites you know aren't going cause any harm, in Internet Explorer you can set and customize your own security levels and can add sites to your list of trusted—or restricted—Web sites.

Set Your Security

1. In Internet Explorer, choose Internet Options from the Tools menu, and click the Security tab of the Internet Options dialog box.

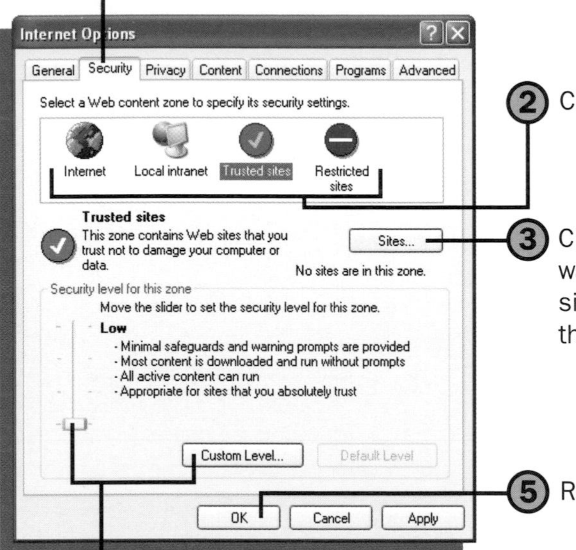

2. Click a zone.
3. Click the Sites button, type or paste an address for a Web site you want to include in that zone, and click Add. Continue adding any other sites you want in that zone, and click OK when you've finished. (Note that you can't add any Web sites to the Internet zone.)
4. Do either of the following:
   - Use the slider to adjust the level of security. If the slider isn't visible, click the Default Level button, and then use the slider.
   - Click Custom Level, and select the options you want in the Security Settings dialog box. Click OK.
5. Repeat steps 2 through 4 for the other zones, and then click OK.

TIP: The Internet Explorer security settings aren't the only means by which content can be restricted. The Windows Firewall also restricts the downloading of potentially dangerous material and restricts access to your computer from the Internet.

SEE ALSO: For information about using parental controls for limiting access to certain types of sites, see "Restricting Internet Access" on the facing page.

For information about security settings using the Windows Firewall, see "Configuring the Windows Firewall" on pages 264–265.

Restricting Internet Access

The Internet provides access to many things—some weird, some wonderful, and some that might not be appropriate for everyone who uses your computer. To restrict access to certain types of sites—those that contain sexually explicit or violent material, for example—you can use Content Advisor.

Set the Restrictions

1. Start Internet Explorer if it isn't already running, choose Internet Options from the Tools menu, and click the Content tab of the Internet Options dialog box.

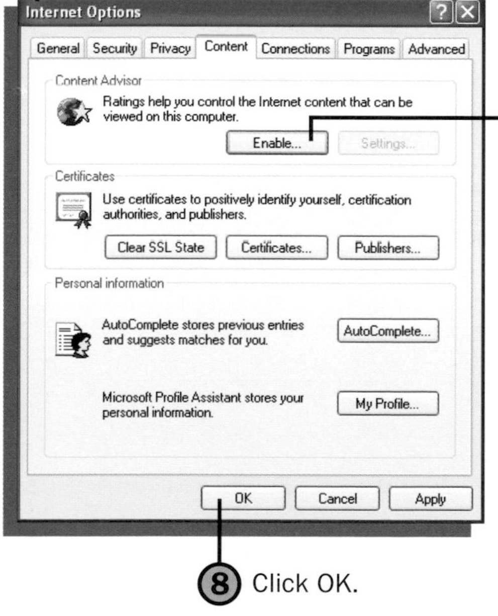

2. Click Enable.
3. In Content Advisor, click a category.
4. Move the slider to adjust the acceptable level of material that can be accessed. Repeat to set levels for the other categories.

5. On the General tab, select or clear check boxes to specify whether unrated sites may be accessed and whether a password may be used to allow access to restricted sites.
6. Click Create Password, enter and confirm your password, provide a hint for the password, and click OK.
7. Click OK.
8. Click OK.

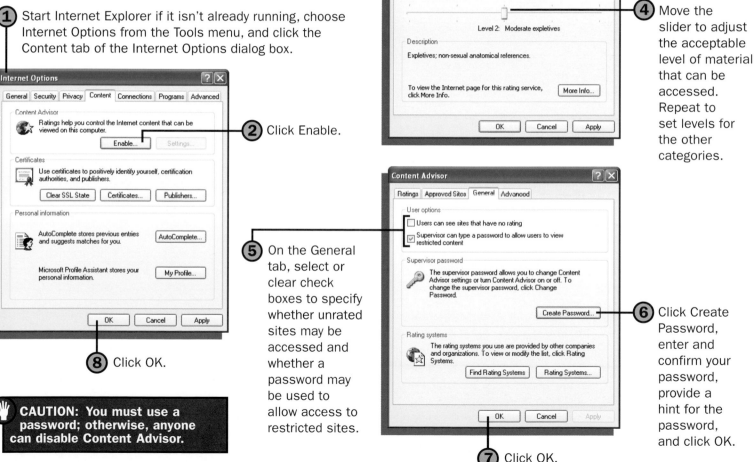

CAUTION: You must use a password; otherwise, anyone can disable Content Advisor.

Maintaining High Security with Service Pack 2 NEW FEATURE

Microsoft Windows XP itself provides your computer with many built-in security features, but, after you've enhanced it with Service Pack 2 (or later), your computer's security will be greatly improved. We've discussed some of these security features in other parts of the book, but now we'll take a look at the big picture to see how Windows with Service Pack 2 enhancements increases your security—and, unfortunately, sometimes complicates your normal computer use.

Closing the Doors to Your Computer

You know that hackers, viruses, worms, spyware, and other evils are lurking out there, making dastardly plans to attack your computer! Fortunately, Windows has come up with several ways of confounding these villains. One such deterrent is the Windows Firewall, which provides superior control of the avenues through which a hacker can access your computer. The hacker's favored avenue of access to your computer is through a gateway, or port, that's left open by a program. The firewall closes any ports that aren't in use and restricts access to others, unless a port has been specifically opened by an authorized program or directly by you. This port patrol adds substantial security, but it can also interfere with the normal operations of certain programs, such as Microsoft NetMeeting. You might need to get specific directions about configuring a particular program, opening ports, or updates for software that doesn't work properly with the firewall.

The firewall also blocks outgoing connections and messages from programs that you haven't authorized to communicate with the outside world. You've probably seen messages that pop up, telling you this or that program is trying to access your network or the Internet and asking you if you want to allow this. Annoying as these seemingly continuous interruptions and questions can be, imagine how much more upsetting it would be to discover that a program was running on your computer without your knowledge, spying on everything you do! When such a program tries to send information to its evil overlords, the firewall detects the attempted outgoing message and tells you about it. Caught in the act!

Avoiding the Troublemakers

Sneaking in via an open port is only one method among many through which nasty programs can invade your computer. Some of these interlopers, particularly viruses and worms, come to you in e-mail messages or attachments, are downloaded from a Web site, or are transferred to you using Windows Messenger. Windows works hard to keep these programs from gate-crashing your computer. Outlook Express checks your attachments, and Windows Messenger and Internet Explorer look for malicious code in any files you transfer. Windows Messenger will block any invalidly signed programs unless they originate from someone in your Contacts list. Internet Explorer also blocks the downloading of ActiveX controls that don't have valid signatures, and it blocks the running of any controls that have previously been disabled. Other security enhancements are extremely technical, including added protection for using Remote Procedure Calls and Distributed Component Object Model items.

Preventing Evil Programs from Running

Windows now provides several ways to protect you from a malicious program that has already made its way onto your computer. For example, whenever you open an attachment or run a downloaded file, Windows checks to see whether the file is a program (that is, an executable file), and, if so, whether the program has been signed by a legitimate publisher. If the program appears not to be legitimate, Windows prevents it from running. There are also several very technical improvements: preventing memory buffer overflows, for example, and, with hardware makers, the development of techniques to prevent executable code from running in parts of the computer's memory designed to store data only.

Doing Your Part

By themselves, these security features can't protect you from every type of mischief. Some of it's up to you. You need to be active in protecting your computer, your data, and your personal information. Here are several things you can do to help improve your security:

- Make sure you have a good, up-to-date anti-virus program installed. This will add protection against viruses and worms that have figured ways around some of the security features.
- In Outlook Express (or in Outlook if you're using Microsoft Office), read your e-mail messages in Plain Text instead of using HTML format. This will prevent any malicious code that's hidden in the HTML code from being executed when you open the message.
- In Outlook Express (or in Outlook if you're using Microsoft Office), don't download pictures and other external HTML content contained on a server. Doing so verifies your e-mail address to any potential authors of spam and can introduce malicious code.
- Make sure that your Web content zones in Internet Explorer are properly set and that you're not using custom settings that provide less protection than the recommended default level.
- In Internet Explorer, make sure you have the pop-up blocker turned on to prevent code from being loaded, to prevent a hacker from stealing information by making the pop-up look like a dialog box or other content that asks for information, and to keep those annoying pop-up ads from showing up.
- In Internet Explorer, use the Add-Ons Manager to disable any add on programs that might be causing problems. If Internet Explorer crashes because an add-on program has caused a problem, use the Internet Explorer Add-On Crash Detection window to determine the culprit, and then use the Add-Ons Manager to disable that add-on.
- Keep Windows up to date with automatic updates. Yes, we ask the same question—will that endless stream of annoying updates never cease?! Remember, however, that each critical update is an urgent fix to outmaneuver a newly detected software vulnerability or to thwart a new method of attacking your computer.
- Use the new Security Center to verify that your basic security settings—Windows Firewall, Virus Protection, and Automatic Updates—are properly configured and up to date.
- Stop and think before you do something you might regret: open an attachment, download a file, install a program, or even answer an e-mail.
- Keep all your important data backed up so that if something nasty sneaks past all your security, you can recover all your data.

Complicated and complex? Absolutely! But don't be intimidated: Windows will take care of most of these issues. You don't need to worry about buffer overflows or spoofed files or any of the other computerspeak techniques of hackers because Windows deals with them swiftly and invisibly. Are you worried because you're not sure how to turn on the Windows Firewall? Don't be: Windows turns it on for you, and you can always check its status in the Security Center. Windows also adjusts many of your default settings to maintain the optimum balance between security and functionality.

Monitoring Your Security Settings ⊕ NEW FEATURE

Although there are many different high-security settings in Windows, there are three big ones: Windows Firewall, Virus Protection, and Automatic Updates. With the new Security Center, you can easily monitor your settings and can adjust them as needed.

Check Your Primary Settings

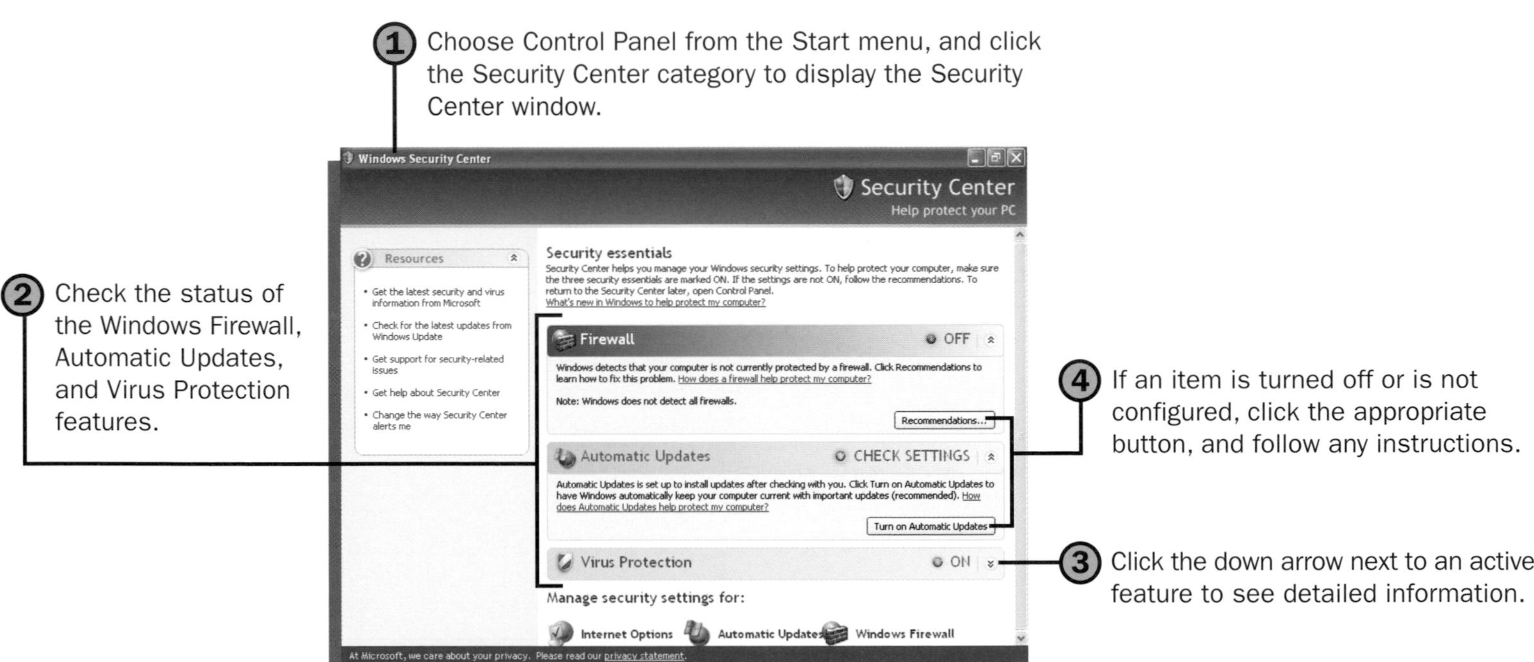

1 Choose Control Panel from the Start menu, and click the Security Center category to display the Security Center window.
2 Check the status of the Windows Firewall, Automatic Updates, and Virus Protection features.
4 If an item is turned off or is not configured, click the appropriate button, and follow any instructions.
3 Click the down arrow next to an active feature to see detailed information.
Windows Security Center
Security Center
Help protect your PC
Resources
Security essentials
Firewall
OFF
Recommendations...
Automatic Updates
CHECK SETTINGS
Turn on Automatic Updates
Virus Protection
ON
Manage security settings for:
Internet Options
Automatic Updates
Windows Firewall

TIP: The Windows Firewall and the Automatic Updates features are part of Windows XP, but the Virus Protection software is provided by third-party software companies. Make sure you've set the anti-virus software to automatically download updated files and to conduct real-time scanning.

SEE ALSO: For information about customizing the Windows Firewall settings, see "Configuring the Windows Firewall" on pages 264–265.

For information about configuring the way automatic updates are downloaded and installed, see "Installing Critical Fixes" on pages 270–271.

Check Your Other Settings

1. Click an item in the Resources section to
   - Go to the Microsoft Security Web page for the latest security information and downloads.
   - Go to Windows Update to manually download critical updates and check for noncritical updates.
   - Go to the Security Support Center Web page for additional information about security.
   - Open the Help And Support Center window for information about using the Security Center.
   - Open the Alert Settings dialog box to specify which security conditions will trigger an alert.

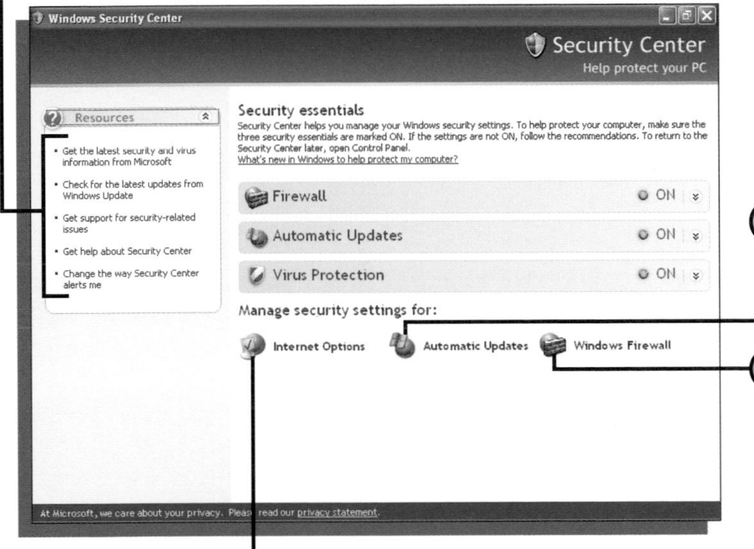

2. Click the Automatic Updates icon to display the Automatic Updates dialog box, from which you can configure your download settings.

3. Click the Windows Firewall icon to display the Windows Firewall dialog box, from which you can configure your settings for the Windows Firewall.

4. Click the Internet Options icon to display the Internet Properties dialog box. Set the security for each Web content zone, set your use of cookies, prevent pop-up windows from appearing, restrict access to certain types of Web sites, and specify the personal data you'll permit to be shared with Web sites.

NEW FEATURE: The Security Center, a feature introduced with Service Pack 2, constantly monitors the status of your security settings. It also provides a central location from which you can adjust your security settings, if necessary.

Configuring the Windows Firewall ⊛ NEW FEATURE

A firewall is a program that's designed to prevent unauthorized and malicious access to your computer over the Internet. In other words, a firewall is your defense against hackers, viruses, Trojan horses, worms, and all the other horrors out there in cyberspace. Unfortunately, a firewall can also block legitimate traffic, so you might need to tweak your settings a bit.

Configure the Firewall

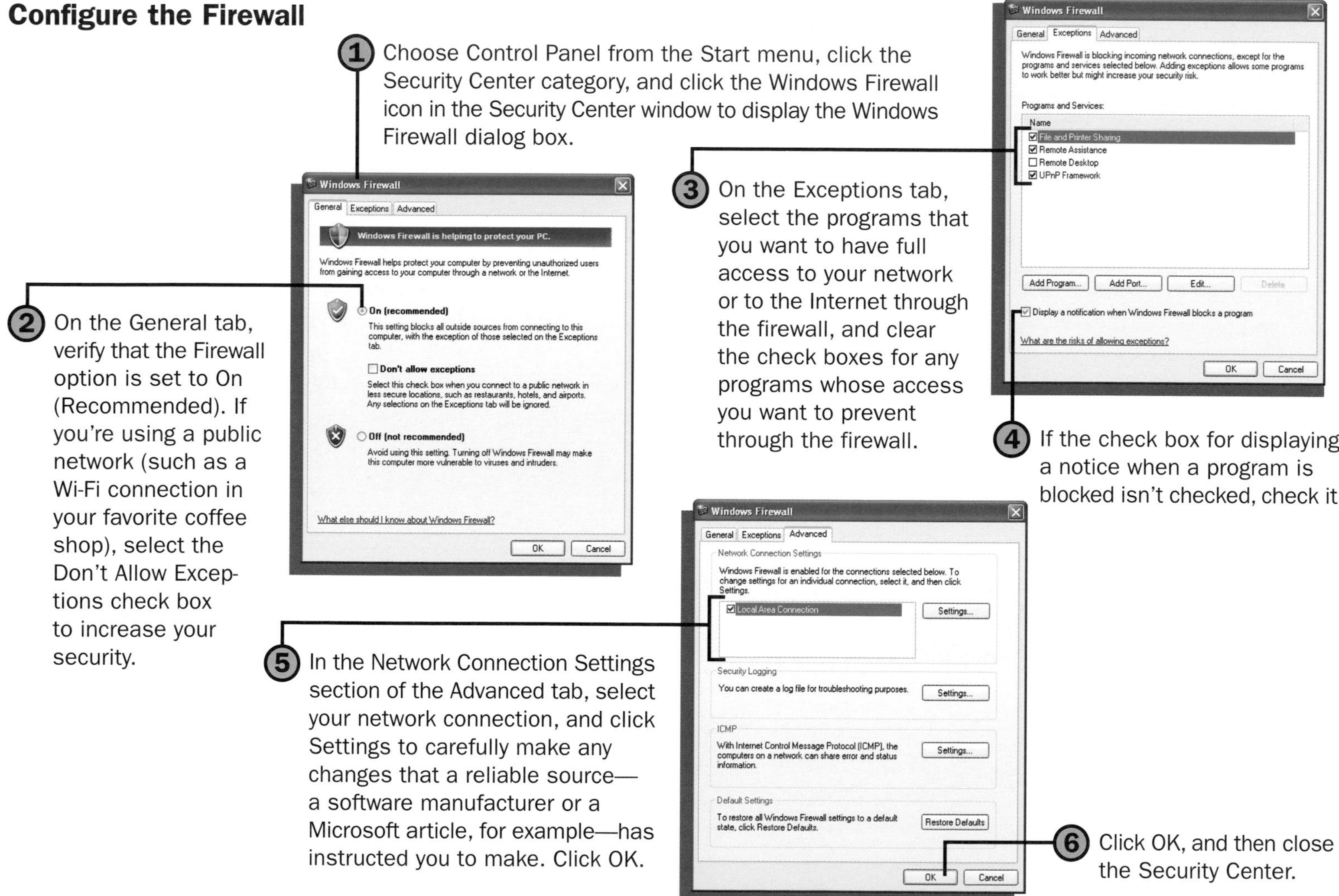

1. Choose Control Panel from the Start menu, click the Security Center category, and click the Windows Firewall icon in the Security Center window to display the Windows Firewall dialog box.
2. On the General tab, verify that the Firewall option is set to On (Recommended). If you're using a public network (such as a Wi-Fi connection in your favorite coffee shop), select the Don't Allow Exceptions check box to increase your security.
3. On the Exceptions tab, select the programs that you want to have full access to your network or to the Internet through the firewall, and clear the check boxes for any programs whose access you want to prevent through the firewall.
4. If the check box for displaying a notice when a program is blocked isn't checked, check it.
5. In the Network Connection Settings section of the Advanced tab, select your network connection, and click Settings to carefully make any changes that a reliable source—a software manufacturer or a Microsoft article, for example—has instructed you to make. Click OK.
6. Click OK, and then close the Security Center.

Allow or Block Program Access

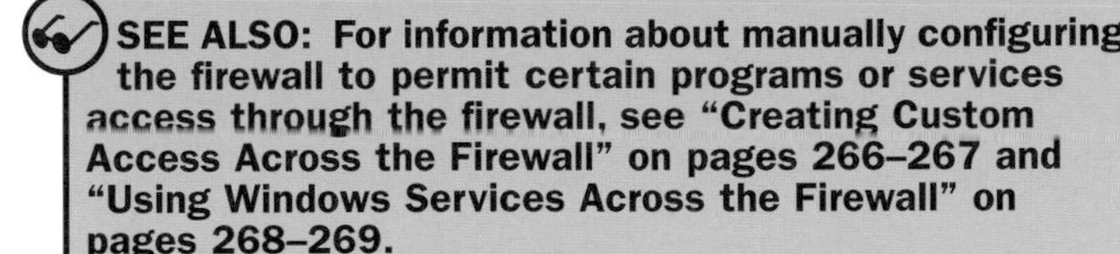

SEE ALSO: For information about manually configuring the firewall to permit certain programs or services access through the firewall, see "Creating Custom Access Across the Firewall" on pages 266–267 and "Using Windows Services Across the Firewall" on pages 268–269.

1. Start the program you want to use. If the program is stopped by the firewall, the Windows Security Alert dialog box will appear.

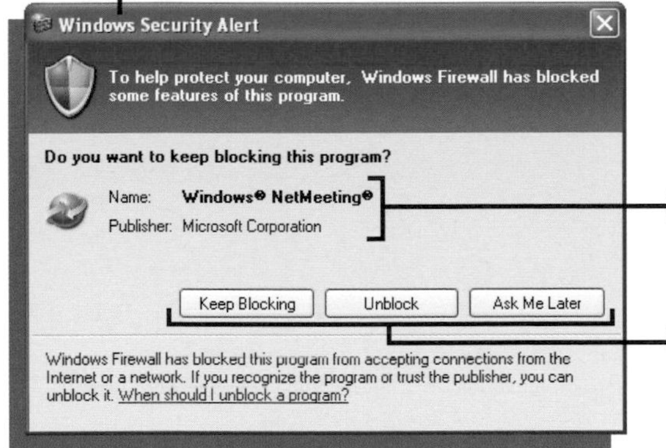

Windows Security Alert
To help protect your computer, Windows Firewall has blocked some features of this program.
Do you want to keep blocking this program?
Name: Windows® NetMeeting®
Publisher: Microsoft Corporation
Keep Blocking
Unblock
Ask Me Later
Windows Firewall has blocked this program from accepting connections from the Internet or a network. If you recognize the program or trust the publisher, you can unblock it. When should I unblock a program?

2. Review the name of the program and its publisher, and decide whether you trust the program and its source.

3. Click the button for the action you want to take:
   - Keep Blocking to deny the program access through the firewall. The Security Alert dialog box won't appear again for this program.
   - Unblock to always allow this program access through the firewall. The program will be added to the Exceptions list for the firewall configuration.
   - Ask Me Later to deny the program access through the firewall this time. The next time the program attempts access through the firewall, the Security Alert dialog box will appear again.

CAUTION: If you've changed the default security settings for the Windows Firewall, the Windows Security Alert dialog box might not be displayed when a program is blocked. Select the Display A Notification When Windows Firewall Blocks A Program check box on the Exceptions tab of the Windows Firewall dialog box if you always want the Windows Security Alert dialog box to be displayed.

TIP: Some program, especially games, might hide the Security Alert dialog box. If necessary, click the Windows Security Alert button on the Windows taskbar, or minimize the program, to access the Windows Security Alert dialog box.

TIP: If the Don't Allow Exceptions check box on the General tab of the Windows Firewall dialog box is checked, access across the firewall will be blocked, and the Windows Security Alert dialog box will not appear.

Creating Custom Access Across the Firewall ⊛ NEW FEATURE

In most cases, when you specify that a program is allowed access to your network or to the Internet through the firewall, the program works perfectly. However, there might be times when a program you're using doesn't work well with the firewall. In that case, you'll need to make some special settings to get the program to work properly, either by manually adding the program to the Exceptions list for the firewall or by adding the port number the program will use.

TIP: A port is an avenue that the computer uses to connect with the world outside the computer. Many programs don't have fixed port numbers, so you'll need to specify the program and let it communicate its port number to the firewall. In some cases, when this communication doesn't work and the program uses a fixed port, you can specify the port number so that the program can use the port to access the network or the Internet.

Add Program Access

1. Choose Control Panel from the Start menu, click the Security Center category, and click the Windows Firewall icon in the Security Center window to display the Windows Firewall dialog box.
2. On the Exceptions tab, click Add Program to display the Add A Program dialog box.
3. Select the program that you want to have access to the network or to the Internet.
4. If the program isn't listed, click Browse, and, in the Browse dialog box, locate and select the program. Click Open.
5. Click Change Scope.
6. In the Change Scope dialog box, select the location of the computers that you'll allow this program to communicate with, or create a custom list of computers by specifying their IP addresses.
7. Click OK.
8. Click OK in the Add a Program dialog box, and then click OK in the Windows Firewall dialog box. Close the Security Center, and then use the program to verify that your settings work.

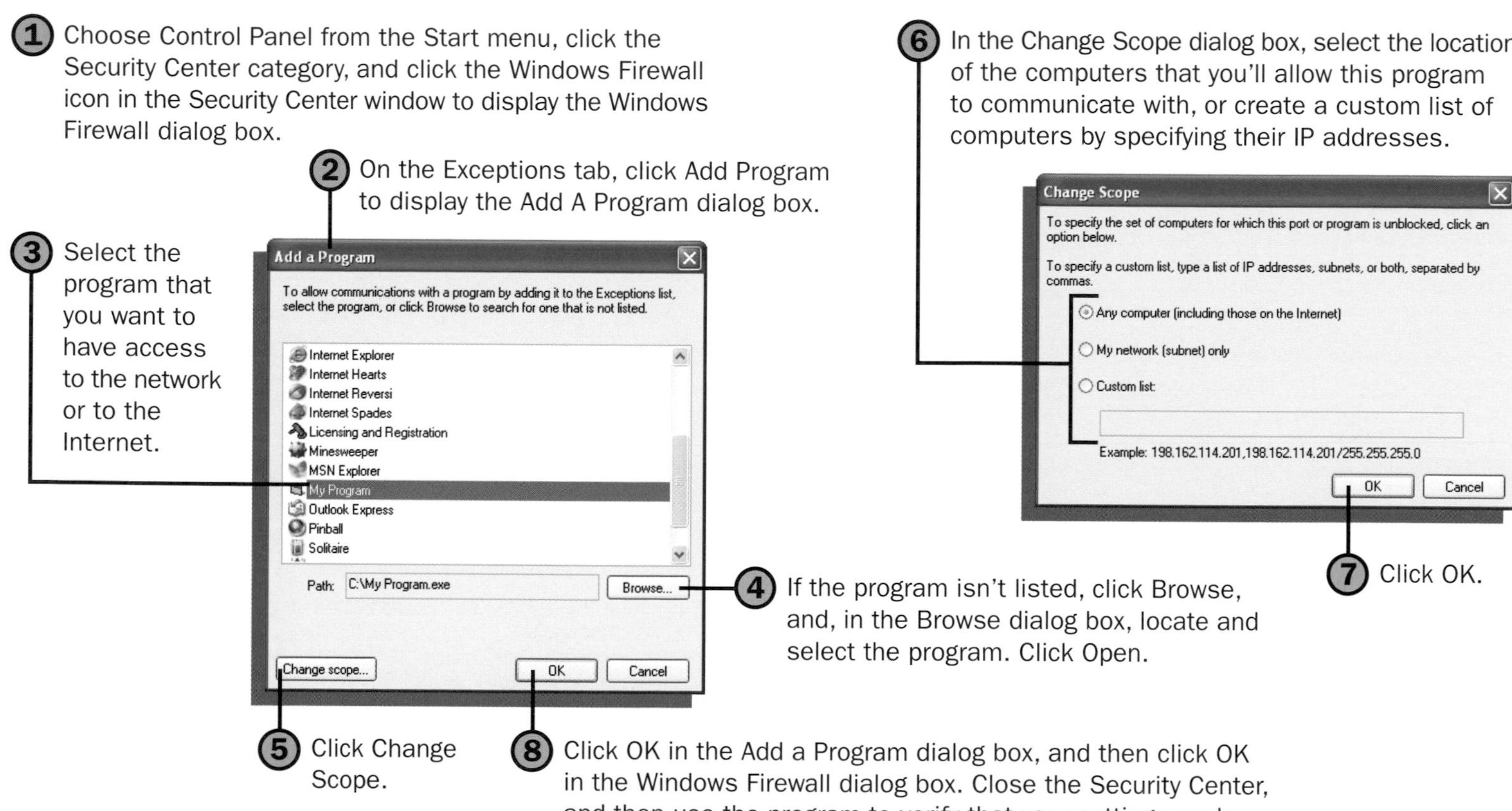

Add a Port

1. Obtain the port number or numbers and the protocol to be used for the program from the program's documentation, the manufacturer's Web site, or a Microsoft article.

2. In the Control Panel, click the Security Center category, and click the Windows Firewall icon in the Security Center window to display the Windows Firewall dialog box.

> **TIP: Just in case you were wondering, TCP is the Transmission Control Protocol that's used in most network configurations, and UDP is the User Datagram Protocol that's used by a network address translation server.**

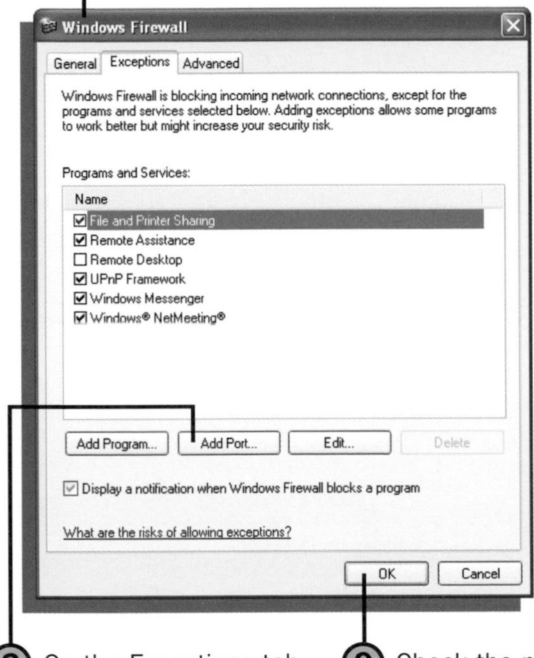

3. On the Exceptions tab, click Add Port.

4. In the Add A Port dialog box, type a common name for the port that will help you identify it later.

5. Enter the port number you want to open.

6. Select the protocol to be used. In most cases, it will be the TCP protocol.

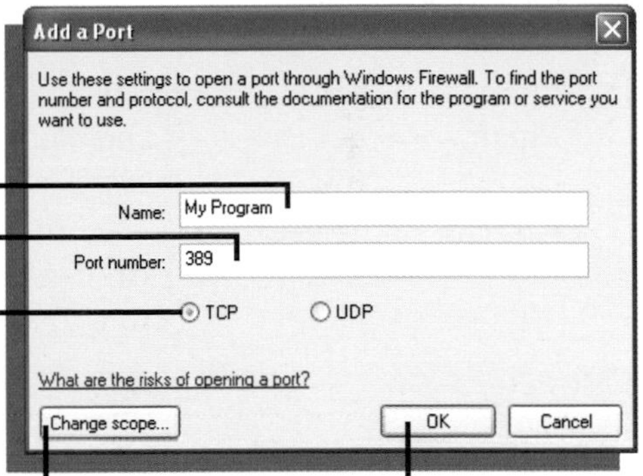

7. Click Change Scope if you want to restrict which computers can communicate through this port.

8. Click OK. Add any additional ports you need for the program.

9. Check the port you added, and then click OK. Close the Security Center, and test the program to see whether you now have access.

> **TIP: Sometimes a program in the Exceptions list or a manually opened port won't be recognized by the firewall until you restart the program. If the program doesn't work after you've made the settings and restarted it, you'll need to restart the computer and try again.**

Using Windows Services Across the Firewall

Your computer can run a variety of services—for example, it can be an FTP server or a mail server. You'll need to tell the Windows Firewall which services you're running so that the firewall will allow the information to pass through. Some services—such as the ICMP (Internet Control Messaging Protocol) services that are usually used to diagnose connection problems—are disabled by default because they have been misused in various ways over the Internet. However, you can enable these if you need them.

CAUTION: The services described here are advanced features and, in most cases, few if any of them will be running on a home computer. Don't change any settings in the dialog boxes shown on these two pages unless you're absolutely certain that you need these services.

Designate the Service

1. Choose Control Panel from the Start menu, click the Security Center category, and click the Windows Firewall icon in the Security Center window to display the Windows Firewall dialog box.
2. On the Advanced tab, select a network connection if you have more than one connection.
3. Click Settings.

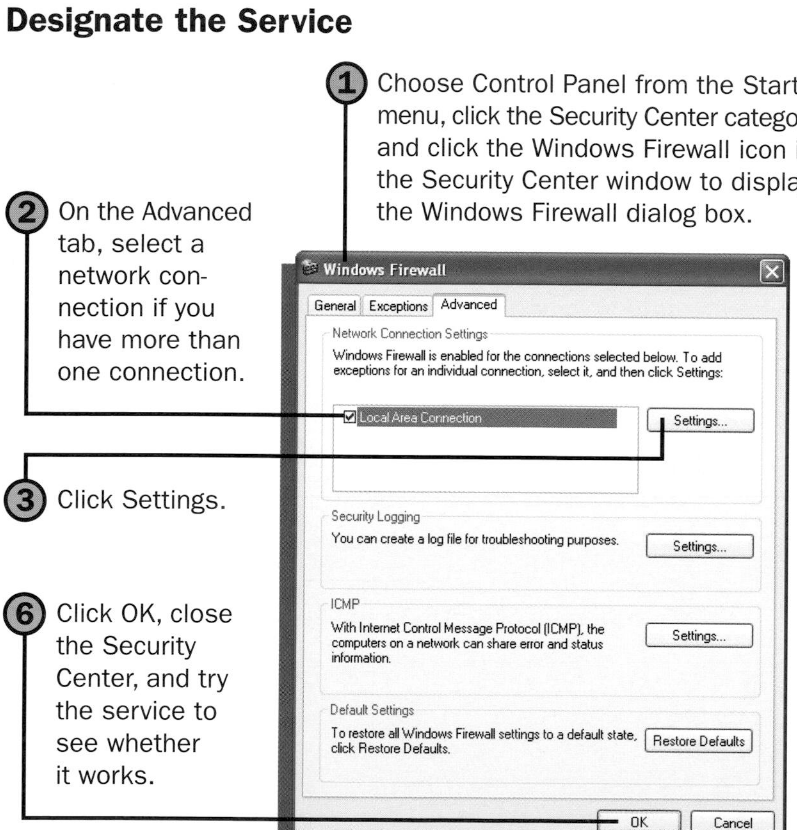

4. On the Services tab, select the check box for each service on your computer that needs to bypass the restrictions of the firewall.
5. Supply the information for each service, and click OK.
6. Click OK, close the Security Center, and try the service to see whether it works.

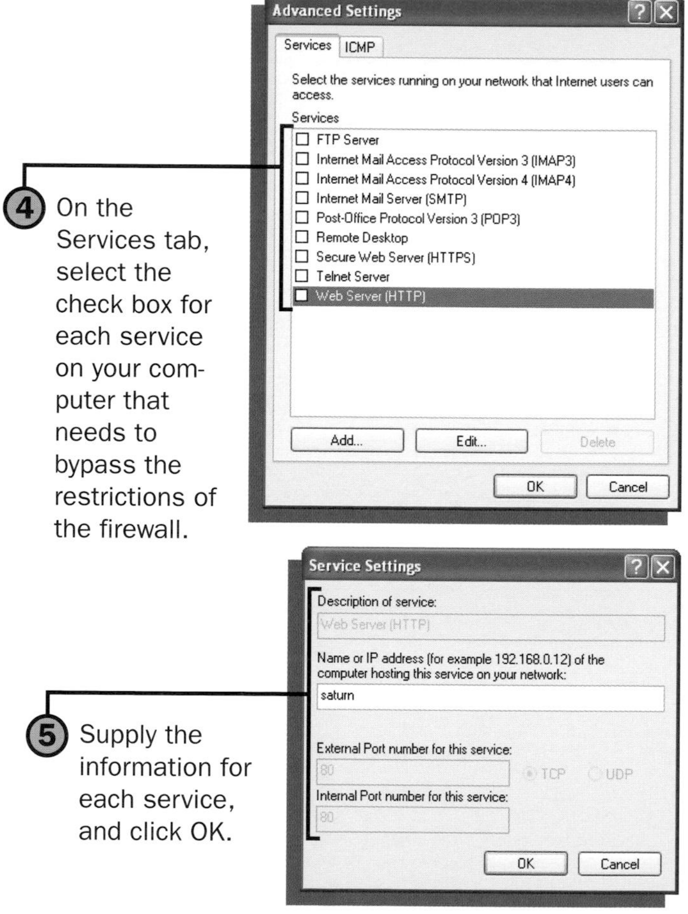

Enable ICMP

1. In the Control Panel, click the Security Center category, and click the Windows Firewall icon in the Security Center window to display the Windows Firewall dialog box.

CAUTION: ICMP requests have been used by those with evil intentions to locate and spy on computers, and are therefore disabled by default. Enable only those requests that you must have open for trouble-shooting or for making improved connections, and be sure to disable any that you're not currently using.

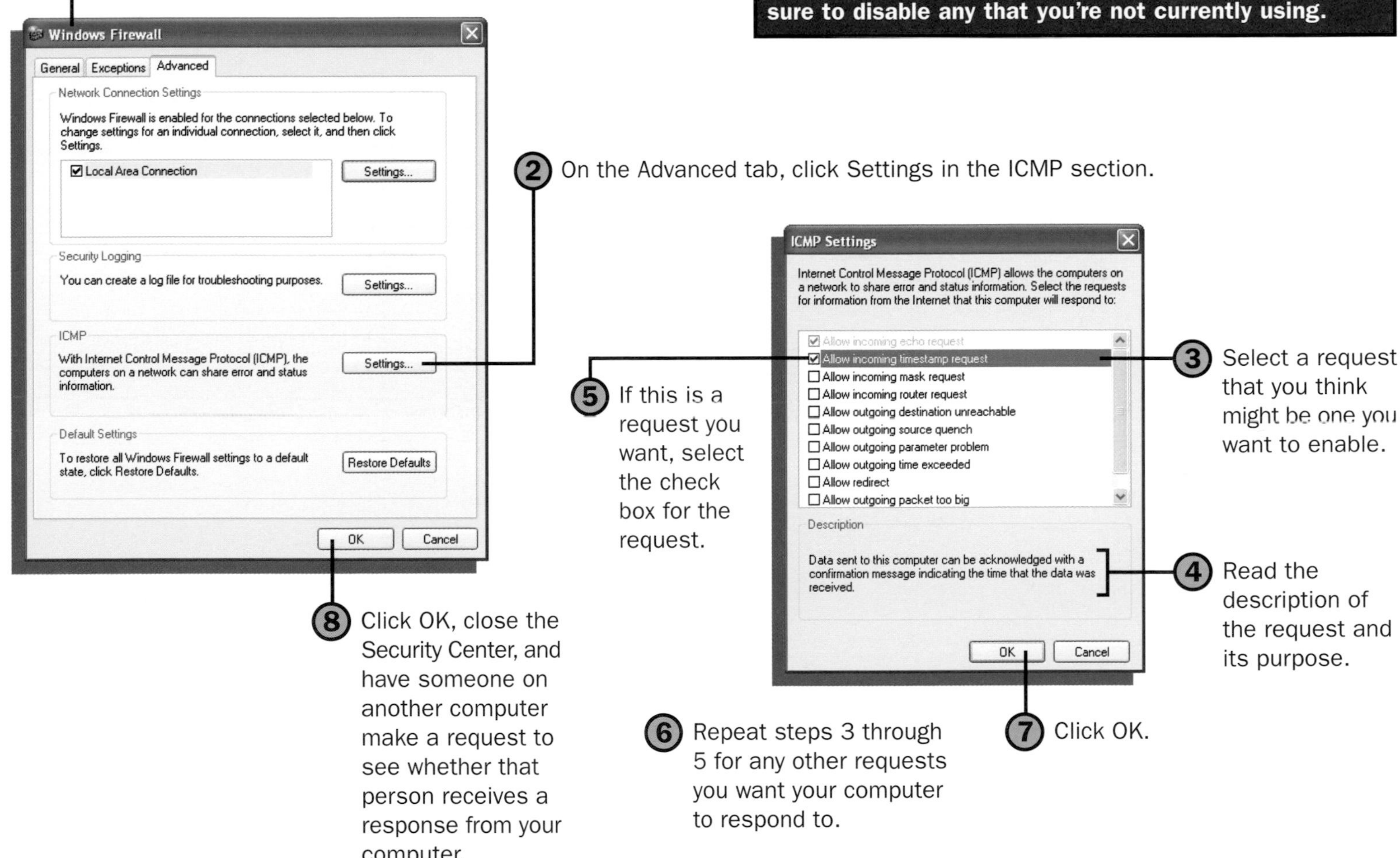

2. On the Advanced tab, click Settings in the ICMP section.
3. Select a request that you think might be one you want to enable.
4. Read the description of the request and its purpose.
5. If this is a request you want, select the check box for the request.
6. Repeat steps 3 through 5 for any other requests you want your computer to respond to.
7. Click OK.
8. Click OK, close the Security Center, and have someone on another computer make a request to see whether that person receives a response from your computer.

Installing Critical Fixes

Microsoft continues to issue updates to Windows, fixing problems and vulnerabilities as they're discovered. To keep your computer running smoothly and to avoid new types of attacks, it's important that you install any critical updates that Microsoft issues as soon as they're available. Fortunately, the Automatic Updates feature in Windows can do most of the work for you. You can choose either to have the updates automatically downloaded and installed or to have them downloaded and/or installed only after you've given Windows permission to do so.

Configure Your Downloading

1. Choose Control Panel from the Start menu, and click the Security Center category to open the Security Center window.

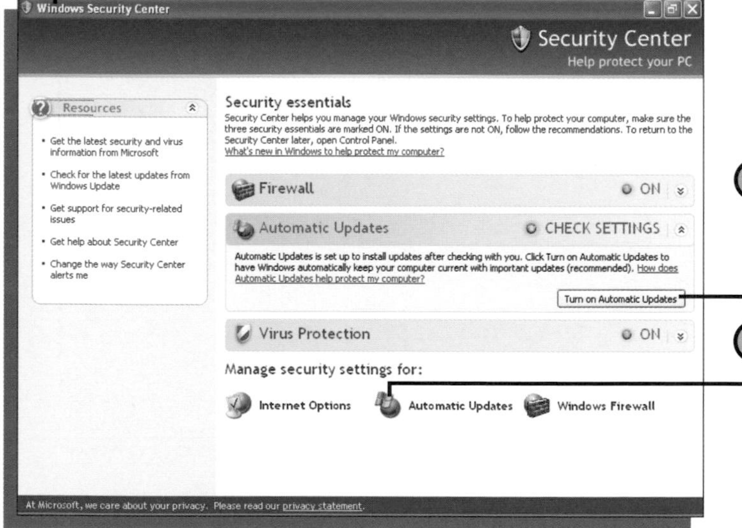

2. If the Automatic Updates section shows that automatic updating is turned off or that updates aren't configured to be installed automatically, click Turn On Automatic Updates to enable automatic downloading and installation.

3. If you want to customize the way updates are downloaded and/or installed, click the Automatic Updates icon, and, in the Automatic Updates dialog box, select one of the following:
   - Automatic (Recommended) to have Windows take care of all the updating automatically. Specify when you want the downloaded files to be installed.
   - Download Updates… to have Windows check for and download any updates, but to wait for your confirmation before installing any files.
   - Notify Me… to have Windows check for updates and to notify you that they're available for download. When they're downloaded, Windows will ask your permission to install the updates.
   - Turn Off Automatic Updates to prevent Windows from checking for updates.

4. Click OK when you've finished.

SEE ALSO: **For information about manually checking for updates, both critical and noncritical, see "Updating Your System" on page 290.**

For information about determining which service packs are installed, the Windows version and build number you're using, and which updates you've installed, see "Checking the Status of Windows" on page 291.

Download an Update

1. If you chose to be notified by Windows to download updates, click the Windows Update icon in the notification area of the Windows taskbar to display the Automatic Updates dialog box.

2. Click an update if there's more than one, and read the description of the update.

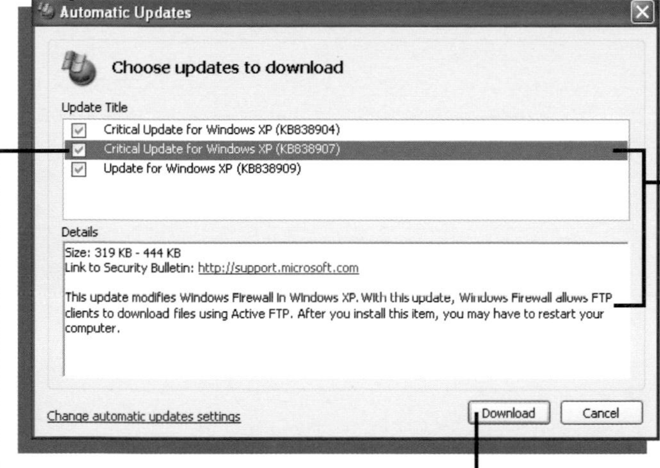

3. If you don't want to download the update, clear its check box.

4. To download the update, click Download, and wait for the Windows Update icon to reappear.

Install an Update

1. Click the Windows Update icon in the notification area of the Windows taskbar to display the Automatic Updates dialog box.

2. Select one of the following:
   - Express Install (Recommended) to have Windows install all the updates.
   - Custom Install (Advanced) to select only the downloads you want to install.

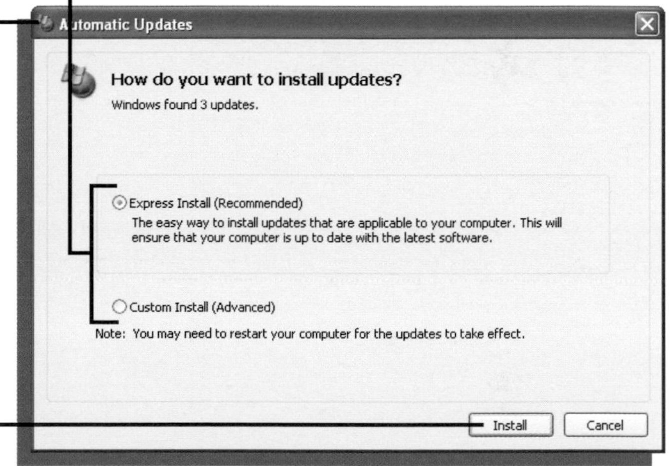

3. Click Install, and wait for the updates to be installed. If you're told that you need to restart the computer, click Restart in the dialog box that appears, or click Close if you have any unsaved information in running programs and you want to save the information before restarting. If you clicked Close, restart your computer after you've closed all your programs.

Using a Digital ID for Secure E-Mail Messages

If you're worried about prying eyes on the Internet, you can protect your e-mail messages by encrypting them so that only people with the correct *digital ID* can read them. You can also digitally sign your messages to authenticate their origin. You obtain your digital ID from a security provider, and then you exchange digital IDs with your intended recipients. You can't send an encrypted message without knowing your recipient's digital ID.

TIP: The digital ID you send out is your "public key." A private key is stored on your computer and is used along with the public key to decrypt messages. The private key exists only on your computer, so you can read encrypted messages only on that computer.

Set Up Your Security

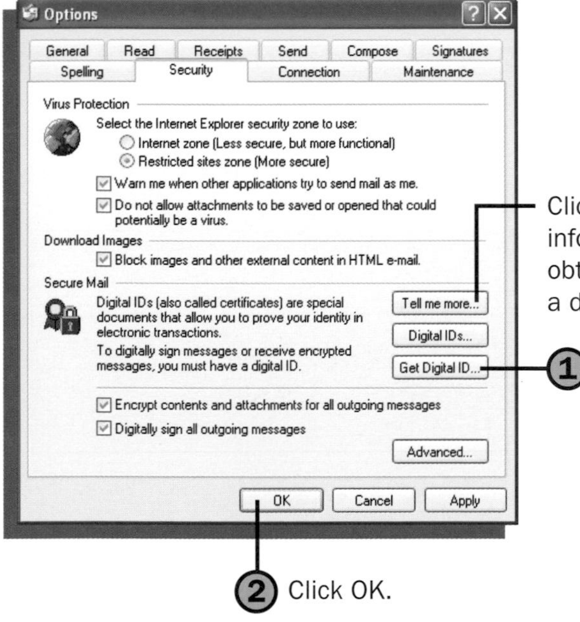

Click to see detailed information about obtaining and using a digital ID.

1. In Outlook Express, choose Options from the Tools menu, and, if you don't already have a digital ID (also called a certificate), click Get Digital ID on the Security tab of the Options dialog box. Follow the instructions provided to install your digital ID.
2. Click OK.

CAUTION: Most digital IDs require a POP3 mail service, so you might not be able to send a digital ID using a Web-based e-mail service such as Hotmail.

3. Choose Accounts from the Tools menu, and, on the Mail tab, select your mail service, and click Properties to display the Properties dialog box.

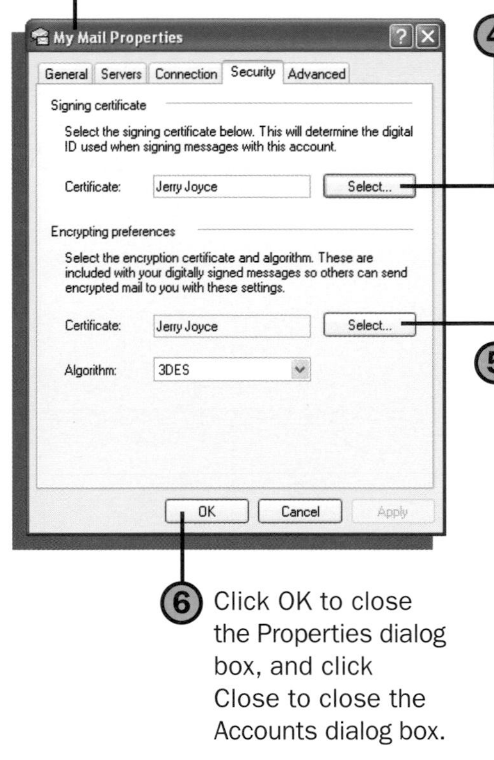

4. On the Security tab, under Signing Certificate, click Select, select the certificate for signing, and click OK.
5. Under Encrypting Preferences, click Select, select the same or a different certificate for encryption, and click OK.
6. Click OK to close the Properties dialog box, and click Close to close the Accounts dialog box.

Exchange Digital IDs

TRY THIS: After you've set up your digital ID, choose Options from the Tools menu, and, on the Security tab of the Options dialog box, select the check boxes for encrypting and signing your outgoing messages. Click the Advanced button, and, in the Advanced Security Settings dialog box, select the check boxes for encrypting mail to yourself, for including your ID, and for adding certificates to your address book. Then select the option to check for revoked IDs, and click OK.

1. Create a message, click the Sign button, and send the message. Have someone send you a digitally signed message.

2. Double-click the digitally signed message you've received to open it, and, in the header of the message window, click the Digital Signature button.

3. On the Security tab of the message's Properties dialog box that appears, click View Certificates.

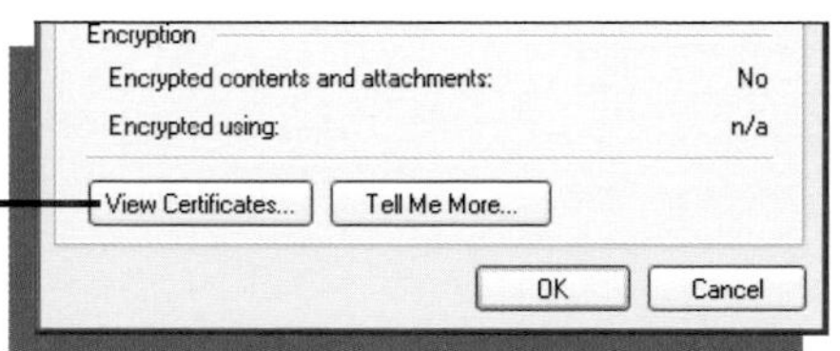

Encryption
Encrypted contents and attachments: No
Encrypted using: n/a
View Certificates...
Tell Me More...
OK
Cancel

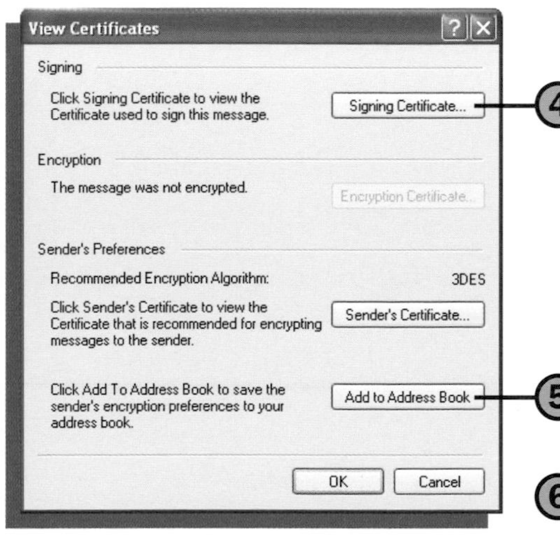

View Certificates
Signing
Click Signing Certificate to view the Certificate used to sign this message.
Signing Certificate...
Encryption
The message was not encrypted.
Encryption Certificate...
Sender's Preferences
Recommended Encryption Algorithm: 3DES
Click Sender's Certificate to view the Certificate that is recommended for encrypting messages to the sender.
Sender's Certificate...
Click Add To Address Book to save the sender's encryption preferences to your address book.
Add to Address Book
OK
Cancel

4. In the View Certificates dialog box, click Signing Certificate to see the information about the certificate. Click OK when you've finished.

5. Click Add To Address Book, and click OK. Click OK again to close the message's Properties dialog box.

6. Create a message addressed to the person with whom you exchanged digital IDs, click both the Sign and the Encrypt buttons on the Standard Buttons toolbar, and send the message to make sure the transfer of IDs was successful.

Securing Your Wireless Network ⊕ NEW FEATURE

Unless your wireless network is properly protected, it can be used by anyone within range of the network. This means that an unscrupulous person could tap into your network to gain access not only to the Internet but to all your personal files! Fortunately, the enhanced security provided by Windows XP with Service Pack 2 can defeat such intrusions by requiring a security key in order to gain access to the network from a wireless computer. You can configure your network security in one of two ways: You can use a USB storage device to transfer the required code to the wireless base station and to each wireless computer and network printer, or you can enter the information manually yourself.

TIP: In case you were wondering, SSID is Service Set Identifier, WEP is Wired Equivalent Privacy security services, and WPA is Wi-Fi Protected Access security protocol. These features are all part of the IEEE 802.11 standard that's used in most wireless networks.

TIP: In the Wireless Network Setup Wizard, select the Use WPA Encryption check box if you need to use the less powerful WPA encription instead of WEP encryption for compatibility with network components.

Configure Your Security

1. With your wireless network already set up and working, choose Wireless Network Setup Wizard from the Communications submenu of the Start menu, and click Next to start the wizard.
2. Enter a name for your network.
3. Specify which way you want to set up your network security key:
   - Automatically Assign A Network Key (Recommended) to automatically create and assign a key
   - Manually Assign A Network Key to create your own key or to use a key that has already been assigned to components on this network
4. Click Next. If you chose to manually assign a network key, enter the key, and then click Next.

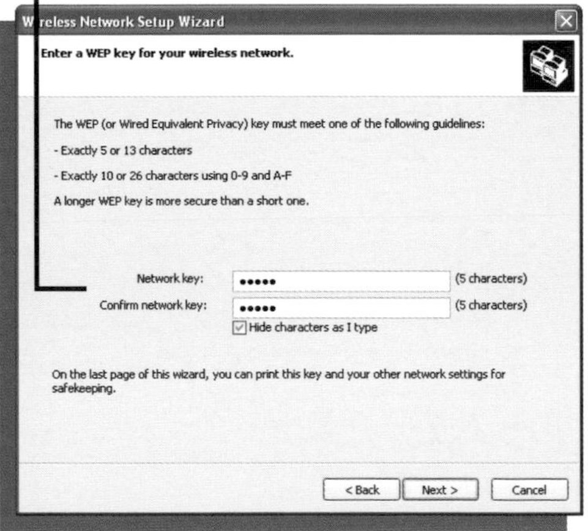

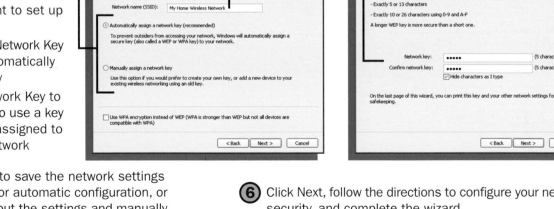

5. Specify whether you want to save the network settings on a USB storage device for automatic configuration, or whether you want to print out the settings and manually configure each device.
6. Click Next, follow the directions to configure your network security, and complete the wizard.

Configure Your Network

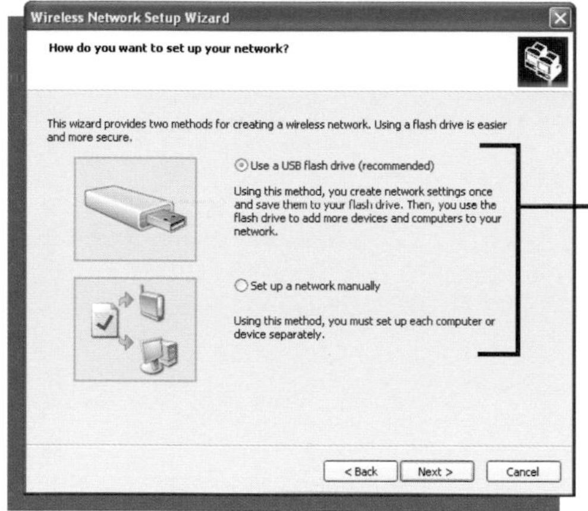

1. If you previously completed the Wireless Network Setup Wizard but you don't have the security settings printed out or saved on your USB storage device, start the wizard again from the Communications submenu of the Start menu. Step through the wizard, and choose to add new computers to your network. Click Next, and choose either to use a USB storage device or to configure each item manually.

2. If you're using a USB storage device, complete the following steps:
   - Insert the USB device into the computer, and download the settings from the wizard to the device.
   - Insert the USB device into the wireless base station, and wait for the network key to be downloaded.
   - Insert the USB device into each computer that will be on the wireless network, and choose to run the Wireless Network Setup Wizard. When prompted, choose Yes to add the computer to the network.
   - Reinsert the USB device into the first computer on which you ran the wizard, click Next, and review the computers that you've added to the network. Print your network settings for safekeeping, and then click Finish.

3. If you chose to manually configure the network, complete the following steps:
   - Choose to print the settings, and, from the Notepad window that appears, print the Wireless Network Settings document.
   - Run the wireless base-station management software from the computer that's connected to the base station. In the wireless security part of the software, enter—and if necessary reenter—the network key, as shown in the Wireless Network Settings document you printed.
   - On each computer, run the Wireless Network Setup Wizard, choose to set up a new wireless network, enter the name of the network, choose to manually assign the network key, and enter and then reenter the network key.

CAUTION: If your wireless network has already been configured, it might currently have a network key in use for security. Use the base-station management software to check the security settings. If a key is already in use, any modifications you make to the security could disable access to the network for some computers.

TIP: The network key is used for security only for the wireless connections on a network that uses a mix of wireless and wired connections.

SEE ALSO: For information about accessing public wireless networks, see "Connecting to a Wireless Network" on pages 204–205.

Foiling E-Mail Viruses ⊛ NEW FEATURE

E-mail is your computer's gateway to the rest of the world, and this gateway is what makes your e-mail one of the prime vectors for the distribution of computer viruses and many other evils. Fortunately, Outlook Express now comes with options that can help you detect and prevent the introduction of viruses onto your computer.

Protect Yourself and Others

1. In Outlook Express, choose Options from the Tools menu, and click the Security tab of the Options dialog box.
2. Select the Restricted Sites Zone (More Secure) option if it isn't already selected.
3. Select this check box, if it isn't already selected, to enable protection from programs already on your computer that want to use your e-mail to infect other computers.
4. Select this check box, if it isn't already selected, to enable inspection of the file type of an attachment and to block any attachment that could be a potential virus. 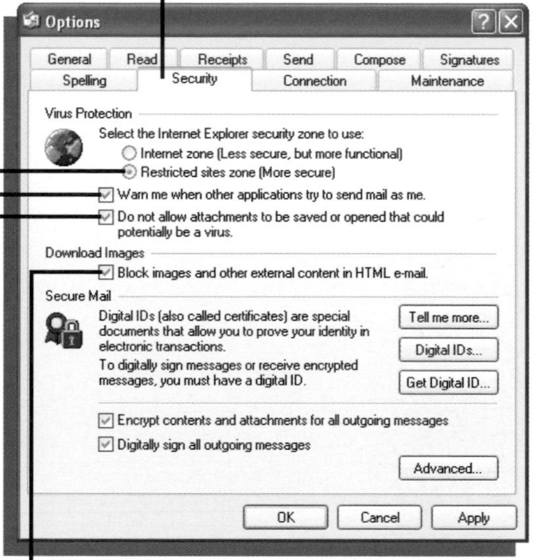
5. Select this check box, if it isn't already selected, to stop your message from requesting additional material from an external server.
6. On the Read tab, select this check box if you want to prevent any hidden code in HTML-formatted messages from gaining access to your computer, provided you don't mind losing the formatting of any HTML-formatted message.

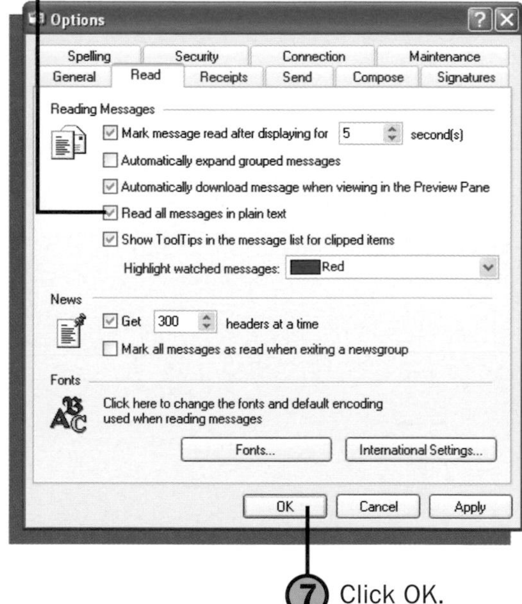

7. Click OK.

TIP: If you choose to read your messages in plain text, you might lose more than just formatting—you could lose some of the message's content. To view a trusted message in HTML format, with the message open, choose Message In HTML from the View menu.

SEE ALSO: For information about displaying pictures that have been blocked, see "Limiting E-Mail Snooping" on page 78.

14 Managing Windows XP

In this section

The beauty of Microsoft Windows XP is the flexibility it gives you to make changes, fix problems, and generally make your computer work better. If your Desktop is a cluttered mess, you can run a wizard that automatically removes Desktop shortcuts you haven't used for the previous 60 days and puts them in a special folder. If you want to squeeze more items onto your Desktop, you can increase its "virtual" size by changing the screen resolution. If the date or time on your computer is inaccurate, it's easy to change it. If your hard disk is NTFS–formatted, you can compress files, folders, or even the entire drive so that you can store more information in the same location. If your disk isn't NTFS–formatted, you can probably convert it to the NTFS format.

Windows XP also provides disk-maintenance tools that help make your computer run better. You can schedule these tools to run periodically—they'll find and re-order bits of files that have become scattered or lost, delete unused files, and so on. Because computers, programs, and peripheral devices are continually changing, we'll show you how to use the Windows Update Web page to update your computer. You'll learn how to avoid common hardware problems and how to remove software programs. If Windows XP won't start properly, you'll find several solutions that will either get it started or help diagnose what's wrong. If you have made changes to your computer and now wish you hadn't, the System Restore tool will restore your previous settings. And we'll show you how to document your system so that if you do encounter serious problems, you can provide a technician with detailed information about your system.

Adding and Deleting User Accounts

If you're a member of the Administrators group—that is, one who has full access to the computer—you can grant other people access to the computer. You grant access by creating a new user account and specifying whether the account grants full or limited access. To keep things tidy, you can also delete accounts that are no longer used.

SEE ALSO: **For information about the access each type of account allows, see "Know Your Rights, Know Your Format" on page 249.**

For information about using the Guest account and about changing the type of account for an existing user, see "Restricting User Rights" on page 254.

Add an Account

1. Choose Control Panel from the Start menu, click the User Accounts category, and click the Create A New Account task to display the User Accounts window.
2. Type a name for the account, and click Next.

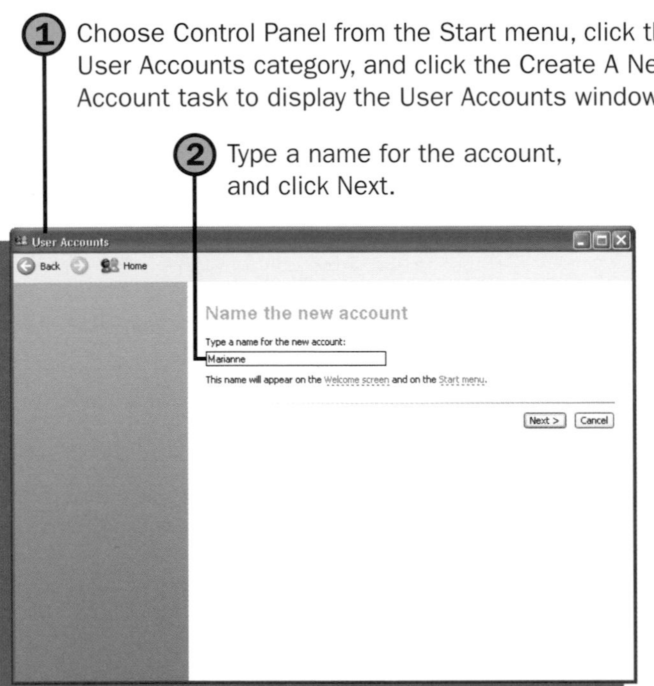

3. Click the Computer Administrator option to grant complete access to the computer; click the Limited option to grant limited access.

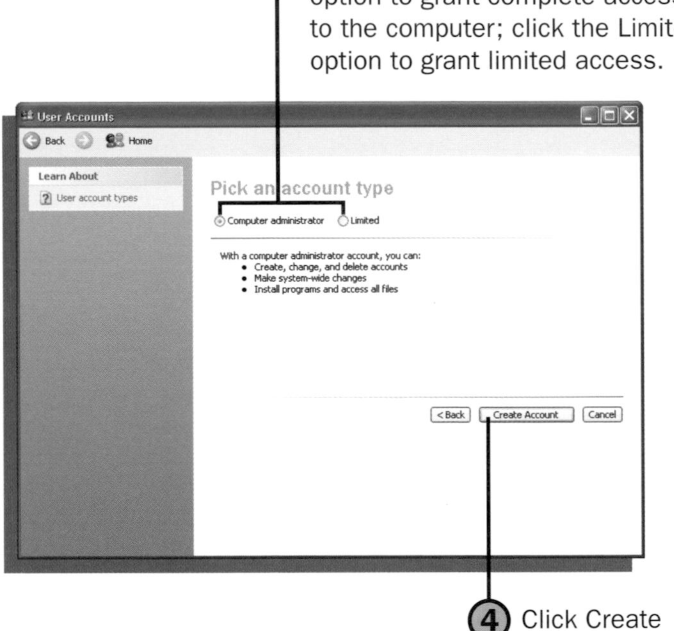

4. Click Create Account.

TIP: If you save a deleted account's files to the Desktop but don't see the folder containing the files on the Desktop, right-click the Desktop, point to Arrange Icons By on the shortcut menu, and choose Show Desktop Icons from the submenu.

TIP: If you want to give someone limited access to the computer for a single session, you don't need to create a new account. Instead, allow the person to log on as a Guest.

Delete an Account

1. If the User Accounts window isn't already open, choose Control Panel from the Start menu, and click the User Accounts category. In the User Accounts window, click the account you want to delete.

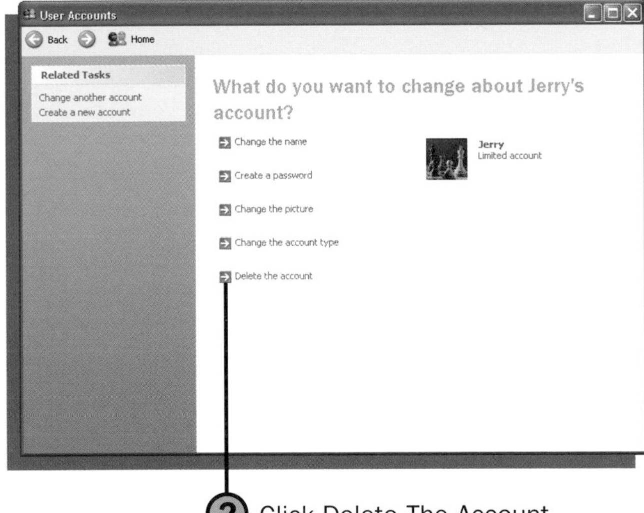

2. Click Delete The Account.

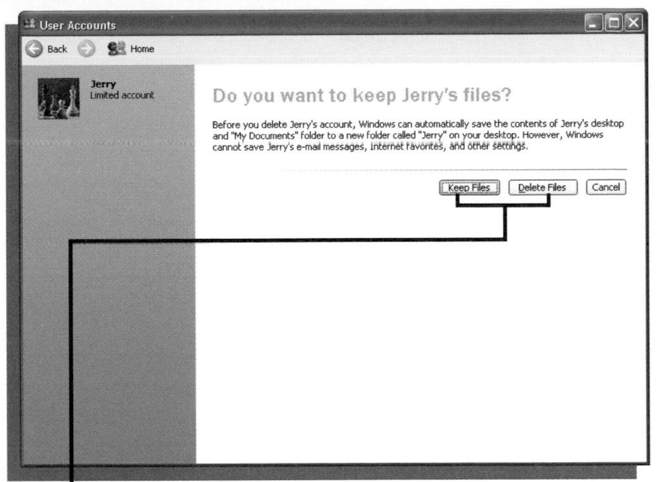

3. Click Keep Files if you want all the files in the account's My Documents folder saved to a Desktop folder, or click Delete Files to delete all the files.

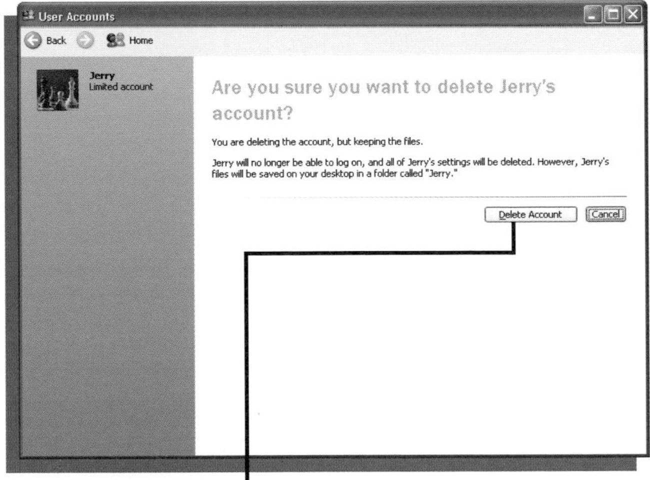

4. Click Delete Account to permanently delete the account.

CAUTION: When you delete an account, its settings, favorites, certificates, and many other items will be lost, even if the items had been saved in the My Documents folder on the Desktop. If you want to preserve those files and settings, use the Files And Settings Transfer Wizard.

SEE ALSO: For information about using the Files And Settings Transfer Wizard, see "Transferring Files and Settings" on pages 208–209.

Tidying Up the Desktop

Although the Desktop is a great place to store shortcuts to files, folders, programs, and Web pages, it can become hopelessly cluttered with items that were probably vital at some point but whose importance is now a vague memory. Do you remember why you placed all those items on the Desktop? Windows XP will take the problem off your hands by removing all the shortcuts that you haven't used for the past 60 days and storing them in a single Unused Desktop Shortcuts folder on your Desktop. You can have Windows run this handy service every 60 days, or you can run the Desktop Cleanup Wizard any time you want.

Start the Cleanup

1. Right-click a blank spot on the Desktop, and choose Properties from the shortcut menu.
2. On the Desktop tab of the Display Properties dialog box, click Customize Desktop to display the Desktop Items dialog box.

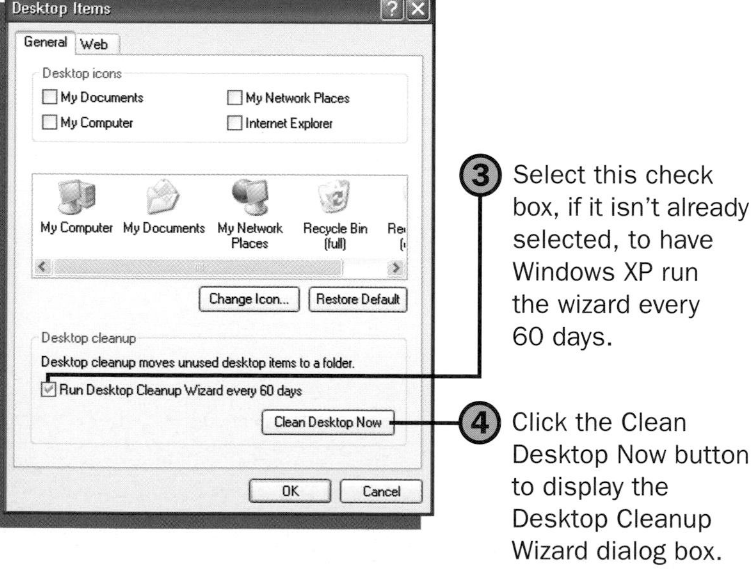

3. Select this check box, if it isn't already selected, to have Windows XP run the wizard every 60 days.
4. Click the Clean Desktop Now button to display the Desktop Cleanup Wizard dialog box.

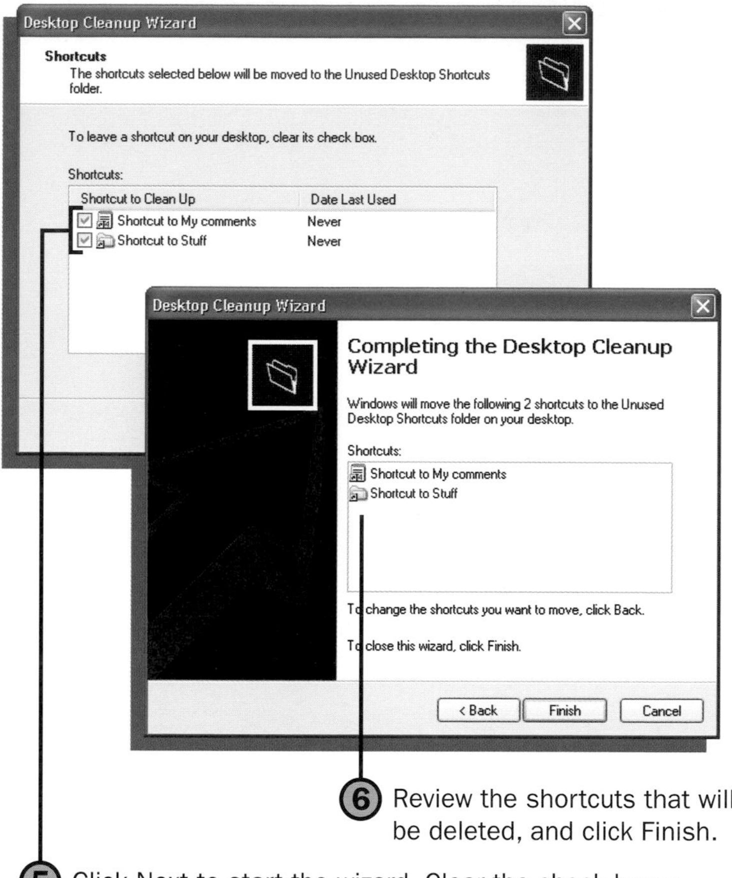

6. Review the shortcuts that will be deleted, and click Finish.
5. Click Next to start the wizard. Clear the check boxes for any shortcuts that you *don't* want removed from the Desktop and placed in the Unused Desktop Shortcuts folder, and click Next.
7. Click OK to close the Desktop Items dialog box, and then click OK to close the Display Properties dialog box.

Changing the Date or Time

Windows XP and your computer keep track of the date and time, using commonly accepted formats to display them. If the date or time on your computer is inaccurate, or if you travel with your computer into different time zones, you can quickly adjust and correct the settings.

Change the Date or Time

1. Double-click the time on the taskbar to display the Date And Time Properties dialog box.
2. If necessary, on the Time Zone tab, select a different time zone, and make sure the Automatically Adjust Clock For Daylight Saving Changes check box is selected or cleared, depending on whether or not the region you're in uses Daylight Saving Time.
3. Click the Date & Time tab, and click the correct month or year in the list if necessary.
4. Click the correct date if necessary.

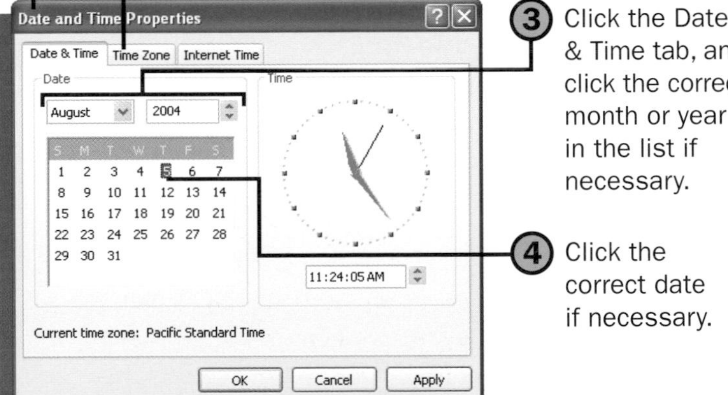

TIP: If the time isn't displayed in the notification area of the taskbar, right-click a blank spot on the taskbar, choose Properties from the shortcut menu, and select the Show The Clock check box.

TIP: Windows XP can link to a time server on the Internet so that the time on your computer is always accurate. If your computer is always connected to the Internet, its time will be adjusted automatically once a week. (If you connect to the Internet manually, you can update the time yourself.)

5. Click the Internet Time tab. If you aren't already connected to the Internet, connect now.
6. Select this check box if it isn't already selected.
7. In the list, click the time server you want to use.
8. Click Update Now, and wait for the time to be updated.
9. Click OK.

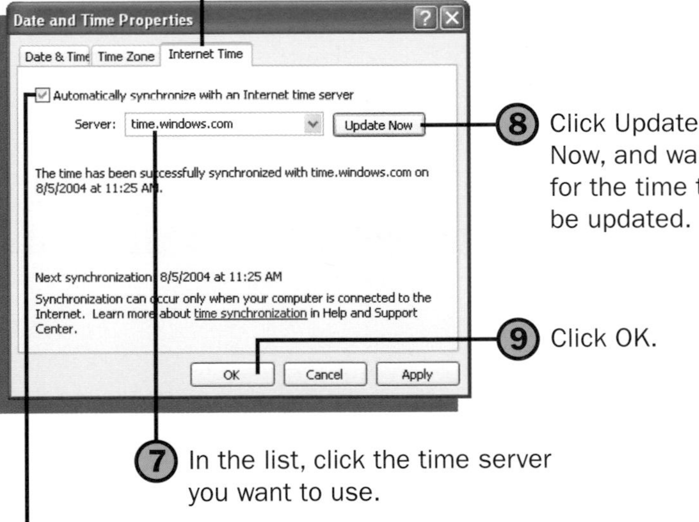

TRY THIS: To manually adjust the time, on the Date & Time tab, in the box that shows the time, click the number for the hour, and then click the up or the down arrow. Click the number for the minutes, and do the same. Finally, click the number for the seconds, and repeat the process.

Changing the Display

If you want to squeeze more items onto your Desktop, you can change its size…sort of. This is one of those "virtual" realities. You "enlarge" the available space by changing the screen resolution, and thereby the *scaling,* which lets you fit more items onto the Desktop even though its area on your screen doesn't get any larger. Your gain in virtual area comes at a cost, though—everything will be smaller and harder to read. Also, the combination of screen resolution and color quality displayed affects how much video memory (the memory on your computer that's dedicated to producing the video image on your monitor) is used. Therefore, you might need to adjust both the screen resolution and the color quality until you're happy with the result.

Increase the Screen Area

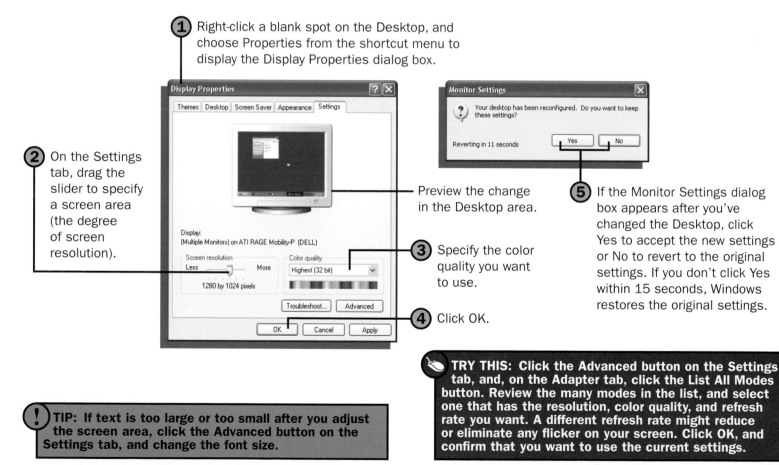

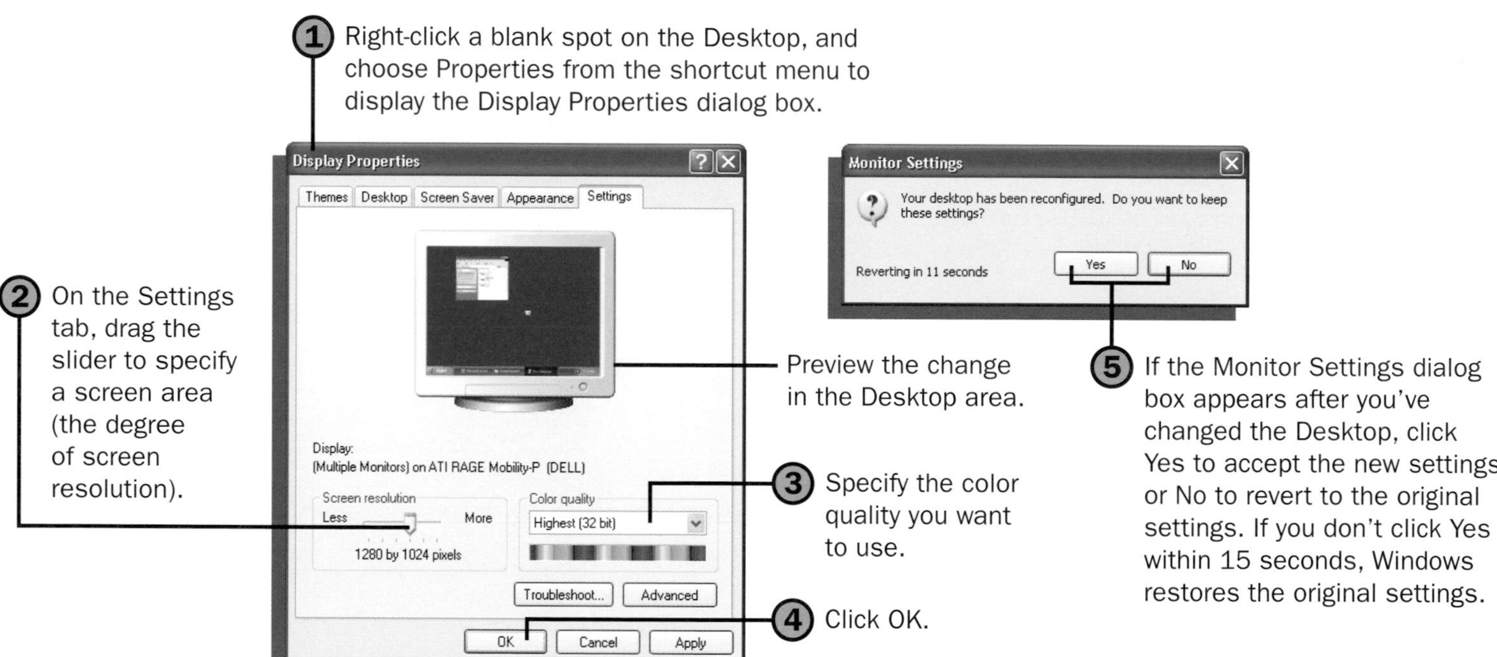

1 Right-click a blank spot on the Desktop, and choose Properties from the shortcut menu to display the Display Properties dialog box.
Display Properties
Themes
Desktop
Screen Saver
Appearance
Settings
Display:
(Multiple Monitors) on ATI RAGE Mobility-P (DELL)
Screen resolution
Less
More
1280 by 1024 pixels
Color quality
Highest (32 bit)
Troubleshoot...
Advanced
OK
Cancel
Apply
2 On the Settings tab, drag the slider to specify a screen area (the degree of screen resolution).
Preview the change in the Desktop area.
3 Specify the color quality you want to use.
4 Click OK.
Monitor Settings
Your desktop has been reconfigured. Do you want to keep these settings?
Reverting in 11 seconds
Yes
No
5 If the Monitor Settings dialog box appears after you've changed the Desktop, click Yes to accept the new settings or No to revert to the original settings. If you don't click Yes within 15 seconds, Windows restores the original settings.

TIP: If text is too large or too small after you adjust the screen area, click the Advanced button on the Settings tab, and change the font size.

TRY THIS: Click the Advanced button on the Settings tab, and, on the Adapter tab, click the List All Modes button. Review the many modes in the list, and select one that has the resolution, color quality, and refresh rate you want. A different refresh rate might reduce or eliminate any flicker on your screen. Click OK, and confirm that you want to use the current settings.

Changing the Disk Format

Windows XP supports three disk formats—FAT, FAT32, and NTFS (NT file system). The NTFS format provides the speed, resources, security, and ability to handle large disks—capabilities that aren't available with the FAT or FAT32 formats. The FAT and FAT32 formats provide compatibility with other operating systems (dual-boot or multi-boot configuration, or the backup of a previous operating system) running on your computer. If your hard disk uses FAT or FAT32, and if you're certain that compatibility won't be an issue, you can convert the disk to the NTFS format.

Convert the Disk

1. Back up your work, and then close all the files and folders on the disk you're going to convert.
2. Click the Start button, point to Programs and then Accessories, and choose Command Prompt from the submenu to display the Command Prompt window.

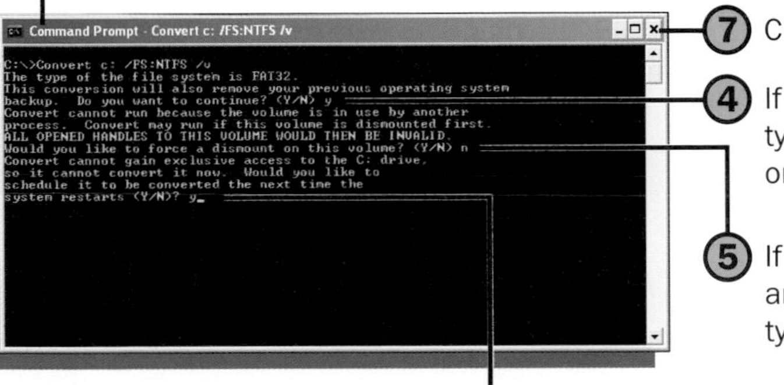

3. At the command prompt, type **Convert drive: /FS:NTFS /v** (where *drive* is the drive letter of the hard disk or drive to be converted), and press Enter.
4. If you upgraded your computer from a previous version of Windows, type **Y** and press Enter to confirm that you want the backup deleted, or type **N** and press Enter to cancel the procedure.
5. If you're notified that the system can't gain access to the drive and are asked whether you want to force a dismount of the drive, type **N** and press Enter.
6. If you're told that the system can't gain exclusive control (as is the case when the drive is the primary drive), type **Y** and press Enter to convert the drive when the system restarts.
7. Close the Command Prompt window.
8. Choose Turn Off Computer from the Start menu, click Restart in the Turn Off Computer dialog box, and wait for the computer to restart and convert the drive.

SEE ALSO: For information about checking the format of the drives on your computer, see "Know Your Rights, Know Your Format" on page 249.

Compressing a Drive or a Folder

When a disk is formatted for NTFS (NT file system), you can compress its files and folders—and even the entire drive—so that you can store even more information in the same location. The cost of compression can be a slightly longer time to access files, which must be decompressed before you can use them. This delay is usually so minor, however, that you won't even notice it on most systems.

TIP: NTFS compression is not the same thing as the Compressed Folders feature that uses ZIP-type compression. NTFS compression is intended for use on your computer only, whereas a compressed folder can be sent to others as a ZIP file.

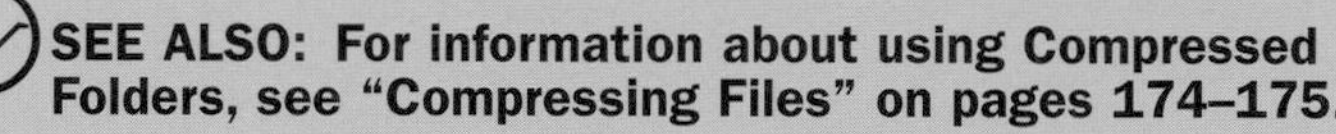

SEE ALSO: For information about using Compressed Folders, see "Compressing Files" on pages 174–175.

Compress a Drive

1. Open the My Computer window, right-click the drive you want to compress, and choose Properties from the shortcut menu to display the drive's Properties dialog box.

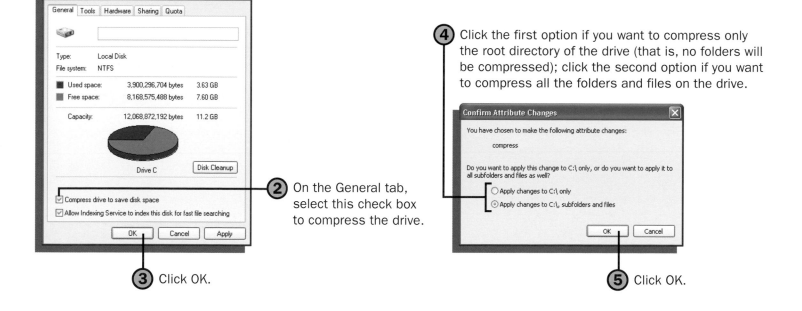

2. On the General tab, select this check box to compress the drive.

3. Click OK.

4. Click the first option if you want to compress only the root directory of the drive (that is, no folders will be compressed); click the second option if you want to compress all the folders and files on the drive.

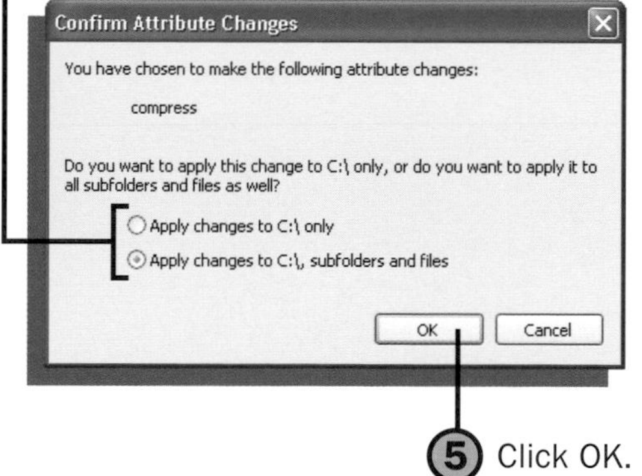

5. Click OK.

Compress a File or a Folder

1. Right-click the file or folder, and choose Properties from the shortcut menu. On the General tab of the Properties dialog box, click the Advanced button to display the Advanced Attributes dialog box.

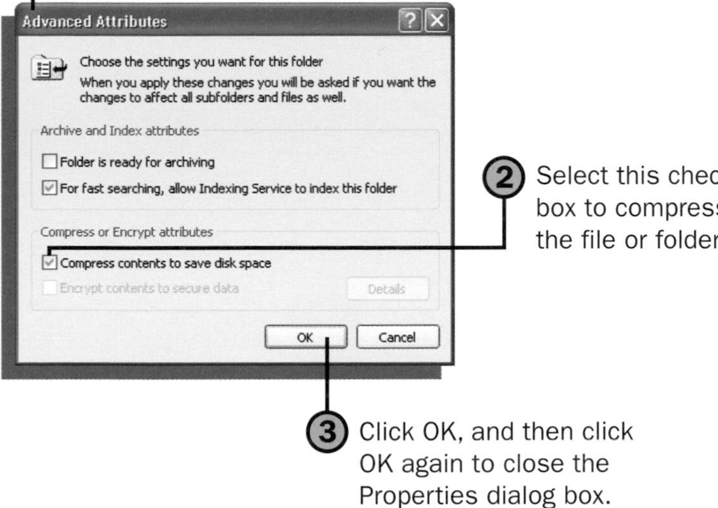

2. Select this check box to compress the file or folder.

3. Click OK, and then click OK again to close the Properties dialog box.

4. Click the first option if you want to compress the folder only; click the second option if you want to compress all the subfolders and files in the folder.

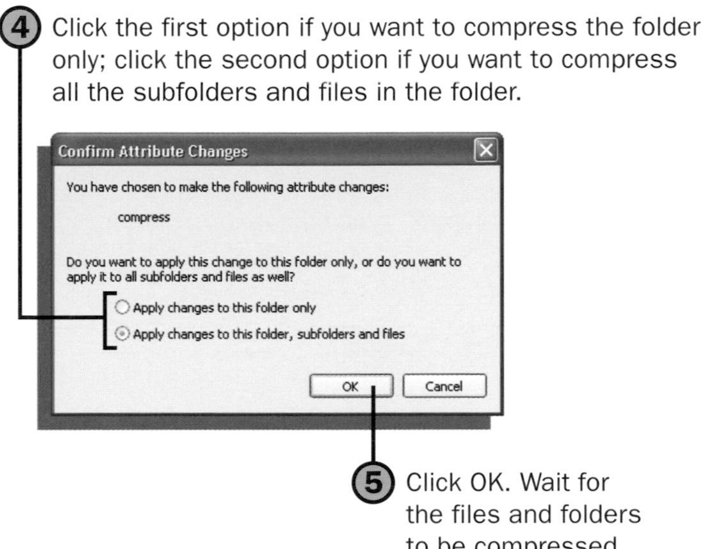

5. Click OK. Wait for the files and folders to be compressed.

TIP: In the Advanced Attributes dialog box, the Folder Is Ready For Archiving check box tags the folder for archiving. This setting is used by certain programs, such as file backup programs, to determine how to handle the folder. The check box for Indexing Service determines whether the content of the folder is indexed to speed up file searching. The Encrypt Contents To Secure Data check box is grayed in Windows XP Home Edition because the required Encrypting File System is available only in Windows XP Professional Edition.

TIP: If the Properties dialog box for a file or a folder doesn't contain the Advanced button, the file or the folder can't be compressed.

Maintaining Your Hard Disk

With time and use, your computer can become a bit disorganized. As the information stored in the computer gets used, moved, copied, added to, or deleted, the computer's hard disk, or drive, can become cluttered with useless or inefficiently organized files. Windows XP provides a group of maintenance tools whose occasional use can make your computer run more smoothly, more efficiently, and (usually) faster. The table at the right describes what each of these tools does.

Maintain a Drive

1. Choose My Computer from the Start menu, right-click the drive that needs attention, and choose Properties from the shortcut menu to display the drive's Properties dialog box.

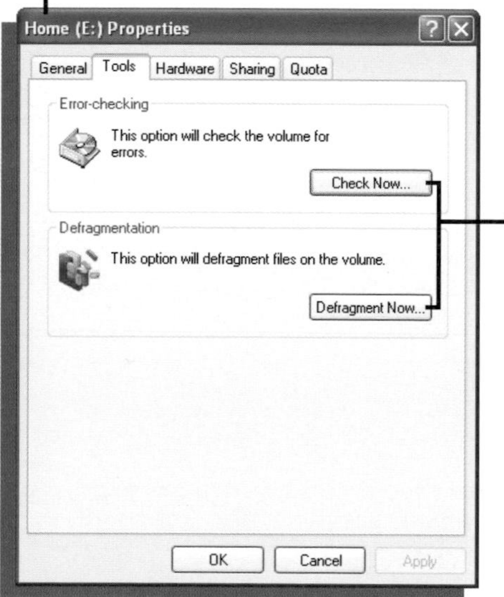

2. Click the appropriate button to use the tool you need, and follow the instructions provided by the program:
   - On the General tab, click Disk Cleanup.
   - On the Tools tab, under Error-Checking, click Check Now.
   - On the Tools tab, under Defragmentation, click Defragment Now.

Disk-Maintenance Tools

Tool	What it does
Disk Cleanup	Checks the disk for unused files that can be deleted.
Error-Checking	Scans the disk to see whether there are disk errors in any files or folders. Optionally, fixes file-system errors and attempts to recover bad sectors on the hard disk. If the disk is in use, error-checking will be scheduled for the next time you log on. For NTFS–formatted disks, records all file-transaction information.
Defragmentation	Analyzes the disk to see whether defragmentation is necessary. Re-orders the items on your disk so that files aren't separated into several noncontiguous parts. Can take a long time to run but speeds up disk performance.

SEE ALSO: For information about managing unused shortcuts on your Desktop, see "Tidying Up the Desktop" on page 280.

For information about backing up your files to another location, see "Backing Up Your Files" on pages 304–305.

Preventing Hardware Problems

Diagnosing hardware problems can be a time-consuming and expensive activity. Instead of checking and modifying settings, uninstalling and reinstalling drivers, and replacing hardware devices that might or might not be incompatible with Windows XP and/or with your computer system, you can avoid most problems by being cautious about any hardware you install, and by using it properly.

Prevent a Problem

1. When buying hardware, make sure that it's certified to work with Windows XP. Many older items and some discounted items aren't designed to be used with Windows XP. To search through a list of devices that have been tested for full compatibility with Windows XP, choose Windows Catalog from the All Programs submenu of the Start menu.

2. Install only hardware drivers for hardware devices that are designed for Windows XP and that are digitally signed (indicating that they're authentic). When you're manually installing a hardware device, you'll be notified if the driver isn't digitally signed.

3. When you're using certain devices, such as some USB (Universal Serial Bus) and SCSI (Small Computer System Interface) devices, you must stop the device before it can be safely removed. To stop a device, click the Safely Remove Hardware icon in the notification area of the taskbar, and then click the device to be stopped and removed.

SEE ALSO: For information about identifying hardware problems, see "Documenting Your System" on page 298 and "Managing Everything" on page 299.

TIP: If a device driver isn't digitally signed, check with the manufacturer for an updated driver. Many drivers that were designed for use with Windows 2000 might work correctly with Windows XP. However, you can't be certain that a device is fully compatible unless it is certified for Windows XP and is digitally signed.

CAUTION: One of the most frequent causes of a sudden hardware problem is something called "surprise removal." This happens when you remove or disable a hardware component when it's in use or when your system thinks it should be available. If you want to undock a portable computer from its docking station, for example, you should either use the Undock Computer command on the Start menu, or shut down the computer and turn it off before you undock it. If you're using a USB hub, don't disconnect its power supply, don't turn off the hub's power, and don't remove any components from the hub while Windows XP is still running.

Controlling the Power Options

Different computers sometimes have different power-management requirements and abilities. You might want the monitor on your main desktop computer to shut down after a few minutes of idleness, but you might also want the hard disk to "stay awake" constantly. On your portable computer, you might want everything to shut down after a few minutes of idleness. Depending on the features and abilities of your computer, you can set these power schemes, as well as some other features.

TIP: Power settings are primarily controlled by the ACPI (Advanced Configuration And Power Interface) features of your computer. Windows XP has very strict standards for supporting ACPI. If, even though your computer is designed to support ACPI, Windows doesn't enable the ACPI features, contact the computer manufacturer for updates that might make your computer's ACPI system work with Windows XP.

Use a Power Scheme

1. Choose Control Panel from the Start menu, click the Performance And Maintenance category, and click the Power Options Control Panel icon to display the Power Options Properties dialog box.

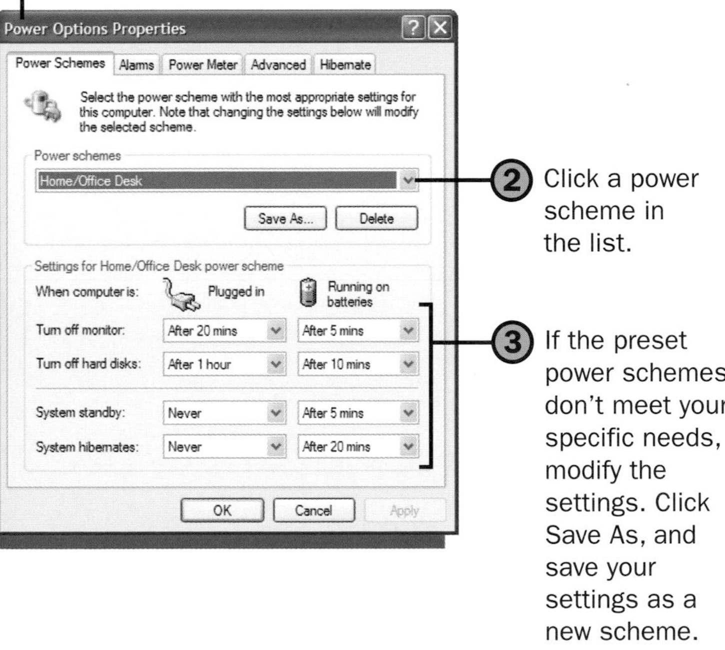

2. Click a power scheme in the list.
3. If the preset power schemes don't meet your specific needs, modify the settings. Click Save As, and save your settings as a new scheme.

Set Advanced Options

1. Click the Advanced tab of the Power Options Properties dialog box.

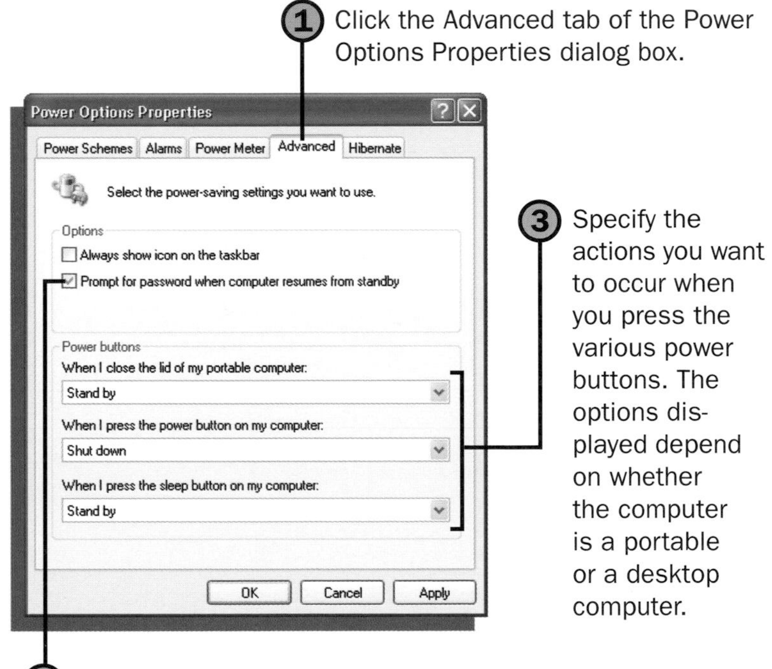

2. Select this check box if you use a password to log on and you want the security of requiring the password to be entered whenever the computer is revived from Standby or Hibernate mode.
3. Specify the actions you want to occur when you press the various power buttons. The options displayed depend on whether the computer is a portable or a desktop computer.

Set Battery Options

1. Click the Alarms tab, and set the battery level at which the computer will take action. Click Alarm Action for each alarm to specify what happens when the battery reaches the specified level.
2. Click the Power Meter tab, and check the current power level of the battery or batteries.

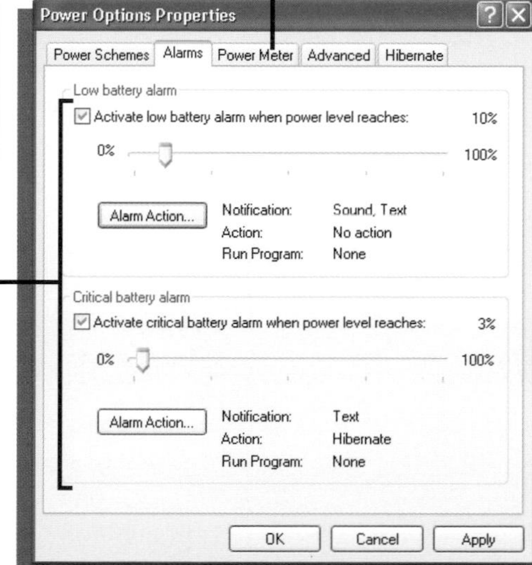

TIP: You'll see the Alarms tab and the Power Meter tab only if your computer is a portable computer with a battery. You won't see the UPS tab on a portable computer. The APM tab appears only on computers that have the APM (Advanced Power Management) feature and don't support the ACPI feature.

Set Other Options

1. Select the appropriate check box on each of the following tabs:
   - APM to enable the APM feature when the ACPI feature isn't available on the computer
   - Hibernate to enable hibernation
   - UPS to configure the settings for any uninterruptible power supply attached to the computer

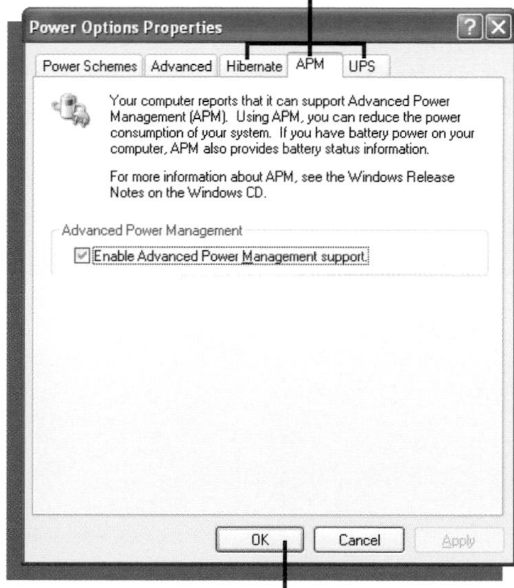

2. Click OK when you've finished.

Updating Your System

As time marches on, Microsoft continues to make improvements, fix problems, and offer new features in Windows. You can easily take care of the critical updates that are necessary to keep your computer running safely and efficiently, as well as those updates that aren't considered critical. At Windows Update, all you need to do is let the system see which updates are available and which you currently have, and then you can install them.

SEE ALSO: For information about using the Automatic Updates feature to install critical updates, see "Installing Critical Fixes" on pages 270–271.

For information about downloading more programs from Microsoft, see "Getting Free Software" on page 292 and "Tweaking Your System" on pages 300–301.

Select Your Updates

1. Choose Windows Update from the All Programs submenu of the Start menu. Connect to the Internet if you aren't already connected. Wait for a scan of your computer to catalog your Windows status and contents and to check for any items available from Windows Update.

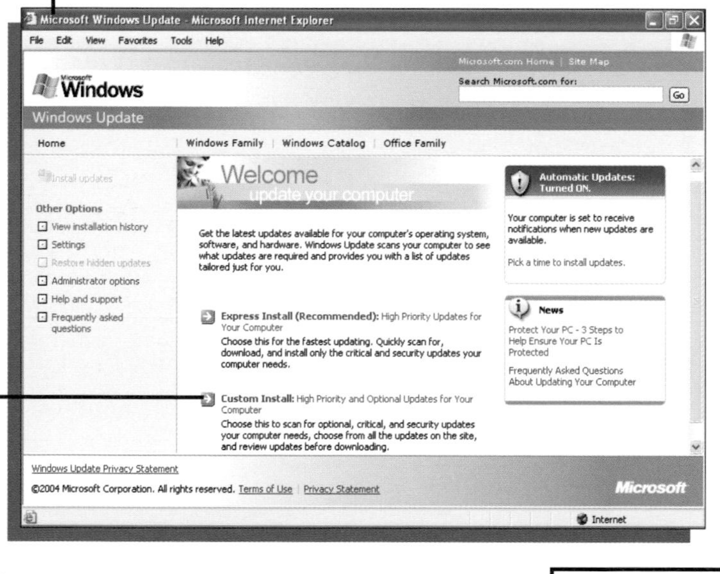

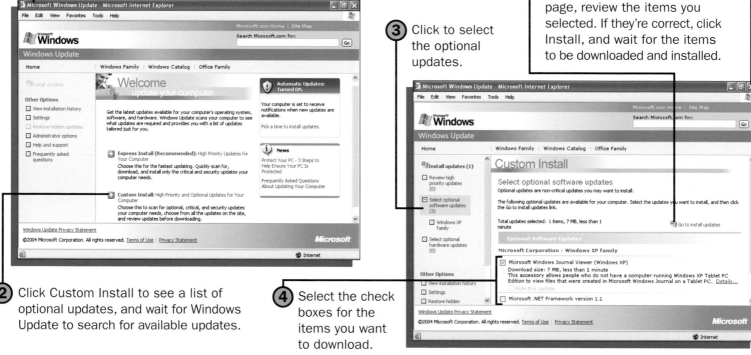

2. Click Custom Install to see a list of optional updates, and wait for Windows Update to search for available updates.

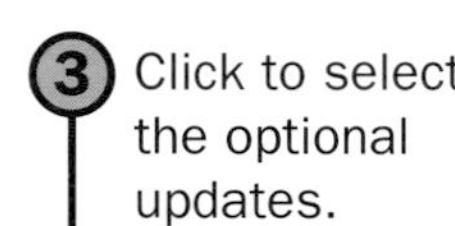

3. Click to select the optional updates.

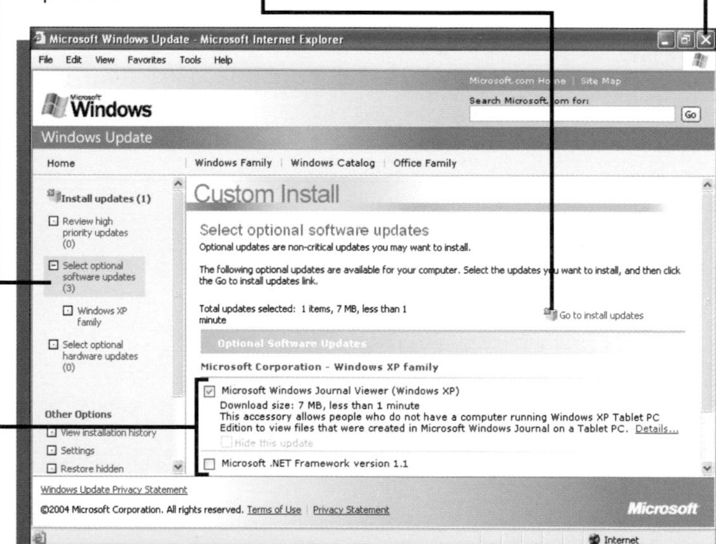

4. Select the check boxes for the items you want to download.
5. Click Go To Install Updates, and, on the Install Updates page, review the items you selected. If they're correct, click Install, and wait for the items to be downloaded and installed.
6. Close the Windows Update Web page when you've finished.

Checking the Status of Windows

Throughout this book we've talked about the increased security provided by Service Pack 2 and the importance of installing critical updates. Although your use of the Automatic Updates feature will keep your computer properly updated, you should also look around to see which service packs and updates are installed on your computer. This information is particularly useful when you need to seek help from another person.

SEE ALSO: For information about using Automatic Updates, see "Installing Critical Fixes" on pages 270–271.

TIP: If Service Pack 2 or a later service pack isn't listed in the About Windows dialog box, the pack has not been installed. Use the Automatic Updates feature to download the update, or obtain it on disc either from Microsoft or from you local software dealer.

Check the Status

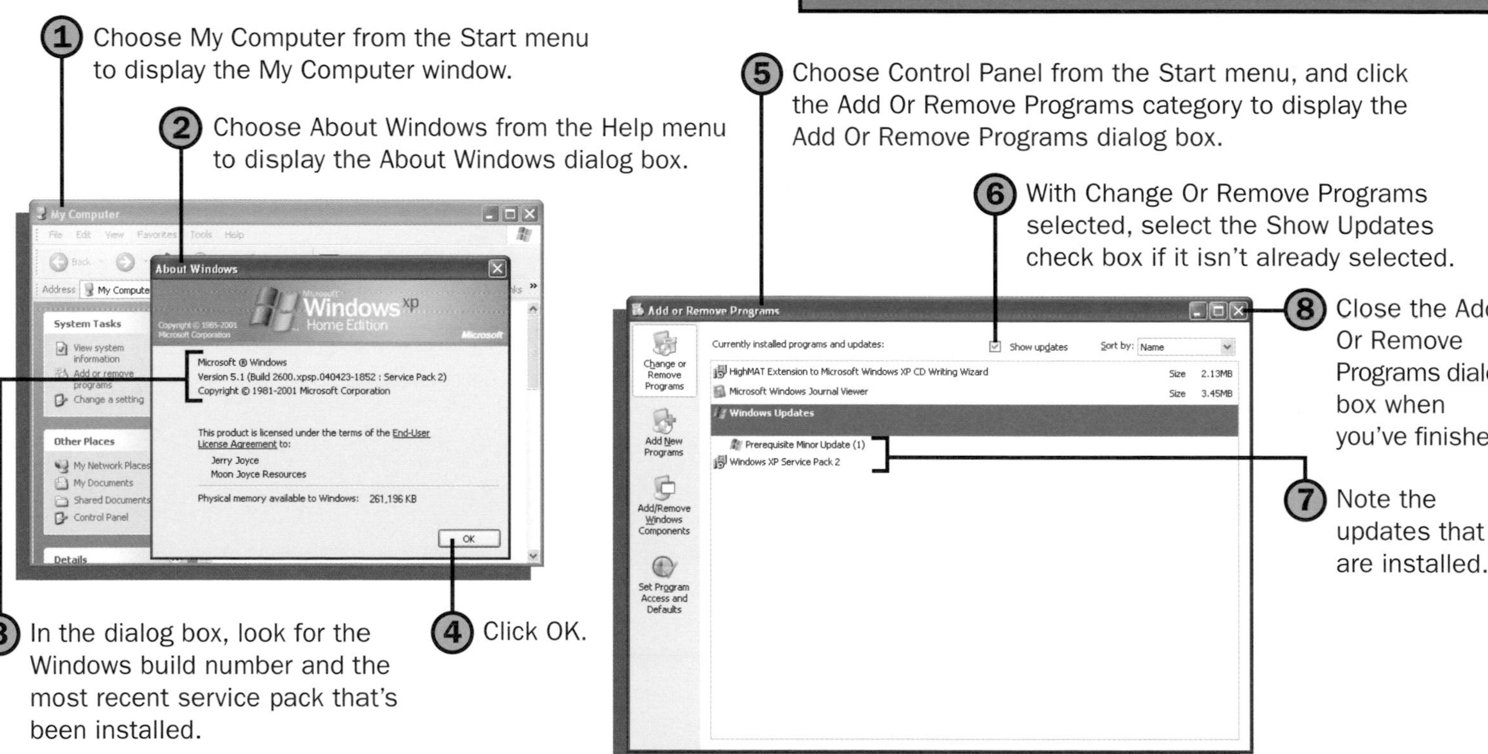

1. Choose My Computer from the Start menu to display the My Computer window.
2. Choose About Windows from the Help menu to display the About Windows dialog box.
3. In the dialog box, look for the Windows build number and the most recent service pack that's been installed.
4. Click OK.
5. Choose Control Panel from the Start menu, and click the Add Or Remove Programs category to display the Add Or Remove Programs dialog box.
6. With Change Or Remove Programs selected, select the Show Updates check box if it isn't already selected.
7. Note the updates that are installed.
8. Close the Add Or Remove Programs dialog box when you've finished.

Getting Free Software

Microsoft and its partners are continually developing tools, utilities, and other items that make it possible for your computer to work better, run more effectively, and just do more things. Many such items are available as free downloads from the Microsoft Web site. True, you'll need to wade through listings of many technical downloads, but it's worth it—your search can yield some pretty interesting items related to just about any Microsoft product, including trial versions of many of Microsoft's games.

Download the Software

1. Use your Web browser to go the main Microsoft Web page *(www.microsoft.com)*, and, in the Resources section, click Downloads to display the Download Center Web page.

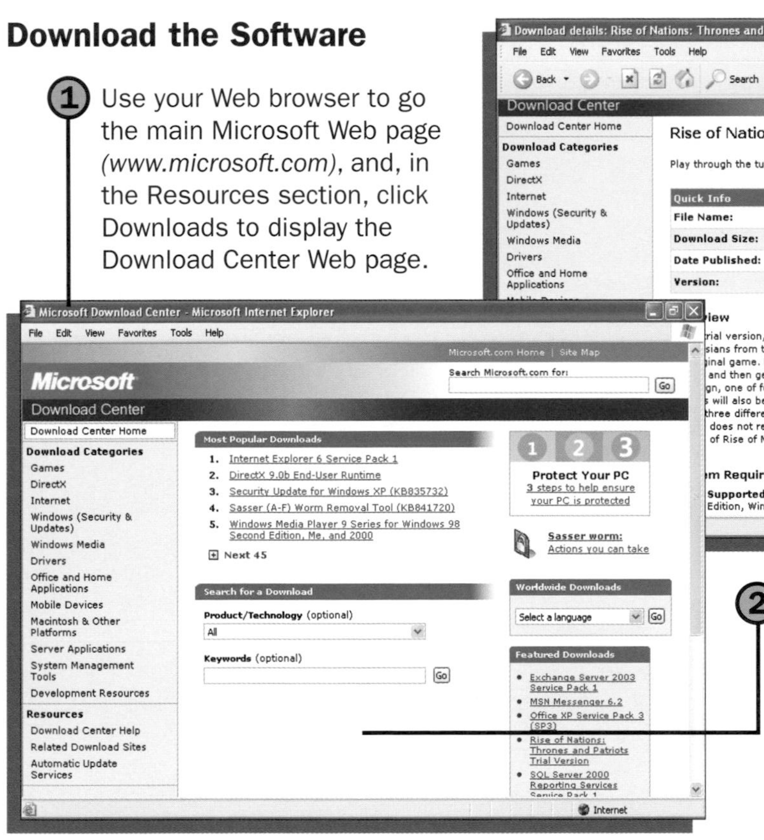

2. Do any of the following:
   - Click a download in the Most Popular Downloads list.
   - Click a category in the Download Categories list, and then click a download in the Most Popular Downloads list.
   - Click a download in the Featured Downloads list.
   - Select an item in the Product/Technology list and/or type a keyword in the Keywords text box, and press Enter. Click the download you want in the Search Results listing that appears.
   - Click Related Download Sites in the Resources section, select a relevant download site, and click the download you want.

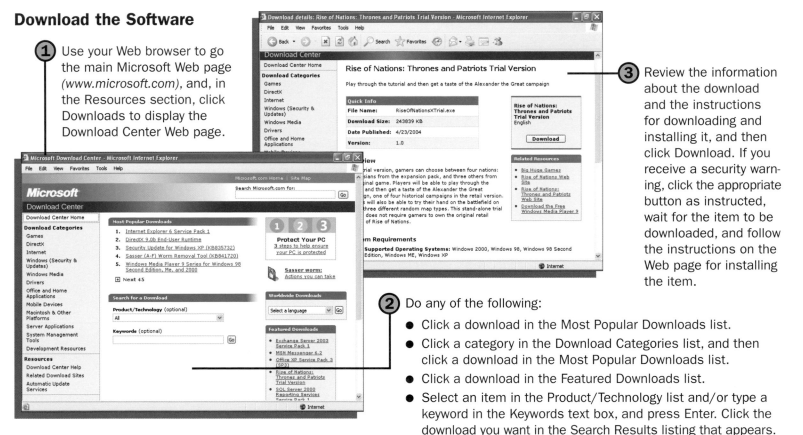

3. Review the information about the download and the instructions for downloading and installing it, and then click Download. If you receive a security warning, click the appropriate button as instructed, wait for the item to be downloaded, and follow the instructions on the Web page for installing the item.

TIP: Some of the most useful free downloads are viewers that are designed to let you view files in specific formats even when you don't have the actual program in which the file was created.

Removing a Software Program

Most programs are *registered* with Windows XP when you install them. You can—and should—use Windows tools when you want to remove a program. If you simply delete the files, you might leave accessory files you don't need, or delete files you need for other programs. When you uninstall a program using Windows tools, Windows keeps track of the files, and only when a file is no longer needed by any of your programs does Windows delete the file.

TIP: Various programs provide different ways to remove or modify an installed program. For example, in some programs you might see a Change/Remove button that starts a setup program so that you can either install only the parts of the program you want or completely remove the program. In other programs you might see a Change button that lets you modify the installation, or a Remove button that simply lets you remove the program.

Uninstall a Program

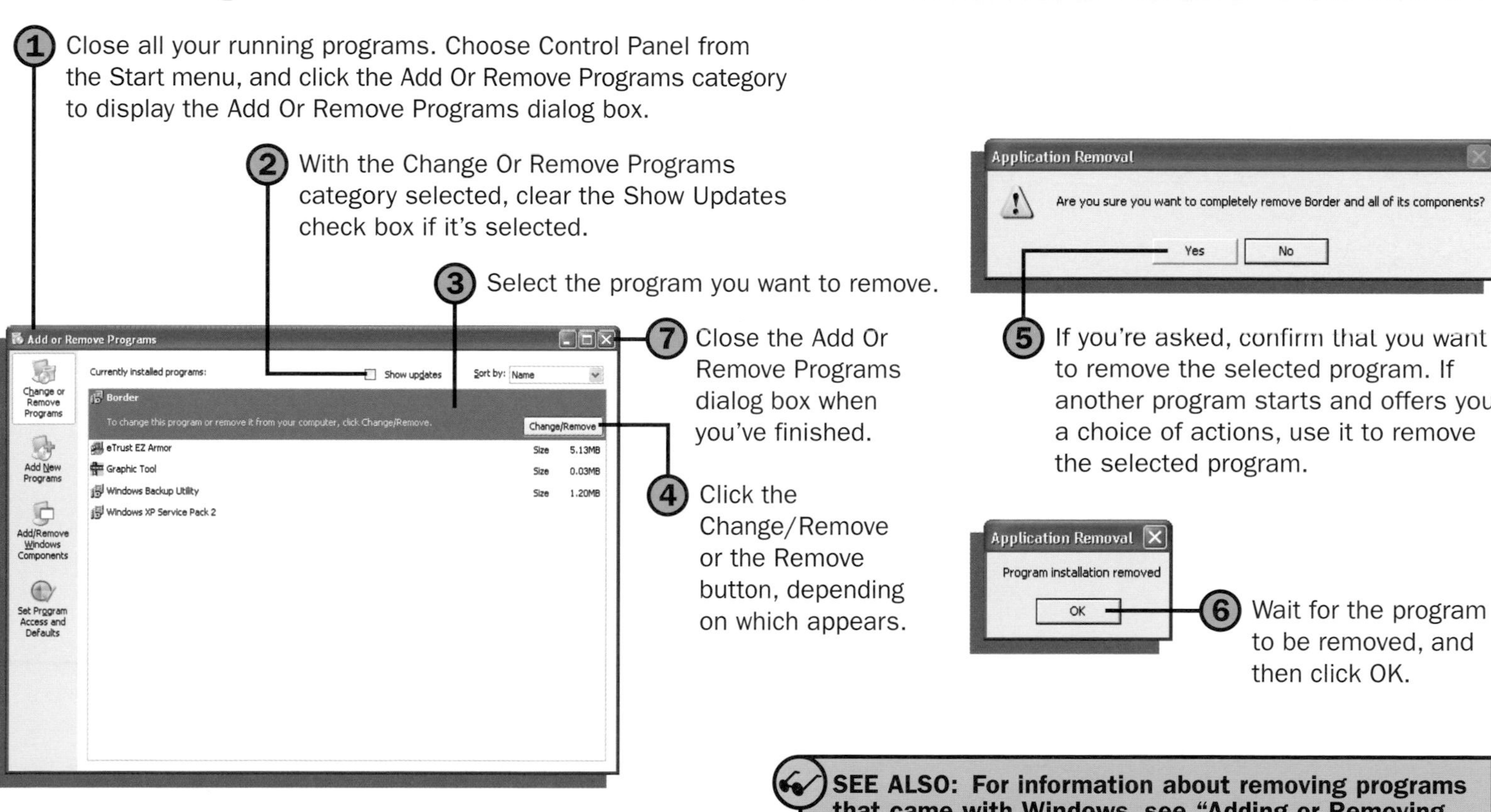

1. Close all your running programs. Choose Control Panel from the Start menu, and click the Add Or Remove Programs category to display the Add Or Remove Programs dialog box.
2. With the Change Or Remove Programs category selected, clear the Show Updates check box if it's selected.
3. Select the program you want to remove.
4. Click the Change/Remove or the Remove button, depending on which appears.
5. If you're asked, confirm that you want to remove the selected program. If another program starts and offers you a choice of actions, use it to remove the selected program.
6. Wait for the program to be removed, and then click OK.
7. Close the Add Or Remove Programs dialog box when you've finished.

SEE ALSO: For information about removing programs that came with Windows, see "Adding or Removing Windows Components" on pages 210–211.

Managing Internet Explorer Add-Ons ❁ NEW FEATURE

Internet Explorer add-ons are programs that provide enhancements to your Internet browser. Unfortunately, some add-ons can cause problems not only with the running of your browser but with Windows itself, and can sometimes even cause serious security problems. You can use the Internet Explorer Manage Add-Ons tool to disable any add-ons that you decide you don't want on your computer.

Manage the Add-Ons

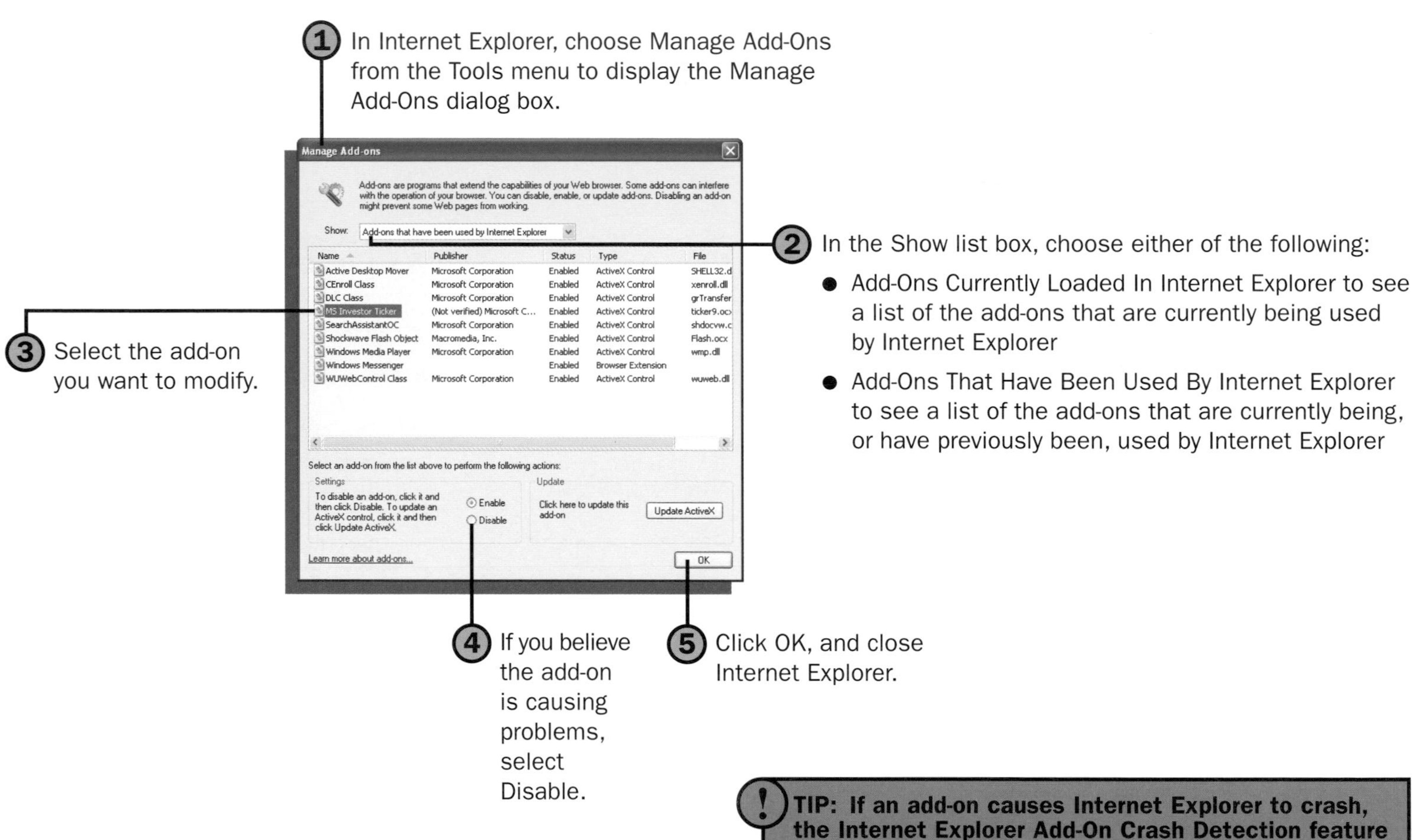

1. In Internet Explorer, choose Manage Add-Ons from the Tools menu to display the Manage Add-Ons dialog box.
2. In the Show list box, choose either of the following:
   - Add-Ons Currently Loaded In Internet Explorer to see a list of the add-ons that are currently being used by Internet Explorer
   - Add-Ons That Have Been Used By Internet Explorer to see a list of the add-ons that are currently being, or have previously been, used by Internet Explorer
3. Select the add-on you want to modify.
4. If you believe the add-on is causing problems, select Disable.
5. Click OK, and close Internet Explorer.

TIP: If an add-on causes Internet Explorer to crash, the Internet Explorer Add-On Crash Detection feature tries to determine which add-on is causing the problem so that you can disable it.

Troubleshoot the Add-Ons

1. Start Internet Explorer, and explore the Web sites where you encountered problems. Note whether you continue to encounter problems.

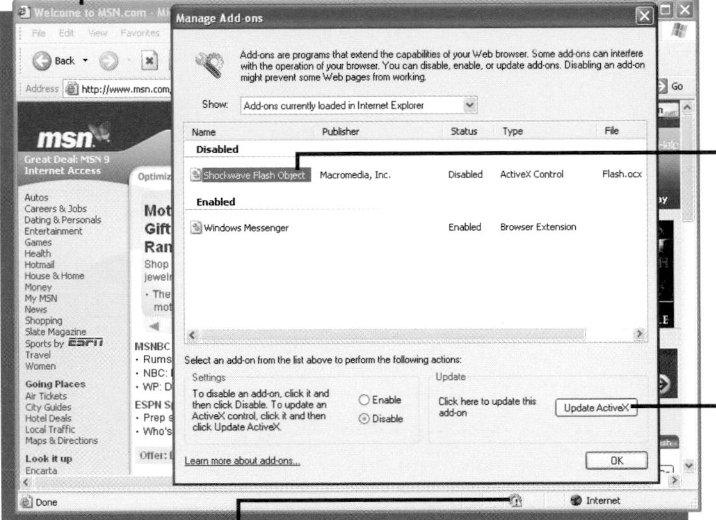

2. If you see a message that an add-on has been disabled, double-click the Manage Add-Ons icon on Internet Explorer's status bar.

CAUTION: Make sure that you allow only the ActiveX controls that display a reputable publisher in the Manage Add-Ons dialog box. Malicious ActiveX controls from unsigned or unknown sources can execute actions on your computer that you really don't want to happen.

3. In the Manage Add-Ons dialog box that appears, select the add-on that was disabled.

4. If you trust the publisher of the add-on, and if the Update ActiveX button is active, click it to try to update the add-on. If there is an update, install it. After you've updated the add-on, enable it, close the Manage Add-Ons dialog box, and see whether you have any problems viewing the Web sites where you previously encountered problems.

5. If you continue to experience the same problems, in the Manage Add-Ons dialog box, deactivate all the other add-ons, and click OK.

6. Close Internet Explorer, and then restart it, exploring the same Web sites and assessing the results as follows:

   - If you have serious problems other than content being blocked because of the deactivated add-ons, your problems are probably not being caused by the add-ons, and you'll need to do other troubleshooting. Use the Manage Add-Ons dialog box to enable the add-ons you disabled.
   - If you're no longer having any problems, open the Manage Add-Ons dialog box, enable one add-on, close the dialog box, and see whether any problems appear. Continue enabling the add-ons one at a time. If or when a problem occurs, deactivate the add-on that caused the problem, and enable all the others.

Starting Up When There's a Problem

If you have a problem starting up Windows XP correctly, you can use one of several startup procedures either to determine what's wrong or to start Windows with minimal features so that you can adjust or restore settings. After you've started Windows, you can use a variety of techniques to fix whatever is wrong with the system.

Control the Startup

1. Restart your computer.
2. After the computer system loads, and as Windows XP starts, hold down the F8 key. (If your computer displays a list of operating systems, press F8 when that list appears.) The Windows Advanced Options menu appears.
3. Use the Up arrow key to select Safe Mode.
4. Press Enter.
5. Make changes to your system to correct the problem.
6. Shut down your computer, and then restart it to see whether it starts correctly now.
7. If the computer doesn't start correctly, repeat steps 1 and 2, and choose a different startup mode to help diagnose the problem.

SEE ALSO: For information about fixing problems by resetting your computer to the previous settings, see "Fixing System Problems" on the facing page.

CAUTION: If Windows XP came preinstalled on your computer, read the computer manufacturer's documentation about fixing problems before you execute any actions.

Startup Options

Option	What it does
Safe Mode	Starts with no network connections and without most of its drivers.
Safe Mode With Networking	Starts with network connections but without most of its drivers.
Safe Mode With Command Prompt	Starts without network connections, without most of its drivers, and with the command prompt only.
Enable Boot Logging	Starts normally; records startup information to the *ntbtlog.txt* file (in the Windows folder).
Enable VGA Mode	Starts normally but uses only the basic VGA video driver.
Last Known Good Configuration	Starts normally, using the settings stored in the Registry when the computer was last shut down properly.
Directory Services Restore Mode	(Not available for Windows XP Home Edition.)
Debugging Mode	Starts normally but sends the debugging information to another computer over a serial cable.
Disable Automatic Restart on System Failure	Prevents the computer from restarting repetitively if a system failure occurs each time the computer restarts.
Start Windows Normally	Starts Windows as if you hadn't pressed the F8 key.
Reboot	Restarts the computer.
Return To OS Choices Menu	Goes to the menu to select the operating system to start.

Fixing System Problems

A fabulous feature of Windows XP is the System Restore tool, which makes it possible for you to undo whatever changes you or programs have made to your system. Periodically, and whenever you make changes to the system, Windows records all the system information. If you've made changes to the system but the effect isn't what you wanted, you can tell Windows to revert to the previous settings.

Restore the System

1. Close all your running programs, and make sure that no one else is logged on to the computer.
2. Choose System Restore from the System Tools submenu of the Start menu to display the System Restore window.

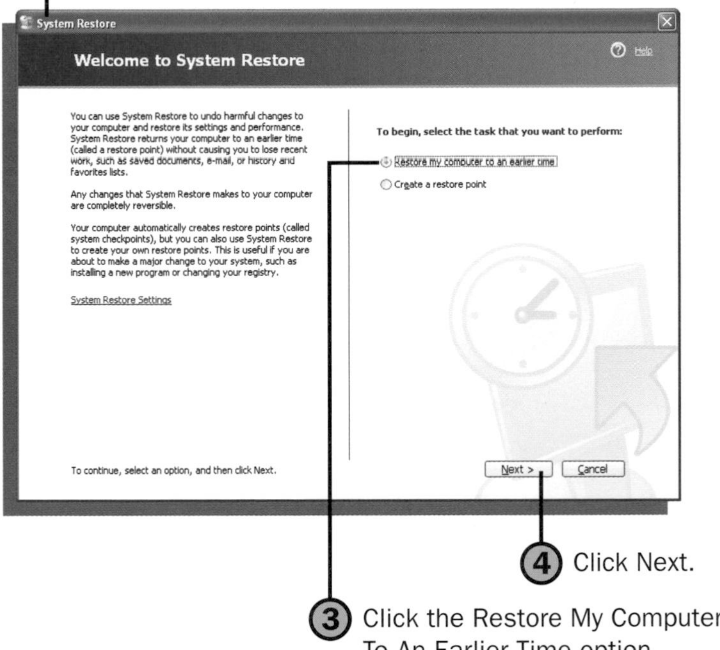

3. Click the Restore My Computer To An Earlier Time option.
4. Click Next.
5. Select a date that contains a restore point. (Only the dates in bold type contain restore points.)
6. Click the restore point you want to use, and click Next.

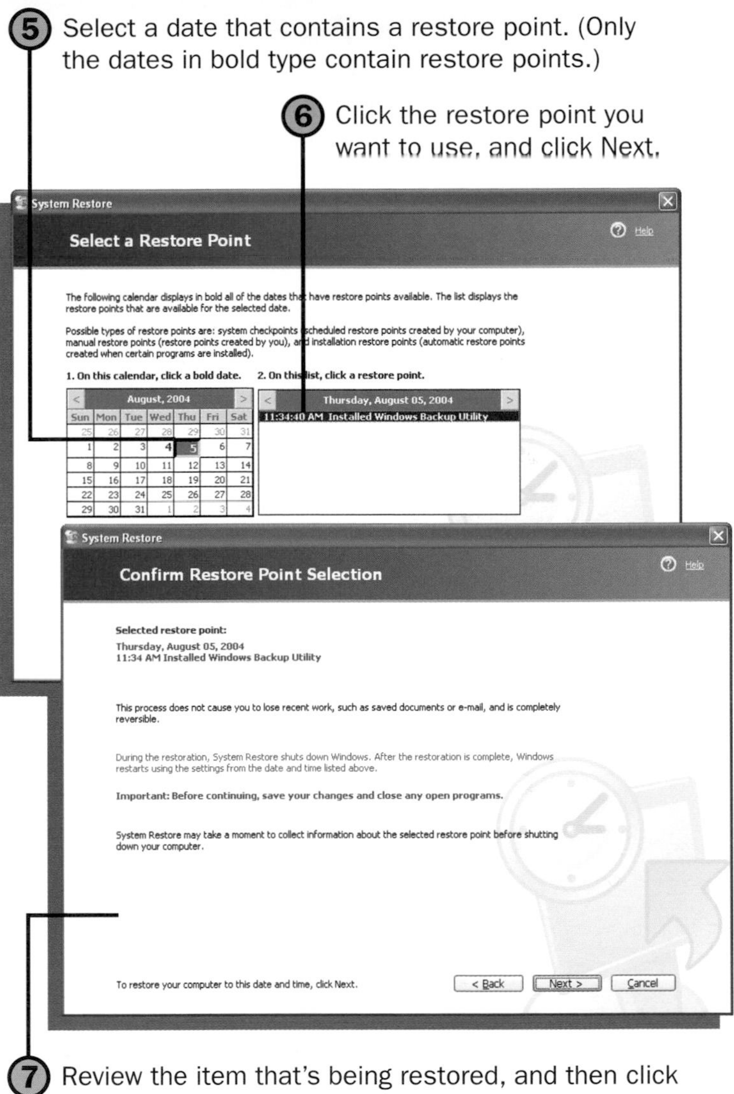

7. Review the item that's being restored, and then click Next to start the restoration process. Wait for the settings and any files to be restored, and log back on when prompted. Click OK when you're notified that the restoration has been completed.

Documenting Your System

Be prepared! Even if your system is working perfectly now, the day might come when you'll encounter a problem that you can't fix yourself. When you need professional assistance, you're going to have to supply a helpful technician with as much information about your system as possible. Windows XP can provide you with a vast amount of information about the system, and you can document some or all of it. Much of the information is indecipherable to the average computer user, but it's invaluable for the support person. Some of the system documentation can be useful to you, though—you might need to refer to it when you're planning to add items to or remove them from the system.

TIP: The Tools menu contains some powerful and advanced tools for monitoring and modifying your system, and you should know how these tools work before you attempt to use them. To learn about them, either search for information in Windows Help And Support, or start the tool and use its Help program.

Get the Information

1. Choose System Information from the System Tools submenu of the Start menu to display the System Information dialog box.

2. To record all the information about your system, click System Summary. To limit the information to a specific component, click that component in the list.

3. Choose Export from the File menu, and save the information as a text file.

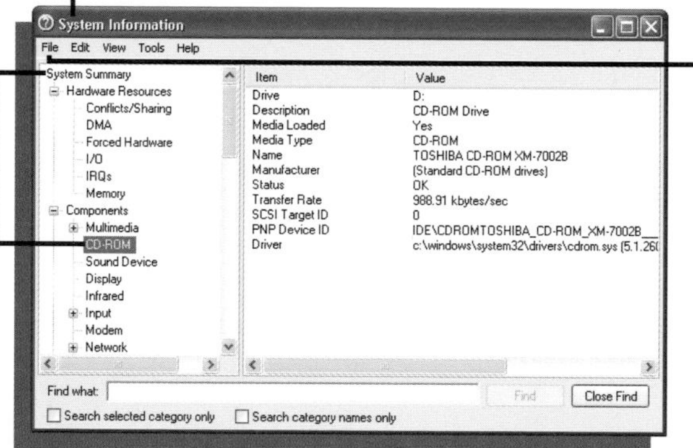

4. Use the text file as your external source of information about your system. You can e-mail the file to a technician, save it on another computer or on a floppy disk, or use Notepad or WordPad to edit, format, and print relevant portions of the report.

Managing Everything

Windows XP provides a powerful administrative tool called the Computer Management Console that gives you access to almost everything on your computer system. You can use this tool to explore your computer and learn about the adjustments you can make, and—armed with a little knowledge—you can then use the tool to maintain and improve your system.

Use the Console

1. Right-click My Computer on the Start menu, and choose Manage from the shortcut menu to display the Computer Management Console.

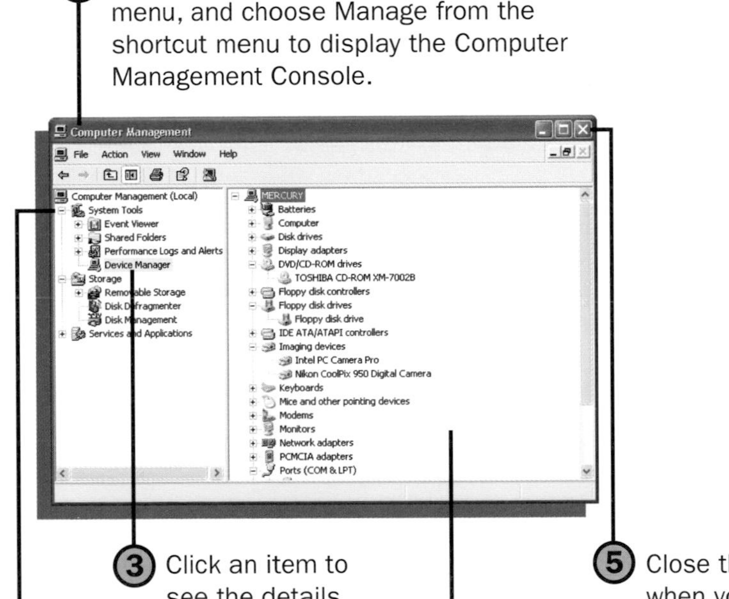

2. Click a plus sign to see a subtopic or category.
3. Click an item to see the details.
4. Use the items in the right pane to gather information or adjust settings.
5. Close the console when you've finished.

Computer Management Console Items

Item	What it does
Event Viewer	Allows you to view logs of events (including errors and warnings) for your applications, security, and the operating system.
Shared Folders	Monitors which items on your computer are shared on the network, who's currently connected to your computer, and which files are being used.
Performance Logs And Alerts	Provides technical data about the running of the computer.
Device Manager	Lists all hardware devices on the system. You can adjust settings, including installing or uninstalling new device drivers.
Storage	Provides information about removable and fixed disks, and allows some management of those disks.
Services And Applications	Lists all the services available on your computer; allows you to manually start or stop services; and provides access to the Indexing Service, where you can manage the service and directly query the index of files on your computer.

Tweaking Your System

Here's a little secret that some computer experts don't want to be widely known: Microsoft has made available a set of free tools that you can use to tweak your Windows system well beyond what you can do using conventional settings. All you need to do is download the correct tool and use it to gain spectacular control of the system. This free tool set is called PowerToys, and the one with the most outstanding power to manage and modify your system is TweakUI.

CAUTION: These tools are powerful, so it's possible to make a real mess of things if you use them without really knowing what you're doing. Microsoft doesn't provide any support for these tools, so be aware that you'll be using them at your own risk!

TIP: If you're using Windows XP Professional instead of the Home edition, you can download the tools from *www.microsoft.com/windowsxp/pro/downloads/powertoys.*

Set Up Your Tools

1. Go to the Microsoft PowerToys For Windows XP Home Edition Web page at *www.microsoft.com/windowsxp/home/downloads/powertoys,* click TweakUI.exe, and follow the directions on the screen to download and install the program.

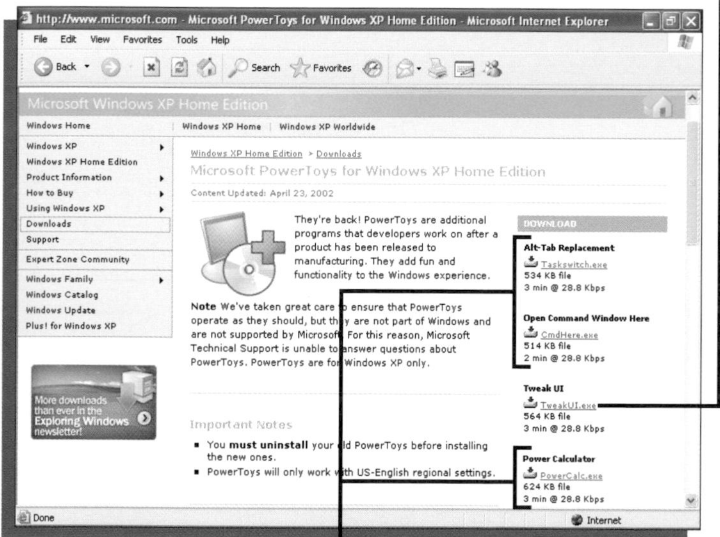

2. From the PowerToys For Windows XP submenu of the Start menu, choose Readme to display the PowerToysReadme Web page. Review the information about the PowerToys, and decide which additional PowerToys you want to use.

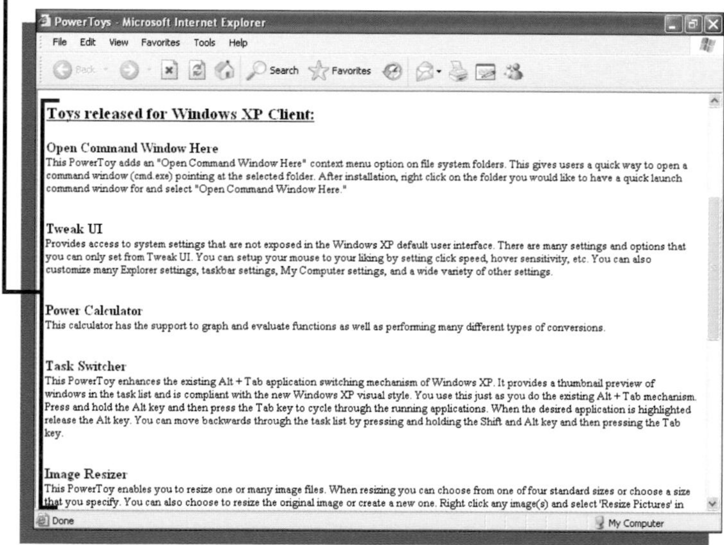

3. Return to the PowerToys download Web page, and download and install any other PowerToys you want to use.

Use the Tools

1. From the PowerToys For Windows XP submenu of the Start menu, choose Tweak UI to display the Tweak UI dialog box.
2. Click a category to make any adjustments or settings for that category.

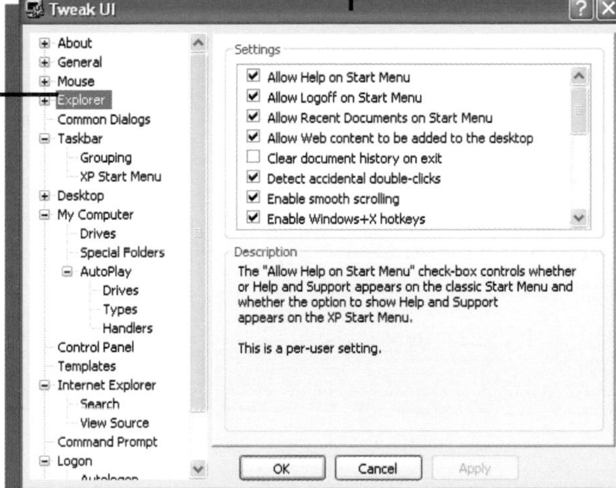

3. If a category has a plus sign next to it, click the plus sign to see the subcategories. Click a subcategory to make changes.

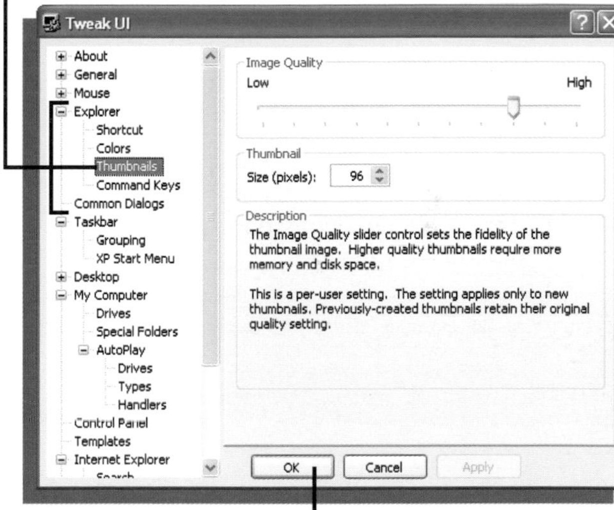

4. Repeat steps 2 and 3 for any other categories you want.
5. Click OK when you've finished.

TRY THIS: In TweakUI, click the plus sign next to the About category, and then click the Tips subcategory. Use the Next Tip and the Previous Tip buttons to read tips for using Windows XP. Then, if you find the tips useful, click the Save Tips button, and save the tips to a text file in your My Documents folder. When you review the tips in a Notepad window, be sure to turn on the Word Wrap option from the Format menu.

TIP: Keep checking the PowerToys Web pages, where new programs are posted occasionally. There's also a PowerToys Fun Pack, which contains two programs: one that lets you use Windows Media video files as your screen saver, and the other that lets you automatically change the wallpaper on your Desktop at whatever interval you set.

Helping Each Other

How many times have you screamed "Help!" (or worse) when your computer was being an uncooperative brat, only to be met by silence? Now your pleas for help won't disappear into the void. Using the Remote Assistance feature, you can contact someone over the Internet for help. Your friend or coworker can view your computer Desktop, review your system information, and even chat with you to help you figure out what's wrong. Likewise, if a friend or colleague has a problem that you know how to solve, you can be the expert who provides the oh-so-welcome assistance.

TIP: To ask for help from someone who isn't in your Contacts list, click the Other tab in the Ask For Remote Assistance dialog box, and type the person's full e-mail address.

Ask for Help

1. Start Windows Messenger if it isn't already running, log on, and open the Windows Messenger window. Choose Ask For Remote Assistance from the Actions menu, and, in the Ask For Remote Assistance dialog box that appears, double-click the name of the contact from whom you want help. Wait for that person to accept the invitation, and then confirm that you want him or her to view your screen and chat with you.

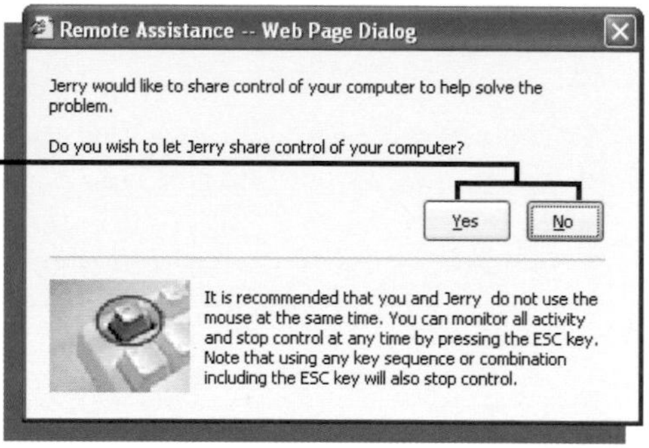

2. When you're connected, type a message to explain your problem, and press Enter.

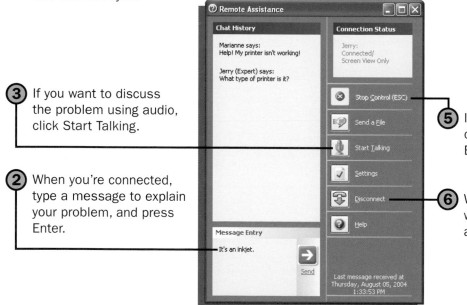

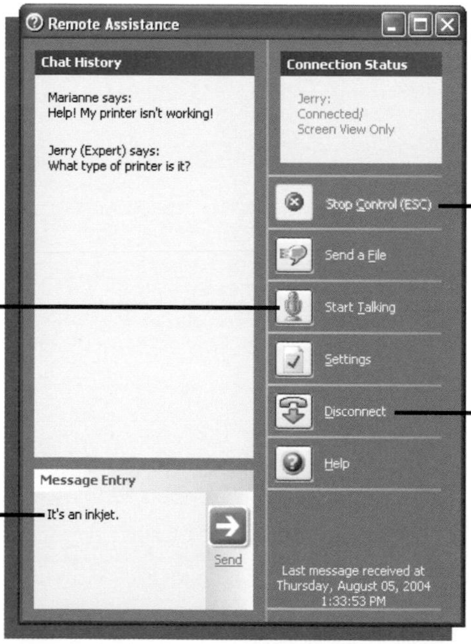

3. If you want to discuss the problem using audio, click Start Talking.

4. If the person asks to take control of your computer, click Yes to allow him or her full access to the computer and permission to make changes to the system. Click No if you want to retain control and make changes or act on suggestions yourself.

5. If you've allowed the other person to take control of the computer, click Stop Control (ESC) or press the Esc key when you want to terminate that control.

6. When you've finished (and solved the problem, we hope!), click Disconnect to end the remote assistance.

Give Help

1. With Windows Messenger running, log on, and wait for the invitation to provide help. When you receive it, accept the invitation, and wait for the Remote Assistance window to appear.

2. If you want to discuss the problem using audio, click Start Talking. Otherwise, use the Chat area to send and read messages.

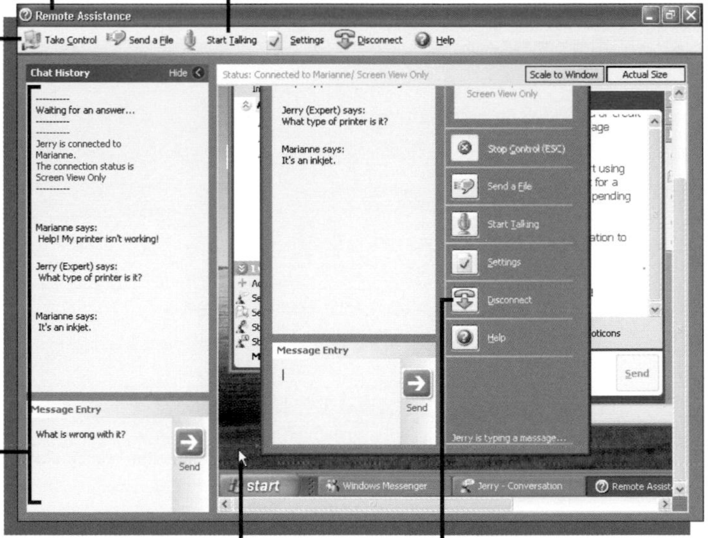

3. Review the Desktop of the person you're helping. All the actions he or she takes will be displayed, including using programs or changing settings.

4. If you want to take control of the other computer, click Take Control. Wait for the other person to confirm that you can take control. Click OK to confirm that you have control, and use your mouse to explore the other computer, open menus and programs, and do whatever troubleshooting and problem-solving you need to do.

5. When you no longer need control, click the Release Control button (the Take Control button changes to the Release Control button after it's clicked), and click Disconnect when the session has been completed.

The Chat area

TIP: In Remote Assistance terminology, the person asking for help is the Novice and the person providing help is the Expert.

SEE ALSO: For information about using Windows Messenger, see "Sending Instant Messages" on page 84.

Backing Up Your Files

With all the security features built into Windows, you'd think you wouldn't need to do anything more. Wrong! What if you have a severe hardware failure—your hard disk just stops, for example—or someone accidentally erases all your files? What if your computer gets hit by lightning? All your work will be gone forever if you haven't backed up your important files. And, with all the right tools readily available, there really is no excuse for not backing up those files periodically.

Back Up Your Files

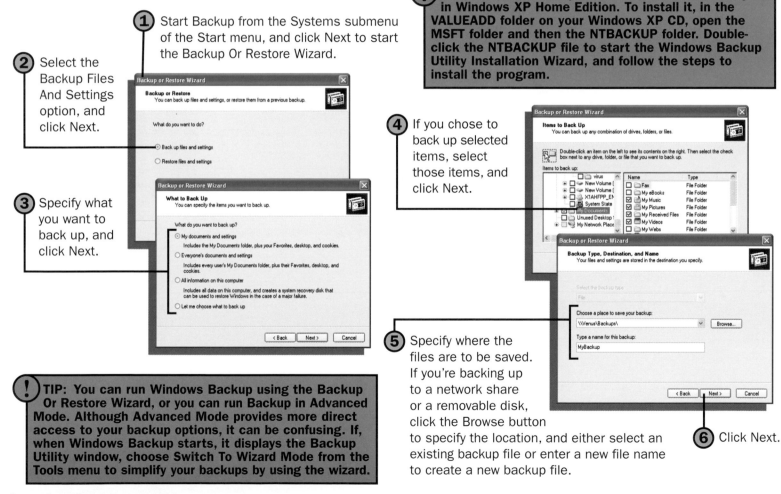

1. Start Backup from the Systems submenu of the Start menu, and click Next to start the Backup Or Restore Wizard.
2. Select the Backup Files And Settings option, and click Next.
3. Specify what you want to back up, and click Next.

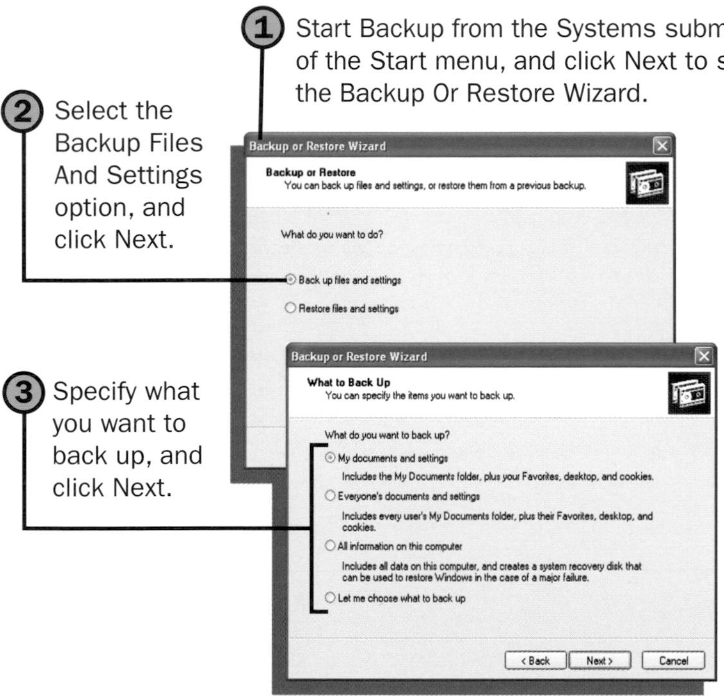

4. If you chose to back up selected items, select those items, and click Next.
5. Specify where the files are to be saved. If you're backing up to a network share or a removable disk, click the Browse button to specify the location, and either select an existing backup file or enter a new file name to create a new backup file.
6. Click Next.

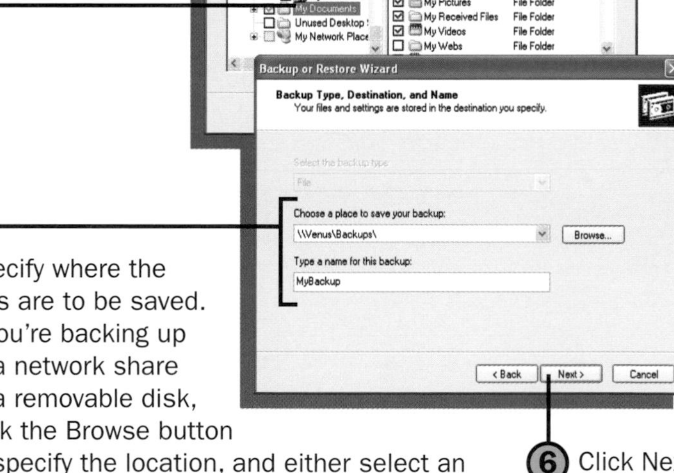

TIP: Windows Backup isn't installed automatically in Windows XP Home Edition. To install it, in the VALUEADD folder on your Windows XP CD, open the MSFT folder and then the NTBACKUP folder. Double-click the NTBACKUP file to start the Windows Backup Utility Installation Wizard, and follow the steps to install the program.

TIP: You can run Windows Backup using the Backup Or Restore Wizard, or you can run Backup in Advanced Mode. Although Advanced Mode provides more direct access to your backup options, it can be confusing. If, when Windows Backup starts, it displays the Backup Utility window, choose Switch To Wizard Mode from the Tools menu to simplify your backups by using the wizard.

Set the Backup Options

1. On the Completing The Backup Or Restore Wizard page of the wizard, click the Advanced button.
2. Specify the type of backup you want, and click Next. Step through the wizard, setting your preferences for verification and compression, appending or replacing the data, and labeling the backup.

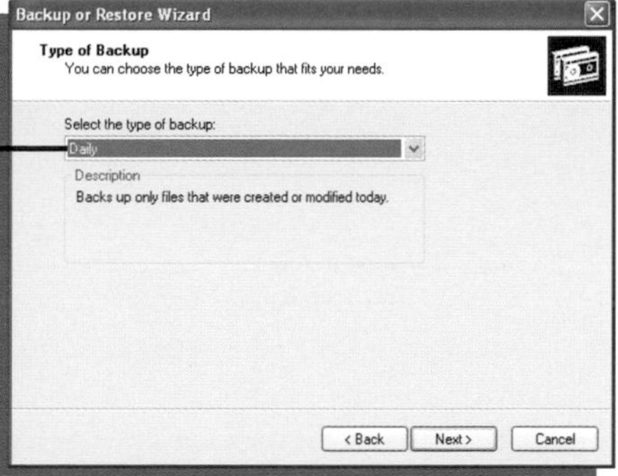

3. Specify when you want the backup to be run. If you choose Later, click the Set Schedule button, and specify whether you want the backup to be run once at a specific time or routinely at specified time increments.

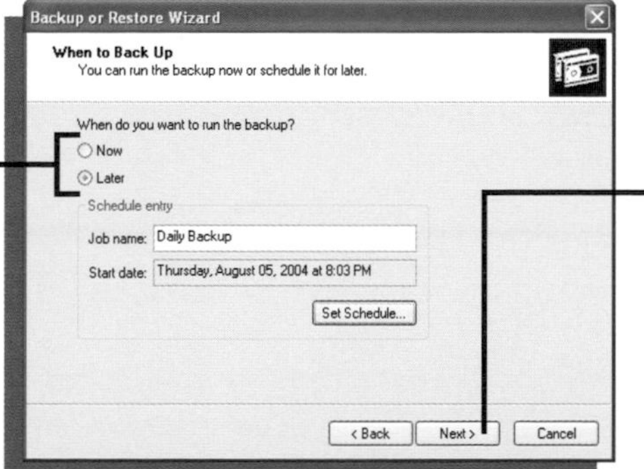

4. Click Next, and complete the wizard.
5. If the backup is set to run immediately, wait for the data to be backed up, and then close both the Backup Progress dialog box and the Backup program when the backup has been completed. If the backup is scheduled to run later, close the Backup program.

TIP: Windows Backup is a useful tool (and it's free!), but if you want more power, including the ability to write the backup files directly to removable media such as CDs or DVDs, you might want to purchase a more sophisticated backup program.

Types of Backup

Type	Files copied
Copy	All files. The files are not marked as backed up.
Daily	Files created or modified on the current day only. The files are not marked as backed up.
Differential	Any files created or modified since the last Normal or Incremental backup. The files are not marked as backed up.
Incremental	Any files created or modified since the last Normal or Incremental backup. The files are marked as backed up.
Normal	All files. The files are marked as backed up.

Restoring Backed-Up Files

Have you deleted or otherwise lost files that you now need? If those files were routinely backed up from your computer, you can restore them from the backup to your computer.

Restore the Files

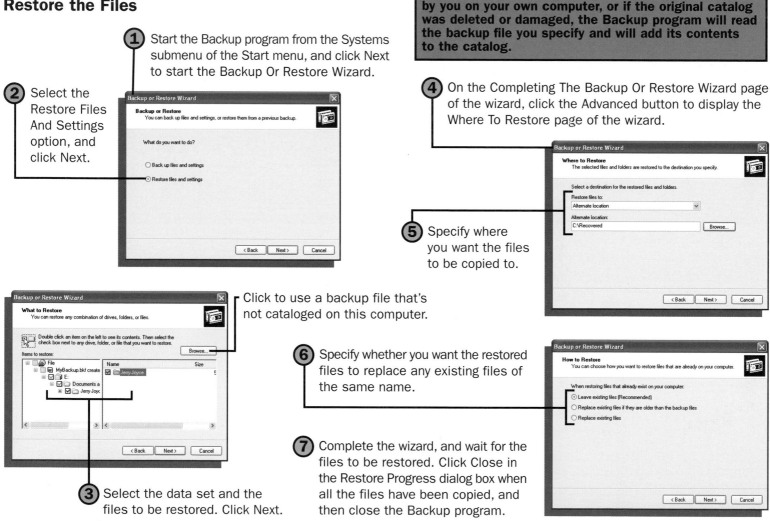

1. Start the Backup program from the Systems submenu of the Start menu, and click Next to start the Backup Or Restore Wizard.
2. Select the Restore Files And Settings option, and click Next.

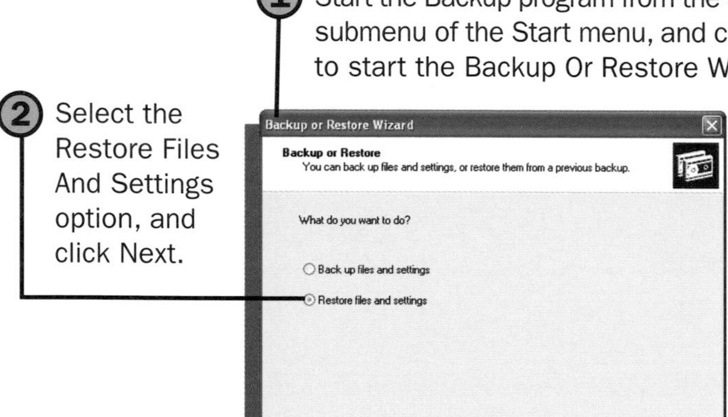

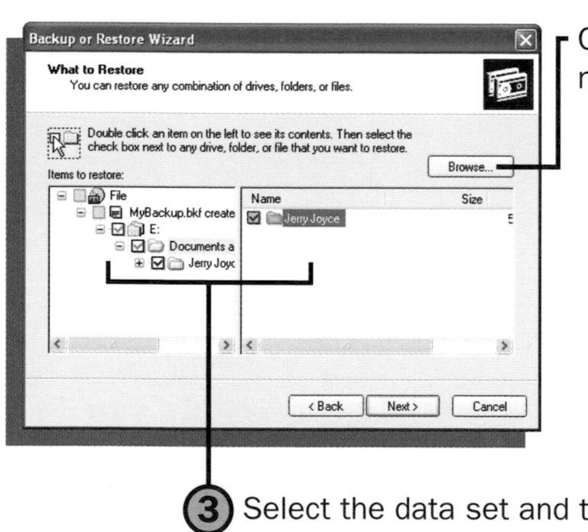

Click to use a backup file that's not cataloged on this computer.

3. Select the data set and the files to be restored. Click Next.

TIP: When a backup is executed, information about the items that were backed up and the storage location of the backup is saved in a "catalog" on your computer. If you're restoring a backup that wasn't created by you on your own computer, or if the original catalog was deleted or damaged, the Backup program will read the backup file you specify and will add its contents to the catalog.

4. On the Completing The Backup Or Restore Wizard page of the wizard, click the Advanced button to display the Where To Restore page of the wizard.
5. Specify where you want the files to be copied to.

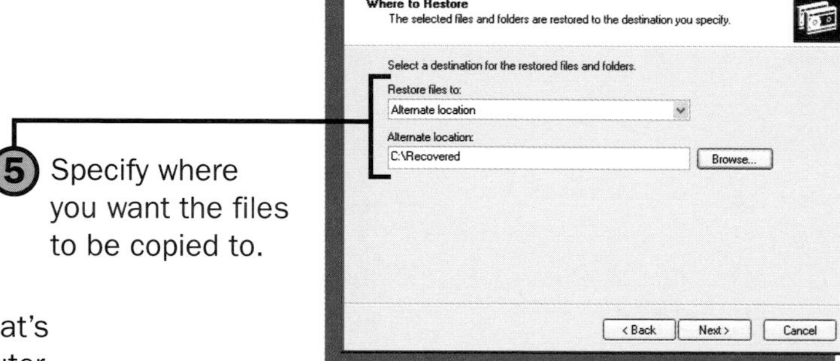

6. Specify whether you want the restored files to replace any existing files of the same name.
7. Complete the wizard, and wait for the files to be restored. Click Close in the Restore Progress dialog box when all the files have been copied, and then close the Backup program.

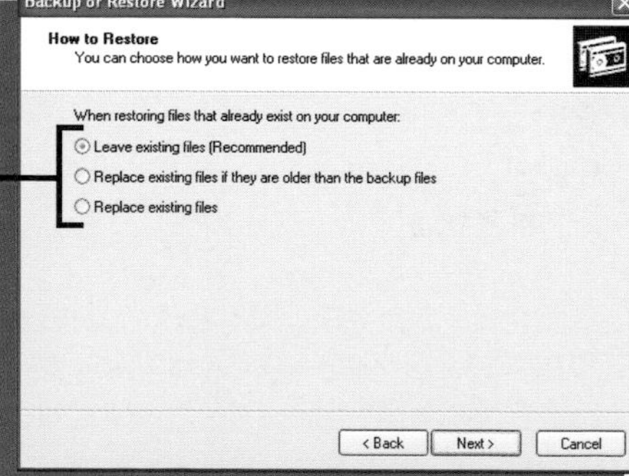

Editing Windows XP Settings

Windows XP uses a database called the *Registry* to keep track of all its settings, including most of the programs that are installed on the system. Occasionally—if there's a problem with your system or with a program, or if you simply want to customize the system—you'll need to modify the contents of the Registry.

CAUTION: Because any modifications to the Registry can cause systemwide problems, you should modify the contents of the Registry only if you have detailed instructions from a reliable source, and—as everyone will warn you—at your own risk and only after you've backed up the Registry.

Edit the Registry

1. Choose Run from the Start menu to open the Run dialog box.
2. Type **regedt32** in the Open box, and click OK.
3. Choose Find from the Edit menu to display the Find dialog box.
4. Type the name of the key you're looking for.
5. Select the Keys check box if it isn't already selected. Clear the check boxes for Values and Data if they're selected.
6. Click Find Next.

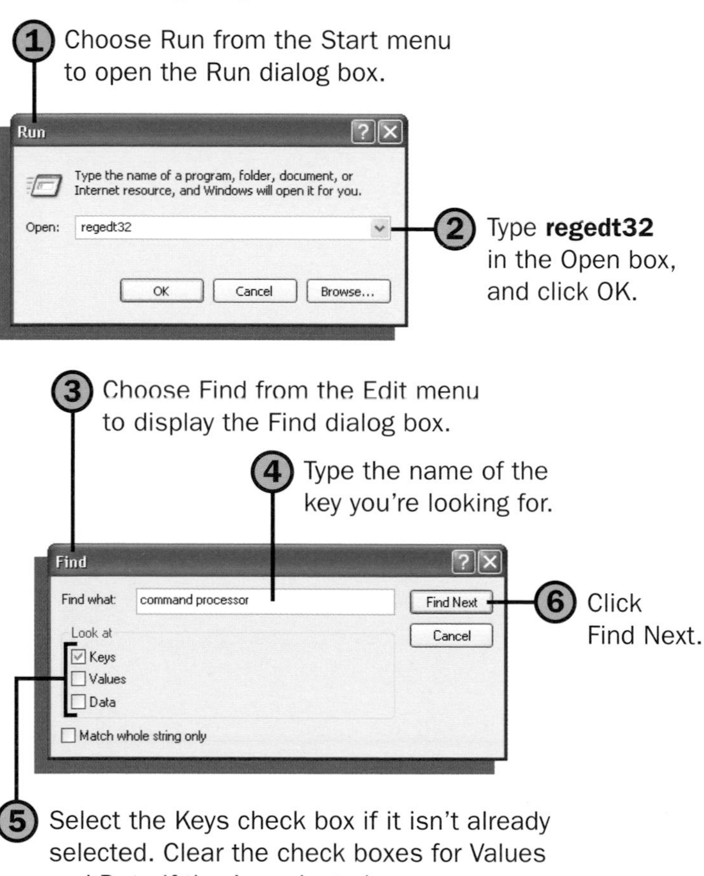

7. Check the directory structure to verify that you have the correct key. If it's not the correct key, choose Find Next from the Edit menu until you've located the correct key.
8. Double-click the item you want to change.
9. Make your changes, and click OK.
10. Close the Registry Editor, and see whether the change works as expected.

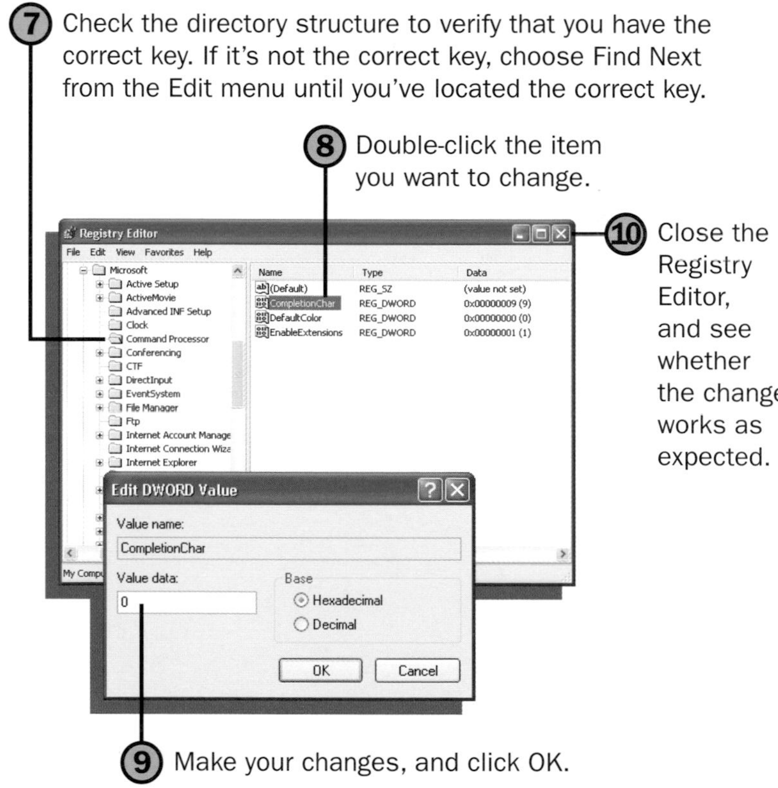

TIP: A key is an identifier for a record or a group of records in the database. The Registry edit shown on this page disables the AutoComplete feature at the command prompt when you press the Tab key.

Index

A

B

C

D

E

F

G

H

I

J

K

L

M

N

Q

R

S

T

U

Z

About the Authors

Jerry Joyce has had a long-standing relationship with Microsoft: He was the technical editor on numerous books published by Microsoft Press, and he has written manuals, help files, and specifications for various Microsoft products. As a programmer, he has tried to make using a computer as simple as using any household appliance, but he has yet to succeed. Jerry's alter ego is that of a marine biologist; he has conducted research from the Arctic to the Antarctic and has published extensively on marine-mammal and fisheries issues. As an antidote to staring at his computer screen, he enjoys traveling, birding, boating, and wandering about beaches, wetlands, and mountains.

Marianne Moon has worked in the publishing world for many years as proofreader, editor, and writer—sometimes all three simultaneously. She has been editing and proofreading Microsoft Press books since 1984 and has written and edited documentation for Microsoft products such as Microsoft Works, Flight Simulator, Space Simulator, Golf, Publisher, the Microsoft Mouse, and Greetings Workshop. In another life, she was chief cook and bottlewasher for her own catering service and wrote cooking columns for several newspapers. When she's not chained to her computer, she likes gardening, cooking, traveling, writing poetry, and knitting sweaters for tiny dogs.

Marianne and **Jerry** own and operate **Moon Joyce Resources,** a small consulting company. They've had a 20-year working relationship and have been married for 13 years. They are coauthors of the following books:

Microsoft Word 97 At a Glance
Microsoft Windows 95 At a Glance
Microsoft Windows NT Workstation 4.0 At a Glance
Microsoft Windows 98 At a Glance
Microsoft Word 2000 At a Glance
Microsoft Windows 2000 Professional At a Glance
Microsoft Windows Millennium Edition At a Glance
Troubleshooting Microsoft Windows 2000 Professional
Microsoft Word Version 2002 Plain & Simple
Microsoft Office System Plain & Simple—2003 Edition
Microsoft Windows XP Plain & Simple

If you have questions or comments about any of their books, you can reach Marianne and Jerry at moonjoyceresourc@hotmail.com.

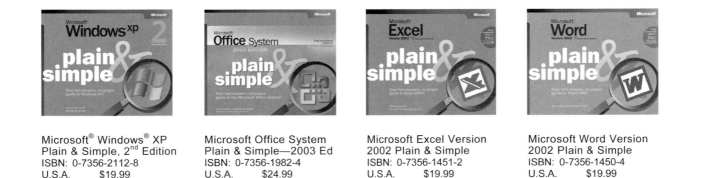